FROMMER'S

BUDGET TRAVEL GUIDE

COSTA RICA, GUATEMALA & BELIZE ON $35 A DAY '93-'94

by Karl Samson

PRENTICE HALL TRAVEL

NEW YORK • LONDON • TORONTO • SYDNEY • TOKYO • SINGAPORE

FROMMER BOOKS
Published by Prentice Hall General Reference
A division of Simon & Schuster Inc.
15 Columbus Circle
New York, NY 10023

ISBN 0-671-84664-7
ISSN 1051-6859

Design by Robert Bull Design
Maps by Geografix Inc.

FROMMER'S COSTA RICA, GUATEMALA & BELIZE ON $35 A DAY

Editorial Director: Marilyn Wood
Senior Editors: Judith de Rubini, Alice Fellows
Editors: Thomas F. Hirsch, Paige Hughes, Sara Hinsey Raveret, Lisa Renaud, Theodore Stavrou
Assistant Editors: Margaret Bowen, Peter Katucki, Ian Wilker
Managing Editor: Leanne Coupe

Special Sales

Bulk purchases of Frommer's Travel Guides are available at special discounts. The publishers are happy to custom-make publications for corporate clients who wish to use them as premiums or sales promotions. We can excerpt the contents, provide covers with corporate imprints, or create books to meet specific needs. For more information write to Special Sales, Prentice Hall Travel, Paramount Communications Building, 15 Columbus Circle, New York, NY 10023

Manufactured in the United States of America

CONTENTS

LIST OF MAPS

INVITATION TO THE READERS

In researching this book, our author has come across many wonderful establishments, the best of which we have included here. We are sure that many of you will also come across appealing hotels, inns, restaurants, guest houses, shops, and attractions. Please don't keep them to yourself. Share your experiences, especially if you want to comment on places that have been included in this edition that have changed for the worse. You can address your letters to:

Karl Samson
Costa Rica, Guatemala & Belize
Prentice Hall Travel
15 Columbus Circle
New York, NY 10023

A DISCLAIMER

Readers are advised that prices fluctuate in the course of time and travel information changes under the impact of the varied and volatile factors that affect the travel industry. Neither the author nor the publisher can be held responsible for the experiences of readers while traveling. Readers are invited to write to the publisher with ideas, comments, and suggestions for future editions.

SAFETY ADVISORY

Whenever you're traveling in an unfamiliar city or country, stay alert. Be aware of your immediate surroundings. Wear a money belt and keep a close eye on your possessions. Be particularly careful with cameras, purses, and wallets, all favorite targets of thieves and pickpockets.

CHAPTER 1

GETTING TO KNOW COSTA RICA

Costa Rica in Spanish means "Rich Coast," which was a misnomer when gold-hungry Spaniards named the country nearly 500 years ago. They found little gold or silver and few Indians to convert and enslave; instead they found a land of rugged volcanic peaks blanketed with dense forests. Costa Rica was ignored for centuries, but today it is beginning to live up to its name. In fact, the country should rightfully be called Costas Ricas since it has two coasts, one on the Pacific and one on the Caribbean. Along these coasts are some of the most beautiful beaches in Central America, and this translates into dollars as resort developments spring up along the shores. The dense forests and rugged mountain ranges that cover much of Costa Rica are also bringing in unexpected revenues. To reduce its national debt, Costa Rica agreed to set aside hundreds of thousands of acres of undisturbed forests as national parks and wildlife preserves. With tropical forests around the world disappearing at an alarming rate, concerned individuals and groups are flocking to Costa Rica to visit and study its pristine wilderness areas.

Costa Rica, bordered by the troubled nations of Nicaragua and Panama, is also a relative sea of tranquility in a region of turmoil. For more than 100 years, the country has enjoyed a stable democracy; in fact, there isn't even a standing army here, which is something that Costa Ricans are very proud of. Former president Oscar Arias Sánchez was awarded the Nobel Peace Prize for his work in implementing a Central American peace plan. With political stability, an educated populace, and vast areas of wilderness, Costa Rica today is a rich coast, indeed.

1. GEOGRAPHY, HISTORY & POLITICS

GEOGRAPHY

Bordered on the north by Nicaragua and on the southeast by Panama, Costa Rica (19,530 square miles) is only slightly larger than Vermont and New Hampshire combined. Within this area are more than 750 miles of coastline on both the Caribbean Sea and the Pacific Ocean. Much of the country is mountainous, with three major ranges running from northwest to southeast. Among these mountains are several volcanic peaks, some of which are still active. Between the mountain ranges there are fertile valleys, the largest and most populated of which is the Meseta

WHAT'S SPECIAL ABOUT COSTA RICA

Beaches
☐ Manuel Antonio National Park, three idyllic beaches set amid jungle-clad hills.
☐ Cahuita National Park on the Caribbean Coast, long deserted beaches and Costa Rica's largest coral reef.
☐ Jacó Beach, an inexpensive resort area with many deserted beaches nearby.
☐ The beaches of Guanacaste, which receive more sunshine than any of the other beaches in the country.

Museums
☐ The Gold Museum in San José, the largest collection of Pre-Columbian gold jewelry and ornaments in the Americas.
☐ The Jade Museum, also in San José, an equally impressive collection of Pre-Columbian jade artifacts and jewelry.

Parks/Gardens
☐ Lankester Gardens, near Cartago, hundreds of species of orchids on display.
☐ National parks, encompassing 11% of Costa Rica's land.

☐ Monteverde Cloud Forest Reserve, a lush jungle that is home to the quetzal, one of the most beautiful birds on earth.

Natural Spectacles
☐ Every year, hundreds of thousands of turtles lay their eggs on Costa Rican beaches.
☐ Arenal Volcano, which erupts regularly and is a spectacular sight at night.

Religious Shrines
☐ The basilica in Cartago, with a statue of the Virgin of Los Angeles said to heal the sick.
☐ The ruins of a church in Cartago turned into a park.

After Dark
☐ San José's National Theater, a stately old opera house with performances almost every night.

Great Adventures
☐ Kayaking and rafting on white-water rivers.
☐ Nature-oriented lodges offering rafting, horseback riding, and bird and wildlife spotting.

Central. With the exception of the dry Guanacaste region, much of Costa Rica's coastal area is hot and humid and covered with dense rain forests. The earliest Spanish settlers found the climate much more amenable in the highlands of the Meseta Central, and to this day most of the population lives in this region.

REGIONS IN BRIEF

The Meseta Central The Meseta Central is characterized by rolling green hills between 3,000 and 4,000 feet above sea level, where the climate has been described as "eternal spring." It is Costa Rica's primary agricultural region, with coffee farms making up the majority of landholdings. The rich volcanic soil of this region makes it ideal for growing almost anything. The country's earliest settlements were in this area, and today the Meseta Central is a densely populated area laced with good roads and dotted with small towns.

The Mountains Surrounding the Meseta Central and extending to Costa Rica's northern and southern borders are three major mountain ranges: the Cordillera Central, the Guanacaste range, and the Talamanca range. Among these mountains are found numerous volcanic peaks, four of which border the Meseta Central. Two of these, Poás and Irazú, are still active and have caused extensive damage during cycles of activity in the past two centuries. Much of the mountainous regions to the north and to the south of the capital of San José have been declared national parks to protect their virgin rain forests from logging.

The Guanacaste Peninsula This northwestern region of Costa Rica is the driest part of the country and has been likened to west Texas. Within this region is one of the last remnants of tropical dry forest left on earth. Because the forest gives way to areas of savannah in Guanacaste, this is Costa Rica's "Wild West," where cattle ranching is the primary occupation.

The Caribbean and the Pacific Coasts On the southern Pacific Coast and the entire Caribbean Coast there are wide, steamy lowlands, much of which have been converted to banana and oil-palm plantations. Lowland rain-forest vegetation predominates where it has not been cleared, and rainfall reaches more than 200 inches per year.

HISTORY & POLITICS

EARLY HISTORY

Little is known of Costa Rica's history prior to its colonization by Spanish settlers. The Pre-Columbian Indians who made their home in this region of Central America never developed the large cities or advanced culture that flowered farther north in what would become Guatemala, Belize, and Mexico. However, from scattered excavations around the country, primarily in the northwest, ancient artifacts have been unearthed that indicate a strong sense of aesthetics. Beautiful gold and jade jewelry, intricately carved grinding stones, and artistically painted terra-cotta ware point toward a highly skilled, if not large, population. The most enigmatic of these ancient relics are carved stone balls, some measuring several yards across and weighing many tons, that have been found along the southern Pacific Coast. The purpose of these stone spheres remains a mystery: Some archeologists say that they may have been boundary markers; others think that they were celestial references.

In 1502, on his last voyage to the New World, Christopher Columbus anchored just offshore from present-day Puerto Limón. Whether it was he who gave the country its name is open to discussion, but it was not long before the inappropriate name took hold. The earliest Spanish settlers found that, unlike the Indians farther north, the native population of Costa Rica was unwilling to submit to slavery. Despite their small numbers and scattered villages, they fought back against the Spanish. However, the superior Spanish firepower and the European diseases that had helped to subjugate the populations farther north conquered the natives. But when the fighting was finished, the settlers in Costa Rica found that there were no more Indians left to oppress into servitude. The settlers were forced to till their own lands, an exercise unheard of in other parts of Central America. Few pioneers headed this way because they could settle in Guatemala, where there was a large native work force. Costa Rica was nearly forgotten, as the Spanish crown looked elsewhere for riches to plunder and souls to convert.

It didn't take long for Costa Rica's few Spanish settlers

DATELINE

- **13,000 B.C.** Earliest record of human inhabitants in Costa Rica.
- **1,000 B.C.** Olmec people from Mexico arrive in Costa Rica searching for rare blue jade.
- **1,000 B.C.– A.D. 1400** City of Guayabo is inhabited by as many as 10,000 people.
- **300 B.C.–A.D. 700** Mysterious stone spheres are carved by inhabitants of southwest coastal areas.
- **1502** Columbus discovers Costa Rica in September, landing at what is now Puerto Limón.
- **1519–1561** Spanish explore and colonize Costa Rica.
- **1563** City of Cartago is founded in Central Valley.
- **1737** San José is founded.
- **Late 1700s** Coffee is introduced as a cash crop.

(continues)

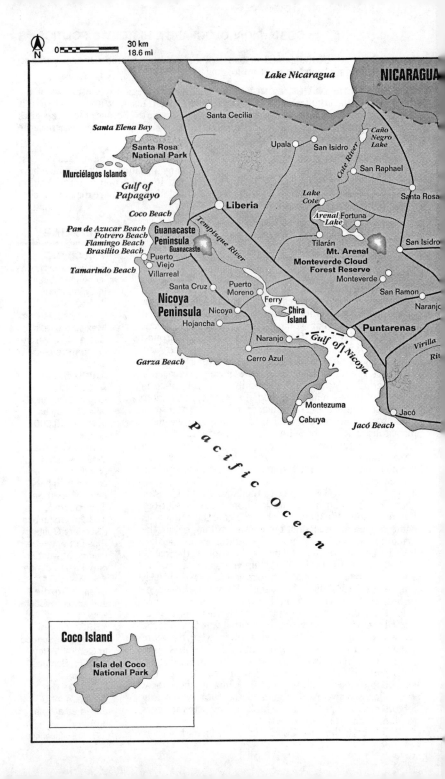

COSTA RICA

Caribbean Sea

San Juan River

Colorado River

Barra del Colorado
National Wildlife Refuge

Tortuguero
National
Park

Mt.
Poas

Mt.
Barva

Braulio Carrillo
National Park

Siquirres

Alajuela

Heredia

San Isidro

Mt.
Irazu

Mt.
Turrialba

Limón

SAN
JOSE

Cartago

Turrialba

Platanillo

Cahuita
National
Park

Cahuita

Orosi

San Ignacio

Orosi Valley

Bribri

Puerto Viejo

Mt.
Chirripó

Telire River

Chirripó
National
Park

Quepos

San Ramon

Manuel Antonio
National Park

Mt.
Dúrika

Mt. Kámuk

PANAMA

San Isidro

Hermosa Beach

Palmar Norte

Coronado
Bay

Golfito

Neily

Caño Island

Corcovado
National
Park

Gulf of Dulce

Jíménez

Canoas

DATELINE

- **1821** On September 15, Costa Rica, with the rest of Central America, gains independence from Spain.
- **1823** Capital is moved to San José.
- **1848** Costa Rica is proclaimed an independent republic.
- **1856** Battle of Santa Rosa; Costa Ricans defeat U.S.-backed proslavery advocate William Walker.
- **1870s** First banana plantations are formed.
- **1889** First election is won by an opposition party, establishing democratic process in Costa Rica.
- **1899** The United Fruit Company is founded by railroad builder Minor Keith.
- **1948** After aborted revolution, Costa Rican army is abolished.
- **1987** President Oscar Arias Sánchez is awarded the Nobel Peace Prize for orchestrating the Central American Peace Plan.

to head for the hills, where they found a climate that was less oppressive than the lowlands and a rich volcanic soil. Cartago, the colony's first capital, was founded in 1563, but it would not be until the 1700s that more cities were founded in this agriculturally rich region. In the late 18th century, the first coffee plants were introduced, and because these plants thrived in the highlands, Costa Rica began to develop its first cash crop. Unfortunately, it was a long and difficult journey transporting the coffee to the Caribbean Coast and thence to Europe, where the demand for coffee was growing.

FROM INDEPENDENCE TO THE PRESENT

In 1821, Spain granted independence to its colonies in Central America. Costa Rica joined with its neighbors to form the Central American Federation, but in 1938 it withdrew to form a new nation and pursue its own interests, which differed considerably from those of the other Central American nations. By the mid-1800s, coffee was the country's main export. Land was given free to anyone willing to plant coffee on it, and plantation owners soon grew wealthy and powerful, creating Costa Rica's first elite class. Coffee plantation owners were powerful enough to elect their own representatives to the presidency.

This was a stormy period in Costa Rican history, and in 1856 the country was invaded by William Walker, a soldier of fortune from Tennessee who had grandiose dreams of presiding over a slavery state in Central America. Prior to his invasion of Costa Rica, he had invaded Baja, California, and Nicaragua. The people of Central America were outraged by the actions of this man, who actually had backing from U.S. president James Buchanan. The people of Costa Rica, led by their own president, Juan Rafael Mora, marched against Walker and chased him back to Nicaragua. Walker eventually surrendered to a U.S. warship in 1857, but in 1860 he attacked Honduras, claiming to be the president of that country. The Hondurans, who had had enough of Walker's shenanigans, promptly executed him.

Until 1890 coffee growers had to transport their coffee either by ox cart to the Pacific port of Puntarenas or by boat down the Sarapiquí River to the Caribbean. In the 1870s a progressive president proposed a railway from San José to the Caribbean Coast to facilitate the transport of coffee to European markets. It took nearly 20 years for this plan to reach fruition and more than 4,000 workers lost their lives constructing the railway, which passed through dense jungles and rugged mountains on its journey from the Meseta Central to the coast. It was under the direction of the project's second chief engineer, Minor Keith, that a momentous deal was made with the government of Costa Rica: In order to continue the financially strapped project, Keith had struck on the idea of using the railway right-of-way (land on either side of the tracks) as banana plantations. The export of this crop would help to finance the railway, and in exchange Keith would get a 99-year lease on 800,000 acres of land with a 20-year tax deferment. In 1878 the first bananas were shipped

❓ DID YOU KNOW . . . ?

- Costa Rica has the oldest democracy in Central America.
- San José, the capital, is farther south than Caracas, Venezuela.
- Costa Rica has no army, navy, air force, or marine corps.
- Costa Rica has 10% of the butterflies in the world and more than the entire African continent, as well as more than 1,200 varieties of orchids and more than 800 species of birds.
- Isla del Coco, the largest uninhabited island in the world, is part of Costa Rica.
- Costa Rica has a mountain from the top of which you can see both the Caribbean Sea and the Pacific Ocean.

from Costa Rica, and in 1899 Keith and a partner formed the United Fruit Company, a company that would eventually become the largest landholder in Central America and cause political disputes and wars throughout the region.

In 1889 Costa Rica held what is considered the first free election in Central American history. The opposition candidate won the election, and the control of the government passed from the hands of one political party to those of another without bloodshed or hostilities. Thus Costa Rica established itself as the region's only true democracy. In 1948 this democratic process was challenged by a former president (who had been president from 1940 to 1944), Rafael Angel Calderón, who lost a bid at a second term in office by a narrow margin. Calderón, who had the backing of communist labor unions, refused to yield the country's leadership to the rightfully elected president, Otilio Ulate, and a revolution ensued. Calderón was eventually defeated. In the wake of this crisis, a new constitution was drafted; among other changes, it abolished Costa Rica's army so that such a revolution could never happen again.

Peace and democracy have become of tantamount importance to Costa Ricans since the revolution of 1948. When Oscar Arias Sánchez was elected president in 1986, his main goal was to seek a solution to the ongoing war in Nicaragua, and one of his first actions was to close down Contra bases inside Costa Rica and enforce Costa Rica's position of neutrality. In 1987 Sánchez won the Nobel Peace Prize for initiating a Central American peace plan aimed at settling the war in Nicaragua.

Costa Rica's 100 years of nearly uninterrupted democracy has helped make it the most stable economy in Central America. This stability and adherence to the democratic process is a source of great pride to Costa Ricans. They like to think of their country as a "Switzerland of Central America" not only because of its herds of dairy cows but also because of its staunch position of neutrality in a region that has been torn by nearly constant civil wars and revolutions for more than 200 years.

2. CULTURAL & SOCIAL LIFE

Art Since the Spanish conquest, Costa Rica's artists have followed European artistic styles. The Museo de Arte Costarricense exhibits works by the country's better-known artists of the last 400 years. Most artistic movements of those years are represented.

Architecture The Pre-Columbian peoples of Costa Rica left few signs of their habitation. The excavations at Guayabo, little more than building foundations and paved streets, are the country's main archeological site. Numerous earthquakes over the centuries have destroyed most of what the Spanish built. One such earthquake, in 1910, halted the construction of a cathedral in Cartago, the ruins of which are now a peaceful park in the middle of town. The ruins of another church, the oldest in Costa Rica, can be found near the village of Ujarrás in the Orosi Valley. This church was built in 1693 and abandoned in 1833 when the village was flooded. The central plaza in Heredia has a historic church built in 1796, and also on this square is an old fortress tower known as El Fortín.

The People   When the first Spaniards arrived in Costa Rica, the small Indian population was further reduced by wars and disease until they became a minority. Consequently, most of the population of Costa Rica today is of pure Spanish descent, and it is not at all surprising to see blond Costa Ricans. There is still a remnant Indian population on reservations in southeast Costa Rica near the town of Limón. This area also has a substantial population of English-speaking black Creoles who came over from Jamaica to work on the railroad and on the banana plantations. They have never moved far inland, preferring the humid lowlands to the cool Meseta Central. For the most part, these different groups coexist without friction. Literacy is high throughout the country, and nearly 50% of the work force is women. There is a large, working middle class, and there is not the gross disparity between rich and poor that you see in other Central American countries. Costa Ricans call themselves *Ticos,* a diminutive form of the term *costarricense.*

Performing Arts and Evening Entertainment   One of the very first things that Costa Ricans did with their newfound coffee wealth in the mid-19th century was to build an opera house. The elite were upset that opera singers were bypassing their country when they toured the Americas. Today that opera house is known as the National Theater and is as popular as it was 100 years ago. Hardly a night goes by that some performance isn't held in the stately theater.
   Mariachi and marimba music have a firm grip on the hearts of all Ticos. In San José there are several 24-hour restaurants where these types of music can be heard live and for free at all hours of the day or night. Discos and casinos are also very popular.

Sports and Recreation   Soccer is the national sport of Costa Rica, but baseball, polo, squash, and handball also are popular. There are currently only three golf courses in Costa Rica: the Cariari Hotel and Country Club in San José, Los Reyes at Guácima in Alajuela, and the Costa Rican Country Club in Escazú. Sportfishing is very popular here, and the waters in and around Costa Rica abound with everything from trout and tarpon to sailfish and marlin. There are fishing tournaments throughout the year and fishing boats for hire on both coasts. You'll need a fishing license (available from your fishing guide).
   Surfing is another sport that has caught on in a big way in Costa Rica. There are excellent surfing waves at various points on both coasts, and many hotels offer off-season discounts to surfers.

3. FOOD & DRINK

Very similar to other Central American cuisines, Costa Rican food is not especially memorable. Perhaps this is why there is so much international food available throughout the country. However, if you really want to save money, you'll find that Costa Rican food is always the cheapest food available. It is primarily served in *sodas,* Costa Rica's equivalent of diners.

FOOD

MEALS & DINING CUSTOMS

Rice and beans are the basis of Costa Rican meals. At breakfast, they're called *gallo pinto* and come with everything from eggs to steak or even to seafood. At lunch or dinner, rice and beans go by the name *casado* (which also means "married"). A casado comes with a cabbage-and-tomato salad, fried plantains (a type of banana), and a meat dish of some sort.

Dining hours in Costa Rica are flexible: Many restaurants in San José are open 24 hours, a sign that Ticos are willing to eat at any time of the night or day. However, expensive restaurants tend to open for lunch between 11am and 2pm and for dinner between 6pm and midnight.

THE CUISINE

Appetizers   *Bocas* are served with drinks in most bars throughout Costa Rica. Often the bocas are free, but even if they aren't, they're very inexpensive. Popular bocas include *gallos* (stuffed tortillas) and *sopa de mondongo* (tripe soup).

Soups   Black bean soup, *sopa negra*, is a creamy soup with a poached or boiled egg soaking in the broth. It is one of the most popular of Costa Rican soups and shows up on many menus. *Olla de carne* is a delicious soup made with beef and several local vegetables, including *chayote, ayote, yuca,* and plantains, all of which have textures and flavors similar to various winter squashes. *Sopa de mondongo* is made with tripe, the stomach of a cow, which some love and others find disgusting. *Picadillo* is a vegetable stew with a little bit of meat in it. It's often served as a side dish with a *casado*.

Sandwiches and Snacks   Ticos love to snack, and there are a large variety of tasty little sandwiches and snacks available on the street, at snack bars and in sodas. *Arreglados* are little meat-filled sandwiches, as are *tortas*, which are served on little rolls with a bit of salad tucked into them. *Gallos* are tortillas stuffed with meat, beans, or cheese. Tacos, tamales, and empanadas also are quite common.

Meat   Costa Rica is a beef country, one of the tropical nations that has converted much of its rain-forest land to pastures for raising beef cattle. Consequently, beef is cheap and plentiful, although it may be a bit tougher than you are used to. Spit-roasted chicken is also very popular here, especially when it is roasted over a coffee-wood fire. It is surprisingly tender.

Seafood   Costa Rica has two coasts, and as you would expect, there is plenty of seafood available everywhere in the country. *Corvina* (sea bass) is the most commonly served fish, and it is prepared innumerable ways, including as ceviche. Surprisingly, although Costa Rica is a major exporter of shrimp and lobster, both are very expensive here. In fact, shrimp is often more expensive than lobster. The reason is that most of the shrimp and lobster are exported, causing them to be very expensive at home.

Vegetables   On the whole, you will find vegetables surprisingly lacking in the meals you are served in Costa Rica. The standard vegetable with any meal is a little pile of shredded cabbage topped with a slice or two of tomato. For a much more satisfying and filling salad, order *palmito* (heart of palm salad). Hearts of palm are considered a delicacy in most places because an entire palm tree (albeit a small one) must be cut down to extract the heart. The heart is a bit like the inner part of an artichoke—many leaves layered around one another. These leaves are chopped into large pieces and served with other fresh vegetables, a salad dressing on top. Even here, where the palms are plentiful, *palmito* is relatively expensive. If you want something more than this, you'll have to order a side dish such as *picadillo*, a stew of vegetables with a bit of meat in it. Most people have a hard time thinking of *plátanos* (plantains) as vegetables, but these giant relatives of bananas are sweet and require cooking before they can be eaten. Fried plátanos are one of my favorite dishes. *Yuca* (manioc root) is another starchy staple vegetable of Costa Rica.

One more vegetable worth mentioning is the *pejibaye*, a form of palm fruit that looks like a miniature orange coconut. Boiled pejibayes are frequently sold from carts on the streets of San José. When cut in half, a pejibaye reveals a large seed surrounded by soft, creamy flesh and looks a bit like an avocado. You can eat it like an avocado, too, by just scooping the flesh out.

Fruits   Costa Rica has a wealth of delicious tropical fruits. The most common are mangos (season begins in May); papayas; pineapples; and bananas, which are oddly unavailable on the Atlantic (Caribbean Sea) Coast near the banana plantations. Other less well-known fruits include the *marañon*, an orange or yellow fruit with a glossy skin that is the fruit of the cashew tree; the *granadilla* (passion fruit); the *mamón chino*, which Asian travelers will immediately recognize as the rambutan; and the *carmabola* (star fruit). When ordering *ensalada de fruita* in a restaurant, make sure that it is made with fresh fruit and does not come with ice cream and Jell-O. What a shock I had when I first received a bowl of canned fruit covered with Jell-O cubes and three scoops of ice cream!

Desserts   *Queque seco*, which literally translates as "dry cake," is the same as pound cake. *Tres leches* cake is a Nicaraguan cake that is so moist you almost need to eat it with a spoon. *Flan de coco* is a sweet coconut flan. There are many other sweets available, many of which are made with milk and raw sugar (rich and sweet).

COSTA RICAN MENU TERMS

Bocas   Appetizers

Casado   Lunch or dinner meal consisting of rice, beans, a main dish, and fried plantains

Ceviche   Marinated seafood salad

Corvina   Sea bass

Gallo pinto   Breakfast dish consisting of rice, beans, and eggs or meat

Horchata   Refresco made with rice flour and cinnamon

Palmito   Heart of palm salad

Pinolillo   Refresco made with roasted corn flour

Plátanos   Plantains, similar to bananas

Refrescos   Water- or milk-based drinks made in a blender with fresh fruit

Tortas   Small sandwiches

DRINKS
WATER & SOFT DRINKS

Although water in Costa Rica is said to be safe to drink, visitors often become ill shortly after arriving in Costa Rica. Play it safe and stick to bottled water, which is readily available. *Agua mineral*, or simply *soda*, is sparkling water in Costa Rica. It's inexpensive and refreshing. Most major brands of soft drinks are also available.

Refrescos, a bit like milk shakes, are my favorite drinks in Costa Rica. They are usually made with fresh fruit juice and milk or water. Among the more common fruits used are mangos, papayas, blackberries (*moras*), and pineapples. Carrot juice (*jugo de zanahoria*) is very common, too. Some of the more unusual refrescos are *horchata* (made with rice flour and a lot of cinnamon) and *pinolillo* (made with roasted corn flour). The former is wonderful; the latter requires an open mind. You might also see egg nog on refrescos lists. Order *un refresco de leche sin hiello* if you are trying to avoid untreated water.

BEER, WINE & LIQUOR

The German presence in Costa Rica over the years has produced several fine beers, which are fairly inexpensive. Heinekin also is available. Costa Rica distills a wide variety of liquors, and you'll save money by ordering these rather than imported brands. Imported wines are available at reasonable prices in the better restaurants throughout the country. You can save a bit of money by ordering a South American wine rather than a European one. Café Rica and Salicsa are two coffee liqueurs made in Costa Rica; the former is very similar to Kahlúa, and the latter is a cream coffee liqueur. Both are delicious.

4. RECOMMENDED BOOKS

General *The Costa Ricans* (Prentice Hall, 1987) by Richard, Karen, and Mavis Biesanz is a well-written account of the politics and culture of Costa Rica.

To learn more about the life and culture of Costa Rica's Talamanca Coast, an area populated by Afro-Caribbean people whose forebears immigrated from Caribbean islands in the early 19th century, pick up a copy of *What Happen, A Folk-History of Costa Rica's Talamanca Coast* (Ecodesarollos, 1977) by Paula Palmer.

The Costa Rica Reader (Grove Weidenfeld, 1989), edited by Marc Edelman and Joanne Kenen, is a collection of essays on Costa Rican topics. For insight into Costa Rican politics, economics, and culture, this weighty book is invaluable.

Natural History *Costa Rica National Parks* (Incafo, 1989), by Mario Boza is published in Madrid and available in both hardbound and softcover editions. It is a beautiful picture book of Costa Rica's national parks. Each of the country's national parks is represented by several color photos and a short description of the park in Spanish and English.

Donald Perry's fascinating *Life Above the Jungle Floor* (Simon & Schuster, 1986) is an account of his research into the life amid the tropical rain-forest canopy. He built a network of trams through the treetops so that he could study this area of great biological and botanical activity.

CHAPTER 2

PLANNING A TRIP TO COSTA RICA

After you decide to visit Costa Rica, you will likely have quite a few questions. This chapter should tell you everything you need to know about planning your trip—from whether you need a visa to how much of an airport tax you'll have to pay when you head home.

1. INFORMATION, ENTRY REQUIREMENTS & MONEY

SOURCES OF INFORMATION

Before you ever leave home, you can get information on Costa Rica by contacting the **Costa Rican National Tourist Bureau** (tel. toll free 800/327-7033).

Once you are in Costa Rica, there are **I.C.T.** (Instituto Costarricense de Turismo) information centers at Juan Santamaría Airport (across from baggage claims and to the left before you go up the stairs after clearing Customs) and beneath the Plaza de la Cultura, Calle 5 between Avenida Central and Avenida 2 (tel. 22-1090). The folks at the latter office are particularly helpful, and they have photo albums from various lodges around the country so you can get an idea of what places look like before you decide to go.

ENTRY REQUIREMENTS

Citizens of the United States, Ireland, Australia, and New Zealand do not need a visa to visit Costa Rica if they intend to stay for 30 days or less. All that is necessary to enter the country is a **Tourist Card,** available on arrival for $2, and proof of citizenship and a photo identity card (driver's license and original birth certificate or voter registration card). A passport is not necessary, but without one you cannot extend your 30-day Tourist Card. If you do have a valid passport and are a citizen of the United States, Australia, New Zealand, or Ireland, you can stay for 30 days without a tourist card. Citizens of Canada and the United Kingdom with valid passports can stay for 90 days without a visa or tourist card. (A passport is necessary if you want to rent a car or change traveler's checks; and it is also much easier to reenter your home country if you have a passport, so I strongly recommend that you acquire one before leaving home.)

In the past it has been very difficult and time consuming to extend a Costa Rican visa. That is easier now, but regulations are still changing. Check with the I.C.T. office in San José to find out what the current regulations are.

MONEY

CASH CURRENCY   The unit of currency in Costa Rica is the colón (¢). In early 1992, there were 135 colónes to the dollar, but because the colón has been devaluing at the rate of about 25 colónes per year, expect the exchange rate to have changed substantially by the time you arrive. Because of this rapid devaluation and accompanying inflation, the Costa Rica section of this book lists prices in U.S. dollars only. In U.S. dollars, prices stay fairly level or increase only slightly from one year to the next.

The colón is divided into 100 centimos. There are notes in denominations of 50, 100, 500, and 1,000 colónes, and coins of 1, 2, 5, 10 and 20 colónes. You might encounter a special issue 5-colón bill that is a popular gift and tourist souvenir. It is valid currency, although it sells for much more than its face value. There are also some older, small-denomination bills and coins floating around.

TRAVELER'S CHECKS   Traveler's checks can be readily changed at banks and hotels. Banks will charge a small commission.

CREDIT CARDS   Major international credit cards accepted readily at hotels throughout Costa Rica include American Express, MasterCard, and VISA. The less expensive hotels tend to take cash only. Many restaurants and stores also accept credit cards. When paying for a hotel room with your credit card, check to see if they charge extra (3 to 5%).

WHAT THINGS COST IN SAN JOSÉ	U.S. $
Taxi from the airport to the city center	12.00
Local telephone call	.02
Deluxe double (at L'Ambiance)	95.00
Moderate double (at Hotel Don Carlos)	57.50
Budget double (at Hotel Bienvenido)	16.10
Moderate lunch for one (at Amstel Grill Room)	6.00
Budget lunch for one (at Soda B & B)	2.50
Deluxe dinner for one, without wine (at Café Parisiene)	20.00
Moderate dinner for one, without wine (at La Cocina de Leña)	10.00
Budget dinner for one, without wine (at Restaurante Campesino)	4.00
Bottle of beer	.80
Coca-Cola	.60
Cup of coffee	.40
Roll of ASA 100 Kodacolor film, 24 exposures	7.25
Admission to the Jade Museum	Free
Movie ticket	1.50
Ticket at Melico Salazar Theater	3.00

2. WHEN TO GO — CLIMATE, HOLIDAYS & EVENTS

CLIMATE Costa Rica is a tropical country and has distinct wet and dry seasons—but some parts are rainy all year and others are very dry and sunny for most of the year. Temperatures vary primarily with elevation, not with season. On the coasts it is hot all year, while up in the mountains it can be quite cool at night any time of year.

Generally speaking, the rainy season is from May to November, and the dry season is from December to April. In Guanacaste, the dry northwestern province, the dry season lasts several weeks longer. Even in the rainy season, days often start out sunny, with rain falling in the afternoon and evening. On the Atlantic (Caribbean Sea) Coast, especially south of Puerto Limón, you can count on rain all year round. The best overall time of year to visit is December and January, when everything is still green from the rains, but the sky is clear.

AVERAGE MONTHLY TEMPERATURES AND RAINFALL IN SAN JOSÉ

Month	Temp [°F]	Temp. [°C]	Days of Rain
Jan	66	19	1
Feb	66	19	0
Mar	69	20.5	1
Apr	71	21.5	4
May	71	21.5	17
June	71	21.5	20
July	70	21	18
Aug	70	21	19
Sept	71	21.5	20
Oct	69	20.5	22
Nov	68	20	14
Dec	67	19.5	4

COSTA RICA CALENDAR OF EVENTS

Because Costa Rica is a Roman Catholic country, most of its holidays and celebrations are church related. The major celebrations of the year are Christmas, New Year's, and Easter, which are celebrated for several days. Keep in mind that Holy Week is the biggest holiday time in Costa Rica, and many families head for the beach (this is the last holiday before school starts). Also, there is no public transportation on Holy Thursday or Good Friday.

MARCH OR APRIL

☐ **Holy Week** (week before Easter), San José and all over the country. Religious processions in the streets.

OCTOBER

☐ **Carnival,** Puerto Limón. For several days leading up to October 12 (Columbus or Discovery of America Day).

DECEMBER

☐ **Carnival,** San José. Last week of December.

HOLIDAYS   Official holidays in Costa Rica include January 1, New Year's Day; March 19, St. Joseph's Day; Thursday and Friday of Holy Week (the week prior to Easter); April 11, Juan Santamaría's Day; May 1, Labor Day; June 29, Saints Peter and Paul Day; July 25, annexation of the province of Guanacaste; August 2, Virgin of Los Angeles's Day; August 15, Mother's Day; September 15, Independence Day; October 12, Discovery of America; December 8, Immaculate Conception of the Virgin Mary; December 25, Christmas Day; December 31, New Year's Eve.

3. HEALTH, INSURANCE & OTHER CONCERNS

HEALTH   Vaccinations   No vaccinations are required for a visit to Costa Rica, Guatemala, or Belize, unless you are coming from an area where yellow fever exists. However, because sanitation is generally not as good as it is in other developed countries, you may be exposed to diseases for which you may wish to get vaccinations: typhoid, polio, tetanus, and infectious hepatitis (gamma globulin). If you are planning to stay in major cities, you stand little risk of encountering any of these diseases, but if you venture out into remote regions of the country, you stand a higher risk.

Malaria is found in the lowlands on both coasts. Although it is rarely found in urban areas, it is still a problem in remote wooded regions. Malaria prophylaxes are available, but several have side effects and others are of questionable effectiveness. Consult your doctor or your local health board as to what is currently considered the best preventative treatment for malaria.

In recent years, an outbreak of cholera has been spreading through Latin America, and though Costa Rica has not been free of this disease, it has one of the lowest incidence levels. This is largely due to an extensive public awareness campaign that has promoted good hygiene and increased sanitation. You need not worry about contracting cholera while you are here; however, it is still advisable to avoid ceviche, the raw seafood salad that is so popular here. Shellfish is a known carrier of cholera; if not properly cooked it can transmit the disease.

INSURANCE   Before leaving on your trip, contact your health-insurance company and find out whether your insurance will cover you while you are away. If not, contact a travel agent and ask about travel health-insurance policies. A travel agent can also tell you about trip insurance to cover cancellations or loss of baggage. If you have homeowner's or renter's insurance, you may be covered against theft and loss even while you are on vacation. Be sure to check this before taking out additional insurance. Some credit cards provide trip insurance when you charge an airline ticket, but be sure to check with your credit-card company. If you decide that your current insurance is inadequate, you can contact your travel agent for information on various types of travel insurance, including insurance against cancellation of a prepaid tour should this become necessary. Or you can contact **Mutual of Omaha,** 3201 Farnam St., Omaha, NE 68131 (tel. toll free 800/228-9792); **Richard Wallach,** P.O. Box 480, Middleburg, VA 22117 (tel. toll free 800/237-6615); or **Access America, Inc.,** 6600 W. Broad St., Richmond, VA 23230 (tel. 804/285-3300 or toll free 800/424-3391).

WHAT TO PACK Clothing Costa Rica is a tropical country, so to stay comfortable bring lightweight, natural-fiber clothing. In the rainy season an umbrella, not a raincoat (which is too hot), is necessary. Nights at any time of year can be cool in San José and in the mountains, so also bring a wool sweater or jacket. Good walking shoes are a must if you plan to visit any of the national park trails.

Other Items A bathing suit is a must, and a mask and snorkel come in handy. Insect repellent is invaluable, and I have heard that citronella-based repellents, available at natural food stores, are sometimes more effective than chemical repellents. Sunscreen, an absolute necessity, is available in Costa Rica but is more expensive than in the United States. Be sure to have waterproof sunscreen if you plan to go rafting. Bring plenty of film and spare batteries for your camera. A water-filter straw, available in camping supply stores, is a convenient way to be sure you always have purified water to drink. The straws are inexpensive and disposable. A Swiss army knife almost always comes in handy at some point in a trip, as does a small sewing kit.

4. TIPS FOR THE DISABLED, SENIORS, SINGLES & STUDENTS

For the Disabled In general, there are few handicapped-accessible buildings in Costa Rica. In San José, sidewalks are crowded and uneven.

For Seniors Many airlines now offer senior-citizen discounts, so be sure to ask about these when making reservations. Due to its temperate climate, stable government, low cost of living, and friendly *pensionado* program, Costa Rica is popular with retirees from North America. There are excellent medical facilities in San José, and plenty of community organizations to help retirees feel at home. If you would like to learn more about visiting or retiring in Costa Rica, contact the **Costa Rican National Tourist Board,** P.O. Box 777-1000, San José, Costa Rica (tel. toll free 800/327-7033).

Because of the long dry season, the beaches and resorts of the Nicoya Peninsula are the most popular places with North American seniors.

Elderhostel, 75 Federal St., Boston, MA 02110 (tel. 617/426-7788), offers very popular study tours for seniors in Costa Rica.

For Singles You'll pay the same penalty here that you would elsewhere: Rooms are more expensive if you aren't traveling in a pair.

For Students Costa Rica is the only country in Central America with a network of hostels that are affiliated with the International Youth Hostel Federation. There are hostels in San José, at Lake Arenal, in Rincón de la Vieja National Park, and at Guayabo National Monument. In San José, there is also a student travel agency: **OTEC,** Edificio Ferencz, Calle 3 between avenidas 1 and 3, 275 meters north of the National Theater (tel. 55-0554 or 22-0866). If you already have an international student identity card, you can use your card to get discounts on hotels, meals, and international flights. If you don't have one, stop by the OTEC office with a passport photo; for a small fee, they'll prepare you one.

Students interested in a working vacation in Costa Rica should contact the **Council on International Educational Exchange (C.I.E.E.),** 205 E. 42nd St.,

New York, NY 10017 (tel. 212/661-1450). This organization also issues official student identity cards and has offices all over the United States.

5. ALTERNATIVE/ADVENTURE TRAVEL

LANGUAGE PROGRAMS

Many people come to Costa Rica to study Spanish. There are several schools in San José that offer courses of varying durations. Spanish schools can also arrange for homestays with a middle-class Tico family that will help you speak only Spanish in your daily life. Classes are intensive and often one-on-one. Listed below are some of the larger and more popular Spanish-language schools.

Forester Instituto Internacional, Apdo. 6945, 1000 San José (tel. 506/25-3155, 25-0135, or 25-1649; fax 506/25-9236), is located 75 meters south of the Automercado in the Los Yoses district of San José. The school offers 2-, 3-, and 4-week programs. Classes start the first Monday of every month, and four hours of class are held five days a week. Prices range from $460 for four weeks (without homestay) to $880 for a 4-week language and culture course (including cultural activities and excursions) with homestay.

Centro Lingüístico Conversa, Apdo. 17, Centro Colón, San José (tel. 506/21-7649 or 33-2418; fax 506/33-2418), provides one of the most attractive environments for studying Spanish at its El Pedregal farm 10 miles west of San José. A 4-week course costs $1,500 for one person and $2,890 for married couples. Price includes instruction, text materials, room and board, laundry services, and even airport pick up and drop off. Courses are offered every month.

Instituto Interamericano de Idiomas (Intensa), Apdo. 8110-1000, San José (tel. 506/24-6353 or 25-6009), is on Calle 33 between avenidas 5 and 7 in the Barrio Escalante neighborhood of San José. It offers 2- to 4-week programs. A 4-week program with homestay costs $765.

Instituto Latinoamericano de Idiomas, Apdo. 1001, San Pedro 2050 (tel. 506/25-2495; fax 506/4765; in the United States, 818/843-1226; in Canada, 416/964-3388), is one block east of the church, then four blocks south and half a block east (no kidding, this really is the street address for the school). Four weeks with homestay here cost $1,015.

Instituto Universal de Idiomas, Apdo. 751-2150, Moravia (tel. 506/57-0441; fax 506/23-9917), is located on Avenida 2 at the corner of Calle 9. The most conveniently located school, it charges only $680 for a 4-week course (only three hours per day) with homestay.

ECOTOURISM & ADVENTURE TRAVEL

Ecotourism (from the term "ecological tourism") is the word these days in Costa Rica. With the growing awareness of the value of tropical forests and the interest in visiting rain forests, dozens of lodges and tour companies have sprung up to cater to the tourists interested in enjoying the natural beauties of Costa Rica. These lodges are located in out-of-the-way locations, sometimes deep in the heart of a forest and sometimes on a farm with only a tiny bit of natural forest. However, they all have one thing in common: They cater to environmentally aware people with an interest in nature. Horseback riding, rafting, kayaking, hiking, and bird-watching are among the popular activities offered at these lodges.

Some U.S. tour operators that offer adventure tour packages to Costa Rica are the following: **Wilderness Travel,** 801 Allston Way, Berkeley, CA 94710 (tel. 510/548-

0420, or toll free 800/247-6700); **Overseas Adventure Travel,** 349 Broadway, Cambridge, MA 02139 (tel. 617/876-0533, or toll free 800/221-0814); **Costa Rica Connection,** 958 Higuera St., San Luis Obispo, CA 93401 (tel. 805/543-8823, or toll free 800/345-7422); and **International Expeditions,** 1776 Independence Court, Birmingham, AL 35216 (tel. 205/870-5550, or toll free 800/633-4734).

There are also dozens of tour companies in San José that offer nature-related tours from one-day rafting trips to week-long adventures. Since their tours are usually held only when there are enough interested people, it pays to contact a few of the companies and find out what they might be doing when you plan to be in Costa Rica. The following is a list of some of the companies.

Costa Rica Expeditions, Calle Central and Avenida 3, Apdo. 6941, San José (tel. 506/22-0333), offers tours of Monteverde and Tortuguero and white-water rafting.

Tikal Tour Operators, Apdo. 6398-1000, San José (tel. 506/23-2811; fax 506/23-1916), offers rafting, diving, and volcano trips and visits to Braulio Carrillo National Park, Rincon de la Vieja National Park, Monteverde and other parks.

Geotour, Apdo. 469 Y-Griega 1011, San José (tel. 506/34-1867; fax 506/53-6338), offers tours of Braulio Carrillo National Park, Carara Biological Reserve, and Cahuita National Park.

If your interest is limited to rafting or sea kayaking, contact **Rios Tropicales,** Apdo. 472-1200, Pavas (tel. 506/33-6455; fax 506/55-4354). This company operates several 1- to 10-day raft trips, as well as sea-kayaking trips at Manuel Antonio.

Sun Tours, P.O. Box 1195, 1250 Escazú (tel. 506/55-2011 or 55-3418; fax 506/55-4410) specializes in small country lodges for nature-oriented travelers.

6. GETTING THERE

BY PLANE

It takes between three and six hours to fly to Costa Rica from most U.S. cities, and as Costa Rica becomes more and more popular with North American travelers, more flights are being added to the San José airport. The following airlines currently serve Costa Rica from the United States, using the gateway cities listed.

American Airlines (tel. toll free 800/433-7300) has daily flights from Miami and Dallas/Fort Worth. **Aviateca-Guatemalan** (tel. toll free 800/327-9832) flies from Los Angeles, Houston, Miami, and New Orleans. **Continental** (tel. toll free 800/231-0856) offers flights daily from Houston. **Lacsa-Costa Rican** (tel. 800/225-2272) has service from New York, Miami, New Orleans, Los Angeles, and San Francisco. **Mexicana** (tel. toll free 800/531-7921) has flights from New York, Chicago, Denver, Miami, Dallas/Fort Worth, San Antonio, Los Angeles, San Jose (California), and San Francisco. **Sahsa-Honduran** (tel. toll free 800/327-1225) flies from Chicago, New York, Houston, and New Orleans. **Taca-El Salvadoran** (tel. toll free 800/535-8780) offers flights from Los Angeles, San Francisco, Houston, New Orleans, Miami, Washington, and New York. **United Airlines** (tel. toll free 800/241-6522) has flights from Miami.

BEST-FOR-THE-BUDGET In recent years airfares have been very unstable. Several major carriers have gone out of business, and the recession has had an adverse effect on airfares. Such instability makes it very difficult to quote an airline ticket price, but at press time, special fares from New York or Los Angeles were between $300 and $350. (Only two months earlier the lowest fares had been between $650 and $850.) Regardless of how much the cheapest ticket costs when you decide to fly, you can bet

FROMMER'S SMART TRAVELER: AIRFARES

1. Check the ads for discounted plane tickets in the Sunday travel section of major-city newspapers. These tickets can be $100 to $200 cheaper than the lowest standard airfare.
2. Try getting a discounted ticket from your departure city to one of the Central American gateway cities (Miami, New Orleans, Houston, or Los Angeles), and combine this with a discount ticket from one of those cities on to Costa Rica.
3. Shop all the airlines that fly to Costa Rica, including the small Central American airlines that travel agents don't usually check.
4. You'll usually save money if you take a "milk run" (flight that makes several stops) rather than a direct flight.
5. Always ask for the lowest-priced fare, which will usually be a mid-week departure. Be flexible and you'll save money.

it will have some restrictions—it will almost certainly be nonrefundable, and you may have to pay within 24 hours of making a reservation. You may or may not have to buy the ticket in advance (anywhere from one week to 30 days). You will also likely have to stay over a weekend and limit your stay to 30 days or less.

BUCKET SHOPS   You can shave a little bit off these ticket prices by purchasing your ticket from what is known as a bucket shop. These ticketing agencies sell discounted tickets on major airlines; although the tickets have as many, and sometimes more, restrictions as an APEX (advance purchase excursion) ticket, they can help you save money. You'll find bucket-shop listings—usually just a column of destinations with prices beside them—in the Sunday travel sections of major-city newspapers. You'll almost never get the ticket for the advertised price, but you will probably get it for less than the airline would sell it to you.

REGULAR AIRFARES   A coach-class seat will run you slightly more than $900, and a first-class seat will cost from $1,200 to $1,600.

BY BUS

There is regular bus service between Panama City, Panama, and Managua, Nicaragua. The former is an 18-hour trip; the latter is only 10 hours. Buses leave Panama City at 10pm and leave Managua at 1, 2, 3, 4, 5, and 6am.

BY CAR

Although it is theoretically possible to travel to Costa Rica by car, in practice it is now very difficult, especially for U.S. citizens. The Interamerican Highway (also known as the Panamerican Highway) passes through El Salvador, Honduras, and Nicaragua after leaving Guatemala and before reaching Costa Rica. All three of these countries can be problematic for travelers because of the continuing internal strife and visa formalities. I do not recommend trying to drive to Costa Rica at this time.

PACKAGE TOURS

It is sometimes cheaper to purchase an airfare-and-hotel package rather than buy an airline ticket only. This is especially true if airfares happen to be in a high period and if you will be traveling with a companion. The best way to find out about these package tours is to contact a travel agent.

Once you are in Costa Rica, there are dozens of tour companies that will arrange overnight and longer tours to remote lodges that cater to ecotourists. For information on some of these companies, see the Alternative/Adventure Travel section above.

7. SUGGESTED ITINERARIES

HIGHLIGHTS

The following are the most important places to visit in Costa Rica:
1. San José
2. Manuel Antonio
3. Monteverde
4. Jacó Beach
5. Cahuita/Puerto Viejo
6. Tortuguero National Park
7. Irazú Volcano
8. Poás Volcano
9. The Nicoya Peninsula
10. Orosi Valley

PLANNING YOUR ITINERARY

IF YOU HAVE ONE WEEK

Day 1: Visit the museums and the National Theater in San José.
Day 2: Make an excursion to the Orosi Valley, Lankester Gardens, and Irazú Volcano.
Days 3 and 4: Travel to Monteverde and spend a day exploring the cloud forest preserve.
Days 5 and 6: Travel to Manuel Antonio National Park and spend a day on the beautiful beaches.
Day 7: Return to San José.

IF YOU HAVE TWO WEEKS

Days 1 and 2: Visit the museums and National Theater in San José.
Day 3: Make an excursion to the Orosi Valley, Lankester Gardens, and Irazú Volcano, or go rafting.
Days 4, 5, and 6: Travel to Monteverde and spend two days exploring the cloud forest.
Days 7 through 9: Explore the beaches and trails of Manuel Antonio National Park.
Day 10: Travel to Lake Arenal.
Day 11: Return to San José.
Days 12 and 13: Travel by canal to Tortuguero National Park and spend a day there.
Day 14: Return to San José.

IF YOU HAVE THREE WEEKS

Follow the outline above for "If You Have Two Weeks." For your third week, explore the many beaches of the Nicoya Peninsula, visit another remote lodge, go rafting, visit more national parks, or spend part of your time on Jacó Beach on the Pacific Coast and part of your time at Cahuita National Park on the Caribbean Sea Coast.

FROMMER'S FAVORITE
COSTA RICA EXPERIENCES

A Day at Manuel Antonio National Park   This idyllic park contains three gorgeous beaches with white sand, turquoise water, and a backdrop of dense jungle-covered hills. Activities here include snorkeling, bodysurfing, and hiking through several jungle trails. Monkeys are often spotted in the trees near the beaches.

Hiking Through the Monteverde Cloud Forest Preserve Cloud forests are to the mountains what the rain forests are to the lowlands: a dense and diverse forest habitat filled with an amazing variety of plant, insect, and animal life, including more than a dozen species of hummingbirds and one of the most beautiful birds on earth, the colorful quetzal.

A Night at the San José National Theater   Built in the late 19th century with money raised through a tax on coffee exports, this classic opera house is still serving up the best cultural performances in the country. The theater is being renovated due to the 1991 earthquake, but hopefully will be open when you visit.

A Trip to the Rim of a Volcano   Drive to the rim of either Poás or Irazú and gaze down into the sulfurous pits. Poás is lush and green, whereas Irazú is gray and barren, but both offer spectacular views if you arrive before the clouds close in.

A Day of White-Water Rafting   Costa Rica offers some of the best white-water rafting opportunities in the world. The water is warm, the mountains are green, and the rapids are as rough as you want.

Cruising the Tortuguero Canals   North of Limón, on the Caribbean coast, there are no roads, only canals through the wilderness. A boat trip through these canals to Tortuguero National Park is as thrilling as exploring the Amazon.

THEMED CHOICES

The most common choice for a themed vacation in Costa Rica is to make it a **naturalist tour** by visiting as many of the national parks and private nature reserves as you can in the amount of time available. Another possible theme would be to sample as many of the different **beaches** as you can.

8. GETTING AROUND

BY PLANE

Surprisingly, getting around by air is one of the most economical ways to see Costa Rica if you plan ahead. Because the country is quite small, the flights are short and, luckily, inexpensive. **Sansa,** the domestic airline of Costa Rica, has flights Monday through Saturday between San José and Quepos (Manuel Antonio); Monday, Wednesday, Friday, and Saturday to Tamarindo (Nicoya Peninsula); and Tuesday, Thursday, and Saturday to Barra Colorado (Tortuguero National Park). The airline's offices are at Calle 24 between Avenida Central and Avenida 1 (tel. 33-3258 or 33-0397). These flights last between 20 and 50 minutes. Fares range from $24 to $50 round-trip. You must check in at the downtown office, from which a free shuttle bus will take you to the airport.

Sansa now has competition from Travelair (tel. 32-7883 or 20-3054), which charges substantially more for flights to the same destinations, but is popular because it flies daily and is extremely punctual. Fares on Travelair range from $60 round-trip to Quepos (Manuel Antonio) to $114 round-trip to Tamarindo.

BY BUS

This is by far the best way to visit most of Costa Rica. Buses are inexpensive, well maintained, uncrowded, and they go nearly everywhere. There are three types of buses: local buses are the cheapest and slowest. They stop frequently and are generally a bit dilapidated. Express buses run between San José and most beach towns and major cities; they sometimes only operate on weekends and holidays. A few luxury buses and minibuses drive to destinations frequented by foreign tourists. For details on how to get to various destinations from San José, see the Getting There heading of each section in the regional chapters.

BY CAR

CAR RENTALS Renting a car in Costa Rica is not something to be entered into lightly. Costa Rica has the second highest accident rate per capita in the world. In addition, since all rental cars in Costa Rica bear special license plates, they are readily identifiable to thieves. Nothing is ever safe in a car in Costa Rica, although parking in guarded parking lots helps. The tourist plates also signal police that they can extort money from unwary tourist motorists. Never pay money directly to a police officer who stops you for any traffic violation. Before driving off with a rental car, be sure that you inspect the exterior and point out to the rental-company representative every tiny scratch, dent, tear, or any other damage. It is a common practice with Costa Rican car-rental companies to claim that you owe payment for damages the company finds when you return the car.

On the other hand, renting a car allows you much greater freedom to explore remote areas of the country, and most roads are in fairly good condition. If after weighing the alternatives, you decide you want to rent a car, read on.

Avis, Budget, Hertz, and **National** car-rental agencies all have offices in Costa Rica. You will save a considerable amount on a car rental if you make a reservation in your home country at least two weeks before you need the car. The least-expensive Budget car available rents for about $250 per week, plus insurance and tax (total of around $385) in San José, but if you book this same car in advance from the United States, you can get it for $175 per week, plus insurance and tax (total of around $300). See the Getting Around section of the San José chapter for details on renting a car in San José. Cars can also be rented in Quepos, Jacó, and Limón.

GASOLINE Regular gasoline is what is most readily available in Costa Rica. Most rental cars take regular.

DRIVING RULES To rent a car in Costa Rica, you must be 25 years old and have a passport. A foreign driver's license is valid for the first three months that you are in Costa Rica. Use of seat belts is required for driver and passengers. Motorcyclists must wear a helmet. Highway police use radar, so keep to the speed limit if you don't want to get pulled over.

MAPS Car-rental agencies and the I.C.T. information centers (see "Information, Entry Requirements & Money" at the beginning of this chapter) at the airport and in downtown San José have adequate road maps.

BREAKDOWNS If your car should break down and you are unable to get it off the road, place a pile of leaves and/or tree branches in the road 100 feet on either side of the car to warn approaching drivers.

BY FERRY

There are two ferries operating across the Gulf of Nicoya between Puntarenas and the Nicoya Peninsula. The car ferry leaves from the north side of the peninsula between calles 33 and 35 and goes to the town of Naranjo. The passenger ferry leaves from behind the market at the north end of Calle 2 and goes to Paquerra. The Paquerra ferry operates only Monday through Saturday.

HITCHHIKING

Although buses go to most places in Costa Rica, they can be infrequent in the remote regions, and consequently local people often hitchhike to get to their destination sooner. If you are driving a car, people will frequently ask you for a ride. If you are hitching yourself, keep in mind that if a bus doesn't go to your destination, there probably aren't too many cars going there either. Good luck.

LOCATING ADDRESSES

There are no street addresses in Costa Rica, at least not often. Addresses are given as a set of coordinates such as "Calle 3 between Avenida Central and Avenida 1." Many addresses include additional information such as the number of meters or *varas* (an old Spanish measurement roughly equal to a yard) from a specified intersection or some other well-known landmark. Often the additional information is only useful if you are familiar with the area. In San José many addresses use distances from the Coca-Cola bottling plant that once stood near the market. The bottling plant is long gone, but the address descriptions remain. In outlying neighborhoods, addresses can become long directions such as "50 meters south of the old church, then 100 meters east, then 20 meters south." Luckily for the visitor, most addresses are straightforward.

9. ENJOYING COSTA RICA ON A BUDGET

In the past, Mexico was where North Americans headed when they wanted an inexpensive yet exotic holiday. Today many cities in Mexico are nearly as expensive as places back home. Costa Rica, on the other hand, is still a travel bargain. It's close to home, and you can still get a bed for $4 a night if that is what you are looking for. If you want to spend more money, there are excellent values to be had throughout the country.

THE $35-A-DAY BUDGET

The premise of this book is that you can enjoy Costa Rica, Guatemala, and Belize on a budget of $35 per day per person. You should have absolutely no problem doing so if you don't need to stay in a first-class high-rise or resort hotel. Keep in mind that the $35-a-day budget covers only lodging and three meals a day, not transportation costs, museum admissions, cost of souvenirs, and so forth. However, all of these are also quite inexpensive, and if you are willing to stay in the lowest-budget accommodations recommended in this book, you should easily be able to include all your transportation and many other costs in your $35 a day.

This is roughly how I break down daily costs: $18 per person (based on double occupancy) for a room, $3 for breakfast, $5 for lunch, and $9 for dinner. Many young travelers can actually get by on about $10 per day. However, a $35 daily budget should allow you to live quite well. For those who prefer a bit more luxury, I have included information on hotels and restaurants that are worth the extra bucks. For those who are traveling on a student's or backpacker's budget, there is also plenty of information.

SAVING MONEY ON ACCOMMODATIONS

Best Budget Bets   Your best way to save money on accommodations in Costa Rica is to choose carefully where you want to go. If you are heading to a beach resort that primarily has expensive rooms and you want one of the handful of budget rooms in town, book early (everybody wants those cheap rooms). Montezuma and Puerto Viejo are the backpackers' hangouts in Costa Rica these days.

Seasonal and Other Discounts   During the rainy season, many hotels offer substantial discounts, especially those at the beaches. Surfers and fishermen get discounts at west coast beach hotels (since they tend to come in the rainy season). Some beach hotels also have weekly rates.

Other Money-Saving Strategies   If you want to go to Manuel Antonio on a backpacker's budget, you'll have to stay in Quepos (or put up with less-than-clean accommodations). If you plan on staying for a month or more, look into renting a room or apartment.

For young travelers, there are a number of **IYHF**-affiliated hostels in Costa Rica.

SAVING MONEY ON MEALS

Best Budget Bets   The cheapest place to eat in Costa Rica will always be a *soda,* the equivalent of a diner in the United States. The food might not be great, but the prices can't be beat. If you like rice and black beans, you can save even more money. Ticos eat rice and beans (with something else on the side) at every meal.

Other Money-Saving Strategies   Quite a few hotels in Costa Rica come with kitchenettes, especially those at the beaches. If you visit the local market and fix your own meals, you can save considerably. I try to buy as much and as many different types of tropical fruits as I can when I'm here. You might want to consider buying a little immersion heating coil and a Costa Rican reusable drip-coffee bag. With these two items and a cup, you can make your own fresh coffee every morning, and the coffee here is as fresh as it comes (you have to wait for them to roast it at the market).

SAVING MONEY ON SIGHT-SEEING & ENTERTAINMENT

Best Budget Bets   Museum admissions in San José are already so low that there is no need to worry about special discounts (there aren't any). Much of the entertainment in San José is free; marimba bands play daily outside the National Theater, and it doesn't cost anything to enjoy the bands at La Esmeralda or the Soda Palace. Even the National Theater is quite cheap if you're willing to settle for a balcony seat; even if you're not and want to hobnob with Costa Rica's landed gentry, the price won't break your bank.

SAVING MONEY ON SHOPPING

Costa Rica doesn't have the wide variety of traditional handicrafts that neighboring countries have (in fact, many Guatemalan crafts and textiles are sold in Costa Rica), so if you're including Guatemala on your trip to Central America, I suggest that you save your money to spend there. There are a few great buys in Costa Rica, though.

Best Buys   One of Costa Rica's best buys is **coffee.** It's hard to get fresher coffee anywhere. The air in the streets around the San José market is redolent with the smell of roasting coffee beans. Stop in at **Café Trebol,** Calle 8 between avenidas Central and 1 (no phone), and you can pick up a pound of beans hot from the roaster for about $1. In tourist shops all over town, this same bag of coffee beans sells for $4 or $5. When buying coffee be sure to buy only bags labeled *100% puro;* otherwise, you will get coffee that has already had sugar added to it (that's the way they like it down here). Also, make sure you buy only whole beans because Costa Rican grinds are too fine for standard drip-filter coffee makers.

Other good buys in Costa Rica are gold and silver reproductions of Pre-Columbian **jewelry,** which you'll find in shops all over San José. You'll probably recognize many of the designs from pieces on display in museums around town. Reproductions of small **carved stone statues** from Pre-Columbian times are additional good buys which are surprisingly light and very authentic looking. You'll also find tropical hardwoods carved into all manner of jewelry, bowls, figurines, and knickknacks. Some are quite expensive, others are quite reasonably priced, but all are beautiful.

Although I personally find them far too gaudy, brightly painted **miniature ox carts** are a symbol of Costa Rica. Once sugarcane was carried on similar ox carts. Today, even though a few ox carts are still used in various parts of the country, painted ones such as these are strictly tourist items. Sarchí is the ox-cart factory capital and is included on many tours. Large wood-and-leather **rocking chairs** also are manufactured in Sarchí.

Markets   Every town in Costa Rica has a market. It may be open only weekly or may be open daily, but it's there. This is the best place to buy fresh fruits and vegetables. Some markets, such as the one in San José, also sell souvenirs and countless other useful items. Take a look in one of the kitchen utensil stalls; you'll probably find dozens of interesting and inexpensive little gadgets. Be sure to keep close tabs on your money at all times because markets are notorious haunts of pickpockets.

Bargaining   You should always try to bargain in markets and with street vendors. It's expected and can save you quite a bit. Tourist prices are always higher, so if you are shopping for souvenirs (especially on the Plaza de Cultura in San José), bargain hard.

SAVING MONEY ON TRANSPORTATION

By Plane   **Sansa,** Costa Rica's domestic airline, is one of the country's best bargains. For around $12 and in only 20 minutes, you can fly to Quepos (for Manuel Antonio National Park beaches). Don't forget to take advantage of the free shuttle bus Sansa runs between their downtown offices and the airport.

By Bus   It is hard to beat the low fares on Costa Rica's intercity buses. The highways are good, so most bus rides are quite comfortable.

By Car   The way to save money on a rental car is to reserve from your home country at least two weeks before you need the car. You can save as much as $85 per week this way. Also check to see if your credit card or auto insurance pays your collision damage waiver. You may not have to buy all that insurance if it does.

SAVING MONEY ON SERVICES & OTHER TRANSACTIONS

Tipping   Tipping is not necessary in restaurants, where a 10% service charge is always added to your bill (along with 10% tax). If service was particularly good, you can leave a little at your own discretion, but it is not mandatory. Porters and bellhops get around 60¢ per bag. Taxi fares must be negotiated prior to getting into a taxi, and therefore tips are unnecessary.

Money Changing and Credit Cards   Although it is illegal to change money on the black market (which offers a slightly better rate than the banks do), it is possible to change money in many hotels and avoid the service charge that banks charge. You may even get a better rate at your hotel. By using your credit card, you can lock in that day's official exchange rate and avoid having to pay bank service charges on changing money.

Telephone   The number for the AT&T USA direct operator is 114. You can place collect and calling-card calls through this English-speaking operator at considerable savings over normal Costa Rican telephone rates.

COSTA RICA

American Express Costa Rica's only American Express office is in San José, Calle 1 between Avenida Central and Avenida 1 (tel. 33-0044). Open Monday to Friday from 8am to 5:30pm.

Business Hours Banks are open Monday to Friday from 9am to 3pm. Bars are open until 1 or 2am. Offices are open Monday to Friday from 8am to 5pm (closed for two hours at lunch). Stores are open Monday to Saturday from 9am to 7pm. Many restaurants stay open 24 hours, while others close between meals.

Camera/Film Most types of film except Kodachrome are available but expensive.

Climate See "When to Go" in this chapter.

Crime See "Safety," below.

Currency See "Information, Entry Requirements & Money" in this chapter.

Customs You can bring in half a kilo of tobacco products, three liters of liquor, and two cameras duty free.

Documents Required See "Information, Entry Requirements & Money" in this chapter.

Driving Rules See "Getting Around" in this chapter.

Drug Laws Drug laws in Costa Rica are strict, so stay away from marijuana and cocaine. You'll also need a prescription from a doctor or lab results to have prescriptions filled in Costa Rica.

Drugstores A drugstore in Costa Rica is a *farmacia*. You'll find at least one in nearly every town.

Electricity The standard in Costa Rica is the same as in the United States: 110 volts.

Embassies and Consulates The **United States Consulate,** in front of Centro Comercial, San José, road to Pavas (tel. 20-3939); **Canadian Embassy,** Calle 3 and Avenida Central, San José (tel. 55-3522); **British Embassy,** Paseo Colón between calles 38 and 40, San José (tel. 21-5566).

Emergencies For an **ambulance** call 21-5818; to report a **fire** call 118; to contact the **police** call 117, or 127 outside cities.

Etiquette Ticos tend to dress conservatively and treat everyone very respectfully. Both sexes shake hands.

Hitchhiking This is permitted. If you're trying to get to remote parks or volcanoes, however, there usually isn't much traffic on such roads. Buses, which are quite inexpensive, go almost everywhere in the country.

Holidays See "When to Go" in this chapter.

Information See "Information, Entry Requirements & Money" in this chapter. Also see individual city chapters for local information offices.

Language Spanish is the official language of Costa Rica. *Berlitz Latin-American Spanish* (Berlitz Guides, 1989) is probably the best phrase book to bring with you.

Laundry For listings of laundromats, see individual city and town sections.

Liquor Laws Alcoholic beverages are sold every day of the week throughout the year, with the exception of the two days before Easter and the two days before and after a presidential election.

Mail Mail to the United States takes about one week. A letter to the United States costs 26¢, and postcards cost 22¢. A post office is called a *correo* in Spanish. You can get stamps either at the post office or at a newsstand.

Theft from the San José post office has become quite common, so do not send anything of value from this post office. Also, before sending a reservation payment to a hotel, find out if they have a U.S. mailing address; many now do.

Maps The **Costa Rican National Tourist Bureau (I.C.T.)** (see "Information, Entry Requirements & Money," above) can provide you with good free maps of both Costa Rica and San José.

Newspapers/Magazines   There are three Spanish-language dailys in Costa Rica and one English-language weekly, the *Tico Times*. In addition, you can get *Time, Newsweek,* and several U.S. newspapers at hotel gift shops and a few of the bookstores in San José.

Passports   See "Information, Entry Requirements & Money" in this chapter.

Pets   If you want to bring your cat or dog, be sure that it has current vaccinations against rabies and distemper.

Police   The number to call for the **Policia de Transito** is 27-7150 or 27-8030.

Radio/TV   Costa Rica has one English-language television station. In addition, satellite cable TV from the United States is available in most hotels. There are more than 100 radio stations on the AM and FM dials.

Restrooms   These are called *servicios sanitarios* and are marked *damas* for women and *hombres* or *caballeros* for men.

Safety   Although most of Costa Rica is very safe, it is known for its pickpockets. Never carry a wallet in your back pocket. In fact, never carry anything of value in pants pockets. A woman should keep a tight grip on her purse (keep it tucked under your arm). Don't leave valuables in your hotel room. Don't park a car on the street in Costa Rica; there are plenty of public parking lots around San José.

Because all rental cars have special plates, they are easily spotted by thieves who know that such cars are likely to be full of expensive camera equipment, money, and so on. Don't ever leave anything of value in a car parked on the street, not even for a moment. Public intercity buses are also frequent targets of stealthy thieves. Never check your bags into the hold of a bus if you can avoid it. If this cannot be avoided, keep your eye on what leaves the hold any time the bus stops. If you put your bags in an overhead rack, be sure you can see the bag at all times. Try not to fall asleep.

Taxes   All hotels charge around 15% tax, and restaurants charge 10% tax and also add on a 10% service charge. There is an airport departure tax of $4.

Telephone   Costa Rica has an excellent phone system, with a dial tone similar to that heard in the United States. Phone numbers in Costa Rica have six digits. There is one telephone book for all of Costa Rica. A pay phone costs ¢2 (2¢), and most accept only 4¢ coins. You can get an AT&T operator to make calling-card and collect calls by dialing 114 (pay phones require deposit of coins). The Costa Rican telephone system allows direct international dialing, but it is expensive.

Time   Costa Rica is on Central Standard Time, six hours behind Greenwich Mean Time.

Tipping   See "Saving Money on Services and Transactions" in this chapter.

Tourist Offices   See "Information, Entry Requirements & Money" in this chapter. Also see specific cities.

Visas   See "Information, Entry Requirements & Money" in this chapter.

Water   Although the water throughout Costa Rica is said to be safe to drink, many tourists do get sick within a few days of arriving in Costa Rica. Play it safe—stick to bottled drinks as much as possible and avoid ice.

SAN JOSÉ

In the center of San José is an open-air market where the air smells of roasting coffee. It's near the Coca-Cola. Of course, everyone knows what the Coca-Cola is: the area where once stood the Coca-Cola bottling plant. The address of every business in this neighborhood—stores, restaurants, hotels, and offices—is measured from the Coca-Cola, even though it's long gone. That's just the way things are in San José. Although it has all the trappings of a modern cosmopolitan city, from an opera house to a McDonald's, there are no street addresses. Everything is "so many *varas*"—an archaic measurement about equal to a yard—"from such-and-such corner" or from the Coca-Cola or from some equally unlikely landmark. Don't worry: If you follow your nose, you'll find the coffee vendor in the market despite the confusing directions.

San José, and modern Costa Rica, was built on coffee. It is one of the country's main exports, along with bananas, and the fortunes that were made shipping coffee to the sleepy souls in Europe helped found San José, which is arguably the most beautiful capital city in Central America. The self-imposed tax on coffee exports helped pay for the National Theater in the latter years of the last century, and coffee revenues provided for the city's university and brought culture to this forgotten backwater of the Spanish empire.

Why does coffee grow so well around San José? The Meseta Central, or Central Valley, in which the city sits, has a perfect climate. At 3,750 feet above sea level, San José enjoys springlike temperatures year round. From nearly any street in the city, you can glance up at lush green mountains planted with coffee. On a clear day, and these are common, the mountains seem close enough to touch. Their patchwork of tiny farms lends San José a small-town feel that lulls visitors into a pleasant sense of familiarity.

1. FROM A BUDGET TRAVELER'S POINT OF VIEW

Budget Bests None of the city's museums charge much in the way of admission; the Jade Museum and the Gold Museum, which are probably the two most impressive museums in Costa Rica, are absolutely free.

Public buses are another of San José's great bargains at only 10¢, and taxis are quite inexpensive, although you must agree on a price before you get in (taxi drivers refuse to use their meters).

When it comes to dining, your best bet for saving money is to look for a *soda*,

WHAT'S SPECIAL ABOUT SAN JOSÉ

Museums
- ☐ The Gold Museum, the largest collection of Pre-Columbian gold jewelry and ornaments in the Americas.
- ☐ The Jade Museum, an equally impressive collection of Pre-Columbian jade artifacts and jewelry.
- ☐ The National Museum, an excellent collection of Pre-Columbian artifacts.

Parks/Gardens
- ☐ Lankester Gardens, near Cartago, with hundreds of species of orchids on display.

Religious Shrines
- ☐ The basilica in Cartago, with a statue of the Virgin of Los Angeles said to heal the sick.
- ☐ The ruins of a church in Cartago turned into a park.

Natural Spectacles
- ☐ Two volcanoes near San José with roads to their rims.

After Dark
- ☐ San José's National Theater, a stately old opera house with performances almost every night.
- ☐ El Pueblo, a shopping, dining, and entertainment complex with nearly a dozen bars, discos, nightclubs, and even a roller-skating rink.

Offbeat Oddities
- ☐ The Serpentarium, a reptilian zoo with dozens of Costa Rica's poisonous snakes on display.

Shopping
- ☐ Fresh-roasted Costa Rican coffee, available by the pound for less than $1.

which serves inexpensive Costa Rican–style meals. But no visit to San José would be complete without having at least one meal at the Gran Hotel's patio buffet (which isn't that expensive by U.S. standards), overlooking the National Theater and all the activity of Plaza de la Cultura.

What's Worth Paying For By all means splurge and buy a ticket for a performance at the **National Theater** (Teatro Nacional). The theater is being renovated due to the 1991 earthquake, but should be open when you arrive. Although you can get a seat for as little as $2 or $3, live it up, hobnob with the elite of Costa Rica (but be sure to look the part). At most it might cost you $15 or $20 to hear the national symphony or see a touring opera company.

You're likely to be bombarded with offers to take this tour or that excursion, but most of them can be done just as easily and at a fraction of the cost on public transport. What you should spring for is a trip to **Tortuguero National Park** if you are interested in seeing nesting sea turtles or visiting a remote jungle. If you've never been **white-water rafting,** you won't find a better place to try a 1-day excursion than San José, and if you dream of spending a day exploring remote islands surrounded by turquoise waters, take one of the day-long cruises around the **Gulf of Nicoya.**

2. ORIENTATION

ARRIVING

BY PLANE Several airlines fly into San José from the United States, Canada, and other Central American countries. You will arrive at the **Juan Santamaría International Airport** near the city of Alajuela, about 20 minutes to downtown San

José whether you take a taxi, car, or bus. A taxi into town will cost around $12 and a bus will cost only 40¢. The Alajuela–San José buses run frequently and drop you on Avenida 2 between calles 12 and 14, which is very convenient to several of the hotels listed in this chapter. There are several car-rental agencies located at the airport, although if you are planning on spending a few days in San José, a car is a liability. However, if you are planning on heading immediately off to the beaches, it is much easier to pick up your car here than at a downtown office. You'll find the car-rental offices and the bus and taxi stands up the stairs and to the left after you clear Customs.

You have several options for **changing money** when you arrive at the airport. If you have cash, you can get colónes at the Tourist Information Desk just past the Customs inspection counter. At the top of the stairs as you exit the terminal, you will be assaulted by money changers; though the black-market exchange is illegal, it is quite common. There is also a bank in the departures hall, open Monday through Friday from 8am to 4pm, where you can change cash or traveler's checks.

BY BUS If you arrived in Costa Rica overland and are coming to San José for the first time by bus, where you disembark depends on where you are coming from. Bus companies have their offices all over downtown San José. To find out where you will be dropped off, see the "Getting There" information which heads the descriptions of destinations outside San José.

TOURIST INFORMATION

There is an **I.C.T. (Instituto Costarricense de Turismo)** desk at Juan Santamaría International Airport, open daily from 8am to 9pm, where you can pick up maps and brochures before you head into San José. You'll find the desk on the left before you come to the stairs after leaving the Customs inspection counter. The main tourist information center is at the Plaza de la Cultura on Calle 5 between Avenida Central and Avenida 2 (tel. 22-1090), beside the entrance to the underground Gold Museum. The people here are very helpful. This office is open Monday through Friday from 9am to 5pm and Saturday from 9am to 1pm.

CITY LAYOUT

MAIN ARTERIES AND STREETS Downtown San José is laid out on a grid. *Avenidas* (avenues) run east and west, while *calles* (streets) run north and south. The center of the city is at **Avenida Central and Calle Central.** To the north of Avenida Central, the avenidas have odd numbers beginning with Avenida 1; to the south, they have even numbers beginning with Avenida 2. Likewise, calles to the east of Calle Central have odd numbers, and those to the west have even numbers. The main downtown artery is Avenida 2, which merges with Avenida Central on either side of the downtown area. West of downtown, Avenida Central becomes Paseo Colón, which ends at Sabana Park and feeds into the highway to Alajuela, the airport, and the Pacific Coast. Calle 3 will take you out of town to the north and put you on the road to the Caribbean Coast.

FINDING AN ADDRESS This is one of the most confusing aspects of visiting San José in particular and Costa Rica in general. There are no street addresses, at least not often. Addresses are given as a set of coordinates such as "Calle 3 between Avenida Central and Avenida 1." It is then up to you to locate the building within that block, keeping in mind that the building could be on either side of the street. Many addresses include additional information, such as the number of meters or *varas* (an old Spanish measurement roughly equal to a yard) from a specified intersection or some other well-known landmark. These landmarks are what become truly confusing for visitors to the city because they are often landmarks only if you have lived in the neighborhood all your life. The classic example of this is the Coca-Cola, one of the most common landmarks used in addresses in the blocks surrounding San José's main market. It refers to a Coca-Cola bottling plant that once stood in this area. Unfortunately, the edifice is long gone, but the address descriptions remain. In outlying neighborhoods, addresses can become long directions such as "50 meters south of the old church, then 100 meters east, then 20 meters south." Luckily for the visitor, most downtown addresses are straightforward. Oh, if you're wondering how mail deliverers manage, you'll be reassured to know that nearly everyone in San José uses a P.O. box. This is called the *apartado* system, abbreviated **Apdo.** on mailing addresses.

NEIGHBORHOODS IN BRIEF   San José is sprawling. Today it is divided into dozens of neighborhoods known as *barrios*. However, because virtually all the listings in this chapter fall within the main downtown area, there is no need to concern yourself with the many outlying neighborhoods.

3. GETTING AROUND

BY BUS

Buses in San José are cheap, only 10¢. The most important buses are those running east and west along Avenida 2 and Avenida 3. The Sabana-Cementerio bus runs from Sabana Park to downtown and is one of the most convenient buses to use. San Pedro buses will take you out of downtown heading east. Unfortunately, taking a bus into town is much easier than taking one out of town, especially if you are trying to catch an outbound Sabana-Cementerio bus. These buses don't run very frequently, and their stops are far apart. Considering this and the congestion on Avenida 3, you'll find that it is generally easier to walk to your destination if it is closer than Sabana Park. Buses are always boarded from the front, and bus drivers can make change. Be especially mindful of your wallet, purse, or other valuables since pickpockets can work the crowded buses. The Alajuela–San José buses that run in from the airport cost 40¢.

BY TAXI

Although taxis in San José have meters (*marías*) the drivers refuse to use them, so you'll have to negotiate the price. The official rate at the time of writing is around 45¢ for the first kilometer and 20¢ for each additional kilometer. If you have a rough idea of how far it is to your destination, you can estimate how much it should cost from these figures. If the first driver gives you a quote that seems way out of line, ask another. You'll find taxis in front of the National Theater (usually at high prices) and around the Parque Central at Avenida Central and Calle Central among other locations.

ON FOOT

Downtown San José is very compact. Nearly everyplace you might want to go is within an area measuring 15 blocks by 4 blocks. Traffic, both vehicular and pedestrian, within this area is heavy. You'll often find it faster to walk than to take a bus or taxi. Avenida Central is a pedestrians-only street for several blocks around Calle Central.

BY CAR

If you decide to rent a car for an excursion out of San José, you have two choices: You can pick up your car downtown and then have to deal with downtown traffic, or you can take a bus out to the airport and pick up your car there. Luckily, many of the car-rental offices are on Paseo Colón, a wide boulevard west of downtown where congestion isn't too bad.

The following international companies have desks at Juan Santamaría Airport: **Avis** (tel. toll free 800/331-1212; tel. in San José 23-9922), **Budget** (tel. toll free 800/527-0700; tel. in San José 23-3284), **Hertz** (tel. toll free 800/654-3131; tel. in San José 23-5959), and **National** (tel. toll free 800/227-7368; tel. in San José 33-4044). These companies also have downtown offices. You will save a considerable amount on a car rental if you make a reservation in your home country at least one week before you need the car. The least-expensive Budget car available rents for about $250 per week, plus insurance and tax (total of around $385) in San José, but if you book this same car in advance from the United States, you can get it for $175 per week, plus insurance and tax (total of around $300). Consult your local *Yellow Pages* for the phone numbers of the above agencies.

There are many other car-rental agencies in San José, some with offices at the airport and others with offices downtown. If you didn't make a reservation before you left home or just want to rent a car for a day, try one of the companies listed below. They charge the same rate (around $40 per day), plus insurance and tax, for their lowest-priced car with unlimited mileage.

Elegante Rent A Car, Calle 10 between avenidas 13 and 15 and Paseo Colón at Calle 34 (tel. 21-0136, 21-0284, or 33-8605).

Tico Rent A Car, Calle 10 between avenidas 13 and 15 or Paseo Colón between calles 24 and 26 (tel. 22-8920 or 22-1765).

FAST FACTS ___ *SAN JOSÉ*

American Express The American Express office is located on Calle 1 between Avenida Central and Avenida 1 (tel. 33-0044). Open Monday to Friday from 8am to 5:30pm.

Babysitters Your only chance for a babysitter in San José is to check with your hotel.

Bookstore The Bookshop, Avenida 1 between calles 1 and 3 (tel. 21-6847), has a wide selection of English-language newspapers, magazines, and books; it's open Monday to Saturday from 9am to 7pm and Sunday from 9am to 2pm. For used books in English, stop by Book Traders (open Monday to Saturday from 9am to 7pm), above the Pizza Hut on Avenida 1 between calles 3 and 5.

Car Rentals See "Getting Around" in this chapter.

Climate See "When to Go" in Chapter 2.

Crime See "Safety," below.

Currency Exchange The best thing to do is ask at your hotel. If they can't change money for you, they can direct you to a private bank where you won't have to stand in line for hours. Avoid changing money on the street.

Dentist If you need a dentist while in San José, your best bet is to call your embassy, which will have a list of recommended dentists.

Doctors Contact your embassy for information on doctors in San José.

Drugstores **Farmacia Fischel,** Avenida 3 and Calle 2, is across from the main post office (tel. 23-7244). Open Monday to Saturday from 8am to 7pm.

Embassies and Consulates **United States Consulate,** in front of Centro Comercial, road to Pavas (tel. 20-3939); **Canadian Embassy,** Calle 3 and Avenida Central (tel. 55-3522); **British Embassy,** Paseo Colón between calles 38 and 40 (tel. 21-5566).

Emergencies In case of **fire** dial 118; for the **police** dial 117; for an **ambulance** dial 21-5818.

Eyeglasses Optica Jiménez, Avenida 2 and Calle 3 (tel. 33-4417 or 22-0233) is open Monday to Saturday from 8am to noon and 2 to 6pm.

Hairdressers/Barbers **El Toque Nuevo,** Avenida 2 between calles 1 and 3 in Edificios Los Arcados (tel. 22-0877), is open Monday to Saturday from 9am to 7pm. It services both men and women.

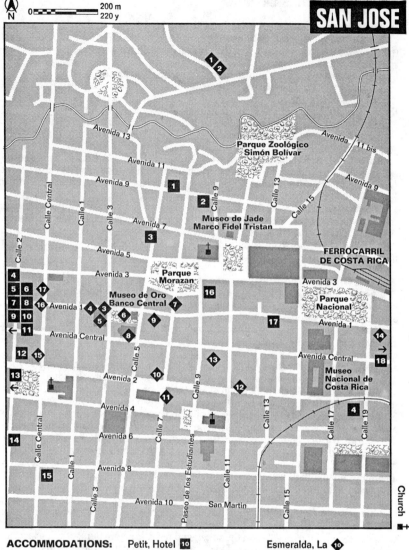

SAN JOSE

0 |======| 200 m
            220 y

N

Avenida 13

Parque Zoológico
Simón Bolívar

Avenida 11

Avenida 11 bis

Avenida 9

Avenida 9

Calle 9

Calle 13

Calle 15

Calle Central

Calle 1

Calle 3

Avenida 7

Museo de Jade
Marco Fidel Tristan

FERROCARRIL
DE COSTA RICA

Avenida 5

Calle 2

Avenida 3

Parque
Morazan

Avenida 3

Parque
Nacional

Museo de Oro
Banco Central

Avenida 1

Avenida 1

Avenida Central

Avenida Central

Museo
Nacional de
Costa Rica

Calle 5

Avenida 2

Calle 9

Calle 7

Avenida 4

Calle 13

Calle 17

Calle 19

Calle Central

Avenida 6

Calle 1

Avenida 8

Calle 3

Paseo de los Estudiantes

Calle 11

Calle 15

Avenida 10

San Martin

Church

ACCOMMODATIONS:
American, Pensión **12**
Alameda, Hotel **5**
Bievenido, Hotel **4**
Cacts, Hotel **6**
Continental, Pensión **15**
Costa Rica Inn, Pensión **16**
Cuesta, Pensión de la **17**
Diplomat, Hotel **2**
Don Carlos, Hotel **7**
Dunn Inn, Hotel **1**
Fortuna, Hotel **14**
Johnson, Hotel **9**

Petit, Hotel **10**
Petit Victoria, Hotel **11**
Plaza, Hotel **8**
Ritz, Hotel **15**
Santo Tomás, Hotel **3**
Talamanca, Hotel **13**
Toruma Youth Hostel **18**
DINING
Amstel Grill Room **7**
B y B, Soda **9**
Campesino, Restaurante **11**
Cocina de Leña, La **1**
Churreria Manolo **13**

Esmeralda, La **10**
Hardee's **3**
Kentucky Fried Chicken **14**
Machu Picchu **16**
McDonald's **6**
Mordisco, Restaurant's **17**
Parisiene, Café **5**
Perla, La **15**
Pueblo, El **2**
Teatro Nacional, Café de **8**
Vilmary's La Casa
   De Sandwich **12**
Vishnu, Soda **4**

Holidays   See "When to Go" in Chapter 2.

Hospitals   **Clinica Biblica,** Avenida 14 between Calle Central and Calle 1 (tel. 23-6422), is conveniently located close to downtown and has several English-speaking doctors.

Information   See "Tourist Information" in this chapter.

Laundry/Dry Cleaning   **Sixaola,** Avenida 2 between calles 7 and 9 (tel. 21-2111), is one of the only places downtown to get clothes cleaned. Unfortunately, their prices are quite high. Ask at your hotel—most offer a laundry service.

Libraries   The **National Library** is at the corner of Avenida 3 and Calle 15.

Luggage Storage/Lockers   Most hotels will store luggage for you while you are traveling around the country.

Newspapers/Magazines   The *Tico Times* is Costa Rica's English-language weekly paper serving the expatriate community and tourists. You can also get the *International Herald Tribune, USA Today, Time,* and *Newsweek,* among other English-language publications.

Photographic Needs   Film is very expensive in Costa Rica, so bring as much as you will need. You can buy film and other photographic equipment at **Dima,** Avenida Central between calles 3 and 5 (tel. 22-3969), open Monday to Friday from 9am to 5pm, Saturday from 8am to noon. I recommend that you wait to have your film processed when you get home.

Police   Dial 117 for the police.

Post Office   The main post office (*correo*) is on Calle 2 between avenidas 1 and 3. It's open Monday to Friday from 6am to midnight, Saturday from 8am to noon for purchasing stamps. For mailing packages, hours are Monday to Friday 7am to 6pm, Saturday 7am to noon.

Radio/TV   There are six Spanish-language TV channels, one English-language channel, and satellite TV from the United States. There are dozens of AM and FM radio stations in San José.

Religious Services   The *Tico Times* has a listing of churches in San José. You can also ask at the tourist office for a list of the city's many churches.

Restrooms   These are known as *sanitarios* or *servicios sanitarios.* They are marked *damas* (women) and *hombres* or *caballeros* (men).

Safety   Never carry anything of value in your pockets or purse. Pickpockets and purse slashers are rife in San José, especially on public buses and in the markets. The Costa Ricans blame the increase in petty crime on all the refugees from Nicaragua and El Salvador. Leave your passport, money, and other valuables in your hotel safe, and carry only as much as you really need when you go out. If you do carry anything valuable with you, keep it in a money belt or special passport bag around your neck. Also be advised that the Parque Central is not a safe place for a late-night stroll.

Other precautions include walking around corner vendors, not between the vendor and the building. The tight space between vendor and building is a favorite spot for pickpockets. Never park a car on the street, and never leave anything of value in a car, even if it's in a guarded parking lot. Don't even leave your car by the curb in front of a hotel while you dash in to check on your reservation. With these precautions in mind, you should have a safe visit to San José.

Shoe Repairs   **Al Instante,** Avenida 1 between calles 5 and 7 (no phone) is open Monday to Saturday from 8am to noon and 1:30 to 6:30pm, Saturday 8am to noon. They'll get you back on your feet in an instant.

Taxes   All hotel bills have an additional tax of around 15% added on; in restaurants, both a 10% tax and a 10% service charge are added to all bills.

Taxis   See "Getting Around" in this chapter.

Telegrams/Telexes   You can send telegrams and telexes from the **I.C.E.** office, Avenida 2 between calles 1 and 3. Open daily from 7am to 10pm.

Telephones   Pay phones are not as common in San José as they are in North American cities. When you do find one, whether on the street or in a restaurant or hotel lobby, it may take coins of various denominations or it may take only 5 colónes.

Pay phones are notoriously unreliable, so it is better to make calls from your hotel, where you will be charged around 100 colónes per call.

Water   The tap water in San José is said to be perfectly fine to drink. Residents of the city will swear to this. However, frequent complaints about intestinal illnesses by tourists make me a bit skeptical about San José's water. I suggest sticking to bottled drinks and *refrescos* with milk as much as possible. *Sin hielo* means "no ice."

4. WHERE TO STAY

Luckily for visitors, there are plenty of good hotel deals to be had in downtown San José. From high-rise hotels to tiny pensións in colonial-style buildings, you'll find a wide variety of budget choices within walking distance of all the city's major attractions. The following are the best of the budget hotels.

DOUBLES FOR LESS THAN $15

PENSIÓN AMERICAN, Calle 2 between Avenida Central and Avenida 2, Apdo. 4853, San José. Tel. 506/21-4171 or 21-9799. 34 rms, none with private bath.
$ Rates: $4.45 single; $8.90 double; $13.35 triple; $17.80 quad. No credit cards.
This is an old favorite with Central American backpack travelers. The prices are about as low as they come in San José, and you don't get much. The rooms are rather dark, the beds vary in quality, and the walls (very thin to begin with) don't go all the way to the ceiling, but the pension stays busy with interesting folks. There's a TV lounge so that you don't have to spend all of your time in your room. The management is friendly and helpful, which is perhaps the reason this place has maintained its good reputation for so many years.

HOTEL BIENVENIDO, Calle 10 between avenidas 1 and 3, P.O. Box 389-2200, San José. Tel. 506/21-1872. 44 rms (all with bath).
$ Rates: $11 single; $14 double; $17 triple. No credit cards.
This new budget hotel has quickly caught on with budget travelers because of its clean rooms and ample hot water. The hotel was created from an old movie theater, and there are still a few architectural details remaining from the building's former

   FROMMER'S SMART TRAVELER: HOTELS

1. Visit in the rainy season (May to November) when rates are often cheaper.
2. To lower your hotel bills, consider taking rooms with shared, rather than private, bathrooms.
3. To avoid a frantic hotel search, make a reservation for your first night in town, especially if you're arriving after dark.
4. Keep your eyes open for new hotels; the tourism industry is booming in Costa Rica and newer hotels often offer good values.

incarnation. This place fills up by early afternoon in the high season, so call ahead for a reservation and ask for a quiet room in the back.

HOTEL JOHNSON, Calle 8 between Avenida Central and Avenida 2a, Apdo. 6638 San José 1000. Tel. 506/23-7633 or 23-7827. Fax 506/22-3683. 57 rms, 3 suites (all with bath).
$ Rates: $8.15 single; $9.65 double; $10.50 triple; $12.95 suite (for five). DC, MC, V.

The lobby of this large, centrally located hotel is on the second floor. You'll find the hotel patronized primarily by Costa Rican businesspeople and families, but it is a good choice for any budget traveler. In the lobby there is a television and several lounge chairs, and on each of the residence floors above there is a sitting area furnished with attractive wicker chairs. On the third floor you'll find one of the most unusual wall decorations I have ever seen in a hotel—a double bass viol. The rooms have tile floors and open onto a narrow air shaft that lets in a bit of light. Bathrooms are relatively clean and roomy. Most rooms come with twin beds (you might want to test a few beds if you're picky about mattresses).

Behind the reception desk there is a breakfast room that serves a limited variety of breakfasts for around $2. Across the lobby is a larger dining room and bar which serves lunch and dinner from an international menu. The special of the day goes for $1.85, while à la carte meals run from $3.50–$5.50. On Friday from 7 to 9pm there is live music here. During happy hour Monday through Saturday from 7 to 8pm, you can get two-for-one drinks.

HOTEL RITZ AND PENSIÓN CONTINENTAL, Calle Central between avenidas 8 and 10, Apdo. 6783-1000, San José. Tel. 506/22-4103. Fax 506/22-8849. 27 rms (10 with bath).
$ Rates: $7 single without bath, $18 single with bath; $12–$20 double without bath, $23.50 double with bath; $15.50 triple without bath, $26 triple with bath; $20.50 quad without bath, $30 quad with bath. AE, MC, V.

These two side-by-side budget hotels are under the same management and together have rooms to fit most budget travelers' needs. There is even a travel agency and tour company on the first floor, so you can arrange all of your travels around Costa Rica without leaving the hotel. Rooms vary greatly in size and comfort levels. If the first room you see isn't to your liking, just ask to see another in a different price category. The current owners are Swiss, so you'll probably meet quite a few Swiss travelers if you stay here.

DOUBLES FOR LESS THAN $30

HOTEL CACTS, Avenida 3 bis No. 2845 between calles 28 and 30, Apdo. 379-1005, San José. Tel. 506/21-2928 or 21-6546. Fax 506/21-8616. 18 rms (all with bath).
$ Rates (including continental breakfast): $25 single with bath; $29 double with bath; $32 triple; $36 quad. No credit cards.

This is one of the most interesting and unusual budget hotels I've ever seen, housed in an attractive tropical contemporary home on a business and residential street. You reach the reception area via a flight of outside steps that lead past a small garden area. Once inside, you are in a maze of halls on several levels (the house is built on a slope). My favorite room is the huge bi-level family room with its high beamed ceiling. The Cacts was in the midst of an ambitious expansion when I last visited and by the time you arrive you should find a rooftop terrace dining area and quite a few more rooms in various price ranges. You can also avail yourself of an airport shuttle, luggage storage room, travel service, and car-rental service.

PENSIÓN COSTA RICA INN, Calle 9 between avenidas 1 and 3, No. 154, Apdo. 10282-1000, San José. Tel. 506/22-5203 or toll free 800/637-

0899 in the U.S.; 318/263-2059 in Canada. Fax 011-506/23-8385. U.S. address: P.O. Box 59, Arcadia, LA 71001. 35 rms. (all with bath).
$ Rates: $18.90 single; $23.90 double; $33 triple. MC, V.
Although most of the rooms are rather small and dark, this little hotel is popular, especially with young travelers. If you're a light sleeper, this is definitely *not* the place for you. The walls are typical of those in old Costa Rican wood buildings—paper thin. There's a small bar that always seems to have a handful of young foreigners hanging around as well as a TV lounge with plenty of couches. The rooms are situated off small courtyards down a maze of narrow hallways. There's no restaurant here, but the staff will do your laundry for you. Recommended for those who like to stay out late.

HOTEL FORTUNA, Avenida 6 between calles 2 and 4, Apdo. 7-1570, San José. Tel. 506/23-5344. Fax 506/23-2743. 30 rms. (all with bath). TEL
$ Rates: $15.25 single; $23.60 double; $27 triple; $30 quad. AE, MC, V.
Located only two blocks from the Parque Central, the Fortuna has a Chinese theme. The second-floor rooms are sunny and warm, and the first-floor rooms are cooler and darker. Floors are of well-worn tile, but each room has a vanity with a Chinese-style chair. The brightness of the rooms makes this place feel much more cheery than other hotels, despite the lack of carpeting.

PETIT HOTEL, Calle 24 between Avenida Central and Avenida 2, Apdo. 7694-1000, San José. Tel. 506/33-0766. 18 rms (14 with bath).
$ Rates: $8 single without bath; $16 single with bath; $16 double without bath, $29 double with bath; $32 quad. No credit cards.
Despite its location (20-minute walk from the Plaza de Cultura), this is one of my favorite bottom-of-the-budget choices in San José. You'll find all sorts of interesting gringos sitting around the television lounge of this mazelike collection of large and small rooms. The management is very friendly and helpful, and the rooms, although basic, are clean and bright. Some rooms have the same highly polished, beautiful hardwood floor as the lounge. You can use the kitchen here for fixing simple meals, and the refrigerator also is available. There is a pot of free hot coffee on the counter at all times of the night or day. The communal toilets are generally clean. If you don't want to carry all your luggage with you while you explore the rest of the country and plan to come back to the Petit after your journeys you can store your excess stuff here.

HOTEL TALAMANCA, Avenida 2 between calles 8 and 10, Apdo. 449-1002, San José. Tel. 506/33-5033. Fax 506/33-5420. 54 rms. (all with bath). TEL
$ Rates: $25 single; $29 double; $41 triple. MC, V. **Parking:** Available for small fee.
This hotel has certainly seen better days, but it is conveniently located and economical and has its own casino which stays open from 2pm to 5am. The rooms will do in a pinch, and if you want to spend a little extra, you can get a TV in your room. Ask for a room on one of the upper floors, and you'll get a view of the surrounding mountains. There is an acceptable restaurant and a disco for those who want to loosen their limbs after sitting too long at the gambling tables. Other attractive features are a discotheque, a restaurant, and room service and laundry service.

DOUBLES FOR LESS THAN $45

HOTEL ALAMEDA, Avenida Central between calles 12 and 14, Apdo. 680. San José. Tel. 506/23-6333 or 21-3045. 50 rms (all with bath). TEL
$ Rates: $26 single; $30–$32 double; $37 triple. AE, DC, MC, V.
This is another of San José's large old hotels, but a recent remodeling of the lobby has given it a very modern feel. One of its greatest assets is that it is only a block away

from the bus stop for the airport. If your flight arrives after dark and you don't have a reservation, this is the first place you should try. Walk around to the side of the block away from the small park and you'll see the Alameda across the street. The rooms are small but carpeted and have clean tiled baths and plenty of closet space.

The second-floor restaurant has two walls of windows and commands an excellent view of the activity on the street. The menu features international and Costa Rican dishes at prices ranging from about $3.35 to $14.80.

There is also laundry and dry cleaning, medical service, and currency exchange.

PENSIÓN DE LA CUESTA, Cuesta de Nuñez, Casa No. 1332, Avenida 1 between calles 11 and 15. Tel. 506/55-2896. Fax 506/23-6808. 4 rms (none with bath).

$ Rates (including continental breakfast): $24.65 single; $38.10 double. No credit cards.

Though these prices may seem a bit steep for a room without a private bathroom, this little bed-and-breakfast is definitely worth considering. It is owned by an artist from the Guanacaste province of Costa Rica, and original artwork abounds. The building itself is also a classic example of a tropical wood-frame home and has been painted an eye-catching pink with blue and white trim. The rooms are a bit dark and are very simply furnished, but there is a very sunny and cheery sunken lounge court area in the center of the house. You'll find this hotel on the hill leading up to the Parque Nacional.

HOTEL DIPLOMAT, Calle 6 between Avenida Central and Avenida 2, Apdo. 6606-1000, San José. Tel. 506/21-8133 or 21-8744. 29 rms. (all with bath).

$ Rates: $22–$35 single; $33–$44 double. AE, MC, V.

It's easy to miss the entrance to this hotel. Watch for it on the east side of the street. The lobby is narrow, and the front door is fairly nondescript. The carpeted rooms are rather small but comfortable nonetheless, and some rooms on the upper floors have nice views of the mountains. The tiled baths are clean, and the water is hot. For $3 extra per night you can get a TV. If you get too claustrophobic in your room, there is a sitting area on each floor. The Diplomat seems to be popular with North American retirees and businesspeople. The hotel's restaurant is a very attractive dark room with pink tablecloths, flowers on every table, and pastel walls. For those seeking an intimate place for dinner, try one of the tiny booths for two. Prices range from $2 for a sandwich to $14.45 for a lobster dinner.

HOTEL PLAZA, Avenida Central between calles 2 and 4, Apdo. 2019 Frente Boulevar, San José. Tel. 506/22-5533 or 22-5605. Fax 506/22-2641. 40 rms. (all with bath) TV TEL

$ Rates: $25.40 single; $34.60 double; $39.25 triple. AE, DC, MC, V.

Downtown hotels in San José tend to be rather nondescript from the outside, and the Plaza is no exception. However, when you step through the doors, you enter a very attractive, newly decorated lobby with richly colored plush carpets, sturdy tropical wicker furniture, and unusual hardwood paneling on both the walls and the ceiling. An added attraction of the Plaza is that it is on the pedestrians-only section of Avenida Central, San José's central shopping district.

You'll find the same unusual paneling incorporated into the guest-room designs. Recessed lighting, colorful bedspreads, and thick carpets make each room a soothing and relaxing place to return to after a long day of touring. There is even remote control for the TV. Bathrooms (shower only) are small but tiled, and the sinks are outside the bathroom door. Room service and laundry service are available.

The second-floor restaurant/bar also features a lot of Costa Rican hardwood, including ramadas (Spanish-style covered patios) over the booths even though there is no direct sunshine in the restaurant. The three-course daily special, which might be something as exotic as Spanish beef tongue with cauliflower salad and pastry, goes for only $5.20. An à la carte meal will run from $3 to $12.60.

A HOSTEL

TORUMA YOUTH HOSTEL, Avenida Central between calles 29 and 31, San José. Tel. 506/24-4085. 70 beds (all with shared bath).

$ Rates: $4.20 per person per night with an IYHF card; $5.60 without IYHF card.

⑤ This attractive old building with a long veranda is the largest of Costa Rica's growing system of official youth hostels. Although it is possible to find other accommodations around town in this price range, the atmosphere here is familiar to those who have hosteled in Europe. The large lounge and dining hall in the center of the building has a high ceiling and a great deal of light. The dorms are 16- to 26-bunk-bed rooms. Guests have use of the kitchen.

WORTH THE EXTRA BUCKS

HOTEL DON CARLOS, Calle 9 between avenidas 7 and 9, No. 779 (mailing address: Dept. 1686, P.O. Box 025216, Miami, FL 33102-5216). Tel. 506/21-6707. Fax 506/55-0828. 16 rms, 9 suites.

$ Rates (including continental breakfast): $40.25–$51.75 single; $46–$57.50 double. No credit cards.

★ If you are looking for a small hotel that is unmistakably tropical and hints at the days of the planters and coffee barons, this is the place for you. Located in an old residential neighborhood only blocks from the business district, the Don Carlos is popular with both honeymooners and businesspeople. A large Pre-Columbian reproduction of a carved stone human figure stands outside the front door of this gray hotel, which was a former president's mansion. Inside you'll find many more Pre-Columbian stone reproductions, as well as orchids, ferns, palms, and parrots. The wicker furniture in the lounge and the small courtyard leading to a sunny deck with a bubbling fountain tempt guests to relax in the tropical breezes after a day of exploring the capital. There is also an intimate TV lounge with a lending library. Most of the rooms are quite large, and each is a little different from the others. If you are going to be there for a while or plan to return after a few days of exploring, you might want to have a look at several rooms and decide which you like best. My personal favorite is room no. 4, a huge suite with polished hardwood floors, a large table with director's chairs around it, a red-velvet couch and love seat, and some attractive paintings by local artists on the walls. This room also has many windows for catching the trade winds. In case you're interested, the paintings throughout the hotel are for sale. There's also a gift shop.

Only breakfast and light meals are served in the Pre-Columbian Lounge, a small dining room with marble-topped tables. Prices for such things as quiche, tamales, and ceviche range from ¢60 to ¢205 (71¢ to $2.41).

HOTEL DUNN INN, Calle 5 and Avenida 11, Apdo. 1584-1000, San José. Tel. 506/22-3232 or 22-3426. Fax 506/21-4596. 10 rms, 1 suite (all with bath).

$ Rates (including continental breakfast): $52.20–$63.80 single or double; $63.80 triple or quad; $102.65 suite. AE, V.

In the same historic neighborhood as the Santo Tomas (below) and the Don Carlos, the Dunn Inn is a noteworthy new small hotel. Housed in a 95-year-old mansion, this hotel offers quiet sophistication at reasonable rates. The courtyard of the old mansion has been partially covered and turned into the dining room and bar, which can get a bit noisy at night. Orchids and bromeliads hang from the brick walls, and a large cage on one side of the room is home to chattering tropical squirrels. A fountain bubbles away beside a huge philodendron vine.

During the restoration, as much of the old hardwood floors was saved as was possible. Consequently, some of the rooms have the original flooring and some are carpeted. All the rooms have overhead fans (air conditioning really isn't necessary in this temperate climate), plenty of windows, and semiorthopedic beds. Although it is quite a bit more expensive than the normal rooms, the one suite is quite luxurious with a whirlpool bath, minibar, hardwood and carpeted floors, potted bromeliads, dual sinks, a lot of sunshine in the bathroom, and paneled walls.

HOTEL PETITE VICTORIA, Paseo Colón, Costado Oeste Sala Garbo, San José. Tel. 506/33-1812 or 33-1813. Fax 506/33-1938. 16 rms (all with bath). MINIBAR

$ Rates: $49 single or double; $59 triple. No credit cards.

One of the oldest houses in San José, this tropical Victorian home was once the election campaign headquarters for Oscar Arias Sánchez, Costa Rica's former president who won a Nobel Peace Prize. Today, after extensive remodeling and restoration, it is one of San José's most interesting little hotels. The big front porch is perfect for sitting and taking in the warm sun, while inside, a circular banquette sits in the middle of a tile-floored lobby. Guest rooms have high ceilings and fans to keep the air cool and medium-to-large tiled bathrooms. Inside, walls are made of wood, so noise can be a bit of a problem, but this is a small price to pay for such old-fashioned elegance. Tour arrangements and a laundry service are also offered.

HOTEL SANTO TOMAS, Avenida 7 between calles 3 and 5, San José. Tel. 506/55-0448. Fax 506/22-3950. 20 rms (all with bath).

$ Rates (including continental breakfast): $42.50 single; $65 double; $75 triple; $85 quad; lower rates May–Sept. No credit cards. **Parking:** Available for small fee.

This is one of the newest little hotels in San José. Even though it is on an otherwise nondescript street, this converted mansion is a real jewel inside. Built around 100 years ago by a coffee baron, the house was recently saved from being bulldozed in order to expand a luxury hotel's parking lot. Under the direction of American Tom Douglas, the old mansion has been restored to its former grandeur. The first thing that you see when you walk through the front door is the beautiful carved desk that serves as the reception area. Throughout the guest rooms you'll find similar pieces of exquisitely crafted antique reproductions made here in Costa Rica from rare hardwoods. The hardwood floors throughout most of the hotel are original and were made from a type of tree that is almost impossible to find today.

The rooms vary in size, but most are extremely large with a small table and chairs. Skylights in the bathrooms will brighten your morning, and queen-size beds will provide a good night's sleep. Maps of Costa Rica hang on the walls of all the guest rooms so you can get acquainted with the country. There are a couple of patio lounges, as well as a television lounge and outdoor bar. A laundry service is available and a casual continental breakfast is served in the little dining room adjacent to the TV lounge in the lobby.

5. WHERE TO EAT

San José has an amazing variety of restaurants in all price ranges. For a true deal, head to a soda, the equivalent of a diner, which serves good and filling Tico food. I have chosen restaurants that are convenient to both hotels and attractions, so that you will never have to go too far for a meal. Two of my favorite places to eat are right on the busy Plaza de la Cultura, the heart of San José.

MEALS FOR LESS THAN $6

SODA B y B, Calle 5 and Avenida Central. Tel. 27-7316.
Cuisine: COSTA RICAN.
$ Prices: Sandwiches 85¢–$2.50; breakfasts $1.15–$1.95. DC, MC, V.
Open: Mon–Fri 8am–10pm, Sat 9am–10pm.

Located on the corner across from the Tourist Information Center on the Plaza de la Cultura, this spot is popular with downtown shoppers and office workers. Service is good, prices (and noise level) are low, and the food is surprisingly good for a sandwich shop. There are high-backed wooden booths and a replica of an overhanging roof along one wall. Try the *chalupa de pollo B y B*. It's a sort of tostada piled high with chicken salad and drenched with sour cream and guacamole.

RESTAURANTE CAMPESINO, Calle 7 between avenidas 2 and 4. Tel. 22-1170.
   Cuisine: COSTA RICAN.
$ **Prices:** $1.25–$4.80. MC, V.
   Open: Daily 10am–midnight.

 This restaurant serves what may be the best chicken I have ever tasted. This is not at all surprising since chicken is just about all they serve, and thus they have had time to perfect its cooking. The secret of this delectable dish is in the wood fire over which the chicken is roasted. The fires are stoked with coffee root wood, which imparts a delicate flavor that has mouths watering all over the globe at the mere thought of a meal here. Unfortunately, the coffee plantations that provide the roots are switching to a new type of coffee tree that produces smaller roots. Campesino chicken may soon become just a memory if this thoughtless upgrading of coffee plantations continues. Oh, well, get it while it's hot. Depending on how hungry you are, you can get a quarter, half, or full chicken. Don't miss the palmito (heart of palm) salad for $2.60. You can't miss this place—watch for the smoking chimney high above the roof, or at street level watch for the window full of chickens rotating over an open fire.

VILMARY'S LA CASA DE SANDWICH, Avenida 2 and Calle 11. No phone.
   Cuisine: SANDWICHES.
$ **Prices:** $1.05–$2.15. No credit cards.
   Open: 24 hours.
No matter what time of the night or day hunger strikes you, you can always get a good cheap sandwich at this little hole in the wall. The different types of sandwiches available are scrawled on every possible bit of wall space, and none of them has a price listed. Never fear: There is a menu with prices on the counter, and besides, there isn't an item on the menu that will break your bank.

CHURRERIA MANOLO, Avenida Central between calles 9 and 11. Tel. 23-4067.
   Cuisine: COSTA RICAN.
$ **Prices:** $1.35–$3.10. No credit cards.
   Open: Daily 7am–11pm.

(F)   FROMMER'S SMART TRAVELER: RESTAURANTS

1. To save money on meals, eat at *sodas*, the Costa Rican equivalent of a diner.
2. Order *gallo pinto* for breakfast and a *casado* for lunch or dinner to economize on meals. These filling Tico standards include rice and beans and either eggs or a main course.
3. You'll get free *bocas* (snacks) when you order a cocktail in most bars. Stay in the bar long enough and you can eat enough to make a light meal.
4. Don't hesitate to try some of the city's many gourmet restaurants—even the most "expensive" restaurant in San José is reasonably priced.

You can't miss this popular sandwich spot: Brass footprints embedded in the sidewalk lead right to the front door. There is also a big glass case full of *churros,* a kind of Latin American doughnut that is a long hollow tube. As the name of the restaurant implies, churros are the specialty here, and you can get them with a variety of fillings. However, the menu lists 128 items, including about 60 different sandwiches. There are daily specials and huge ice-cream plates. If you don't understand the Spanish menu, walk over to the case full of premade sandwiches and bocadillos (Costa Rican appetizers) and point to the ones that you want.

LA PERLA, Avenida 2 and Calle Central. Tel. 22-7492.
   Cuisine: INTERNATIONAL.
   $ Prices: $1.10–$6.10; 10% extra 10pm–6am. AE, MC, V.
   Open: Daily 24 hours.
It's easy to walk right past this place (I did) the first time that you try to find it. The entrance is on the corner looking across to Parque Central and the restaurant itself is a little bit below street level. La Perla is not long on atmosphere, but the food is good and the portions are huge. The special here is paella, a Spanish rice-and-seafood dish for only $4.25. It is almost impossible to finish the plate that they bring you unless you are absolutely ravenous. You can even get it with extra seafood for $5.55. Another excellent choice is the huevos à la ranchera for $2.95, which is prepared a bit differently than it is in Mexico and makes a filling meal at any time of the night or day. Be sure to try a delicious refresco, made with water or milk and fresh fruit whirred in a blender. *Mora* (blackberry) is my favorite.

CAFÉ DE TEATRO NACIONAL, Teatro Nacional, Avenida 2 between calles 3 and 5. Tel. 33-4488.
   Cuisine: INTERNATIONAL.
   $ Prices: $1.85–$2.95. No credit cards.
   Open: Mon–Fri 8am–6pm, Sat 11am–6pm.
This is absolutely my favorite place to eat in all of San José. Even if there is no show at the Teatro Nacional during your visit, you can enjoy a meal or a cup of coffee here and soak up the neoclassical atmosphere. The theater was built in the 1890s from the designs of European architects and the art nouveau chandeliers, ceiling murals, and marble floors and tables are purely Parisian. There are even changing art displays by local artists. The menu is limited to a few sandwiches, pastas, cakes, and special coffees, but the ambience is classic French café. However, the marimba music drifting in through the open window will remind you that you are still in Costa Rica.

SODA VISHNU, Avenida 1 between calles 1 and 3. Tel. 22-2549.
   Cuisine: VEGETARIAN.
   $ Prices: $1.50–$2.95. No credit cards.
   Open: Mon–Fri 8am–9pm, Sun 9am–7pm.
Vegetarians may find themselves eating all their meals at this bright and modern natural foods eatery. There are booths for two or four people and photo murals on the walls. At the cashier's counter you can buy natural cosmetics, teas, and bags of granola. However, most people just come for the filling *plato del dia* that includes soup, salad, veggies, an entrée, and dessert all for around $2.50. There are also bean burgers and cheese sandwiches on whole-wheat bread. There is another Vishnu around the corner on Calle 3 between Avenida Central and Avenida 1.

MEALS FOR LESS THAN $12

AMSTEL GRILL ROOM, Avenida 1 and Calle 7. Tel. 22-4622.
   Cuisine: AMERICAN/CONTINENTAL/COSTA RICAN.
   $ Prices: Menu of the day $4.45–$5.20; entrées $4.10–$13.35. AE, MC, V.
   Open: Daily 6:30–11am, 11:30am–3pm, 6–10pm.
Ask anyone in San José for a restaurant recommendation, and this hotel dining room will always be at the top of the list. For years the Grill Room has maintained its high standards and its atmosphere of quiet sophistication.

White-jacketed waiters move unobtrusively between tables, making sure that all the diners are happy. Businesspeople and well-dressed matrons are the primary customers, but tourists in casual attire receive the same careful attention. Lunch here, the most popular meal of the day, is a real bargain. For $4.45 to $5.20, you can order the special of the day or the deluxe special of the day—the only difference between the two is that the deluxe is served with a fish main course. Soup or salad and a dessert round out the meal. Should you choose to order à la carte, try one of the choice steaks of Costa Rican beef or fresh shrimp. In addition to the Continental and American dishes on the menu, there is also a plato tipico that comes with the Tico standby of beans and rice.

LA COCINA DE LEÑA, El Pueblo. Tel. 55-1360.
Cuisine: COSTA RICAN.
$ Prices: Entrées $2.20–$20.75. AE, DC, MC, V.
Open: Lunch daily 11:30am–3pm; dinner daily 6–11:30pm.

La Cocina de Leña (The Wood Stove) bills itself as "the best typical restaurant in the country," and I would have a hard time arguing with them on that claim. Although almost every restaurant in Costa Rica offers *tipico* meals, few serve the likes of green banana ceviche or palmito ceviche, $2.10 and $3. After such unusual appetizers, you might wonder what could come next. Perhaps oxtail soup served with yuca and platano for $4.80 might appeal to you; if not, there are plenty of steaks and seafood on the menu. If you are an adventurous eater, you will need several trips to this cozy restaurant to try all that appeals to you. I recommend the *chilasuilas,* delicious tortillas filled with fried meat, for $4.45. Black bean soup with an egg is a Costa Rican standard available everywhere, but corn soup with pork for $2.95 is equally satisfying. For dessert there is tres leches cake for $2.10, as well as the more unusual sweetened *chiverre,* which is a type of squash that looks remarkably like a watermelon, for the same price.

Located in the unusual El Pueblo shopping, dining, and entertainment center, La Cocina de Leña has a rustic feel to it, with firewood stacked on shelves above the booths, long stalks of bananas hanging from pillars, tables suspended by heavy ropes from the ceiling, and most unusual of all—menus printed on paper bags. Don't miss it.

CAFÉ PARISIEN, Gran Hotel Costa Rica, Avenida 2 between calles 1 and 3. Tel. 21-4011.
Cuisine: INTERNATIONAL.
$ Prices: Sandwiches $1.80–$3.80; appetizers $1.50–$14.55; entrées $2.60–$15.55. AE, MC, V.
Open: Daily 24 hours.

The Hotel Gran Costa Rica is the grande dame of hotels and as such is considerably outside your budget. However, its picturesque patio café right on the Plaza de la Cultura is a surprisingly inexpensive place to dine (if you stay away from the shrimp and lobster). A wrought-iron railing, white columns, and arches create an old-world atmosphere. There is almost no hour when there isn't something interesting going on in the plaza. Stop by this sophisticated café for the $5.55 breakfast buffet and fill up as the plaza's vendors set up their booths, peruse the *Tico Times* over coffee while you have your shoes polished, or simply bask in the tropical sunshine. For lunch or dinner, you can get steak or corvina for around $6.50. There is also a dinner buffet featuring classic Continental dishes, such as escalopine de milanesa for $6.90. If ordering à la carte, be sure to try the black-bean soup with an egg for $1.20.

LA ESMERALDA, Avenida 2 between calles 5 and 7. Tel. 21-0530.
Cuisine: COSTA RICAN.
$ Prices: Entrées $3.35–$14.45. AE, MC, V.
Open: Mon–Sat 24 hours.

No one should visit San José without stopping in at La Esmeralda at least once, the later at night the better. This is much more than just a restaurant serving Tico food: It is the Grand Central Station of Costa Rican mariachi bands. In fact, mariachis and other bands from throughout Central America and Mexico hang out here every night waiting for work. While they wait they often serenade diners in the cavernous open-air dining hall of the restaurant. Friday and Saturday nights are always the busiest, but you'll probably hear a lot of excellent music any night of the week. The classic Tico food is quite good, with heart of palm salad for $4.60, corvina (sea bass) for $4.60, and shrimp for a pricey $14.45. The tres leches cake for $1.10 just might be the moistest cake on earth. Try it.

MACHU PICCHU, Calle 32 between avenidas 1 and 3. Tel. 22-7384.
   Cuisine: PERUVIAN/CONTINENTAL.
$ Prices: Appetizers $1.30–$6.65; entrees $2.95–$8.15. No credit cards.
   Open: Lunch Mon–Sat 11:30am–3pm; dinner Mon–Sat 6–10pm.
Located just off Paseo Colón near the Kentucky Fried Chicken, Machu Picchu is an unpretentious little restaurant which has become one of the most popular places in San José. Operated by twin brothers who make every customer feel welcome, the restaurant is always busy. The menu is primarily seafood and consequently most dishes tend toward the upper end of the menu's price range, but all are well worth the price. A couple of my favorites are the *causa Limeña*, which is lemon-flavored mashed potatoes stuffed with shrimp, and the *aji de gallina*, a dish of chopped chicken in a fragrant cream sauce. Be sure to ask for one of the specialty drinks.

RESTAURANTE MORDISCO, Paseo Colón, next to Mercedes Benz. Tel. 55-2448.
   Cuisine: VEGETARIAN.
$ Prices: Appetizers $1.50–$1.60; main dishes $2.10–$5.20. AE, MC, V.
   Open: Mon–Sat 9am–10pm.
Though there are other vegetarian restaurants around town, none of them offer as wide a variety of delicious dishes as this one. You'll find such meatless favorites as miso soup, sesame noodles, tofu and bean sprout salad, as well as Central American dishes such as *pozole*, a corn soup, and campesino casserole, which is made with plantains, beans, avocado, and cheese. The desserts make excellent use of local fruits in such creations as coconut flan and guanabana delight. There are also lots of fresh juices and various types of fruit shakes and smoothies. The restaurant's main dining room is a sort of shady greenhouse with lots of plants and filtered yellow light coming through the roof. The restaurant is in the same building as Rios Tropicales, in case you are in the mood to book a rafting trip.

SPECIALTY DINING

LOCAL BUDGET BETS/FAVORITE MEALS Wherever you go in Costa Rica, the cheapest places to eat are always called *sodas,* which usually serve the Tico standards of rice and beans in different guises. If you can cultivate a taste for this simple meal, you can save a bundle on your food bills. Rice and beans are called gallo pinto when served for breakfast and may come with anything from fried eggs to steak. At lunch and dinner, those very same rice and beans are called casado and served with a salad of cabbage and tomatoes, fried bananas, and a main dish. Gallo pinto might cost $1.10 to $1.85, and a casado might cost $1.50 to $2.60.
   Another favorite of Ticos, and tourists, is the refresco. A refresco is a bit like a fresh-fruit milk shake without the ice cream; when made with mangos, papayas, or any of the other delicious tropical fruits of Costa Rica, it is pure ambrosia. Refrescos also are made with water (con agua), but these are not nearly as good as those made with milk (con leche). Despite all the assurances that the water in San José is safe to drink, you're better off avoiding it as much as possible.

FAST-FOOD CHAINS Many of the largest North American fast-food chains have restaurants in San José, with prices that are only slightly lower than those in the United States. Among the chains represented here are **McDonald's,** at Plaza de la Cultura (tel. 57-1112) and also at Calle 4 between Avenida Central and Avenida 1 (tel. 21-3632); and **Hardee's,** Avenida Central and Calle 3 (tel. 23-4646). **Kentucky Fried Chicken** seems to have restaurants all over the city these days (there's one midway down Paseo Colón and another on Avenida Central between calles 29 and 31). **Pizza Hut** is at Paseo Colón, near Kentucky Fried Chicken (tel. 35-1222).

A DINING COMPLEX   Hop in any taxi and say "El Pueblo," and within a few minutes you'll be dropped at the entrance to a maze of Spanish-style buildings filled with restaurants, bars, nightclubs, discos, and exclusive shops. If you are feeling like a splurge, there are dozens of restaurants here to accommodate you. My favorite is **La Cocina de Leña,** which I described above.

STREET FOOD   On almost every street corner in downtown San José, you'll find a fruit vendor. If you're lucky enough to be in town between April and June, you can sample more varieties of mangoes than you ever knew existed. I like buying them already cut up in a little bag. They cost a little more this way, but you don't get nearly as messy. Be sure to try a green mango with salt and chili peppers. That's the way they seem to like mangoes best in the steamy tropics—guaranteed to wake up your taste buds.

Another common street food that you might be wondering about is called *pejibaye,* a bright-orange palm nut about the size of a small apple. They are boiled in big pots on carts. You eat them in much the same way you would an avocado, and they taste a bit like squash.

LATE NIGHT/24 HOURS   San José has quite a few all-night restaurants— including **La Perla, La Esmeralda, Vilmary's La Casa de Sandwich,** and **Café Parisien,** all of which are described above. Another popular place, which is almost exclusively for men, is the **Soda Palace** on Avenida 2 and Calle 2 (see the "Evening Entertainment" section in this chapter for more information).

6. ATTRACTIONS

With its near-perfect climate, compact size, and numerous museums and parks, San José is a delightful city to explore. The museums here are the most modern in Central America and hold a wealth of Pre-Columbian artifacts despite the fact that Costa Rica had a very small Pre-Columbian Indian population.

SUGGESTED ITINERARIES

IF YOU HAVE ONE DAY   Start your day with breakfast at Café Parisien on the Plaza de la Cultura. Then visit the **Gold Museum** and see if you can get tickets for a performance that night at the **Teatro Nacional.** From the Plaza de la Cultura, stroll up Avenida Central to the **Museo Nacional.** After lunch, head over to the **Jade Museum** if you have the energy for one more museum. After all this culture, a stroll through the chaos of the **Central Market** is in order. Well worth a stop in this area is the coffee-roasting shop **Café Trebol,** where you can pick up freshly roasted coffee for about $1 per pound. Try dinner at Restaurante Campesino before going to the Teatro Nacional. After the performance, you absolutely must swing by **La Esmeralda** for some live mariachi music before calling it a day.

IF YOU HAVE TWO DAYS   Follow the itinerary above. On day two, visit the **Serpentarium** and the **Costa Rican Art Museum** and any sights that you missed the day before.

IF YOU HAVE THREE DAYS   Follow the itinerary for the two days outlined above. On day three, head out to the **Irazú Volcano, Orosi Valley, Lankester Gardens,** and **Cartago.** Start your day at the volcano and work your way back toward San José.

IF YOU HAVE FIVE DAYS   Follow the itinerary for the three days outlined above. Then spend days four and five on other excursions from San José. You can go white-water rafting or horseback riding for a day if you are an active type. If you prefer less strenuous activities, try a cruise around the Gulf of Nicoya.

THE TOP ATTRACTIONS

MUSEO NACIONAL DE COSTA RICA, Calle 17 between Avenida Central and Avenida 2. Tel. 57-1433.

Costa Rica's most important museum is housed in a former army barracks that was the scene of fighting during the civil war of 1948, after which the Costa Rican army was disbanded. You can still see hundreds of bullet holes on the turrets at the corners of the building. Inside this traditional Spanish-style courtyard building, you will find displays on Costa Rican history and culture from Pre-Columbian times to the present. In the Pre-Columbian rooms, you'll see a 2,500-year-old jade carving that is shaped like a seashell and etched with an image of a hand holding a small animal. Among the most fascinating objects unearthed at Costa Rica's many small archeological sites are many *metates*, or grinding stones. This type of grinding stone is still in use today throughout Central America. However, the ones on display here are more ornately decorated than those that you will see anywhere else. Some of the metates are the size of a small bed and are believed to have been part of funeral rites. A separate vault houses the museum's small collection of Pre-Columbian jade jewelry and figurines.

Some of the most celebrated Pre-Columbian artifacts in Costa Rica are the almost perfectly spherical carved stone-balls that have been found in the southwest part of the country. These spheres can be as large as 9 feet across and weigh 16 tons. No one is sure how they were carved so perfectly or what purpose they served. Several small spheres are on display here.

One room is dedicated to former president Oscar Arias Sánchez, who won the Nobel Peace Prize for orchestrating the Central American Peace Plan to bring peace to a region that has been rocked by revolutions and civil wars for centuries. Another room chronicles the people and history of Costa Rica from the Conquest to the present, utilizing photographs, illustrations, and objects of historical significance.

Admission: 40¢.
Open: Tues–Sat 8:30am–4:30pm, Sun 9am–4:30pm. **Bus:** San Pedro.

MUSEO DE ORO BANCO CENTRAL [GOLD MUSEUM], Calle 5 between Avenida Central and Avenida 2. Tel. 23-0528 or 33-4233, ext. 282.

Located directly beneath the Plaza de la Cultura, this unusual underground museum houses one of the largest collections of Pre-Columbian gold in the Americas. On display are more than 20,000 troy ounces of gold in more than 2,000 objects. The sheer number of small gold pieces can be overwhelming in this ultramodern museum; however, the unusual display cases and complex lighting system show off every piece to its utmost. This museum includes a gallery for temporary art exhibits and a numismatic and philatelic museum.

Admission: Free.
Open: Fri–Sun 10am–5pm. **Bus:** Sabana-Cementerio.

MUSEO DE JADE MARCO FIDEL TRISTAN [JADE MUSEUM], Avenida 7 between calles 9 and 9B, 11th floor, INS Building. Tel. 23-5800, ext. 2581.

Among the Pre-Columbian cultures of Mexico and Central America, jade was the most valuable commodity, worth more than gold. This modern museum displays a huge collection of jade artifacts from throughout Costa Rica's Pre-Columbian archeological sites. Most of the jade pieces are large pendants that were parts of necklaces and are primarily human and animal figures. A fascinating display illustrates how the primitive people of this region carved this extremely hard stone. Of particular interest are the stones that were intricately carved with string saws coated with quartz sand abrasive. Most of the jade pieces date from 330 B.C. to A.D. 700.

In addition to the jade collection, there is an extensive collection of Pre-Columbian

polychromed terra-cotta vases, bowls, and figurines. Some of these pieces are amazingly modern in design and exhibit a surprisingly advanced technique. Particularly fascinating are three vases: one that incorporates real human teeth, one that shows how jade was imbedded in human teeth merely for decorative reasons, and one that resembles a frog-faced human being. Most of the identifying labels and explanations are in Spanish, but there are a few in English.
Admission: Free.
Open: Mon–Fri 9am–3pm.

MUSEO DE ARTE COSTARRICENSE, Calle 42 and Paseo Colón, East Sabana Park. Tel. 22-7155 or 22-7247.
This small museum at the end of Paseo Colón in Sabana Park houses a collection of works in all media by Costa Rica's most celebrated artists. On display are many exceptionally beautiful pieces in a wide range of artistic styles. This exciting collection demonstrates how Costa Rican artists have interpreted the major European artistic movements. In addition to the permanent collection of sculptures, paintings, and prints, there are regular temporary exhibits. If the second floor is open during your visit, be sure to go up and have a look at the conference room's unusual bas-relief walls, which chronicle the history of Costa Rica from Pre-Columbian times to the present with evocative images of the people. On weekends local artists sell their art out on the plaza in front of the museum.
Admission: Mon–Sat 75¢; Sun free.
Open: Tues–Sun 10am–5pm. **Bus:** Sabana-Cementerio.

MORE ATTRACTIONS

PARQUE ZOOLÓGICO SIMÓN BOLÍVAR, Avenida 11 and Calle 11. No phone.
I don't think that I have ever seen a sadder zoo than this little park tucked away beside the polluted Río Torres. It is a shame that a country that has preserved so much of its land in national parks would ignore its only public zoo. The cages here are only occasionally marked, and many are dirty and small. The collection includes Asian, African, and Costa Rican animals. There are rumors that a new zoo is to be built or that this one is to be renovated. Hopefully something will be done soon about this disgraceful situation.
Admission: 30¢.
Open: Wed–Fri 8am–3:30pm; Sat–Sun 9am–4:30pm.

SERPENTARIUM, Avenida 1 between calles 9 and 11. Tel. 55-4210.
The tropics abound in reptiles and amphibians, and the Serpentarium is an excellent introduction to all that slithers and hops through the jungles of Costa Rica. The live snakes, lizards, and frogs are kept in beautiful large terrariums that simulate their natural environments. Poisonous snakes make up a large part of the collection, with the dreaded fer-de-lance pit viper being the star attraction. Also fascinating to see are the tiny, brilliantly colored poison arrow frogs. Iguanas and Jesus Christ lizards are two of the more commonly spotted of Costa Rica's reptiles, and both are represented here. Also on display is an Asian import—a giant reticulate python, which is one of the largest I have ever seen. This little zoological museum is well worth a visit, especially if you plan to go bashing about in the jungles, because it will help you identify the numerous poisonous snakes that you'll want to avoid.
Admission: $1.50.
Open: Daily 10am–7pm.

WALKING TOUR — DOWNTOWN SAN JOSÉ

Start: Plaza de la Cultura.
Finish: Plaza de la Cultura.

Time: Allow a full day for this tour, although most of your time will be spent touring the three museums mentioned.

Best Time: Sunday, when artists and street performers perform at the Plaza de la Cultura.

Worst Time: Monday, when museums are closed. Because San José is so compact, it is possible to visit nearly all of the city's major sites in a single day's walking tour. Begin your tour on the **Plaza de la Cultura,** perhaps after having breakfast at the Gran Hotel Costa Rica.

Begin by walking to:

1. **Teatro Nacional,** which faces the entrance to the Gran Hotel Costa Rica. Be sure to take a tour of this baroque masterpiece.
2. **The Gold Museum** is built beneath the Plaza de la Cultura to the left of the Teatro Nacional and houses the largest collection of Pre-Columbian gold in Central America.
3. **The National Cathedral** is a neoclassical structure with a tropical twist. The roof is tin, and the ceiling is wood. A statue of the Virgin Mary is surrounded by neon stars and a crescent moon.
4. **Melico Salazar Theater** is diagonally across the street from the cathedral. This theater has an impressive pillared facade, though the interior is not nearly as impressive. Continue down Avenida 2 and turn right on Calle 6. In two blocks, you will be in:
5. **The Central Market,** a fragrant district of streets crowded with produce vendors. A covered market, with its dark warren of stalls, takes up an entire block and is the center of activity. Beware of pickpockets in this area. Head back toward the Teatro Nacional on Avenida 1, and in seven blocks you will come to an excellent place for lunch.

REFUELING STOP One of the best lunches in San José is at the **Amstel Grill Room,** Avenida 1 and Calle 7. White-jacketed waiters attend to your every need. Prices are reasonable; the cuisine is American, Continental, and Costa Rican.

From the restaurant, walk up Calle 7 to Avenida 3, and you will find yourself in:

6. **The Parque Morazán,** a classically designed park that was restored to its original configuration in 1991. At the center of the park is a large bandstand modeled after a music temple in Paris.
7. **Escuela Metálica,** Avenida 5 and Calle 9, is one of the most unusual buildings in the city. It is made of metal panels that are bolted together and was manufactured in Europe late in the last century. In the park across the street is a beautiful music temple.
8. **The Jade Museum** is one block over on Avenida 7 in the high-rise office building. The cool, dark exhibit halls are filled with jade pendants. Great views of the city!
9. **Casa Amarilla,** across Calle 11 from the Jade Museum, is an interesting building housing the Ministry of Foreign Affairs. It was donated, along with the park across the street, by Andrew Carnegie.
10. **Parque Nacional,** at Avenida 3 and Calle 15, has an impressive monument to the nations that defeated William Walker's attempt to turn Central America into a slave state. Across Avenida 1 is a statue of **Juan Santamaría,** who gave his life to defeat Walker.
11. **Museo Nacional,** Calle 17 between avenidas Central and 2 is housed in a former army barracks that still shows signs of the 1948 revolution.

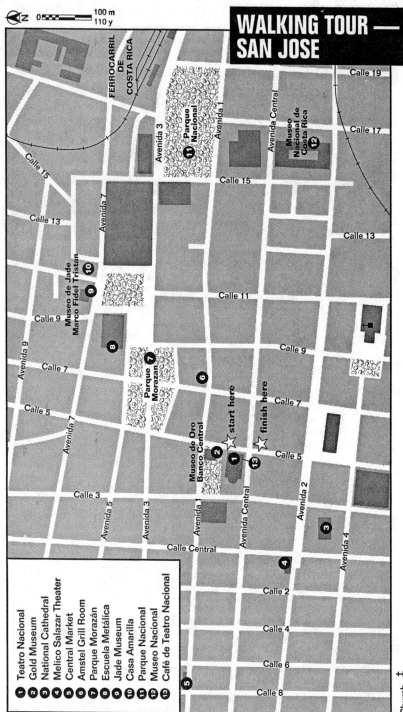

WALKING TOUR — SAN JOSE

N 0 ▭▭▭▭ 100 m
              110 y

FERROCARRIL DE COSTA RICA

Calle 19

Avenida 1

Avenida Central

Museo Nacional de Costa Rica **⑫**

Calle 17

Avenida 3

Parque Nacional **⑪**

Calle 15

Calle 15

Calle 13

Avenida 7

Calle 13

Calle 11

Museo de Jade Marco Fidel Tristan **⑩ ⑨**

Calle 9

Avenida 9

Calle 9

Calle 7

⑧

Calle 7

Parque Morazán **⑦**

⑥

Calle 9

Avenida 7

Calle 5

☆ start here

☆ finish here

Calle 7

Calle 5

Museo de Oro Banco Central

Avenida 7

② ①

⑬

Avenida 1

Avenida Central

Avenida 2

Calle 3

Avenida 5

Avenida 3

③

Avenida 4

Calle Central

④

Calle 2

Calle 4

Calle 6

⑤

Calle 8

① Teatro Nacional
② Gold Museum
③ National Cathedral
④ Melico Salazar Theater
⑤ Central Market
⑥ Amstel Grill Room
⑦ Parque Morazán
⑧ Escuela Metálica
⑨ Jade Museum
⑩ Casa Amarilla
⑪ Parque Nacional
⑫ Museo Nacional
⑬ Café de Teatro Nacional

Church ✝

FINAL REFUELING STOP Without a doubt, San José's most elegant place to have a light meal, snack, or coffee and cake is **Café de Teatro Nacional,** Plaza de la Cultura.

ORGANIZED TOURS

There are literally dozens of tour companies operating in San José, and the barrage of advertising brochures can be quite intimidating. There really isn't much reason to take a tour of San José since it is so compact—you can easily visit all the major sites on your own. However, if you want to take a city tour, which will run you about $18, here are some companies that you can contact.

Otec Tours, Edeficio Ferencz, Calle 3 between avenidas 1 and 3, Apdo. 323-1002 (tel. 55-0554 or 22-0866).

TAM, Calle 1 between Avenida Central and Avenida 1, Apdo. 1864-1000 (tel. 23-5111).

Panorama Tours, Calle 9 between Avenida Central and Avenida 1, Apdo. 7323 (tel. 33-3058).

Swiss Travel Service, Hotel Corobici, Apdo. 7-1970 (tel. 31-4055), has several offices around San José. The most convenient is in the Hotel Amstel at Calle 7 and Avenida 1.

SPECIAL/FREE EVENTS

San José is a conservative city and doesn't stage many public festivals or events. Those it does have are strictly religious in nature: The days between Christmas and New Year's and the week prior to Easter are the city's two top periods of celebration. During these times there are parades, dances, and other special events.

On Sundays throughout the year there are often free classical music concerts on the Parque Central and the Parque Morazán.

SPORTS/RECREATION

Sabana Park, formerly San José's airport, is the city's center for sports and recreation. Here you'll find everything from jogging trails and soccer fields to the National Stadium. For information on horseback riding and white-water rafting trips from San José, see "Easy Excursions" at the end of this chapter.

If you like to swim and would like to spend an afternoon relaxing in a spring-fed swimming pool, head out to Ojo de Agua, which is just beyond the airport near Alajuela. The crystal-clear waters are cool and refreshing, and even if it seems a bit chilly in San José, it is always several degrees warmer out here. Admission is $1.10 and there are express buses from San José Monday through Saturday both in the morning and in the afternoon. These buses depart from Avenida 1 between calles 20 and 22.

7. SAVVY SHOPPING

In Costa Rica, you probably won't be overwhelmed with the desire to buy things, as you might be in Guatemala. In fact, for lack of its own handcrafts, Costa Rica does a brisk business selling crafts and clothes imported from Guatemala.

THE SHOPPING SCENE

Shopping in San José centers around the parallel streets of Avenida Central and Avenida 2, from about Calle 14 in the west to Calle 13 in the east. For several blocks east of the Plaza de la Cultura, Avenida Central is a pedestrians-only street where you'll find store after store of inexpensive made-in-Costa Rica clothes for men, women, and children. Most shops in the downtown shopping district are open from 8am to noon and from 2 to 6pm. When you do purchase something, you'll be happy to find that there is no sales tax.

There are several markets around downtown San José, but by far the largest is the **Mercado Central,** which is located between Avenida Central and Avenida 1 and calles 6 and 8. Inside this dark maze of stalls you'll find all manner of vendors. Although this is primarily a food market, you can find a few vendors selling Costa Rican souvenirs. Be especially careful about your wallet or purse because this area is frequented by very skillful pickpockets. All the streets surrounding the Mercado Central are jammed with produce vendors selling from small carts or loading and unloading trucks. It is always a hive of activity, with crowds of people jostling for space on the streets. In the hot days of the dry season, the aromas can get quite heady.

BEST BUYS
COFFEE

Two words of advice—buy coffee. Buy as much as you can carry. Coffee is probably the best shopping deal in all of Costa Rica. Although the best Costa Rican coffee is supposedly shipped off to North American and European markets, it is hard to beat coffee that is roasted right in front of you. **Café Trebol,** on Calle 8 between Avenida Central and Avenida 1, is highly recommended as a place to buy coffee. They'll pack the beans for you in whatever size bag you want. Be sure to ask for whole beans; Costa Rican grinds are too fine for standard coffee filters. Best of all is the price: One pound of coffee sells for about $1! It makes a great gift and keeps for a long time in your refrigerator or freezer. If you should happen to buy prepackaged coffee in a supermarket in Costa Rica, be sure that the package is marked *puro;* otherwise, it will likely be mixed with a good amount of sugar—the way Ticos like it.

HANDCRAFTS

If your interest is in handcrafts, there are several places for you to visit. The most appealing artisans market is the daily one on the Plaza de la Cultura. Prices here tend to be high and bargaining is necessary, but there are some very nice items for sale. If you prefer to do your craft shopping in a flea-market atmosphere, head over to **La Casona** on Calle Central between Avenida Central and Avenida 1. The Hotel Don Carlos, Calle 9 between avenidas 7 and 9, has an excellent gift shop too.

Several other shops around San José sell a wide variety of crafts—from the truly tacky to the divinely inspired. Here are some of the places to look for such items.

MERCADO DE ARTESANOS CANAPI, Calle 11 and Avenida 1. Tel. 21-3342.

Inside you'll find a wide variety of typical Costa Rican handcrafts, including large, comfortable woven rope hammocks; reproductions of Pre-Columbian gold jewelry and pottery bowls; coffee-wood carvings; and many other wood carvings from rare Costa Rican hardwoods. The most unusual crafts for sale are the brightly painted miniature ox carts that are almost the national symbol. These ox carts are made in the small town of Sarchí, which is mentioned under "Easy Excursions" in this chapter.

Open: Mon–Fri 9am–noon and 1–6pm; Sat 9am–noon.

MERCADO NACIONAL DE ARTESANIAS, Calle 11 and Avenida 4 bis. Tel. 21-5012.

Similar crafts at similar prices are available from this shop, which is located only two blocks away from the CANAPI store.

Open: Mon–Fri 9am–12:30pm and 1:30–6pm, Sat 9am–12:30pm and 1:30–5pm.

ANTIC, EDIFICIO LAS ARCADAS, Avenida 2 and Calle 1. Tel. 33-4630.

Located in the building to the left of the Gran Hotel Costa Rica, this tiny shop has—among other things—carved stone reproductions of the Pre-Columbian figures on display in the National Museum and Jade Museum. Antic sells crafts from all over Central America, and it is a good place to pick up a *mola,* the appliquéd panels from Panama.

Open: Mon–Fri 9am–noon and 2–6pm; Sat until 5pm.

SURASKA, Calle 5 and Avenida 3. Tel. 22-0129.

If you haven't been impressed with the quality of Costa Rican handcrafts found elsewhere, save your money for a visit to this store. Of particular note are the wood carvings by Barry Biesanz and Jay Morrison. These two North American artists turn out exquisite pieces of finely worked hardwood. One of Biesanz's pieces was even given to the Reagans as a gift. Woods used for these works of art include purple heart, rosewood, and lignum vitae, among others. Be forewarned, however, that these pieces sell for hundreds of dollars.

Open: Mon–Fri 8:30am–12:30pm and 1:30–5:45pm, Sat 8:30am–12:30pm.

ATMÓSFERA, Calle 5 between avenidas 1 and 3. Tel. 22-4322.

Even if you can't afford anything in this shop, it is worth a visit just to see the best of Costa Rican arts and crafts. From naive paintings to skilled turned-wood bowls, this store simply has the best. There are several small rooms on two floors, so be sure you explore every nook and cranny. You'll see stuff here that is not available anywhere else in town.

Open: Mon–Sat 8:30am–6:30pm.

8. EVENING ENTERTAINMENT

To find out about the entertainment scene in San José, pick up a copy of the *Tico Times* (English) and *La Nación* (Spanish). The former is a good place to find out where local expatriates are hanging out; the latter's "Viva" section has extensive listings of everything from discos to movie theaters to live music.

THE PERFORMING ARTS

TEATRO NACIONAL, Avenida 2 between calles 3 and 5. Tel. 21-1329.

Financed with a self-imposed tax on coffee exports, this grand baroque theater was completed in 1897. Muses representing Music, Fame, and Dance gaze off into the distance from the roof, while statues of Beethoven and Calderón de la Barca flank the entrance. The lobby is simple and elegant. Marble floors, frescoes, and gold-framed Venetian mirrors offer cultured Ticos a grand foyer in which to congregate prior to performances by the National Symphony Orchestra, ballet companies, opera companies, and all the other performers who keep this theater busy almost every night of the year. Within the hall itself, there are three tiers of seating amid an elegant gilt-and-plasterwork decor, and of course the wealthy patrons have their private box seats. Marble staircases are lined with sculptures; the walls are covered with murals and changing art exhibits. The symphony season begins in late April, shortly before the start of the rainy season, and continues on until November. Performances are on Thursday and Friday. The Café de Teatro Nacional, just off the lobby, is open daily and is the most elegant café in the city.

The Teatro Nacional was badly damaged by an earthquake in 1991 and has been undergoing renovation since then. Hopefully the theater will be once again hosting performances when you visit.

Tours: Mon–Sat 9am–5:30pm for $1.10.

Prices: $1.50–$5.20, purchasers of cheaper tickets must use side entrance. **Bus:** Sabana-Cementerio.

TEATRO MELICO SALAZAR, Avenida 2 between Calle Central and Calle 2. Tel. 21-4952.

Just a few blocks away from the Teatro Nacional, and directly across the street from the Parque Central, is this 1920s neoclassical theater. Though the facade is far more impressive than the interior, it is still a grand old theater. "Fantasia Folklorico," which features modern dance, pantomime, and traditional dances that together tell the history of Costa Rica, is staged every Tuesday night at 8pm. The box office is open daily from 9am to noon and from 2 to 8pm.

Prices: $1.10–$3.70. **Bus:** Sabana-Cementerio.

THE CLUB & MUSIC SCENE

Salsa is the music of young people in San José, and on any weekend you can join the fun at half a dozen or more high-decibel nightclubs around town. The "Viva" section of *La Nacion* newspaper has weekly performance schedules.

The best place to sample San José's nightclub scene is in El Pueblo, a shopping, dining, and entertainment complex done up like an old Spanish village. It's just across the river to the north of town. The easiest way to get here is by taxi; all the drivers know El Pueblo well. Within the alleyways that wind through El Pueblo are a dozen or more bars, clubs, and discos. There is even a roller-skating rink. **Salon Musical Lety** offers live Latin music nightly, **Cocolocos** features nightly "fiestas," and **Discoteque Infinito** has three different ambiences under one roof. **Manhattan** is a piano bar, and the **Tango Bar** is just what its name implies.

THE BAR SCENE

The best part of the varied bar scene in San José is something called a *boca,* the equivalent of a *tapa* in Spain, a little dish of snacks that arrives at your table when you order a drink. In most bars, the bocas are free; but in some, where the dishes are more sophisticated, you'll have to pay for the treats. Also, with the exception of Key Largo, drinks are very reasonably priced at 80¢ to $1.20.

LA ESMERALDA, Avenida 2 between calles 5 and 7. Tel. 21-0503.

A sort of mariachi Grand Central Station, La Esmeralda is a cavernous open-air restaurant and bar that stays open 24 hours a day. In the evenings, mariachi bands park their vans out front and wait to be hired for a moonlight serenade or perhaps a surprise party. While they wait, they often wander into La Esmeralda and practice their favorite melodies. If you've never been serenaded at your table before, this place is a must.

SODA PALACE, Calle 2 and Avenida 2. Tel. 21-3441.

Mostly a men's hangout, this dingy but brightly lit bar hardly lives up to its name. It opens directly onto busy Avenida 2 and is open 24 hours a day. Men of all ages sit at the tables conversing loudly and watching the world pass by. You never know what might happen at the Palace. Mariachis stroll in, linger for a while, then continue on their way. Legend has it that the revolution of 1948 was planned right here.

KEY LARGO, Calle 7 between avenidas 1 and 3. Tel. 21-0277.

Housed in one of the most beautiful old buildings in San José, Key Largo is elegant and expensive. It is worth a visit just to see the interior of the building, but be forewarned—this is known as San José's number-one prostitute hangout.

CHARLESTON, Avenida 4 between calles 7 and 9. No phone.

Jazz lovers will enjoy this relaxed bar with a 1920s theme. Great recorded jazz music plays on the stereo all day and night. There are occasional live bands.

EL CUARTEL DE LA BOCA DEL MONTE, Avenida 1 between calles 21 and 23. Tel. 21-0327.

This very popular bar is reputed to have the best bocas in San José, although you'll have to pay for them. Their cocktails are also famous. Just look around and see what sort of amazing concoctions people are drinking and ask for whichever one strikes your fancy.

NASHVILLE SOUTH, Calle 5 between avenidas 1 and 3. Tel. 33-1988.

As its name implies, this is a country-and-western bar. It's very popular with homesick expatriates and has a friendly atmosphere and fun music.

MORE ENTERTAINMENT

MOVIE THEATERS   Even if you aren't interested in what's playing at one of the downtown theaters, it's worth the $1.50 admission just to gain entrance to one of these old palaces. The screens are huge, and on a weeknight you might have the theater almost to yourself. Check the "Viva" section of *La Nacion* or the *Tico Times* for movie listings and times.

GAMBLING CASINOS   Gambling is legal in Costa Rica, and there are casinos at virtually every major hotel. In most of these hotel casinos, you'll need to get dressed up; but at the casino in the lobby of the Gran Hotel Costa Rica, at Calle 3 between Avenida Central and Avenida 2, on the Plaza de la Cultura, there doesn't seem to be any dress code.

9. EASY EXCURSIONS

San José makes an excellent base for exploring the beautiful Meseta Central and the surrounding mountains. Probably the best way to make most of these excursions is by car, though public transportation is available.

For many years the most popular excursion from San José was the so-called jungle train which chugged from San José to Limón amid rugged and remote scenery. Since the earthquake of April 22, 1991, the railroad has been closed except for a short section that is kept open as a tourist route. This abbreviated jungle train tour is quite expensive for what you get (a lot of time on buses), so I no longer recommend the trip.

Rates for various excursion tours from San José are pretty much standardized; if, say, you book a cruise through the Gulf of Nicoya with one company, you will take the same cruise being offered by many other companies. Generally the rates are rather high, with half-day trips costing $25 to $30 and full-day trips costing $65 to $75. Several companies offer cruises to remote islands in the Gulf of Nicoya, and these excursions include gourmet buffet meals and stops at deserted (until your boat arrives) beaches. Companies offering these trips include **Calypso Island Cruise** (tel. 33-3617) and **Fantasia** (tel. 55-0791).

If you enjoy horseback riding, you have your choice of fascinating locations for day-long trips not far from downtown San José. Contact **L.A. Tours** (tel. 24-5828 or 21-4501) for rides on the beach or through a cloud forest. Rates are around $70 for a day of riding, including hotel pick up and lunch.

Cascading down from Costa Rica's mountain ranges are dozens of tumultuous rivers, several of which have become very popular for white-water rafting and kayaking. For about $75 you can spend a day rafting through lush tropical forests. Contact **Rios Tropicales** (tel. 33-6455), **Costaricaraft** (tel. 25-3939), or one of the tour companies listed under "Organized Tours" in the "Attractions" section. If I were to splurge on just one San José excursion, rafting would be it. There are few other experiences as exciting or as refreshing.

If rafting doesn't interest you, consider kayaking the Sarapiquí River. This is a quiet river fed by clear mountain streams, and the scenery is a combination of forests and farms. Trips can be arranged through **Rancho Leona,** La Virgen de Sarapiquí, Heredia (tel. 71-6312). For $75 you get a day of kayaking plus two nights lodging in shared accommodations (bunks) at the ranch's private hostel. Meals such as eggplant parmesan and hamburgers are available. Lunch on the day of your kayak trip is included in the price, but other meals are not. You can reach Rancho Leona by taking a Río Frío bus from Calle 12 between avenidas 7 and 9 in San José. Buses leave at 6am, noon, 1, 3, and 4pm. The fare is around $3 and the trip takes about 3½ hours. It is also possible to take a taxi from San José, but this will cost around $50. Longer trips can also be arranged.

Of all the possible excursions from San José, none is more enjoyable than a visit to Lankester Gardens with a trip up to the top of Irazú Volcano, a stop in Cartago, and a drive through the Orosi Valley.

LANKESTER GARDENS

There are more than 1,200 varieties of orchids in Costa Rica, and no less than 800 species are on display at this botanical garden in Cartago province. Created in the 1940s by English naturalist Charles Lankester, the gardens are now administered by the University of Costa Rica. The primary goal of the gardens is to preserve the local flora, with an emphasis on orchids and bromeliads. Paved trails wander from open sunny gardens into shady forests. In each environment, different species of orchids are in bloom. Be sure to bring lots of color film for your camera. The only disappointment in a visit to Lankester Gardens is that you are allowed to visit for only one hour before you have to leave. There are free guided tours, or you can wander on your own.

Admission is $1.50. The gardens are open Tuesday through Sunday 8:30am to 3:30pm with tours every hour on the half hour. To get there take a Cartago bus from San José. In Cartago, cross to the south side of the Central Park and catch a Paraíso bus to Campo Ayala. From this stop, walk 500 yards to the gardens. Alternatively, you can take a taxi from Cartago for between $2.50 and $4. If you're driving, take the Paraíso road out of Cartago and watch for a 3-foot-tall blue-green cube on the right side of the road.

CARTAGO

Located about 15 miles southeast of San José, Cartago is the former capital of Costa Rica. Founded in 1563, it was Costa Rica's first city—and was in fact its only city for almost 150 years. Irazú Volcano looms up from the edge of town; although it is quiescent these days, it has not always been so peaceful. Earthquakes have damaged Cartago repeatedly over the years, so that today there are few colonial buildings left standing. In the center of the city are the ruins of a large church that was destroyed in 1910, before it was ever finished. Construction was abandoned after the quake, and today the ruins are a neatly manicured park.

Cartago's most famous building, however, is the **Basílica de Nuestra Señora de Los Ángeles** (the Basilica of Our Lady of the Angels), which is dedicated to the patron saint of Costa Rica and stands on the east side of town. Within the walls of this Byzantine church is a shrine containing the tiny figure of La Negrita, the Black Virgin, which is nearly lost amid its ornate altar. This statue was found at a spring that now bubbles up at the rear of the church on the right side. Miraculous healing powers have been attributed to La Negrita, and over the years thousands of pilgrims have come to the shrine seeking cures for their illnesses and difficulties. The walls of the shrine are covered with a fascinating array of tiny silver images left as thanks for cures affected by La Negrita. Amid the plethora of diminutive arms and legs, there are also hands, feet, hearts, lungs, kidneys, eyes, torsos, breasts—and, peculiarly, guns, trucks, beds, and planes. There are even dozens of sports trophies which I assume were left in thanks for helping teams win big games. August 2 is the day dedicated to La Negrita. On this day thousands of people walk from San José to Cartago in devotion to this powerful statue.

If you'd like to soak in a warm-water swimming pool, head 2½ miles south of Cartago to Aguas Calientes.

Buses for Cartago leave San José frequently from Avenida Central between calles 13 and 15 and cost 35¢. The length of the trip is 45 minutes.

IRAZÚ VOLCANO

Located 20 miles north of Cartago, 11,260-foot-tall Irazú is one of Costa Rica's three active volcanoes (at this time it is dormant). It last erupted on March 19, 1963, on the day that President John F. Kennedy arrived in Costa Rica. The eruption showered ash on the Meseta Central for months after, destroying crops and collapsing roofs but enriching the soil. There is a good paved road right to the rim of the crater. At the top, amid desolate expanses of gray sand, few plants grow. The air smells of sulfur, and clouds descend by noon each day. From the parking area, a short trail leads to the rim of the volcano's two craters, its walls a maze of eroded gullies feeding onto the flat floor far below. If you arrive early enough, before the clouds close in, you may be treated to a view of both the Pacific Ocean and the Caribbean Sea. There are also magnificent views of the fertile Meseta Central and Orosi Valley as you drive up from Cartago. It is officially open only from 8am to 4pm, but there is nothing to stop you from visiting earlier. Don't forget to wear warm clothes. This may be the tropics, but it's cold up at the top. In the busy season, an admission of 75¢ is charged. Plan to arrive at the rim as early as possible, then, on your way down, stop for breakfast at **Restaurant Linda Vista** (tel. 25-5808). It's on the right as you come down the mountain and is open daily from 7:30am to 6pm. At 10,075 feet, it claims to be the highest restaurant in Central America; there are walls of windows looking out over the valley far below. A hearty Tico breakfast of gallo pinto with ham will cost about $2.25.

Buses leave for Irazú Volcano Wednesday, Saturday, Sunday, and holidays from Avenida 2 between calles 1 and 3 (in front of the Gran Hotel Costa Rica). The fare is around $2.50 and the trip takes about 1½ hours. To make sure the buses are running, you can phone 34-0344. If you are driving, head northeast out of Cartago toward San Rafael, then continue driving uphill toward the volcano, passing the turnoffs for Cot and Tierra Blanca en route.

OROSI VALLEY

The Orosi Valley, southeast of Cartago, is called the most beautiful valley in Costa Rica. The Reventazón River meanders through this steep-sided valley until it collects in the lake formed by the Cachí Dam. There are scenic overlooks near the towns of Orosi, at the head of the valley, and Ujarrás, on the banks of the lake. Near Ujarrás are the ruins of Costa Rica's oldest church, whose tranquil gardens are a great place to sit and gaze at the surrounding mountains. Across the lake is a popular recreation center, called Charrarra, where you'll find a picnic area, swimming pool, and hiking trails. In the town of Orosi itself is a colonial church built in 1743. A small museum here displays religious artifacts.

It would be difficult to explore this whole area by public bus, since this is not a densely populated region. However, there are buses from Cartago to Ujarrás as well as buses to the town of Orosi. These buses leave from a spot one block east and one block south of the church ruins in Cartago. A bus that will drop you at the Orosi lookout point leaves from the same vicinity. If you are driving, take the road to Paraíso from Cartago, head toward Ujarrás, continue around the lake, then pass through Cachí and on to Orosi. From Orosi, the road leads back to Paraíso. There are tours of this area from San José.

POÁS VOLCANO

This is another active volcano accessible from San José in a day trip. It is 36 miles from San José on narrow roads that wind through a landscape of fertile farms and dark forests. As at Irazú, there is a paved road right to the top. The volcano stands 8,800 feet tall and is located within a national park, which preserves not only the volcano but also dense stands of virgin forest. Poás's crater is nearly a mile across and is said to be the second-largest crater in the world. Geysers in the crater sometimes spew steam and muddy water 600 feet into the air, making this the largest geyser in the world. There is an information center where you can see a slide show about the volcano, and marked hiking trails through the cloud forest that rings the crater. About 20 minutes from the parking area, along a forest trail, is an overlook onto beautiful Botos Lake, which has formed in one of the volcano's extinct craters.

IMPRESSIONS

. . . below us, at a distance of perhaps two thousand feet, the whole country was covered with clouds . . . the more distant clouds were lifted, and over the immense bed we saw at the same moment the Atlantic and Pacific Oceans . . . This was the grand spectacle we had hoped . . . It is the only point in the world which commands a view of two seas . . .
—J.L. STEPHENS, *INCIDENTS OF TRAVEL IN CENTRAL AMERICA, CHIAPAS AND YUCATAN,* 1841

Because the sulfur fumes occasionally become dangerously strong at Poás, the park is sometimes closed to the public. Before heading out for the volcano, contact the tourist office to make sure that the park is open. The admission fee is 75¢.

There is an excursion bus on Sunday leaving from the corner of Calle 12 and Avenida 2 at 8:30am and returning at 2pm. The fare is $2.60 for the round trip. The bus is always crowded, so arrive early. Other days it is possible to get as far as the town of San Pedro de Poás, but from there you will have to hitchhike or take a taxi ($20 round trip), which makes this alternative as costly as a tour. All the tour companies in San José offer tours to Poás, although they often don't arrive until after the clouds have closed in. If you're traveling by car, head for Alajuela and continue on the main road through town toward Varablanca. Just before reaching Varablanca, turn left toward Poasito and continue to the rim of the volcano.

HEREDIA, ALAJUELA, GRECIA, SARCHÍ & ZARCERO

All of these cities and towns are northwest of San José and can be combined into a long day trip, perhaps in conjunction with a visit to Poás Volcano.

Heredia was founded in 1706. On its central park stands a colonial church dedicated in 1763. The stone facade leaves no questions as to the age of the church, but the altar inside is decorated with neon stars and a crescent moon surrounding a statue of the Virgin Mary. In the middle of the palm-shaded park is a music temple, and across the street, beside several tile-roofed municipal buildings, is the tower of an old Spanish fort. Of all the cities in the Meseta Central, this is the only one that has even the slightest colonial feeling to it.

Alajuela is one of Costa Rica's oldest cities, only 12 miles from San José. Although it is an attractive little city filled with parks, there isn't much to see or do here. The **Juan Santamaría Museum,** Avenida 2 between Calle Central and Calle 2 (tel. 41-4775), commemorates Costa Rica's national hero, who gave his life defending the country against a small army led by William Walker, a U.S. citizen who invaded Costa Rica in 1856 with the goal of setting up a slave state in Central America. Open Tuesday through Sunday 2 to 9pm.

From Alajuela, a narrow, winding road leads to the town of **Grecia,** which is noteworthy for its unusual metal church, painted a deep red with white gingerbread trim. The road to Sarchí is to the right as you go around the church.

Sarchí is Costa Rica's main artisans town. It is here that the colorfully painted miniature ox carts you see all over Costa Rica are made. Ox carts such as these were once used to haul coffee beans to market; today they are entirely decorative and have become a well-known symbol of Costa Rica. Many other carved wooden souvenirs are made here with rare hardwoods from the nation's forests. There are dozens of shops in the town, and all have similar prices. The other reason to visit Sarchí is to see its unforgettable church. Built between 1950 and 1958, the church is painted pink with aquamarine trim and looks strangely like a child's birthday cake. This outrageously decorated church is the largest pink building I have ever seen. There is even an ox-cart wheel atop one of the church's towers.

Beyond Sarchí, on picturesque roads lined with cedar trees, you will find the town of **Zarcero.** In a small park in the middle of town is a menagerie of topiary sculptures (sculpted shrubs) that includes a monkey on a motorcycle, people and animals dancing, an ox pulling a cart, and a man wearing a top hat. It is well worth the drive to see this park.

The road to Heredia turns north off the highway from San José to the airport. To reach Alajuela from Heredia, take the scenic road that heads west through the town of San Joaquín. To continue on to Sarchí, it is best to return to the highway south of Alajuela and drive west toward Puntarenas. Turn north to Grecia and then west to Sarchí.

CHAPTER 4

GUANACASTE AND THE NORTHWEST

The northwest of Costa Rica is the country's "Wild West." It is the driest region and toward the end of the dry season resembles west Texas. This resemblance is further accentuated by the presence of large cattle ranches where gigantic, flop-eared white Brahma cattle graze in the fields. The Guanacaste Peninsula, which is divided from the mainland by the Gulf of Nicoya, is where most tourists coming in this direction are headed. Because of its long dry season and relatively dry rainy season (only 65 inches per year), the Guanacaste Peninsula has been targeted for major resort developments. In addition to the towns and beaches mentioned in this chapter, there are many remote beaches, some accessible only by plane, where there are small, but expensive, resorts. Down at the southern tip of the peninsula is an area, Playa Montezuma, that has a few backpacker-type cabinas, but it is very difficult to reach. In upcoming years, all of these beaches should become more accessible; as they do, they will be included in future editions of this book.

1. MONTEVERDE

90 miles NW of San José; 35 miles NW of Puntarenas

GETTING THERE By Bus Express buses leave San José Monday through Thursday at 2:30pm and Saturday and Sunday at 6:30am from the corner of Calle 14 between avenidas 9 and 11. The trip takes 3½ hours; the fare is $4.45. There is also a daily bus from Puntarenas to Santa Elena, which is only a few miles from Monteverde. These buses leave at 2:15pm from the stop across the street from the San José station in Puntarenas. Costing $1.18, this trip takes 2½ hours. One other option is to take Costa Rica Expeditions' van from San José. The one-way fare is $30. Phone 57-0766 or 22-0333 to make a reservation.

By Car Take the Interamerican Highway toward Puntarenas and follow the signs for Nicaragua. Turn off to the right shortly before Puntarenas and head north. In about 25 miles (41km), watch for the Rio Lagarto bridge. Just before the bridge is a dirt road to the right. Turn here. From this turnoff, it's another 19 miles (1½ to 2 hours) to Monteverde, but the going is very slow because the road is so bad. Don't try

WHAT'S SPECIAL ABOUT THE NORTHWEST

Beaches
☐ The beaches of Guanacaste, with more sunshine than any of the other beaches in the country.

Parks/Gardens
☐ Monteverde Cloud Forest Reserve, a lush jungle that is home to the quetzal, one of the most beautiful birds on earth.
☐ Rincón de la Vieja and Santa Rosa national parks, unique habitats including tropical dry forest and a geyser field.

Natural Spectacles
☐ Every year, hundreds of thousands of turtles lay their eggs on beaches in Santa Rosa National Park.
☐ Arenal Volcano, with a large artificial lake at its base.

Activities
☐ Sportfishing for billfish off the northwest coast.

it in the rainy season unless you have four-wheel drive. If you reach the turnoff from the highway before the afternoon bus passes through, you will likely be hailed by people wanting a ride. If your car can handle the additional load, a lift will be greatly appreciated. On remote sections of road throughout Costa Rica, hitchhiking is quite common because buses are often infrequent or nonexistent. One more thing: Be sure you have plenty of gas in the car before starting up to Monteverde. This grueling road eats up fuel, and the one gas station in Monteverde doesn't always have gas.

DEPARTING   The express bus to San José leaves Tuesday, Wednesday, and Thursday at 6:30am, Friday, Saturday, and Sunday at 3pm.
 The bus from Santa Elena to Puntarenas leaves daily at 6am.
 To get to Manuel Antonio, take the 6am Santa Elena–Puntarenas bus and then catch the 2:30 bus for Quepos. It makes for a long day, but is the only choice you have unless you want to go back to San José and catch the 3pm plane (Monday through Saturday only), which will save you only a couple of hours if any.
 To reach Liberia, take the Santa Elena–Puntarenas bus at 6am and get off at the Rio Lagarto bridge, where the bus reaches the paved road. You can then flag down a bus bound for Liberia (almost any bus heading north).

ESSENTIALS   Orientation   Monteverde is not a village in the traditional sense of the word. There is no center of town, only dirt lanes leading off from the main road to various farms. This main road has signs for all the hotels and restaurants mentioned here and dead-ends at the reserve entrance.
 A taxi between Santa Elena and Monteverde costs $4.45 to $7.40.

In the past few years, ecotourism has become big business in Costa Rica, and nowhere is this more apparent than in the tiny village of Monteverde. "Green Mountain" is how the Spanish name translates, and that is exactly what you will find up here at the end of a long, rutted dirt road that passes through mile after mile of pastures. All those pastures were once covered with dense forest, but only a small piece of it now remains. That piece of forest has been preserved as the **Reserva Biologica Bosque Nuboso Monteverde,** the Monteverde Cloud Forest Biological Reserve.
 The village of Monteverde was founded in the 1950s by Quakers from the United States. They wished to leave behind the constant fear of war and the obligation to

support continued militarism through U.S. taxes. They chose Costa Rica because it was committed to a nonmilitaristic economic path. Since its founding, Monteverde has grown slowly as other people who shared the ideals of the original Quaker founders moved to the area. Although the original founders came here to farm the land, they recognized the need to preserve the rare cloud forest that covers the mountain slopes above their fields.

A cloud forest is much like a rain forest, but much of the moisture comes not from falling rain but from the condensation left by the nearly constant cloud cover that blankets the tops of mountains in many parts of the tropics. Monteverde Reserve covers 26,000 acres of forest, including several different life zones that are characterized by different types of plants and animals. Within this small area are more than 2,000 species of plants, 320 bird species, and 100 different species of mammals. It is no wonder that the reserve has been the site of constant scientific investigations since its founding.

WHAT TO SEE & DO

Don't expect to see all those plants and animals during your visit because many of them are quite rare or elusive. However, with a guide hired through your hotel or with one of the reserve guides who lead 2- to 3-hour tours of the reserve, you can see far more than you could on your own. At $12 per person, the tours are expensive, especially after you pay the $5 reserve entrance fee, but I strongly recommend that you go with a guide. I went into the reserve twice in the same morning—once on my own and once with a guide—and with the guide I saw much more and learned much more about cloud forests and their inhabitants. On the other hand, while alone I saw a rare bird, a guan, that I didn't see when walking the trails with a dozen or more other interested visitors. There is much to be said for walking quietly through the forest on your own.

The preserve is open daily from 7am to 4pm. Because only 100 people are allowed into the preserve at any one time, you may be forced to wait for a while before being allowed in. Rubber boots rent for less than $1 and are a very good idea here. The mud gets quite deep on some trails.

Before venturing into the forest, have a look around the information center. There are several guidebooks available, as well as posters and postcards of some of the reserve's more famous animal inhabitants. Perhaps the most famous resident of the cloud forests of Costa Rica is the quetzal, a robin-sized bird with iridescent-green wings and a ruby-red breast, which has become extremely rare due to habitat destruction. The male quetzal also has two long tail feathers that make it one of the most spectacular birds on earth. The best time to see quetzals is early to midmorning, with March and April (mating season) being the easiest months to spot these magnificent birds.

Other animals that have been seen in Monteverde include jaguars, ocelots, and tapirs. After the quetzal, Monteverde's most beautiful resident *was* the golden toad (*sapo dorado*). However, due to several years of low precipitation, the golden toad seems to have disappeared from the forest, which was its only home in the world. There has been speculation that the toad was adversely affected by a natural drought cycle, the disappearing ozone layer, or acid rain. Photos of the golden toad abound in Monteverde, and I'm sure you'll be as saddened as I was by the disappearance of such a beautiful creature.

Because the vegetation in the cloud forest is so dense, with hundreds of species of epiphytic plants such as orchids and bromeliads hanging from almost every imaginable square inch of tree limb, none of the forest's animal residents is very easy to spot. If you were unsatisfied with your sightings, even with a naturalist guide leading you, you might want to consider attending a slide show of photographs taken in the reserve. These slide shows are presented by the **Hummingbird Gallery** (tel. 61-1259) daily at 4:30pm. Admission is $3.50. The gallery is just outside the park entrance. Hanging from trees outside the gallery are several hummingbird feeders that attract more than seven species. At any given moment, there might be several dozen hummingbirds buzzing and chattering around the building. Inside you will, of course, find a lot of beautiful mounted and unmounted color prints of hummingbirds. There are also many other beautiful photos from Monteverde available in prints or postcards. The gallery is open daily from 9:30am to 5pm.

Birds are not the only colorful fauna in the Monteverde cloud forest. Butterflies abound here, and the **Butterfly Garden,** located near the Pensión Monteverde Inn, displays many of Costa Rica's most beautiful species. Besides the hundreds of preserved and mounted butterflies, there are also gardens and a greenhouse where you can watch live butterflies. The gardens are open daily from 9:30am to 4pm and the admission is $5, which includes a guided tour. The best time to visit is between 11am and 1pm, when the butterflies are most active.

Hiking opportunities can also be found outside the reserve boundaries. The **Bajo Tigre Trail** is a 1-mile-long trail that's home to different bird species than are found within the preserve. The trail starts near the Pensión El Quetzal and is open daily from 8am to 4pm. There is a $1.50 charge to hike this privately owned and maintained trail. Guided night tours are another fascinating way to experience the world of the cloud forest. These tours are led by Tomas Guindon (tel. 61-1008). Glowworms, walking sticks, and luminescent fungi are among the flora and fauna to be seen at night.

When you feel like you've had enough hiking, you might want to try exploring the area on a **horse** or **bicycle.** Most of the hotels here can arrange horseback rides with a guide for around $7 to $10 per person per hour. Or you can contact Meg (tel. 61-0952), who rents horses at similar rates. If mountain bikes are more your style, contact Mountain Cycling Adventures Monteverde, across from the Hotel Tucan in Santa Elena (tel. 61-1007 or 61-0957). The owner, Adrian Mendez, rents bikes for $3 per hour, and also leads tours around the area. Tours range in price from $3 per person for a sunset ride up to $10 per person for a full day tour.

If you're in the mood for shopping, stop in at **CASEM** (tel. 61-2550), on the right just past Restaurant El Bosque. This crafts cooperative sells souvenirs made from local hardwoods, embroidered clothing, T-shirts, posters and postcards with photos of the local flora and fauna, hats, and many other items to remind you of your visit to Monteverde. CASEM is open Monday through Saturday from 8am to noon and 1 to 5pm, and on Sunday from 10am to 4pm (closed Sundays May through November).

You might also want to stop by the **Cheese Factory,** which is on the main road on the left after you pass CASEM and before you cross the stream. You can observe the cheese-making process and then buy some cheese for lunch or a snack. The factory and store are open Monday through Saturday from 7:30am to 4:30pm, and on Sunday from 7:30am to 12:30pm.

WHERE TO STAY

When choosing a place to stay in Monteverde, be sure to check whether the rates include meals or not. In the past all the lodges operated on the American plan (all three meals included). This practice is on the wane, though, so rates can be misleading if you don't read carefully.

DOUBLES FOR LESS THAN $30

EL IMAN, Santa Elena, Puntarenas. Tel. 506/61-1255. 8 rms (1 with bath).
$ Rates: $5 single; $10 double. No credit cards.
This extremely basic pension on the outskirts of Santa Elena, which is almost two miles from Monteverde, is one of the only choices in the area for those traveling in Costa Rica on a very limited budget. Rooms here are far from immaculate, but if this is your price category, you haven't got too many choices.

HOTEL TUCAN, Santa Elena, Puntarenas. Tel. 506/61-1007. 15 rms, 8 with bath.
$ Rates (including two meals): $15 single without bath, $20 single with bath; $30 double without bath, $40 double with bath. No credit cards.
This hotel is little more than a pension and is downhill toward Monteverde from

Santa Elena's main intersection. Though the rooms without bath are only slightly larger than closets, they are fairly clean. Wooden walls and floors give the main building a rustic feel. Rooms with private bathrooms are in a separate building and are slightly larger. Costa Rican–style meals are served in a very basic dining room on the ground floor. Keep in mind that it is a long walk to the park from here.

DOUBLES FOR LESS THAN $45

EL BOSQUE, Monteverde, Puntarenas. Tel. 506/61-1258. Fax 506/61-2559. 20 rms (all with bath).
$ Rates: $23 single; $28.75 double. No credit cards.
Hidden down the hill behind El Bosque restaurant (on the main road to the preserve), the rooms here are arranged in a semicircle around a minimally landscaped garden in what may have once been a pasture. The setting is not the best in town, but the rates are quite reasonable for what you get. Rooms have high ceilings, picture windows, double beds, stucco walls, and cement floors. It's a few hundred yards up a dirt road, down a path, and across a jungly ravine on a footbridge to the restaurant, which makes going for breakfast nearly an adventure in itself. The restaurant is open daily from 7am to 9:30pm serving Tico standards and international dishes including steaks and fish filets. Prices range from $2.90 to $12.60. This is the most centrally located restaurant in Monteverde.

PENSIÓN FLOR MAR, Apdo. 10165, San José. Tel. 506/61-0909. 13 rms (3 with bath).
$ Rates (including three meals): $22 single without bath, $25 single with bath; $44 double without bath, $50 double with bath. No credit cards.
Researchers have been coming to the Monteverde Cloud Forest Reserve since it was created, and for much of that time they have been staying here at the Flor Mar. Obviously, scientists and students are not overly concerned with their accommodations. There are no stunning views, and the rooms are simply furnished. Business is still derived primarily from study groups, and several rooms have bunk beds. There is even one tiny single room that reminds me of a monk's cell. This lodge is close to the park entrance. The dining room is large and dark, but there is a much more appealing lounge in the lower of the lodge's two main buildings.

PENSIÓN MONTEVERDE INN, Apdo. 10165-1000 San José. Tel. 506/61-2756. 14 rms (all with bath).
$ Rates (including three meals): $22.40 single; $44.80 double. No credit cards.
David Savage and his family are the owners of this simple rustic lodge on a farm between Monteverde and Santa Elena. This is the most economical of the lodges in Monteverde, and although it is a bit of a walk up to the park entrance, this is a good choice for those who have to watch their colónes. The rooms are small and come with two twin beds or a double bed. Hardwood floors keep the rooms from seeming too spartan. There are plans to open an inexpensive hostel charging around $10 per person per night.

PENSIÓN EL QUETZAL, Apdo. 10165-1000, San José. Tel. 506/61-0955. 10 rms (7 with bath).
$ Rates (including three meals): $30 single without bath, $35 single with bath; $44 double without bath, $50 double with bath. No credit cards.
One of the oldest and most popular of Monteverde's rustic lodges, the Quetzal is nearly always full in the busy season (December to May), so be sure to make your reservations well in advance. Staying here is like staying with friends. There are plenty of chairs and lots of reading material around for those who want to brush up on their cloud-forest ecology. The rooms are in the main house or in separate buildings, with three or four rooms in each building. Pastures and dark forests surround the buildings. Less than 100 yards away is an informative nature trail operated by the Monteverde Conservation League. If you are coming with a group of four or more, ask for the large room with the sleeping loft. The sign for the Quetzal is on the right not far past the Hotel de Montaña Monteverde (below).

All guests eat together in a small dining room that adjoins the living room.

DOUBLES FOR LESS THAN $60

HOTEL BELMAR, Monteverde, Puntarenas. Tel. 506/61-1001. Fax 506/61-1001. 18 rms (all with bath).
$ Rates: $45.20 single; $56.50 double; $67.80 triple. Meals are an additional $20.40 per person per day. No credit cards.

You'll think that you're in the Alps when you stay at this beautiful Swiss chalet–style hotel. Set at the top of a grassy hill, the Belmar has stunning views all the way to the Nicoya Gulf and the Pacific Ocean. Afternoons in the dining room or lounge are idyllic, with bright sunlight streaming in through a west-facing wall of glass that provides a grandstand seat for spectacular sunsets. Most of the guest rooms come with wood paneling, French doors, and little balconies that open onto splendid views. Meals usually live up to the surroundings. The Belmar is up a road to the left of the gas station as you come into the village of Monteverde.

EL ESTABLO, Apdo. 549-2050, San Pedro. Tel. 506/61-2851 (in San José 25-0569). Fax 506/61-2851. 19 rms (all with bath).
$ Rates: $46.55 single; $52.40 double; $64 triple; $69.85 quad. No credit cards.
El Establo is one of the newer hotels at Monteverde, and as its name implies, it plays on the stable theme. Though the hotel is next to the road, there are 120 acres of farm behind it, and half of this area is in primary forest. Most of the rooms are situated off a large enclosed porch that contains plenty of comfortable chairs and a fireplace. Guest-room doors look as if they were salvaged from a stable, but inside, the rooms are carpeted and have orthopedic mattresses and modern bathrooms, though with showers only. Photos of local flora and fauna hang on the walls. The end rooms have a bit more light than other rooms. There are even two rooms in the actual stable. Of course the hotel has plenty of horses for rent at $7 per hour with a guide. Meals in the hotel's dining room cost $6.10 for breakfast and $9.15 for lunch or dinner, but they'll pack you a box lunch for $5.50.

HOTEL FONDA VELA, P.O. Box 10165, San José. Tel. 506/61-2551. 23 rms (13 with bath), 4 suites.
$ Rates: $41.40 single; $48.30 double. Meals are an additional $22 per person per day.
Located on the right after the sign for the Pensión Flor Mar, the Fonda Vela is one of my personal favorites in Monteverde. Guest rooms are housed in several buildings scattered among the forests and pastures of this former farm, and most have views out to the Nicoya Gulf. Lots of hardwood has been used throughout and there are flagstone floors in some rooms. About half of the rooms have bathtubs, a rarity in Costa Rica. There are also safes in all the rooms. At the time of my last visit, several large suites—two of which even had sleeping lofts—were under construction. The dining room, which offers great sunset views, serves delicious three-course dinners with occasional live musical accompaniment. You'll also find a bar and a gift shop here, and laundry service and horse rentals are available.

HOTEL DE MONTAÑA MONTEVERDE, Apdo. 70, Plaza G. Víquez, San José. Tel. 506/33-7078. Fax 506/22-6184 or 61-1846. 29 rms (all with bath).
$ Rates: $42.55 single; $57.50 double; $71.30 triple. Meals are an additional $28 per person per day. AE, MC, V.
This long, low, motel-style building is one of the oldest hotels in Monteverde and is frequently filled with tour groups from San José. The hotel is surrounded by 15 acres of farm and woods that are ideal for quiet strolls or bird watching and there are horses available for rent. Rooms are rustic with wood paneling and hardwood floors and come with double or twin beds; there are even a few rooms with queen-size beds and carpeting. If the nights are a bit chilly for you, warm up in the sauna or hot tub.

The rustic glass-walled dining room offers excellent views. Meals are not mandatory, but a meal plan is available. Attached to the restaurant is a small bar that is always busy in the evening, when people sit around swapping stories of their day's adventures and wildlife sightings.

EL SAPO DORADO, Apdo. 10165, San José. Tel. 506/61-2952. Fax 61-2952. 10 rms (all with bath).

$ Rates: $51.75 single; $63.25 double; $74.75 triple. No credit cards.

Located up a steep hill from the main road between Santa Elena and the preserve, El Sapo Dorado (named for Monteverde's famous "golden toad") offers attractive cabins with good views. The cabins are built of hardwoods both inside and out and are surrounded by a grassy lawn. Big windows let in lots of light, and high ceilings keep the rooms cool during the day. The hotel's restaurant is open to the public and serves three meals daily (breakfast 7 to 10am; lunch noon to 4pm; dinner 6 to 10pm). The dinner menu changes nightly, but among the regular offerings are chicken with olive sauce, sailfish niçoise, and filet mignon with pepper cream sauce. Prices range from $5 to $8.90. There is a large patio terrace from which you can watch the sun set while listening to classical music. The bar here stays open until 11pm and is usually fairly quiet. To find the hotel and restaurant, watch for the sign on the main road to the preserve.

WHERE TO EAT

Though most lodges in Monteverde no longer require you to take all your meals in their dining room, it is still encouraged and is certainly the most convenient option. Since the lodges are scattered across more than three miles, it can be a long hike to eat a meal if you don't have your own vehicle. The food at the different lodges is generally comparable, so it doesn't make too much sense to go traipsing off to a distant lodge. One exception is El Sapo Dorado, where the menu shows a bit more imagination. See the lodge listing above for details.

2. TILARAN & LAKE ARENAL (NORTH END)

118 miles NW of San José; 12 miles NW of Monteverde; 42 miles SE of Liberia

GETTING THERE By Bus Express buses leave San José daily at 7:30am, 12:45, 3:45, and 6:30pm from Calle 14 between avenidas 9 and 11. The trip takes 4 hours and the fare is $2.05. There are also morning and afternoon buses from Puntarenas to Tilaran, which take 3 hours and cost $1.20. From Monteverde (Santa Elena), there is a bus daily at 7am which takes 3 hours and costs 75¢.

By Car From San José, take the Carretera Interamericana, and at Cañas turn east toward Tilaran. The drive takes 4 hours.

DEPARTING Direct buses to San José leave at 7 and 7:45am, and 2 and 4:55pm; the trip lasts 4 hours and the fare costs $2.05. Buses to Puntarenas leave at 6am and 1pm. Costing $1.20, the ride takes 3 hours. There is also a bus to Monteverde (Santa Elena) daily at noon. The 3 hour trip costs 75¢.

ESSENTIALS Tilaran is about 3 miles from Lake Arenal. All roads into town lead to the central park, which is Tilaran's main point of reference for addresses. If you need to change money, check at one of the hotels listed here. If you need a taxi to get to a lodge on Lake Arenal, phone 69-5324.

Lake Arenal, a man-made lake with an area of 33 square miles, is the largest lake in Costa Rica and is surrounded by rolling hills that are partly pastured and partly forested. At the opposite (south) end of the lake from Tilaran is the perfect cone of Arenal Volcano, which is still very active. The volcano's barren slopes are a stunning sight, especially when reflected in the waters of the lake. The north side of Lake Arenal is a dry region of rolling hills and pastures, distinctly different from the lusher landscape at the south end.

Until recently the area saw few visitors, but when the international boardsailing set caught wind of the sailing conditions here, Tilaran and Lake Arenal suddenly became known all over the world. Tilaran is still little more than a quiet farm community serving the surrounding fincas (ranches), and though there are *For Sale* signs all over the landscape, there are still few hotels or other developments. If you aren't a rabid boardhead (fanatical sailboarder), you still might enjoy hanging out by the lake in hopes of catching a glimpse of Arenal volcano.

WHAT TO SEE & DO

Windsurfers aren't the only people who have discovered this interesting region of Costa Rica. Anglers have known of the great fishing in Lake Arenal for years; volcanologists have been studying the eruptions of Arenal Volcano; and now curious visitors from around the world are descending on the lake to enjoy the setting, the nighttime light show (eruptions) from the volcano, and the nearby hot springs. These latter activities, however, are best pursued using the town of Fortuna as a base. Fortuna is at the south end of the lake; it's in a different section of this book because it's not easily accessible from Tilaran due to the poor road around the lake.

If you want to try windsurfing, you can rent equipment from **Tilawa Viento Surf** (tel. 69-5050), which has its facilities on one of the lake's few accessible beaches about 5 miles from Tilaran on the road around the west end of the lake. Windsurfers rent for $35 to $45 per day and lessons are also available. If you'd rather stay on dry land, you can rent a horse for $10 per hour by phoning 69-5050. Another excursion is to the smaller Coter Lake over on the north side of the lake. A taxi to Coter Lake will cost around $12.

WHERE TO STAY
DOUBLES FOR LESS THAN $16

CABINAS MARY, costado sur del parque Tilaran, Tilaran, Guanacaste. Tel. 506/69-5479. 16 rms (12 with bath).
$ Rates: $3 single with shared bath, $3.70 single with private bath; $6 double with shared bath, $7.40 double with private bath. No credit cards. **Parking:** Available.
Located right on Tilaran's large and sunny central park, Cabinas Mary is a very basic, but fairly clean hotel. It's upstairs from the restaurant of the same name and has parking in back. Rooms are large and have plenty of windows. You even get hot water here, which is a surprise at this price. The restaurant downstairs is the most popular place in town with travelers. It's open daily from 7am to 10pm; meals cost between $2 and $5.

CABINAS EL SUEÑO, Tilaran, Guanacaste. Tel. 506/69-5347. 12 rms (all with bath).
$ Rates: $9 single; $15 double; $18 triple; $21 quad. MC, V.
Right in the middle of this small town, Cabinas El Sueño is a simple two-story hotel, but it is clean and bright, and the management is friendly. There is parking in back of the hotel and a small courtyard complete with fountain on the second floor of the building. Downstairs there is a restaurant and bar.

DOUBLES FOR LESS THAN $32

PUERTO SAN LUIS, 3 miles from Tilaran á Tronadora, Tilaran, Guanacaste. Tel. 506/69-5572. Fax 506/69-5750. 15 rms (all with bath). TV
$ Rates: $25 single; $30 double; $35 triple. MC, V.
Located on a small bay of Lake Arenal 3 miles from Tilaran, Puerto San Luis is popular both with windsurfers and vacationing Ticos. The two-story white building sits on a grassy slope overlooking the lake and green hills beyond. The setting is very

tranquil during the week, though on weekends it can get a bit noisy with speedboats racing around the lake. All the rooms here have been recently remodeled and have small refrigerators, carpeting, and tiled bathrooms. There is a bar and restaurant where the house specialty is sautéed tilapia (a farm-raised freshwater fish). Meal prices range from $2 to $5. The hotel also has fishing gear and water skis for rent and offers boat trips and trips to the foot of Arenal Volcano. A taxi from Tilaran to Puerto San Luis will cost you $3 (phone 69-5324 in Tilaran). Windsurfers receive a $5 discount at this hotel.

ALBERGUE TILARAN, Santa Ana, San José, Apt. 147, P.O. 6150. Tel. 506/82-7555. 4 rms (all with shared bath).
$ Rates: $12 per person ($7 with youth hostel card). No credit cards.
This small hostel is on the edge of town near where the road heads north to the lake. The four rooms are in a fairly modern house with a central lounge and dining area. Guests can use the kitchen and there is plenty of space for storing Windsurfers. The folks here can also arrange tours of the lake and to the volcano.

WORTH THE EXTRA BUCKS

ROCK RIVER LODGE, P.O. Box 2907-1000, San José. Tel. 506/22-4547. Fax 506/21-3011. 16 rms (all with bath).
$ Rates: $35 single or double. V.
Set high on a grassy hill above the lake, this small lodge looks as if it might have been transported from Hawaii. The guest rooms are housed in a long low lodge set on stilts. Walls and floors are made of hardwood and there are bamboo railings along the veranda. Wind chimes let you know when the winds are up, and there are sling chairs on the porch. Rooms are of medium size and have double beds and bunk beds, as well as modern tiled bathrooms. This is by far the most attractive lodge in the area and should be your first choice. However, it is a long walk down (and then back up) to the lake. Meals will cost you around $25 per person per day, with American and Tico meals served in the large open-air restaurant where there is even a stone fireplace.

3. LA FORTUNA

87 miles NW of San José; 38 miles E of Tilaran

GETTING THERE   By Bus   A bus leaves San José daily at 6am from Calle 16 between avenidas 1 and 3. The trip takes 4½ hours and costs $2.30. Alternatively, you can take a Ciudad Quesada bus from the same location in San José and then take a local bus from Ciudad Quesada to La Fortuna. Ciudad Quesada buses leave San José daily every hour from 5am to 7:30pm. The trip takes 3 hours, costing $1.50. Buses leave Ciudad Quesada for La Fortuna at 6 and 9:30am and 3 and 6pm; this trip takes 1 hour and costs 75¢.

By Car   There are a couple of routes to La Fortuna from San José. The most popular is to head west on the Interamerican Highway and then turn north at Naranjo, continuing north to Ciudad Quesada (San Carlos). From Ciudad Quesada one route goes through Jabilos while the other goes through Muelle. Alternatively it is a little quicker to go first to Alajuela and then head north to Varabanca and then to San Miguel where you turn west toward Rio Cuarto and Aguas Zarcas. From Aguas Zarcas, continue west through Muelle to the turnoff for La Fortuna. Travel time either way is around three hours. A new route from San Ramon (west of Naranjo) north through La Tigra is being paved and may be open when you arrive.

DEPARTING   There is a bus to San José daily at 2:30pm. A bus leaves for Tilaran daily at 8am. There are also buses to Ciudad Quesada (San Carlos) at 5:15, 6:30, and 7:30am. From there you can catch one of the hourly buses to San José.

ESSENTIALS   Fortuna is only a few streets wide, with almost all the hotels, restaurants, and shops clustered along the main road. There is a little information and tour booking office, open daily from 7am to 7:30pm, next door to La Central restaurant.

Watching a volcano is mesmerizing. Seeing Mother Earth churn out new land in a spectacular display of fire and brimstone never ceases to amaze people. Hearing the earth explode like a hydrogen bomb may be disconcerting at first, but when you realize you're in no danger, the explosions become fascinating. This is the allure of La Fortuna. Though the little town was a sleepy farming hamlet until a few years ago, it has rapidly become very popular with tourists who come to ooh and aah at the daily show given by Arenal Volcano. Rising disturbingly close to town, Arenal is a perfect cone-shaped volcano which reaches a height of 5,400 feet and is ranked as one of the most active volcanoes in the world.

WHAT TO SEE & DO

The first thing you should know is that you can't climb Arenal Volcano. It is not safe due to the constant activity and several foolish people who have ignored this warning have lost their lives. Watching Arenal Volcano spewing red hot lava rocks into the air is the main activity in La Fortuna and is best done at night when the orange lava glows against the starry sky. Though it is possible to simply look up from the middle of town and see Arenal erupting, it is more fun to take one of the **night tours** that includes a swim in a thermal river as well as a view of the volcano. These tours cost $11.10 and can be booked at the information center next to La Central restaurant.

There are also a few activities to keep you busy during the day. The first thing you might do is hike out to the **Río Fortuna waterfall.** It's about 3½ miles outside of town in a lush jungle setting. There is a sign in town to indicate the road that leads out to the falls, and as you hike along this road, you'll probably be offered a lift. If this seems like too much exercise, you can rent a horse and guide for four hours for $14.80. Stop by the information center next to La Central to arrange your ride. When you've finished your ride or hike, you'll probably like a soak in a hot spring. If so, head out to **Tabacón,** a hot spring resort about 7½ miles from La Fortuna toward Lake Arenal. This resort was in the process of being upgraded when I last visited and may now be a bit pricey. However, demands by local residents that part of the thermal river running through Tabacón be made affordable may have been answered. Ask in town before heading out this way. At the Burio Inn you can arrange to spend the day tubing on the **Río San Carlos** for $22.25, including transportation. At this same inn, you can rent boats and fishing equipment on Lake Arenal for $30 to $35 per hour.

WHERE TO STAY

La Fortuna's popularity with international travelers has grown so quickly that, when I last visited, there was a shortage of rooms. If this happens to you, stop by the information center next door to La Central restaurant and they'll try to arrange you a stay with a local family.

DOUBLES FOR LESS THAN $15

HOTEL/RESTAURANT LA CENTRAL, La Fortuna, San Carlos. Tel. 506/ 47-9004. 16 rms (1 with bath).
$ Rates: $3.70 single; $7.40 double; $11.10 triple; $14.80 quad. MC, V.
This is the cheapest and most basic hotel in La Fortuna, and though there is only one room with a private bathroom, the rest are small but clean (usually). Floors are hardwood and the walls are painted blue. The hotel is upstairs from the restaurant of the same name. You'll usually find lots of foreigners hanging out there waiting for

meals. The service in the restaurant is notoriously bad so be sure to plan at least 45 minutes for your meal. The restaurant is open from 6am to 11pm daily. La Central is a white wooden building on a corner of the main street through town.

HOTEL SAN BOSCO, La Fortuna, San Carlos. Tel. 506/47-9050. 27 rms (all with bath).
$ Rates: $7.75 single; $13.35 double; $15.85 triple; $20.90 4–5 people. No credit cards.

Located on a quiet residential street a block off La Fortuna's main street, the San Bosco was in the process of adding 16 new rooms when I last visited. These rooms have hot water and are bigger than the old rooms, so they'll probably cost more. The new building also has an observation deck for viewing Arenal Volcano. There are also plans to add a pool sometime in the near future. The old rooms here are very basic, with cement floors, bright-blue bedspreads, and tile showers.

WORTH THE EXTRA BUCKS

ALBERGUE BURÍO, P.O. Box 1234, 1250 Escazú. Tel. 506/47-9076 or 28-0267. Fax 506/47-9045. 8 rms (all with bath).
$ Rates (including continental breakfast): $23 single; $46 double; $69.60 triple. MC, V.

This small lodge is operated by the same folks who run the much more expensive Arenal Lodge. Located on the main road through La Fortuna, the Burío is set back from the street behind some shops. There is a grassy garden, a small breakfast room, and the owners are very friendly and helpful. Guest rooms are attractively decorated with lace curtains, big windows, and lots of polished hardwood. If you have a reservation you must arrive by 4pm, or they'll rent your room. However, if you arrive and the hotel is full, they'll also try to find you a room in a private home. There are plans to open a youth hostel charging $5 to $7 per person per night.

ARENAL LODGE, P.O. Box 1139, Escazú 1250, San José. Tel. 506/28-2588 or 46-1881, or toll free 800/235-3625 in the U.S. Fax 506/28-2798. 16 rms (all with bath).
$ Rates: $46–$69 single; $69–$92 double; $97.75–$115.00 suite. MC, V.

Located a couple of miles from Lake Arenal, Arenal Lodge is first and foremost a fishing lodge. However, its location in the hills above the lake gives it an exceptional view of the volcano that has made it popular with nonanglers as well. Guest rooms range from fairly basic rooms in the old house to a luxurious and expensive suite. Situated in the middle of a macadamia plantation between two strips of virgin forest, the lodge has several trails that are great for bird watching. The rooms in the old house open onto a covered garden that is filled with orchids, and inside the house you can enjoy a game room, library, and sitting room. The lodge arranges fishing and other trips in the surrounding area.

NEARBY PLACES TO STAY

After visiting La Fortuna, you might want to consider a side trip to the Sarapiquí River region. This area of lowland forests is home to several remote lodges that are set up primarily for naturalists (both amateur and professional). You could also visit this area before going to La Fortuna: both lodges offer package tours that include the cost of transportation. It is also possible to take a bus from San José to Puerto Viejo de Sarapiquí. Buses leave from Calle 12 between avenidas 7 and 9 at 7 and 9am and 1, 4, and 5pm. The ride takes four hours, costing $3.

EL GAVILAN LODGE, P.O. Box 445-2010, San José. Tel. 506/34-9507. Fax 506/53-6556. 13 rms (all with bath).
$ Rates (including breakfast): $25 single; $50 double; $75 triple. MC, V.

Located on the banks of the Sarapiquí River just outside the town of Puerto Viejo de Sarapiquí, El Gavilan is surrounded by 250 acres of forest reserve (secondary forest). Directly adjacent to the lodge is a 12½-acre garden that makes a stay here pleasant even for non-naturalists. However, people with an interest in the outdoors and nature are the ones who will most enjoy a stay here. Guided hikes through the forest, horseback rides, and river trips are all offered. Guest rooms are simply furnished, but do have fans and hot water. There is also a whirlpool spa out in the garden. Meals are served buffet style and there are always plenty of fresh fruits and juices (though no alcohol is served, so bring your own). Lunch and dinner each cost $8.

ORO VERDE STATION, P.O. Box 7043, 1000 San José. Tel. 506/23-7479. Fax 506/23-7479. 14 rms (all with bath).
$ Rates (including breakfast): $35 single; $45 double; $55 triple.
Surrounded by nearly 20,000 acres of private reserve (3,000 acres of which is virgin forest) and bordering the Barra del Colorado National Wildlife Refuge, the Oro Verde Station is primarily a facility for researchers and students but is also open to the public. The nearest road is 30 miles away, so the lodge can only be reached by boat. The lodge's several high-peaked thatched roof buildings lend a very tropical air to the facilities. Guest rooms are fairly basic, as you might expect at a research facility, but meals are well prepared and filling. Both lunch and dinner are in the $5 to $15 range. There are plenty of hiking trails; river trips and guided hikes can be arranged. This lodge is under the same management as the Playa Chiquita Lodge near Puerto Viejo de Limón.

4. LIBERIA

145 miles NW of San José; 83 miles NW of Puntarenas

GETTING THERE   By Bus   Express buses leave San José from Calle 14 between avenidas 1 and 3 daily at 7, 9, and 11:30am and 3, 4, 6, and 8pm. Duration: 4 hours. Fare: $2.50. From Puntarenas, buses leave at 5:30, 7, and 9:30am and noon. Duration: 2 hours. Fare: $1.50.

By Car   Take the Carretera Interamericana from San José. Follow the signs for Nicaragua. Duration: 4 hours without stops.

DEPARTING   The Liberia bus station is at the northwest corner of the town's main square, which is about 300 yards from the highway.
   The express buses for San José leave at 4:30am, 6am, and 7:30am and 12:30, 2, 4, and 6pm.
   To reach Monteverde take any bus leaving before 1pm for Puntarenas or San José. Get off at the Rio Lagarto and catch the Puntarenas-Santa Elena bus around 3:15pm.
   See the specific beach section below for information on how to get to the beach.

ESSENTIALS   There is a small **tourist information center** (tel. 66-1606) three blocks south of the modern white church on the park in the center of town. However, if you don't speak Spanish, you may not learn much here. The center is open Tuesday through Saturday from 9am to noon and 1 to 6pm, and on Sunday from 9am to 1pm.

Orientation   The highway passes slightly to the west of town. At the intersection with the main road into town, there are several hotels and gas stations. If you turn east into town, you will come to the central square after less than half a mile.

Liberia itself isn't much of a town. There isn't anything to see here, but there are several fine budget hotels out on the highway at the turnoff for the beaches of the northern Guanacaste Peninsula. Also reachable from Liberia in a day trip are Santa Rosa National Park and Rincón de la Vieja National Park. Accommodations at the beaches range from basic to luxury, with little in between that would fall within your budget. The hotels I have listed here are much better than those charging the same rates right on the beach. If you are more interested in seeing the country than in being on beaches, this is the place for you. Besides, if you want a truly tropical beach experience, I recommend Manuel Antonio National Park to the south.

WHAT TO SEE & DO

Most people who come up this way are heading to the beaches. Guanacaste is well known as the sunniest and dryest part of Costa Rica, and consequently it is rapidly growing as a tourist resort destination. I prefer the beaches of the southern Pacific Coast and the Caribbean Coast—they are much lusher and have more of that tropical feel that people up north expect of a beach in these latitudes. However, if you can't tolerate the least bit of rain on your holiday in the sun, the beaches up here are where you'll want to be. If you have made it this far north, there are also a couple of national parks that you should not miss.

Santa Rosa National Park is about 20 miles north of Liberia on the Panamerican Highway. The park, which covers a large peninsula jutting out into the Pacific Ocean, has both historic and environmental significance. Santa Rosa was Costa Rica's first national park. However, it was not founded to preserve the land but to preserve a building, known as La Casona, which has played an important role in Costa Rican independence.

Rincón de la Vieja National Park is an area of geothermal activity similar to Yellowstone National Park in the United States. Fumaroles, geysers, and hot pools cover a small area of this park, creating a bizarre other-worldly landscape. There is a youth hostel near the park for adventurous types who want to explore the area for a few days. Contact the Toruma Youth Hostel, Avenida Central between calles 29 and 31 (tel. 506/24-4085), in San José for details.

WHERE TO STAY

IN TOWN

Doubles for Less Than $30

HOTEL BRAMADERO, Carretera Interamericana, Liberia. Tel. 506/66-0371. 25 rms (all with bath).

$ Rates: $13.15 single, $18.40 single with A/C; $19 double, $27.30 double with A/C; $25.20 triple, $31.75 triple with A/C. AE, MC, V.

There isn't much parking at this small, motel-style place, but the rates are good and the rooms are clean if simply furnished. Behind the restaurant is the hotel's small pool, wonderfully cooling in an area that is the hottest, dryest, and dustiest in Costa Rica. Rooms around the pool can be noisy at night, especially on the weekends, when families from San José flee the cool elevations for the warmth of the lowlands. Most of the rooms have air conditioning.

There is a large open-air restaurant and bar in front of the hotel. Unfortunately, the food here is not worth recommending.

HOTEL LA SIESTA, Apdo. 15-5000, Liberia. Tel. 506/66-0678. Fax 506/65-2532. 24 rms. (all with bath). A/C.

$ Rates: $20.35 single; $29.65 double; $35.20 triple. AE, MC, V.

Unlike the other hotels listed here, this one is actually in town. Turn right at the highway crossroads and right again at the Farmacia Lux. Although it is quite small, La Siesta has its own pool. The basic rooms are clean and come with either two twin beds or a double and a twin.

There is a restaurant and bar serving the standard Tico menu of steaks, fried chicken, sea bass, and shrimp. Prices range from $2.50 to $6.90.

Doubles For Less Than $40

HOTEL EL SITIO, about 80 yards west of the fire station on the road to the beaches, Liberia. Tel. 506/66-1211. 52 rms (all with bath).

$ Rates: $30.50 single, $36.16 single with A/C; $37.30 double, $45.20 double with A/C. AE, MC, V.

This is the newest of Liberia's hotels—and as such is one of the nicest—but all the hotels here seem to follow the same basic Spanish-influenced plans. There are red-tile floors, lots of potted plants, and original paintings of local

Guanacaste scenes on the walls. A wagon-wheel chandelier hangs from the high ceiling of the lobby. All the rooms are carpeted and very clean, and you have your choice of twin or double beds. The air conditioners can be noisy, so check before agreeing to a room (eighteen rooms have air conditioners). The pool area is shady (a welcome relief from the strong Guanacaste sun), and there is even one of those famous Pre-Columbian basalt balls by the pool.

NEW HOTEL BOYEROS, Carretera Panamericana, Apdo. 85, Liberia. Tel. 506/66-0995 or 66-0722. Fax 506/66-2059 or (in San José) 33-6883. 60 rms (all with bath). A/C
$ Rates: $23.05 single; $32 double; $35.95 triple; $39.90 quad. AE, MC, V.
Arches with turned wooden railings and a red-tile roof give this two-story motel-style building a Spanish feel. Between the reception area and the simple restaurant is a huge convention room. Hopefully your visit won't coincide with that of a rowdy convention. In the courtyard of the hotel are two pools, one for adults and one for children, and a thatch-roofed bar. All the rooms have a private balcony or patio overlooking the pool and gardens. Although the bathrooms are small, there is plenty of closet space.

The small restaurant, which happens to have a few tables on a terrace under a huge "rubber" tree (actually a type of ficus or fig), serves meals ranging in price from $2.95 to $5.80.

NEAR RINCÓN DE LA VIEJA NATIONAL PARK
Doubles For Less Than $40

HACIENDA LODGE GUACHEPELIN, P.O. Box 636, Alajuela. Tel. 506/41-6545 or 41-6994. Fax 506/42-1910. 10 rms (none with bath).
$ Rates: $13.85 single; $34.60 double; $41.50 triple. Meals are additional $16 per person per day. No credit cards.
Located 14 miles northeast of Liberia on the edge of Rincón de la Vieja National Park, this basic lodge is housed in a 112-year-old ranch house. The ranch is still in operation today and in addition to exploring the park, you can ride horses, and commune with the pigs, dairy cows, and beef cattle. It isn't easy to get out here and once you're here you'll need a few days to explore the park, so plan on taking all your meals here and going on a few guided tours. A horseback tour with bilingual guide will cost around $30 per person. Reservations are a must here and when you contact the lodge you can arrange to be picked up in Liberia for $10 per person. To reach the lodge, drive about 3 miles north of Liberia and turn right on a dirt road. Continue on this road for about 8 miles to Curubande, and pass through the gate to the lodge.

Worth The Extra Bucks

SANTA CLARA LODGE, Apdo. Box 17, Quebrada Grande de Liberia, Guanacaste. Tel. 506/66-2596 or 26-1494. 5 rms (none with bath), 1 cabin.
$ Rates: $23.05 per person. Meals are additional $22 per person per day. No credit cards.
Santa Clara Lodge is located on a working finca (ranch) in the foothills of the mountains. With shady grounds on the banks of a small river, the setting is quite tranquil. You can sit beneath the palapa sipping a drink and listen to the chickens clucking in the yard or go for a swim in the mineral-water pool. The lodge is well suited for exploring the region if you have your own car or want to arrange tours. Santa Rosa, Guanacaste, and Rincón de la Vieja national parks are all within an hour's drive. You can also hike through field and forest to four different waterfalls. Guided hikes and horseback rides can be arranged, and the trip to the hot springs is particularly recommendable. Rooms are simply furnished, as you might expect on a working ranch, and meals are filling Tico fare such as rice and beans, steaks, chicken and fries, salads, and fruits. To reach the lodge, head north from Liberia for about 15 miles and turn right on the road to Quebrada Grande. In Quebrada Grande, turn right at the soccer field and continue for another 2½ miles.

WHERE TO EAT

You don't have too many choices for dining in Liberia, so your hotel dining room is certainly going to be the most convenient. However, the hotels serve standard fare at best. For meals a cut above what you would expect in this cow town, try the following restaurant.

RESTAURANTE PÓKOPÍ, no address. Tel. 66-1036.
   Cuisine: CONTINENTAL.
$ **Prices:** Entrées $1.50–$9.05. AE, MC, V.
   Open: Sun–Thurs 10am–10pm, Fri–Sat 10am–midnight.

It doesn't look like much from the outside, but this tiny restaurant has a surprising amount of class inside. An even more pleasant surprise is the unusual (for rural Costa Rica) variety of Continental dishes offered on the menu. Order one of the delicious daiquiris from the bar while you peruse the menu, which is on a wooden cutting board. You have your choice of dolphin (the fish not the mammal) prepared five different ways, pizza, chicken Cordon Bleu, chicken in wine sauce, and other equally delectable dishes. However, for a real surprise, order the chateaubriand for $12.40. It comes to your table with great flare, surrounded by succulent fresh vegetables and a tomato stuffed with peas. Don't miss this treat. Attached to the restaurant there is even a disco that swings into action at 9pm on the weekend, with a $1.50 to $2.20 cover charge. And you thought you were out in the sticks.

5. PLAYA DEL COCO

156 miles NW of San José; 11 miles W of Liberia

GETTING THERE   By Bus   There is one express bus daily from San José, leaving from Calle 14 between avenidas 1 and 3 at 10am. Duration: 5 hours. Fare: $2.65. From Liberia, buses leave at 5:30am, 12:30, 2, and 4:30pm.

By Car   Follow the directions for getting to Liberia, then turn west at the Liberia intersection for the road to Nicoya and the beaches. Follow the signs.

DEPARTING   Buses for Liberia leave at 7 and 9:15am and 2 and 6pm. Duration: 30 minutes. Fare: 75¢.
   The bus for San José leaves daily at 9:15am. Duration: 5 hours. Fare: $2.65.

ESSENTIALS   Orientation   Playa del Coco is a tiny village with most of the hotels and restaurants right on the water.

This is one of the most easily accessible of the Guanacaste beaches, with a paved road right down to the water; it has long been a popular destination with middle-class Ticos from San José. Unfortunately, most of the hotels right in town are quite run-down, and the water doesn't look too clean (this is a busy fishing port). The crowds that come here like their music loud and constant, so if you are in search of a quiet retreat, stay away. On the other hand, if your quest is for a cheap place to stay right on the beach, with plenty of cheap food and cheap beer nearby, you'll probably like Playa del Coco.
   The water's quite wide at low tide and comes almost to the tree line at high tide. The beach is a grayish brown sand, and trash is a bit of a problem right in town. However, if you walk down the long curving beach to the north of town, you're bound to find a nice clean spot to unfold your blanket.

WHAT TO SEE & DO

There is not much to do here except lie on the sand, hang out in the *sodas*, or go to the discos. If you are interested, you might be able to join a soccer match (the soccer field is in the middle of town).

WHERE TO STAY

DOUBLES FOR LESS THAN $16

CABINAS EL COCO, Playa del Coco, Guanacaste. Tel. 506/67-0167, 67-0110, or 67-0276. 76 rms (all with bath).
$ Rates: $9.85 single; $12.40 double; $15 triple; $20.95 quad. No credit cards.
If you're a light sleeper, stay away from this super-budget choice. Next door to the hotel is a disco that seems to be in a constant competition with the hotel's restaurant to see who can play louder music. The rooms are pretty dreary, and even the pricier ones with ocean views also have a dirty parking lot right outside their windows. This place is definitely a last resort, and then only for the hardiest of backpackers.

CABINAS LUNA TICA, Playa del Coco, Apdo. 67, Guanacaste. Tel. 506/67-0127 or 67-0279. 37 rms (all with bath).
$ Rates: $15.55 single or double; $19.25 triple; $25.20 quad; $28.15 for 1–4 people with A/C. No credit cards.
These basic rooms are in two buildings on opposite sides of a street that runs parallel to the beach south of the main square. The annex, across the street from the beach, has newer and slightly nicer rooms, including three with air conditioning. The rooms in the older building are quite dark and set up so that they *don't* catch the nearly constant breezes that blow across the peninsula. It is fairly quiet down at this end of town, and the hotel is right on the beach. If you want to be on the beach and spend as little money as possible, this is the place for you.

DOUBLES FOR LESS THAN $25

CABINAS CHALE, Playa del Coco, Guanacaste. Tel. 506/67-0036 or 67-0303. 17 rms (all with bath).
$ Rates: $22.20 double; $25.65 triple; $29.05 quad. No credit cards.
$ Located down a dirt road to the right as you are coming into town, this small motel is quite a bit better than those right on the beach and also much quieter. Your only company as you stroll down to the beach may be a herd of grazing cattle. The rooms are simply furnished with double beds, overhead fans, and tile floors, and each comes with a Tico clothes-washing sink called a *pila*. There is no sign out front so watch for the wrought-iron and white cinder-block wall.
There is a spartan, screen-walled bar that is open only during the busy season (November to April).

DOUBLES FOR LESS THAN $45

COSTA ALEGRE, Playa del Coco, Guanacaste. Tel. 506/67-0218 (in San José 57-1939). 14 rms (all with bath).
$ Rates: $44.45 1–5 people. No credit cards.
About half a mile before the turnoff for Playa Hermosa, you'll see on your left another new hotel that is also popular with Tico families. The apartments here come with full kitchen but sleep only five people. Otherwise, the facilities are very similar— swimming pools, soccer field, volleyball court. The rooms have high ceilings and fans to keep you cool, and there are plans to add air conditioning in the future. A lively (and noisy) atmosphere prevails on the weekends.
Although Costa Alegre is several miles from the beach, it does have a large open-air restaurant and even a barbecue where you can grill any fish you might have caught. Meals in the restaurant average around $3.70 to $8.90.

PIRATES COVE HOTEL, Apdo. 188-5019, Playa del Coco. Tel. 506/67-0367. Fax 506/67-0117. 21 rms (all with bath).
$ Rates: $44.85 single or double; $51.75 1–4 people. MC, V.

This was the newest hotel in town when I last visited and was by far the best deal around. Operated by Canadians, the Pirates Cove has a skull-and-crossbones theme. The large guest rooms have modern bathrooms with bamboo accents, double beds, and ceiling fans. Window seats, big picture windows (with no view), wall sconces, vanities, and pastel colors round out the decor. There were plans to add a few rooms with air conditioning and telephones. An open-air restaurant completes the picture.

WORTH THE EXTRA BUCKS

HOTEL RESORT LA FLOR DE ITABO, Apdo. 32, Playa del Coco, Guanacaste. Tel. 506/67-0292 or 67-0011. 22 rms (all with bath).

$ Rates: $45–$55 single; $45–$60 double; $80 triple or quad. AE, MC, V.

If you have a little extra money to spend, this is the place to stay. The grounds are lushly planted, and there are two pools, one for adults and one for kids. Toucans and parrots squawk and talk amid the flowers, adding their own bright colors to an already colorful garden. Stone reproductions of Pre-Columbian statues add a touch of the mysterious to this quiet retreat. With barely a dozen rooms, service here is intimate. The rooms are spacious (especially the bungalows) and attractively decorated and housed in beautiful two-story houses.

Italian dishes are the specialty of the restaurant, with prices ranging from $3.35 to $7.40 for entrées. The bar is decorated with flags from all over the world and there is a TV in the lobby.

WHERE TO EAT
MEALS FOR LESS THAN $6

RESTAURANT-BAR EL OASIS, Calle Principal across from the soccer field. No phone.

$ Prices: $2.10–$6.50. No credit cards.

Open: Daily 10am–10pm.

On the right as you approach the beach is one of Playa del Coco's better restaurants. In the one large room of the restaurant, you'll find a long table for groups and several other smaller tables. There are traditional Tico-style wrought-iron bars on the windows for a touch of colonial atmosphere; otherwise, this is a very simple place. Meals are all Costa Rican, with an emphasis on seafood and broiled chicken.

RESTAURANT GUAJIRA, on beach opposite the soccer fields. No phone.

$ Prices: $2.60–$11.10. No credit cards.

Open: Wed–Mon 10am–10pm.

This breezy family restaurant is right on the beach, so you can watch fishermen bring in the catch while you dine. You know the fish served here is fresh because you can watch them clean it on a picnic table in back of the restaurant. Late at night, the party crowd takes over—and it can get pretty noisy. The standard Tico seafood fare includes corvina (sea bass) prepared in different sauces, lobster or shrimp in garlic and butter, and casados with fried fish.

---

6. PLAYA HERMOSA

160 miles NW of San José; 15 miles W of Liberia

GETTING THERE   By Bus   An express bus leaves San José daily at 3:30pm from Calle 12 between avenidas 5 and 7. Duration: 5 hours. Fare: $5.90. Buses leave from Liberia at 11:30am and 7pm. Duration: 30 minutes. Fare: 75¢.

By Car   Follow the directions for getting to Playa del Coco, but take the right fork (at the rock quarry) as you approach Playa del Coco.

DEPARTING   The express bus back to San José leaves Playa Hermosa just after

5am. The bus from Playa Panamá to Liberia leaves at 6am and 4pm, stopping in Playa Hermosa a few minutes later. Ask at your hotel where to catch the bus. Duration: 30 minutes. Fare: 75¢.

To reach San José, take the bus to Liberia and then catch one of the many express buses to San José.

ESSENTIALS   Orientation   There is no real town here, just a few houses and hotels on and near the beach.

Playa Hermosa means "beautiful beach," an appropriate name. Surrounded by dry rocky hills, this curving gray sand beach is long and wide and rarely crowded, despite the presence of a new luxury condominium development on the hill behind. There are a few Tico-style *sodas* right on the beach, but little else. Green trees come right down to the edge of the sand, even in the driest months of the year. At both ends of the beach rocky headlands jut out into the surf. At the base of these rocks, you will find tide pools that are fun to explore.

WHAT TO SEE & DO

The tourist information center and water-sports equipment rental center for Playa Hermosa is **Aqua Sport** (tel. 67-0050 or 67-0158). Kayaks, sailboards, canoes, bicycles, beach umbrellas, snorkel gear, and parasails are all available for rental at fairly reasonable rates. This is also where you'll find the local post office, public phones, and a restaurant (see "Where to Eat" below).

Beyond Playa Hermosa, where the paved road ends, you'll find one more appealing and even more secluded beach—Playa Panamá. This big bay is lined with dense vegetation now but is scheduled for development in the near future. In fact, the signs are already up announcing the new resorts that will be built. When you visit, you might still be able to find a stretch of beach all to yourself, where you can sit back and watch the pelicans feeding just offshore.

WHERE TO STAY

DOUBLES FOR LESS THAN $30

CABINAS PLAYA HERMOSA, Apdo. 117, Liberia, Guanacaste. Tel. 506/67-0136. 20 rms (all with bath).
$ Rates: $15.95 single; $28.15 double; $35.20 triple; $42.20 quad. No credit cards.

This little hotel tucked away under shady trees and surrounded by green lawns is run by Italians who make sure that their guests enjoy the quiet vacation they dreamed about before leaving home. Each large room has a pair of Adirondack chairs on its front porch, and the beach is only a few steps away. Rooms, even though rather dark, are large and have a lot of closet space and double beds. You can also rent snorkeling gear and bicycles here, but you'll find that they are cheaper up the beach at Aqua Sport. To find the hotel, watch for the white archway over the driveway after the curve to the right on the dirt road. The turnoff from the main road is well marked.

The open-air restaurant has a rustic tropical feel to it, with unfinished tree trunks holding up the roof. Seafood and homemade pasta are the specialties here. Menu prices range from $4.45 to $14.80.

DOUBLES FOR LESS THAN $56

LOS CORALES, Apdo. 1158-1002, San José. Tel. 506/67-0255 or 57-0259 in San José. Fax 506/55-4978. 12 rms (all with bath). A/C
$ Rates: $55.55 1–6 people; $62.95 7–8 people. MC, V.

This is one of the newer hotels in Playa Hermosa and it does not have any shade. It's in the middle of a large field set back from the beach about 200 yards. If you're down here with your family or a group of friends, you might want to consider staying here. All the accommodations are large two-bedroom apartments that come complete with full kitchen and can sleep up to eight people. There are pools for adults and children, a hot tub, and a volleyball court.

WHERE TO EAT

AQUA SPORT, on the beach. Tel. 67-0158.
  Cuisine: CONTINENTAL.
$ **Prices:** $5.20–$11.10. MC, V.
  Open: Daily 9am–9pm (noon–9pm in rainy season).
Part of the Aqua Sport market and equipment rental shop is a small open-air restaurant with booths of polished hardwood. The beach is only steps away, and the atmosphere is very casual. The food, however, is much better than what you would expect from such a place. The focus is on Continental—with paella for $7.40, lobster provençal for $11.10, and shrimp à la diabla for $10.35. You'll also find a variety of crêpes on the menu.

7. PLAYAS BRASILITO, FLAMINGO, POTRERO & PAN DE AZUCAR

165 miles NW of San José; 35 miles SW of Liberia

GETTING THERE   By Air   Even though there are no regularly scheduled flights to the airstrip at Playa Flamingo, it is possible to charter a plane to these beaches.

By Bus   The express bus from San José leaves from the corner of Calle 20 and Avenida 3 daily at 10:30am. Duration: 6 hours. Fare: $3.25. Buses also run from the central park in Santa Cruz, which is south of here on the Nicoya Peninsula. These buses leave at 6:30am and 3pm. Duration: 2½ hours. Fare: $1.10. If you are coming from Liberia, take a Santa Cruz or Nicoya bus (which run almost hourly) and get off in the village of Belén, which is south of Filadelfia.

By Car   Follow the directions for getting to Liberia, then take the road toward Nicoya. After about 24 miles you will see the turnoff for Playa Flamingo and Playa Tamarindo. After another 12 miles, take the right fork for Playa Flamingo and Playa Brasilito.

DEPARTING   To reach Liberia, buses leave from Potrero village at 5:30am, 12:30 and 5pm. They pass by Playa Potrero, the turnoff for Playa Flamingo, and Brasilito a few minutes later. Ask at your hotel where the best place is for catching the bus. Get off the bus at Belén and wait for a bus going north to Liberia.
   To reach San José the express bus leaves from Playa Flamingo daily at 9am, stopping in Brasilito at 9:15am. You must buy your ticket in advance (in San José, tel. 21-7202). Duration: 6 hours. Fare: $3.25. You can also take the buses to Liberia and then transfer to an express bus to San José.

ESSENTIALS   Orientation   These four beaches are strung out over several miles of dirt roads. Hotels are generally well marked, but if you arrive after dark, you'll find it very difficult to find anything.

Almost at the westernmost point of the Nicoya Peninsula are a string of beaches that are rapidly gaining popularity with international sunseekers and North American retirees. The beaches are along two bays separated by a small peninsula, and each has its own very different personality.

WHAT TO SEE & DO

On **Playa Brasilito** you will find one of the only two real villages in the area. The village of Brasilito will give you some idea of what this entire coast was like not too long ago. The soccer field is the center of the village, and there are a couple of little *pulperias* (general stores). There is a beach, but it is not very appealing—gray sand, with the decrepit village right on the beach—and I can't recommend either of the very basic accommodations here. If you have come this far, you owe it to yourself to stay someplace a little bit more attractive, so read on.

Only a few miles away and at the opposite end of the scale is the luxury resort beach called **Playa Flamingo.** This is one of Costa Rica's top resort beaches, with luxury hotels, a marina, a private airstrip, retirement and vacation homes, and, best of all, one of the only white-sand beaches in the area. In fact, the old name for this beach was Playa Blanca, which made plenty of sense. When the developers moved in, they needed a more romantic name than White Beach, so it became Playa Flamingo, even though there are no flamingos. You probably won't be able to afford any of the hotels here, but you should definitely plan to spend plenty of time on this beautiful beach.

Playa Flamingo is on a long spit of land that forms part of Potrero Bay, or Bahia Flamingo, as the developers wish it to be known. On the ocean side of the peninsula, there is the long white-sand beach, behind which is a dusty road and then a mangrove swamp that is still home to a few caymans (relatives of alligators). If you are not staying on Playa Flamingo, you should know that there are parking spots all along the beach road where you can park your car for the day. There is, however, little shade on the beach, so be sure to use plenty of sunscreen and bring an umbrella if you can. The bay side of the peninsula is where the marina is located.

If you continue along the unpaved road from Brasilito without taking the turn for Playa Flamingo, you will soon come to **Playa Potrero.** The sand here is a brownish gray, but the beach is long, clean, and deserted. You can see the hotels of the Playa Flamingo resort complex across the bay.

Playa Pan de Azucar is the last and prettiest of these beaches. As the name implies it is as white as sugar. The little crescent of sand is surrounded by steep, rugged hills covered with chaparral-type shrubs. In the rocky cove, there is very good snorkeling and swimming. Because the Hotel Sugar Beach takes up the entire cove, you will have to stay here if you want to use this beautiful beach.

WHERE TO STAY
DOUBLES FOR LESS THAN $30

CABINAS CRISTINA, Playa Potrero, Santa Cruz, Apdo. 121-Santa Cruz. Tel. 506/67-4006. 3 rms (all with bath).

$ Rates: $19.25 single; $24.45 double; $30.40 triple; $35.55 quad. No credit cards.

Although it isn't right on the beach, Cabinas Christina is a great value in this area of high-priced hotels. The rooms are spacious and very clean (and fill up fast) with hot plates, refrigerators, dressers, bars with stools, tiled baths, and double and bunk beds. On the veranda there are large rocking chairs. The friendly owner, Daniel Boldrini, speaks some English. There is a small pool in the middle of a grassy green yard and a thatched-roof palapa. The beach is a five-minute walk away down a dirt road, and Restaurant Las Perlas is only 50 yards away (see "Where to Eat" below).

LONG-TERM STAYS

If you are interested in splurging a bit or have a group of friends or large family, you might want to consider renting a house here. They rent for anywhere between $55 and $450 per day. Fred Schultz is the person to contact at Apdo. 77, Santa Cruz, Guanacaste (tel. 506/67-4007), for reservations or more information.

WORTH THE EXTRA BUCKS

BAHIA FLAMINGO BEACH RESORT, Playa Flamingo, Apdo. 45-5051 Santa Cruz, Guanacaste. Tel. 506/67-4183. 14 rms (all with bath).

$ Rates: $48.30–$64.40 single; $56.35–$64.40 double; $77.05 triple; $90.85 quad. MC, V.

Despite its name, this little beach hotel is in fact on Playa Potrero. You'll see the resorts of Playa Flamingo across the bay when you stand on the beach. Set in a green garden with a white wooden fence round the property, the Bahia Flamingo feels like a private home in the country. A laid-back atmosphere prevails—with hammocks for dozing, a pool, and miles of nearly deserted beach for strolling and swimming. Most of the rooms have kitchenettes, two double beds, good-sized bathrooms with counter space and hot water, tile floors, and ceiling fans. Fishing and snorkeling trips can be arranged. Watch for the sign pointing down a road to the left a mile or so after you pass the turnoff for Playa Flamingo. The hotel's restaurant is a breezy, high-ceilinged room with a colorful mural over the bar and it has a nice view of green lawns, white fence, and blue ocean. Meals average $4.80 to $8.15.

HOTEL SUGAR BEACH, Playa Pan de Azucar, Guanacaste. Tel. 506/67-4242. 25 rms (all with bath).

$ Rates: $85 single or double. No credit cards.

⭐ Just as the name implies, the Hotel Sugar Beach is located on a white-sand beach—one of the few in the area and therefore one of the most attractive in my opinion. The beach is on a small cove surrounded by rocky hills. Unfortunately, the hills become very brown and desolate in the dry season (which is when most tourists come to visit), so don't expect the verdant tropics if you come down here in March or April. The hotel itself is perched high above the water on a gentle slope. The managers Julie and Bill Enell have several pet macaws, a few of which are quite gabby and keep the guests entertained. Nature lovers will be thrilled to find wild howler monkeys and iguanas almost on their doorsteps. Snorkelers will also be happy here because the cove here has some of the best snorkeling on the west coast. All but one of the rooms have air conditioning, hot water, and two double beds, and all are spacious and comfortable and have porches in front so that you can sit back and watch birds right from your room. Hammocks under the trees provide a great way to while away a hot afternoon.

The open-air dining room and bar are in a circular building with a panoramic vista of ocean, islands, and hills. The dining room serves up excellent Costa Rican and international meals. The special of the house is jumbo shrimp for $14, while other meals range from $5 to $10. Scuba diving ($75), horseback riding ($5/hour), and fishing boat charters ($250/½ day) can be arranged.

WHERE TO EAT

HAL'S AMERICAN BAR & GRILL, between the turnoff for Playa Flamingo and Playa Potrero. Tel. 67-4213.
   Cuisine: INTERNATIONAL.
$ Prices: $3.75–$5.95. AE.
   Open: Mon–Thurs 4–11pm, Fri–Sun 11am–11pm.

I guess it had to happen sooner or later—a miniature golf course has opened at Playa Flamingo, though it is doubling as a restaurant as well. Pasta, burgers, and steaks are the staples, but there is also a long list of side orders that includes such offerings as stuffing, french fries, roast peppers, buffalo wings, and a Greek salad. The roast chicken is the specialty of the house. A round of miniature golf costs $2.95 for adults and $1.50 for children. The restaurant operates a free shuttle bus to Playa Flamingo at 6:30 and 8pm.

MARIE'S, Playa Flamingo near the Marina Hotel. Tel. 67-4136.
   Cuisine: SANDWICHES/SEAFOOD.
$ Prices: $1.95–$6.50. AE, MC, V.
   Open: Daily 7am–9pm. Closed Tues May–Sept.

★ Right in the middle of all the luxury hotels at Playa Flamingo is a great little place for a snack and a swim. This is the only restaurant I have ever visited that had its own swimming pool. Forget what you learned about not swimming after eating; here it's encouraged. Luckily the pool is quite small, so you don't have to worry about drowning from cramps. The menu is primarily sandwiches and other lunch foods, but on the blackboard behind the bar you'll find daily specials such as mahi-mahi (called dorado down here) and, from August to December, lobster and conch. The owners are from Alaska and England, but they have mastered many Tico favorites, such as heart of palm salad (palmito). Tables in the open-air restaurant are made from slabs of tree trunks. Be sure to try the three-milks cake (a Nicaraguan specialty), which just might be the moistest cake on earth.

RESTAURANT LAS PERLAS, Playa Potrero, at the corner near Cabinas Christina. No phone.
    Cuisine: AMERICAN.
$ Prices: $1.10–$2.60. No credit cards.
    Open: Daily 7am–1pm.
Las Perlas, an unusual open-air restaurant with chain-link fencing for walls, is primarily the local community center, but also serves up decent breakfasts and lunches. You can chat with a parrot as you wait for your meal.

---

8. PLAYA TAMARINDO

184 miles NW of San José; 45 miles SW of Liberia

GETTING THERE **By Air** Sansa flies from San José Monday, Wednesday, Friday, and Saturday at 8:45am. Duration: 50 minutes. Fare: $25.90. Travelair (tel. 32-7883 in San José) flies to Tamarindo daily at 1:30pm from the Pavas Airport near San José. Duration: 50 minutes. Fare: $57.

By Bus An express bus leaves San José daily at 3:30pm from the corner of Calle 14 between avenidas 3 and 5. Duration: 5½ hours. Fare: $3.35. Another express bus leaves from Calle 20 and Avenida 3 (also in San José) at 4pm, but you must buy your ticket in advance. Duration: 5½ hours. Fare: $3. From Santa Cruz, there are buses daily at 4:30, 6:30, 8:30, and 11:30am and 1pm.

By Car The most direct route is by way of the Tempisque ferry, Nicoya, and Santa Cruz. The turnoff for the ferry is at La Irma, about midway between Puntarenas and Liberia. Once you're across on the ferry, turn right in Mansión and head north through Nicoya and Santa Cruz to the beach turnoff at Belén.

DEPARTING Sansa flights leave for San José at 9:35am Monday, Wednesday, Friday, and Saturday. Travelair flights leave at 2:40pm daily. An express bus leaves for San José daily at 5:45am, on Sunday it leaves at 1:45pm. Duration: 5 hours. Fare: $3.35. The Tralapa express bus (in San José, tel. 21-7202), for which you must buy your ticket in advance, leaves for San José daily at 6:45am.

ESSENTIALS **Orientation** The unpaved road leading into town runs parallel to the beach and dead-ends at Cabinas Zully Mar. You'll find virtually all of Tamarindo along this one road.
    There is a public phone with international service at the Fiesta del Mar restaurant (see "Where to Eat" below) at the end of the road. The phone is available from 6am to 9pm.

Tamarindo is a long swath of white sand that curves gently from one rocky headland to another at the far end. Behind the beach are low, dry hills that can be a very dreary brown in the dry season but instantly turn green with the first brief showers of the rainy season. With only one major resort hotel in town, Tamarindo is still a quiet little fishing village. The fishing boats bob at their moorings at the south end of the beach, and brown pelicans fish just outside the breakers. A sandy islet offshore makes a great destination if you are a strong swimmer; if you're not, it makes a great foreground for sunsets.

WHAT TO SEE & DO

The beaches near Tamarindo are one of the last nesting sites for the giant leatherback turtle, which is the largest turtle in the world. The turtles nest between August and February—during this time there are usually lots of night tours to see nesting turtles. The tours cost anywhere between $10 and $25 per person, but when I last visited there was a movement to end the tours because the flashlights on the beach are confusing the turtles and preventing them from nesting properly. Before going on one of these tours, try to find out if precautions are being taken to protect the turtles.

You have to be careful when and where you swim on Tamarindo Beach. There are rocks just offshore in several places, some of which are exposed only at low tide. An encounter with one of these rocks could be nasty, especially if you were bodysurfing.

Papagayo Excursions (tel. 68-0859 or 68-0652), which has its office at the Hotel Tamarindo Diriá, offers folks a chance to go after the big ones that abound in the waters offshore. From here it takes only 20 minutes to reach the edge of the continental shelf and the waters preferred by marlin and sailfish. Although fishing is good all year, the peak season for billfish is between mid-April and August. Rates are $250 to $450 for a half day and $350 to $700 for a full day for the boat. If you aren't an angler, you can arrange to go horseback riding. Rates for horses, with a guide, are $25 for two hours. They also offer two-hour boat tours of the nearby estuary for $25 per person and two-tank scuba diving trips for $60.

Tamarindo Turicentro, which is on the right as you come into town, rents scooters, bodyboards, beach chairs, and beach umbrellas at reasonable rates. They're open daily from 8am to 1pm and from 4 to 6pm.

WHERE TO STAY

DOUBLES FOR LESS THAN $25

CABINAS MARIELOS, Playa Tamarindo, Guanacaste. Tel. (in Alajuela) 506/41-4843. 8 rms (all with bath).
$ Rates: $18.50 1–3 people. No credit cards.
This place is located down a palm-shaded driveway across the street from the beach and Pensión Doly. Rooms are clean and fairly new, though small and simply furnished. There are tile floors and wooden chairs on the patios. The bathrooms have no door on them but are otherwise quite acceptable. There is even a kitchen that guests can use. The garden was only recently planted but is already providing a bit of shade. You can rent a bike here for $5.90 per day.

HOTEL POZO AZUL, Playa Tamarindo, Santa Cruz, Guanacaste. Tel. 506/68-0147 or 68-0412. 27 rms (all with bath).
$ Rates: $24.45 1–3 people, $31.20 1–3 people, with A/C; $38.10 quad with A/C. No credit cards.
This is the first hotel you'll spot as you drive into Tamarindo. It's on the left side of the road and therefore is not on the beach. There isn't much shade on the grounds, but there are swimming pools for adults and kids. In the 17 rooms with air conditioning, there are also hot plates, refrigerators, tables and chairs, large windows, and *pilas* (sinks) for washing clothes. Some rooms have covered parking to keep your car out of the blistering heat. There is no restaurant here, so you'll have to either cook your own meals or travel into town to one of the few restaurants.

CABINAS ZULLY MAR, Tamarindo, Guanacaste. Tel. 506/26-4732. 27 rms (all with bath).
$ Rates: $18.05–$21.20 single or double, $35.30 single or double with A/C. MC, V.

⑤ The Zully Mar has long been a favorite of budget travelers staying at Tamarindo Beach, and with the addition of eight new rooms with air conditioning, the hotel has only gotten better. Rates are still reasonable, and there are even plans to add a swimming pool. The new rooms are in a two-story white-stucco building with a wide curving staircase on the outside. The doors to the guest rooms are hand-carved with Pre-Columbian motifs. There are high ceilings with fans; tile floors; a long veranda; and large, clean bathrooms. Although there are mango trees out front for shade, there is little other landscaping, and the sandy grounds look a bit unkempt. Don't let this bother you: Miles of beach are just across the street, and even the older rooms are clean and pleasant.

WORTH THE EXTRA BUCKS

LAGARTILLO BEACH HOTEL, P.O. Box 1584-1000, Avellana Beach, Guanacaste. Tel. 506/57-1420. Fax 506/21-5717. 6 rms (all with bath).
$ Rates: $50 single or double. MC, V.
This small hotel is not actually in Tamarindo, and it will cost you a bit for a taxi if you don't have your own car, but it is well worth the expense. The rooms are fairly basic with cement porches, cinder-block walls, bunk beds and a double bed, and a modern tile bathroom with cold water only. There is an open-air bar and dining area beside the small pool. If it weren't for the radio in the bar, it would be tranquil out here; it is miles from the nearest village and just down a path is your own private beach. There are dry forests nearby where you're likely to see monkeys and plenty of birds. Meals run $3.50 to $5 for breakfast and $5 to $10 for lunch or dinner.

PUEBLO DORADO HOTEL, Tamarindo, Guanacaste. Tel. 506/22-5741. Fax 506/22-5741. 22 rms (all with bath). A/C
$ Rates: $59.80 single; $69 double; $80.50 triple.
This two-story, blindingly white hotel has a central garden courtyard and looks a bit like a Los Angeles apartment building. There's a small pool at the back of the garden and above the pool is an open-air restaurant and bar serving meals in the $3.75 to $7.50 range. Guest rooms are done in white tile and have big bathrooms and double beds. In the guest rooms and elsewhere around the hotel there are huge stone masks mounted on the walls, reproductions of Pre-Columbian stone carvings. Though this hotel is across the road from the beach, it still offers the best deal if you want a place with air conditioning and a swimming pool.

WHERE TO EAT

FIESTA DEL MAR, at the end of the road. No phone.
Cuisine: STEAK/SEAFOOD.
$ Prices: $3.35–$13.35. V.
Open: Mon–Fri 5–10pm, Sat–Sun 7:30am–10pm.
Across the circle from the Zully Mar, the Fiesta del Mar specializes in steak and seafood cooked over a wood fire. Try the grilled steak in garlic sauce for $8.90, and be sure to finish off any meal with the coconut flan for $1.85. After a filling meal, you might want to relax in one of the hammocks the restaurant has strung in the shade for its clients. The open-air dining area is edged with greenery, and there are more of those interesting Pre-Columbian stone statue reproductions. There is also a public phone with international service, available from 6am to 9pm daily.

EL MILAGRO, on the left as you enter town. No phone.
Cuisine: CONTINENTAL/COSTA RICAN.
$ Prices: Main dishes $4.45–$16.29. AE, MC, V.
Open: Daily 11am–10:30pm.
Lush gardens, wide terraces, and live music in the evenings should make this your first choice for dinner in Tamarindo. Reproductions of Pre-Columbian stone statues stand in the gardens and the bar has carved wood columns. On those rare occasions when it is raining, you can retreat to one of the indoor dining rooms. Though the emphasis here is on seafood, you'll also find such unexpected offerings as beef fondue for two,

melon cocktail, peach Melba, crêpes with ice cream, and hot fruits and amaretto sauce.

RESTAURANT ZULLY MAR, at the end of the road. No phone.
Cuisine: COSTA RICAN.
$ Prices: Meals $2.95–$12.60. No credit cards.
Open: Daily 7:30am–10pm.

This restaurant, opposite the hotel of the same name, is right on the beach at the end of the road that leads into Tamarindo. It's a basic Tico-style open-air restaurant, but the food is good, and the view can't be beat. Sit and watch the waves crash over the rocks just offshore while you dine on fresh fish sautéed in garlic for $4.10. The fruit salads here are quite large and delicious and make a wonderful afternoon snack or dessert for $1.85. The bar is a popular hangout with locals and tourists.

PICNIC FARE

If you are in the mood for a picnic or are doing your own cooking, be sure to get your bread at **Panadería Johan,** a Belgian-run bakery on the outskirts of town. There are always fresh-baked goodies here, although what you might find on any given day is never certain. Possibilities include croissants, pizzas, chocolate éclairs, and different types of bread. A whole pizza goes for $6.50. There are also a couple of tables where you can eat your pizza. Johan's is open daily from 6am to 8pm.

For other picnic essentials, try the **Supermercado** on the right a little farther into town. Watch for the Tamarindo Turicentro sign. The market is open Monday to Saturday from 8:30am to 5pm.

9. PLAYA NOSARA & PLAYA SÁMARA

Distances to Playa Nosara: 40 miles SW of Nicoya;
165 miles W of San José.
Distances to Playa Sámara: 28 miles S of Nicoya;
152 miles W of San José.

GETTING THERE By Air Flights on Sansa leave San José for Nosara and Sámara on Monday, Wednesday, and Friday at 6am. Duration: 35 minutes to Nosara, 1 hour and 35 minutes to Sámara. Fare to Nosara or Sámara: $25.92.

By Bus A direct bus leaves San José for Sámara daily from Calle 14 between avenidas 3 and 5 at noon. Duration: 6 hours. Fare: $3.35. To reach Nosara, you must first take a bus to the town of Nicoya. These buses leave San José from Calle 14 between avenidas 3 and 5 daily at 6, 8, and 10am, noon, and 1, 2:30, 3, and 5pm. Duration: 6 hours. Fare: $3.25. Nosara-bound buses leave Nicoya daily at 1pm. Duration: 2½ hours. Fare: $2.50.

By Car From San José, take the Interamerican Highway to La Irma and turn west following signs for the Tempisque ferry. After taking the ferry, continue to Nicoya, where the paved road ends. From Nicoya, follow the signs south out of town for either Sámara or Nosara.

DEPARTING Buses leave Sámara daily at 4am for San José. Buses leave Nosara for Nicoya daily at 6am. Buses leave Nicoya for San José daily at 4, 7:30, and 9am, noon, and 2:30 and 4pm. See above for fares and travel times.

ESSENTIALS The village of Nosara is about 3 miles inland from the beach. To find the hotels listed here, drive through the village and watch for the hotel's signs. Sámara is slightly larger and is right on the water.

These two beaches have yet to see the sort of development that is hitting other Costa Rican beaches because they are so difficult to reach. The best way to get here is to fly, and with only a few flights a week, you had better plan to stay put for awhile. There are plans to pave the roads in this area, and perhaps by the time you arrive driving times and conditions will be much improved. Nosara has long been popular with North American retirees who have built houses hidden in the trees. Sámara on the other hand is a fishing village that is a popular vacation spot with Ticos.

WHAT TO SEE & DO

As far as I can tell, the area around Nosara is the greenest area of the Nicoya Peninsula, so if you are looking for reliably sunny winter weather and a bit of tropical greenery, this is a good bet. Unfortunately, there are only a couple of hotels here and only one is close to the beach. There are actually several beaches at Nosara, but my favorite is **Playa Pelada.** This is a little white-sand beach lined with sea grasses and mangroves. However, there isn't too much sand at high tide. At either end of the beach there are rocky outcroppings that contain tide pools at low tide. Surfing and bodysurfing are both good here. Because the village of Nosara is several miles inland, these beaches are very clean, secluded, and quiet.

Sámara sits right on a horseshoe-shaped bay. It sees a lot of weekend visitors and consequently can get a bit dirty. However, it is excellent for **swimming** because the rocks across the mouth of the bay break the waves. A small rocky island and steep cliffs on the far side of the bay make this a very attractive spot, and the beach is long and wide. Directly behind the main beach is a wide, flat valley that stretches far inland.

WHERE TO STAY
PLAYA NOSARA

RANCHO SUIZO LODGE, Apdo. 14, Bocas de Nosara, Guanacaste 5233. No phone. Fax 506/25-1493. 10 rms (all with bath).
$ Rates: $23 single; $35 double. No credit cards.
To reach this peaceful lodge, follow the signs from the village of Nosara toward the beach. The lodge is situated on grassy grounds a 5-minute walk down a trail from the beach. At the center of the grounds is a large conical restaurant with a thatch roof. Inside, the decor is tropical Swiss. The guest rooms are in several little cabins and are fairly small; they have double beds, bamboo furniture, a porch, and a big window. Bathrooms have cold-water tiled showers. The owner's aviaries, full of exotic birds, are outside the lodge. Only breakfast and dinner are served in the restaurant, with prices ranging from $2.65 to $2.90 for breakfast and around $7.75 for dinner, which must be reserved by 2pm.

ESTANCIA NOSARA, Nosara, Guanacaste. No phone. 8 rms (all with bath).
$ Rates: $40 single; $46 double; $54 triple; $62 quad. No credit cards.
Although this hotel is a mile or so from the beach, it's set amid shady jungle trees and has a swimming pool and tennis court. By the time you arrive there should be a restaurant as well. There's a man-made waterfall tumbling from a small hill of stones near the pool and reproductions of Pre-Columbian stone statues in the lush garden. The guest rooms are in two buildings and have red-tile floors, kitchenettes, high ceilings, overhead fans, showers with hot water, and plenty of closet space, so you can move in for a long stay if you're so inclined. You can even rent horses here and ride to the beach. But with the surroundings so idyllic, with lots of shade, big trees, and tropical birds singing overhead, you may never make it to the *playa.*

PLAYA SÁMARA

HOTEL MARBELLA, P.O. Box 490, 3000 Heredia. Tel. 506/33-9980. Fax 506/33-9980. 17 rms (all with bath).
$ Rates: $28.15 single; $35.55 double; $42.95 triple. AE, MC, V.
Though it is a bit of a walk to the beach and the immediate surroundings are none too

appealing, this small German-run hotel is properly tropical in decor. You'll find the Marbella just around the corner from the road that leads down to the soccer fields and the beach. Guest rooms are fairly large and have red-tile floors and woven mats for ceilings. There are open closets and modern bathrooms with hot water. There is a small swimming pool in a gravel courtyard and a second-floor dining room with rattan chairs and bamboo-fronted bar. All the rooms have a balcony or porch, though not necessarily any sort of a view. There is a thatch roof over the dining room where the menu focuses on seafood and changes daily. Prices are in the $6-to-$15 range. You'll also find a bar and snack bar here.

HOTEL LAS BRISAS DEL PACIFICO, Apdo. 129-6100, Ciudad Colón. Tel. 506/55-2380 or 68-0876. Fax 506/55-2380 or 68-0876. 24 rms (all with bath).

$ Rates: $40–$48 single; $40–$60 double; $60–$70 triple. AE, MC, V.

Though it is a bit pricey, this is your best bet in Sámara. Located on the same road as the Marbella, this hotel is set amid very shady grounds right on the beach and backs up to a steep hill. The less expensive rooms are up a long and steep flight of stairs at the top of the hill, where there is an excellent view of the bay. These rooms have large balconies and walls of glass that take in the views. The most expensive rooms are near the pool in stucco duplexes with steeply pitched tile roofs and red-tile patios. Rooms have cold-water showers only, but it's never warm enough here to warrant hot showers. There is a small pool with a cold-water whirlpool area only a few steps from the beach. The open-air restaurant is breezy, surrounded by lush garden plantings. The menu changes daily but ranges from $6 to $13.35. The management here is German as are many of the guests.

WHERE TO EAT

There are a couple of *sodas* in the village of Nosara where you can get a cheap Tico meal, and down at the beach there's **Olga's Bar,** which serves three meals daily, including the biggest plate of bacon I've ever been served with breakfast. Meals at Olga's range from $2.95 to $5.20 and are served from 7am to 9pm daily.

10. PLAYA MONTEZUMA

105 miles W of San José (not including the ferry ride); 24 miles SE of Paquera; 39 miles S of Naranjo; 120 miles S of Liberia.

GETTING THERE   By Bus and Ferry   If you are traveling from San José by public transportation, it will take you two buses and a ferry ride to get to Montezuma. This can require spending a night in Puntarenas, so don't plan on heading out this way unless you have plenty of time. First take a Puntarenas bus from the corner of Calle 12 and Avenida 9; these buses leave hourly from 6am to 6pm. Duration: 2 hours. Fare: $1.90. From Puntarenas take the *lancha* (not the ferry, which is for cars and goes to the town of Naranjo further to the north), which leaves from the pier behind the market at 6:15 and 11am and 3pm. Duration: 1½ hours. Fare: $1.40. The Montezuma bus will be waiting to meet the lancha when it arrives in Paquera. Duration: 1½ hours. Fare: $2.20.

By Car   Take the Interamerican Highway from San José to Puntarenas and catch the Naranjo ferry (you'll probably have to arrive the night before and put your car in line to assure a space on the ferry the next morning. The ferry leaves daily at 7 and 11am and 4pm. Duration: 1½ hours. Fare: $4.80 for cars, 65¢ for adults, and 40¢ for children. From Naranjo, head south. It should take you at least two hours to get to Montezuma from the ferry landing. Alternatively you can continue north on the Interamerican Highway to La Irma and then turn west, taking the Tempisque ferry and continuing to the town of Mansión. From Mansión, head south and follow the signs for Naranjo.

DEPARTING   The Paquera bus leaves at 5:30 and 11am and 2:30pm and meets the Paquera ferry, which leaves for Puntarenas at 8am and 12:30 and 5pm. Total duration: 3½ hours. Fare: $3.65.

ESSENTIALS   There is a tour and tourist information desk in a little shack in the center of the village. The bus stops at the end of the road into the village. From here, hotels are scattered up and down the beach and around the village's few sand streets.

Before I came to Montezuma, I had heard different opinions about this beach at the southern tip of the Nicoya Peninsula. Some people, mostly European budget travelers, thought it was the best beach in Central America. Other people, those who prefer a few more amenities, thought it would be a great beach in a few years when it had some decent accommodations and restaurants. After spending some time there myself, I have to agree with all of them. Montezuma has its charms and its drawbacks, not least of which is a problem with untreated sewage flowing onto the beach from some of the establishments in the village. Unfortunately, Montezuma has gained popularity far faster than local restaurants and hotels can cope with the growing sanitary needs. This problem is further aggravated by the large numbers of people who camp on the beach. There is a severe shortage of rooms here—if you don't show up with reservations, you better have a tent or hammock. And even if you do manage to get a room in the village, don't expect to go to sleep early; a disco and a bar, side by side, blast their respective music for hours on end. Head out of town if peace and tranquillity are what you're seeking.

On the other hand, the water here is a gorgeous royal blue, though the waves can occasionally be too rough for casual swimming and you need to be aware of stray rocks at your feet. Be sure you know where the rocks are before doing any bodysurfing. In either direction from Montezuma are a string of sandy coves separated by outcroppings of volcanic rock that form tide pools.

WHAT TO SEE & DO

Mostly you just hang out on the beach, hang out in a restaurant, hang out in a bar, or hang out in front of the disco. However, if you're interested in more than just hanging out, you can rent a horse for around $5 an hour or take a 4-hour **horseback tour** for $20. Luis, whose rental place is down the road that leads out of town to the left, is a reliable source for horses. Right in the center of the village, you can **rent a bicycle** for $11.10 per day. There are also a number of tours possible from Montezuma. You can visit nearby **Cabo Blanco Preserve** for $14.80, which includes breakfast, or **Tortuga Island** for $25.95, also including breakfast (this is a savings of about $40 over the similar tours sold in San José).

Just outside of town to the south (toward Cabo Blanco), there are a couple of **waterfalls** with pools that are perfect for a refreshing afternoon dip. Watch for the trail just after you cross the stream. Five miles to the north is another waterfall, but this one empties directly into the sea. The best way to reach this latter waterfall is by horse. Seven miles south, at the southernmost point of the Nicoya Peninsula, is the Cabo Blanco Preserves, open from 8am to 4pm daily with an admission charge of 75¢. The preserve is a nesting site for brown pelicans, magnificent frigate birds, and brown boobies. Howler monkeys are often seen (and heard!). You can hike through the preserve's lush forest right down to the deserted, pristine beach.

WHERE TO STAY
DOUBLES FOR LESS THAN $10

PENSIÓN ARENAS, Montezuma, Cobano de Puntarenas. No phone. 14 rms (none with bath).
$ Rates: $4.25 single; $8.50 double.
This is the backpackers' first choice in Montezuma. If they haven't got a room for you, you can pitch a tent or hammock on the sand in front of the pension. Rooms are split

between an old wooden house and a newer cement building, though the end rooms on the second floor of the house are probably the best and they catch the breezes. This place is about as basic as it gets in Costa Rica, although there are toilet seats (some places don't even have that). Most of the rooms have fans.

HOTEL MONTEZUMA, Montezuma, Cobano de Puntarenas. Tel. 506/61-1122, ext. 258. 28 rms (23 with bath).
$ Rates: $4.25 single without bath, $6.80 single with bath; $8.50 double without bath, $13.65 double with bath. V.

Located right in the center of the village across the street from the disco, the Hotel Montezuma offers basic but clean rooms with fans. Some of the rooms are upstairs from the hotel's noisy bar and restaurant. If you like to go to sleep early, try to get a room at the back of the hotel's building across the street. The walls here don't go all the way to the ceiling, which is great for air circulation but lousy for privacy.

DOUBLES FOR LESS THAN $30

CASABLANCA, Montezuma, Cobano de Puntarenas. No phone. 6 rms (2 with bath).
$ Rates (including breakfast): $18.50 1–3 people (slightly more with private bath). No credit cards.

Just to the left as you enter the village of Montezuma, you'll see this large white house. Because the management is German, you're likely to hear that language more than English or Spanish here. The rooms are arranged around the spacious second-floor porch, which has a small library of books, some hammocks and comfortable chairs, and flowering vines growing up the walls. In fact there are vines all over Casablanca, which gives it a tropical, yet gothic feel. Guest rooms are of average size and have wood walls that don't go all the way to the ceiling, which improves air circulation but reduces privacy. There is also a kitchen, including refrigerator available to guests, and lunch and dinner are served at reasonable prices.

HOTEL MONTEZUMA PACIFIC, Montezuma, Cobano de Puntarenas. Tel. 506/61-1122, ext. 200. 11 rms (10 with bath). A/C
$ Rates (including breakfast): $20 single; $25–$40 double; $40 triple or quad. AE

Located down a narrow road to the left before you reach the center of the village, the Montezuma Pacific is one of the few hotels in Montezuma that offers air conditioning. Ceramic tiles seem to be cheap in Costa Rica—the lobby is done in a crazy quilt of tiles. Guest rooms are small and have double beds. By the time you visit, they should have their terrace restaurant in operation, as well as a fountain. Montezuma's colorful church is directly across the street.

DOUBLES FOR LESS THAN $40

AMOR DE MAR, Montezuma, Cobano de Puntarenas. Tel. 506/61-1122, ext. 262. 10 rms (5 with bath), 2 cabins.
$ Rates: $30 single or double with shared bath; $35 single or double with private bath; $50 single or double in cabin. No credit cards.

You'll find the Amor de Mar just past the stream on the far side of the village from where the bus stops. With its wide expanse of neatly trimmed grass sloping down to some tide pools and hammocks slung from the mango trees, this is the perfect place for families who want to do a bit of serious relaxing. If you'd rather play, they have plenty of different lawn games available. The current owners extensively remodeled the hotel and there are a lot of unusual touches like railings made from twisted branches and vines. On the second floor of the main building, there is a big porch overlooking the ocean. There is even a private saltwater swimming pool of sorts—a tide pool that has been enlarged and deepened. Only breakfast is served, but don't pass up the chance to have some homemade whole-wheat French bread.

EL SANO BANANO, Montezuma, Cobano de Puntarenas. Tel. 506/61-1122, ext. 272. 16 cabins (13 with bath).

$ Rates: $35 single or double with shared bath; $45–$55 single or double with private bath. AE, MC, V.

Located about a 10-minute walk up the beach to the left as you enter the village, El Sano Banano is the sort of tropical retreat budget travelers dream about. There are two types of cabins here—octagonal hardwood Polynesian-style buildings and white ferrocement geodesic domes that look like igloos. There are also a few rooms in the main building. All the rooms are set amid a lush garden planted with lots of banana and elephant ear plants. There are big rocks scattered beneath the shady old trees, and from your front porch you can sit and listen to the waves crashing on the beach a few feet away. El Sano Banano restaurant, which serves excellent vegetarian meals, is back in the village across from the bus stop.

WHERE TO EAT

EL SANO BANANO, on main road into village. Tel. 61-1122, ext. 272.
   Cuisine: VEGETARIAN.
$ Prices: $2.95–$8.85. No credit cards.
   Open: Daily 7am–9pm.

Delicious vegetarian meals including nightly specials, sandwiches, and salads are the specialty of this ever-popular Montezuma restaurant. You can even order a pizza with cheese from the cheese factory in Monteverde. The day's menu specials are posted on a blackboard out front early in the day so you can be savoring the thought of dinner all day. El Sano Banano also doubles as the local movie house. They show nightly films on a large screen and have a library of more than 300 movies. After the film, you can step across the street to the disco for a Montezuman night on the town.

LAS CASCADAS, on the road out of town toward Cabo Blanco. No phone.
   Cuisine: COSTA RICAN/SEAFOOD.
$ Prices: $2.75–$6.65. No credit cards.
   Open: Daily 6:30am–9pm.

This little open-air restaurant is built on the banks of the stream just outside of the village and takes its name from the nearby waterfalls. The short menu offers fresh fish filets, whole red snapper, and pork chops in a green salsa. You'll sit at a picnic table beneath a thatched roof and listen to the stream flowing past. Service here is often surprisingly better than most restaurants in Costa Rica.

CHAPTER 5

THE PACIFIC COAST

From the steamy seaport of Puntarenas to the jewel of Manuel Antonio and beyond, the climate of the Pacific Coast is humid, and frequently it will be sunny here when it is raining in San José. Greater numbers of tourists gravitate to the Pacific Coast than the Caribbean Coast, making tourist amenities more available.

Manuel Antonio Park is gaining fame, but luckily it's still not overrun with tourists. Truly adventurous travelers who don't need to be pampered will enjoy exploring the remote southern coast.

1. PUNTARENAS

68 miles W of San José; 70 miles S of Liberia;
37 miles N of Jacó Beach; 75 miles N of Manuel Antonio

GETTING THERE   By Bus   Express buses leave San José daily every hour on the hour from 6am to 6pm from the corner of Calle 12 and Avenida 9. Duration: 2 hours. Fare: $1.90.

By Car   Head west on Paseo Colón and follow the signs for Alajuela and the airport. These will take you to the Interamerican Highway. After about 50 miles you will see signs for Puntarenas.

By Ferry   The passenger ferry from Paquera, on the Nicoya Peninsula, operates daily at 8am and 12:30 and 5pm. Duration: 1½ hours. Fare: $1.40. The car ferry from Naranjo, also on the Nicoya Peninsula, operates daily at 9am and 1 and 6pm. Duration: 1½ hours. Fare: cars, $4.80; adults, 65¢; children, 40¢.

DEPARTING   The ferry to Paquera leaves daily at 6:15 and 11am and 3pm. One-way fare is $1.40. This is a passenger ferry only, but it connects with buses waiting in Paquera to take you to other towns on the Nicoya Peninsula.

The large car ferry to Playa Naranjo leaves daily at 7 and 11am and 4pm. The trip takes 1½ hours. Fares are 40¢ for children, 65¢ for adults, and $4.80 for cars.

The bus to San José leaves every hour on the hour between 6am and 7pm. Fare is $1.90. The bus station is a block down from the Hotel Imperial, which is in front of the old main pier.

The bus to Santa Elena leaves daily at 2:15pm from a stop across the railroad tracks from the San José bus station. Duration: 3¼ hours. Fare: ¢100 ($1.18).

ESSENTIALS   Orientation   Puntarenas is built on a long, narrow sand spit that stretches 3 miles out into the Gulf of Nicoya. It is only 5 streets wide at its widest. The ferry docks for the Nicoya Peninsula are near the far end of the town, as are the bus station and market. The north side of town faces an estuary, while the south side faces the mouth of the gulf. The Paseo de los Turistas is on the south side of town,

WHAT'S SPECIAL ABOUT THE PACIFIC COAST

Beaches
- ☐ Manuel Antonio National Park, three idyllic beaches set amid jungle-clad hills.
- ☐ Jacó Beach, an inexpensive resort area with many deserted beaches nearby.

Activities
- ☐ Sportfishing near Puntarenas.

- ☐ A day-long cruise around the Gulf of Nicoya.

Parks
- ☐ Carara Biological Reserve, a transitional forest between wet and dry regions.
- ☐ Corcovado National Park on the Osa Peninsula, one of Costa Rica's most remote national parks.

beginning at the pier and extending out to the point. If you need a taxi, phone 61-0053 or 63-0250.

Puntarenas was once Costa Rica's busiest port, but it was recently replaced by nearby Puerto Caldera. In the manner of all good port towns, it is hot and dirty. Although this is the easiest beach to reach from San José and is popular on weekends with holidaying Ticos, it is not the kind of place that you would want to waste any time in when there are so many other beautiful beaches in the country. The water is polluted, and swimming is not recommended. Thieves work the beach, making it impossible to leave anything unattended. Hopefully these dire warnings will convince you that you don't want to visit Puntarenas. Now the sad part: You may get stuck here against your wishes. Puntarenas is a transfer point for buses going north or south along the coast and is where you catch ferries to the Nicoya Peninsula. You may be forced, due to a missed connection, to spend a night here. I have included enough information to make your stay bearable.

WHAT TO SEE & DO

Take a walk along the Paseo de los Turistas and notice how similar this side of town is to a few Florida towns 50 years ago. If you want to go swimming, head out to the end of the peninsula to the **Balneario Municipal,** the public pool. It is huge, has a great view (albeit through a cyclone fence), and is surrounded by lawns and gardens. Entrance is only 75¢ for adults and 35¢ for children. Open from 9am to 4:30 Tuesday through Sunday.

If you want to get out on the water, there are several options. You can hire a water taxi from **Taximar** (tel. 61-0331 or 61-1143). The taxis charge $40 per hour and can carry up to six passengers. If you want to do some **fishing,** contact Fred Wagner (tel. 63-0107). If you have four people in your group, it will cost each of you $135 for a day of fishing. The waters off these shores have some of the best sailfish and marlin fishing in the world. Prices are not cheap.

The most popular water excursions from Puntarenas are yacht cruises among the tiny uninhabited islands of the Guayabo, Negritos, and Pájaros Islands Biological Reserve. These cruises include a gourmet seafood buffet and a stop at beautiful and undeveloped Tortuga Island, where you can swim, snorkel, and sun. The water is clear blue, and the sand is bright white. Several companies offer these excursions, often with round-trip transportation from San José, so you don't even have to spend the night in Puntarenas. **Calypso Tours** (tel. 55-3022 or 33-3617) and **Fantasy Fun**

Cruise (tel. 55-0791 or 22-4752) offer similar tours and will pick you up at your hotel in San José. The price for one of these trips is a steep $60 (or $70 with transportation to and from San José). Calypso Tours also offers sunset trips from 5:30 to 7:30pm with music, bocas, and a bar.

WHERE TO STAY
DOUBLES FOR LESS THAN $18

HOTEL AYI CON, Apdo. 358, Puntarenas. Tel. 506/61-0164 or 61-1477. 44 rms (20 with bath).
$ Rates: $3.50 single without bath, $4.95–$5.95 single with bath; $7 double without bath, $9.90–$11.90 double with bath; $10.50 triple without bath, $14.85–$17.85 triple with bath; $14 quad without bath, $19.80–$23.80 quad with bath. No credit cards.

Centrally located near the market and the ferryboat docks, the Ayi Con is your basic low-budget Tico hotel. It's above a row of shops in a very busy shopping district of Puntarenas and is frequented primarily by Costa Ricans. Backpackers will find that this is probably the best and the cleanest of the cheap hotels in Puntarenas. If you're just passing through and have to spend a night in town, this place is convenient and acceptable.

GRAN HOTEL IMPERIAL, Paseo de los Turistas, frente al Muelle, Apdo. 65, Puntarenas. Tel. 506/61-0579. 28 rms (10 with bath).
$ Rates: $6.15 single without bath, $7.40 single with bath; $12.30 double without bath, $16.30 double with bath; $16.15 triple without bath, $18.60 triple with bath. No credit cards.

Don't be fooled by the grandiose name—this is about as basic a hotel as you'll ever want to stay in. However, I have to include it here because of its amazing atmosphere: It is located directly across the street from the now-little-used main shipping pier for the port of Puntarenas. In its heyday, this long, green wooden building with rusting corrugated-metal roof must have been home to countless sailors and their escorts. The architecture is classic Caribbean, with high ceilings, wide halls, wooden walls that don't go all the way to the ceiling, and bathrooms down the hall. It looks like a huge solid building from the front, but there is actually a narrow courtyard inside (there are even plants growing). It can get noisy, so light sleepers should look elsewhere. However, if you have ever dreamed of stepping onto the set of a Tennessee Williams play or onto the page of an Ernest Hemingway story, this is the place.

DOUBLES FOR LESS THAN $36

HOTEL LA PUNTA, Apdo. 228, Puntarenas. Tel. 506/61-0696. 10 rms.
$ Rates: $21 single; $30 double; $37 triple; $44 quad. AE, DC, MC, V.
This somewhat new hotel is located out at the far end of the Puntarenas peninsula 100 yards south of the car ferry terminal, which makes it a great choice for anyone heading over to the Nicoya Peninsula with a car. A covered sidewalk leads from the street to the open-air bar/restaurant that also serves as reception area. Out in back of the two-story hotel, there is a small swimming pool. Rooms vary in size, with huge rooms for four or five people. Some rooms have balconies and one has air conditioning.

HOTEL TIOGA, Paseo de los Turistas, Apdo. 96. Tel. 506/61-0271. Fax 506/61-0127. 46 rms (all with bath). A/C
$ Rates (including breakfast): $24.60–$36.90 single; $30.75–$46.15 double; $46.15–$60 triple. AE, MC, V.

This 1950s modern-style hotel is on the Paseo de los Turistas, the wide boulevard that runs along Puntarenas's beach. When you walk through the front door, you enter a courtyard with a pool that has been painted a brilliant shade of blue. There is even a little island with a tree in the middle of the pool. The four-story hotel is built around this pleasant setting. Rooms vary in size, and some come with cold-water showers only, so if you must have hot water (not really necessary in these hot regions), be sure to request it. The larger rooms are very attractive—with huge closets and modern bathrooms. The smaller, less expensive rooms have louvered, frosted-glass windows to let in lots of light and air while maintaining some privacy. There is a cafeteria and bar on the second floor and a breakfast room and lounge on the fourth floor. You'll be able to look out across the water as you enjoy your complimentary breakfast.

DOUBLES FOR LESS THAN $45

HOTEL LAS BRISAS, Apdo. 132, Paseo de los Turistas, Puntarenas. Tel. 506/61-2120. 19 rms (all with bath). A/C

$ Rates: $35.55 single; $42.95 double; $50.35 triple. No credit cards.

Out near the end of the Paseo de los Turistas, you'll find a very clean new hotel with large air-conditioned rooms and a small pool out front. All the rooms have tile floors, double or twin beds, and small tables. Large picture windows let in a lot of light. If you're traveling with children, they can stay in your room for free. The owner of the hotel is a friendly Italian man who speaks a bit of Spanish and a bit of English.

You'll find some unusual offerings on the menu of the small open-air dining room in front of the hotel. Smoked pork chops with pineapple, raisins, and wine for $4.80 is just one example. It's worth staying here just to enjoy the food.

CLUB-HOTEL COLONIAL, Apdo. 368, Puntarenas. Tel. 506/61-1833 or 61-1834. Fax 506/61-2969. 56 rms (all with bath). A/C

$ Rates: $25.90 single; $44.50 double; lower rates in off season. AE, DC, MC, V.

This large hotel on the outskirts of Puntarenas is a popular weekend getaway for wealthy Ticos from San José. The two-story building is surrounded by spacious grounds filled with palms that rustle constantly in the trade winds. Guest rooms are about what you would expect from an interstate motel—carpets, two double beds, medium-sized baths with tubs, and air conditioning—although they also have balconies for enjoying the breezes. Of course, since this is primarily for vacationing families, there is plenty to keep everyone happy: two pools (one for adults, one for children), a tennis court, a game room, and a bar and restaurant (both with TV). If you feel like taking to the water, you can hire a water taxi for a trip around the bay or up an estuary for a bit of bird watching.

Meals in El Bambu restaurant range from $3.70 to $14.05 for primarily seafood dishes. In addition to this restaurant, there is a less formal bar and café.

WORTH THE EXTRA BUCKS

HOTEL PORTO BELLO, Apdo. 108, Puntarenas. Tel. 506/61-1322 or 61-2122. Fax 506/61-0036. 35 rms (all with bath). A/C TEL

$ Rates: $45 single; $58 double; $68 triple. AE, MC, V.

Almost next door to the Colonial (above), the Porto Bello is a slightly more luxurious, although similar, weekend escape resort. The stucco walls of the hotel are almost blindingly white, tempered by the lush overgrown garden that surrounds the buildings. The modern rooms have high ceilings, red-tile floors, attractive teak-and-cloth headboards, and balconies or patios that are often hidden by the shrubbery. There are pools for adults and kids, with a poolside bar, and even a small beach. You can hire a water taxi for a spin around the bay or book an all-day cruise to some of the remote and picturesque islands out in the gulf.

The open-air restaurant is breezy and cool, with a high ceiling and stucco walls that harken back to local Indian architectural designs. Grilled meats and seafood are the specialties here—with a range of $6 to $16.

WHERE TO EAT

Without a doubt, your hotel restaurant is going to be the best place to eat. At the **Club-Hotel Colonial,** you can listen to live mariachi music while you dine on fresh seafood. At the **Porto Bello,** the grilled steaks are particularly good. Since you are in a seaport, you should be sure to try the national fish dish of Costa Rica—corvina—at least once.

One other option is to pull up a table at one of the half-dozen open-air snack bars along the Paseo do los Turistas. They have names like Soda Rio de Janeiro and Soda Acapulco and serve sandwiches, drinks, ice cream, and other snacks. Sandwiches are priced at around a dollar.

2. JACÓ BEACH
67 miles W of San José; 37 miles S of Puntarenas

GETTING THERE   By Bus   Buses leave daily at 7:15am and 3:30pm from Calle 16 between avenidas 1 and 3. Duration: 2½ hours. Fare: $1.65.

By Car   Although it is not as direct as taking the bus, you can take the Puntarenas highway from San José and turn south on the Costanera, the coastal road to Puerto Caldera, Jacó, and Manuel Antonio. This is an excellent road. The alternative is to take the narrow and winding old highway, which turns off the Interamerican Highway just west of Alajuela near the town of Atenas.

DEPARTING   To reach Manuel Antonio, you can catch buses that are en route between either San José or Puntarenas and Quepos. The bus stop is near Restaurant El Jardin. Buses stop around 6 and 8am and 2, 2:30, and 8pm. Since schedules can change it is best to ask at your hotel about current times of departures. Duration: 1½ hours. Fare: 55¢. Two buses a day run between Quepos and Puntarenas at 6am and 4:30pm, with a stop in Jacó. Duration: 1 hour. Fare: $1.10. The bus for San José leaves daily at 5am and 3pm from the corner of the main street and the road past the airport. Duration: 2½ hours. Fare: $1.65.

ESSENTIALS   Orientation   Jacó Beach is a short distance off the southern highway. One main road runs parallel to the beach, 100 or 200 yards inland from the shore. Off this road branch many narrow, often unpaved, roads leading down to the beach. It is on these side roads that you will find most of the hotels and restaurants. When you stand on the beach here, you are facing almost due south, not west as you might think.

There is an informal **information center** (tel. 64-3248) across from the supermarket in the center of town which occasionally has maps of Jacó available. You'll find a coin-operated laundry, open daily from 8am to noon and 1 to 8pm, just west of the Hotel Cocal on the main drag. You can rent a car from either Budget, which has its office right on the main street in the center of town, or Elegante (tel. 64-3224). Expect to pay around $50 per day.

There's a bank in the middle of town on the main road. Botiquín Garabito, the town's pharmacy, is down the street from the bank. There is a gas station out by El Bosque restaurant at the south end of town. The health center and post office are at the Municipal Center at the south end of town, across from El Naranjal restaurant.

Jacó Beach is currently the most touristy beach in Costa Rica, almost exclusively the turf of Canadian charter tour groups that fly down weekly all winter and occupy most of the higher-priced rooms in town. If you want to stay here, book well in advance. Jacó is on the edge of a wide plain surrounded by high forested hills. The land inshore from the beach is primarily pastures and farms up to the foot of the hills. Despite its discovery by charter tours, Jacó still has a very small-town, undiscovered feel to it. Best of all, it is the first beach on Costa Rica's Pacific Coast that actually feels tropical. Flowers bloom profusely, and tiny streams form pools just behind the beach before they empty into the ocean. At night, the frogs in these pools strike up a symphony.

WHAT TO SEE & DO

Unfortunately, the water here has a nasty reputation for riptides, as does most of the water of Costa Rica's Pacific Coast. Even strong swimmers have been known to drown in the powerful rips. Storms far offshore often cause huge waves to pound on the beach, making it impossible to go in the water. You'll have to be content with the hotel pool (if your hotel has one) most of the time. However, if you happen to be a surfer, those same powerful waves and dangerous rip currents spell excitement. This is a popular surfing beach, and there are several even better surfing beaches nearby. Those who want to challenge the waves can rent surfboards for $2.20 an hour and body-boards for $1.50 an hour. If you would rather stay out of the surf but still want to get some exercise, you can rent a bike for $4.45 per day or $11.10 for a two-seater. Both bikes and boards are available from several places along the main road.

For nature lovers, the nearby **Carara Biological Reserve** has several miles of trails. There is a loop trail that takes about an hour and another trail that is open only to tour groups. Among the wildlife you might see here are caymans, coatimundis, armadillos, pacas, peccaries, river otters, kinkajous, and, of course, hundreds of species of birds. Admission is 75¢. The reserve is open from 8am to noon and from 1 to 4:30pm daily. No camping is allowed. There are several companies offering tours to Carara Biological Reserve for around $30. Check with your hotel for details.

Horseback riding tours are also very popular. These trips give you a chance to get away from all the development in Jacó and see a bit of nature. Contact Sánchez Madrigal Bros. (tel. 64-3203), AFA Tours (tel. 64-3215), or Viti Tours (tel. 64-3248) to make a reservation. Tours lasting three to four hours cost around $22.

WHERE TO STAY
DOUBLES FOR LESS THAN $25

CABINAS ALICE, Playa de Jacó. Tel. 506/64-3061 or 37-1412. 22 rms (all with bath).
$ Rates: $12.20–$15.00 single; $24.45–$29.95 double; $30.10–$35.60 triple. No credit cards.

Set beneath the shade of large old mango trees, this motel-style place is right on the beach. The newer five rooms in back are one of the best deals in Jacó; each comes with a carved wooden headboard and matching nightstand, a tile floor, a large shower, and even potted plants. The other rooms are pretty basic, with nothing but a double and a single bed in the room. There is even a tiny aboveground pool here. The road down to Cabinas Alice is across from the Red Cross center. Meals are served in a little dining room. You can get a fish filet fried in garlic and butter for under $4.80.

CABINAS EL BOHIO, Playa de Jacó. Tel. 506/64-3017. 15 rms (all with bath), 7 apartments.
$ Rates: $18.50 1–4 people; $37 apartment; discounts June–Nov. No credit cards.
Popular with a young crowd, the Bohio has a slightly run-down air about it, but the rooms are quite acceptable. Little care is paid to the garden, and there is almost no shade. There is, however, a small pool and a thatched-roof bar and restaurant that frequently plays very loud rock music. Each room has two double beds, a ceiling fan, a refrigerator, a kitchenette, and a bar. Connecting 12 of the rooms is a long porch with comfortable chairs and tables made from tree trunks. Recommended for groups of young people planning to stay here for a while.

CABINAS GABY, P.O. Box 20, 4050 Alajuela. Tel. 506/64-3080 or 41-9926. Fax 506/41-5922. 12 rms (all with bath).
$ Rates: $25.65 single or double; $34.20 triple. AE, MC, V.
Located at the far west end of the beach, this is almost the last accommodation before you hit the forest. The location makes it a bit quieter down here, though the hotel's popularity with Tico families means there are always a lot of kids around. The grounds are very shady and extend right down to the edge of the beach. The large guest rooms have kitchens. Some have separate sleeping rooms, and a few have air conditioning, though none have hot water. There are picnic tables and barbecue grills

in the gardens, a small swimming pool for adults, and three pools for kids. All the rooms also have patios with rocking chairs.

CABINAS LAS PALMAS, Playa de Jacó. Tel. 506/64-3005. 23 rms (all with bath).
$ Rates: $18.50–$27.80 single; $21.65–$36 double. No credit cards.
Although all the rooms here are acceptable, the newer ones are a bit nicer. Some rooms come with refrigerators, hot plates, kitchen sinks, laundry sinks, and tables with four chairs so you can set up housekeeping and stay a while. All the rooms have tile floors and very clean bathrooms, and most have two double beds. There are lots of flowers in the garden, and the location down a narrow lane off the main road makes Las Palmas a quiet place. The owner, Leonid Kudriakowsky, is from Canada and speaks English, Russian, German, and Spanish. If you're coming from San José, take the Jacó exit from the Costanera and go straight through the first (and only) intersection you come to. Take a right on the narrow lane just past Cabinas Antonio.

CHALET SANTA ANA, Playa de Jacó. Tel. 506/64-3233. 8 rms (all with bath).
$ Rates: $22.20 single; $29.65 double. No credit cards.
Located at the quiet east end of the beach across from the Jacó Fiesta resort, Chalet Santa Ana is a two-story blue-and-beige building. Guest rooms sleep up to five people and have kitchenettes. Though the bathrooms are small and may not have showerheads, the rooms are otherwise quite acceptable and clean. The second-floor rooms have the added advantage of high ceilings and a large veranda with chairs. Though the surroundings are not too attractive, this is a good deal for Jacó.

DOUBLES FOR LESS THAN $45

HOTEL COCAL, Playa de Jacó. Tel. 506/64-3067. 26 rms (all with bath).
$ Rates: $27–$31 single; $39–$45 double; $46–$54 triple. AE, MC, V.
No children are allowed at this hotel right on the beach, so the atmosphere is peaceful. The building is done in colonial style, with arched porticos surrounding the courtyard. In that courtyard you'll find two medium-size pools, a few palapas for shade, and a thatched-roof bar. You can lie on the beach all day reading a book; when you finish that one, trade it for another from the hotel's book swap. Each guest room is well proportioned with a tile floor, a double and a single bed, a desk, and a porch or balcony. The rooms with ocean views get the best breezes and cost the most. Because this is one of the hotels used by Canadian charter tours, it fills early. The Cocal is on one of the streets leading down to the beach in about the middle of town. Watch for the sign.
There are two dining rooms (one on each floor) serving three meals a day. The upstairs dining room has a wonderful view of the beach. Service is generally quite good, and so is the food. Prices range from $5.50 to $14.05.
A charter fishing boat is available for $650 per day.

VILLAS MIRAMAR, Playa de Jacó. Tel. 506/64-3003. 10 rms (all with bath).
$ Rates: $40 single or double; $45 triple. MC, V.
Located down a narrow lane off the main road through town, the Miramar is about 100 feet from the beach, though it also has its own small pool surrounded by a terrace. There is a snack bar by the pool and barbecues in the gardens in case you'd like to grill some fish or steaks. Guest rooms sport a Spanish architectural style with arched doorways, wrought-iron wall lamps, and red-tile floors throughout. There are large patios and all the rooms have kitchenettes. The spacious rooms are clean and can sleep up to six people.

HOTEL ZABAMAR, Playa de Jacó. Tel. 506/64-3174. 19 rms (all with bath).
$ Rates: $31.10–$53.35 single; $35.55–$60.45 double; $41.80–$66.65 triple. No credit cards.
The Zabamar is set back a little from the beach in an attractively planted compound. The rooms have red-tile floors, small refrigerators, ceiling fans, and hammocks on their front porches. There are also 10 rooms with air conditioning. There are even

pilas (laundry sinks) in little gravel-and-palm gardens behind each room. Some rooms have rustic wooden benches and chairs. There are three pools (two for kids). Surfers get a 10% discount and prices for everyone are lower from April 15 to December 15. A little open-air bar/restaurant serves inexpensive seafood.

CAMPING

There are several campgrounds in or near Jacó Beach. **Madrigal,** at the south end of town at the foot of some jungly cliffs, is my favorite. The campground is right on the beach and has a bar/restaurant that is open from 7am to midnight. **El Hicaco,** in town and close to the beach, is right next door to an open-air disco, so don't expect much sleep if you stay here. Campsites are around $1.50 per night.

WORTH THE EXTRA BUCKS

APARTOTEL GAVIOTAS, Playa de Jacó. Tel. 506/64-3092. Fax 506/64-3054. 12 apartments.
$ Rates: $50 1–6 people. AE, DC, MC, V.

Although it's on the inland side of the main road and is a bit of a walk from the beach, this is one of the nicest places in town. These cheerful little apartments are intended for families or groups who plan to stay for a week or more but are a great bargain even for two people in the off-season. Each apartment has a front wall of windows looking onto the little pool, a cathedral ceiling with a clerestory for light, and a fan. Floors are tile, as are the kitchen counters. The couch in each living room is a bright blue, and there is a double bed and a bunk bed. In each bathroom, you'll find an elegant scalloped sink. There is a little bar beside the pool.

APARTAMENTOS EL MAR, Playa de Jacó. Tel. 506/72-1098 or 64-3165. 12 apartments.
$ Rates: $55 2–5 people. MC, V.
At the east end of town, not far from the beach, is a grouping of attractive apartments built in a C shape around a small pool and colorful garden. The apartments are new, clean, and spacious. Each comes with a unique hardwood refrigerator, two couches, a double and a single bed, and a complete kitchen. Overhead fans and high ceilings keep the rooms cool. There is no restaurant since most guests do their own cooking. If you feel like going bicycling, they have a few bikes for rent.

POCHOTE GRANDE, Apdo. 42, Jacó. Tel. 506/64-3236 or 32-0094. 24 rms (all with bath).
$ Rates: $57.50 1–4 people. MC, V.
Named for a huge old *pochote* tree on the grounds, this very attractive hotel is located right on the beach at the west end of town near the San José bus stop. The grounds are shady and there is a small pool. Guest rooms are large enough to sleep four comfortably and have kitchenettes. Though all the rooms have white tile floors and a balcony or patio, the second-floor rooms also have high ceilings. The restaurant and snack bar serve a mixture of Tico, German, and American meals (the owners are German by way of Africa). Prices for meals range from $2.50 to $7. There is also a gift shop.

WHERE TO EAT

Most of the accommodations in Jacó come with kitchenettes, and if you want to save money on meals, I advise shopping at the local *supermercado* and fixing your own. Those hotels that don't have kitchenettes in the rooms usually have small restaurants. One of the best restaurants in town is the dining room at the **Hotel Cocal.** The menu includes such dishes as chateaubriand for two, wienerschnitzel, and pepper steak.

MEALS FOR LESS THAN $10

EL BOSQUE, 27 yards south of the gas station. Tel. 64-3009.
Cuisine: INTERNATIONAL. **Reservations:** Suggested on weekends.

$ Prices: Entrées $3.50–$10.35. AE.
Open: Tues–Sun 11am–11pm.

⭐ Located on the highway leading south to Manuel Antonio, El Bosque (The Forest) is set amid shady mango trees. The dining room itself is a small open-air building with hanging fern baskets and nests of oropendula birds used as decorations. The furnishings are heavy colonial reproductions. Shrimp or lobster is a pricey $10.35, but you can get a delicious corvina filet for only $3.50. If you are not in the mood for seafood, you can try a very popular Tico dish—beef tongue in salsa. There is a long list of refrescos to choose from. Besides being a good place to come for breakfast or dinner if you're staying in town, El Bosque makes a great meal stop if you are on your way back from Manuel Antonio.

RESTAURANT GRAN PALENQUE, next to the Hotel Jacó Beach. Tel. 64-3023.
   Cuisine: COSTA RICAN/SEAFOOD.
$ Prices: Appetizers $2.05–$11.50; main dishes $2.95–$12.60. MC, V.
   Open: Tues–Sun 11am–10:30pm.
Hopefully when you visit this restaurant it will still be just a restaurant and not a full-fledged resort. Gran Palenque is set amid spacious and shady grounds where palm trees rustle in the breeze. The large restaurant is a huge thatch-roofed, open-air structure that is known as a *palenque* here in Costa Rica. The beach is only steps away, with an unobstructed view of the ocean. The menu is the standard seafood-and-steaks Tico menu, but everything is well prepared and the prices are quite reasonable. You can get a filet mignon with mushrooms for only $5.90 or lobster for $12.60. There are also daily specials.

RESTAURANT OCEANO PACIFICO, west of the Hotel Jacó Beach. Tel. 64-3116.
$ Prices: Main dishes $2.40–$10.35. No credit cards.
   Open: Mon–Fri 10am–10pm, Sat 6am–10pm, Sun 6am–3pm.
If you follow the main road through town all the way west (past the San José bus stop), you'll come to this little open-air restaurant. Come during the day and you'll have a view of a steep, jungly hillside across an estuary. Weekends can be a bit noisy here because there is a pool right beside the restaurant. However, the view is great and the food is good and inexpensive. Try the palmito (heart of palm) appetizer, it's a Tico treat that you don't often find up north. If you like submarine sandwiches, try the Costa Rican version, which is called a *lápiz* (pencil). The dinner menu is primarily seafood.

EVENING ENTERTAINMENT

There are a couple of discos in Jacó that stay busy several nights each week. My favorite is the **Disco La Central** (tel. 64-3067), which is right on the beach near the east end of town. The disco is complete with flashing lights and a mirrored ball in a huge open-air hall. A garden bar in a thatched-roof building provides a slightly quieter place to have a drink. **Foxy's** (tel. 64-3002), out on the road to the airport, is another favorite. Both are open Thursday through Sunday with a very low admission and reasonably priced drinks.

EXCURSIONS

It is possible, although expensive, to arrange excursions to almost anywhere in Costa Rica from Jacó. However, for do-it-yourself jaunts, you are pretty limited. You might want to visit **Carara Biological Reserve** (mentioned previously in "What to See and Do") or make day trips to other nearby beaches, of which there are many in the vicinity. **Playa Esterillos,** 14 miles southwest of Jacó, is long and wide and almost always nearly deserted. **Playa Hermosa,** six miles southeast of Jacó, where sea turtles lay eggs from July to December, is also well known for its great surfing waves. **Playa Herradura,** about four miles northwest of Jacó, is ringed by lush hillsides and has a campground and a few very basic cabinas. All of these beaches are beautiful and easily reached by car or possibly by bicycle.

3. QUEPOS & MANUEL ANTONIO

87 miles SW of San José; 20 miles S of Jacó Beach

GETTING THERE   By Air   Flights on Sansa leave from the Juan Santamaría International Airport in San José Monday through Saturday at 8:00am and 3pm. Duration: 20 minutes. Fare: $11.10. There are also daily flights from Pavas Airport near San José on Travelair (tel. 32-7883 or 20-3054 in San José) at 7am and 4:10pm. Duration: 20 minutes. Fare: $30.

By Bus   Direct buses to Quepos leave San José daily at 6am, noon, and 6pm from Calle 16 between avenidas 1 and 3. Duration: 3½ hours. Fare: $4.10. There is also a luxury bus between San José and Manuel Antonio which leaves San José Monday, Wednesday, and Friday from the Gran Hotel Costa Rica at 7am and returns at 3pm. The fare is an astronomical $55 round-trip (more than airfare on Sansa), but included in the price are coffee and a continental breakfast. The bus even has a bar!

By Car   Take the Puntarenas highway from San José and turn south on the Costanera, the coastal road to Puerto Caldera, Jacó, and Manuel Antonio. This is an excellent road to just beyond Jacó, but then it becomes a rutted and often very muddy washboard road frequented by heavy trucks, making for slow driving. An alternative is to take the narrow and winding old highway, which turns off the Interamerican Highway just west of Alajuela near the town of Atenas and joins the Costanera north of Jacó. You'll still have to drive that rutted road between Jacó and Quepos.

DEPARTING   Sansa flights for San José leave Monday through Saturday at 8:35am and 3:35pm. Their office is beneath the Hotel Quepos across from the soccer field in Quepos (tel. 71-0161). They're open Monday through Saturday from 7 to 11:30am and 1:30 to 5pm. Flights to San José on Travelair (tel. 77-0505 in Quepos) depart at 7:40am and 4:50pm.

Buses leave from the bus station in the market, which is two blocks from the water and one block before the road to Manuel Antonio. Express buses leave at 6am, noon, and 5pm. Duration: 3½ hours. Fare: $4.10. Local buses that take five hours leave at 7 and 10am and 2 and 4pm. In the busy winter months, get your ticket several days in advance.

Any bus headed for San José will let you off in Jacó Beach.

Buses for Puntarenas leave daily at 4:30am and 1:30pm. Duration: 2½ hours. Fare $1.95.

ESSENTIALS   Orientation   Quepos is a small port town at the mouth of the Boca Vieja Estuary. After crossing the bridge into town, follow the road through town and turn left on the road to Manuel Antonio. This road winds through town a bit before starting over the hill to the national park beaches.

Getting Around   A taxi between Manuel Antonio and Quepos, or vice versa, costs $2.95. The bus from Quepos to Manuel Antonio takes 15 minutes and departs at 5:45, 8, and 10:30am and 12:30, 3, and 5pm, returning 15 minutes later. Fare: 20¢.

If you'd like to zip around as you wish, you can rent a moped or bicycle in Quepos from Pico Rent-a-Moto (tel. 77-0125), across from the Hotel Malinche. Mopeds rent for $25 per day, $15 for a half day, or $5 per hour. You can also rent a car for around $50 a day from Elegante Rent A Car (tel. 77-0115).

Fast Facts   You'll find a laundry around the corner from the Restaurant Isabel. Open Monday to Friday from 8am to 4pm, Saturday from 8am to noon. They'll even pick up and deliver for $2.75 per kilo. There's a pharmacy called Botíca Quepos on the corner of the main street where you make the turn for Manuel Antonio (tel. 77-0038). Open daily from 7am to 6pm.

Searching for the perfect tropical beach? Manuel Antonio National Park, just over the hill from the small town of Quepos, is a strong contender. It's hot and humid and tends to rain a lot (even in the dry season), but this wouldn't be the tropics if things were otherwise. Imagine lush green mountains covered with dense rain forests, where misty clouds drift slowly down the valleys. Imagine a cool stream flowing over the beach to empty into the bathwater-warm ocean. Imagine a string of beaches connected by trails through forests inhabited by orange-and-purple crabs, three-toed tree sloths, and chipper squirrel monkeys leaping from branch to branch. Imagine islets just offshore and Technicolor sunsets. Imagine perfect waves for board surfing and bodysurfing on one beach and good snorkeling on another only a 10-minute walk away. Sounds idyllic, right? So, what's the catch?

One catch is that more and more people are discovering this gem. It can get crowded on weekends with vacationers from San José. Luckily, the Costa Rican government had the foresight to preserve it as a national park before the developers got hold of it. The other catch is that only two hotels that I know of are right on the beach (and only one is really suitable for anyone but travel-hardened backpackers), so you're going to have to walk or use a vehicle of some sort to get to the beach each day. A small price to pay for such a paradise.

The town of Quepos is just a quiet little port. To the north of town are miles and miles of oil-palm plantations. This land was once where Chiquita bananas were grown, but disease wiped out the banana plantations, and they were replaced by palm plantations. It's recently been discovered that palm oil is one of the unhealthiest oils humans can consume, so who knows what might be growing here in a few years.

WHAT TO SEE & DO

Manuel Antonio National Park is probably Costa Rica's most popular park and a leading destination for international tourists. It was established in 1972, about 4½ miles south of Quepos. The park is not very large, but within its boundaries are three of the prettiest little beaches I know of. The road from Quepos dead-ends at the long Playa Espadilla (Espadilla Beach), which is just outside the park. To reach the park itself, you must cross a small stream that is little more than ankle deep at low tide but can be knee or even waist deep at high tide. Just after crossing the stream, you will have to pay the entrance fee of ¢100 (80¢). Playa Espadilla Sur is the first beach, just inside the park boundaries. You can walk along the beach or follow a trail inside the forest behind the beach. At the far end there is a short connecting trail to Playa Manuel Antonio. A branch trail from this one leads up and around Punta Catedral (Cathedral Point), where there are some spectacular views. If you take this trail, wear good shoes. You're likely to spot monkeys up on Cathedral Point. From the second beach there is another, slightly longer, trail to the third beach, Puerto Escondido. There is a blowhole on this beach that sends up plumes of spray at high tide. Beyond here, at Punta Serrucho, there are some sea caves. Two other trails wind their way inland from the trail between Playa Manuel Antonio and Puerto Escondido. It's great to spend hours exploring the steamy jungle and then take a refreshing dip in the ocean. The best beach for snorkeling is the second, Playa Manuel Antonio, although the water is often too murky to see much. The park is open daily from 7am to 4pm.

On Playa Espadilla, just a short distance outside the park, there is a little shop on the water that rents surfboards and body-boards.

If you're staying in Quepos and don't want to go all the way up the hill to the park, you can swim and lounge at **Nahomi,** Quepos's public swimming pool. You'll find this pool on a tiny peninsula at the end of the road that parallels the water. Admission is 75¢ and the pool is open daily from 7am to 10pm. The rocky promontory on which the pool is built feels like an island and is surrounded by the turquoise waters of a small cove.

If your tropical fantasy is to **ride a horse** down the beach with a jungle on one side and the ocean on the other, contact Punta Quepos Trail Rides (tel. 77-0371) and ask for Erick. They offer half-day trail rides with lunch on the beach. A multilingual naturalist accompanies every trail ride, pointing out monkeys, sloths, and birds. The charge is $10 per person per hour. If you'd rather **hike,** you can arrange a 3-hour guided tour for $20 per person through the jungle with Leo, who works at the Hotel Mariposa (tel. 77-0355). Rios Tropicales (tel. 77-0574) offers **sea-kayak trips** among the islands of Manuel Antonio National Park, with stops on the beach of course. Another trip explores the Isla Damas estuary.

If you're into **sportfishing** and happen to be here between December and April, contact La Buena Nota (tel. 77-0345), where you can arrange a fishing charter for $290 per day. Another company to try is Skip's Sportfishing (tel. 77-0275), which charges $200 for a half day and $300 for a full day of fishing. Sailfish, marlin, and tuna are all common in these waters.

The main evening entertainment at Manuel Antonio is the disco that appears after dark at Restaurant Mar y Sombra. If this one is too crowded, the one next door is usually empty. You can also hang out at the **Vela Bar,** which is up the road to the left just before you reach Manuel Antonio, or meet interesting gringos at the **Barba Roja,** which is across from Hotel Divisamar.

For shopping, **La Buena Nota,** on the left just over the bridge as you enter Quepos (tel. 77-0345), is an informal information center for the area. They also sell beachwear, U.S. newspapers and magazines, and souvenirs. If you'd like to find out about renting a house or chartering a fishing trip, this is the place to ask.

The market (two blocks in from the main road into town) sells lots of delicious fruit. If you're doing your own cooking, this is the place to shop. **Super Mas** is a general store on the main street near the corner where you turn to head out to Manuel Antonio.

WHERE TO STAY

DOUBLES FOR LESS THAN $21

Quepos

HOTEL CECILIANO, Apdo. 16, Quepos. Tel. 506/77-0192. 20 rms (12 with bath).

$ Rates: $18.50 double without bath, $25.90 double with bath; $25.90 triple without bath, $33.35 triple with bath; $40.75 quad with bath. No credit cards.

This is an excellent low-budget choice in Quepos. It is run by the mother of the woman who runs the Hotel Quepos (below). Mom must have taught her daughter everything she knows about running a budget hotel because the high standards of cleanliness and friendly service apply here as well. The only drawback is that this newer building is a bit darker than the Quepos. The Ceciliano is about a block before the Hotel Quepos on the same road.

HOTEL MALINCHE, Quepos. Tel. 506/77-0093. 12 rms (all with bath).
$ Rates: $7.40 single; $14.80 double. No credit cards.
Another good choice for backpackers, the Hotel Malinche is located on the first street to your left as you come into Quepos. You can't miss the arched brick entrance. Inside you'll find bright rooms with louvered windows but no screens, so be sure to buy some mosquito coils (mosquito-repelling incense coils, available in drugstores and general stores) before night falls. The rooms are small but have hardwood floors and clean bathrooms.

HOTEL QUEPOS, Apdo. 79, Quepos. Tel. 506/77-0274. 23 rms (13 with bath).
$ Rates: $9.65 single without bath, $14.80 single with bath; $18.50 double without bath, $25.90 double with bath; $25.90 triple without bath, $33.35 triple with bath. No credit cards.

If you're traveling on a rock-bottom budget, you'll get a whole lot more for your money by staying in Quepos and taking the bus to the beaches at Manuel Antonio every day. The rooms here at the Quepos may be small, but they are much cleaner and more appealing than those available in this price category on the other side of the hill. There are hardwood floors, ceiling fans, a large sunny TV lounge, even a parking lot and laundry service. The management is very friendly, and downstairs from the second-floor hotel is the Sansa airlines office, a souvenir shop, and a charter fishing office. This hotel is across from the soccer field on the way out of town toward Manuel Antonio.

Between Quepos & Manuel Antonio

CABINAS PEDRO MIGUEL, Manuel Antonio, Quepos. Tel. 506/77-0035. 6 rms (all with bath).
$ Rates: $15.10 single; $20.10 double; $24.35 triple. No credit cards.
A little way out of town as you climb the hill to Manuel Antonio, this small place offers very basic rooms that are large but could stand a good cleaning. In classic tropical budget style, the floors are cement, and the walls are cinder block. There are picnic tables on the long veranda that connects the five rooms, and one room has its own kitchen (but no utensils). There is a tiny swimming pool and a terrace restaurant under the trees.

Near Manuel Antonio

CABINAS MANUEL ANTONIO, Manuel Antonio, Quepos. Tel. 506/77-0212 or 77-0255 (53-2103 in San José). 17 rms (all with bath).
$ Rates: $12.90 double; $15.45 triple. No credit cards.
I don't know how much longer this old cinder-block hotel is going to be around because when I last visited, the waves were lapping at the foundations at high tide. Until it is claimed by the Pacific, it will continue to be popular with the backpacking crowd. Even if it isn't very clean or cheery, it's cheap and right on the beach. How many places in the world will travelers wanting to pay the least amount of money get the prime beachfront location? This is a great place for groups of young people traveling together since many of the rooms are quite large. Be sure to check the fan before you accept a room—not all of them work.

DOUBLES FOR LESS THAN $36

Near Manuel Antonio

CABINAS LOS ALMENDROS, Manuel Antonio, Quepos. Tel. 506/77-0225. 21 rms (all with bath).
$ Rates: $35–$51 1–3 people. No credit cards.
If you continue past the Vela-Bar, you'll come to another good deal among the hotels of Manuel Antonio. The rooms are nothing fancy, but they are clean, roomy, moderately priced, and, best of all, close to the beach. Most rooms have air conditioning and either three single beds or a double and twin. Bathrooms are small but tiled, and there are chairs on the front porch of each room. The only drawback here is the lack of circulation, so rooms without air conditioning can get a bit stuffy in the hot season. Look up from the grassy lawn between the long row of guest rooms and the open-air restaurant and you'll see nothing but jungle-covered hills. The restaurant is one of the better ones around, with prices that are quite reasonable: from $2.95 for pork chops to $10.35 for shrimp.

CABINAS ESPADILLA, Manuel Antonio, Quepos. Tel. 506/77-0416. 16 rms (8 with kitchenette, all with bath).
$ Rates: $17.05–$17.50 single; $21.50–$25.55 double; $25.55–$29.80 triple; $29.80–$34.05 quad. No credit cards.
There isn't much shade around these cabinas, but they are clean and close to the beach. The rooms are spacious even though there isn't much in the way of decor or closet space in any of them. Each sleeps up to four people with a double bed and a bunk bed, with high ceilings and fans to keep each cool. If you plan to stay for a while and want to save some money on meal expenses, you can get a room with a small refrigerator and equipped kitchenette. There are even *pilas,* clothes-washing sinks, in each room. Bars on the windows ensure security.

CABINAS PISCIS, Apdo. 219, Quepos. Tel. 506/77-0046. 6 rms (all with bath).

$ Rates: $30 double; $40 triple; $50 quad. No credit cards.
If you want to be within walking distance of the park, but out of hearing range from the discos' booming speakers, and you don't want to spend a lot of money, try staying at this place, located on the beach side of the road just before you reach Cabinas Ramirez. The rooms are basic but clean, and the management is very friendly. It's a short walk to the beach down a forest trail and there is a small, open-air restaurant and bar that serves very good and inexpensive meals.

CABINAS RAMIREZ, Manuel Antonio, Quepos. Tel. 506/77-0003. 18 rms (all with bath).
$ Rates: $20.75 single; $25.95 double or triple; $33.35 quad. No credit cards.
Dark and damp or shady and cool, it's all in the eyes of the beholder. This older low-budget hotel, under the trees just before the road reaches the beach, is popular with backpackers and surfers. There are fans but few toilet seats. Some of the rooms have metal gates on their porches so that you can leave your surfboard out front and still have it locked up. There are several brightly painted cement picnic tables out front and a popular inexpensive restaurant next door. The restaurant is also the local disco and gets so noisy at night that it is impossible to sleep.

CABINAS VELA-BAR, Apdo. 13, Manuel Antonio, Quepos. Tel. 506/77-0413. 7 rms (all with bath), 1 apt, 1 house.
$ Rates: $15–$30 single; $22–$35 double; $40–$50 triple; $55 quad. AE, MC, V.
You have a wide variety of choices at this small hotel up a dirt road to the left just before you reach the end of the road to Manuel Antonio. You can stay in a tiny room or a spacious one-bedroom house with tile floors and arched windows. There are double beds and tiled bathrooms in the rooms. The open-air restaurant/bar is deservedly very popular. Although meals are not cheap, they are a welcome change from rice and beans, fried chicken, and steaks. Check the chalkboard for the day's special. Prices range from $3.70 to $18.50, with shrimp the highest. A typical day's choices might include fish in sherry or wine sauce. The restaurant is open daily from 7 to 10am, 11:30am to 2:30pm, and 5:30 to 11pm, but does not serve lunch during the low season (June through Nov).

DOUBLES FOR LESS THAN $48

Between Quepos & Manuel Antonio

HOTEL PLINIO, Apdo. 71, Quepos. Tel. 506/77-0055. 9 rms, 5 suites (all with bath); 1 small house.
$ Rates (including full breakfast): $45 double; $75 suite. AE, MC, V.
The Plinio has long been a favorite with budget travelers to Manuel Antonio. The hotel is built into the side of a steep hillside, so it's a steep walk from the parking lot up to the restaurant, which is on the third floor. Once you are up top, though, you'll think you are in a tree house. There are also lots of hanging plants to add to the tree-house feeling. Floors and walls are polished hardwood, and there are even rooms with tree trunk pillars. Take a book off the book exchange shelf and slip into one of the hammocks for a relaxing day on the veranda. There is a huge map of Costa Rica for you to study before you continue to explore other parts of the country. There are now some pricier suites, some of which have sleeping lofts, however, my favorite room is the jungle house, which is set back in the forest and also has a sleeping loft and a huge bathroom. The view from the open-air dining room is across the treetops. The restaurant serves a variety of good Italian food for $5.20 to $7.40.

HOTEL MIRADOR DEL PACIFICO, Apdo. 164, Quepos. Tel. (and Fax) 506/77-0119. 8 rms (all with bath).
$ Rates: $46–$74.75 single or double; $57.50–$86.25 triple. AE, MC, V.
Located 200 yards up the road from the Plinio, this new tastefully designed and decorated lodge is set amid shady trees on a steep hillside. The lodge consists of a

single two-story building with a long veranda along the front of each floor. From the veranda you can look out over the forest to the ocean far below. Guest rooms have a Central American touch, with Guatemalan rugs and placemats on the bedside stands. There are paintings by local artists on the walls, and a few rooms have fake stuffed parrots hanging from their ceilings. The smaller, less expensive rooms have twin beds, while the larger more expensive ones have doubles. The German owner has had a fascination with funiculars (cable cars) for years, and has built one of his own. It carries guests to a tiny bar at the top of the property. From here there is a magnificent view of the mountains, forests, and ocean.

LONG-TERM STAYS

If you decide that you don't want to leave, contact **Blue Marlin** (tel. 77-0295), **La Buena Nota** (tel. 77-0345), or **Manuel Antonio House Rentals** (tel. 77-0560) for information on renting anything from a simple single room to a luxurious house for 12.

WORTH THE EXTRA BUCKS

APARTOTEL EL COLIBRI, Apdo. 94, Manuel Antonio, Quepos. Tel. 506/77-0432. 8 rms (all with bath), 2 apartments.
$ Rates: $51.75 single; $63.25 double; discount May–Nov. V.

If you have dreams of a secluded, tranquil retreat where you can laze in a hammock and watch hummingbirds sipping nectar from crimson flowers, this hotel is for you. The eight elegant rooms are set amid a garden that would have kept Monet or Gauguin happy for years. Narrow paths wind up a hill through lush vegetation that completely hides the rooms from the street. You'll feel as though you have the whole place to yourself in these cozy duplex rooms, each of which has a king-size bed with Guatemalan bedspread, high ceilings with overhead fans, screen-and-cinder-block walls that make the most of the prevailing breezes, red-tile floors, framed posters of Costa Rican wildlife, and French doors leading to a patio. The spacious patios make the rooms seem much larger than they are and come with hammocks, tables and chairs, and barbecues for grilling any fish you might catch. There are even rooms with beautiful kitchenettes with blue-and-white-tile counters and espresso coffee makers. True tropical elegance.

HOTEL DIVISAMAR, Apdo. 82, Quepos-6350, Tel. 506/77-0371. Fax 506/77-0525. 30 rms (all with bath). A/C.
$ Rates (including breakfast): $85 single or double; $100 triple. No credit cards.
It can get pretty hot and sticky here at Manuel Antonio, but if you can't handle the heat, you can return to your air-conditioned room. Not many hotels here offer the luxury of air conditioning, so of course the rooms don't come cheap. The hotel is midway between the town of Quepos and the beaches of Manuel Antonio, with a local bus running regularly to the beach. Although you are high on a hill here, you don't get views of the ocean, but you do get a small pool and sunny, neatly manicured grounds. The rooms have tile floors, high ceilings to maintain coolness even when you don't run the air conditioner, colorful floral bedspreads, and unusually artistic towels for wall decorations.

There are bright floral tablecloths on all the tables in the open-air restaurant. The menu features Costa Rican and international dishes—with prices ranging from $3.35–$5.95. Be sure to try the heart of palm omelet.

KARAHÉ, Apdo. 100-6350, Manuel Antonio, Quepos. Tel. 506/77-0170. 9 rms (all with bath).
$ Rates (including breakfast): $70–$100 double; $90–$125 triple. AE, MC, V.
You have to be in good shape to stay at this attractive hotel because the guest rooms are built on a steep hillside and are up a steep flight of steps from the reception area. However, once you've climbed the steps, you might not want to leave your room. The beds, either double or twin, have wicker headboards and floral-print spreads. There are ceiling fans to keep you cool, bathtubs for warm soaks, and refrigerators to cool

your drinks. Best of all, most of the rooms have spectacular views over the treetops to the ocean below. The lush gardens are planted with ginger plants, whose red flowers often attract hummingbirds. When you do choose to leave your room, you can go for a swim in the pool or walk down the hill to the beach.

The restaurant is built at treetop level too, so your view is of lush tropical vegetation. Wide-plank hardwood floors, unusual ship models in the bar, and bright flowers on every table decorate the dining room. The specialty of the house is shish kebabs cooked over an indoor barbecue for $7.75.

LA QUINTA, Apdo. 76, Manuel Antonio, Quepos. Tel. 506/77-0434. 7 rms (all with bath).

$ Rates: $50–$65 single or double; $60–$75 triple; $70–$85 quad. No credit cards.

It may be a distance to the beach, but the vistas from the lawns and bungalows of this secluded hilltop hotel are fabulous. All the rooms are spacious and have large blue-and-white-tiled bathrooms with a lot of counter space. Each comes with a small table where you can have breakfast (not included in room rates). The triple and quad rooms come with their own refrigerators and hot plates. If you don't feel like going all the way down the hill to the beach, you can get in a little swimming in the hotel's pool, which is set into the hillside. There are also hammocks beside the pool for those who want to spend their days swinging in the breeze. Watch for the hotel's sign by El Brise restaurant.

WHERE TO EAT

For the cheapest meals around, head to one of the dozen or so open-air shacks near the side of the road just before the circle at the entrance to the park. The standard Tico menu prevails with prices in the $2.25 to $10.35 range. Though these little places lack atmosphere, they do have a view of the ocean and the service is often better than in more formal restaurants.

Three of the better places to eat in the Manuel Antonio area are the restaurants at **Cabinas Vela-Bar** (good Continental meals), **Hotel Plinio** (Italian), and **Cabinas Los Almendros** (Costa Rican). See the hotel listings above for more information.

MEALS FOR UNDER $10
Quepos

RESTAURANT ISABEL. Tel. 77-0137.
   Cuisine: STEAKS/COSTA RICAN.
$ Prices: Sandwiches $1–$2.95, full meals $2.60–$9.65. MC, V.
   Open: Daily 7:30am–10pm.

Located on the main street as you come into town from the north, the Isabel is a favorite with budget travelers. The restaurant is a large, sparsely furnished place with lots of tourist information plastered on the walls. The jukebox plays North American oldies, and the TV plays North American cable programming. You can get a variety of steaks, including T-bone with mushrooms; BLTs; seafood soup; and an assortment of breakfasts, from corn flakes to gallo pinto.

LA TORTUGA, Isla Damas. No phone.
   Cuisine: SEAFOOD.
$ Prices: Main dishes $2.95–$10.35. V.
   Open: Daily 9am–8pm.

This is one of the most unusual restaurants in Costa Rica and should not be missed. To reach it, you must first drive north out of town toward Jacó Beach. Watch for the signs for the new Complejo Turistico sign and turn west for another mile or so. When you reach the water, you'll find a boatman waiting to take you out to the restaurant, which is a large converted boat. If there is no boatman around flash your lights and beep your horn; someone will soon come for you. The menu is primarily fish, and the owner seems to always have the very best catches of the day. The great seafood, exhilarating boat ride, and the view across the estuary to the forested mountains beyond make this place well worth the effort.

Near Manuel Antonio

RESTAURANT MAR Y SOMBRA, Tel. 77-0412.
   Cuisine: COSTA RICAN.
$ Prices: Full meals $2.60–$13.33. No credit cards.
   Open: Daily 8am–10pm.

⑤ Since there is little need for walls here in the tropics, many restaurants do without. This is a classic example of a Tico restaurant—a cement floor, some tables, and a roof over your head. There are no attempts at style here, but the shady trees and crashing surf a few steps away fill the gap. You can sit at a table on the edge of the room and watch hummingbirds sipping nectar from hibiscus flowers. Despite the lack of decor, this restaurant is very popular, especially on weekends, with the influx of folks from San José. The food is mostly unmemorable, but there are a few exceptions—such as Spanish-style shrimp, heart of palm salad (always delicious), and fish in salsa. This is also a good place for breakfast. You can take an early stroll down the beach and stop here for gallo pinto or a Spanish omelet. Mar y Sombra is on the right where the road from Quepos reaches the beach at Manuel Antonio.

WORTH THE EXTRA BUCKS

BARBA ROJA, Quepos-Manuel Antonio Rd. Tel. 77-0331.
   Cuisine: SEAFOOD/CONTINENTAL.
$ Prices: Appetizers $2.20–$13.35, entrées $4.65–$11.65; sandwiches $2.20–$2.95. No credit cards.
   Open: Tues–Sun 7am–midnight.

★ This is the place for an extra-special sunset splurge. Perched high on a hill with stunning views over jungle and ocean, the Barba Roja is the kind of restaurant that you would go back to time and again if you could afford it. The rustic interior is done with local hardwoods that give the dining room a warm glow. Take a seat at the counter, and you can sit for hours gazing out at the view. If you tire of the view, glance around at some of the original art by local artists. There is even a gallery attached to the restaurant and a few tables outside where purple-and-orange crabs scuttle about. Best of all is the food. There are daily specials on the blackboard such as grilled fish steak served with a salad and baked potato. The restaurant is open for breakfast and serves delicious whole-wheat french toast. For lunch, there are a number of different sandwiches, all served on whole-wheat bread. If you are in the mood to hang out and meet interesting people from all over the world, spend some time at the bar sipping a piña colada or margarita.

4. DOMINICAL

22 miles SW of San Isidro; 106 miles S of San José

GETTING THERE   By Bus   Buses for San Isidro del General leave San José daily every hour from 5:30am to 5pm (leave no later than 10:30 if you want to catch the 2:30 bus to Dominical). Duration: 3 hours. Fare $2.75. From San Isidro del General, buses leave for Dominical at 6:30am and 2:30pm. Duration: 2 hours. Fare: $2.65.

By Car   From San José, head south (toward Cartago) on the Interamerican Highway. Continue on this road all the way to San Isidro del General, where you turn right and head down toward the coast.

DEPARTING   Buses leave Dominical for San Isidro del General daily at 7:30am and 3pm. Buses leave San Isidro for San José throughout the day.

ESSENTIALS   Dominical is a small village on the banks of the Baru River. The village is to the right after you cross the bridge. The center of the village is the soccer field and general store, where there is a public telephone.

The coastline becomes rocky again about 40 miles south of Manuel Antonio, as the mountains meet the sea. Tide pools and tiny coves line the shore and a wide gravel road runs above the water. Dominical is the largest village in the area and has several small lodges both in town and along the beach to the south. The village enjoys an enviable location on the banks of the Barú River, which at this point, just before emptying into the ocean, is a wide lagoon. There is good bird watching along the banks of the river. Life is still slow in Dominical. Soccer games are always the biggest events in town. Expect this to change in the near future as more people discover the beauty of this region.

WHAT TO SEE & DO

Although the beaches stretching south from Dominical should be beautiful enough to keep most people content, there are lots of other things to do. Several local *fincas* (farms) offer **horseback tours** through forests and orchards; at some of these farms you can spend the night. Hacienda Barú (tel. 71-1903, leave message) offers several different **hikes and tours,** including a walk through mangroves and along the river bank (good bird watching), a rain-forest hike through 100 acres of virgin jungle, an all-day trek from beach to mangrove to jungle that includes a visit to some Indian petroglyphs, an overnight camping trip, and a tour of a hacienda's cocoa plantation. Tour prices range from $7 to $60 per person (the more people there are in your group, the less the per person cost).

Finca Brian y Milena (tel. 71-1903, leave message) offers **day and overnight trips** to their farm in the hills outside of Dominical, where you can bird-watch, explore the tropical rain forest, and visit a working farm where tropical fruits, nuts, and spices are grown. If you stay for several nights, you can visit several different waterfalls by horseback. Rates range from $36 for a day trip for two people to $160 for two people for four days and nights. Horse rentals are additional.

Pisces Pacific Boat Tours (tel. 71-1903, leave message) offers **fishing charters and sight-seeing cruises.** If you have four to six people, these trips are a great way to see this beautiful section of coast. Trips cost $325 for a full day or $200 for a half day.

WHERE TO STAY
DOUBLES FOR LESS THAN $20

ROCA VERDE, Dominical. Tel. 506/71-1414 or in the U.S. 408/684-0600. 11 rms (3 with bath).
$ Rates: $8.90 single, double, or triple without private bath; $14.80 single, double, or triple with private bath. No credit cards.
This is the best of the basic hotels in Dominical, and though it is a couple of miles out of town, they do have a restaurant where you can get equally inexpensive meals. The setting is superb—on a little cove with rocks and tide pools at the near end. If you're driving, you'll only be able to take the back road from town at low tide since the road goes out on the beach. The cheaper rooms are very basic, with wooden walls, a fan, one small window, and a couple of beds. The shared toilets and showers are what you would expect from a campground. The more expensive cabins have private baths and a decidedly tropical feel.

ALBERGUE WILLDALE, Playa Dominical. Tel. 506/71-1903 (leave message) or 71-0866. 7 rms (all with bath).
$ Rates: $18.50 single or double. No credit cards.
The best in-town choice, this place is located directly across from the soccer field. Behind the lodge is the river, where you can go swimming, fishing, or paddling around. The owners of this lodge are friendly folks from Virginia, and they'll gladly fill you in

on all there is to do in the area. The rooms are large and have big windows and patios. There are reading lights, fans, and even hot water. If you are interested in staying for a while, the Dales also rent a house for $100 a night.

DOUBLES FOR LESS THAN $30

CABINAS RIO MAR, Apdo. 487-8000, San Isidro, P.Z. Tel. 506/71-2333. Fax 506/71-2455. 8 rms (all with bath).
$ Rates: $20 single; $25–$35 double; $80 1–4 people in room with kitchen. No credit cards.

Located up river from town, this lodge is set amid a clearing that's not very appealing, but the river is at the edge of the property and there is a dense forest flanking the road into town. There's no restaurant here, but there are hot plates in the rooms. If you don't cook your own meals, you'll have to hike or drive into town. The guest rooms are of different sizes, but all have tile floors, fans, basic bathrooms, and small patios. You can arrange tours here to the private Hacienda Barú Private Nature Reserve for $15 per person.

DOUBLES FOR LESS THAN $40

CABANAS ESCONDIDAS, Apdo. 364, San Isidro del General. Tel. 506/71-1903. Fax 506/71-0735. 3 rms (all with bath).
$ Rates (including breakfast): $30 double; $40 triple. No credit cards.

Travelers with a New Age outlook will want to make Cabañas Escondidas their first choice in Dominical. The spiritual folks who operate this casual bed-and-breakfast prefer guests with a similar outlook on life. Most mornings will find guests meditating on the porch of their cabin or doing tai chi chuan in the garden. You really need to have your own car if you plan to stay here, because meals other than breakfast are not always available. The three cabins are situated high on a hill overlooking the Pacific Ocean and two of them have sleeping lofts. The cabins are spread out so each one is very private. Down below is a beautiful little cove with tide pools and safe swimming. There are 80 acres of virgin rain forest surrounding the lodge and tours can be arranged for $10 to $15 per person. You'll find Cabañas Escondidas about 4 miles south of Dominical.

PUNTA DOMINICAL, Apdo. 196 (8000), San Isidro de El General. Tel. (in San José) 506/25-5328. Fax 506/53-4750. 4 cabins (all with bath).
$ Rates: $35 double; $65 1–6 people in large cabin. No credit cards.

Located about 3 miles south of Dominical on a rocky point, this place has a stony cove on one side and a sandy beach on the other. The cabins and restaurant are set among shady old trees high above the surf with excellent views of either cove. The best views are to be had from the cabins higher up the hill, but all have good views. The cabins, built on stilts and constructed of dark polished hardwood, all have big porches with chairs and hammocks. Screened and louvered walls are designed to catch the breezes. The bathrooms are large and have separate changing areas. Meals in the open-air restaurant range from $2.60 to $11.10, with an emphasis on seafood.

5. DRAKE BAY & THE OSA PENINSULA

190 miles S of San José; 20 miles SW of Palmar

GETTING THERE **By Plane** Sansa (tel. 33-3258 or 33-0397, in San José) flies from San José to Palmar Monday, Wednesday, and Friday at 10:30am. Duration: 35 minutes. Fare: $18.50. Travelair (tel. 32-7883 or 20-3054, in San José) flies daily to Palmar. Duration: 35 minutes. Fare: $50. From the Palmar airport, a taxi will take you to the town of Sierpe for around $15. From Sierpe, a boat can be hired to take you down river to Drake Bay for $15.

By Bus From San José, there are daily express buses to Palmar. They leave from

Avenida 18 between calles 2 and 4 at 5, 6:30, 8:30, and 10am and 2:30 and 6pm. Duration: 5 hours. Fare: $5. From Palmar, you must take a taxi to Sierpe for $15. In Sierpe, you can hire a boat to take you down the river for $15.

DEPARTING Arrange your boat trip back at your lodge, and in Sierpe, hire a taxi to take you to Palmar where you can catch either a bus or plane.

ESSENTIALS Because Drake Bay is so remote and only accessible by water or chartered plane, it is imperative that you have a reservation before arrival.

_____

The Osa Peninsula is one of Costa Rica's most beautiful regions, yet it is also one of its least accessible. Corcovado National Park covers a large portion of the peninsula and contains the largest virgin lowland forest in Central America. For this reason, Corcovado is very popular with naturalists and researchers studying rain-forest ecology. And rest assured it does rain here—some parts receive more than 250 inches per year. This precipitation has produced an amazing variety of plants and animals: more than 140 species of mammals, 267 species of birds, and 117 species of amphibians and reptiles make their home on the peninsula. There are also miles upon miles of deserted beaches, tide pools, waterfalls, and spring-fed rivers.

If such a paradise appeals to you and you don't mind roughing it a bit, Drake Bay is where you'll want to make your base. Located on the edge of the national park, Drake Bay is little more than a collection of lodges catering to naturalists, anglers, scuba divers, and assorted vacationers. All the lodges produce their own electricity from generators and communication is by radio-telephone. The only way in or out is by boat or chartered plane to a nearby dirt airstrip, although there is talk of putting a road through. If you long to travel beyond the reach of automobiles, check out Drake Bay, but do it soon. Life here will change quickly if a road ever reaches this remote spot.

WHAT TO SEE & DO

Beaches, forests, and solitude are the main attractions of Drake Bay, with **Corcovado National Park** the star attraction. Within the park are many miles of trails through lowland rain forests, mountain cloud forests, swamps, beaches, and numerous other habitats. The tallest tree in Costa Rica, a 230-foot-tall silk-cotton tree, is located within the park, as is Costa Rica's largest population of scarlet macaws (parrots). Other inhabitants here include jaguars, tapirs, giant anteaters, sloths, and crocodiles. All of the lodges listed below offer guided excursions into the park and you can also camp in the peninsula (but first contact the park headquarters in Puerto Jimenez, tel. 78-5036, or the national parks headquarters in San José at Avenida 9 between calles 17 and 19, tel. 33-6701).

Only 12 miles offshore the Osa Peninsula, the **Caño Island Biological Reserve,** preserves a unique habitat and the remains of a Pre-Columbian culture. Of the latter all that remains are a cemetery and several enigmatic stone spheres. What makes Caño Island unique is its geological isolation: due to plate tectonics, the island has remained separate from the rest of Central America for more than 40 million years. The dominant tree species on the island is the huge cow or milk tree, which produces a milky sap that can be drunk. Few animals or birds live on the island, but the coral reefs just offshore teem with life and are the main reason most people come here. All of the lodges listed below offer trips to Caño Island for between $35 and $55 per person.

WHERE TO STAY

None of the four lodges listed here fall within our budget, but because the location is so idyllic and remote, I think it's worth splurging a bit. In addition to the lodges below, there are a few basic places that offer lower rates. If you like to live dangerously and want to head down here without a reservation, you might be able to find a room at one of the simple lodges. If this is your plan, consider bringing a hammock or tent with you. You might be able to find out more about other basic lodges at Drake Bay by contacting Pedro Garro (tel. 506/53-6909 or 24-8000).

EL CABALLITO DE MAR, P.O. Box 025216-Dept 8, Miami, FL 33102-5216. Tel. 506/31-5028. Fax 506/31-5028. 7 rms (all with bath).
$ Rates (including three meals): $88 single; $143 double; $180 triple. MC, V.
Though the rates here are a bit high, the views are well worth the price. Situated high on a hill overlooking Drake Bay and the Pacific Ocean, El Caballito de Mar (The Little Seahorse), is an idyllic retreat. With only seven rooms, you are assured of personal service. The dining room takes full advantage of the views and you'll likely find yourself lingering over the family-style meals. All the guest rooms have hardwood floors, ceiling fans, and excellent views. A thermos of fresh-brewed coffee will be set by your door at 5am, so early-rising bird-watchers can be assured of being alert as they scan the trees. Tours to Corcovado National Park and Isa del Caño can be arranged, as can scuba diving and fishing trips. Hiking trails lead into the surrounding rain forest from the lodge and canoes and sailboards are available.

DRAKE BAY WILDERNESS CAMP, Palmar Norte, Osa, Apdo. 988150. Tel. 506/71-2436. Fax 506/71-2436. 19 rms (all with bath), 4 tent cabins.
$ Rates (including three meals): $69 single; $138 double; $207 triple. No credit cards.
Directly across the Río Agujitas, this place offers thatched-roof cabins with verandas overlooking the water. For those who prefer the ambience of camping, there are even a few tents for rent. This lodge enjoys an enviable position on a narrow peninsula between the river and Drake Bay, so on one side you have freshwater swimming and on the other side you have saltwater and tide pools. Ten acres of forest surround the lodge and the view across the bay is of virgin forests. Meals are filling, with an emphasis on fresh seafood and fresh fruits. Horseback riding, canoeing, snorkeling, hiking, and fishing are what keep people busy here, but tours farther afield can also be arranged.

MARENCO BIOLOGICAL STATION, Centro Comercial El Pueblo, Local No. 36, San José. Tel. 506/21-1594 or 33-9101. Fax 506/55-1340. 10 rms (all with bath).
$ Rates (including three meals): $75 single; $150 double; $225 triple. No credit cards.
Though some scientists stay here, Marenco is mostly filled with tour groups organized by various environmental organizations. This means you'll be associating with a lot of interesting and well-educated people at meals, which makes this lodge a fascinating place even without the surrounding biological diversity. Accommodations are fairly simple, with bunk beds in the small wood-paneled rooms. However, all the rooms have large decks that take in the views across the forest to the sea. There are 2½ miles of hiking trails on the lodge's property, so bird-watchers can stay busy without having to walk very far at all. Meals are served family-style in an open-air dining room.

RIO SIERPE LODGE, Box 818-1200, Pavas. Tel. 506/20-2121. Fax 506/32-3321. 10 rms (all with bath).
$ Rates (including three meals): $55 single; $110 double; $165 triple. No credit cards.
Slightly more rustic than the above mentioned lodges and located across the bay, the Rio Sierpe Lodge is, nonetheless, another good choice for a quiet getaway. Hiking trails lead from the lodge to a couple of very secluded beaches, and an excursion to the Violin Island Biological Reserve is included in the rates. Meals in the dining room feature international cuisine with an emphasis on fresh fruits, fish, and chicken. Naturalists, anglers, and scuba divers are all catered to here. Adventurous types can spend two days horseback riding in the area. Note that taxi and river transfers between Palmar and the lodge are included in the rates, which makes this place slightly more economical than the other lodges I've listed.

6. FARTHER SOUTH

The southern Pacific coast of Costa Rica remains undeveloped, but as the northern beaches become crowded (at least by Costa Rican standards), travelers seeking tranquillity have headed ever farther south. South of the secluded beaches of the Osa Peninsula are the port of Golfito and its nearby beaches. Playa Zancudo has already developed a reputation among surfers and a few basic accommodations have sprung up in the past few years. If you have time on your hands, and feel like doing a bit of exploring, you're likely to turn up a few new and surprisingly pleasant lodges down this way. It's a long bus ride to Golfito, but there are also flights to Golfito's airstrip.

CHAPTER 6

THE CARIBBEAN COAST

1. LIMÓN &
   TORTUGUERO
   NATIONAL PARK
 • WHAT'S SPECIAL
   ABOUT THE
   CARIBBEAN COAST
2. CAHUITA
3. PUERTO VIEJO

The jungle-covered lowlands of the Caribbean Coast seem wilder and more remote than the Pacific Coast; a modern highway to the Caribbean did not open until 1987. Many of the people who live on the Caribbean Coast are descendants of Jamaicans who came here to work on the banana plantations or to cultivate their own cacao farms. They still celebrate their Afro-Caribbean culture in their festivities and language.

---

1. LIMÓN & TORTUGUERO NATIONAL PARK

100 miles E of San José (Limón); 156 miles NE of San José (Tortuguero)

GETTING THERE   By Air   Sansa operates one flight a day on Tuesday, Thursday, and Saturday at 6am to Barra del Colorado. Duration: 35 minutes. Fare: $22.20. From Barra you must take a boat to Tortuguero National Park. There are no flights to Limón. Travelair (tel. 32-7883 in San José) flies from San José to Barra del Colorado daily at 8:30am. Duration: 35 minutes. Fare: $57. Departures are from the Pavas Airport.

By Bus   Express buses leave San José every hour on the hour daily from 5am to 7pm from the corner of Calle 21 and Avenida 3. Duration: 2½ hours. Fare: $2.20. There is no bus service to Tortuguero.

By Car   The Guápiles Highway heads north out of San José before turning east and passing under the Barva Volcano and through Braulio Carillo National Park en route to Limón. There are no roads to Tortuguero.

DEPARTING   The bus stop for Cahuita is located one block north of the municipal market. Buses leave daily at 5 and 10am, 1 and 4pm. Duration: 1 hour. Fare: 60¢.
 The bus stop for San José is one block east and half a block south of the municipal market. Buses leave daily every hour on the hour from 5am to 7pm. Duration: 2½ hours. Fare: $2.20.

ESSENTIALS   Orientation   Nearly all addresses in Limón are measured from the market or from Parque Vargas. The train station is at the west end of town about six blocks from the municipal market. The bus station for buses to San José is on the street between Parque Vargas and the market. The bus stop for Cahuita and Puerto Viejo is a block north of the market. The stop for buses out to Playa Bonita is just around the corner to the north of the Cahuita bus stop. At the east end of town is Parque Vargas, with an old seawall running north.

In 1502, on his fourth and last voyage to the New World, Christopher Columbus anchored just offshore from what is now Limón and christened this newfound land

WHAT'S SPECIAL ABOUT THE CARIBBEAN COAST

Beaches
☐ Cahuita National Park, with long, deserted beaches and Costa Rica's largest coral reef.
☐ Puerto Viejo surfing.

Natural Spectacles
☐ The Tortuguero Canals, which will make you feel like you're cruising deep in the Amazon.

Parks
☐ Tortuguero National Park, known for the turtles that lay their eggs on the beaches.

Costa Rica ("Rich Coast"). In the 1800s black and Chinese laborers were brought to this area to work on the railroad and the banana plantations. The blacks were of African-Caribbean heritage, accustomed to this hot and humid coastal region, and they stayed on long after the railroad was completed. Laws prevented them from moving into the highlands so here they stayed, creating their own unique Costa Rican culture with more ties to the islands of the eastern Caribbean than to the Spanish culture of Costa Rica's central valleys. Today Limón is a busy port city that ships millions of pounds of bananas northward every year.

There is virtually nothing to see or do in Limón, except during the annual October Carnival. For a week around October 12 (Columbus Day), Limón wakes up, and the citizens don costumes and take to the streets in a nonstop bacchanal orchestrated to the beat of reggae, soca, and calypso music. If you want to experience this carnival, make hotel reservations early.

Should you be stuck here in transit from San José to Tortuguero National Park or to Cahuita, here are a few lodging choices. I recommend hopping in a taxi or a local bus and heading out toward Playa Bonita, a small public beach park. Although the water isn't very clean and I don't recommend swimming, the setting is much more attractive than downtown.

WHERE TO STAY & EAT

DOUBLES FOR LESS THAN $12

PARK HOTEL, Avenida 3 between calles 1 and 3, Apdo. 35, Limón. Tel. 506/58-3476. 25 rms (all with bath).
$ Rates: $8.50–$13.65 single; $11.95–$17.05 double; $13.65–$20.45 triple. No credit cards.
You can't miss this pink, yellow, and turquoise building across the street from the fire station. It's certainly seen better years, but in Limón there aren't too many choices. Be sure to ask for a room on the ocean side of the hotel because these are brighter, quieter, and cooler than those on the side of the hotel that faces the fire station.

The large sunny dining room off the lobby serves standard Tico fare at very reasonable prices. The daily specials are $2.95 and $3.70.

DOUBLES FOR LESS THAN $26

In Town

HOTEL ACON, Avenida 3 and Calle 3, Apdo. 528, Limón. Tel. 506/58-1010. 39 rms (all with bath). A/C TEL
$ Rates: $19.70 single; $25.75 double; $30.40 triple. AE, MC, V.

⑤ This older in-town choice is the best you can do in Limón. The rooms, all of which are air conditioned (almost a necessity in this muggy climate), are clean and have two twin beds and a large bathroom.

The restaurant on the first floor just off the lobby is a cool, dark haven on steamy afternoons, highly recommended for lunch or as a place to beat the heat. Prices range from $3.70 to $11.10. The second-floor discotheque stays open late on weekends, so don't count on a quiet night.

On the Road to Playa Bonita

CABINAS COCORI, Apdo. 1093, Playa Bonita, Limón. Tel. 506/58-2930. 6 apartments.
$ Rates: $44.70 1–5 people. MC, V.
Located on the water just before you reach Playa Bonita, these apartments command a fine view of the cove and crashing surf. The grounds are in need of landscaping, but the rooms are quite nice. A two-story white building houses the apartments, each of which has a kitchenette with hot plate and refrigerator, two bedrooms, and a bathroom. A long veranda runs along both floors. Staying at this location is far preferable to staying in town. You can get here by bus or taxi.

WORTH THE EXTRA BUCKS

HOTEL MATAMA, Apdo. 686, Limón. Tel. 506/58-1123. 16 rms (all with bath). A/C
$ Rates (including breakfast): $45 single; $55 double; $67.50 triple; $80 quad. AE, MC, V.

★ On the same road as Cabinas Cocori and Hotel Las Olas, the Matama is in a class by itself. The hotel consists of several multiplex buildings set amid dense tropical vegetation across the road from the ocean. The strikingly modern design of the buildings, both inside and out, is a welcome surprise in an area of generally unmemorable accommodations. Each room is decorated with attractive matching drapes and bedspreads and has comfortable wicker furniture and, best of all, large bathrooms with solarium gardens that bring the jungle right into your bath. There are even some units with lofts. Splashing around in the small pool, you'll be surrounded by the sounds of the jungle, and if you want to explore nearby jungles further, you can arrange trips here at the hotel.

Seafood is the specialty of the large open-air restaurant, with prices ranging from $3.65 to $14.05. The meals are well prepared and elegantly served, but the service can be a bit slow.

EXCURSIONS
TORTUGUERO NATIONAL PARK

The name refers to the giant Atlantic green sea turtles (tortugas) that come up on the beaches here to lay their eggs every year between June and November.

Located on the remote northeastern coast of Costa Rica, this is one of the country's most popular national parks. Until last year it was fairly easy and inexpensive to reach this remote region, but when the mailboat that used to make regular runs up and down the rivers and canals died, tourists were left with only one feasible choice—take a tour. You will be bombarded with brochures about Tortuguero tours from the moment you set foot in Costa Rica. Tour prices currently range from $150 to $300 per person for a 3-day, 2-night tour, based on double occupancy. No matter which tour you choose, it is going to cost more than your normal daily budget if you are using this book. However, if it is egg-laying season for sea turtles, this trip might well be worth the splurge. Outside of egg-laying season, I would think long and hard about making this expensive and time-consuming trip, especially if your time is limited. Here is the information that you'll need to make your decision.

Where to Stay

HOTEL ILAN-ILAN, Apdo. 91-1150, San José. Tel. 506/55-2262 or 55-2031. Fax 506/55-1946. 20 rms (all with bath).

$ Rates: $180 per person, including meals, for three days and two nights. AE, MC, V.

Currently the best deal on a tour to Tortuguero National Park is offered by this newer lodge. Guest rooms are large, with either a double and a single bed or three singles. Overhead fans will keep you cool in this steamy region. Tico meals are served in the small dining room, and there is a bar where you can meet other adventurers. The tour includes a brief stop at Braulio Carillo National Park en route from San José to Limón by bus, so you actually get two park visits for the price of one. There are bilingual guides to point out wildlife and answer questions.

JUNGLA LODGE, Apdo. 26-1017, San José 2000. Tel. 506/33-0155 or 33-6579. Fax 506/22-0568. 17 rms (all with bath).

$ Rates: $150 per person for three days and two nights. AE, MC, V.

Located on the river about half a mile from Tortuguero National Park, this simple lodge is your next best bet. The Jungla Lodge's 3-day, 2-night tours starting on Tuesdays and Fridays include bus transportation to the coast and the trip up the canals to the park, all meals, bilingual guides, a tour to the park, and a night tour during turtle egg-laying season. The lodge itself is rustic with simply furnished rooms and a spartan dining hall. Guest rooms have wood-paneled walls and come with twin beds. Arranged in long narrow buildings that resemble mobile homes, the rooms share a common porch that has chairs for relaxing after a day of exploring the region's waterways. Dugout canoes with outboards and paddles are available.

RIO COLORADO LODGE, Apdo. 5094, San José. Tel. 506/32-4063. Fax 506/31-5987. 18 rms (all with bath).

$ Rates (including three meals per day): $115 single; $140 double. AE, MC, V.

Though it bills itself as the "world headquarters for tarpon and snook" and is first and foremost a fishing lodge, the Rio Colorado also offers tours to Tortuguero National Park, which is 25 miles to the south. Clinging to the banks of the Rio Colorado, the lodge offers comfortable accommodations with private baths, hot and cold water, and family-style meals in their rustic dining room. A small menagerie here guarantees that you'll see some of the region's fascinating wildlife, even if they elude you in the wild. A recreation room and lounge, complete with satellite TV, provides an excellent environment for socializing in the evenings. There is also daily laundry service here. Fishing boats and guides are included in fishing packages.

TORTUGA LODGE, Avenida 3 and Calle Central, Apdo. 6941, San José 1000. Tel. 506/22-0333 or 23-9975. Fax 506/57-1665. 25 rms (all with bath).

$ Rates: $299 per person, including meals, for double occupancy for a 3-day, 2-night tour. AE, MC, V.

Though more expensive than the Ilan-Ilan or Jungla Lodge, the Tortuga Lodge offers far more tropical atmosphere, and by that I don't mean that the air is more humid here. The lodge is constructed of tropical hardwoods and thatch with lush flowering plants in the neatly manicured garden. Guest rooms and the dining room/bar are all done in equally rustic, tropical decor. Though motorboats interrupt the quiet occasionally, the solitude and tranquillity here are almost palpable.

2. CAHUITA

125 miles E of San José; 26 miles S of Limón

GETTING THERE By Bus From San José, there are direct express buses leaving daily at 6am and 2:30 and 4:30pm from Avenida 11 between Calle Central and Calle 1. Duration: 3½ hours. Fare: $4.65. Or you can take a Limón bus from San José and then catch a Cahuita-bound bus from Limón. San José–Limón buses leave from the corner of Calle 21 and Avenida 3 every hour on the hour daily from 5am to 7pm. Duration: 2½ hours. Fare: $2.20. From Limón, buses leave from one block north of the municipal market at 5 and 10am and 1 and 4pm daily. Duration: 1 hour. Fare 60¢.

By Car Take the Guápiles Highway out of San José bound for Limón. From Limón, head south on the road that runs along the beach and past the airport.

DEPARTING Buses from Limón stop in Cahuita on their way to Puerto Viejo and Sixaola, which is on the Panamanian border. They stop here around 6 and 11am and 2 and 5pm. Buses to Limón leave daily at 6:30 and 10am, noon, 1:30, and 5pm.

The express buses from Sixaola to San José stop here around 6:30 and 9:30am and 4pm, but check with locals to be sure the schedule hasn't changed. There are rarely any seats left by the time this bus reaches Cahuita. This bus takes four hours and costs $4.65. It's probably more comfortable if you take the local bus to Limón and then catch a bus from there to San José. Buses from Limón leave for San José every hour between 5am and 7pm daily.

ESSENTIALS   Orientation   There are only eight sand streets in Cahuita, so you shouldn't get lost. Two roads lead into town from the highway. Buses usually take the road that leads into the heart of town and drop their passengers at the Salon Vaz bar. An alternate route bypasses town and heads toward Black Beach, which is just north of town. If you come in on the bus and are staying at Black Beach, head out of town on the street that runs between Salon Vaz and the small park. This road will curve to the left and continue a mile or so out to Black Beach. The village's main street deadends at the entrance to the national park (a foot bridge over a small stream).

If you need to have some laundry done, watch for signs around town since local women often take in laundry. The police station is located where the road from Playa Negra turns into town. The post office, next door to the police station, is open Monday to Friday from 7 to 11am and noon to 4pm.

If you're traveling on a student budget and seeking cut-rate accommodations and a peaceful environment, look no further: You have arrived. Not too many years ago, backpackers in Costa Rica headed to Manuel Antonio, but then that beach was "discovered" and room rates skyrocketed—this is now one of their destinations. Cahuita village traces its roots to Afro-Caribbean fishermen and laborers who settled in the region in the mid-1800s. Today the population is primarily English-speaking blacks whose culture and language set them apart from other Costa Ricans.

The main reason people come to Cahuita, other than its laid-back atmosphere, are its miles of pristine beaches that stretch from the south end of town. These beaches, the forest behind them, and the coral reefs beneath the waters offshore are all part of the Cahuita National Park. It is here that you will find Costa Rica's only coral reef (which is not nearly as spectacular as the reefs in Belize).

WHAT TO SEE & DO

You'll immediately feel the call of the long scimitar of **beach** that stretches south from the edge of town. You can walk on the beach itself or follow the **trail** that runs through the forest just behind the beach. This trail is great for bird-watching, and if you're lucky, you might see some monkeys or a sloth. The loud whooping sounds you hear off in the distance are the calls of howler monkeys, who can be heard more than a mile away. Nearer at hand, you are likely to hear crabs scuttling about amid the dry leaves on the forest floor. There are half a dozen or so land crabs living in this region. My favorites are the bright orange-and-purple ones. The trail behind the beach stretches a little more than 4 miles to the southern end of the park at **Puerto Vargas,** where you will find a beautiful white-sand beach, the park headquarters, and a primitive campground with drinking water and outhouses. The reef is off the point just north of Puerto Vargas. There is a small fee for camping, but daily admission is free. The national park is open daily from dawn to dusk.

If you want to find out where the best **diving spots** are (there is even a sunken ship you can visit), I suggest a snorkeling trip by boat. There are two companies running boats out to the reef. **Moray's** (tel. 58-1515, ext. 216), on the road to Playa Negra near the police station and post office, charges $14.05 with gear, or $5.20 for snorkeling gear alone. **Cahuita Tours & Rentals** (tel. 58-1515, ext. 232), around the corner on the village's main street, charges $14.80 for a 3½-hour glass-bottom boat ride with snorkel gear. If you want just to rent snorkeling equipment here, it will cost $3.70. You can also rent horses, bicycles, and binoculars. Sportfishing and tours by Jeep also are available. Moray's arranges river trips and boat trips to Tortuguero for $65 (not including meals or lodging for the night) if you have enough people. **Brigitte** (watch for the sign on Playa Negra) rents horses for $2.95 per hour or $14.80 for a 4-hour guided jungle tour. The best places for swimming are on Playa Negra, behind Letty Grant's in the little cove, and beyond the mouth of the Peresoso River inside the national park.

Please keep an eye out for poisonous snakes around here. I was almost bitten by one on a path on Playa Negra. If you aren't a herpetologist, assume that all snakes here are poisonous and thus give them a wide berth.

As you might have guessed, Cahuita is not exactly a shopper's paradise. However, there is one interesting shop that you should be sure to visit while in town. **Tienda de Artesania,** in a small yellow house on the road to Playa Negra, is a women's craft cooperative headed by Letty Grant. She and her group of five or so women paint T-shirts and make coconut jewelry. The store is open Monday through Friday from 8am to 5pm. Miss Letty also rents out a few rooms, so if you're planning on staying a while, you might want to ask her about these.

At Restaurant Vaz and a couple of other places around the village, you can pick up a copy of Paula Palmer's *What Happen, A Folk-History of Costa Rica's Talamanca Coast* (Ecodesarollos, 1977). The book is a history of the region based on interviews with many of the area's oldest residents. Much of it is in the traditional Creole language, from which the title is taken. It makes fun and interesting reading, and you just might bump into someone mentioned in the book.

For evening entertainment, the **Salon Vaz,** a classic Caribbean bar, is the place to spend your nights (or days for that matter) if you like cold beer and very loud reggae and soca music. Located right across the street from Cahuita's central park, Salon Vaz doubles as the bus stop and community meeting point. There are always folks hanging out on the front porch or steps with a 5-foot-tall speaker blaring in back of them. At night the back room of this bar becomes a very lively disco complete with flashing lights and mirrored ball. If this isn't quite your scene, there is a much quieter little bar just up the road toward Black Beach. Other options for evening entertainment in Cahuita include playing dominoes at Cabinas Surfside or sloth watching.

In terms of excursions, you might want to get a group together and organize a trip from here to Tortuguero. See the folks at **Moray's** (tel. 58-1515, ext. 216) to arrange things. They can also arrange other types of tours here and at **Cahuita Tours and Rentals,** around the corner.

WHERE TO STAY
DOUBLES FOR LESS THAN $18

CABINAS BLACK BEACH, Cahuita. Tel. 506/58-2251. 4 rms (all with bath).
$ Rates: $12.90 single or double; $16.35 triple; $19.80 quad. No credit cards.
Although there are only four rooms here, this is one of the most unusual hotels in Cahuita. The four rooms are in two two-story cabins with stone foundation walls and polished hardwood walls above. The downstairs rooms are cool and dark, and the upper rooms have balconies. Lattice-and-screen walls help let in every little breeze.

The cabinas are across a dirt road from a black-sand beach, as their name implies, with a long green lawn between. It's a long walk back into town, but because it is, this place is quiet at night.

The restaurant, which specializes in Italian food, is tiny, with hardwood floors, no walls, and tables with built-in checkerboards.

CABINAS SOL Y MAR, Cahuita. Tel. 506/58-2037. 8 rms (all with bath).
$ Rates: $11.10–$14.80 single or double; $13.35–$17.05 triple; $15.55–$19.25 quad. No credit cards.

The more expensive rooms here are the ones upstairs, which have more light and catch more of the breezes, an important factor in these hot, humid, and cloudy climes. However, all the rooms are large and quite clean and have fans. There isn't much decor, but you're only steps from the park entrance and the beach. Because of the nearby restaurants, it can be a little noisy here at night.

CABINAS VAZ, Cahuita. Tel. 506/58-2218. 14 rms (all with bath).
$ Rates: $10.35 single; $12.88 double; $15.45 triple; $17.95 quad; $20.50 quint. No credit cards.

Only steps from the park entrance, Cabinas Vaz is one of the more popular places in town, especially with folks from San José, which means that it can get pretty noisy on the weekends. The rooms are in an *L*-shaped building behind the Restaurant Vaz, with a few located directly above. I recommend asking for a room as far from the restaurant as possible because the tape player stays on loud from dawn until long after dark. Rooms are simple but clean, and they have fans and large wardrobes.

DOUBLES FOR LESS THAN $26

HOTEL CAHUITA, Cahuita. Tel. 506/58-2201. 23 rms (all with bath).
$ Rates: $11.10–$14.45 single; $22.20 double; $33.35 triple; $44.45 quad. AE, MC, V.

Across the street from Cabinas Vaz, the Cahuita looks quite run-down from the street, but it is not nearly as bad once you get inside. The better rooms, those in the new building, have private baths, abundant light, and good ventilation. Still, they're none too special. Those in the older section of the hotel are rather gloomy. Ask for one of the rooms with a private bath.

CABINAS MARGARITA, Cahuita. Tel. 585-2205. 11 rms (all with bath).
$ Rates: $15 single; $20 double; $30 triple. No credit cards.

Though the surroundings are not very attractive (little in the way of landscaping), the rooms themselves are clean and there is hot water. Located in a few small cinder-block buildings, the rooms have tile floors and fans. The yellow-and-red color scheme really makes this place stand out. There are some cement garden tables where you can sit and read or have a picnic, though the wooden chairs in the shade of the verandas are more inviting on a hot day. You'll find Cabinas Margarita down the road leading out to the highway from the Black Beach area.

CABINAS PALMER, Apdo. 865, Limón. Tel. 506/58-2243. Or Apdo. 1445-1002, P. Estudiantes, San José. Tel. 506/27-0927. 22 rms (all with bath).
$ Rates: $18 single; $20 double; $23 triple; $26 quad. AE, MC, V.

Down the street from the bus stop, toward the water, is another good choice for backpackers and other ultralow-budget travelers. The management at Cabinas Palmer is very friendly and helpful and dedicated to providing folks with decent inexpensive accommodations. The rooms in the newer cinder-block building are large and have bathrooms shared with one other room; some have kitchenettes. All of these rooms have back doors that open onto a sunny garden where you can sunbathe in privacy. Look for the white building with the blue roof on the right as you walk toward the water from the bus stop.

SEASIDE JENNY'S, Cahuita. Tel. 506/58-2256. 9 rms (all with bath).
$ Rates: $20–$25 single or double. No credit cards.

Located 200 yards straight ahead (toward the water) from the bus stop, Jenny's place has been popular for years, and her newer rooms are some of the best in town in this price range. They're right on the water so you can listen to the waves. The more expensive rooms, on the second floor, have a better view. The rooms have shuttered windows, high ceilings (on the second floor), and sling chairs and hammocks on the porches. There are a couple of rooms in an older building, which, though it has a big porch and plenty of Caribbean atmosphere, is not quite as nice as the newer building. There is also a little boutique here.

SURF SIDE CABINS, Apdo. 360, Limón. Tel. 506/58-2246. 19 rms (all with bath).

$ Rates: $10.25–$12.75 single; $21.30 double or triple. No credit cards.

Despite its name, this hotel is not right on the water; however, it is one of the nicer places in Cahuita. All the rooms are clean and have been recently painted. Louvered windows let in a lot of light and air. There are rooms with double beds, twin beds, and bunk beds.

The restaurant is popular with locals, who sit and play dominoes for hours, and it can get noisy at times. Prices for Tico meals range from $2.60 to $11.85. While I was eating here one night, a large sloth crawled into the open-air restaurant from an adjacent tree. With entertainment like that, it's hard not to recommend this place.

CABINAS TITO, Cahuita. Tel. 506/58-2286. 4 rms (all with bath).

$ Rates: $20 double; $25 triple; $30 quad. No credit cards.

Located down a grassy path off of the road to Black Beach, these little cabins are quiet and comfortable. They're surrounded by a shady yard, and the owner's old Caribbean wood-frame house is to one side. The cabins are made of cement block with tin roofs, but they have tile floors and front porches with a couple of chairs. Two of the cabins have little refrigerators. There are plans to build a few more cabins. The good value and pleasant surroundings have made this place an instant hit with budget travelers.

DOUBLES FOR LESS THAN $36

CABINAS ATLANTIDA, Cahuita. Tel. 506/58-2213. 20 rms (all with bath).

$ Rates: High season $30 single; $35 double; $40 triple. MC, V.

Set amid lush gardens and wide green lawns and run by a French Canadian the Atlantida is my favorite hotel in Cahuita. You'll find it beside the soccer field out by Black Beach (Playa Negra), about a mile out of town. The guest rooms are done in a style reminiscent of local Indian architecture, with thatch-covered roofs and pale yellow stucco walls. All rooms have a patio with bamboo screen divider for privacy, and when you sit there, you'll be gazing into a flourishing garden where a pet toucan and parrot flit from tree to tree. There was also a pet monkey when I last visited, as well as a large aviary full of toucans that were rescued after an earthquake a few years ago. Although only breakfast is included in the rates above, you can also order dinner for around $6. The meals are served in a thatch-roofed, open-air dining room (a *rancho*). Breakfasts include fresh fruit and fresh juice, rolls and homemade marmalade, and there is free coffee all day long. Dinners are primarily Continental and are some of the best in town, though they are only available to hotel guests. A couple of different tours can be arranged using the hotel's Land Rover.

WORTH THE EXTRA BUCKS

HOTEL JAGUAR CAHUITA, Cahuita. Tel. 506/26-3775. 22 rms (all with bath).

$ Rates (including breakfast and dinner): $30.35 single; $55.20 double. MC, V.

If this ambitious hotel ever gets completed, it will be the largest hotel in Cahuita, but for now it consists of two long buildings and several partially completed foundations. Rooms are designed with solar principles in mind to stay cool and make the most of prevailing breezes, consequently, you'll find neither air conditioning nor fans here. Half the rooms face the water across a sandy road, while the rest are set back on the far side of a wide lawn. Surrounding the hotel are 17 acres of forest and brush with a short nature trail leading through it. You're almost certain to see at least one sloth on a morning walk here. Meals are served in an open-air dining area beneath an old house that is built on stilts. Many of the ingredients used in the meals come from trees on the hotel property.

LONG-TERM STAYS

CHALET HIBISCUS, Apdo. 943, Limón. Tel. (in San José) 506/39-4485.
1 house, 3 cabins (all with bath).
$ Rates: $75 1–6 people in the house; $20–$30 single or double in cabins. No credit cards.

⭐ If you're planning a long stay in Cahuita, I advise checking into this beautiful chalet. Although it is about two miles from town on the road along Black Beach, it is well worth the journey. The house has two bedrooms that sleep up to six people, with hardwood paneling all around, a full kitchen, hot water, red-tile floors, a *pila* for doing your laundry, and even a garage. A spiral staircase leads to the second floor, where you'll find ornate Nicaraguan rocking chairs and hammocks on the balcony, which looks over a green lawn to the ocean. There are also a couple of attractive little cabins with wicker furniture and walls of stone and wood. If you ever wanted to be marooned on the Mosquito Coast, this is the place to live out your fantasy. The chalet is both simple and elegant, the setting, serene and beautiful.

If you're staying down the beach and decide to check this place out, be sure to ring the bell outside the gate—there are guard dogs on the grounds.

WHERE TO EAT

There are several restaurants near the entrance to Cahuita National Park. They all serve the standard Tico menu (casados, fried fish, pork chops, steaks, and so on) at low prices. However, if you'd like to try some of the local foods, check out the little shack just before the bridge leading into the national park. The folks here sell meat and vegetable turnovers (called patties) for about 75¢, as well as delicious coconut tarts, and various stews with coconut rice, and a refreshing tamarind drink that's a bit like lemonade. Also, local women cook up pots of various local specialties (including stewed pigs' feet) and sell them from the front porch of Salon Vaz (the disco) on Friday and Saturday nights. A full meal will cost you about $2.25.

For snacks, there is a tiny bakery on the left side of the main road as you head toward Black Beach. The coconut pie, brownies, ginger snaps, banana bread, and corn pudding are all delicious. Prices range from 55¢ to 75¢.

PIZZERIA EL CACTUS, on the road from Black Beach to the highway. No phone.
Cuisine: ITALIAN.
$ Prices: Pizza or spaghetti $2.95–$4.45. No credit cards.
Open: Tues–Sun 4–9pm.
There are only a couple of tables at this small open-air restaurant, so be sure to arrive early if you have your heart set on pizza. Try the pizza Cahuita, which is made with tomatoes, mozzarella, salami, green peppers, olives, and oregano. There's also one made with conch and shrimp. The pizzas are just the right size for one person. Also on the menu are four types of spaghetti, salads, fruit plates, and ice cream.

RESTAURANT EDITH, by the police station. No phone.
Cuisine: SEAFOOD.
$ Prices: $2.60–$6.65. No credit cards.
Open: Mon–Sat 7am–10pm, Sun 2–10pm.
It is a mystery to me why this place is so popular, but it is and has been for several years. If you don't get here very early (before 6pm), you may have to wait an hour for your meal. Miss Edith is a local lady who decided to start serving up home-cooked meals to all the hungry tourists hanging around. While Miss Edith's daughters take the orders, Mom cooks up a storm out back. The menu, when you can get ahold of it, is long, with lots of local seafood dishes. After you've ordered, it is usually no more than 45 minutes until your meal arrives. It's always crowded here, so don't be bashful

about sitting down with total strangers at the big table. To find Miss Edith's, head down to the opposite end of the road that ends at the park entrance and turn right. It's a few steps down on the left.

RESTAURANT VAZ. Tel. 58-2218.
   Cuisine: COSTA RICAN.
$ **Prices:** $2.20–$15.55. No credit cards.
   Open: Daily 6am–10pm.

If you don't mind loud music while you eat, you might enjoy having a meal here. The menu is the standard Cahuita seafood and casados menu. The pancake with fresh fruit makes a delicious and filling breakfast for $1.65. They also have an interesting assortment of refrescos. If you have had enough fried food lately, try the baked redfish. There's not much atmosphere in this basic Tico restaurant.

3. PUERTO VIEJO

135 miles E of San José; 34 miles S of Limón.

GETTING THERE   By Bus   You can get off the Sixaola-bound express bus from San José out on the highway at El Cruce (the crossroad) and walk into town, but it is a 3-mile hike. (If you plan to take the express bus from San José, be sure to ask the hotel you will be staying at to arrange for a taxi to pick you up at El Cruce; you'll need to know which bus you'll be on.) This bus leaves San José from Avenida 11 between Calle Central and Calle 1. Duration: 4½ hours. Fare: $4.65. If you take one of the hourly buses from San José to Limón, which leave from Calle 21 and Avenida 3 every hour between 5am and 7pm, and then transfer in Limón to a Puerto Viejo–bound bus, you will get dropped right in the village. These buses leave Limón from the block north of the municipal market at 5 and 10am and 1 and 4pm. Duration: 1½ hours. Fare: 95¢ or $1.50.

By Car   To reach Puerto Viejo, continue south from Cahuita for another 10 miles. Watch for a gravel road that forks to the left from the paved highway. This road will take you into the village after another 3 miles.

DEPARTING   The local bus from Puerto Viejo to Limón leaves daily at 6 and 9am and 1, 4:30, and 5pm, but check to make sure that the schedule hasn't changed.

   The direct bus to San José leaves El Cruce (the highway crossroad) at 5 and 9am and 3:30pm. Duration: 4 hours. Fare: $4.65. Alternatively, you can take a local bus to Limón and then transfer to a San José bus.

ESSENTIALS   Orientation   The dirt road in from the highway runs parallel to Playa Negra just before entering the village of Puerto Viejo. There are about six dirt streets. The sea will be on your left and forested hills on your right as you come into town. Public phones are located at Hotel Maritza and Pulpería Manuel León. The nearest bank is in Bribri, about 6 miles away. There is a Guardia Rural police post near the park on the beach.

Even smaller than Cahuita, Puerto Viejo is where you go if you think that Cahuita has been spoiled and is too crowded with tourists. Accommodations here are even more spartan than those in Cahuita (with several exceptions). The road into town from the highway leads through old cacao plantations, which have been all but abandoned due to a blight that has killed off most of the trees.

WHAT TO SEE & DO

Most people who show up in this remote village have only one thing on their mind—surfing. Just offshore from the village park is a shallow reef where powerful storm-generated waves sometimes reach 20 feet. These waves, known locally as *salsa brava*, are the biggest and most powerful on the Atlantic Coast. Even when the waves are small, this spot is recommended only for very experienced surfers because of the danger of the reef. For swimming, head out to **Playa Negra,** along the road into town, or to the beaches south of town where the surf is much more manageable.

If you aren't a surfer, there isn't much else for you to do here. The same activities that prevail in Cahuita are the norm here as well. Read a book, take a nap, or walk on the beach. However, if you have more energy, you can rent a bicycle (watch for signs) or a horse (from Antonio at Tropical Paradise) and head down the beach toward Punta Uva, which is a little less than 5 miles down a dirt road.

If you have an interest in medicinal plants, ask around for Miss Dolly, a local expert who enjoys sharing her knowledge with interested visitors.

Souvenirs Denise, across the street from Soda Tamara, sells hand-painted T-shirts and coconut shell jewelry. There are also a couple of *pulperías* (general stores) in the village.

WHERE TO STAY
DOUBLES FOR LESS THAN $20
In Town

CABINAS JACARANDA, Puerto Viejo. No phone. 5 rms (1 with bath).
$ Rates: $8.15 single; $10.40–$13.35 double; $14.80 triple; $16.30 quad. No credit cards.

This basic backpackers' special has a few nice touches that set it apart from the others. The floors are cement, but there are mats, with Japanese paper lanterns covering the lights and mosquito nets hanging over the beds. The Guatemalan bedspreads add a dash of color and tropical flavor, as do the tables made from sliced tree trunks. If you are traveling in a group, you'll enjoy the space and atmosphere of the big room. The Garden Restaurant, adjacent to the rooms, serves the best food in town.

HOTEL MARITZA, Puerto Viejo, Limón. Tel. 506/58-3844. 24 rms (14 with bath).
$ Rates: $3.70 single or double without bath; $18.50 double or triple with bath. AE, MC, V.

This very basic hotel is upstairs from a popular restaurant, which also happens to have one of the only public phones in town. The rooms are just what you would expect from such a place: Not overly clean, rather small, and dark. But if you're here for the surf or want your money to last as long as possible, there's not much to complain about. The jukebox in the restaurant downstairs gets played a lot at night and is a very important factor when you consider whether you want to stay here.

HOTEL PUERTO VIEJO, Puerto Viejo, Limón. No phone. 20 rms (none with bath).
$ Rates: $3.70 single; $7.40 double; $11.10 triple; $14.80 quad. No credit cards.

Although it is managed by locals, this backpackers' hotel is owned by an avid surfer from California; consequently, the hotel is frequented by like-minded young people. The rooms are extremely basic (there aren't even fans) with nothing but beds and a light in them, but the communal toilets and showers are fairly clean. When surf is all you can think about, where you sleep is rarely of any concern. The new two-story building is an eclectic blend of Caribbean traditional wood and modern tropical concrete block. The first-floor restaurant is cheap and popular.

HOTEL PURA VIDA, Puerto Viejo, Limón. Tel. 506/58-3844 (leave message). 7 rms (none with bath).
$ Rates: $12.80 single; $17.05 double. No credit cards.

You'll find the Pura Vida around the corner from Cabinas Jacaranda and facing the soccer field. This pink and pale green cement and wood building is a sprawling structure with several cool and breezy covered patios, and the second floor, where the guest rooms are located, has a veranda on three sides. Guest rooms have high ceilings, fans, and sinks, though the clean tiled bathroom is down the hall. Walls are made of wood, so sounds carry. Down in the shade of the patios there are hammocks for those who want to laze away the days.

North of Town

CABINAS BLACK SANDS, Puerto Viejo, Limón. No phone. 3 rms (none with bath).
$ Rates: $10 single; $14 double; $40 6 people. No credit cards.

The owners of this rustic beachside thatch house are refugees from chilly Wisconsin. They offer basic accommodations in a secluded spot on a long black-sand beach. Three of the rooms are in one building, which has a communal kitchen and dining-room table. If there are six of you, you can rent the entire house. If you don't have the whole place to yourself, remember that the folks next door can hear everything you say because the walls don't go all the way to the ceiling. It's wonderfully tranquil out here, but it's a long walk to the nearest restaurant; it's better if you plan to do your own cooking.

If arriving by bus, be sure to get off at the Pulperia Violeta before the road reaches the beach. Otherwise it's a long walk back out from the bus stop in town.

CABINAS CHIMURI, Lista de Correos, Puerto Viejo, Limón. Tel. 58-3844 (leave a message). 4 cabins (none with bath).
$ Rates: $20 double; $30 quad. No credit cards.

If you don't mind being a 15-minute walk from the beach, I'm sure that you'll enjoy this rustic lodge. It is built in traditional Bribri Indian–style with thatched-roof A-frame cabins in a forest setting. In fact, it is a short stroll down a trail from the parking lot to the lodge buildings, and there are other trails on the property as well. This lodge is definitely for nature lovers who are used to roughing it: Accommodations are very basic, but there is a kitchen for guests to use. The lodge also runs several different hiking trips into the rain forest and the adjacent Bribri Indian Kékoldi Reserve. Trips range from one to three days of hiking. If arriving by bus, be sure to get off at the trail to Cabinas Chimuri before the road reaches the beach. Otherwise it's a long walk from the bus stop in town.

DOUBLES FOR LESS THAN $32

CABINAS PLAYA NEGRA, Puerto Viejo, Limón. Tel. 506/56-1132 or 56-6396. 5 rms (none with bath).
$ Rates: $30 1–4 people. No credit cards.
These colorfully painted two-story buildings, on a side road as you come into Puerto Viejo, have a very Caribbean flavor. Each duplex shares one bathroom; the rooms are large and sunny. Screened porches with rocking chairs are a pleasant place to spend an afternoon if it isn't too hot, which it often is in the hot season. The beach is about 200 yards down a narrow dirt road.

WORTH THE EXTRA BUCKS

EL PIZOTE, P. O. Box 230-2200, Coronado. Tel. 506/58-1938. Fax 506/29-1428. 8 rms (none with bath), 6 bungalows.
$ Rates: $28.75 single without bath, $69.60 single with bath; $41.75 double without bath, $69.60 double with bath; $55.65 triple without bath, $83.50 triple with bath; $62.60 quad without bath, $91.10 quad with bath. No credit cards.

Although it bills itself as a surf resort, this comfortably rustic little resort would be ideal for anyone who simply wants to get away from it all. Located about a half mile outside of town, El Pizote is set back from the black-sand beach that runs beside the dirt road into town. The name El Pizote is Spanish for "coatimundi," a raccoonlike creature that is common in Costa Rica. They have a few in a cage near the restaurant.

The rooms are in two beautiful, unpainted wooden buildings that are completely hidden from the road or even from the parking lot. You have to walk through a dense grove of dracaena plants, which you might recognize as a common houseplant. The rooms are cool—with polished wood walls, double beds, and absolutely beautiful bathrooms that have wood slat floors in the showers and huge screen windows looking out on dense jungle. There are unusual burlap-and-bamboo window shades, ceiling fans, and reading lamps. For activity, there are hiking trails into the forest, the beach, and the volleyball court.

The restaurant serves breakfast ($6) and dinner ($12), but drinks are available all day. There is a set menu each evening, which might be lobster with broccoli or an equally delectable fish plate.

If arriving by bus, ask the bus driver to let you off at the entrance to the lodge. It's on the stretch of road that runs along the beach just before entering town.

DOUBLES FOR LESS THAN $32
South of Town

ESCAPE CARIBEÑO, Puerto Viejo, Limón, Tel. 506/58-3844 (leave message). Fax 506/40-9648. 6 rms (all with bath), 1 apartment.
$ Rates: $25.20 single; $28.90 double; $32.60–$47.40 triple; $34.80–$49.65 quad; $40.75 apartment (1–4 people). No credit cards.

Just outside of Puerto Viejo on the road to Punta Uva, Escape Caribeño consists of six little white cabins with brick pillars and tiled patios. With clerestory windows, vertical blinds, and rather fancy hardwood furniture, these cabins are a step above the basic places in this price range. Though the fans are a bit noisy, there are reading lamps by the beds and small refrigerators in every room. The gardens have been planted with bananas and palms. It's a 5-minute walk into town or out to an excellent beach with a small island just offshore.

MIRAFLORES LODGE, Playa Chiquita, Puerto Viejo, Limón. Tel. 506/33-5127 or 58-0854. Fax 506/33-5390. 4 rms (2 with bath).
$ Rates (including breakfast): $23 single without bath, $40.25 single with bath; $28.75 double without bath, $40.25 double with bath; $40.25 triple without bath, $54.65 triple with bath. No credit cards.

Located a few miles south of Puerto Viejo on the road to Punta Uva, Miraflores Lodge is basically a private home with a few rooms available. Because it is a private home, the decor is far more attractive than other lodges in the area. The large second-floor porch, which is virtually an open-air living room, is decorated with wood carvings, masks, and Panamanian and Guatemalan textiles. Huge vases hold fresh flowers and there is a free-form table made from a slice of tree trunk. Surrounding the lodge is a flower farm where heliconias, ginger, banana, anthurium, and orchids are grown. The guest rooms with private bath are very large and can sleep up to six people in two sleeping areas. Walls and doors are faced with cane, and there are hardwood floors in the second-floor rooms. Full payment is required on making reservations during the December-to-April busy season (40% deposit the rest of the year); these deposits are nonrefundable.

WORTH THE EXTRA BUCKS

LAS PALMAS RESORT, Edificio Cristal, Avenida 1 between calles 1 and 3, P.O. Box 6942-1000, San José. Tel. 506/55-3939. Fax 506/55-3737. 20 rms (all with bath).
$ Rates: $23 single; $46 double; $69 triple. AE, MC, V.

Five miles south of Puerto Viejo in the village of Punta Uva, Las Palmas Resort is one of the only true beachfront hotels in the area. The only drawback is that the guest rooms face an unkempt gravel parking lot. Snorkeling is good among the coral just offshore and the beach stretches for miles. There isn't much shade here though so bring plenty of sunscreen. Guest rooms are clean and comfortable, though not very attractive. Basically what you're paying for here is the location, not the atmosphere or decor. The open-air restaurant serves Tico and Continental meals, with an emphasis on lobster and seafood. There are plans to add a swimming pool, though when this happens, you can expect the rates to go up.

PLAYA CHIQUITA LODGE, Avenida 2 between calles 17 and 19, P.O. Box 7043-1000, San José. Tel. 506/23-7479. 13 rms (all with bath).
$ Rates (including breakfast): $40.25 single; $51.75 double; $63.25 triple. AE, V.
This place just oozes jungle atmosphere and is sure to please anyone searching for a steamy retreat on the beach. Note: credit cards can only be used if you book reservations in San José. Set amid the shade of large old trees a few miles south of Puerto Viejo toward Punta Uva (watch for the sign), the lodge consists of unpainted wooden buildings set on stilts and connected by wooden walkways. There are wide verandas with rocking chairs and seashell mobiles hanging everywhere. Rooms are dark and cool with wide-board floors and paintings by local Indian artists. The top of the bathroom wall is completely screened so you can gaze out into the jungle as you shower. There is a short trail through the jungle and across a marsh to a private little swimming beach with beautiful turquoise water, as well as tide pools. Meals here cost from $5 to $14 and choices range from spaghetti to lobster; since the management is German you can expect a few German dishes as well. Throughout the day there are free bananas and coffee. On weekend evenings there is live calypso music. This lodge is affiliated with another jungle lodge in the Sarapiquí region of Costa Rica and many guests split their trip between the two—both are very popular with naturalists.

WHERE TO EAT

To really sample the local cuisine, you need to look up a few local ladies. Ask around for Miss Dolly and see if she has anything cooking. Her specialties are bread (especially banana) and ginger biscuits, but she will also fix a special Caribbean meal for you if you ask a day in advance and she has time. Miss Sam makes pineapple rolls, plantain tarts, and bread. Miss Daisy makes pan bon, ginger cakes, patties (meat-filled turnovers), and coconut oil (for tanning). Julia and Mateo bake whole-wheat bread. Just ask around for these folks and someone will direct you to them.

GARDEN RESTAURANT, Cabinas Jacaranda. No phone.
   Cuisine: CARIBBEAN/ASIAN.
   $ Prices: Main dishes $3.15–$4.40. No credit cards.
   Open: Thurs–Tues 7–11:30am (light snacks until 3:30pm), 5:45–9pm.
Located near the soccer field a couple of blocks from the water, this restaurant serves the best food in Puerto Viejo. The co-owner and chef is from Trinidad by way of Toronto. You'll find such surprising offerings as chicken saté (a Thai dish), yakitori (Japanese), Jamaican jerk chicken, calypso curry chicken, and chicken Bangkok. There are also daily specials and tasty sandwiches such as a cheese sandwich spread with pesto. There are delicious fresh juices and ambrosial desserts made with local fruits, as well as such delights as ginger spice cake and macadamia chocolate torte. Every dish is beautifully presented, usually with edible flowers for garnish.

CAFE PIZZERIA CORAL, on the road to the soccer field. No phone.
   Cuisine: PIZZA.
   $ Prices: Pizza $3.25–$5.40; pasta $2.95–$3.70. No credit cards.
   Open: Tues–Sun 7am–noon and 6–10pm.
Though the owner here is from El Salvador, she cooks a great pizza. She also bakes the perfect peanut butter cookie! Some of the goodies not to be missed are the pumpkin soup, the tomato and green peppercorn pizza (the peppercorns are grown locally), the summer wine (a bit like sangría), and of course the peanut butter cookies (though the key lime pie is great too). The dining room is up a few steps and has hardwood floors and wood railings. The restaurant is just down the street from Cabinas Jacaranda and about two blocks from the water.

SODA TAMARA, one block from the end of the road into town. No phone.
   Cuisine: COSTA RICAN.
   $ Prices: $1.50–$4.05. No credit cards.
   Open: Wed–Mon 6:30am–9:30pm.
This little Tico-style restaurant has become a popular spot with budget-conscious travelers and has begun upgrading its image. There is now a small patio dining area in

addition to the dark dining room. The white picket fence in front gives the restaurant a very homey feel. At the counter inside, you'll find homemade cocoa candies and unsweetened cocoa biscuits. These are made by several ladies in town, but unfortunately, for several years, the cocoa trees in this area have been dying from some type of blight.

SOUTH OF TOWN

NATURALES, Punta Uva. No phone.
   Cuisine: COSTA RICAN.
$ Prices: Main dishes $3.70–$14.80. No credit cards.
   Open: Thurs–Tues 7:30am–noon and 2–9pm.
Located south of Playa Chiquita on the road to Punta Uva, Naturales is built into a hillside at the top of a steep flight of 49 steps. From this tree house–like vantage point there is a great view of Punta Uva beach and the surrounding forests. The short, simple menu is posted on a blackboard. There are daily specials, whatever fish happens to be available that day, and spaghetti. The owner is both cook and waitress so don't expect fast-food service. Relax, have a fresh fruit juice, enjoy the view, and soon enough, your food will come. A tip: If everyone in your group orders the same thing, you'll usually get served sooner.

EXCURSIONS

The most interesting excursion from Puerto Viejo is a hiking trip to the nearby **Kékoldi Indian Reservation** (tel. 58-3844). These trips are led by Mauricio Salazar, who also runs Cabinas Chimuri. On these 1-day trips, you ride through virgin forest where you are likely to see dozens of species of birds and perhaps a sloth or two or some monkeys. Keep a watch out for the magnificent keel-billed toucans that frequent this region. Mauricio will tell you about the customs of the Bribri and Cabécar people who inhabit the reservation. Although the native peoples have adopted western dress, they still maintain their religious beliefs and closeness to nature. The trips cost about $22.25. If you are interested in heading deeper into the forest, longer trips also can be arranged.

You should be able to arrange for someone in town to take you out fishing or snorkeling for a reasonable price.

If you continue south on the coast road from Puerto Viejo, you will come to a couple of even smaller villages. **Punta Uva** is 5 miles away, and **Manzanillo** is just over 9 miles away. There is the trail along the beach from Barra Cocles to Manzanillo, a distance of about 6 miles. Another enjoyable hike is from Monkey Point to Manzanillo (about 3½ miles). There is a reef offshore from Manzanillo that is good for snorkeling. In Manzanillo, ask for Willie Burton, who rents snorkeling equipment and will take you out in his boat to different locations.

Still farther south is the **Manzanillo-Gandoca Wildlife Refuge,** which extends all the way to the Panamanian border. Within the boundaries of the reserve live manatees and crocodiles and more than 350 species of birds. The reserve also includes the coral reef offshore. On one 5½-mile-long beach within the reserve, four species of sea turtles nest from March to July.

CHAPTER 7

GETTING TO KNOW GUATEMALA

- **WHAT'S SPECIAL ABOUT GUATEMALA**
- **1. GEOGRAPHY, HISTORY & POLITICS**
- **DATELINE**
- **2. ART, ARCHITECTURE & LITERATURE**
- **DID YOU KNOW . . . ?**
- **3. CULTURAL & SOCIAL LIFE**
- **4. FOOD & DRINK**
- **5. RECOMMENDED BOOKS & FILMS**

Guatemala: The very name sounds exotic as it rolls off the tongue. Even though it is possible to drive there by way of Mexico, Guatemala seems worlds away. The name conjures up images of lost cities in the steamy jungle and colorfully clothed Mayan Indians. These are here, yes, but there is more. Guatemala is also a country rich in Spanish history, the history of the Conquest. Colonial architecture—with its arches, porticos, stucco walls, and cobblestone streets—has been preserved in the city of Antigua, once the capital of all Central America. Ruins of churches, monasteries, and universities have become parks, giving the late 20th century a glimpse of the greatness of Central America in earlier times.

With nearly 50% of the population claiming Indian ancestry and clinging to ancient customs and costumes, Guatemala is culturally fascinating. Spanish is the official language, but ancient Indian languages such as Quiché and Mam are still spoken in the highlands. Primitive rituals and masked dances are the last vestiges of the once-great Mayan culture.

Guatemala has been called "the land of eternal spring" because of the nearly perfect weather that the highlands enjoy throughout the year. It was this gentle climate that first attracted Spanish settlers, and today it is this same climate (and the stunning setting) that attracts tourists from all over the world to Lake Atitlán, which is encircled by volcanoes and which many claim is the most beautiful lake in the world. Why, then, has Guatemala not become overrun with tourists? Politics. Central America in the last 20 years became a terra incognita for citizens of the United States. Nicaragua and El Salvador have given the entire region a bad name. Civil wars, revolutions, death squads, and communist guerrillas throughout the narrow strip of land connecting North and South America made the headlines and stopped the once-growing flow of tourists to the region. Guatemala, suffering plenty of its own internal strife, became one of those places that only soldiers of fortune and journalists wanted to visit.

But things have changed in Guatemala, and things remain the same. Ancient cultures with ties to the mysterious Mayan civilization of more than 1,000 years ago survive, although these Indian peoples continue to struggle for land reform and a better standard of living. There is still occasional guerrilla activity in remote regions of Guatemala, but these are generally far from anyplace a tourist would likely venture. Every year, more tourists discover the ancient Mayan ceremonial center of Tikal; Antigua, once the capital of Central America; the stunning vistas of Lake Atitlán; and the fascinating Indian cultures and crafts of the Guatemalan highlands. From the jungled plains of El Petén to the volcanoes of the Sierra Madre, Guatemala offers a diversity of natural beauty unrivaled anywhere in Central America.

WHAT'S SPECIAL ABOUT GUATEMALA

Great Towns/Villages
- ☐ Antigua, one of Guatemala's colonial capitals, with beautiful architecture, atmosphere, and many ruins.
- ☐ Chichicastenango, famous for great shopping and rituals performed by local Indians.

Mayan Ruins
- ☐ Tikal, the largest Mayan city yet excavated.
- ☐ Copán (actually in Honduras), nearly as impressive as Tikal.
- ☐ Quiriguá, known for its intricately carved stelae (record-keeping stones).

Natural Spectacles
- ☐ Lake Atitlán, said to be the most beautiful lake in the world.
- ☐ Volcanoes, live or dormant, that you can climb.
- ☐ Semuc Champey cataracts and the quetzal preserve near Cobán.

Museums
- ☐ The Museum of Archeology and Ethnology in Guatemala City, Central America's finest collection of Pre-Columbian artifacts.
- ☐ The Ixchel Museum in Guatemala City, dedicated to the indigenous clothing of Guatemala.
- ☐ The Popol Vuh Museum in Guatemala City, small but contains many beautiful terra-cotta artifacts.

Offbeat Oddities
- ☐ The Mayan god Maximón, also known as San Simón, who is worshiped in Zunil and Santiago Atitlán by blowing cigar smoke in his face and pouring liquor into his mouth.

- ☐ Pascual Abaj, another Mayan god, who is worshiped in Chichicastenango, where he has an altar on a hill outside of town.

Events/Festivals
- ☐ Holy Week (the week before Easter) in Antigua, celebrated with daily processions through the streets.
- ☐ Ancient Indian dances performed in towns and cities around the country.

Religious Shrines
- ☐ The basilica in Esquipulas, with a statue of Christ that is the object of a massive pilgrimage every year.
- ☐ Antigua's Church of San Francisco, with the remains of Hermano Pedro, who is said to heal the sick.

Architectural Highlights
- ☐ Ruins of colonial churches, monasteries, convents, universities, and government buildings all over the town of Antigua.

Shopping
- ☐ The Chichicastenango market on Sunday and Thursday, flooded with vendors selling beautiful Guatemalan textiles at the best prices in the country.
- ☐ Panajachel's Calle Santander, lined on both sides with vendors selling "gringo" fashions in Guatemalan fabric.

1. GEOGRAPHY, HISTORY & POLITICS

GEOGRAPHY

Guatemala is the northernmost country of Central America, bordered on the north and west by Mexico; on the south by the Pacific Ocean, El Salvador, and Honduras; and on the east by the Caribbean Sea and Belize. Covering 42,000 square miles,

Guatemala is roughly the size of the state of Tennessee. Stretching from northwest to southeast are several volcanic mountain ranges that form the backbone of the country.

To the south of the mountains lies the Costa Sur, the South Coast, a narrow strip of plains. To the northeast is El Petén, a vast, high, jungle-covered rolling plain. This is the most remote and least developed region of Guatemala and was at one time the heart of the Mayan culture.

DATELINE

- **200 B.C.** Earliest record of inhabitants at Mayan city of Tikal.
- **A.D. 600–A.D. 900** Mayan civilization reaches its zenith.
- **1523** Pedro de Alvarado, under command from Hernán Cortés, marches into Guatemala with an army of Spanish and Indian troops.
- **1524** Iximché becomes the first Spanish capital of Guatemala and is renamed Santiago (St. James).
- **1527** The capital is moved to the Valley of Almolonga at the foot of Agua Volcano and given the name of Santiago.
- **1541** Pedro de Alvarado dies from injuries sustained when a horse falls on him. His second wife, Doña Beatriz, proclaims herself captain general, becoming the first female head of a government in the Americas. The second Santiago (today's Ciudad Viejo) is destroyed by a flood.

(continues)

HISTORY

The earliest Mayan culture dates back to the Formative Period (in Mesoamerican civilizations) from 300 B.C. to A.D. 100, but it did not fully flower until the Classic Period (A.D. 200 to 925). By A.D. 600 the Mayas were the most important culture in Mesoamerica. The advanced culture of Teotihuacan was declining, while the Mayas were rising intellectually and artistically to a height never before reached by the natives of the New World. In Guatemala and the Yucatán peninsula, the Mayas built magnificent ceremonial centers; carved intricate hieroglyphic stelae; and developed superior astronomical, calendrical, and mathematical systems.

Then in the Late Classic Period, around A.D. 790, the Mayan civilization began to decline. Over the next 40 to 100 years, one village after another was abandoned, until by the end of the 9th century, the last chapter of this brilliant civilization was closed. Why? No one is certain. Was it the population explosion? The misuse of land? The northern barbarians who were roaming Mesoamerica? Whatever the reason, the Postclassic Period, from A.D. 900 up to the Spanish Conquest, shows the loss of splendor and the beginning of a polity of class systems (priests, merchants, and serfs), government regulation and taxation, trade guilds, and a primitive but productive agriculture.

In 1519 Hernán Cortés conquered Mexico, and in 1523 he sent his chief lieutenant, Pedro de Alvarado, to explore the region of Guatemala. Alvarado led an expedition against the Quiché people (then the most powerful and wealthy tribe in Guatemala). In the words of a 16th-century Spanish historian, Alvarado was "reckless, merciless and impetuous, lacking in veracity if not common honesty, but zealous and courageous." It wasn't long before Alvarado had conquered the indigenous peoples and was named representative of the sovereign power of Spain. He set about establishing a typical Spanish colonial empire, founding cities and towns throughout Central America, and converting the Indians to Catholicism. But unlike Mexico, Central America did not yield vast amounts of gold and silver for the conquerors and was thus somewhat of a disappointment. Many of the Spaniards stayed on, however, to carve out large coffee plantations using the Indians as laborers.

The Spanish made their first capital at Iximché, a Cakchiquel Maya city; after forming an alliance with the Cakchiquels they renamed the city Santiago (St. James). In 1527, they built a new capital at the foot of Agua volcano

GUATEMALA: GEOGRAPHY, HISTORY & POLITICS • 129

in the Almolonga Valley. This city, also called Santiago, lasted only until 1541 when it was destroyed by a flood. In 1543, the capital was moved a few miles away to what was thought a safer location in the Panchoy Valley. Once again the city was called Santiago (de los Caballeros). This city, now known as Antigua, was a religious and cultural center even before the arrival of the Spaniards. The friars established universities and monasteries, building grand edifices to rival any in colonial Mexico or Peru. Between 1543 and 1773, the city flourished and the city's population rose to 55,000. From Santiago, the Spanish governed a vast dominion that stretched from southern Mexico to Costa Rica.

However, this capital, too, was ill fated. Between 1543 and 1717 it suffered numerous floods, earthquakes, and fires. Then, in 1773, a series of devastating earthquakes virtually destroyed the city, and in 1775, the capital was moved once again—this time to the Ermita Valley. This new capital, now known as Guatemala City, proved just as prone to natural catastrophes as the three previous cities, but it has remained the capital.

Early in the 19th century, Guatemalan and other Central American leaders followed the lead of other Latin American states and declared their independence from Spain. The captain-general of Guatemala became the chief executive. But in Mexico the empire of Agustín Iturbide had been formed, and conservative Guatemalan leaders voted for annexation to the empire. This political arrangement didn't last. A republican Federation of Central American States was formed in 1823. The federation lasted some 15 years but was continually torn by internecine battles, both political and military. By 1840 Central America had taken the political form it has today, and political struggles were confined to the large towns. As a result, except for Guatemala City and the provincial capitals, "progress" is a stranger to much of the country, leaving it untouched and incredibly beautiful.

POLITICS

Throughout its history, Guatemala has been subjected to tumultuous political upheavals. Even before the Spanish Conquest, the various Indian tribes of the highlands had been constantly at war. When Pedro de Alvarado marched into the country with his armies, he utilized these feuds to his advantage, playing one tribe against the other and eventually conquering the entire country. During the colonial period, priests from various Catholic sects were busy converting (and virtually enslaving) the Indian population that remained after the wars, and European diseases took their toll (between 75 and 90% of the native population was lost after the Conquest). The church and the wealthy Spanish landowners thus had a ready, if unwilling, work force at their command. They used this conscripted work force to make themselves wealthy.

Pure Spanish blood is rare in Guatemala today, but the

DATELINE

- **1542** The capital is moved to the site of present-day Antigua.
- **1696** Tikal is discovered by a Franciscan friar seeking to convert Indians to Christianity.
- **1773** Antigua is destroyed by a series of earthquakes.
- **1775** The capital is moved again, this time to the Valley of Ermita (the hermitage), site of today's Guatemala City.
- **1821** Guatemala, along with the rest of Central America, gains independence from Spain.
- **1847** Guatemala becomes an independent nation separate from the other Central American nations.
- **1870s** Coffee becomes the main export of Guatemala.
- **1944** Period known as "10 years of spring" begins, and the country experiences fair elections and peace.
- **1952** Land reform policies cause United Fruit Company, a foreign-owned company and the largest landowner in Guatemala, to lose much of its land.

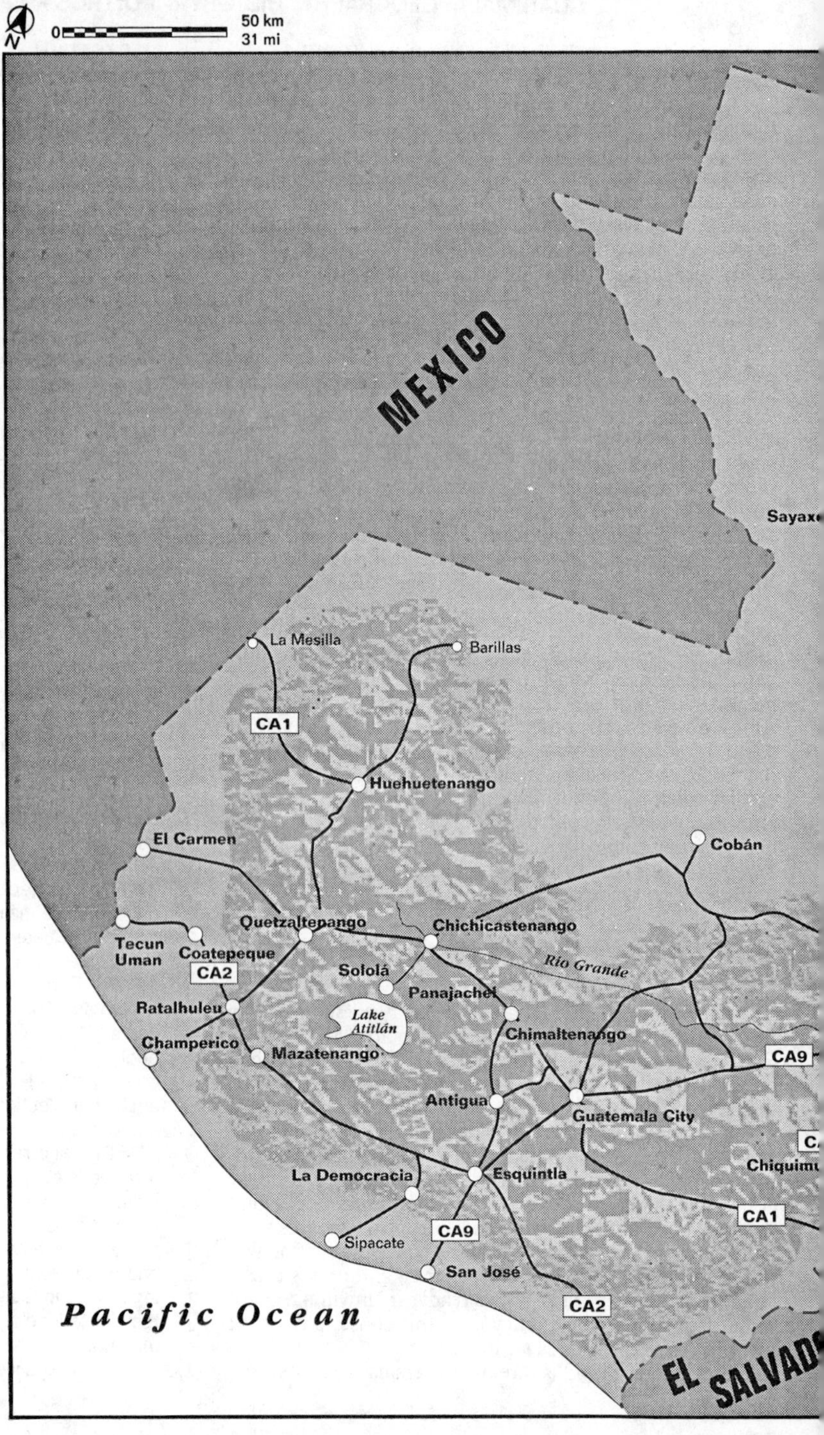
0
50 km
31 mi
MEXICO
Sayax
La Mesilla
Barillas
CA1
Huehuetenango
El Carmen
Cobán
Tecun Uman
Coatepeque
Quetzaltenango
Chichicastenango
Río Grande
CA2
Sololá
Panajachel
Ratalhuleu
Lake Atitlán
Chimaltenango
Champerico
Mazatenango
CA9
Antigua
Guatemala City
Chiquim
La Democracia
Esquintla
CA1
CA9
Sipacate
San José
CA2
Pacific Ocean
EL SALVAD

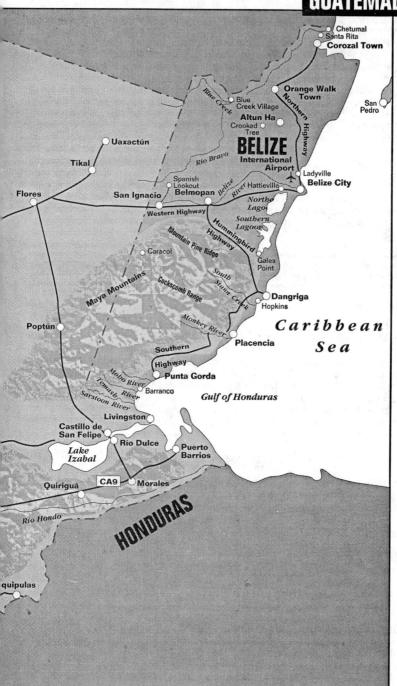

DATELINE

• **1954** CIA-
backed Guatemalan
exiles invade Gua-
temala from Hon-
duras and
overthrow govern-
ment.

• **1950s–
Present** Scattered
guerrilla activity
continues.

Ladino population, which is descended from marriages of Indians and Spaniards, are firmly in control of the government. Those of Indian ancestry (generally defined as anyone who wears traditional attire and farms on subsistence plots) have almost no power. Although Guatemala is ostensibly a democracy (with elections held every four years), the military wields a great deal of power. Throughout the past 100 years, the military has often taken control of government, suspending the constitution as necessary to maintain its power. There is a great disparity between the rich and the poor. Wealthy landowners own nearly all of the land in the country, with peasants forced to farm small plots on the least productive land. This disparity has led to constant conflicts for nearly 200 years as the liberal parties have tried to wrest power from the wealthy and the church.

Today there is still guerrilla activity throughout much of Guatemala, but on a relatively small scale. The guerrillas, primarily poor, rural Indians from the highlands and left-wing intellectuals, continue to demand land reform.

2. ART, ARCHITECTURE & LITERATURE

ART

The Mayas, who reached a cultural peak around A.D. 600, have left an amazing legacy of intricately beautiful works of art. Stone carvings, pottery, and gold and jade jewelry give us some idea of the high level of artistic ability reached by this ancient culture. The stylized figures depicted on many works of Mayan art are actually historical records. Through these images, archeologists have been able to deduce a great deal about Mayan culture. The Museum of Archeology and Ethnology in Guatemala City has the most outstanding collection of Pre-Columbian art in all of Central America, and the Popul Vuh Museum, also in Guatemala City, has a smaller but equally interesting collection.

ARCHITECTURE

As long ago as 2000 B.C., the Mayas were building at Tikal, an ancient religious center in the remote Petén region of Guatemala. Today the hundreds of pyramids, temples, and palaces that have been excavated make this one of the great archeological finds of the New World. Using limestone, the Mayas at Tikal erected one pyramid after another, often building directly on top of previously existing structures. Many of these buildings incorporated what has come to be known as the Mayan, or corbelled, arch. Although not a true arch (a keystone is not used), the Mayan arch allowed ancient architects to build structures entirely of stone, structures that have withstood the ravages of time and today are a testament to the architectural skills of Mesoamerica's greatest civilization. In 1979, Tikal was declared a "World Cultural and Natural Monument" by UNESCO.

With the Spanish Conquest came an entirely new form of architecture: Moorish influences, interpreted by Spanish architects, were incorporated into the many colonial cities erected by the Spanish throughout Guatemala. Unfortunately, Guatemala is a land of volcanic activity and is subject to earthquakes of devastating magnitude, so much of the country's colonial architecture has been destroyed over the years. However, the city of Antigua, once the capital of all Central America, although

- Tikal is the largest excavated Mayan ruin.
- Antigua was once the capital of all of Central America.
- There is a town on the Caribbean Coast where the people are predominantly black, with English as their mother tongue.
- The quetzal, described as the most beautiful bird in the world, is the national bird of Guatemala.
- Manatees live in the Río Dulce, a river that drains into the Caribbean Sea.
- The United Fruit Company was once the largest landholder in Guatemala.
- The Indians of the Guatemalan highlands still practice rituals passed down from the ancient Mayas.
- Lake Atitlán was formed by the crater of a giant extinct volcano.
- Guatemala City is the fourth capital of Guatemala; the others were destroyed by earthquakes, volcanic eruptions, and floods.

destroyed several times by earthquakes and floods, still preserves its colonial heritage. It was named a "Heritage of Humanity" by UNESCO in 1979. At one time, the city was the grandest in all the Americas, but after the devastating earthquake of 1773 many of the most grandiose churches, universities, and convents were destroyed. Today the ruins of these buildings have been turned into parks and museums, giving Antigua much of its charm. Regulations prohibiting obtrusive signs and advertising help the city retain its 17th-century atmosphere. There are literally dozens of colonial and colonial-style buildings of architectural interest here.

Guatemala City, on the other hand, has few historical buildings since over the years the city's colonial buildings were destroyed by earthquakes. Guatemala City's most architecturally noteworthy buildings are those of the Centro Civico and the Centro Cultural Miguel Angel Asturias, constructed in the 1950s and 1960s. The façades of the former buildings are covered with murals, while the latter is designed to resemble the superstructure of a luxury cruise ship.

LITERATURE

The single most significant piece of literature produced in Guatemala is the *Popol Vuh,* a history of the Quiché people written in the Mayan language sometime shortly after the Conquest. Although the original accordian-pleated codex is housed in a museum in Dresden, Germany, there is a beautiful reproduction in the Popol Vuh Museum in Guatemala City. It is an exact copy in every detail, down to the type of tree used to produce the paper. The book consists of both Mayan glyphs and small, colorful paintings. The original was discovered in the early 18th century in Chichicastenango and was translated into Spanish. Numerous editions of the *Popol Vuh* are now available in both Spanish and English and offer fascinating reading.

Nobel laureate Miguel Angel Asturias is known and loved for his novels and translations into Spanish of ancient Indian legends. Otto René Castillo is a revolutionary poet whose works are unavailable in Guatemala but are popular outside the country.

3. CULTURAL & SOCIAL LIFE

Guatemalan cultural life is decidedly stratified. The population of the country is almost evenly divided between the indigenous peoples (Indians) and the *ladinos* (those who can trace their ancestry to Spain). However, these are becoming very loose terms. Today an Indian who moves to the city and gives up his or her traditional dress in favor of North American or European fashions becomes a ladino; an Indian who becomes wealthy and gives up farming also may be labeled a ladino, as may any Indian who is educated. The term *indigeno* has come to refer almost exclusively to the poor

GUATEMALAN TERMS

ARCHEOLOGICAL

Corbeled arch   False arch used in construction of Mayan buildings

Stela[e]   Stone with carved figures (usually of warriors, princes, or kings) and glyphs, erected as a record of a historic event

Pre-Classic Period   Mayan period from 300 B.C. to A.D. 300

Early Classic Period   Mayan period from A.D. 300 to 600

Late Classic Period   Mayan period from A.D. 600 to 900

Post-Classic Period   Mayan period from A.D. 900 to the Conquest

MUSIC AND DANCE

Marimba   Instrument related to the xylophone and also the music performed on this instrument—the most popular music in Guatemala

Palo Volador   "Flying pole," an acrobatic performance that has been popular in Guatemala since Mayan times; men spin from ropes tied to their ankles as they descend from a tall pole.

RELIGIOUS

Anda   Float carried in Holy Week processions

Cofrade   Member of a cofradía

Cofradías   Indian religious organizations that oversee various rituals in villages around the country.

Maximón   Mayan god who is found in several towns around the highlands, dressed in jacket, pants, and hat with a wooden mask for a face; Indians believe he answers their prayers

Pascual Abaj   Another Mayan god whose shrine is on a hill near Chichicastenango

MENU SAVVY

Cak ik   Mayan stew made with turkey or chicken, plantains, and vegetables

Licuado   Milk- or water-based drink made in a blender with fresh fruit

Pepian   Thick stew made with chicken, vegetables, and pumpkin seeds

Plátanos   Plantains, similar to bananas

peasants who cling to their traditional ways and still farm the rugged mountains of the Guatemalan highlands.

Down on the Caribbean Coast is yet a third culture, that of the English-speaking blacks who migrated from Jamaica in the 18th century. These people have nothing in common with the rest of Guatemala's population and maintain their isolation in the small town of Lívingston, which can be reached only by boat. In Lívingston, the sound of the marimba band, ubiquitous in the rest of the country, is replaced by reggae music from the Caribbean islands and, increasingly, by rap music from the United States.

Religion, Myth & Folklore   The melding of ancient Mayan traditions and religious beliefs with Roman Catholicism has created a singular form of Catholicism that is filled with obscure rituals and the worship of Mayan gods thinly disguised as saints. The Mayan religion was pantheistic, and many of the gods demanded human sacrifices. When Spanish priests arrived preaching the worship of yet another god, the Mayas of Guatemala were amenable and readily accepted Catholicism but continued to worship their old gods. Over the years, the old gods became associated with Catholic saints, and today every village and town has its patron saint, whose feast day is cause for great celebration. An important part of many fiestas is masked dancing. Several of these dances depict historical events. See "Performing Arts and Evening Entertainment" in this chapter for more information on masked dances.

In several towns in the highlands, a strange cult holds sway over the people. In these villages, the Indians turn to a god known as Maximón, or San Simón, for intervention in their lives. Maximón, although he looks like little more than a mannequin wearing a hat, is a very real god to these people, and he may be derived from the ancient Mayan god Mam. The people come to him to solve their problems, to protect them, to find them a wife or husband, and to bring them wealth. It is the way in which they worship Maximón that is the strangest: Cigar smoke is blown into his face, and liquor is poured into the mouth of the mask that serves as his face. There are Maximóns in Santiago Atitlán and Zunil, among other places. Should you go looking for Maximón, be sure to bring a gift—money, liquor, and cigars are probably the safest offerings.

Guatemalans as a rule are extremely devout, and nowhere is this devotion to the Catholic church more evident than in Antigua during Semana Santa (Holy Week), the week prior to Easter Sunday. During this week, solemn processions march through the streets of the city. Intricate "carpets" made of colored sawdust, flowers, and pine needles are constructed in the streets, only to be trampled by men and women who march through the city carrying massive wooden floats atop which stand sculptures of Christ, the Virgin Mary, and various saints. Men dressed as Roman soldiers and mourners in black or purple robes commemorate the death and resurrection of Christ amid clouds of incense and doleful music played by marching bands. The pageantry of these processions is unsurpassed anywhere in Latin America, and the devout march through the streets from morning until late at night. Even though the processions in Antigua are the largest and draw immense crowds of spectators, nearly every town and village in Guatemala has similar processions during Holy Week.

Performing Arts & Evening Entertainment   The sound of the marimba, a large wooden xylophone played with rubber mallets, permeates Guatemala just as mariachi music prevails in Mexico. The instrument is often so large that it takes several people to play it. The rhythms that are produced are complex and hypnotic. You'll find marimba bands performing at nearly all celebrations, in restaurants, and on the radio (there are all-marimba radio stations).

Celebrations in Guatemala often include masked dances that have their basis in ancient Mayan customs. The most popular dance is the dance of the conquistadors, in which dancers dressed as Pedro de Alvarado and Tecún Umán symbolically reenact the battle that brought about the downfall of the Quiché people and the eventual conquest of Guatemala. By far the most famous "dance," if it can be called that, is the *palo volador* (the flying pole). In this breathtaking acrobatic display, two men climb to the top of a 60-foot pole, attach ropes to their ankles, and "fly" to the ground as the rope unwinds from the top of the pole. This ancient ritual is staged several times a year in different parts of the country, including Guatemala City and Chichicastenango.

Evening entertainment in Guatemala is pretty much restricted to going to the movies (U.S. movies dubbed in Spanish or with subtitles), hanging out in bars (a male-dominated activity), and going to discos (mostly in the capital only).

Sports and Recreation   The national sport of Guatemala is soccer (here known as *futbol*). In 1990 the national team even made it to the World Cup playoffs in Italy, an event that caused much talk and elicited great pride from the team's fans. Bicycle racing is also a very popular sport, and cyclists are frequently seen, especially on Sunday, puffing up the hill on the highway between Guatemala City and Antigua. Keep an eye out for cyclists when driving, especially if you are still on the road after dark, because some races go far into the night and the roads are not lit.

One favorite recreational activity among Guatemalans and tourists alike is volcano climbing. There are several volcanoes in the country that can easily be climbed in a day, and the views from the tops of these peaks can be spectacular if the weather is clear. Perhaps the most popular climb is up Pacaya Volcano, near Lake Amatitlán. It is possible to climb within about 100 yards of the cone of this active volcano (on a separate cone) and watch it erupt every few minutes.

4. FOOD & DRINK

FOOD Traditional Guatemalan cuisine is very similar to Mexican food in many ways. The staples are beans (here they are black beans) and corn in the form of tortillas. To this are added rice and perhaps a bit of stewed chicken. Such meals are not often found in restaurants, except in the simplest of *comedores* (basic food stalls most often found in or near markets). Restaurants throughout Guatemala lean heavily toward international food—with everything from chow mein to spaghetti showing up at nearly every meal.

There are a few exceptions to the generally lackluster Guatemalan cuisine. In El Petén, wild game, including venison and turkey, is readily available. Because the country has two coasts, it is not surprising that throughout Guatemala, good and inexpensive seafood is readily available. However, I suggest that you stay clear of any freshwater fish, which tend to have a muddy flavor and may come from very polluted rivers and lakes.

Pepian is the de facto national dish of Guatemala. It is a thick, often grainy, stew made with chicken, vegetables, and toasted pumpkin seeds. *Cak ik* is a specialty of Cobán, a stew made with turkey or chicken, plantains (similar to bananas), and vegetables.

DRINKS Water and Soft Drinks Tap water in Guatemala is generally not safe to drink unless you treat it yourself. Hotels and restaurants often have large bottles of purified water on hand, from which they fill pitchers for their guests. If you have doubts about the water, it is best to avoid it. Tikal is one place where the water is notorious for making people sick. Bottled water, although relatively expensive, is readily available throughout the country, as is *agua mineral,* which is club soda. All major brands of soft drinks also are available. However, while in Guatemala you should take advantage of the delicious fresh juices and *licuados* (fruit juice blended with ice and water or milk), which are wonderful and very cheap. You can get a tall glass of fresh-squeezed orange juice for 40¢ in some places. Some of my favorite licuados are those made with milk and papaya or mango. It is usually a good idea to get your licuado with milk and no ice to avoid consuming the water.

Beer, Wine, and Liquor Several brands of locally brewed beer are available at very reasonable prices throughout Guatemala. Virtually all the wines are imported and consequently are expensive; those imported from South America are the cheapest and often are quite good. All types of hard liquor are manufactured in Guatemala, with rum being the most popular.

IMPRESSIONS

The market at Guatemala is the only place where I have seen reality outdoing a Dutch still life.
—ALDOUS HUXLEY, *BEYOND THE MEXIQUE BAY,* 1934

5. RECOMMENDED BOOKS & FILMS

BOOKS The *Popol Vuh* (Simon & Schuster, 1986) is one of the only records we have of Mayan life before the Conquest. It provides fascinating insights into the history, culture, and religion of these Pre-Columbian people.

If you can find any English translations, or if you read Spanish, the novels and Indian legends translated into Spanish by Miguel Angel Asturias offer insight into Guatemalan life. Asturias won the Nobel Prize for Literature in 1967.

To learn more about the history of Central America, try *A Brief History of Central America* (University of California Press, 1989) by Hector Perez-Brignali, who is himself a Central American. If you want to gain a better understanding of the plight of Guatemalan Indians, *A Cry from the Heart* (Health Institutes Press, 1990) by V. David Schwantes will certainly enlighten you.

The classic travelogue to this region is Aldous Huxley's *Beyond the Mexique Bay*, a narrative of his travels through Guatemala, Belize, and Mexico in 1934; it's out-of-print, but your local library should have it. *Time Among the Maya* (Henry Holt, 1991) by Ronald Wright is an interesting account of Wright's travels among the Mayas of Guatemala, Belize, and Mexico. Both contemporary and ancient Mayan life are explored.

FILMS *When the Mountains Tremble* (1983) is an excellent documentary about the struggle of Guatemala's Indian peasants. Directed by Thomas Sigel and Pamela Yates, the film depicts the experiences of a young Indian woman named Rigoberto Menchu. Gregory Nava directed *El Norte* (1984), a very moving portrayal of two Guatemalan youths who leave their country in search of a better life in the United States.

CHAPTER 8

PLANNING A TRIP TO GUATEMALA

Once you have decided to visit Guatemala, you're likely to have a lot of questions: How much is it going to cost? When should I go? Where in Guatemala should I plan to go? How do I get there? How do I get around once I get there? Will I be able to communicate with people there? These are some of the many questions that this chapter will answer for you. In addition, you'll find information on health precautions that you should take before and during your visit, saving money on flights to Guatemala, studying Spanish in Guatemala, arranging alternative vacations, and finding more information before you leave home and after you arrive. In short, you'll find all the information that you'll need to make your visit as easy and enjoyable as you dreamed it would be.

1. INFORMATION, ENTRY REQUIREMENTS & MONEY

SOURCES OF INFORMATION

For information on Guatemala before you leave home, you can contact the **Guatemalan Tourist Commission,** 299 Alhambra Circle, Suite 510, Coral Gables, FL 33134 (tel. 305/442-0651 or 442-0412; fax 305/442-1013). Within Guatemala, you will find **INGUAT** (Guatemalan Tourist Commission) offices or desks in Guatemala City (downtown and at the airport), Antigua, El Petén (Santa Elena Airport), Panajachel, and Quetzaltenango. See the appropriate chapters for details.

ENTRY REQUIREMENTS

DOCUMENTS   To enter Guatemala, U.S. citizens will need a passport and either a visa or Tourist Card. Visas are only available at embassies and consulates and cost $10. However, they are valid for repeated entries for up to five years, so if you are planning to pass through Guatemala more than once during your travels, it makes sense to get a visa. If you are just coming down for a few weeks and don't anticipate repeated visits, a Tourist Card, which costs $5, is all you need. Tourist Cards are available from airlines flying into Guatemala City—be sure to ask about getting one when you first check in. If you don't get your Tourist Card before arriving, you can ask at the Tourist Information desk just before Immigration in the arrivals terminal of Guatemala City's La Aurora Airport. If you are entering the country by land or sea, you can get your Tourist Card at the border. If you are a citizen of the United Kingdom, Canada, Ireland, or Australia, a visa is required and is only valid for 30 days.

CUSTOMS   When you enter Guatemala, Customs may or may not search your bags. You can legally bring in two bottles of liquor, two cartons of cigarettes, one still camera plus six rolls of film (rarely if ever enforced), and one movie camera.

MONEY

CASH CURRENCY   The unit of **currency** in Guatemala is the quetzal (Q). It's named after Guatemala's national symbol, the freedom-loving quetzal bird, which was revered by the ancient Mayas. One quetzal is divided into 100 centavos. There are 1-, 5-, 10-, and 25-centavo coins and bills in denominations of 50 centavos and 1, 5, 10, 20, 50, and 100 quetzals. At this writing, $1 U.S. will buy you Q5, so each quetzal is worth about 20¢, and one centavo is worth a fifth of a penny.

American dollars can be exchanged for Guatemalan quetzals ("quetzal*es*" in Spanish) easily and legally in many hotels as well as at banks. If a bank isn't open, ask at a hotel. However, banks always give a better rate. You will get better rates of exchange the closer you are to Guatemala City. Ask around. The dollar-to-quetzal exchange rate began climbing late in 1989 and has been variable since, although from one week to the next there are only slight changes. It is a good idea not to change too much at one time just in case the rate changes to your benefit.

If you need to exchange other foreign currency (Canadian dollars, German marks, English pounds, and so forth), you'll find it most convenient to exchange it at a bank. Banks are found nearly everywhere that you are likely to go, except at Tikal; if you are staying at one of the three Tikal hotels, you can change traveler's checks or dollars at the hotel.

By the way, in Guatemalan villages you may hear the Maya words *pisto* for money (quetzals) and *leng* for centavos.

It's good to have $25 or so in U.S. dollars of small denominations with you at all times for emergencies (most places will take them if you don't have the proper local currency).

TRAVELER'S CHECKS   Traveler's checks drawn in U.S. dollars are only slightly more difficult to change than cash dollars. You can change them at banks and hotels all over Guatemala, although hotel rates are usually not very good. Even bank rates vary considerably, so it is a good idea to shop around. It can take quite a while to change traveler's checks at a bank, so go as early in the day as possible, when the lines are shorter.

WHAT THINGS COST IN GUATEMALA CITY	U.S. $
Taxi from the airport to the city center	7.00
Local telephone call	.02
Double at Camino Real Hotel (deluxe)	140.00
Double at Hotel Pan American (moderate)	64.35
Double at Chalet Suizo (budget)	12.30
Lunch for one at Altuna (moderate)	5.00
Lunch for one at Cafetería el Roble (budget)	1.20
Dinner for one, without wine at Teppanyaki (deluxe)	20.00

	US$
Dinner for one, without wine at El Gran Pavo (moderate)	10.00
Dinner for one, without wine at Restaurant Ruby (budget)	4.00
Bottle of beer	1.20
Coca-Cola	.70
Cup of coffee	.50
Roll of ASA 100 Kodacolor film, 36 exposures	6.00
Admission to the Popul Vuh Museum	1.00
Movie ticket	1.10
Theater ticket to the National Theater	1.00–20.00

CREDIT CARDS   The major international credit cards most widely accepted in Guatemala are MasterCard, VISA, Diners Club, and American Express. Very low-budget hotels and restaurants rarely accept credit cards, but moderate or expensive ones usually do. There are some exceptions. As in most places, it is very difficult to rent a car without a major credit card.

CURRENCY EXCHANGE CHART

Q	U.S. $	Q	U.S. $
1	.20	200	40.00
2	.40	250	50.00
3	.60	300	60.00
4	.80	350	70.00
5	1.00	400	80.00
6	1.20	450	90.00
7	1.40	500	100.00
8	1.60	550	110.00
9	1.80	600	120.00
10	2.00	650	130.00
15	3.00	700	140.00
20	4.00	750	150.00
25	5.00	800	160.00
30	6.00	850	170.00
35	7.00	900	180.00
40	8.00	950	190.00
45	9.00	1,000	200.00
50	10.00	2,000	400.00
75	15.00	3,000	600.00
100	20.00	4,000	800.00

2. WHEN TO GO — CLIMATE, EVENTS & HOLIDAYS

CLIMATE   The conditions in Guatemala are similar to those in Costa Rica, with basically two seasons: The rainy season, from May to October, is called *invierno* (winter), and the dry season, from November to April, is called *verano* (summer). In the rainy season, it rains virtually every day, sometimes all day but sometimes only in the afternoon. It will also be chillier in the highlands and muggier in the lowlands during these months. During the dry season, the sun shines nearly every day, and there is almost never any rain. Days, even high in the mountains, are warm, but nights can be quite cold.

Average annual temperatures in Guatemala's highlands are 64° to 68°F; in Guatemala City, 68° to 72°F; in El Petén and along the Atlantic Highway, 77° to 86°F.

AVERAGE MONTHLY TEMPERATURES AND RAINFALL IN GUATEMALA CITY

Month	Temp. [°F]	Days of Rain
Jan	63	2
Feb	65	2
Mar	69	2
Apr	69	5
May	73	8
June	71	20
July	70	17
Aug	70	16
Sept	70	17
Oct	67	13
Nov	65	6
Dec	64	2

GUATEMALA CALENDAR OF EVENTS

MARCH OR APRIL

⊙ **SEMANA SANTA (HOLY WEEK) PROCESSIONS** *Devout Roman Catholics, many dressed in robes, carry huge floats through the streets of the city. Streets are decorated with "carpets" made from flowers, colored sawdust, and pine needles.*

Where: Antigua. When: The week leading up to Easter. How: Make hotel reservations months in advance and reconfirm often.

NOVEMBER

☐ **All Saints' Day,** Santiago Sacatepequez. Giant kites are flown from the graveyard. November 1.

☐ **All Saints' Day,** Todos Santos Cuchamatán. Horse races and the dance of the Conquest. November 1.

HOLIDAYS Official holidays in Guatemala include January 1, New Year's Day; Holy Thursday; Good Friday; May 1, Labor Day; June 30, Army Day; August 15, Assumption of the Virgin Mary; September 15, Independence Day; October 20, Revolution Day; November 1, All Saint's Day; December 24, Christmas Eve; December 25, Christmas; December 31, New Year's Eve.

3. HEALTH, INSURANCE & OTHER CONCERNS

See Chapter 2, "Planning a Trip to Costa Rica," for information.

4. WHAT TO PACK

CLOTHING Bring extra-warm clothes for the mountain towns, which can get quite cold at night at any time of year. Good walking shoes are an absolute necessity here, because even sidewalks in Guatemala City can be rough and uneven; in smaller towns, the streets are often cobblestone, which is hard on the feet no matter what kind of shoes you are wearing. Last, a good pair of walking shoes is essential to enjoying the Mayan ruins of Tikal. You want good traction when climbing steep pyramids. An umbrella in the rainy season is much more useful than a raincoat, which will cause you to sweat in the heat. You'll end up just as wet as if you hadn't worn the raincoat at all.

OTHER ITEMS Plenty of insect repellent for the lowland towns will help keep mosquitoes off you at night—very important, since malaria is still found in many parts of Guatemala. Sunscreen for your nose is necessary if you plan to spend a lot of time outdoors in the mountains, where the sun is much stronger. Although the water is supposedly safe to drink in cities and towns, I prefer not to take chances, especially in remote areas. I now carry a filter straw with me whenever I travel to places where the water is questionable. These straws are available in stores that sell camping equipment and are good for filtering about 30 gallons of water before they have to be thrown away. An alternative is to carry a bit of iodine, an eye dropper, and a water bottle for purifying your own water.

A few other items that have proven invaluable through countless trips all over the world are a Swiss army knife, a collapsible umbrella (great for rain or to keep off the tropical sun), a small flashlight, and a travel alarm clock or a watch with an alarm. In addition, I always wear a watch with a tiny built-in calculator, which can cost as little as $30 and is great for making quick exchange-rate calculations.

5. TIPS FOR THE DISABLED, SENIORS, SINGLES & STUDENTS

For the Disabled Guatemala is not an easy country for the disabled to get around in. The streets are often narrow, with broken or nonexistent sidewalks, and in some cases they are even of cobblestone. Public transit is overcrowded, so a private vehicle is an absolute necessity. Few if any hotels or public buildings are accessible to the handicapped. However, don't be put off if you have your heart set on visiting Guatemala. I once met a man in a wheelchair on the remote Río Dulce. He had hired a boat to take him from Livingston on the coast to the old Spanish fort of San Felipe, three hours up river.

For Seniors You won't find senior-citizen discounts in Guatemala, but the prices are so low that they really aren't necessary. .

For Singles   Though single travelers are discriminated against in hotel pricing just as they are in so many other places, if you are traveling on a budget, you will find that room rates are surprisingly low.

For Students   Students may want to look into studying Spanish for a while in Antigua (see "Language Programs," below) or Quetzaltenango. The courses are quite inexpensive and you can save more by staying with a local family.

6. ALTERNATIVE/ADVENTURE TRAVEL

LANGUAGE PROGRAMS

Every year, thousands of people come to Guatemala from Europe and North America to study Spanish in Antigua. There are literally dozens of schools offering courses and one-on-one tutoring at very reasonable prices. Some people make Antigua their first stop in Latin America so that they can learn some Spanish before traveling on to other countries. Listed below are some of the better schools in Antigua. When choosing a Spanish school, you should make sure how many hours of study you will receive each day, whether this is one-on-one or group instruction, clarify whether you want to study grammar or conversation, have a look at the textbooks that will be used to see if they seem well written, and find out whether the price includes meals and accommodations with a local family. In addition to the schools listed below, there are others in Quetzaltenango and Huehuetenango, but Antigua is such a beautiful town that I strongly recommend you attend classes there.

   Proyecto Linguistico Francisco Marroquin, Apdo. 237, 4a Av. Sur No. 4, Antigua (tel. 320-406), is one of the oldest and most respected of the Spanish schools. It offers 4-week intensive courses (six hours of study daily) for Q2500 ($500), which includes room and board. A $125 nonrefundable deposit is required, but this money is then applied toward your tuition. This is the only school in Antigua that is certified in Washington, D.C., to administer the Foreign Service Institute's examination for fluency in Spanish.

   Centro Linguistico Maya, 5a Calle Poniente No. 20, Antigua (tel. 320-656). Weekly rates, including room and board, start at Q450 ($90) for four hours of study five days a week.

   Centro Linguistico Antigua, 6a Av. Norte No. 25, Antigua (Fax 323-091). Weekly rates, including room and board, start at Q450 ($90) for four hours of study five days a week.

   Academia de Español Tecún Umán, 6a Calle Poniente No. 34, Apdo. 68, Antigua (tel. 322-792). Rates, including room and board, start at Q425 ($85) for four hours of study five days a week.

   Professional Spanish Language School, 2a Av. Sur No. 11, Apdo. 230, Antigua (tel. 322-349), is affiliated with the Shawcross Aid Programme for Highland Indians. Profits from the school go to this program, which is providing teachers, potable water systems, clothing, medicine, and food to Indians in remote villages. Rates start at Q395 ($79) for four hours of study five days a week.

RIVER TRIPS

The ancient Mayas of El Petén had a far-flung empire that was connected by river routes, the old Mayan trade routes, that cross El Petén and extend into Mexico. Trips on these rivers include days of river travel by outboard-powered boats through jungles, with stops at several remote Mayan ruins. **Maya Expeditions,** 15 Calle 1-91, Zona 10, Edificio Tauro, Loc. 104, Guatemala City (tel. 502/374-666), offers rafting trips from 3 to 11 days long on the Cahabon and Usumacinta rivers. Prices range from $315 for a 3-day trip up to $1,395 for an 11-day expedition. Other companies sometimes offer river trips in El Petén using outboard-powered boats. These trips follow ancient Mayan trade routes with stops at several remote ruins. The best way to find out about such trips is to contact a travel agent in Antigua or Guatemala City or head for Flores in El Petén and start asking around.

7. GETTING THERE

BY PLANE

For airlines serving **La Aurora Airport** in Guatemala City, see the "Getting There" section of Chapter 2. The same airlines that fly to San José also fly to Guatemala City, and often at almost the same price.

Flores Airport, which is the gateway to Tikal ruins, has service from Chetumal and Cancun, Mexico, on Aerocaribe, from Cancun on Aviateca, and from Belize City, Belize, on Aerovias. See Chapter 11 for details.

BEST FOR THE BUDGET These days there doesn't seem to be any particular airline that offers consistently lower prices. When rates at one airline go up, rates at all the other airlines follow, and vice versa. However, it pays to check the various Central American airlines, which tend to charge a bit less because their flights make more stops.

In 1992 the lowest airfares to Guatemala City from most North American cities ranged from $300 during a "fare war" to $750 when the airlines were convinced that if people weren't flying, then prices should be raised higher than ever. You can only hope that when you decide to fly south, there will be a fare war going on.

Bucket Shops In my opinion, there is almost no reason to pay the regular full airfare for any international ticket. In nearly every major city in the United States and Britain, there are now discount ticket agencies known as bucket shops or ticket

---

🅕 FROMMER'S SMART TRAVELER: AIRFARES

1. Check the ads for discounted plane tickets in the Sunday travel section of major-city newspapers. These tickets can be $100 to $200 cheaper than the lowest standard airfare.
2. Consider getting a discounted ticket from your departure city to one of the Central American gateway cities (Miami, New Orleans, Houston, or Los Angeles), and combine this with a discount ticket from one of those cities on to Guatemala.
3. Check out the small Central American airlines that fly to Guatemala.
4. You'll usually save money if you take a "milk run" (flight that makes several stops) rather than a direct flight.
5. Make domestic flight reservations for Tikal as far in advance as possible; these flights book up quickly.
6. Always ask for the lowest-priced fare, which will usually be a mid-week departure. Be flexible and you can save money.

consolidators. These companies sell airline tickets on major carriers at a substantial discount over what you would pay the airline for the same ticket. In many cases, low-cost tickets that would be nonrefundable through an airline are refundable with a $100 penalty through a bucket shop. You'll find bucket shops advertised in major newspapers (which are often available at your local library, even if you live in a small town). These ads often are misleading because the price listed may be available only to students and does not include taxes; but even when all the additional charges are included, you almost always save money at a bucket shop.

REGULAR AIRFARES Regular, full-price airfares are often two to four times the lowest fare ($800 to $900) and first-class fares are usually about five time the lowest fare ($1,200 to $1,600).

BY BUS

There are four bus routes into Guatemala, three from Mexico, and one from Belize. Buses leave San Cristobal de las Casas, Mexico, for the border station at Ciudad Cuauhtemoc, in the mountains. After border formalities, passengers board a Guatemalan bus for the rest of the journey. This bus leaves the Guatemalan border station at La Mesilla and heads for Huehuetenango and Guatemala City. The bus from the border will drop you at transfer points for Chichicastenango or Quetzaltenango if you wish. If you are coming from Tapachula, Mexico, you can take a bus from the downtown bus station or catch a minibus to the border crossing at either Talisman or Tecún Umán. As in La Mesilla, there will be buses waiting on the Guatemalan side of the border. These buses are bound for Guatemala City with a connection to Quetzaltenango if desired. From Belize, you can catch a bus bound for the border town of Benque Viejo, Belize, in either Belize City or San Ignacio. Depending on which bus you catch, you may be taken all the way to the border station or may be dropped at the bus station in Benque Viejo, in which case you will need to take a taxi (inexpensive) the rest of the way. This route is favored by those wishing to visit the impressive Mayan ruins at Tikal. After border formalities, cross the bridge and walk up to the intersection, where a bus will likely be waiting. You then continue, down a very rough dirt road, in a Guatemalan bus to the city of Flores. If you leave early enough in the morning, it is possible to get off this bus at El Cruce and catch a connecting bus directly to Tikal. You will be approached by money changers at all of these border stations; although these changers don't give very favorable rates (unless you have dollars or traveler's checks), they often are the only choice you have.

You can shorten procedures at the border a bit by getting your Tourist Card or visa in advance at a Guatemalan consulate, but don't spend a day doing it. If you're near a consulate (hours are usually 9am to 2pm weekdays) it's a good plan; if not, you can always get a Tourist Card at the border. The best place to get a Tourist Card or visa in advance is the Guatemalan Embassy in Mexico City or Belize City or the Guatemalan Consulate in Tapachula. Tourist cards cost $5.

BY CAR

The same routes that apply to buses also are available to cars. However, keep in mind that if you're driving from Belize, you're going to travel some of the worst roads that you have ever seen between the Guatemalan border and El Cruce 65 miles away. Even after you reach the city of Flores, you have an equally bad road to take to get to the rest of Guatemala. This route is nearly impassable in the rainy season and very difficult during the rest of the year. Only try it if your car has high clearance and, preferably, four-wheel drive. From Tehuantepec, Mexico, you can head either to Tapachula and the Pacific Slope road to Guatemala City or to Tuxtla Gutierrez and San Cristobal de las Casas for the high mountain road to Guatemala City. The low road along the

Pacific Slope goes through lush tropical country and a few pretty towns. Straighter and faster than the high road, it still has several disadvantages: It's heavily trafficked (especially when the sugarcane harvest is on) and hot and muggy all the time and, except for the lushness, there's not much to stop and see along the road. The high road, by contrast, is reached by going through San Cristobal, one of the prettiest places in Mexico; there is virtually no traffic for the first 100 miles into Guatemala; the mountain scenery is breathtaking; and interesting towns and villages abound all along the road. Perhaps you can see that I prefer the high road, despite its disadvantages: some landslides in the rainy season (late May to October), even though they are cleared away pretty quickly by road crews, and a curvy (but very good and safe) 40-m.p.h. mountain road.

The border-crossing procedures are the same at both posts. See the preceding section, "By Bus," for information on shortening border procedures.

The road from San Cristobal de las Casas, Mexico, is fairly fast. It's slightly over 100 miles from San Cristobal to Ciudad Cuauhtemoc, the border station, and you should be able to cover it in about 2½ hours. After winding through the mountains east of San Cristobal, you descend to a plain before heading into the mountains that mark the border. The first Customs post you'll come to is where you hand in your car papers and Tourist Card (you fill out a new one when you return from Guatemala). Go on to the border proper, about a mile down the road, and pass the barrier into Guatemala.

You must get a Guatemalan Tourist Card ($5) right across the border, if you don't already have a visa. After getting your card (have your passport), drive on for a mile or so to the Customs inspection station, where you'll get your car papers, usually after a fairly serious look at the car and its contents. You may have to open a few bags, but it's wise just to follow the inspector around and do exactly and only what he or she asks.

While you're getting your car papers, someone will wash your tires with a disinfectant solution. This fumigation is required and costs a few dollars—a bothersome but fairly minor nuisance. The entire border crossing takes about an hour. The officials are businesslike, sometimes even friendly (especially if you show an interest in Guatemala), and the whole procedure is quite painless. The Guatemalan border stations keep regular business hours: 8am to noon and 2 to 6pm Monday through Friday, 8am to noon on Saturday. You can cross at other hours and on Sunday, but you'll end up paying a little extra. All in all, expect to pay between $10 and $20 to get across the border.

Note that Mexican auto insurance is not valid in Guatemala. Buy Guatemalan insurance through your agent at home, or through the AAA, or within Guatemala. It is usually available at border crossings.

PACKAGE TOURS

Clark Tours, 9 Boston St., Suite 10, Lynn, MA 09104 (tel. 617/581-0844, or toll free 800/223-6764), has been organizing tours to Guatemala since 1929.

8. SUGGESTED ITINERARIES

HIGHLIGHTS

The following are Guatemala's top tourist destinations.
1. Antigua
2. Chichicastenango
3. Panajachel

4. Quetzaltenango
5. Tikal
6. Guatemala City

PLANNING YOUR ITINERARY

IF YOU HAVE ONE WEEK

Day 1: Spend one day in Guatemala City visiting the museums.
Days 2 and 3: Settle into Antigua and explore this beautiful little colonial town for two days.
Day 4: Visit Chichicastenango if it is market day and spend the night there. If it is not market day, arrange your schedule accordingly.
Day 5: Return by way of Panajachel and beautiful Lake Atitlán, spending a day there.
Days 6 and 7: Spend your last two days visiting the Mayan ruins in Tikal. This is a rushed itinerary, but you will get an overview of Guatemala, its people, its history, and its landscape.

IF YOU HAVE TWO WEEKS

With two weeks, you can spend more time in some of Guatemala's many beautiful locations.

Days 1 and 2: So that you won't have to carry your purchases around with you, head first to Tikal for two days. Don't buy anything here because prices are much lower in Chichicastenango and Panajachel.
Days 3 through 6: Make Antigua your base of operations for the next four days. Spend three days enjoying colonial Antigua, with perhaps a trip to climb a volcano or a visit to a nearby village. Take a day trip to Guatemala City to see the museums.
Day 7: From Antigua, head to Chichicastenango for market day and spend the night there.
Days 8 through 10: Continue on to Quetzaltenango, the heart of the highlands, the next day. Spend three days exploring the Indian villages near Quetzaltenango.
Days 11 through 14: By now you should be ready for a rest, so head to Panajachel and relax on the beach of this volcanic lake for four days, taking ferries to the little villages that ring the lake.

IF YOU HAVE THREE WEEKS

Days 1 and 2: Head first to Tikal for two days.
Days 3 and 4: After returning to Guatemala City, take a bus to Cobán for two days and visit the quetzal preserve and other natural wonders of this mountainous region.
Days 5 through 8: Continue toward the Caribbean Coast, but turn north to Río Dulce and take a boat down the river to Lívingston. You will probably have to spend the night in Río Dulce. Spend a couple of days in Lívingston or Puerto Barrios.
Day 9: Head back toward Guatemala City, with a stop at the ruins of Quiriguá.
Day 10: Spend a day visiting the museums of Guatemala City, then head for Antigua.
Days 11 through 13: Spend three days exploring Antigua.
Day 14: Go to Chichicastenango for market day and spend the night.
Days 15 through 17: Continue on to Quetzaltenango. Spend three days there visiting small villages on their market days.
Days 18 through 21: Head to Panajachel and Lake Atitlán for four days of rest and recreation.

FROMMER'S FAVORITE
GUATEMALA EXPERIENCES

A Boat Ride Down the Río Dulce   Long narrow boats with outboard motors carry passengers between Río Dulce and Lívingston, stopping at a manatee preserve en route. Forested mountains rise up on either side of the river, and along its banks are the huts of fishermen for whom the river is the only link to the outside world.

Chichicastenango on Market Day   Guatemalan textiles are some of the most beautiful in the world, and Chichicastenango is the place to buy them. The local Indians wear colorful traditional costumes, and age-old rituals based on Mayan rites are performed in front of the town's main church and on a hillside just outside of town. There are great deals here late in the afternoon, when vendors are packing up their goods.

Antigua During Semana Santa   During the week prior to Easter, Antigua's cobblestone streets are the scene of religious processions in which thousands of people participate, carrying heavy religious floats on their shoulders as they march slowly through incense-filled streets.

Dawn and Dusk in Tikal   At the opening and close of each steamy day, the ruins come alive with the roar of howler monkeys, the chatter of spider monkeys, the squawking of parrots and toucans, and the songs of countless species of other birds. If you're lucky, you might even see a "herd" of coatimundis.

Climbing Pacaya Volcano   This is one of the few active volcanoes in the world that you can hike to the top of while it's exploding and spewing out molten rock, but hiking to the top of Pacaya is not for the faint of heart. The last bit of climbing to reach the peak of the volcano's quiet cone (it has two cones) can be extremely difficult when the winds are strong.

THEMED CHOICES

Archeology buffs will want to take in Guatemala's many Mayan ruins, which include Tikal and several smaller and more remote sites in the Petén region. You might end up spending a week or more in this area. After flying back to Guatemala, you should head next for the ruins in Copán, Honduras, just over the border from Guatemala. This will probably take you another two or three days. Three much less impressive sites are Iximché near Lake Atitlán, Quiriguá near Puerto Barrios, and Zaculeu outside Huehuetenango. The huge carved-stone heads in La Democracia also are worth an excursion.

9. GETTING AROUND

BY PLANE

Tikal is probably the only place in Guatemala that you will want to reach by air. Airfare between Guatemala City and Flores (the closest city to the Tikal ruins) is $53.50 each way. There are daily flights on Aviateca, Aerovias, and Tapsa. If you are a very serious student of archeology, you may want to charter a plane to reach some of the remote Mayan sites. Such a charter flight, in a small plane, can work out to be fairly inexpensive if you have enough people to fill the plane.

BY BUS

Every town of any size in Guatemala has several bus companies that operate to surrounding towns and to the capital; minibus services connect the smaller villages or run the very frequent services between towns a short distance apart.

BY CAR

The main roads in Guatemala are better than the main roads in Mexico—with smoother, harder surfaces; gentler curves; and better maintenance.

CAR RENTALS Car rentals are available in Guatemala City, Antigua, and Flores/Santa Elena. See Chapter 9, "Getting Around," for more information.

GASOLINE Unleaded gasoline is rarely available in Guatemala. Rental cars use regular gasoline. If you're from the U.S., expect gasoline to cost slightly more than you are used to paying.

DRIVING RULES The most important driving rule here is to stop for police and military checkpoints and blockades, which you will encounter frequently. Present the officer with your driver's license (international driver's licenses are best but not necessary), your vehicle registration papers, and perhaps your rental agreement. You should get everything back within a minute and be on your way. *Remember:* Never drive without your passport. Occasionally, it is not the police, but leftist guerrillas, who have barricaded the road. Should you encounter one of these barricades, do as you are instructed and you will likely be sent on your way unharmed. Otherwise, driving rules in Guatemala are basically the same as they are in the United States, except that you must be 18 years old to drive. Also keep in mind that if you see a pile of leaves, grass, or branches from a tree or bush piled in the road, it is a signal that there is a vehicle stopped on the road ahead.

SAFETY Bandits are a bigger problem than guerrillas these days. During my last visit several carloads of tourists were robbed on the road from the Belize border to Tikal. No one was harmed by the armed bandits, but the incidents reinforced the fact that Guatemala can be a dangerous place, especially if you are driving your own car. Always ask in San Ignacio, Belize, if there have been recent robberies before heading out on this road. Though these armed robberies are mostly confined to remote areas of the country, they can happen almost anywhere. Just do as you are told and you won't be harmed. I suggest getting a good travel insurance policy that covers you for theft, and make sure that the company does not exclude Guatemala because of the guerrilla activity that has been going on there for decades.

MAPS Ask for a map when you rent a car. These maps are about the best that are available. If you want to get a map before you arrive, contact an INGUAT (Guatemalan Tourist Commission) office. See "Information, Entry Requirements & Money" in this chapter for addresses and phone numbers.

BREAKDOWNS If you should have a breakdown, immediately pile some branches in the road at least 100 feet on either side of your car. Wait for help from the national police or flag down a bus and ride to the nearest town in search of a mechanic.

BY FERRY

There are a few ferries in Guatemala that you should know about. It is possible to enter the country from Belize on a ferry that plies between Punta Gorda, Belize, and Puerto Barrios, Guatemala. The ferry makes the trip a couple of times a week. Another ferry also runs between Puerto Barrios and Livingston, across the mouth of the Río Dulce. There is a mail boat that makes a regular run between Livingston and the town of Río Dulce, which is several hours up the river. There are also several ferries that operate on Lake Atitlán, providing service between Panajachel and several small villages on the shore of the lake. See the pertinent chapters for details on these ferries.

HITCHHIKING

Because buses in Guatemala are so cheap and go nearly everywhere in the country, you should not need to hitchhike. However, if you're driving a car, you will often notice hitchhikers. It is very common for hitchhikers to wait at toll booths and highway police check points. Often you will be asked by an officer if you can give someone a ride.

FINDING AN ADDRESS

The street-numbering system in Guatemala is logical, easy to use, and found in every town. In fact, the system is so good that there's almost no excuse for getting lost anywhere but in Guatemala City! Once you get the hang of it, you'll be on your way to the exact location of any hotel or restaurant. Here's how it works: Every town is planned on a grid with avenidas running roughly north to south and calles running east to west. Addresses are given in the following form: 2a. Av. 4-17, which means that the place you're after is on 2nd Avenue, at 4th Calle, number 17 (2a is "Spanish" for 2nd, 3a for 3rd, and so on). You can even tell what side of the street the building will be on. If the street number is even, it'll be on the right side; if the number is odd, it'll be on the left—as you walk along the avenida toward higher-numbered calles. You can guess, then, that 3a. Av. 5-78 will be on 3rd Avenida between 5th and 6th calles (closer to 6th, as the house number is a high one), on the right side. Once you get the hang of it, you'll see that it's a marvelous system.

One last note: Each town is also divided into zones, but in the small towns (everywhere but Guatemala City), almost every important place is in Zona 1. If a zone number does not appear as a part of any address given in this book, you can assume that the place you're looking for is in Zona 1.

10. ENJOYING GUATEMALA ON A BUDGET

SAVING MONEY ON ACCOMMODATIONS

Whether you are traveling on $10 a day or $100, you can almost always find a place to your liking in cities throughout Guatemala. However, when you start venturing off into small towns and villages, you can expect the quality of accommodations to be fairly low. Though it is possible to pay anywhere from $2 to $200 a night for a room in Guatemala, most hotels are in the $15-to-$60 range. Within this range of prices are some of the best hotel deals in the world, but there are also some overpriced losers. You can be sure that if it is recommended in this book it is the best that you can do in a given price range, unless a new hotel has opened since the book was updated.

Because maintenance of budget hotels is often minimal to nonexistent, what was a wonderful and clean new hotel two years ago could have become dirty and run down by the time you visit. Keep your eyes and ears open for new hotels, these are often the best deals around, because hotels frequently open with low prices in order to develop a word-of-mouth following. If you do stumble across some very fine new accommodations, please let me know by writing to the address in the front of this book.

To give you some idea of what to expect from Guatemalan hotels, in the lowest price range you'll likely get a bed and a bare light bulb, that's it. What you'll also get in the lowest price range is a lot of free noise, so be sure to bring some earplugs. Cheap hotels tend to be near discos, bars, and bus stops. Moving up a bit, say to $15 a night for a double, you can expect a fairly clean bathroom, a fan, a window, and a bedside stand or table, and usually, a quiet night's sleep. For $25 to $30, expect a spacious room with a bit of style, perhaps a bit of colonial-style furnishings or a good view. For $50 to $100, you might find antiques and a bit of thought given to interior decor. Above $100 you move into the domain of international standards, where a hotel room will look roughly like any other hotel room in the world and service will be just what you would expect from an international hotel chain. These high-priced hotels generally are not a very good value in Guatemala.

Best Budget Bets The cheapest accommodations in Guatemala are usually called *pensiónes*. *Albergue* and *posada* are other titles often attached to budget lodgings in place of the word "hotel." In Antigua, a very popular tourist town, there are a few apartment hotels that represent an excellent value since each apartment comes with a kitchenette that allows you to do your own cooking.

Seasonal Discounts Keep in mind that nearly everyone in Guatemala goes on holiday during Semana Santa (Holy Week), the week prior to Easter. Not only are rooms difficult to find, but room rates are nearly double. Rates are also higher at Christmas and New Year's.

Other Money-Saving Strategies Although our budget in Guatemala allows us the luxury of a private bath, if you're willing to forsake this and walk down the hall, you will save considerably on your hotel bills. Rooms with air conditioning are also much more expensive and rarely necessary. If there are two of you traveling together, getting one double room instead of two singles will save you money. Getting a *cama matrimonial* (double bed), instead of two twin beds, will also save you money in many cases. If there is a view from the hotel, you will pay for it; take a room without the view to save even more money.

SAVING MONEY ON MEALS

The *plato del dia* is the way to save money in Guatemala. This lunch special is usually a large three-course meal for much less than you would pay for just an entrée at regular prices. These meals are served until the pot is empty. Breakfasts are usually surprisingly expensive, but if you stop by the market and buy some fruit and pick up some bread at a *panaderia,* you will need only a cup of tea or coffee to put together a tasty breakfast.

SAVING MONEY ON SIGHT-SEEING & ENTERTAINMENT

You won't find any special discount days at museums, and there aren't discount tickets to theaters. However, because the prices are so low in Guatemala already, it hardly matters.

SAVING MONEY ON SHOPPING

Best Buys Guatemala's best buy is in textiles. Most visitors come here because they are fascinated by the colorful cotton textiles woven by the highland Indians. Brilliant colors in bold stripes are the norm. These beautiful fabrics are sewn into a wide variety of traditional and modern fashions and are considerably less expensive than they are back home. The best place to buy textiles is always in the villages where they are manufactured. There are several villages near Quetzaltenango that are known for different textiles. You can make trips to the different villages on their respective market days and bargain for beautiful pieces of cloth. For ready-made fashions, the best places to shop are in Chichicastenango and Panajachel. The stores in Antigua tend to be expensive, although they sell contemporary designs.

Another good buy is jade, which was highly valued by the Mayas. Their jade quarries were lost for hundreds of years but were rediscovered several years ago. Beautiful jade jewelry is available at several shops in Antigua. The prices are high, but the jade is of the highest quality.

Stay away from any Pre-Columbian artifacts that are offered to you as being *originales.* It is against the law to buy, sell, or export original Pre-Columbian art. It is also very doubtful whether anything offered to you truly is an original. High-quality fakes are common, and many people have been taken when they "got a great deal" on a piece of ancient Mayan pottery.

Markets   Every town and village in Guatemala has its market day. Once or twice a week, people from all over the region will come into town to buy and sell their wares. The most famous market in the country, and now a major tourist destination, is the one at Chichicastenango. It takes place on both Thursday and Sunday; the Sunday market is larger and more colorful. You will always get a better deal in a market than you will in a tourist shop, and often they have the same items for sale. The market in Antigua is a prime example of this, so be sure to visit this market before making any purchases in Antigua. Calle Santander in Panajachel isn't really a market, but it is lined with vendors' stalls that offer those beautiful Guatemalan textiles at some of the best prices in the country.

Bargaining   When making purchases in markets, especially when buying tourist items, be sure to bargain hard. The prices can be inflated several hundred percent if you look like you have the money to pay. Try to avoid looking "rich" and you'll save money; if you're wearing expensive jewelry and watches, you'll automatically be charged a high price. Bargaining is much easier late in the day when the vendors are packing up and will often lower their prices far below midday quotes. If you ask the price of something, you have expressed an interest in buying it and will be expected to negotiate for the item. This can be very frustrating if you're trying to do a little comparison shopping. If you ask the price and don't buy, you'll have to learn to live with the intimidating stares. It is much harder to bargain in shops, but it is possible, especially if you are buying several items. More and more shops are displaying "Fixed Prices" signs.

SAVING MONEY ON TRANSPORTATION

By Plane   There is only one domestic flight of concern to visitors to Guatemala—the flight between Guatemala City and Flores, El Petén. Tapsa and Aerovias both charge $53.50 each way, while Aviateca charges a bit more. The flights are often booked up by large tour groups, so try to reserve in advance. See Chapter 11 on El Petén for details.

By Bus   Although cleaner and more comfortable, first-class buses are more expensive and run less often than the second-class buses known to travelers as "chicken buses." Whether this name derives from the livestock carried among the passengers or the disquieting passing habits of the drivers is a matter for speculation. Chicken buses almost always leave from the market of a town and are for those seeking adventure.

By Car   To save money on a rental car, reserve at least one week ahead with a company in your home country. Once in Guatemala, the best way to save money on car rentals is to drive one with a stick shift and forsake air conditioning, which isn't really necessary in most of the country. Be sure to ask for a free road map when you pick up your car. When filling up the gas tank, ask for regular. *Lleno* means "full."

SAVING MONEY ON SERVICES & OTHER TRANSACTIONS

Tipping   Bellhops: Q1 to Q2 (20¢ to 40¢) per bag. Waiters/waitresses: 10 to 15%, but only in more expensive restaurants. Taxi drivers: not necessary. Porters: Q1 (20¢) per bag.

Money Changing and Credit Cards   Currency exchange rates vary from bank to bank in Guatemala, so it pays to check with a few banks before changing money. *Prensa Libre,* the daily newspaper, publishes a list of exchange rates at various Guatemala City banks. Although hotels will often change money, they tend to give very low rates. By using your credit card to pay hotel and restaurant bills, you will be locking in the bank exchange rate for the day the bill is submitted to a bank. This can work to your advantage and save you money if the value of the quetzal is falling rapidly against the dollar (that is, you're getting more quetzals for your dollar each day). However, make sure that you aren't charged a higher rate for using your credit card.

Telephones   You'll save money on local phone calls by going to a phone booth rather than by calling from your hotel; budget hotels in Guatemala rarely have phones in the rooms anyway. For international calls, I suggest using AT&T USA Direct. By dialing 190, you will reach an English-speaking AT&T operator. However, only calling-card and collect calls can be made this way. You'll save time, money, and aggravation by making your call to the United States this way.

FAST GUATEMALA

American Express   The only office is in Guatemala City at Avenida La Reforma 9-00, Zona 9 (tel. 311-311).

Business Hours   Banks are generally open Monday to Friday from 9am to 3pm, with *ventanillas especiales* (special windows) open longer hours. Bars generally stay open until 2am, except on Sunday, when they close at midnight. Office hours are Monday to Friday from 8am to 4:30pm. Less expensive restaurants tend to be open all day, while more expensive ones tend to close for a couple of hours between meals. Shops are generally open Monday to Friday from 9am to 12:30pm and 3 to 7pm, Saturday from 9am to noon. Shops catering primarily to tourists usually have longer hours and stay open on weekends.

Camera/Film   Color print and Ektachrome film are readily available, but more expensive than in the United States. It's best to bring your own. If your camera requires odd-size batteries, be sure to bring some spare ones with you. You can get a camera repaired in Guatemala City, but I can't vouch for the quality of service.

City Code   If dialing Guatemala City phone numbers from outside Guatemala, it is necessary to dial "2" after the country code (502).

Climate   See "When to Go" in this chapter.

Crime   See "*Safety*," below.

Currency   See "Information, Entry Requirements & Money" in this chapter.

Customs   See "Information, Entry Requirements & Money" in this chapter.

Documents Required   See "Information, Entry Requirements & Money" in this chapter.

Driving Rules   See "Getting Around" in this chapter.

Drug Laws   Although marijuana and cocaine are readily available, the drug laws are strict, and there is nothing your embassy can do to get you out of jail. If you take prescription drugs, play it safe and bring your prescription with you. Most prescription drugs are actually available over the counter in Guatemala.

Drugstores   Drugstores here are called *farmacias*.

Electricity   The current is 110 volts.

Embassies and Consulates   Canada: Embassy and consulate, 7a Avenida 11-59, Zona 9, Edificio Galerías España (tel. 321-411 or 321-413). United Kingdom: Embassy and consulate, 7a Avenida 5-10, Zona 4, Edificio Centro Financiero, Torre II, Nivel 7, (tel. 321-612, 321-604, or 321-606).

United States: Embassy and consulate, Avenida La Reforma 7-01, Zona 10 (tel. 311-541 to 311-555).

Emergencies   Emergency phone numbers are different in each city. Check the appropriate chapter.

Hitchhiking   See "Getting Around" in this chapter.

Holidays   See "When to Go" in this chapter.

Information   See "Information, Entry Requirements & Money" in this chapter. Also see individual city chapters for local information offices.

Language   Spanish is the national language; many different Indian dialects derived from ancient Mayan languages also are spoken, primarily in the mountains. A good phrase book to take with you is the *Berlitz Latin-American Spanish for Travelers* (Berlitz Guides, 1989).

Laundry For listings of laundromats, see individual city chapters.

Liquor Laws Officially you must be 18 years old to buy alcoholic beverages in Guatemala.

Mail Mail to the United States takes anywhere from one to two weeks. A postcard to the United States costs 20 centavos (4¢); a letter costs 20 (4¢) centavos for the first five grams, 10 centavos (2¢) for each additional gram. Stamps often are available at hotel desks; otherwise, you'll have to go to a post office. It is always a good idea to make sure that the stamps on your letter get canceled. If you want to ship a package home, it is best to use one of the shipping companies in Antigua or Panajachel; otherwise, you must go to the Central Post Office in Guatemala City. Don't close the package until after it has been inspected. Surface mail can be very slow (a month or more). Air mail is much faster.

Maps Road and city maps are available from INGUAT offices and car-rental agencies (if you're renting one of their cars).

Newspapers/Magazines You'll find several U.S. newspapers and magazines available at major hotels throughout the country, although these newspapers may be a day or two old and are expensive. *Prensa Libre* is Guatemala's most popular daily paper.

Passports See "Information, Entry Requirements & Money" in this chapter.

Pets Rabies is common in Guatemala, so it is best to leave your pet at home. If you must bring it, your dog must have vaccinations for rabies, distemper, leptospirosis, hepatitis, and parvovirosis, while your cat must have vaccinations against rabies, distemper, and hepatitis. Please do not buy any parrots that you are offered. These beautiful birds are disappearing in the wild due to hunting for the live bird trade.

Police The phone number for the Policia Nacional is different in every town. You will find it in the phone book at the beginning of the section for each town or city. In Guatemala City, dial 120; in Antigua, dial 320-251; in Panajachel, dial 621-120.

Radio/TV There are plenty of AM and FM radio stations throughout the country. You're never far from a marimba music station. Most expensive hotels have satellite cable TV either in the rooms or in a TV lounge, so you can keep in touch with U.S. programming. A TV schedule is published daily in the newspaper *Prensa Libre*.

Restrooms These are known as *servicios* or *servicios sanitarios*. Public toilets, rarely clean, are free or cost a few centavos. However, you will have to buy your own toilet paper from the restroom attendant at a table outside the door.

Safety The government of Guatemala continues to wage a small-scale war against rebel guerrillas in the highlands. You will see gun-carrying soldiers almost anywhere you go in the country, but the main tourist areas are kept free of fighting; if I didn't tell you, you probably would not know that there was any fighting going on here at all.

Of greater importance is protecting yourself against pickpockets. I suggest getting a money pouch that you can wear under your clothes, either around your neck or around your waist. Be cautious with your bags when traveling by bus. Bags have been known to disappear from the roofs of buses, so try to keep your bag inside the bus with you.

Petty crime, armed robberies, and violent crime all seem to be on the rise in Guatemala, especially in Guatemala City and El Petén. When planning a trip to Guatemala, be sure to contact the **U.S. Department of State's Citizens' Emergency Service** (tel. 202/647-5225) in Washington, D.C., weekdays between 8:15am and 10pm for a recorded report of current travel advisories for Guatemala. If you are already in Guatemala, it is a good idea to ask about safety measures at your hotel or at your embassy. You should never hike alone in Guatemala, especially on the volcano trails. Hikers are frequently robbed on the trail up Pacaya Volcano, so if you make this hike, go with a group and don't carry any money. It is a good idea to carry as little cash as possible wherever you go in Guatemala, and if you are particularly concerned about theft, take out some travel theft insurance before you leave home.

Taxes   The Guatemalan government levies a 17% room tax on each night you spend in a hotel. When a hotel receptionist quotes you the room price, the tax may or not be included in the quotation. Ask to make sure. In this book I will quote room prices with the tax included, so that you'll know the total charge you will have to pay for a room.

Telephone   The dial tone in Guatemala is a long, low tone similar to that heard in the United States. Telephone numbers vary in the number of digits that they have—usually four, five, or six digits. There is only one telephone book for all of Guatemala. You'll find several copies available at Guatel (the national telephone company) offices.

A pay phone in Guatemala is called a *telefono monedero*, but it is not very common. A 3-minute local call will cost you 10 centavos (2¢). Machines accept various coins but do not give change.

The best way to make a long-distance call is to call collect or to use an AT&T calling card by dialing 190. This number connects you directly to an English-speaking AT&T operator and is much faster than trying to make a call through a Guatel office. If you must pay for the call yourself, you will need to go to a Guatel office and wait in line or pay a premium and call from your hotel. Calls have a tendency to go through better early in the morning.

Time   Guatemala is six hours behind Greenwich Mean Time, which is the same as Central Standard Time.

Tipping   See "Saving Money on Services & Transactions" in this chapter.

Tourist Offices   See "Information, Entry Requirements & Money" in this chapter. Also see specific cities.

Visas   See "Information, Entry Requirements & Money" in this chapter.

Water   Consider all tap water unfit for drinking. Bottled water, although expensive, is readily available. I carry a filter straw that filters bacteria from water. These straws are available at stores that sell camping equipment and can filter up to 30 gallons before they have to be thrown away. An alternative is to carry a little bottle of iodine, an eye dropper, and a water bottle for purifying water.

GUATEMALA CITY

The Guatemalan capital is a city of over two million souls. It's the biggest and most modern city in the country—indeed, in all Central America—and is the headquarters for companies, airlines, and government. However, it is not a major point of attraction for anyone who visits Guatemala for pleasure rather than for business. After the spectacular beauty of the countryside, the clean air and relative quiet of the provincial towns, the capital almost puts you off: The decibel level and pollution index go up almost as soon as you leave Antigua and start on the Guatemala City road.

But since all roads lead to the capital, it's the transportation hub of the nation, and chances are you'll find occasion to pass through. Here's the information that you'll need to make a short visit pleasant.

1. FROM A BUDGET TRAVELER'S POINT OF VIEW

Budget Bests   There are plenty of hotels offering good value at moderate prices, and restaurant prices are still quite low. You can confidently walk into almost any restaurant in the city without having to worry about how much you are spending—and that includes major hotel restaurants. Taxis charge about what you would expect to pay in other major cities around the world, but public buses are a super deal at only 40 centavos (7.5¢).

Discount Opportunities   The only people who get any sort of discounts in Guatemala City are students and children, who get a reduction on museum admissions. However, admission fees are already so low that these discounts hardly matter.

What's Worth Paying For   The only thing that I can really say is worth paying for in Guatemala City is a plane ticket to Flores in El Petén, which is where the famous Mayan ruins of Tikal are located. The 1-hour flight costs around $50 and saves up to 18 hours of grueling bus travel over one of the worst roads I have ever traveled.

2. ORIENTATION

Guatemala City can be a confusing place, but with a little information, getting there and getting around can be quite painless and inexpensive.

WHAT'S SPECIAL ABOUT GUATEMALA CITY

Museums
- ☐ The Museum of Archeology and Ethnology, Central America's finest collection of Pre-Columbian artifacts.
- ☐ The Ixchell Museum, dedicated to the indigenous clothing of Guatemala.
- ☐ The Popol Vuh Museum, small but containing many beautiful terra-cotta artifacts.

Events/Festivals
- ☐ The ancient Indian dances performed several times a year.

Architectural Highlights
- ☐ The Centro Cultural Miguel Angel Asturias, which resembles a luxury cruise ship.

- ☐ The Centro Cívico, with high-rise buildings covered with murals.

Churches
- ☐ The Yurrita Chapel, a fascinating mixture of architectural styles.

Offbeat Oddities
- ☐ The Mapa en Relieve, a huge relief map of Guatemala.

Ancient Ruins
- ☐ Kaminal Juyú ruins on the outskirts of the city.

ARRIVING

BY PLANE If you fly to Guatemala, you will arrive at the capital's La Aurora International Airport, in the southern part of the city only about 15 or 20 minutes from the center by taxi. La Aurora is small but modern and pleasant, equipped with a bank, dozens of interesting craft and clothing shops, several small cafeterias, and snack bars. Before you pass through Customs and Immigration, you will come to an INGUAT Tourism Information Desk staffed by an English-speaking agent. Guatemalan Tourist Cards can be obtained here or on board your plane before you arrive, at the cost of $5. Also available are a few brochures.

If the Banco de Guatemala in the arrivals hall is closed when you arrive, ask at the souvenir shops to find someone who will change U.S. dollars into Guatemalan quetzals for you.

Outside the lower level of the terminal building are car-rental booths and taxi ranks. Taxi fare from the airport to Zona 9 or 10 is Q20 to Q25 ($4 to $5); to Zona 4 is Q30 ($6); and to Zona 1, the very center, is Q35 ($7). A small tip is appreciated but not required. You should have chosen your desired hotel by this time; examine the address and find its zone number so that you'll know what the taxi fare will be.

It is also possible to get into town on a public bus for only 40 centavos (8¢). There is a bus stop on the near side of the road directly in front of the terminal. The black no. 5 (as opposed to the red no. 5, which runs a similar route but does not go all the way to the airport) "Aeropuerto" bus comes by frequently. Other buses also head downtown to the *parque,* and you can take any of these. The trip downtown will take about 30 minutes.

For those going directly from the airport to Antigua or Panajachel, there is another option. You can take a minibus operated by **Buses Inter-Hotel y Turismo** (tel. 322-664 or 953-574), which makes two runs daily from the airport to Antigua and continues on once a day to Panajachel. Because their schedule is constantly changing, be sure to ask for a current schedule at the information desk inside the terminal. The trip takes two hours, due to numerous stops at Guatemala City hotels. In Antigua, the minibus drops passengers at several of the top hotels. The fare of Q35 ($7) to Antigua is considerably more than that of a local bus leaving from downtown (see below), but it is only about a quarter of the taxi fare to Antigua. If there are four of you, you might want to look into hiring a taxi. The official fare is Q125 ($25).

BY BUS Unfortunately, because intercity bus routes are handled by dozens of bus companies, there is no single terminal at which you will arrive. You have to know which company you are traveling with to know where you will be arriving. The list of bus companies, routes, and times at the end of this chapter should help you to figure out where you are when you arrive. Then you can walk to your destination (fairly easy in most cases if you're not carrying too much luggage and can find an intersection with both street names posted), catch a local bus (difficult because buses must use streets outside the main hotel and restaurant district), or hail a taxi (easiest). In the general chaos and disorientation of your first arrival in Guatemala, I suggest that you take a cab, even if you're on the tightest of budgets. It will save you much frustration and aggravation. Be sure to agree on a fare before getting into the cab. I have found that most taxi drivers in Guatemala City are pretty honest about their fares. Tipping is not necessary.

BY CAR If you're driving into Guatemala City, you'll probably come in on the Carretera al Atlántico or the Pan American Highway. There are few signs when you come into town on the former: You suddenly find yourself no longer on a highway and surrounded by traffic. The heart of the city is to the south (left). Your best bet is to take 8a Avenida into downtown. If you're coming in on the Pan American Highway, just continue straight into town, following the signs, and you'll find yourself on 5a Avenida. There is also a ring road (Anillo Periférico) that will help you avoid downtown if you just want to get around the city. To connect between the Carretera al Atlántico and Pan American Highway, take the ring road around the north side of the city.

Most of Guatemala is easy to drive in, with good, uncrowded roads and fairly courteous drivers. All that changes in the capital, where streets are narrow and crowded or wide and fast.

TOURIST INFORMATION

Contact **INGUAT**, the **Instituto Guatemalteco de Turismo** (Guatemalan Tourist Commission), 7a Av. 1-17, Zona 4 (tel. 311-333 or 311-347), in the Centro Cívico (Civic Center) complex. The entrance to the INGUAT building, marked by a blue-and-white sign bearing the letter *i*, is just south of the railroad viaduct on 7a Avenida. It's open weekdays from 8am to 4pm, on Saturday from 8am to 1pm; closed Sunday.

CITY LAYOUT

MAIN ARTERIES AND STREETS Although Guatemala City is the largest city in all Central America, most visitors need to familiarize themselves with only a small portion of it. Plaza Mayor, between 5a and 7a avenidas and 6a and 8a calles, is the heart of the city. From here south on 6a Avenida, you'll find the city's greatest concentration of stores. The sidewalks are always jammed with pedestrians and vendors. Most of the buses you will want to use run on 7a and 10a avenidas. Avenida La Reforma, which is the most attractive avenue in the city, is a southern extension of 10a Avenida and divides Zona 9 and Zona 10.

FINDING AN ADDRESS The street-numbering system in Guatemala City, at least within the downtown area, is logical and easy to use. Once you get the hang of it, you'll be on your way to the exact location of any hotel or restaurant. Avenidas run roughly north to south, and calles run east to west. Addresses are given in the following form: 2a Av. 4-17, which means that the place you're after is on 2nd Avenida, at 4th Calle, number 17 (2a is "Spanish" for 2nd, 3a for 3rd; however, after 10, numbers are simply written 11, 12, and so on). You can even tell what side of the street the building will be on. If the street number is even, it'll be on the right side; if the number is odd, it'll be on the left—as you walk along the avenida toward higher-numbered calles. You can guess, then, that 3a Av. 5-78 will be on 3rd Avenida between 5th and 6th calles (closer to 6th, as the house number is a high one) on the right side. Once you get the hang of it, you'll find that it's a marvelous system. Unfortunately, the city sprawls beyond the practical limits of the plan, so you find within the downtown area an address such as 14 Av. "A" 2-31, 14—"A" being a short street or alley between, and parallel to, 14th and 15th avenidas. Outside the downtown area of the capital, you'll also run into diagonales, rutas, vias, and other designations.

In an attempt to remedy this situation, all addresses in Guatemala City also have a "zona" designation. A zona is a section of the city. Most of downtown is within Zona 1. The system works well here, but when you cross into another zona, you may find that the numbering system has started all over again. Such is the case in Zona 10. Here you may find the address 4a Av. 16-27, Zona 10, but there may also be a 4a Av. 16-27, Zona 1. Always be sure that you are in the right zona.

NEIGHBORHOODS IN BRIEF   **Zona 1** is the downtown shopping, hotel, and restaurant district. Starting at the Plaza Mayor in the north, Zona 1 extends to the Centro Cívico in the south.

Zonas 9 and 10 are the prettiest residential neighborhoods and flank Guatemala City's **Zona Viva,** the upscale hotel, restaurant, nightlife, and boutique district. The Zona Viva centers around the wide Avenida La Reforma, the capital's most attractive avenue and actually the southern continuation of 10a Avenida. Avenida La Reforma divides zonas 9 and 10, with Zona 9 to the west and Zona 10 to the east. It's here that you'll find most of the city's well-to-do residents, as well as the best hotels, the most important embassies, various corporate headquarters, and also several of the city's finest museums.

Zona 13, in the southern part of the city, is where you'll find the large Parque Aurora, just west of the airport. The park holds Guatemala City's museums of modern art, archeology, and natural history, as well as its zoo, hippodrome (racetrack), and a government crafts market. There's also an amusement park amid towering, shady trees. It's a pleasant place.

STREET MAPS   The tourist office and car-rental agencies have free or very inexpensive maps of Guatemala City.

3. GETTING AROUND

BY BUS

Public buses in Guatemala City are incredibly cheap—only 40 centavos (8¢). However, city buses are rolling wrecks, often without windows and desperately in need of paint, muffler work, seat cushions, and the like. At busy times they can be wall-to-wall in human flesh. Bus stops are not well marked. But outside of peak times, for all their discomforts and unsightliness, these buses do provide very cheap and quite convenient transportation up and down the long north-to-south avenidas.

To reach Parque Aurora, take bus no. 6, which leaves from 8a Calle across the park from the National Palace. The bus travels down 8a Avenida to 18 Calle, and you can pick it up anywhere along its route. Bus no. 5 ("Parque Aurora"), which travels up and down avenidas 5, 7, and 8, will also get you there. It's a 20-minute trip; get off the bus two stops after you pass the zoo, and you'll find the museums on your left. Keep in mind that there are two no. 5 buses—the red no. 5 and the black no. 5—and only the black no. 5 goes to Parque Aurora and the airport.

Bus routes are subject to change, so the best course is to ask a hotel clerk, shopkeeper, police officer, or passerby which bus to take to your destination.

BY TAXI

Taxis are surprisingly expensive in this city, with an average ride in town costing around $3 or $4—almost the same as in a large American city. A taxi to the airport is Q35 ($7).

ON FOOT

You will probably find yourself doing a lot of walking in Guatemala City—and it won't be easy. The sidewalks are crowded, the traffic is loud, and diesel exhaust fumes fill the air. Buses run primarily north to south and vice versa; if you're going east to west or vice versa, you'll have to hoof it. I have chosen hotels and restaurants for their proximity to one another so as to minimize your time on the streets. All the city's major sights are out along the Avenida La Reforma and in the Parque Aurora, which are both a long bus ride from downtown.

BY CAR

International car-rental agencies with desks at La Aurora Airport and in downtown Guatemala City include **Avis,** 12 Calle 2-73, Zona 9 (tel. 316-990; tel. toll free in the U.S. 800/331-1212); **Budget,** Avenida La Reforma 15-00, Zona 9 (tel. 316-546; tel. toll free in the U.S. 800/527-0700); **Dollar Rent a Car,** Avenida La Reforma 6-14, Zona 9 (tel. 348-285; tel. toll free in the U.S. 800/800-4000); **Hertz,** 7a Avenida 14-76, Zona 9 (tel. 322-242; tel. toll free in the U.S. 800/654-3131); and **National Car Rental,** 14 Calle 1-42, Zona 10 (tel. 680-175; tel. toll free in the U.S. 800/227-7368).

You will save a considerable amount if you make your reservation in your home country at least two weeks ahead of time. Weekly rates for such advance bookings are around $300 dollars, including tax and insurance for the smallest car available. This same car will cost you between $350 and $400 a week if you book it when you're already in Guatemala.

Daily rates are higher than weekly; about $50 or $60 a day when you add in fees, insurance, mileage charges, and gas. Also, you cannot get insurance to cover all losses by collision or theft. You will usually be liable for something like $600 to $1,500 on any car, unless you take an additional insurance at about $2 per day. This extra insurance reduces your responsibilities to about $250. This is scary, but if you take precautions (park the car in a safe space at night and so forth) things should work out all right.

The minimum age for renting a car is usually 25 years; have a valid driver's license with you, as well as your passport and credit card.

It is not unusual for all the rental cars in the city to be booked up, so you'd be well advised to reserve in advance. If the big companies have no more cars, try calling **Tabarini Rent-a-Car,** 2a Calle "A" 7-30, Zona 10 (tel. 316-108), or **Tally Renta Autos,** 7a Av. 14-60, Zona 1 (tel. 514-113 or 23-327). The cheapest vehicles these companies offer are pickup trucks, which rent for around $45 including insurance and 100 free kilometers (62 miles).

FAST GUATEMALA CITY

American Express The American Express office (the only one in the country) is located at Avenida La Reforma 9-00, Zona 9 (tel. 311-311 or 347-463). Open weekdays only.

Area Code The area code for Guatemala City is 5022.

Bookstores The Book Exchange, 12 Calle 6-14, Zona 9 (tel. 319-923), has a good selection of books in English and Spanish, but you'll do better to do your book shopping in Antigua.

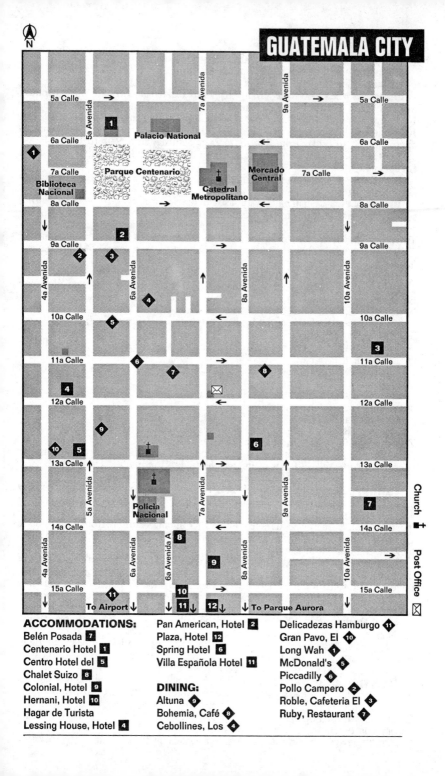

GUATEMALA CITY

N

5a Calle
7a Avenida
9a Avenida
5a Calle

5a Avenida
6a Calle
1
6a Calle

Palacio National

7a Calle
Biblioteca Nacional
1
Parque Centenario
Mercado Central
7a Calle

Catedral Metropolitano
8a Calle
8a Calle

9a Calle
2
4a Avenida
9a Calle
2
3
6a Avenida

4
8a Avenida

10a Calle
5
10a Calle

11a Calle
6
3
11a Calle
10a Avenida
7
8

4
12a Calle
12a Calle

9
6
13a Calle
10
5
13a Calle

Policia Nacional
5a Avenida
7a Avenida
9a Avenida

14a Calle
7
14a Calle
4a Avenida
6a Avenida
8
6a Avenida A
8a Avenida
10a Avenida

9

15a Calle
11
10
15a Calle
To Airport
11
12
To Parque Aurora

Church ✠
Post Office ✉

ACCOMMODATIONS:
Belén Posada **7**
Centenario Hotel **1**
Centro Hotel del **5**
Chalet Suizo **8**
Colonial, Hotel **9**
Hernani, Hotel **10**
Hagar de Turista
Lessing House, Hotel **4**

Pan American, Hotel **2**
Plaza, Hotel **12**
Spring Hotel **6**
Villa Española Hotel **11**

DINING:
Altuna **9**
Bohemia, Café **8**
Cebollines, Los **4**

Delicadezas Hamburgo **11**
Gran Pavo, El **10**
Long Wah **1**
McDonald's **5**
Piccadilly **6**
Pollo Campero **2**
Roble, Cafeteria El **3**
Ruby, Restaurant **7**

Car Rentals See "Getting Around" in this chapter.

Climate See "When to Go" in Chapter 8.

Crime See "*Safety*," below.

Currency Exchange Many banks in Guatemala City are open Monday through Friday between 8:30 or 9am and 7 or 8pm and on Saturday between 9 or 10am and 1 or 2pm. The Banco del Quetzal, also called Banquetzal, has an office at 10a Calle 6-28, Zona 1 (tel. 512-153 or 512-055), near the Hotel Ritz Continental—open Monday to Friday from 8:30am to 7pm, Saturday from 9am to 1pm.

Dentist Contact your embassy for a list of English-speaking dentists in Guatemala City.

Doctors Contact your embassy for a list of English-speaking doctors in Guatemala City.

Drugstores Guatemala City uses a duty-pharmacy (*farmacia de turno*) system. Ask for directions to the nearest pharmacy, then look in the window for the address and telephone number of the nearby pharmacy that is open that day or night. Two conveniently located drugstores are the Pharmacia Klee, 6a Avenida and 12 Calle, Zona 1 (tel. 23-905 or 20-060); and the one at 6a Avenida and 14 Calle, Zona 1 (tel. 23-906).

Embassies and Consulates Canada: Embassy and consulate, 7a Av. 11-59, Zona 9, Edificio Galerías España (tel. 321-411 or 321-413). United Kingdom: Embassy and consulate, 7a Av. 5-10, Zona 4 Edificio Centro Financiero, Torre 11, Nivel 7 (tel. 321-612 or 321-604).

United States: Embassy and consulate, Avenida La Reforma 7-01, Zona 10 (tel. 311-541 or 311-555).

Emergencies For fire department call 123; for the national police call 120; for an ambulance call 125.

Eyeglasses Get your glasses repaired or replaced at Nacional Optica, 6a Av. 14-55, Zona 1.

Hairdressers/Barbers Salon Ramiro, 5a Av. 140-02, Zona 1, is a conveniently located hairdresser.

Holidays See "When to Go" in Chapter 8.

Hospitals Two good private hospitals are the Centro Medico, 6a Av. 3-47, Zona 10 (tel. 323-555), and Hospital Herrera Llerandi, 6a Av. 8-71, Zona 10 (tel. 366-771 or 366-775). For the names and addresses of others, consult your embassy or consulate or the *Yellow Pages* of the telephone directory under "Hospitales."

Information See "Tourist Information" in this chapter.

Laundry/Dry Cleaning First check with your hotel—most offer laundry service and can tell you where the nearest dry cleaner (*lavanderia seca*) is located. If you still need to find someplace, try these two: Lavanderia Cisne, Ruta 7, 7-34, Zona 4 (tel. 316-756), is open weekdays from 8am to 7pm and Saturday from 8am to 6pm; Centro, 9a Calle 6-65, Zona 1 (tel. 24-641), is open weekdays from 8am to 1pm and 3 to 7pm, Saturday from 8am to 2pm.

Libraries Biblioteca Nacional, 4a Avenida and 8a Calle, doesn't have much of interest unless you're a student who wants to do research. It's an incredibly large building. The student library is on the 5a Avenida side off 8a Calle, and as you enter you'll notice a controversial, high-relief sculpture done by artist Efraín Recinos. To the right is Centenario Park, where the Declaration of Independence was signed.

Lost Property You can contact the police or tourist office, but neither is really set up to handle lost and found.

Luggage Storage Your only choice if you want to leave a bag is to ask at your hotel; if you need to leave the bag for only a few hours, ask at the INGUAT (Tourist Information Center), 7a Av. 1-17, Zona 4.

Newspapers/Magazines Try the lobbies of major hotels for current editions of U.S. newspapers and magazines. They usually have *USA Today*, the *International Herald Tribune*, the *New York Times*, *Time*, and *Newsweek*. Guatemala's most popular daily newspaper is *Prensa Libre*, in which you'll find information on cultural events around town.

Photographic Needs There are one-hour to 24-hour film processing centers all over downtown these days, but I still recommend waiting until you get home to have your processing done. Film is expensive.

Police   See "Emergencies," above.

Post Office   The central post office is at the corner of 12 Calle and 7a Avenida in Zona 1—open weekdays from 8am to 6pm, Saturday from 8am to 3pm; closed Sunday. It has no sign to identify it. Look for the men selling postcards in large racks—that's the front door. Other post offices are generally open weekdays from 7:30am to 12:30pm and 1 to 2:30pm.

Radio/TV   Marimba is the national music and is heard on many radio stations. Many hotels now have satellites and offer U.S. programming.

Religious Services   Guatemala is a Roman Catholic country, in which there are dozens of Catholic churches, many of them old and beautiful. Some conveniently located churches include Catedral Metropolitana, 7a Avenida between 6a and 8a calles, Zona 1; Capuchinas, 10a Avenida and 10a Calle, Zona 1; and Nuestra Señora de la Merced, 11 Avenida and 5a Calle, Zona 1.

Restrooms   In Guatemala, public restrooms are called *servicios* or *servicios sanitarios*. Men are *caballeros* and women are *damas*. There aren't many public toilets around, but you will find them in restaurants and the lobbies of large hotels.

Safety   Guatemala City is very urban, with all the problems you would expect in a densely populated area. Petty crime and armed robberies are on the rise here so it's a good idea not to walk the streets alone after dark. Even daytime crime is on the rise, so don't carry large amounts of cash on your person. Take extra precautions with your money, credit cards, traveler's checks, and passport whenever you are out, especially if you are in a market or a crowded bus or on a busy sidewalk. It is best to wear a money belt large enough to hold your money and passport under your clothes. I like the type that you wear around your neck; they're easier to get at when you need them. Carry only as much cash as you think you'll need when venturing out of your hotel and try to keep it in a buttoned pocket so you don't have to pull your money belt out in public. The areas around 7a Avenida and 18 Calle and 18 Calle between 4a Avenida and 8a Avenida are well known as haunts of pickpockets, so try to avoid these areas. If you are driving a car, never park it on the street. There are plenty of public parking lots available for only a few cents an hour. Look for signs reading *estacionamentos*.

Taxes   The 17% hotel tax is included in hotel room rates quoted in this book.

Taxis   See "Getting Around" in this chapter.

Telegrams   To send a telegram dial 127. International telegrams are handled by the Guatel, the Guatemalan telephone company. The main office is at 7a Avenida 12-39, Zona 1 (tel. 80-598). All other telegrams are handled by post offices.

Telephones   Most telephone numbers in Guatemala City have six digits, but a few old ones have only five. Special information and emergency numbers have only three digits. For intercity long-distance calls, dial 121; for international calls, dial 171. Directory assistance is 124; the correct time is 126. A pay phone in Guatemala is called a *telefono monedero*.

Water   Although the tap water in the capital is chlorinated and presumably safe, it's probably a good idea to stick to bottled mineral water, soft drinks, wine, beer, and the like.

4. WHERE TO STAY

Just as you would expect in a large cosmopolitan city, Guatemala City has a wide variety of hotels in various price categories. Those at the low end of the budget tend to be concentrated in the area within a few blocks of 6a Avenida between 6a Calle and 16 Calle in Zona 1. You'll find a couple at the top end of your budget in Zona 4, but nearly all of the city's luxury hotels are in zonas 9 and 10. It is relatively safe (though street crime is on the rise), but Zona 1 is hardly what you might call an attractive neighborhood, and there is little of interest to see or do. Most visitors to Guatemala spend as little time as possible in the capital, and I suggest you follow suit. However, if you're forced to spend a night here, try these suggestions.

DOUBLES FOR LESS THAN Q75 [$15]

CHALET SUIZO, 14 Calle 6-82, Zona 1, Guatemala City. Tel. 502/513-786. 44 rms (13 with bath).
$ Rates: Q46 ($9.20) single; Q61.50–Q87.75 ($12.30–$17.55) double; Q79–Q105.30 ($15.80–$21.05) triple; higher prices are for rooms with baths. No credit cards.

The Chalet Suizo is a longtime favorite of budget travelers. Though there are a few older rooms left in the hotel, most rooms are either new or remodeled. Shared bathrooms are large and clean, while private bathrooms are not quite so roomy. Street-side rooms can be a bit noisy; the quieter rooms with shared bath happen to be the oldest rooms. The entire hotel also seems to have a mosquito problem, but nonetheless the Chalet Suizo is still a good choice. There is a small café just inside the front door, and in the evenings, Indian women sell huipiles and traditional textiles.

HOTEL HERNANI, 15 Calle 6-56, Zona 1, Guatemala City. Tel. 502/22-839. 20 rms.
$ Rates: Q21.10 ($4.20) single; Q35.10 ($7) double; Q49.10 ($9.80) triple. No credit cards.
This dignified small hotel in a fairly good location is another fine choice for those watching every penny. Many rooms here have private bathrooms, but the baths are separate from the rooms—the bathroom down the hall is yours only, but it's not connected to your room.

HOGAR DEL TURISTA, 11 Calle 10-43, Zona 1, Guatemala City. Tel. 502/25-522. 10 rms (all with bath).
$ Rates: Q70.20 ($14.05) single; Q93.60 ($18.70) double; Q117.00 ($23.40). No credit cards accepted. **Parking:** Free.
The street may look rather depressing and industrial, but once inside the hotel you'll forget the outside world. A simple converted city house, the Hogar del Turista is very popular with budget travelers. Two narrow courtyards provide light and sun, and two bright, pleasant local ladies keep everything clean. Native blankets cover the beds, and Guatemalan crafts decorate the walls. Most rooms have windows opening onto the courtyards to provide light, but there are a few dolorous rooms without any windows at all. Breakfast can be had for Q15–Q20 ($3–$4).

HOTEL LESSING HOUSE, 12 Calle 4-35, Zona 1, Guatemala City. Tel. 502/513-891. 8 rms (all with bath).
$ Rates: Q23.40 ($4.70) single; Q35.10 ($7) double; Q46.80 ($9.35) triple. No credit cards.

Located on one of the better streets in downtown Guatemala City, the tiny Lessing House is tucked into a narrow building that is easy to miss. The rooms here all sport a bit of local crafts for decoration, which helps the hotel seem a bit better than basic. Each room has two or three beds and a private bathroom with hot-water shower.

SPRING HOTEL, 8a Avenida 12-65, Zona 1, Guatemala City. Tel. 502/ 26-637, 514-207, or 514-876. 29 rms (11 with bath).

$ Rates: Q23.80 ($4.75) single without bath; Q38.71 ($7.75) double without bath, Q47.85 ($9.50) double with bath. DC, MC, V.

A fairly good location, decent rooms in an old-style building converted for use as a hotel, and a sunny little courtyard make this an acceptable rock-bottom choice. The rooms are not fancy and might have a bit of peeling paint, but they are large.

DOUBLES FOR LESS THAN Q175 [$35]

POSADA BELEN, 13 Calle "A" 10-30, Zona 1, Guatemala City. Tel. 502/29-226, 534-530, or 513-478. 9 rms (all with bath).

$ Rates: Q130 ($26) single; Q155 ($31) double; Q175 ($35) triple; lower rates in May and September. AE, MC, V.

This small family run pension has long enjoyed an excellent reputation. Since the Belen is on a little downtown side street, its rooms are quiet, and the quiet is further encouraged by a policy of discouraging guests with children under five years of age. The pension has a charming, sunny courtyard with tropical plants; parrots; a fountain; much wrought-iron decoration; many fine examples of local textiles, including weavings and native blankets; a cozy breakfast room; and a rack of used books for exchange. The price is a bit high, but the Belen is certainly a unique place. The rooms are attractively appointed with lots of local arts and crafts. There are even skylights in the bathrooms. Francesca Sanchinelli, your hostess, speaks excellent English.

Breakfast and lunch are served; if you let them know in advance, dinner also is served. Prices range from Q15 ($3) for a continental breakfast to Q45 ($9) for a full dinner. Add 7% to your bill if you're paying by credit card.

HOTEL CENTENARIO, 6a Calle 5-33, Zona 1, Guatemala City. Tel. 502/80-381 to 80-383. Fax 502/82-039. 43 rms (all with bath).

$ Rates: Q111.15 ($22.25) single; Q134.55 ($26.90) double; Q157.95 ($31.60) triple. AE, DC, MC, V.

Want to stay right near the National Palace? This old-fashioned hotel is right on the main square, almost next door to the National Palace. Built at least 50 years ago, the Centenario has been well maintained and recently redecorated. It's a modest place, but the staff is particularly helpful, providing carafes of drinking water, free ice, maps of the city, and pocket calendars. The rooms are simple but nice enough, many with good beds (often there's a double and a single bed in a room). The private baths have showers that are well worn but tidy.

HOTEL COLONIAL, 7a Avenida 14-19, Zona 1, Guatemala City. Tel. 502/26-722, 22-955, or 81-208. 42 rms (34 with bath).

$ Rates: Q60 ($12) single without bath, Q83.25 ($16.65) single with bath; Q83.25 ($16.65) double without bath, Q107.45 ($21.50) double with bath; Q107.45 ($21.50) triple without bath, Q131.40 ($26.30) triple with bath. No credit cards.

If you'd like to stay in a grand old mansion converted into a hotel, try the Colonial. The pleasant interior court has been covered over with translucent plastic panels to let the sun in but to keep the rain out; the walls are of

IMPRESSIONS

I could see the volcanoes from the window of my hotel room . . . They were tall volcanoes and looked capable of spewing lava. Their beauty was undeniable; but it was the beauty of witches. The rumbles from their fires had heaved this city down.
—PAUL THEROUX, THE OLD PATAGONIA EXPRESS, 1979

frighteningly tactile stucco; and the parlor is furnished in ponderous neocolonial pieces. The guest rooms gleam and shine—there is nothing tattered or worn here. Carved bedsteads and huge old wardrobes, although not antique, are properly colonial. Most rooms have baths, and some rooms are more luxurious than others, so examine several before taking your pick.

WORTH THE EXTRA BUCKS

HOTEL DEL CENTRO, 13 Calle 4-55, Zona 1, Guatemala City. Tel. 502/81-281 or 81-282. Fax 502/22-705. 60 rms (all with bath) TV
$ Rates: Q210.60 ($42.12) single; Q228.15 ($45.65) double; Q245.70 ($49.15) triple. AE, DC, MC, V.

(S) If you can spend a bit more, this is perhaps the all-around best place to stay when considering its location, services, comforts, and price. A five-story building with colonial-inspired modern decor, the Del Centro has all the comforts and conveniences—from thick carpets and plush furniture to large, light, and airy guest rooms with two double beds, separate seating areas, big color TVs, and small but new and very clean tile bathrooms. Although there is a bit of street noise, this hotel offers one of the best values in the city and has been doing so dependably for several decades.

In the Del Centro's second-floor restaurant, a typical daily special meal might be soup, German-style pork chops, potatoes and fresh vegetables, dessert, and coffee for Q20 ($4), plus drink, tax, and tip.

HOTEL PAN AMERICAN, 9a Calle 5-63, Zona 1, Guatemala City. Tel. 502/26-807, 26-808, or 26-809. Fax 502/26-402. 60 rms (all with bath). TV TEL
$ Rates: Q280.75 ($56.15) single; Q321.75 ($64.35) double; Q362.75 ($72.55) triple. AE, DC, MC, V. **Parking:** Q5 ($1).

(★) This is a colonial-style hotel in the very midst of Zona 1. The spacious interior courtyard is now covered, equipped with a fountain, decorated with framed huipiles, and set with tables and chairs to serve as a dining area. Waiters and waitresses are in traditional country garb. With the soothing sound of water from the fountain, it's a very enjoyable place for lunch. In keeping with the 1930s decor, there is one elevator, manned by an operator, to take you upstairs. The rooms seem not to have changed much since the hotel's heyday and, although quite clean and tidy, are still furnished the same way. If you're an art deco aficionado, you'll be in heaven. The clean private bathrooms have tubs and showers, and each room has a large cable color TV. Rooms facing the street can be noisy, but those overlooking the courtyard are quiet.

Even if you don't plan to stay here, come by for the set-price lunch, which might be a Guatemalan plate of chuchitos (tamales à la Chichicastenango), black beans, and fried bananas; a tropical fruit plate; or a beef pot roast. The portions are huge, and the prices are a reasonable Q30 ($6) to Q50 ($10), plus drink, tax, and tip.

HOTEL PLAZA, Via 7, 6-16, Zona 4, Guatemala City. Tel. 502/316-337 or 310-396. 64 rms (all with bath).
$ Rates: Q257.40 ($51.50) single; Q292.50 ($58.50) double; Q327.60 ($65.50) triple. AE, DC, MC, V.

(S) The Plaza is not downtown, but in Zona 4, south of the Civic Center. It's located just off busy 7a Avenida, but most of the rooms are quiet. This pleasant hostelry might best be described as a Spanish Bauhaus motel, with echoes of old Spain coming through the clean lines and curves of the Bauhaus idiom—you'll see what I mean. Two motel-style floors are arranged facing the enclosed parking lot or the courtyard's heated swimming pool. The guest rooms are comfy and well kept, with good baths. The Plaza is within walking distance of the Zona 4 bus terminal if your bags are light; you will have to ask your way frequently to get through the maze of streets. Ask for Septima Avenida, and once you get to that major avenue, the Plaza isn't far away. There's a nice restaurant and bar where a meal will run around Q25 ($5).

HOTEL VILLA ESPAÑOLA, 2a Calle 7-51, Zona 9, Guatemala City. Tel. 502/323-362, 323-381, or 318-503. 64 rms, 3 suites (all with bath). TEL
$ Rates: Q257.40 ($51.50) single; Q292.50 ($58.50) double. AE, DC, MC, V.
Parking: Free.

This Spanish colonial–style motel, just south of downtown in Zona 4, could easily have been transported from a Texas interstate. All the expected amenities are here, except the swimming pool. Rooms are carpeted and have one or two double beds. For a little bit extra, you get a TV in your room. You'll even find a tub in the bathroom, not just a shower. There is also laundry service.

Down in the bright basement of the hotel, you'll find a large dining room decorated with colonial reproductions. The menu, which features both Guatemalan and international cuisine, is varied and reasonably priced—with meals ranging from about Q25 ($5) to Q75 ($15). There is also a small bar down here.

5. WHERE TO EAT

For the best food at the best price in the most pleasant surroundings, the thing to do in Guatemala City is to dine at one of the better hotels. The Hotel Del Centro and the Hotel Pan American all have good dining rooms serving tasty food in large portions at surprisingly reasonable prices, usually around Q25 ($5) to Q50 ($10) for an entire meal. Refer to the descriptions of those hotels given above for details. For more reasonably priced meals, you might try the following.

MEALS FOR LESS THAN Q20 [$4]

DELICADEZAS HAMBURGO, 15 Calle 5-34, Zona 1. Tel. 81-627.
  Cuisine: GUATEMALAN/GERMAN.
$ Prices: Breakfasts Q3–Q8 (60¢–$1.60), main dishes Q9–Q32 ($1.80–$6.40). No credit cards.
  Open: Daily 7am–10pm.

On the south side of the always busy Parque Concordia you'll find this typical Guatemalan diner. The lunch counter and display case full of rainbow Jell-O may say small town America, but the menu is sprinkled with German dishes—a reminder of old German coffee-growing days. Service is surprisingly good. Try the garlic soup if you're a fan of the fragrant cloves.

RESTAURANT LONG WAH, 6a Calle 3-70, Zona 1. Tel. 26-611.
  Cuisine: CHINESE.
$ Prices: Main dishes Q11–Q24 ($2.20–$4.80). No credit cards.
  Open: Daily 11am–11pm.

This noisy restaurant is in the midst of Guatemala City's tiny Chinatown district, a few blocks west of the Parque Central on 6a Calle at 4a Avenida, along with several other Chinese restaurants bearing names such as Felicidades and Palacio Real and China Hilton. The five rooms at the Long Wah, done in the predictable gold lanterns, red booths, and black wainscoting, are often bustling with diners out for a change of pace. Adapt the Spanish transliterations on the menu slightly, and you'll see that "chaw mein" is chow mein, "wantan" is wonton, and so forth. The most expensive dishes are those with shrimp for Q24 ($4.80). Beer is served.

RESTAURANTE PICCADILLY, 6a Avenida 11-01, Zona 1. Tel. 511-468.
  Cuisine: ITALIAN.

$ Prices: Pasta Q6.10–Q7.25 ($1.20–$1.45); pizza Q9.95–Q17.95 ($2–$3.60); main dishes Q11.75–Q17.95 ($2.35–$3.60). No credit cards.
Open: Daily 7am–midnight.

Watch for the take-out window at the corner of 11 Calle and 6a Avenida. You can grab a slice of pizza to go for only Q1.40 (30¢), or you can take a seat inside amid modern decor. A red neon sign glares on the wall of the first dining room, but the back room is more subdued. In addition to the Italian dishes, there are also shish kebabs and burgers. The spaghetti al pesto, though light on basil, is still quite good.

RESTAURANT RUBY, 11 Calle 6-56, Zona 1. Tel. 26-438.
Cuisine: CHINESE.
$ Prices: Main dishes Q8–Q20 ($1.60–$4). No credit cards.
Open: Daily noon–8:45pm.

For Chinese food closer to the Hotel Ritz Continental, try Ruby. The menu is suitably bewildering, running to 133 items, but the special plates (large or small) give you samplers of the best items. Ruby is one high-ceilinged corridor, a lunch counter, and several rear dining rooms that are always busy. The menu is in Chinese, Spanish, and English, and a number of new-world dishes make it into the list.

MEALS FOR LESS THAN Q30 [$6]

RESTAURANT ALTUNA, 5a 12-31, Zona 1. Tel. 20-669.
Cuisine: SPANISH.
$ Prices: Main dishes Q16–Q40 ($3.20–$8). AE, DC, MC, V.
Open: Tues–Sun noon–4pm and 6:30–11:30pm.

Just a few steps north of the Hotel Del Centro is a big restaurant with lots of dining rooms done in European style—with dark-wood furniture, white tablecloths, and formal but pleasant and unobtrusive decor. The service is smooth and polished, and the specialties are Spanish cuisine and seafood, with fish and squid, shrimp, steaks, chicken, and even doves cooked in sherry on the menu. A full meal here, all included, will come to about Q35 ($7) per person. Popular with local businesspeople at lunch.

LOS CEBOLLINES, 6a Avenida 9-75, Zona 1. Tel. 27-750.
Cuisine: MEXICAN.
$ Prices: Appetizers Q3.50–Q10 (70¢–$2); main dishes Q5.50–Q15.95 ($1.10–$3.20). No credit cards.
Open: Mon–Sat 6am–midnight, Sun 6am–10pm.

This restaurant, one of a popular chain, takes its name from the grilled green onions that are served with almost every dish. According to legend cebollines were first served to Pancho Villa, who went nuts for them. My favorite way to dine here is to order from the long appetizer list, trying whatever sounds different or unusual. When I'm full I stop trying new dishes. I've never gone wrong. More traditional diners will find a wide range of regional Mexican cuisines, including Especialedades Norteños—burritos, fajitas, Mexipizza, and Mexiburguesas. The mixed drinks here come in huge glasses and there always seems to be a daily drink special.

EL GRAN PAVO, 13 Calle 4-41, Zona 1. Tel. 510-933 or 29-912.
Cuisine: MEXICAN.
$ Prices: Main dishes Q20–Q40 ($4–$8). AE, DC, MC, V.
Open: Daily 9am–12:30am.

Plain but clean and cheerful, El Gran Pavo (the "big turkey") adjoins the Hotel Del Centro and is fairly large, with several dining rooms. A long menu tries admirably to cover every variety of Mexican cuisine, from Veracruz seafood and mole poblano through panuchos yucatecos to cabrito al horno. The antojito (appetizer) menu alone is enough to keep adventurous diners busy for weeks. The range of prices is as wide as the menu selections. A big Mexican combination plate, drink, tax, and tip will cost about Q30 ($6). That unusual beribboned umbrella just inside the door is actually a design based on a Guatemalan kite. There's another branch on 12 Calle 6-54, Zona 9 (tel. 313-976).

SPECIALTY DINING

A LOCAL BUDGET BET

CAFETERÍA EL ROBLE, 9a Calle 5-46, Zona 1. No phone.
  Cuisine: GUATEMALAN.
$ Prices: Q4.50–Q6 (90¢–$1.20). No credit cards.
  Open: Mon–Sat 8:30am–6pm.

If your budget is really low, take a look at this little place across from the entrance to the Hotel Pan American. A cafetería in Guatemala is not a place where you stand in line with a tray while a surly food-service worker ladles unidentifiable stuff onto your plate. There are cafeterías all over town; they're where local office workers go when they're tired of fried chicken and burgers. This clean little café is nothing fancy, but you can get breakfast here for less than a dollar and lunch for only slightly more.

FAST-FOOD CHAINS

Guatemala City has a full assortment of international fast-food restaurants. Downtown along 6a Avenida, you'll find **McDonald's** (also at 10a Calle and 5a Avenida), **Burger King,** and even **Taco Bell.** There are also plenty of local fast-food restaurants serving hamburgers, hot dogs, and fried chicken. The following is one of the most popular fast-food chains in Guatemala.

POLLO CAMPERO, 9a Calle and 5a Avenida, Zona 1. No phone.
  Cuisine: CHICKEN.
$ Prices: Full meal Q7.20–Q12 ($1.45–$2.40). No credit cards.
  Open: Daily 7:30am–10:30pm.

Imitations of Colonel Sanders' eateries have sprung up all over Guatemala in recent years. For a taste of fried chicken Guatemalan-style, seek out a branch of Pollo Campero, which is bright and cheery with orange-and-yellow tables and burnt-orange floor tiles. You'll feel as though you're back home at your favorite chicken restaurant. A lunch consisting of two pieces of chicken, french fries, and a soft drink or coffee costs Q9 ($1.80); supper, with one more piece of chicken plus salad, costs Q12 ($2.40). There are branches at 6a Avenida and 15 Calle, Zona 1 and 8a Calle 9-29, Zona 1.

PASTRIES

CAFÉ BOHEMIA, 11 Calle 8-48. Tel. 82-474.
  Cuisine: PASTRIES.
$ Prices: 30 centavos–Q2 (6¢–40¢). No credit cards.
  Open: Mon–Fri 8:30am–6pm, Sat 8:30–noon.

When you're hungry for cakes and pastries, seek out this little café where Central European country furniture and aproned waitresses put you in the mood for the selection of bakery treats in the display cases. Coffee and pastry should cost less than a dollar; if you're a bit hungrier, you can get a ham-and-cheese sandwich, a filled croissant, or a whole cake.

6. ATTRACTIONS

The largest city in Central America, Guatemala City, spreads across a narrow plateau cut by deep ravines. The old downtown section of the city, Zona 1, is centered on the Palacio Nacional (National Palace), the Catedral Metropolitana (Metropolitan Cathedral), and the Biblioteca Nacional (National Archives and Library), all of which face the Parque Central. Start your tour here, then work your way south to see the city's other sights, all the way to the Parque Aurora, near the airport at the southern end of town in Zona 13.

SIGHT-SEEING STRATEGIES

IF YOU HAVE ONE DAY Head first to the Museum of Archeology out near the airport. Then head over to the Paseo de la Reforma area to visit the Popol Vuh Museum and the Ixchel Museum. These three museums should just about fill your day.

IF YOU HAVE TWO DAYS On your second day, visit the Mapa en Relieve and the Parque Central, where you will find the Metropolitan Cathedral and the National Palace. After lunch, stroll down 6a Avenida for a bit of shopping. You might also hop a bus and visit the Yurrita Chapel.

IF YOU HAVE THREE DAYS Visit the ruins of Kaminal Juyú on the outskirts of the city and perhaps the Museo de Artes e Industrias Populares.

IF YOU HAVE FIVE DAYS If you have this much time, you should spend at least two days in Antigua, which is much more interesting than Guatemala City and is only an hour away.

THE TOP ATTRACTIONS

MUSEO DE ARQUEOLOGÍA Y ETNOLOGÍA, Building No. 5, Parque La Aurora, Zona 13. Tel. 720-489.
   The beautiful stark-white Moorish building in Parque La Aurora is the Archeological and Ethnological Museum, which boasts the largest and most spectacular collection of Mayan carvings in the world. One of the more famous pieces now on display is the throne from Piedras Negras, which you should not miss.
   As you wander through the archeological section of the museum, you'll see beautiful black ceramic vessels from excavations in Zaculeu (Preclassic Period, A.D. 200); an outstanding collection of clay masks (Postclassic Period, A.D. 925 to 1200), and artifacts of shell, alabaster, obsidian, and flint (Classic Period, A.D. 200 to 925).
   There is also an ethnological section in the museum, with a textile room in which 150 native costumes are displayed. Moving through the other ethnological rooms, you'll see a glass rotunda exhibiting the types of dwellings the Indians used, and exhibits of nutrition (foods that originated in America) and industry (baskets, ceramics, weaving, and so on).
   Admission: Q1 (20¢).
   Open: Tues–Fri 9am–4pm; Sat–Sun 9am–noon and 2–4pm. **Bus:** Black no. 5.

MUSEO POPOL VUH, EDIFICIO GALERIA REFORMA, 6th floor, Avenida La Reforma 8-60, Zona 9. Tel. 347-121.
   In 1977 Jorge and Ella Castillo donated their personal collection of Mayan art to the Universidad Francisco Marroquin, which now cares for it in the Museo Popol Vuh, named for the sacred "painted book" of the Quiché Mayans, now known as the Dresden Codex. There is a copy of this unique book on display in the museum.
   The immense collection of Mayan art is arranged by region and period, as is a smaller collection of colonial religious and secular art. Some of the Mayan pieces are simply gorgeous: polychrome vases, huge burial urns, incense burners, and ceramic figurines. The religious art, mostly of the 16th to 18th centuries, includes some handsome altars in wood with silver trim. You'll find folk art here as well: face masks, which are still made and used in many regions, and mannequins wearing regional costumes. This collection is perhaps the finest in the city.
   There's a good museum shop here, with an excellent bookstore and a nice crafts

collection. On the ground floor in the same building is the Café Reforma, good for a light lunch, snack, or pick-me-up beverage.
Admission: Q5 ($1) adults; Q3 (60¢) college students; Q1 (20¢) secondary-school students; 25 centavos (5¢) children under 12; Q5 ($1) to take photos.
Open: Mon–Fri 9am–5pm, Sat 9am–4pm. **Bus:** Any Avenida La Reforma bus.

MUSEO IXCHEL DE TRAJE INDÍGENA (Ixchel Native Dress Museum), 4a Avenida 16-27, Zona 10. Tel. 680-713.

Ixchel, wife of the Mayan sky god Itzamna, was goddess of the moon and protectress of women in childbirth. The museum bearing her name is dedicated to the woven art of Guatemala's Mayan women and to their village life-style. It's a private, nonprofit museum established in a large house in this luxury neighborhood, within walking distance from the Museo Popol Vuh. From the Popol Vuh, walk south on Avenida La Reforma about seven blocks, past the Camino Real Hotel, and turn left (east) onto 16 Calle. Go a few blocks along 16 Calle to 4a Avenida and turn right (south), and the museum will be on your left.

The two floors of the house are filled with exquisite examples of Guatemalan traditional weaving from the various sections of the country. Artful use of mannequins has created lifelike situations that work well to give you a feeling for the creative, hardworking indigenous people of Guatemala. Several figures represent members of the cofradías, the traditional village socioreligious groups whose duties and beliefs bridge the gap between traditional Mayan and Roman Catholic religion. Other exhibits demonstrate the weaving process through the use of looms, diagrams, and photographs. There are also exhibits showing tie-dyeing, which is done in Huehuetenango and some other towns. Signs on the exhibits are in English as well as in Spanish.

On the ground floor, the museum has a nice shop selling books, crafts, and textiles.
Admission: Q5 ($1) adults; Q1 (20¢) college students; 50 centavos (10¢) children.
Open: Mon–Fri 9am–5:30pm, Sat 9am–1pm. **Bus:** Any Avenida La Reforma bus.

PALACIO NACIONAL, Plaza Mayor, 6a Calle between 6a and 7a avenidas. No phone.

The heart of Guatemala's governmental power is here in the Palacio Nacional (National Palace), built at a cost of Q2,800,000—when that amount had a much higher exchange rate than today—by Gen. José Ubico, president from 1939 to 1943. The palace has three entrances you can use; the fourth, on the back, is for VIPs, whose darkened, bulletproof cars bristling with radio antennas wait in readiness there. The main entrance facing the Parque Central is the site of exhibits that change from time to time; it's the two side entrances that will take you inside the palace. You will catch the mood of the palace as you climb the brass-and-wood stairways up through three levels of beautiful wood-beamed ceilings, hand-carved stone-and-wood columns, frescoed arches, large wrought-iron-and-glass lanterns, tile floors, and numerous murals by Alfredo Galvez Suarez. It's fascinating, with all the interest of a museum yet not so overpowering as to be an unlivable place. There's a sense of harmony about the palace which you don't often find in government buildings. The two side entrances lead up to symmetrical floors, both of which overlook separate courtyards on the ground floor.
Admission: Free.
Open: Mon–Fri 9am–5pm; Sat 10am–noon. **Bus:** Any bus that stops at Plaza Mayor.

MAPA EN RELIEVE, Parque Minerva, 11 Calle and 6a Avenida at the end of Avenida Simeon Cañas, Zona 2. No phone.

Guatemala City's Relief Map is a scale model of the entire country. It's 40 by 80 yards, with a depth of 2 yards; the proportions of the mountains (especially the volcanoes) have been exaggerated so that the topography of the country is readily apparent. You can observe the map from ground level or climb up one of the observation platforms for a look at Guatemala from the air. The major towns and features are marked by labels and little pennants. It's nice that Guatemala is small and distinct enough that such a map could be built. Francisco Vela, the engineer who created the map, had to traverse the country by donkey to collect all the information necessary to construct the map in 1904. The map is several dozen blocks to the north of the National Palace. To reach it, follow 7a Avenida north to its very end, where it joins Avenida Simeon Cañas near the Parque Minerva.

In recent years, visitors to the Relief Map have been the victims of robberies, so be sure to ask at your hotel or at the INGUAT information center if it is currently safe to visit the map. In particular, visitors are being told to avoid the observation tower.

Admission: Free.

Open: Daily 9am–5pm. **Bus:** Nos. 1 and 18.

MORE ATTRACTIONS

RUINS OF KAMINAL JUYÚ, Zona 7. Tel. 516-224.

Kaminal Juyú was a very early Mayan city (300 B.C. to A.D. 900), flourishing before the classic Mayan cities of Tikal and Palenque. The earliest people (the Miraflores) planted crops and made excellent ceramics and carved jade. They seem to have been dominated by the priestly class that held all the power. By A.D. 300 Kaminal Juyú had been conquered by the people of Teotihuacan (near Mexico City), but the rulers who came here from Mexico were "Mayanized" over the years. The remains of the Intermediate Period (the Esperanza Period), before the peoples were completely assimilated, show a strange mixture of Mayan and Teotihuacan art and culture.

The Spanish conquerors who came in the 1500s make no mention of Kaminal Juyú, probably because the city had been burned and destroyed when it was abandoned in A.D. 900. It wasn't until the late 18th century that mounds were discovered, and only in 1899 did Maudslay begin the first excavations. About 200 mounds have been found here—some from the Miraflores' time, when structures were built of adobe and pumice, others from the later Esperanza Period, when the inhabitants built pyramids and temples of limestone. Archeologists have found traces of Teotihuacan influence, such as stepped temple platforms called *tablero y talud* covered in red stucco, slit-eyed figurines, and three-legged pottery cylinders, and also of influence from Monte Alban (Tlaloc figures with large headdresses). In the tombs here were the finest jade objects found in all Guatemala, and in fact these people valued jade more than they did gold. The objects found in the tombs, which include precious stones, pottery, terra-cotta figurines, and incense burners, are in the Archeological Museum and the Museo Popol Vuh, as are the stelae carved with hieroglyphs, earlier than any stelae found in the Petén (before A.D. 290).

Urban development has covered or destroyed much of the ancient city, and what you see today are substructures of buildings from various periods, built mostly of ordinary clay and rubble. There are a few of limestone covered in a lime wash, which is not too impressive a sight.

Basically, there isn't much to see at Kaminal Juyú—a trip out here will likely be of interest only to serious archeology students.

Admission: Free.

Open: Daily 8am–6pm. **Bus:** Take bus BC, "Kaminal Juyú," to the intersection of Diagonal 24 and 24a Avenida; the entrance is just west of Diagonal 24.

CATEDRAL METROPOLITANA, Plaza Mayor, 7a Avenida between 6a and 8a calles. No phone.

Despite its look of antiquity, the Metropolitan Cathedral, on the east side of the Parque Central, was built between 1782 and 1815. The wrought-iron gates into the cathedral precincts are locked every day between 1 and 3pm (the caretaker's lunch, I suppose). Don't enter with expectations of seeing a gorgeous symphony of gleaming gold and flowery decoration. As with many Guatemalan churches, this national symbol is quite plain, even severe, inside. The Archbishop's Palace is next to the cathedral.

Admission: Free.

Open: Daily 8am–7pm. **Bus:** Any bus that stops at Plaza Mayor.

CAPILLA YURRITA, Ruta 6 8-52, Zona 4. Tel. 363-514.

Located in a newer section of town, amid car dealers and offices, this is one of the most architecturally unusual churches in Guatemala City. If you have been through this part of town already, you may have noticed the tall steeple and wondered what it was. The chapel, built in 1928, is a bizarre structure worthy of Bavaria's mad king Ludwig. It draws on numerous architectural styles, including Gothic and Russian Orthodox church architecture. Notice the work lavished on the front doors. This is a privately owned family chapel, but the public is welcome to visit.
Admission: Free.
Open: Tues–Sat 8am–noon and 3:30–6pm; Sun 8am–1pm and 4–7pm. **Bus:** Red or black no. 5.

MUSEO DE ARTES E INDUSTRIAS POPULARES, 10a Avenida 10-72, Zona 1. Tel. 80-334.

This small downtown museum is housed in an old colonial-style house. The collection includes naïve art paintings of processions and dances by Guatemalan artists. There are also examples of indigenous handcrafts, including carved and painted gourds, tin candle holders, and masks for the dances of the highland villages. There is also a large collection of antique musical instruments.
Admission: 25 centavos (5¢).
Open: Tues–Fri 9am–4pm; Sat–Sun 9am–noon and 2–4pm.

MUSEO DE HISTORIA, 9a Calle 9-70, Zona 1. Tel. 536-149.

To learn more about the history of Guatemala, stop by this museum. It has been undergoing renovation in recent years and is slowly taking on a modern appearance inside, although the exterior still looks quite decayed. The collection covers Guatemalan history from prehistory through the discovery, conquest, and colonization by Spain. Exhibits are more extensive for the period beginning after the country's independence in 1821. In these rooms you'll learn how the economic, social, and cultural life of the nation was shaped.
Admission: Free.
Open: Tues–Sun 8:30am–4pm.

MUSEO NACIONAL DE ARTE MODERNA, Building No. 6, Parque La Aurora, Zona 13. Tel. 720-467.

This small museum is located directly across the street from the Archeological Museum. The interior of the building is striking, with a high wooden rosette ceiling and white plaster walls. The museum was founded in 1934 and contains paintings and sculpture from the late 18th century up to the present. Some well-known Guatemalan painters, such as Carlos Merida and Garavito, are represented here. The historical section is smaller, the exhibit of greatest interest here being a collection of coins from the colonial period. There are sometimes temporary exhibits here that cause the permanent collection to be closed off. Call first.
Admission: Free.
Open: Tues–Fri 9am–4pm. **Bus:** Black no. 5.

CENTRO CÍVICO, 21 Calle between 6a and 7a avenidas, Zona 1.

The central part of the city holds the Centro Cívico and Ciudad Olímpica, important complexes of buildings dedicated to city and national government and to sports. This is the pride of Guatemala City because of its modern architecture. City officials claim that it is "the most advanced architecture in Latin America." The center includes the well-known (and always hopelessly crowded) Bank of Guatemala, the Social Security Building (IGSS), and Olympic City. Much of the exterior relief sculpture is the work of artists Efraín Recinos and Carlos Merida. As you enter the complex (at the intersection of 6a Avenida and Diagonal 2), you'll see a statue of a wolf with Romulus and Remus underneath; the statue is inscribed "From Eternal Rome to Immortal Guatemala." To the right as you face the statue is city hall and directly ahead of you in the distance is the Bank of Guatemala, constructed from 1962 to

1966. The high-relief murals in concrete are by Dagoberto Vasquez and depict the history of Guatemala. The Social Security Building behind city hall was designed by Roberto Aycinena and Jorge Montes; the enormous mosaic, completed in 1959, is by Carlos Merida. On the hill behind you is the Fortress of San José and the National Theater, which looks a lot like a blue-and-white ocean liner. Olympic City, farther to the east, is an enormous building that houses the Mateo Flores Stadium (named after the athlete who won the Boston Marathon in 1952), the National Gymnasium, a swimming pool, tennis courts, and a Boxing Palace.

COOL FOR KIDS

If you have your kids with you, then you should definitely plan on spending a lot of time at Parque la Aurora. The kids will definitely enjoy the amusement park and zoo and maybe even the Museum of Archeology.

WALKING TOUR — Downtown

Start: Plaza Mayor.
Finish: Centro Cívico.
Time: 3 hours.
Best time: Mon–Fri 8am–6pm.

Begin your tour on the Plaza Mayor, Guatemala City's central square.

1. **Palacio Nacional,** the seat of government in Guatemala, is on the north side of the square.
2. **Catedral Metropolitana** is on the east side.
3. **Biblioteca Nacional** is on the west.
4. **Mercado Central,** most of which is beneath a small open square, is in the block behind the Catedral Metropolitana. After you have visited these sites, stroll down busy 6a Avenida, the city's main shopping street. Take your time, stop and shop, and have a bite to eat.

REFUELING STOP   A short way down 6a Avenida is one of my favorite Guatemala City restaurants, **Los Cebollines,** at 6a Avenida 9-75.

5. **Centro Cultural Miguel Angel Asturias,** one of the most unusual buildings I've ever seen, is at the southern end of 6a Avenida. From the east and west, it resembles the superstructure of an ultramodern ocean liner. The cultural center houses three theaters.
6. **Centro Cívico and Ciudad Olímpico,** which both feature equally interesting architecture, are a block to the east.

WALKING TOUR — The Zona Viva

Start: Museo Popol Vuh.
Finish: Parque Aurora Zoo.
Time: All day.

The Zona Viva is where the wealthy of Guatemala eat, shop, and live. It is also home to the city's most interesting museums.

1. **Museo Popol Vuh,** on Avenida La Reforma, is one of the city's best museums, with an excellent collection of Pre-Columbian art. From here head south to 16 Calle, where you should turn left. It is a rather long walk, but the avenue is shady and there are plenty of restaurants and shops to visit. Walking past the walled

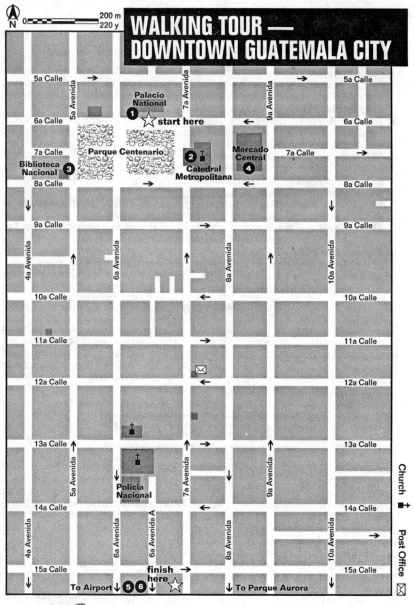

WALKING TOUR —
DOWNTOWN GUATEMALA CITY

0 ____ 200 m
____ 220 y

N

5a Calle
5a Avenida
Palacio National
① ☆ start here
6a Calle

Parque Centenario

7a Calle
Biblioteca Nacional ③
② ✝ Catedral Metropolitana
Mercado Central ④
7a Calle

8a Calle

9a Calle
4a Avenida
6a Avenida
8a Avenida
10a Avenida
7a Avenida
9a Calle

10a Calle

11a Calle

⊠
12a Calle

✝

13a Calle
5a Avenida
7a Avenida
9a Avenida
✝ Policia Nacional
13a Calle

14a Calle
4a Avenida
6a Avenida
6a Avenida A
8a Avenida
10a Avenida
14a Calle

15a Calle
finish here ☆
To Airport ↓ ⑤ ⑥
To Parque Aurora
15a Calle

Church ■✝

Post Office ⊠

GUATEMALA CITY

Downtown

① Palacio Nacional
② Catedral Metropolitana
③ Biblioteca Nacional
④ Mercado Central
⑤ Centro Cultural Miguel Angel Asturias
⑥ Centro Cívico and Ciudad Olímpica

compounds of 16 Calle, you will get an idea of how the wealthy live here. When you reach 4a Avenida, turn right. A few houses down on the left is the:

2. **Museo Ixchel de Traje Indígena,** where you can learn to recognize all the beautiful costumes of the native peoples of Guatemala. Head back out to Avenida La Reforma when you are done here and carefully cross the busy road. Continue down 14 Calle several more blocks until you come to another wide boulevard, Diagonal 12. Across it is the entrance to:

3. **Parque Aurora.** You will be crossing under an old aqueduct built several hundred years ago by the Spanish as you enter the park. Just inside the park, you will see on your right the:

4. **Mercado de Artesanía,** where the prices tend to be high and the handcrafts seem less authentic than those at the downtown Mercado Central. There is a little restaurant here where you can get lunch. Turn right just past the Mercado and you will be within two long blocks of the:

5. **Museo de Arqueología y Etnología,** which has a huge collection of Pre-Columbian artifacts. Across from this museum is the:

6. **Museo de Arte Moderno.** If you still have time or energy after this, you can walk north on the Avenida del Observatorio to the:

7. **Parque Zoológico La Aurora,** which is only about five minutes away. In front of the zoo is a large statue of Tecún Umán, the Mayan chieftain who fought the last great battle against the conquistadores. From here you can catch a taxi or take a black no. 5 bus back downtown.

ORGANIZED TOURS

There are no organized tours of Guatemala City that I can recommend. Although there are tours offered by several companies, the tours do not visit the city's three best museums—the Museum of Archeology, the Popol Vuh Museum, and the Ixchel Museum. You would spend your time here much more wisely if you simply went to these museums, perhaps following the walking tour outlined above, and then took a taxi to the Plaza Mayor and the Mapa en Relieve.

7. SAVVY SHOPPING

The savvy shopper in Guatemala City should save every last penny to spend in the shopper's heavens of Chichicastenango and Panajachel. However, if for some reason you are not headed to either of these places but would still like to buy some of those beautiful Guatemalan textiles, head for the **Mercado Central.** Before the earthquake of 1976, the area directly behind the Catedral Metropolitana was the city's central market. It was ruined in the quake, and a new one was built that has most of its shopping space below street level (they're not going to let a quake "bring it down" again!). Walk through the huge market to see selections of cloth (both handwoven and machine-made), leather goods, wood carvings, metalwork, baskets, and other handcrafts. It's worth at least a stroll through. All of the streets near the market are devoted to shopping as well. Be especially careful with your valuables: Pickpockets and purse slashers make a very good living here. Open Monday to Saturday from 9am to 6pm, Sunday from 9am to noon.

The **Mercado de Artesanía** (Handcrafts Market), located in Parque Aurora, is an outdoor area with vendors' stalls, a small courtyard, and a modern restaurant. The products on sale represent a good portion of Guatemala, and the prices are not bad. They have leather goods, woven cloth, huipiles (blouses), ceramics, baskets, and hand-painted terra-cotta figurines. If you're traveling extensively throughout Guatemala, you'll find these products elsewhere, but it's probably worth a trip to see what they have here. Although prices are a little higher here than at the shops in Mercado Central, this is a very pleasant place, and you may even be entertained by a marimba

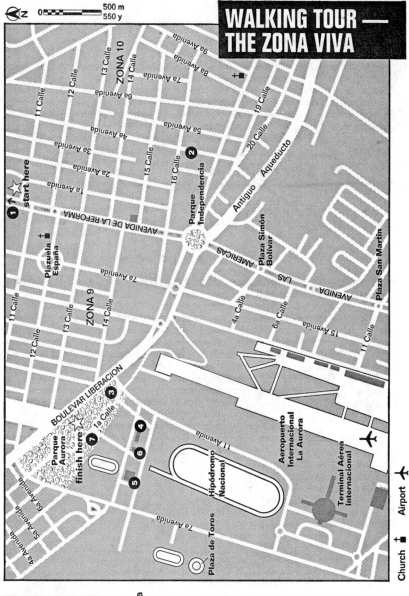

N

0 ⌀⌀⌀⌀⌀ 500 m
         550 y

ZONA 10

13 Calle

12 Calle

11 Calle

9a Avenida

8a Avenida

7a Avenida

6a Avenida

5a Avenida

4a Avenida

3a Avenida

2a Avenida

1a Avenida

14 Calle

15 Calle

16 Calle

19 Calle

20 Calle

ZONA 9

13 Calle

14 Calle

11 Calle

12 Calle

① ↑ start here

AVENIDA DE LA REFORMA

Plazuela
España

Parque
Independencia

②

Antiguo   Aqueducto

Plaza Simón
Bolívar

AVENIDA   LAS   AMERICAS

Plaza San Martin

7a Avenida

4a Calle

6a Calle

15 Avenida

11 Calle

BOULEVAR LIBERACION

Parque
Aurora

finish here

⑦   1a Calle

③

④

⑥

⑤

11 Avenida

Hipódromo
Nacional

Aeropuerto
Internacional
La Aurora

Terminal Aérea
Internacional

7a Avenida

Plaza de Toros

6a Avenida

5a Avenida

4a Avenida

Church ✝ ■   Airport ✈

GUATEMALA
CITY

The Zona Viva

① Museo Popol Vuh
② Museo Ixchel
   de Traje Indígena
③ Parque Aurora
④ Mercado de
   Artesanía
⑤ Museo de
   Arqueología
   y Etnología
⑥ Museo de
   Arte Moderno
⑦ Parque Zoológico
   La Aurora

band. As for the quality of the merchandise, it's good—with the exception of woven goods, especially huipiles, which are of higher quality in the villages. Open Monday to Saturday from 9am to 6pm, Sunday 9am to 1pm.

If you're in the market for cheap clothing and cheap shoes, head for 6a Avenida. For higher quality and correspondingly higher prices, visit the many boutiques in the Zona Viva along Avenida La Reforma.

If you're buying large quantities and want to ship things home, your best bet is to use one of the shipping companies in Antigua or Panajachel. This will save you the aggravation of dealing with the post office and all its paperwork.

8. EVENING ENTERTAINMENT

Although it is the largest city in Central America, Guatemala City has very little in the way of an entertainment scene. If you crave cultural programs or lively nightlife, you're out of luck here.

THE PERFORMING ARTS

CENTRO CULTURAL MIGUEL ANGEL ASTURIAS, 24 Calle 3-81, Zona 1. Tel. 24-041 or 24-044.

Perched high atop a hill overlooking the Centro Cívico is a dramatic blue-and-white building that looks strangely like a luxury cruise ship. Don't worry—the polar ice caps haven't melted; this is the city cultural center, home to three theaters. Inaugurated in 1978, the building is the work of Guatemalan artist Efraín Recinos. The Gran Teatro seats more than 2,000 people. The much smaller Teatro de Cámara is for chamber music concerts, while the Teatro al Aire Libre, an open-air theater, stages everything from music to dance to drama. Check *Prensa Libre,* the city's daily newspaper, for information on performances.

Prices: Q5–Q100 ($1–$20), depending on performance and seat.

THE BAR, CLUB & MUSIC SCENE

The best place to look for active nightlife is in the Zona Viva, the area along Avenida La Reforma in Zona 9 and Zona 10. Here you will find the city's greatest concentration of expensive restaurants, bars, discos, and nightclubs. Probably your best bet will be to head to one of the major hotels in this area. Both the Hotel Conquistador Sheraton and the Westin Camino Real Hotel have popular discos frequented by locals and tourists. **Kahlua,** 1a 13-29, Zona 10, is another popular disco.

9. EASY EXCURSIONS

LA DEMOCRACIA

GETTING THERE By Bus In Guatemala City, Chatia Gomerana, Muelle Central, Terminal de Buses, Zona 4, has buses every 30 minutes from 6am to 6:30pm. Duration: 1½ hours. Fare: Q2 (40¢). You can also take a bus to Siquinalá and then get a local bus to La Democracia.

By Car If you're coming from the west on the Pacific Highway, turn right in Siquinalá. From Guatemala City, take the Carretera al Pacífico to Siquinalá and turn left.

DEPARTING   You can catch a bus to Siquinalá and then transfer to a Guatemala City bus, or catch one of the less frequent buses that stop in La Democracia on their run from Sipacate to Guatemala City.

Fifty seven miles southwest of Guatemala City, the tiny town of La Democracia is famous for strange boulder-sized Preclassic Mayan (sometimes called Pre-Olmec) statues and artifacts found at a nearby farm, Finca Monte Alto. When you get to La Democracia, follow the signs for "El Museo." The museum is on the town's main square (two blocks east of the main road). The plaza is simple but has a pleasant cement gazebo built around a large ceiba tree, and several of the large stone sculptures decorate the square.

WHAT TO SEE & DO

La Democracia Museum was built in 1967 to house the numerous objects found during excavations at Finca Monte Alto and the smaller fincas of Río Seco, La Gomera, and Ora Blanca. The museum (open Tuesday to Sunday from 9am to noon and 2 to 5pm; closed Monday and holidays) is not large, so you should be able to see everything in an hour or so. Unfortunately, organization and classification are not the museum's high points, so you'll see primitive pottery and terra-cotta figurines (mostly female); obsidian blades, spears, and knives; and curious zoomorphic jars all mixed together, the primitive with the sophisticated. Some of the figurines have elaborate headdresses similar to those found in Zapotec Monte Alban (Mexico). There are several stone "yokes" and stone replicas of mushrooms, which immediately suggest that hallucinogenic mushrooms and their replicas were used in ceremonies by these people.

Outside the museum, in front of it, and in the plaza are the great Buddha-like stone figures and heads carved from boulders—11 of these have been found to date. Just what they represent is a mystery: Similar crude carvings have been found in El Salvador and as far north as Chiapas in Mexico—but are they deities, chiefs, or local dignitaries? Professor Edwin Shook, who headed the excavations here from 1968 to 1970 under the auspices of the National Geographic Society and Harvard's Peabody Museum, says that they were made during the period from 300 B.C. to the birth of Christ. He maintains that they were carved by a Mayan people, not "Pre-Olmecs" as many others thought; the Olmecs carved much more sophisticated heads, complete with headbands and ornaments, while these are really very crude images chipped out of the sides of boulders. His theory is that they were carved by a Preclassic Mayan people who settled at Monte Alto about 1000 B.C., reached the peak of their civilization from 300 B.C. to A.D. 1, and then declined by about A.D. 300. If this is so, these people would be very early Mayas, earlier than the people who settled at Tikal and Palenque, but so far no Mayan glyphs—which would be proof of their race—have been found at Monte Alto. Perhaps some will turn up, for found at Kaminal Juyú (in Guatemala City) were glyphs that predate those found at Tikal; therefore it's thought that Mayan hieroglyphic writing may have started here on the Pacific Slope and then progressed north and east to the Petén and Yucatán.

The town of La Democracia itself is not what I'd call wildly interesting, unless you're an anthropologist who loves sticky heat, so plan on a quick visit to the museum and the plaza and then a quick retreat back up into the mountains to Guatemala City.

LAKE AMATITLÁN

GETTING THERE By Bus   There are buses every 30 minutes from the Terminal de Buses in Zona 4 in Guatemala City. Duration: 30 minutes. Fare: Q1 (25¢).

By Car   Take the Carretera al Pacífico south and watch for the turnoff to Lake Amatitlán.

DEPARTING   Catch a bus from the public beach back into Guatemala City. They run every 30 minutes throughout the day.

ESSENTIALS Orientation   The lake, 17 miles south of Guatemala City, is

7½ by 2½ miles, with villas and vacation homes surrounding it. At the northwest end of the lake, near the highway, is one of the only public beaches on the lake.

Don't confuse this small lake with Lake Atitlán to the northwest; the latter is a spectacular sight, whereas this one, Lake Amatitlán, is not as interesting. If you're driving, after exiting from the highway, bear left at the gas station, then left again at the *T,* then right down the wide, straight street to the lakefront.

WHAT TO SEE & DO

The government has built a park here on the shore with little stone thatch-roofed changing cubicles, picnic tables, and the like. The swimming at this beach is not great because the water tends to be dirty, so your best bet for a dip would be either to walk along the road to the left past the villas and cottages to a rock outcrop or to rent a rowboat for an hour, row out a short distance, and swim. Near the entry road where you came in are various little restaurants and soft-drink stands that will do nicely for lunch. As for a hotel, the one that's here is more on the order of a thermal spa, not really suitable for 1-night stays. As I said, the lake is mostly a place for denizens of the capital to cool off in for a day. Don't plan an extended stay.

You may notice several *balnearios* (warm spring swimming pools) in the area. This is an area of much geothermal activity. There are hot springs at various places around the edges of the lake, and even the bottom of the lake itself is filled with hot springs. Perhaps this is why the ancient Mayas of this region used the lake for making offerings to the gods. The soft, hot mud of the lake bottom has preserved most of these offerings, and divers continue to recover amazing terra-cotta pots and urns, many of which are on display at the Popol Vuh Museum in Guatemala City.

Warning: In recent years, pollution from Guatemala City has been contaminating this small lake. It is questionable whether you should swim here at all. Definitely do not eat any fish that was taken from the lake.

10. MOVING ON — TRAVEL SERVICES

If you don't already have a ticket out of the country, you can contact **Viajes Internacionales Paco Sandoval,** 6a Av. 9-62, Zona 1 (tel. 510-522 or 533-477), or **Clark Tours,** 7a Av. 6-53, Zona 4 (tel. 310-213), both of which are conveniently located.

BY PLANE   When the time comes for your flight out, take a taxi or the black no. 5 "Aeropuerto" bus out to the airport, leaving an hour or more for check-in, Customs, and immigration. There are a few duty-free shops past the immigration desks, but the shops in the main check-in are much more interesting.

Here are some of the most-used airlines serving the country; all have offices and counters at La Aurora Airport, and some have ticket offices downtown as well.

Aerovias, Avenida Hincapié and 18 Calle, Zona 13, Hangar no. 8 (tel. 319-663 or 325-686).

American Airlines, Avenida La Reforma 15-54, Zona 9, Edificio Reforma Obelisco, Office 401A-D (tel. 311-361, 347-415, or 347-316).

Aviateca, 10a Calle 6-39, Zona 1 (tel. 81-479 or 81-415).

Continental, 12 Calle 1-25, Zona 10 (tel. 353-208 or 353-209).

Iberia, Avenida La Reforma 8-60, Zona 9 (tel. 373-911).

Lacsa, 7a 14-44, Zona 9, Edificio La Galería (tel. 373-905 or 346-905).

Mexicana, 12 Calle 4-55, Zona 1 (tel. 518-824 or 518-834).

Sahsa, 12 Calle 1-25, Zona 10, Edificio Geminis 10, Local 208 (tel. 352-671).

Taca, 7a 14-35, Zona 9 (tel. 322-360).

Tapsa, Avenida Hincapié, Hangar 14, Aeropuerto La Aurora, Zona 13 (tel. 314-860 or 319-180).

CHAPTER 10
THE GUATEMALAN HIGHLANDS

The Guatemalan highlands are a convoluted quilt of cultivated hillsides. The land has been turned on its side, but the tenacious Indians cling to the steep mountains and plant their corn as they have for thousands of years. Narrow roads wind through the mountains, and around nearly every bend is another breathtaking vista. Picture-perfect volcanic peaks, some sitting in silent grandeur, others providing explosive reminders of their presence, rise up above the surrounding mountains. However, it is the people of these mountains that capture the heart and imagination of the visitor to this country. Descended from the ancient Mayas, the indigenous people of the Guatemalan highlands pursue a way of life entirely separate from the life of the *ladinos,* the more Spanish inhabitants of this country's cities and towns. The Indians cling to their age-old traditions, many of which have been incorporated into Roman Catholic rituals. Most of the men and women of this region also continue to wear their very colorful traditional attire. In this often dry and dusty landscape, their skirts and huipiles (blouses), pants and jackets are bold splashes of unlikely colors—lime green and cherry red, indigo and purple, and magenta and fuchsia. Every village has its own styles and colors, so that when people leave their village, they can be recognized wherever they go. Nowhere is this more apparent than around the banks of Lake Atitlán, which many people claim is the most beautiful lake in the world. Every village around the lake has a slightly different fashion, which makes excursions around the lake particularly interesting.

Nestled at the base of these rugged mountains, in the shadow of a perfectly shaped volcano, is Antigua, the colonial capital of Guatemala. Amid the ruins of Spanish churches, monasteries, and convents, this city goes about its quiet life, attracting people from all over the world to enjoy its cobblestone streets and stucco walls.

---

1. ANTIGUA

28 miles SW of Guatemala City; 62 miles E of Panajachel

GETTING THERE By Bus Buses leave Guatemala City from 15 Calle 3-65, Zona 1, every 30 minutes between 7am and 7pm. Duration: 1½ hours. Fare: Q2.50 (50¢). If you are coming from anywhere in the highlands, your best bet is to catch any bus headed toward Guatemala and get off at Chimaltenango. Here you can catch a

WHAT'S SPECIAL ABOUT THE GUATEMALAN HIGHLANDS

Great Towns/Villages
☐ Antigua, one of Guatemala's colonial capitals, with beautiful architecture, atmosphere, and many ruins.
☐ Chichicastenango, famous for its shopping and rituals performed by local Indians.

Natural Spectacles
☐ Lake Atitlán, said to be the most beautiful lake in the world.
☐ Volcanoes, live or dormant, that you can climb.

Events/Festivals
☐ Holy Week (the week before Easter) in Antigua, celebrated with daily processions through the streets.
☐ Ancient Indian dances performed in towns and cities around the country.

Religious Shrines
☐ The Church of San Francisco, with the remains of Hermano Pedro, who is said to heal the sick.

Architectural Highlights
☐ Ruins of colonial churches, monasteries, convents, universities, and government buildings all over the town of Antigua.

Shopping
☐ The Chichicastenango market on Sunday and Thursday, flooded with vendors selling beautiful Guatemalan textiles at the best prices in the country.
☐ Panajachel's Calle Santander, lined on both sides with vendors selling "gringo" fashions in Guatemalan fabrics.
☐ Villages around Quetzaltenango, with colorful markets on different days of the week.

bus down to Antigua. Turansa (tel. 322-928 in Antigua or 953-574 in Guatemala City) operates a tourist van shuttle between Panajachel and Antigua on Wednesday, Friday and Sunday. Fare: Q45 ($9). This company also operates a similar shuttle daily between Guatemala City and Antigua. You can catch this latter van at the Hotel Panamerican at 6:15am or 5:15pm or at the airport at 7:15am or 6:15pm. Fare: Q35 ($7).

By Car The road to Antigua heads northwest out of Guatemala. The junction for Antigua is in San Lucas Sacatepequez, which is a short distance over the hill that the road climbs as it leaves Guatemala City.

DEPARTING Buses run very frequently between Antigua and Guatemala City, and minibuses shuttle between Antigua and Chimaltenango, on the Pan American Highway, all day long. Buses trundling along the Pan American Highway will stop in Chimaltenango and take you on to your final destination, whether it be the capital or the Mexican border.

Buses Inter-Hotel y Turismo (tel. 320-011 to 320-015 in Guatemala City) runs comfortable scheduled minibuses on a circular route past many of Guatemala City's luxury hotels (El Dorado, Conquistador Sheraton, Cortijo Reforma, Fiesta, Camino Real), and La Aurora airport, then out Bulevar Tecún Umán to Antigua, stopping at various spots in town and terminating at the Ramada Hotel. The return run from Antigua to Guatemala City starts at the Hostal Tetuan, goes to the Ramada, the Hotel Antigua, the Posada de Don Rodrigo, the Restaurant Doña Luisa, and the Hotel Aurora, before heading out of town to the airport and the capital. Schedules are set up to get you to the airport in time for a flight to Tikal or a flight home. Cost for a one-way ticket is Q20 ($8), more than for the normal bus but substantially less than for a taxi. Check at any of the aforementioned establishments for the latest fares and schedules.

Antigua's bus station is located in the market.

Buses for Guatemala City leave every 30 minutes between 7am and 7pm. Duration: 1 hour. Fare: Q1.50 (38¢).

To get to Panajachel by bus, you must first catch one of the frequent buses to Chimaltenango. In Chimaltenango, you can flag down one of the hourly Guatemala-Panajachel buses. Duration: 3 hours. Fare: Q4 ($1).

To reach Chichicastenango, first catch a bus to Chimaltenango, then flag down one of the half-hourly buses that make the run from Guatemala City to Chichicastenango. Duration: 3½ hours. Fare: Q5 ($1.25).

To reach Quetzaltenango again, you must first catch a bus to Chimaltenango, then flag down a bus from Guatemala City. They pass by around 6:30 and 9:30am, noon, and 3:30, 6, 8, and 10pm. Duration: 4 hours. Fare: Q6 ($1.50).

ESSENTIALS Orientation Unlike most Guatemalan towns, Antigua has a street numbering system that includes compass designations; the central point for the plan is the city's main plaza, called the Parque Central. Calles run east to west, and so 4a Calle west of the Parque Central is 4a Calle Poniente; avenidas run north to south, and thus 3a Avenida north of the Parque Central is 3a Avenida Norte. Remember your directions here: norte (north), sur (south), oriente (east), poniente (west).

Fast Facts Antigua's tourist office is in the Palacio de Gobierno, at the southeast corner of the Parque Central, next to the intersection of 4a Avenida Sur and 5a Calle Oriente (tel. 320-763). It is open daily from 8am to 5:30pm. The Banco g&t, on the west side of the Parque Central, is open Monday from 9am to 3pm, Tuesday through Friday from 9am to 7pm, and Saturday from 10am to 3:30pm. The post office (Correos)—open Monday to Saturday from 8am to noon and 2 to 8pm (closed Sunday)—is at 4a Calle Poniente and the Alameda de Santa Lucia, west of the Parque Central near the market. The Guatel telephone office is just off the southwest corner of the Parque Central, at the intersection of 5a Calle Poniente and 5a Avenida Sur.

For books in English and Spanish, visit Un Poco de Todo, on the Parque Central at the northwest corner—open Monday to Friday from 9:30am to 1pm and 3 to 6pm. Another shop, selling Spanish and English books, postcards, maps, and photocopies, is Casa Andinista, at 4a Calle Oriente no. 5, just a few steps off the Parque Central. The market here is held daily. Feast day is first Friday of Lent.

Officially called Antigua Guatemala, this well-preserved colonial city (alt. 5,020 feet; pop. 27,000) was the capital of the country from 1543 to 1773. Even before it was the capital, however, it was on the way to becoming the cultural and religious center of the country. Pedro de Alvarado encouraged the Dominican, Mercedarian, and Franciscan friars to come and teach here, and the church spent a great deal of money in subsequent centuries to make this the most impressive city in Central America.

As the capital of the Captaincy-General of Guatemala, Antigua's official name was La muy Noble y muy Leal Ciudad de Santiago de los Caballeros de Goathemala, or Santiago for short, and from here orders went out to all parts of the region (which included the present-day nations of Guatemala, Belize, Honduras, El Salvador, and Costa Rica). The city's population peaked at 55,000, and the citizens could boast that they lived in the third-oldest Spanish city in America (founded in 1542) and that they had the first Pontifical University in the hemisphere (founded in 1675). It remains impressive to this day, still beautiful and much-visited by tourists, even though the ravages of the earthquakes of 1773 and 1976 are plain to see, along with the effects of 14 smaller quakes, fires, and floods that damaged the city between 1540 and 1717. Some buildings have been in ruins since the quake of 1773; in the quake of 1976, some of the finest churches were badly damaged, but reconstruction efforts are now complete. The San Francisco church, virtually ruined in earlier quakes, was barely touched in the recent one. If you look at the photographs of the reconstruction work on display in the church, you'll see why: Modern construction methods using steel reinforcing rods kept everything in place.

Coming down into the valley of Antigua from Guatemala City, you'll see Antigua's impressive setting, surrounded by three magnificent volcanoes named Agua, Fuego, and Acatenango—Agua is the grand one to the south, visible throughout the town; Fuego is the middle one, which is always smoking.

Antigua is packed full during the week before Easter because of its unique pageantry during Holy Week, so if you plan to be here at that time be sure to reserve your room weeks (even months) in advance. At other times of year, Antigua is one of the most delightful towns to make your base, greatly preferable in all ways to Guatemala City, though even Antigua gets crowded on weekends. I highly recommend that you settle in at Antigua and make day trips to the capital, rather than vice versa.

WHAT TO SEE & DO

Antigua is one of the most pleasant towns to stroll around in: It's quiet because there are few cars, and the buses are routed outside the main area; the air is clean (no exhaust fumes), with an occasional smell of wood smoke; and there are beautiful colonial buildings at every corner. You can see some 35 churches and monasteries in Antigua. The best thing is to meander through the lovely cobbled streets and see what you discover. The following are the high points.

While you're on the main square (Parque Central), take a look at the **Palacio de Gobierno,** officially named the Palace of the Royal Audiencia and the Captaincy-General of Guatemala. Construction was begun in 1543, but earthquakes and the ravages of time destroyed almost everything but the facade on the park. Most of what you see was rebuilt about 100 years ago. The facade bears the insignia of the Bourbons and the name of the monarch reigning at the time, Charles III.

Also on the plaza, on the north side at 4a Calle Oriente, is the **Museo de Santiago,** which was set up a few years ago to preserve some of Guatemala's history. On display in the 16th-century building, which once was the palace of the Council of the Realm of Guatemala, are cannons, guns, swords, religious articles, and an old Quiché marimba. Not terribly exciting, but certainly worth the 25 centavo admission. Note the barred rooms that were used as cells when the palace was converted to a prison in the 19th century. Admission is free on Sunday and holidays. It's open Tuesday through Friday from 9am to 4pm, Saturday and Sunday from 9am to noon and from 2 to 4pm.

Of the other notable buildings, the **University of San Carlos** comes next. The university was founded in 1676 and was the third university (after those in Mexico and Lima) in Spanish America. Much of the building you'll see was built around 1763 after the previous structure was damaged by the inevitable earthquake. Today the university building serves as the Colonial Museum, open Tuesday through Friday.

As you enter the university, you can almost feel a change in time period. You come first to a beautiful open courtyard with a fountain, peaceful except for the sound of running water. Off to the right is the first of nine salons decorated in 17th- and 18th-century style, hung with paintings and dotted with the statuary of the period. One of the foremost painters of the time, Thomas de Meilo (1694–1739), is well represented, and although the museum is not slick, or even well run, the atmosphere succeeds in giving you a taste of old Antigua. The last of the rooms is the library (*biblioteca*).

CHURCHES

Of the churches, one of the best is the **Convent and Church of Our Lady of Mercy,** called simply La Merced by local people. It's at the end of 5a Avenida Norte, and the facade is something to behold—you'll see what I mean. Legend has it that the 12 sprays in the church's foundation are symbolic of the Apostles, which makes sense.

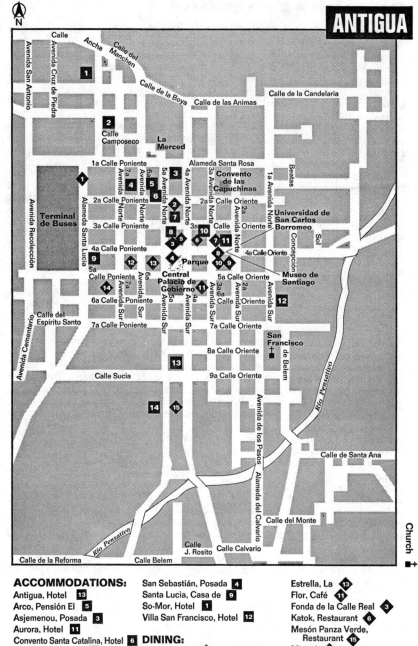

ANTIGUA

ACCOMMODATIONS:

Antigua, Hotel **13**
Arco, Pensión El **5**
Asjemenou, Posada **3**
Aurora, Hotel **11**
Convento Santa Catalina, Hotel **6**
Descanso, Hotel El **8**
Don Rodrigo, Posada de **7**
Placido, Hotel **2**
Rosario Lodge, El **14**
San Francisco, Posada **10**

San Sebastián, Posada **4**
Santa Lucia, Casa de **9**
So-Mor, Hotel **1**
Villa San Francisco, Hotel **12**

DINING:

Capuchino, El **12**
Cenicienta Pasteles, El **5**
Don Rodrigo, Posada de **2**
Doña Luisa, Restaurant **7**
Doña Maria Gordillo Dulces Típicos **10**

Estrella, La **13**
Flor, Café **11**
Fonda de la Calle Real **3**
Katok, Restaurant **6**
Mesón Panza Verde, Restaurant **15**
Mistral **9**
Peroleto **1**
Sereno, El **14**
Sueños del Quetzal **4**
Zen **8**

La Merced is much more of an attraction than the cathedral on the main square, but the latter has the distinction of being the church in which were buried such illustrious figures of Guatemalan history as Pedro de Alvarado, discoverer of the country, and one of his wives; and Bernal Díaz de Castillo, whose day-to-day account of the conquest of Mexico and Guatemala has become a classic (it's available in Penguin paperback). Back in the 16th century, some 180,000 gold pieces went toward the construction of this cathedral. Inside are 68 vaulted arches carved with angels and coats-of-arms. The dome is 70 feet high; the altar is decorated with gold and lacquer. Unfortunately, very little remains intact of this once-opulent cathedral, but it is presently under reconstruction to repair the sections that collapsed with the earthquakes. Since the quake of 1976, entrance to the cathedral has been limited to Tuesday to Sunday from 8am to noon; closed Monday.

The **Convent of the Capuchinas,** 2a Avenida Norte and 2a Calle Oriente, was built by the monastic order for the sisterhood of the Capuchins in 1736. The nuns were invited to come here from Madrid by the bishop of Santiago (Antigua). Earthquakes have destroyed a good part of the building, but what remains is fascinating. As you enter, you'll find a plan of the convent to your right and the central court to your left. Notice the unusual pillars, rather squat and wider at the base than at the top. At the west end of the court is the bath and laundry room, made of beautiful pink stone, and next to it is a stairway leading down into the crypt. There's a small museum, on the right as you enter, in which you can see tiles and ceramics from excavations done in 1974 and 1975 on several churches in Antigua; some of the relics found in these excavations date as far back as 400 B.C.

When leaving the museum, turn right and walk through a small patio and take the first left, to where a large white tunnel leads to a lower-level room that must be seen to be believed: It is ring-shaped, with a large concave pillar in the middle. Any sound reverberates for a long time. Although I'd like to think some sort of religious rite took place here, it seems that this was a *bodega* (wine cellar).

Go back upstairs and turn right to the central courtyard, turn left, and go upstairs to get to the monastic cells, complete with a mock-up of a nun saying her vespers. In the central courtyard, two stairways lead to an upper level from which you can get a good idea of the layout of the convent and the surrounding area.

The **Church of San Francisco,** at 7a Calle Oriente and 2a Avenida Sur, was once a very beautiful building and is still fine, but earthquakes destroyed a lot of the best work on the facade. The church was built through the wish of one Fray Toribio de Benavente Motolinia, a Franciscan friar who arrived in Guatemala in 1544. Of the original church about all that survives is a single chapel, and that houses the remains of Hermano Pedro de Betancourt, a Franciscan who came to Antigua in about 1650 and later established a hospital where he cared for the sick and the poor for 15 years. He is remembered as an unselfish and saintly man, and people still come to solicit his help for cures. The walls around his resting place hold the most fantastic array of testimonial plaques, letters, photos, and memorabilia. You may see someone quietly praying before his crypt, gently knocking on it to let Hermano Pedro know that he's needed.

The church was restored in 1961 using modern methods, and this helped it to survive the 1976 quake; only rubble remains of the convent of the Franciscans to the south of the church.

THE MARKET AREA

The market is located between Alameda de Santa Lucia and Alameda de la Recoleccion. It is a busy market selling everything from vegetables and baskets to huipiles (Guatemalan handwoven, embroidered blouses) and beautiful cloth. The village women file in early every day (except Sunday, when the market is closed) with their wares of jackets, huipiles, and rugs.

To buy local silverwork, you can go to the nearby village of San Felipe, where there's a silver factory. Catch a bus near the market in Antigua for the 1¼-mile ride, and when you get to the village, ask for the factory—there are no street signs.

Also near the market, at the western end of 5a Calle Poniente, is the Monumento a Landívar, a set of five colonial-style arches set in a little park next to the bus station. Rafael Landívar, a Jesuit priest and poet, lived and worked in Guatemala during the mid-1700s. After the Jesuits were expelled from New Spain, he returned to Italy, where he wrote the works that Guatemalans continue to value as the best poetry of the colonial period. The house in which Landívar lived while in Antigua (then the capital of Guatemala, of course) was nearby on 5a Calle Poniente.

HOLY WEEK

The week between Palm Sunday and Easter Sunday, called Semana Santa throughout the Spanish-speaking world, is a time for solemn religious processions throughout Guatemala, but nowhere is this spectacle more elaborate than in Antigua. Throughout the week women and men dressed in purple robes carry massive carved wooden floats (*andas*) through the streets of the city. Atop these floats stand statues of Jesus, the Virgin Mary, and other saints. People pay for the privilege of carrying the heavy andas (through these payments the churches raise funds). Sign-up sheets are circulated months in advance and people usually are only allowed to help carry the anda for a block or two.

The andas can weigh several tons and are carried by as many as 40 bearers, who walk slowly and rhythmically. In front of each anda young boys swing censers that waft clouds of incense smoke into the streets. Marching brass bands play doleful hymns and the crowds of pilgrims from all over the world gaze with amazement and reverence. As Easter Sunday approaches the stages of the Passion of Christ are reenacted. Men on horseback and on foot and dressed in the raiment of Roman soldiers march through the streets. Men in chains representing the thieves who were crucified with Christ are led through the town, and a criminal is even set free from the local jail.

On Good Friday, Antigua's cobblestone streets are blanketed with *alfombras,* carpets made of colored sawdust, flowers, pine needles, and the huge flowers of a special palm tree. Neighborhoods, schools, wealthy families, and shops all try to outdo one another in creating the most beautiful alfombras, some of which are hundreds of feet long, take all night to create, and look like colorful cake decorations. This beauty is ephemeral, though, for within a few hours, the processions shuffle dolorously across the works of art, turning them into a tossed salad of bright colors.

The ritual continues on into the night, with andas illuminated by lights hooked up to gasoline generators. Each day, various churches parade different statues through the streets. Before and after the processions, the statues are placed on altars and surrounded by heaps of flowers and fruit.

Because of the large crowds of tourists and pilgrims, pickpockets and purse slashers are out in force during the processions. Do not leave anything of value in your pockets or purse. Be sure to wear a money belt or a neck pouch inside your clothing.

Again, this festival is very popular and packed with Guatemalans and foreigners who have come to enjoy the ceremonies. *You'll need hotel reservations well in advance.*

A brochure listing the events during Holy Week can be obtained through the Tourism Office, but here is a quick rundown on the processional times: **Palm Sunday** (3 to 10pm), leaves from La Merced; **Holy Thursday** (4 to 9:30pm), leaves from the Church of San Francisco; and **Good Friday** (8am to 3pm), leaves from La Merced and (4:30 to 11:30pm) from Escuela de Cristo.

SPANISH LANGUAGE SCHOOLS

Antigua is almost as well known for its Spanish schools as it is for its ruins. There are dozens of large and small schools all over town and they vary greatly in the quality of their teaching programs. If you decide that you'd like to study Spanish in Antigua, you might want to first try one of the schools listed under "Alternative/Adventure Travel" in Chapter 8.

WHERE TO STAY

DOUBLES FOR LESS THAN Q50 [$10]

POSADA SAN FRANCISCO, 3a Calle Oriente No. 19, Antigua. Tel. 502/320-266. 15 rms (8 with bath).

$ Rates: Q15 ($3) single without bath, Q25 ($5) single with bath; Q30 ($6) double without bath, Q50 ($10) double with bath. No credit cards.

A good choice for those traveling on a very low budget, the Posada San Francisco offers basic, but clean, rooms with red-tile floors. You'll find the rooms down a hall and up a few steps from street level; they're on two floors and surround a small courtyard. Some of the double rooms are fairly large so ask to have a look before taking one. Bathrooms are functional but certainly not spacious.

HOTEL VILLA SAN FRANCISCO, 1a Avenida Sur No. 15, Antigua. No phone. 9 rms (4 with bath).

$ Rates: Q23.40–Q29.25 ($4.70–$5.85) single without bath, Q35.10 ($7) single with bath; Q35.10–Q40.95 ($7–$8.20) double without bath, Q46.80 ($9.35) double with bath. No credit cards.

Down at the very end of 6a Calle Oriente, you'll find a good budget choice that is popular with Peace Corps workers (who receive discounts). Villa San Francisco is an imposing classical two-story building with wrought-iron balconies and a monstrously big front door covered with brass knobs. The guest rooms are a bit larger than you would expect for such prices, and though spartan, are generally clean. On the premises, you'll find a video bar and a Spanish school.

DOUBLES FOR LESS THAN Q100 [$20]

POSADA ASJEMENOU, 5a Avenida Norte No. 31, Antigua. Tel. 502/ 322-832. 10 rms (4 with bath).

$ Rates: Q41 ($8.20) single or double without bath, Q53 ($10.60) single or double with bath; Q63 ($12.60) triple without bath, Q79 ($15.80) triple with bath. V.

A few doors past the arch on 5a Avenida you'll find one of the best deals in town (at least as long as these prices hold out). The hotel is situated in an old colonial home and the guest rooms surround two very tranquil courtyards. In one there is a fountain and colorful garden, in the other a traditional clothes-washing basin (*pila*). Pale yellow walls, squeaky tile floors, and open porticoes all evoke Antigua's colonial heritage. On

---

Ⓕ FROMMER'S SMART TRAVELER: HOTELS

1. Make your room reservations up to a year in advance if you want to be in Antigua for Semana Santa (Holy Week), which is the week before Easter. Rates then are as much as 50% higher than normal.
2. If you're coming here to study Spanish, check with your Spanish school about a homestay plan, the cheapest way to stay in Antigua. You'll also be able to practice your Spanish with the host family.
3. Check the bulletin board at Dona Luisa, 4a Calle Oriente no. 12, for information on apartments for rent.
4. Get a room close to the Parque Central so you'll be close to the best restaurants and can easily stroll the square after dinner.
5. Once you arrive in town, keep your eyes open for new lodges and hotels; they often offer excellent value.

the other hand, there are very contemporary tables and chairs in the porticoes and even a television lounge. Decorative pottery braziers are replicas of Mayan urns. The rooms themselves are only slightly more than basic but the serene surroundings more than make up for that.

HOTEL EL DESCANSO, 5a Avenida Norte no. 9., Antigua Guatemala. Tel. 502/32-0142. 4 rms (all with bath).
$ Rates: Q45 ($9) double; Q67.50 ($13.50) triple; Q90 ($18) quad. No credit cards.
Waiting for you only a half block north of the Parque Central, in the building facing the restaurant called Café Café, is a little pension with only four rooms. This place is nothing fancy, just a place to rest, as the name implies. The rooms vary in size and the amount of light they get, but they are all fairly comfortable. This is a sort of Guatemalan homestay, and you'll feel like part of the family by the end of your visit. The hotel entrance is through a shop.

EL ROSARIO LODGE, 5a Avenida Sur 36, Antigua Guatemala. Tel. 502/32-0336. 10 rms (all with bath).
$ Rates: Q93.60–Q117 ($18.72–$23.40) single or double. No credit cards.
Antigua is not a very noisy town, but the quietest of the quiet places is five blocks south of the Parque Central, down 5a Avenida Sur. El Rosario is just about at the end of the paving, on the right side. Although it's a short walk from the plaza, the pleasant setting amid shady trees makes it worthwhile. The rooms come in a variety of shapes and sizes and have many extras, such as native blankets and craftwork decorations; some rooms have terraces and fireplaces. Furnishings have a Teutonic accent because the ownership here was German for many years.

CASA DE SANTA LUCIA, Alameda de Santa Lucia 5, Antigua Guatemala. No phone. 12 rms (all with bath).
$ Rates: Q40 ($8) single; Q50 ($10) double; Q75 ($15) triple. No credit cards.
The Casa de Santa Lucia is located in Antigua's busiest street, only two blocks from the bus station, but most of the rooms are quiet enough for sleeping and studying. The decor here is modern colonial with a lot of dark wood, much of it shaped on the lathe, creating a good atmosphere in the public rooms even though this is a very inexpensive pension. The guest rooms are quite plain and simple and have seen some wear, but the tiled showers always seem to have hot water.

DOUBLES FOR LESS THAN Q175 [$35]

HOTEL AURORA, 4a Calle Oriente 16, Antigua Guatemala. Tel. 502/32-0217. 16 rms (all with bath).
$ Rates: Q140.40 ($28.10) single; Q157.95 ($31.60) double; Q181.35 ($36.30) triple. No credit cards.
An old favorite in the moderate range, even though it has become considerably more expensive in recent years, the Aurora is housed in a traditional colonial building. A grassy courtyard decorated with flowers and graced by a fountain is surrounded by a portico set with wicker furniture and paved in shiny tiles. For cool evenings, there's a snug parlor with a fireplace. The guest rooms are lofty and airy but a bit dark (as befits their colonial style), with odd bits of furniture both antique and not. All is in good condition. Breakfasts, costing Q6–Q9 ($1.20–$1.80), are taken in a grand old-fashioned dining room.

HOTEL CONVENTO SANTA CATALINA, 5a Avenida Norte No. 28, Antigua. Tel. 502/323-080. 10 rms (all with bath).
$ Rates: Q117 ($23.40) single; Q140.40 ($28.10) double; Q163.80 ($32.76) triple. No credit cards.
As its name implies, this hotel was once a convent—in fact it is the convent for which Antigua's famous arch was built. The arch was meant to hide the temptations of the

world from cloistered nuns as they crossed the street between convent buildings. Today the hotel's rooms surround a garden courtyard in the center of which is a bubbling fountain. The wide porticoes are set with tables and chairs and serve as the hotel's dining room, although there is also an indoor eating area as well. You'll have a strong sense of the history of Antigua if you stay here. Right next door, and blending into the hotel, are the ruins of the rest of the convent. The rooms, though dark, are high-ceilinged and spacious, with tile floors, old wooden wardrobes, and heavy wooden bed frames. Bathrooms are also quite large.

POSADA SAN SEBASTIÁN, 7a Avenida Norte No. 67 (Calle San Sebastián), Antigua Guatemala. Tel. 502/32-0465. 7 rms (all with bath).
$ Rates: Q130 ($26) single; Q150 ($30) double. No credit cards.

On a quiet street about 10 minutes from the Parque Central you'll find a tranquil little hotel. Luis Mendez Rodriguez, the English-speaking owner, takes pride in his accommodations—and it shows. All the rooms have two double beds, some with Momostenango blankets on them, and the bathrooms are modern and clean. The floors are of highly polished tile that squeaks when you walk across it. The grassy courtyard also serves as a parking area, and there's an old orange grove in back of the house and a community room with a fireplace and a TV. An annex is located at 3a Avenida Norte No. 4.

There's a breakfast room where breakfast will cost you Q15 ($3). Laundry service is available.

HOTEL SOL-MOR, Avenida El Desengaño no. 26, Antigua Guatemala. Tel. 502/032-2312 or 502/920-809. 5 rms (all with bath).
$ Rates (including breakfast): Q139.40 ($27.88) single; Q173 ($34.60) double; Q196.40 ($39.30) triple. MC, V.

A 10-minute walk from the Parque Central, the Sol-Mor is directly across the street from another pretty little park filled with tall palm trees. This hotel is housed in a 160-year-old building, and many interesting architectural touches from that period remain. In the breakfast room, there are old laundry tanks the likes of which you can still see women using around town. This one has been turned into a planter and fountain. The rooms are built around a courtyard and a back garden. In the first courtyard, you'll find the hotel's name spelled out in living red-leafed plants in the grass. The back garden has a tiny pool, a parking area, and a few white wrought-iron tables and chairs for relaxing on sunny days. On the roof there is a terrace where you can enjoy the views and the sunshine. All five rooms have carpeting, but the furnishings are simple. This is one of my favorite hotels in Antigua.

SUPER-BUDGET CHOICES

Antigua has many little family pensions where tourists (often students learning Spanish) can stay for rock-bottom rates. The tourist office has information on how to get in touch with willing families. However, for a similar experience, try one of these popular pensions.

PENSIÓN EL ARCO, 5a Avenida Norte no. 32, Antigua Guatemala. No phone. 10 rms (none with bath).
$ Rates: Q17.50 ($3.50) single; Q29 ($5.80) double. No credit cards.
Just north of the arch, this old colonial building has been divided up, and a smiling señora rents very plain rooms without baths. Some of the rooms are sort of claustrophobic, with no windows (but, oddly, there are screens on the doors), so it's a good idea to look at your room before you rent it.

HOTEL PLACIDO, Avenida el Desengaño no. 25, Antigua Guatemala. No phone. 15 rms (4 with bath).
$ Rates: Q20 ($4) single without bath, Q30 ($6) single with bath; Q30 ($6) double without bath, Q40 ($8) double with bath; Q40 ($8) triple without bath, Q50 ($10) triple with bath. No credit cards.
Spartan and dark but probably acceptable to hardy young travelers here to study

Spanish on a limited budget, the Placido is on a busy street. Take a room at the back and the buses on the street out front shouldn't disturb you too much. There's a tiny religious grotto under the stairs leading to the second floor and colorful framed Guatemalan towels decorating the walls. The rooms with baths are the better deal. Try to get a room with a window.

WORTH THE EXTRA BUCKS

HOTEL ANTIGUA, 8a Calle Poniente no. 1, Antigua Guatemala. Tel. 502/32-0331 or 32-0288. In Guatemala City, tel. 502/532-490 or 27-575. Fax 502/032-0807 or 535-482. 60 rms (all with bath).

$ Rates: Q450.45 ($90.10) single; Q497.25 ($99.45) double; Q544.05 ($108.80) triple. AE, DC, MC, V.

This hotel, most favored by Guatemala's wealthy residents, is an expansive place only two blocks from the Parque Central. The hotel takes up an entire city block between 5a Avenida Sur and 4a Avenida Sur, and the block north of it serves as its parking lot. As you enter the colonial portal between two lion's-head fountains, you'll find what might best be termed a Spanish colonial country club, with beautiful lawns and a large heated swimming pool, patios with café tables, a children's playground, sun decks, and red-tile porticos over the low buildings surrounding the courtyard. These buildings hold the guest rooms, each with a fireplace and many with two double beds. From the grounds, you get surprising views of the ruined colonial church of San José, across 5a Avenida to the west. Keep in mind that prices are nearly double during Semana Santa.

The dining room is suitably large and elegantly colonial, and the loungelike Conquistador Bar is woody and masculine. You might want to come for a drink in the bar even if you can't afford to splurge on a room.

HOTEL POSADA DE DON RODRIGO, 5a Avenida Norte no. 17., Antigua Guatemala. Tel. 502/32-0291 or 32-0387. 33 rms (all with bath).

$ Rates: Q351 ($70.20) single; Q397.80 ($79.55) double; Q421.20 ($84.25) triple. AE, DC, MC, V.

Guests here can easily conjure up the life-style of the captains-general of Guatemala. The hotel is arranged around two courtyards, both very beautiful, the hind court having a tinkling fountain to entertain diners in the hotel's restaurant. The guest rooms have period furnishings: brass or carved-wood bedsteads, beamed ceilings, woven floor mats, and other antique or "antiqued" furnishings. The 24-hour hot water is sometimes little more than a warm trickle, but aside from this one drawback, the hotel is a rough-cut jewel. Rates are occasionally lower than those listed above, so be sure to ask for their best rates.

The main dining room and the bar of the open-air patio restaurant keep up the theme of colonial opulence, and marimba music entertains guests each afternoon.

WHERE TO EAT

Antigua is an excellent place to enjoy a meal. Although elegant dining is to be had only at the three top hotels and a couple of the "Worth the Extra Bucks" restaurants (described below), there's plenty of good food—and good value—here. By and large, restaurants don't have telephones in this town, and there's little need for them in any case.

MEALS FOR LESS THAN Q25 [$5]

RESTAURANT DOÑA LUISA, 4a Calle Oriente no. 12. No phone.
  Cuisine: INTERNATIONAL.
$ Prices: Breakfast Q3–Q11.50 (60¢–$2.30); sandwiches Q6–Q14 ($1.20–$2.80). No credit cards.
  Open: Daily 7am–10pm.

This busy two-story café is the town's traditional and very popular meeting place, and it is not far off the main square. Enter the building, and you'll see a small central courtyard set with dining tables, but there are more dining rooms and porticoes on the upper level. Doña Luisa's is frequented almost exclusively by gringos; the newsy bulletin board bears messages in both Spanish and English, with a few notices in French and German thrown in for good measure. The menu is eclectic—with sandwiches of many varieties (made on good bread baked right here), yogurt, chili, cakes and pies, and also more substantial fare. Alcohol is served, as is excellent Antigua coffee.

LA ESTRELLA, 5a Calle Poniente no. 6. Tel. 320-480.

Cuisine: CHINESE.

$ Prices: Main dishes Q11–Q26 ($2.20–$5.20). No credit cards.

Open: Daily noon–10pm.

There are 102 items on the menu here, not including the extensive cocktail menu, so if you can't find something that strikes your fancy, you just aren't trying. The most enjoyable part of eating here, or at any Chinese restaurant in Guatemala, for that matter, is translating the menu. *Tacos chinos* are egg rolls; anything *agridulce* is sweet and sour; and *salsa de soya* is soy sauce. You get the picture. There is little in the decor to lead you to believe that this is a Chinese restaurant, but the food, if not inspired, is recognizably Chinese. The bowls of soup here are huge, and the meal portions also are generous. Most dishes, including 18 shrimp entrées, are Q11 to Q15 ($2.20 to $3).

CAFÉ FLOR, 4a Avenida Sur no. 1. No phone.

Cuisine: MEXICAN.

$ Prices: Main dishes Q8–Q14.50 ($1.60–$2.90). No credit cards.

Open: Daily 9am–10pm.

It is difficult to think of Mexican food as exotic and foreign when you are this far south of the border, but that is exactly what it is in Guatemala. Locals and tourists alike put away plates of tacos, burritos, and enchiladas. You can have yours made with beef, chicken, pork, or tofu. The restaurant is on two levels, with a couple of window tables that are sunny spots for lunch. The restaurant occasionally shows videos.

FONDA DE LA CALLE REAL, 5a Avenida Norte no. 5. No phone.

Cuisine: GUATEMALAN/INTERNATIONAL.

$ Prices: Full meal Q10–Q27 ($2–$5.40).

Open: Daily 7am–10pm.

 Popular as a hangout and meeting place for Spanish students, the Fonda is known for its delicious *caldo real*—a delicious chicken soup that comes with tortillas and a condiment tray of oregano, cilantro, lime slices, chopped onions, and ground chili pepper—for Q9 ($1.80). Although the restaurant doesn't look like much at street level, upstairs there are 30 tables where you can sit comfortably and order roast chicken, fondues, steaks, and chops prepared by several busy señoras working hard in the downstairs kitchen. Steaks are the most expensive items.

Ⓕ FROMMER'S SMART TRAVELER: RESTAURANTS

1. Be sure to ask if there's a *plato del día*, which is always the best deal on the menu.
2. Some of Guatemala's best restaurants are in Antigua, so if you can afford a splurge or two, this is the place for it.
3. Check the opening time for a restaurant before heading off for your coffee and breakfast. Many restaurants don't open until fairly late in the morning.
4. You'll beat the dinner crowds, which can be particularly bad on weekends, if you eat dinner early, say between 5:30 and 6:30pm.

MISTRAL, 4a Calle Oriente no. 7. Tel. 323-228.
Cuisine: GUATEMALAN/INTERNATIONAL.
$ Prices: Licuados Q3.50–Q7 (70¢–$1.40); main dishes Q7.50–Q30 ($1.50–$6).
AE, DC, MC, V.
Open: Daily 11:30am–10pm.

For the best licuados in Guatemala, stop in here at any time of day. Mistral specializes in freshly prepared juices of fruits and vegetables, many of which are served in huge glasses known as *globos*. Watermelon and strawberry with milk is my favorite. They also have a complete menu that includes sandwiches and crêpes. The room in front is a noisy TV lounge and bar, but there is also a nice partially covered courtyard and several small dining rooms in the back.

PEROLETO, Calzada de Santa Lucia No. 36. No phone.
Cuisine: JUICE BAR/SNACKS.
$ Prices: Licuados Q2.25–Q4.75 (45¢–95¢), sandwiches Q4–Q5.50 (80¢–$1.10). No credit cards.
Open: Daily 7am–8pm.

You're almost sitting in the street at this slightly sunken juice bar and snack shop just up from the market and bus terminal, and the noise of the buses roaring by can be a bit deafening. However, there's no place better for a quick, early breakfast or a cheap, fast lunch. If the noise is too much for you, they have an enclosed dining room right next door to the juice bar. Granola with yogurt, *ceviche,* burgers, and hot dogs are the staples on the menu here. The juices and licuados are excellent. Try the orange and carrot juice mix.

SUEÑOS DEL QUETZAL, 5a Avenida Norte No. 3. No phone.
Cuisine: VEGETARIAN.
$ Prices: Main dishes Q11–Q18 ($2.20–$3.60). No credit cards.
Open: Daily 7am–10pm.

With one of the only balconies in town, Sueños del Quetzal enjoys an enviable location. If you can manage to grab one of the two balcony tables while it is free, sit back for a leisurely meal and enjoy the view of the street activity below. An international vegetarian menu made this restaurant an instant hit with young travelers and students staying in Antigua. On the menu, you'll find 12 different breakfasts, listed by nationality (including Australian). In addition to veggie standards such as tabouli, hummus, and veggie burgers, there are some local dishes cooked without the meat and daily casserole specials.

ZEN, 3a Avenida Norte No. 3. Tel. 323-293.
Cuisine: JAPANESE.
$ Prices: Main dishes Q9–Q17 ($1.80–$3.40). No credit cards.
Open: Thurs–Tues noon–10pm.

Antigua has become very cosmopolitan over the years and there is quite an array of international restaurants around town. If you've a hankering for some good vegetable soup or noodles with vegetables, try Zen. Though the cooking here seems a touch more Chinese than Japanese, it is still a welcome change from the standard meat-beans-and-tortillas diet so familiar to Guatemalan travelers. Chicken teriyaki and even teppanyaki with shrimp, chicken, beef, and vegetables are some of the better dishes on the menu. You can sit outside in the patio or inside near the bar.

MEALS FOR LESS THAN Q50 [$10]

RESTAURANT ITALIANO EL CAPUCHINO, 6a Avenida Norte no. 8. Tel. 320-613.
Cuisine: ITALIAN.
$ Prices: Main dishes Q13–Q50 ($2.60–$10). No credit cards.
Open: Daily 10am–10pm.

Between 4a and 5a calles Poniente, 1½ blocks from the Parque Central, you'll find one of Antigua's popular Italian restaurants. The facade of the restaurant doesn't look like much, but there is a covered interior court and arcade, with simple dining tables set out. Homey rather than fancy, the restaurant features a long menu of Italian food: pizzas, chicken cacciatore, lasagne, ravioli, spaghetti bolognese, and all the other favorites. Most meals here will not run over Q35 ($7). In the evening, mariachi bands often stop by the restaurant; for a small tip, they will serenade you.

POSADA DE DON RODRIGO, 5a Avenida Norte no. 17. Tel. 320-613.
   Cuisine: GUATEMALAN/INTERNATIONAL.
$ Prices: Main dishes Q28–Q52 ($5.60–$10.40). AE, DC, MC, V.
   Open: Daily 6am–9:30pm.

Although this is a splurge hotel, you can enjoy lunch here even if you're on a tight budget. You can order a filling platillo chapín (plate of Guatemalan specialties), including carne asada (grilled beef), guacamole, and frijoles refritos with rice and cheese, for Q39 ($7.80); with a drink, tax, and service, the bill may come to Q50 ($10). The menu also features a vegetarian plate, fish filets, chicken, pork, and tenderloin of beef (*lomito*). Even a full à la carte meal will cost only Q60 ($12). The setting is pleasant, and the staff (dressed in traditional costumes) is accommodating and helpful.

RESTAURANT KATOK, 4a Avenida no. 7. No phone.
   Cuisine: GUATEMALAN/INTERNATIONAL.
$ Prices: Main dishes Q17.50–Q42 ($3.50–$8.40). DC, MC, V.
   Open: Daily 10am–10pm.

Antigua is full of delightful little restaurants, and this is one of my favorites, located a block away from the Parque Central in a colonial building. You can dine in one of several dining rooms or out on the portico beside a lush little garden. There are beautiful old black-and-white photos of Antigua on the walls (they're for sale if you're interested). Fresh flowers grace every table, and waiters in black jackets make sure that everything is to your satisfaction. The plato típico especial Katok is a bounteous platter that includes two types of sausage, steak, ham, beans, cheese, fried bananas, salad, potatoes, and fried green onion—all for Q23 to Q26 ($4.60 to $5.20). The parrillada Katok is similar but feeds two people for Q48 ($9.60). Soups here are excellent and can be enough for a light meal. There's even a children's menu on Sunday. Also, there's a wide assortment of cocktails, beer, and wine.

SWEETS & PASTRIES

DOÑA MARÍA GORDILLO DULCES TÍPICOS, 4a Calle Oriente no. 11. No phone.
   Cuisine: SWEETS.
$ Prices: 30 centavos–Q1 (6¢–20¢). No credit cards.
   Open: Mon–Sat 9am–6pm.

Located across the street from the Hotel Aurora, this shop—filled with all sorts of sweets, desserts, and confections made from milk, fruit, eggs, marzipan, chocolate, and sugar—brings a bit of heaven to earth. Some local crafts are on sale as well. There is always a crowd of loyal customers filling the shop. Note that the treats here are for take-out only—there's no place to sit and munch. Since few if any of these sweets will be familiar to you, your best bet is to try a little of whatever looks good until you find the one that you can't live without.

LA CENICIENTA PASTELES, 5a Avenida Norte no. 7. No phone.
   Cuisine: PASTRIES.
$ Prices: Cake Q2–Q5 (40¢–$1) per slice. No credit cards.
   Open: Daily 8am–8pm.

With local textiles on the walls and a display case full of delectable cakes and pastries, Cenicienta is always jammed with young students indulging themselves. The daily menu includes quiche Lorraine and quiche chapín (Guatemalan style), yogurt and fruit, New York cheesecake, and numerous licuados. Don't be discouraged by the crowd in the front room; there is another dining area in the courtyard out back. You also can get anything to go.

WORTH THE EXTRA BUCKS

RESTAURANT MESÓN PANZA VERDE, 5a Avenida Sur no. 19. Tel. 322-925.
   Cuisine: CONTINENTAL.
$ Prices: Appetizers Q15–Q40 ($3–$8); main dishes Q36–Q44 ($7.20–$8.80). No credit cards.
   Open: Tues–Sat noon–3pm and 6:30–10pm; Sun noon–4pm.
If you want to be pampered and surround yourself with elegance, head out 5a Avenida Sur to one of Antigua's classiest little restaurants. The European owner knows how to make his guests happy. You might start your meal with six snails for Q22 ($4.40), then order a perfectly done steak with béarnaise, wine, or chile sauce for Q44 ($8.80). Top it off with chocolate mousse or peach Melba for Q15 ($3). There are also daily specials that include such tempting courses as cream of tomato soup, smoked salmon, and lobster thermidor. Your bill might come to around Q100 ($20), which is a fraction of what you would pay for this same meal back home.

EL SERENO, 6a Calle Poniente no. 30. Tel. 320-073.
   Cuisine: INTERNATIONAL. **Reservations:** Recommended, especially at dinner.
$ Prices: Appetizers Q8.50–Q20 ($1.70–$4); main dishes Q30–Q50 ($6–$10). AE, MC, V.
   Open: Wed–Sun noon–3pm and 6:30–9:30pm.
   ⭐ Between the Alameda de Santa Lucia and 7a Avenida Sur, next door to the Tecún Umán School of Spanish, is one of Antigua's finest restaurants. Within this colonial house are several small dining rooms. There are corner fireplaces, original oil paintings (many for sale), a small open-air portico, and carefully tended plants here and there. A doorman will welcome you, and a barman awaits your order in the small old-fashioned bar. The service is as refined as the cuisine. You might start with potage au pistou and go on to chicken Florentine, ham in a sauce of crème de cassis and mustard, or filet mignon with mushrooms. Desserts in this land of German influence are rich and delicious. The menu changes weekly, with new items being added all the time. With a glass of house wine, a full dinner might cost as little as Q75 ($15) per person—but it could be as high as Q115 ($23) per person, or perhaps even a bit higher, depending on your wine selection. Whatever you pay, you won't soon forget your meal here.

EVENING ENTERTAINMENT

Because most people in Antigua are here studying Spanish, this is generally an early-to-bed, early-to-rise town. There are, however, several bars that are popular with both Spanish students and their instructors. Spending time in the bars is almost a requirement for some students who actually learn most of their Spanish in that less structured environment. However, these bars change names frequently, so it's best to ask around for the current hangouts.

SHOPPING

Antigua has recently become a very reputable jade center: An ancient Mayan quarry near Nejar was rediscovered in 1958 and has been reopened. Jade from this quarry was sent to the Smithsonian Institution, which verified that the stones are jadeite, the highest quality of jade and equal to Chinese jade. Buying jade is a tricky business, for unless you're an expert, you may end up buying low-quality stones pawned off as the real thing. Jadeite is characterized by its hardness (6.5 to 7), which differs from many other stones and can easily be distinguished from softer stones. If a stone can be scratched with a pocketknife, then it isn't jadeite.
   The quality of jade is also differentiated as gemstones and carving stones. The gemstones are the most valuable and are rated according to their purity and the intensity of their color and translucency. A good gemstone jade can be more valuable than a diamond, and because of its hardness, it can take a jade carver half a day to

carve just one simple pendant. Therefore, know that if you go looking at the real things, you'll be looking at price tags in the $100-and-up bracket.

Two dealers in jade with good reputations and experience, not to mention beautiful collections, are **La Casa de Jade** (that's pronounced "ha-deh" not "jayd"), 4a Calle Oriente 3; and **Jades** ("ha-dess"), 4a Calle Oriente 34.

ONE-DAY EXCURSIONS

You can get a fine **panorama** of the city of Antigua by walking along La Avenida Norte northward to the outskirts of town. Pretty soon you'll come to a path leading uphill to a small park and a cross mounted on a pedestal. The walk takes only 20 to 30 minutes and is well worth it for the view. Go around to the back of the hill and see Ciudad Vieja, the town that was the forerunner of Antigua. Women should *never* make this trip without one or more large male escorts. In fact, it is questionable whether anyone should venture up here anymore. Rapes and robberies on this deserted hill have become far too commonplace. Before heading up here, ask around or check the bulletin boards around town for recent reports.

Ambitious mountaineers can climb up **Agua,** the impressive volcano that rises just beyond the outskirts of town. Start by taking the bus from behind the Antigua market to Santa María de Jesus. After a 20-minute ride, the bus will drop you in the main square of the village of that name; from the square, a road leads out of town and up the volcano. It's a fairly easy hike (not a climb) to the top for someone who's used to hiking. The free bonuses are everywhere: lovely wildflowers, fragrant aromas, lots of forest, and more mist the higher up you get. You can reach the top in four hours if you push it, five hours if you don't. *Remember:* The air's thinner here than at sea level. When you reach the top, you'll see the crater and a magnificent view (if it's a clear day and the clouds don't shut you off).

If you've ever wanted to climb an active volcano, this is the place to do it. A 2½-hour drive from Antigua is **Pacaya,** a live volcano that can be climbed by anyone in good health. Every few minutes the volcano erupts, spewing red-hot rocks into the air. A nearby dormant cone serves as a perfect vantage point for observing the eruptions. Keep in mind that, although the hike up is strenuous, the last few hundred yards to the top of the crater, across loose lava rocks and up a steep slope, can be very difficult. Winds can be strong and the footing is always slippery. Also, keep in mind that for several years now bandits have been robbing people on the slopes of Pacaya. Do not carry any cash or other valuables with you if you climb this volcano. If you go with a guide from Antigua, the price of the trip should include security measures as well. To find a group going up the volcano, just check out the bulletin boards at Doña Luisa or Casa Andinista. One more thing, if you're only interested in seeing the volcano erupt, be sure it's active before making the climb. Many adventurous types camp out near the peak to watch the eruptions at night; others simply make the hike a day trip. For day trips, check the bulletin boards around town. There are often enterprising folks organizing trips for around Q75 ($15).

---

2. LAKE ATITLÁN & PANAJACHEL

75 miles W of Guatemala City; 50 miles SE of Quetzaltenango;
25 miles S of Chichicastenango

GETTING THERE   By Bus   Rebuli buses from Guatemala City leave from 21 Calle 1-34, Zona 1 daily every hour from 5am to 3:45pm. Duration: 4 hours. Fare: Q8 ($1.60). From Quetzaltenango or Chichicastenango, take a bus to Los Encuentros, then change to a bus for Panajachel (you may have to change buses in Sololá).

By Car   Lake Atitlán can be reached from either the north or the south, although the southern route is not recommended due to frequent rebel activity in that area. Coming from Guatemala City, take the Patzún turnoff and continue down to Panajachel. Coming from Quetzaltenango, take the Sololá road. If you're coming from Chichicastenango, you must first turn west onto the highway before turning south a few miles later for Sololá and Panajachel.

DEPARTING If you're headed for Antigua, you'll have to take a bus bound for Guatemala City as far as Chimaltenango. In Chimaltenango, you'll catch another bus to Antigua. The ride to Chimaltenango takes about 2½ hours; from Chimaltenango to Antigua takes about 30 minutes. Total fare: Q10 ($2). Rebuli and Higueros buses make the trip to Guatemala City almost hourly between 5am and 3pm. Duration: 4 hours. Fare: Q8 ($1.60). On Thursday and Sunday mornings at 6:45am there is a direct bus to Chichicastenango. Otherwise you'll have to take any bus going to Los Encuentros and then transfer to a Chichi-bound bus. Duration: 2–2½ hours. Fare: Q3 (60¢). If you are headed to Quetzaltenango, look for a Higueros or Morales bus. Duration: 3 hours. Fare: Q10 ($2).

There are also tourist vans that head up to Chichi for market days. Ask around in town for the name of a company offering these trips. Expect to pay around Q50 ($10) for the round-trip fare. Turansa (tel. 322-928 in Antigua or 953-574 in Guatemala City) operates a shuttle between Panajachel and Antigua on Wednesday, Friday, and Sunday. The shuttle van stops at the Panajachel INGUAT office at the corner of Calle Principal and Calle Santander at 12:10pm. Fare: Q45 ($9).

ESSENTIALS Orientation Panajachel lies on the northern shore of Lake Atitlán, at the foot of the mountains. Coming into town from Sololá, you descend the mountainside along a serpentine road; you might like to stop at the scenic overlook. Near the bottom of the hill, you pass the turnoff on the right for the deluxe Hotel Atitlán, then for the Hotel Tzanjuyu, and next for the Cacique Inn, before continuing into town along the Calle Principal, the main street. There's a grocery store on the right, then a Texaco service station. Finally you come to the heart of town: the intersection of the Calle Principal and the Calle Santander, where you will see the INGUAT tourist office, the Banco Agricola, and the Hotel Mayan Palace. Calle Santander, on the right, goes down to the beach and the Hotel Monterrey.

Farther along, the Calle Principal holds several more hotels, restaurants, and shops and also the post and telegraph offices and the church. By the church is the town hall, the police station, and the marketplace, busiest on Sunday, but with some activity on weekdays from 9am to noon.

Parallel to Calle Santander, going from the center of town to the beach at the Hotel del Lago, is the Calle Rancho Grande.

Fast Facts The INGUAT Tourism Office is in the center of town on the Calle Principal near the Hotel Mayan Palace. It's open Friday to Tuesday from 8am to noon and 2 to 6pm, Wednesday from 8am to noon; closed Thursday.

Near the Circus Bar on Calle Santander is the Gallery Bookstore, where you can find new and used books in English, Spanish, and other languages. It also has maps of Guatemala, local art, and Guatemalan coffee. If you've bought more stuff than you can carry, you can use the shipping service here to send your purchases home.

The town's handiest bank is the Banco Agricola, on Calle Principal in the center of town—open Monday to Friday from 9am to 3pm (to 3:30pm on Friday), but note that currency-exchange hours are 9am to noon only! If the bank is closed, see if you can change money at your hotel or at some other hotel.

Bicycle rentals ($1 per hour) are available from a shop on Calle Santander just around the corner from Calle Principal heading away from the beach.

Market day is Sunday. Feast days are October 2 to 6.

The road from the main highway winds through the mountains and then descends to the lake through the provincial capital of Sololá (alt. 6,825 feet; pop. 9,000). Before you reach this town, however, you get glimpses of one of the most beautiful lakes in the world, a clear-blue mirror more than a mile above sea level, ringed by near-perfect-shaped volcanoes. The lake is not heavily settled or developed, so much of its natural beauty remains in pristine condition. Fishing, swimming, boating (some waterskiing), and hiking along the shore keep most lake visitors busy, and there are some restaurants and even a nightspot or two to keep people from going to bed too early. A good selection of hotels in all price ranges completes the picture.

Sololá has been here a long time, since 1547 to be exact. Even earlier than that, it was a Mayan town. Stop to inspect the ornate cathedral facade (Sololá has a bishop) and for the fabulous market (on Tuesday and Friday). The most exciting day of the year in Sololá is August 15, date of the annual festival. If you're anywhere nearby on that date, don't miss it.

From Sololá, head down the hill for Panajachel (that's "Pahn-ah-ha-chell"—alt. 5,150 feet; pop. 5,000), the resort town on the lakeshore. This is where you'll want to make your headquarters, not in Sololá. Market day in Panajachel is Sunday.

WHAT TO SEE & DO

It's only a 10- or 15-minute walk to the beach from any of the hotels mentioned below, and the beach is hardly ever crowded, perhaps because the water's a little chilly. There are beach cubicles for changing clothes, and several little eateries and soft-drink stands serve up snacks advertised on signboard menus. The one indispensable activity in Panajachel is sitting at one of the eateries along the beach, sipping a cool drink, and looking out over the water to the clouds scraping the tops of the volcanoes—you'll never forget the scene.

One of the main activities in Panajachel is shopping for clothes made from Guatemalan fabrics. All along Calle Santander, from Calle Principal to the beach, are vendors' stalls. After a while the riot of colors becomes overwhelming, so be sure to buy early in your stay before you get burned out on all the típico clothing. Remember: Back home this stuff is not very common and twice as expensive.

WHERE TO STAY

Because Panajachel is one of Guatemala's major tourist destinations and is, in fact, the country's top beach resort, there is a wide selection of accommodations available.

DOUBLES FOR LESS THAN Q80 [$16]

HOTEL FONDA DEL SOL, Calle Principal, Panajachel, Sololá. Tel. 502/ 62-1162. 20 rms (10 with bath).
$ Rates: Q35 ($7) single without bath. Q50–Q75 ($10–$15) single with bath; Q50 ($10) double without bath, Q75–Q100 ($15–$20) double with bath; Q75 ($15) triple without bath, Q100–Q125 ($20–$25) triple with bath. AE, DC, MC, V.
The most expensive rooms are in a new wing that offers some of the most attractive rooms in town. Patchwork quilts cover the beds, and there are brick floors and stone walls that have been stuccoed over. The doorways are arched and there are marble bathrooms and big windows. The cheapest rooms benefit from modern clean shared bathroom facilities. Laundry service is available.

HOTEL GALINDO, Calle Principal, Panajachel, Sololá. Tel. 502/62-1168. 18 rms (all with bath).
$ Rates: Q40 ($8) single; Q66 ($13.20) double; Q90 ($18) triple. MC, V.
Though the rooms may leave something to be desired in many cases, the setting is as idyllic as you'll find in any budget accommodation in Guatemala. The front of the hotel affects a colonial mood with arches and wrought iron, and behind this facade, through the dining room, is a riotously overgrown garden full of flowering shade trees. You can sit on the veranda and listen to dive-bombing hummingbirds or stretch out on one of the garden hammocks. Rooms are a bit dark, but if you stay out in the garden, it shouldn't matter too much. Laundry service is available.

HOTEL MAYA KANEK, Calle Principal, Panajachel, Sololá. Tel. 502/62-1104. 29 rms (13 with bath).
$ Rates: Q23.55–Q41.20 ($4.70–$8.25) single; Q41.20–Q58.85 ($8.25–$11.75) double. No credit cards.

Among this town's cheaper hotels is the Maya Kanek, just down from the church. It's a motel-style arrangement, with simple, fairly well-used quarters facing a cobbled court with a small garden. Twin beds, small showers, and dim light bulbs make this a fairly basic place to put up. One advantage is that you can park your car in the safety of the courtyard. Although there's more noise in the rooms above the reception desk, these are relatively new.

HOTEL MAYAN PALACE, Calle Principal, Panajachel, Sololá. Tel. 502/ 62-1028. 24 rms (all with bath).
$ Rates: Q52.65 ($10.55) single; Q70.20 ($14.05) double; Q87.75 ($17.55) triple. AE, DC, MC, V.

On the intersection of Calle Principal and Calle Santander at the heart of Panajachel you'll find a good choice in the bottom end of this price category. The rooms are fairly clean and were recently remodeled. They all have large windows looking out onto the open hallway that runs the length of the hotel. You'll have a nice view of the hills behind town from here, and you can watch the action in the street below. Several rooms have color TVs and most have some antique furniture.

HOTEL PRIMAVERA, Calle Santander, Panajachel, Sololá. Tel. 502/62-2052. 8 rms (all with bath).
$ Rates: Q46.80 ($9.35) single; Q64.35 ($12.90) double. AE, DC, MC, V.

One of Panajachel's newest little budget hotels is a German-owned place at the end of Calle Santander, farthest from the beach. The two-story hotel has a pretty little garden in the courtyard out back. The rooms are simple but clean and very appealing because they are new. The bathrooms in some of the rooms have skylights. Run with German efficiency, this is an excellent choice. There's even a sauna here.

Meals in the first-floor German restaurant range from Q20 to Q30 ($4 to $6).

DOUBLES FOR LESS THAN Q185 [$37]

HOTEL MONTERREY, Panajachel, Sololá. Tel. 502/62-1126. 30 rms (all with bath).
$ Rates: Q117 ($23.40) single; Q163.80 ($32.75) double; Q181.35 ($36.25) triple. No credit cards.

Hidden away on a dirt lane a few hundred yards off Calle Santander is a rather stark blue-and-white, two-story motel-style establishment. Don't be put off by the dry and dusty parking lot. Facing the lake across its own lawns, which extend down to the beach, the Monterrey offers you clean and cheerful accommodations in pleasant surroundings.

HOTEL PLAYA LINDA, Calle Rancho Grande, Panajachel, Sololá. Tel. 502/62-1159. 19 rms (all with bath).
$ Rates: Q117–Q146.25 ($23.40–$29.25) single; Q175.50–Q210.60 ($35.10–$42.10) double. DC, MC, V.

If you want to be as close to the lakeshore as possible, take a look at this hotel. A semi-modern building of brick, stone, white stucco, and dark wood, it has a small lawn, an aviary, lots of bougainvillea, and an assortment of guest rooms

---

IMPRESSIONS

. . . you see Lake Atitlan . . . Nothing can ever come up to this first moment of seeing it below you at its widest expanse, two thousand feet down, unruffled, blue as a peacock's breast . . .
—SACHEVERELL SITWELL, *GOLDEN WALL AND MIRADOR*, 1961

priced according to what sort of view they have. Rooms 1 through 5 are the best, on the second floor facing the lake; rooms 6 through 14 have no views but are a bit cheaper; rooms 1B through 4B are suites, and 5B is a large family suite. The one drawback here is that the area in front of the hotel is a large, noisy parking lot on weekends and holidays, spoiling the wonderful views. If you're paying by credit card, add 5% to your hotel bill. Meals in the open-air restaurant, with a fabulous view, cost around Q25 ($5).

RANCHO GRANDE INN, Calle Rancho Grande, Panajachel, Sololá. Tel. 502/62-1554. In Guatemala City, tel. 502/764-768. 11 rms (all with bath).
$ Rates (including breakfast): Q125 ($25) single; Q175 ($35) double; Q275 ($55) triple. DC, MC, V.

Founded several decades ago, the Rancho Grande was conceived as an inn of German country-style architecture in a tropical Guatemalan setting. Since 1975 the inn has been owned by Marlita Hannstein, who has preserved the lovely white-stucco cottages with red-tile or thatched roofs and small sitting porches, all set in emerald lawns beneath towering palm trees. All the rooms are different and feature Danish modern furniture. It's a quiet place, equally convenient to town and to the beach, where you'll receive a warm welcome. The bungalows can hold as many as five people, which makes them an excellent choice for families. However, the rooms tend to be in great demand. Highly recommended.

HOTEL REGIS, Calle Santander, Panajachel, Sololá. Tel. 502/62-1149. Fax 502/62-1152. 20 rms (all with bath).
$ Rates: Q157.95 ($31.60) single; Q181.35 ($36.25) double; Q204.75 ($40.95) triple. DC, MC, V.

Opposite the Guatel office on Calle Santander, which is the road from the center of town to the beach, stands this pretty hotel. The small, colonial-style complex is set back from the street across a lush lawn shaded by palms and equipped with a children's swimming pool and a small playground (swings and slide). The reception area and dining room are decorated with lots of local crafts. The guest rooms are in long, low buildings and separate bungalows, each with a nice veranda facing the lawn. There are also two rooms that have kitchenettes if you plan to be staying a while and want to save money by doing some of your own cooking. Some rooms have a TV and phone, as well as a small refrigerator. There is a small gift shop in the hotel lobby.

SUPER-BUDGET CHOICES

Besides the hotels below, Panajachel abounds in very simple, extremely cheap family pensions. You'll see them all along the Calle Santander and in other parts of town. Bath facilities may consist of a cold-water tap and primitive shower, but the price per person is usually only Q10 ($2), which is about as cheap as you can find anywhere in the world these days.

HOSPEDAJE CABANA COUNTRY CLUB, Calle Rancho Grande, Panajachel, Sololá. No phone. 22 rms (none with bath).
$ Rates: Q10 ($2) single without bath; Q20 ($4) double without bath. No credit cards.

Near the Rancho Grande Inn you'll find the most unusual of this type of rock-bottom pension. Despite its name, the Hospedaje Cabana is a low-budget accommodation. The rooms are arranged along a central courtyard parking area and are built to resemble long cabins. Each is just large enough to hold two twin beds. Sheets and blankets are included in the price.

HOSPEDAJE SANTA ELENA ANNEXO, Panajachel, Sololá. No phone. 8 rms (none with bath).
$ Rates: Q17.80 ($3.55) single; Q23.50 ($4.70) double. No credit cards.
Here you get a bed, one sheet, no blankets, a light, and a small table—period. But the señora keeps it all tidy. There are little tables in the modest courtyard (which you

share with banana plants and parrots) and there is a cold-water shower and toilet. The Annexo is off Calle Santander on the road to the Hotel Monterrey. The original Hospedaje Santa Elena is closer to the center of town, on the path up to the lookout.

WORTH THE EXTRA BUCKS

HOTEL ATITLÁN, Panajachel, Sololá. Tel. 502/62-1416, 62-1441, or 62-1429. 65 rms (all with bath).
$ Rates: Q292.50 ($58.50) single; Q321.75 ($64.35) double; Q409.50 ($81.90) triple. AE, DC, MC, V.

About 1½ miles (a 15- or 20-minute walk or a $2 taxi ride) from the center of town is one of Panajachel's more exclusive and expensive hotels. This is a fairly lavish Guatemalan-style establishment with spacious grounds and various tropical gardens filled with bougainvillea, ivy, and geraniums. The rambling three-story colonial-style hotel has gleaming tiled floors, antique wood carvings, and exquisite local craft pieces as decoration, as well as an experienced and obliging staff. The guest rooms have nice baths, twin beds, local craft decorations, and shady balconies from which to enjoy the view of the grounds and the lake.

Dining/Entertainment: A good restaurant with a long wall of glass providing a stunning view of lake and volcanoes and a nice open-air patio looking across the swimming pools to the lake are great places for a meal, whatever the weather might be. In the cool months, a fire burns in a large fireplace in the dining room. In the evening, the cozy bar is the perfect place for a drink before heading off to the dining room and a table by the fireplace. Meals are in the Q30 to Q40 ($6 to $8) range.

Facilities: Swimming pool and private beach.

CACIQUE INN, Calle Embarcadero, Panajachel, Sololá. Tel. 502/62-1205. 35 rms (all with bath).
$ Rates: Q204.75 ($40.95) single; Q234 ($46.80) double; Q263.25 ($52.65) triple. No credit cards.

Another excellent, quiet choice, this hotel is off Calle Principal at the western edge of town. A *cacique* is a native chieftain, and the inn has been hosting notables—both native and foreign—for many decades. In its own walled compound not far from the lakeshore, the inn has a spacious court planted with tropical shrubs and trees and green lawns and furnished with a tidy little swimming pool. The guest rooms, dining room, bar, souvenir shop, and reception desk are in low, rustic-inspired buildings facing the court. Lots of rounded stone, tree trunks, and other country touches were used in construction. The rooms are large, each with a fireplace (with wood laid, ready to light), two double beds with locally made blankets, and odd sliding glass-and-wrought-iron doors that take some getting used to. It's a welcoming place, obviously with a history all its own.

Lunch or dinner in the simple but light and airy dining room can be ordered à la carte; the table d'hôte dinner is about Q25 ($5).

HOTEL TZANJUYU, Panajachel, Sololá. Tel. 502/62-1318. In Guatemala City, tel. 502/310-764. 35 rms (all with bath).
$ Rates: Q204.75 ($40.95) single; Q234 ($46.80) double; Q263.25 ($52.65) triple. MC, V.

Located at the western end of town off Calle Principal, the Tzanjuyu was Panajachel's prime place to stay several decades ago, and it still has an old-fashioned air about it. If other hotels are full, you can get a passable, tidy room here with private tiled bath and a view of the lake. Room 30, with a curved wall of windows is my favorite. The lawns here are not kept up as well as those at some of the other, more expensive hotels, and there is little shade. There is, however, a nice little pool.

In the large restaurant/bar, the waiters wear jackets and ties. A meal will run you less than Q35 ($7).

HOTEL VISION AZUL, Panajachel, Sololá. Tel. 502/62-1426 or 62-1419. In Guatemala City, 41a Calle 18-67, Zona 12, Guatemala City. Tel. 502/761-483. 25 rms, 8 bungalows (all with bath).

$ **Rates:** Q257.40 ($51.50) single; Q292.50 ($58.50) double; Q327.60 ($65.50) triple or bungalow. AE, DC, MC, V.

⭐ A short distance outside of town on the road to the Hotel Atitlán, you'll find this very attractive white-stucco hotel with brick arches and volcanic stone accents. It is built into the hillside with a view across grassy lawns and through a grove of trees to the lake. Set in the midst of those lawns is a sunny swimming pool. Unfortunately, between you and the lawns and lake is a dusty dirt road that gets a lot of traffic on the weekends. Otherwise, the location is quiet. There is little to disturb you in one of the main building's big, bright guest rooms with a spacious terrace. The bungalows are small and located on the road so that they are not really a very good deal. Verdure is everywhere: bougainvillea, bananas, and ivy. The chirp of the birds is the loudest noise, except for the rumble of passing cars going to the Hotel Atitlán.

The Vision Azul has a decent restaurant, where lunch or dinner will cost around Q40 ($8).

WHERE TO EAT

The best dining is in the fancy hotels. For more modest meals, Panajachel has numerous places to offer, many of which are run by foreigners looking for a way to stay in Panajachel. These restaurants often go out of business within a year of opening. Often some other foreigner moves in, renames the restaurant, changes the menu, and tries to make a go of it. Consequently, you might find that a restaurant recommended here no longer exists but another restaurant occupies the same location. Give it a try as long as you're there—it may be the next "in" restaurant, and you'll have helped discover it.

MEALS FOR LESS THAN Q20 [$4]

LA HAMBURGUESA GIGANTE, Calle Santander. No phone.
   Cuisine: BURGERS/GUATEMALAN.
$ **Prices:** Q5–Q22 ($1–$4.40). No credit cards.
   Open: Daily 8am–10pm.
This is a long-time favorite in Panajachel, a congenial place with dependably tasty burgers, steaks, shrimp, chicken, and fish at moderate prices. Try the grilled chicken, for about Q15 ($3). Breakfast is served here as well.

RANCHÓN TÍPICA ATITLÁN, Calle Santander. No phone.
   Cuisine: GUATEMALAN.
$ **Prices:** Main dishes Q12–Q22 ($2.40–$4.40). No credit cards.
   Open: Daily 8am–11pm.
Ⓢ Another currently popular place is opposite the Hotel Regis. The walls are of rough-hewn logs, and the floor is of cobblestone. The specialty here is fish fresh from the lake for Q18 ($3.60). Although the service can be slow, you're likely to be entertained by young vendors who wander into the restaurant every few minutes. You can also order roast chicken for Q15 ($3). The restaurant is open from breakfast until late in the evening.

MEALS FOR LESS THAN Q30 [$6]

AL CHISME, Calle Los Arboles. Tel. 62-2063.
   Cuisine: INTERNATIONAL.
$ **Prices:** Breakfast Q6–Q13 ($1.20–$2.60); main dishes Q18–Q28 ($3.60–$5.60). MC, V.
   Open: Thurs–Tues 7am–11pm.
With an excellent assortment of salads and pastries, it is no wonder this restaurant was an instant hit in Panajachel. The meal includes all manner of European and

American favorites, such as crêpes, pastas, salads, and chicken Cordon Bleu. The music on the stereo is what you would expect if this restaurant were in Seattle or Miami. The narrow patio out front has a nice view of the steep hills outside town. You'll really get a sense of being inside a volcano when you gaze up at those walls.

PARADISE GARDEN RESTAURANT, Calle Principal. Tel. 62-1231.
   Cuisine: GUATEMALAN/INTERNATIONAL.
$ **Prices:** Main dishes Q12–Q40 ($2.40–$8). DC, MC, V.
   Open: Daily noon–10pm.

Set back from the road in a large grassy garden is a little Spanish-style house that has been converted into a simple-but-chic restaurant (by Panajachel standards). Within the dark dining room are several unusual lamps and sculptures made from old automobile parts. There are also a few tables on the veranda and out in the garden, where you can watch a pet parrot preening. The menu includes *pepian de pollo,* the Guatemalan national dish, a stew with a thick dark gravy. There are plenty of seafood entrées and a few dishes made with black bass from the lake.

EL PATIO, Calle Santander. No phone.
   Cuisine: INTERNATIONAL/GUATEMALAN.
$ **Prices:** Breakfast Q8–Q15 ($1.60–$3); lunch and dinner Q12–Q25 ($2.40–$5). DC, MC, V.
   Open: Sun–Fri 7am–9pm; Sat 7:30am–10pm.

As its name implies, this popular restaurant does indeed have a streetside patio for dining, plus a bright and attractive interior room. Quiet music soothes your spirit as you order from the menu, which includes a good assortment of sandwiches and *platos fuertes* (main courses) such as pepian de pollo (Guatemala's national dish), Szechuan chicken, cassoulet, roast pork, Virginia-style ham, chicken à la king, and filet mignon. Drinks are served.

TOCOYAL, Calle Rancho Grande. Tel. 62-1555.
   Cuisine: GUATEMALAN/INTERNATIONAL.
$ **Prices:** Main dishes Q12–Q40 ($2.40–$8). DC, MC, V.
   Open: Daily 7am–9pm.

Down at the end of Calle Rancho Grande, right on the beach, is this restaurant with one of the best views in the world. Take a seat on one of the restaurant's two terraces or inside the thatched-roof dining room with sliding glass walls and gaze across the lake at the volcanoes. It would be a crime not to have at least one sunset dinner here during your stay—in fact, you might want to eat here every evening. With views like these, it doesn't really matter what the food is like, but luckily meals here are tasty, and the service is good. The menu includes fresh lake fish and seafood, international pasta dishes, sandwiches, and that Guatemalan carnivore's delight, the *parrillada*. There is live music here on Saturday evening.

MEALS FOR LESS THAN Q40 [$8]

CASABLANCA, Calle Principal. Tel. 62-2025.
   Cuisine: INTERNATIONAL.
$ **Prices:** Soups and salads Q8–Q18 ($1.60–$3.60); entrees Q16–Q49 ($3.20–$9.80). MC, V.
   Open: Daily noon–9:30pm (sometimes later).

With the opening of this classy restaurant/bar, Panajachel emerged into the world of upscale resort towns. Mellow jazz music plays on the stereo, and on the weekend this place has live jazz, reggae, and salsa. Contemporary art hangs from the walls, sunshine filters through skylights, and diners on two floors gaze out at pedestrians through the large windows. Young and hip waiters in bow ties hurry between the kitchen and the tables. And, of course, it couldn't be called Casablanca without a few ceiling fans. If your German is good, you can grab a German magazine off a table here and spend the evening brushing up on world events. Daily specials for about Q25 ($5) are the best deal here, but if you're in the mood for a splurge, you can dine on steak or lobster. Try the shrimp-stuffed avocado salad for a starter. If you aren't in the mood for a big meal, you can get a sandwich (I'd stay away from the steak tartare sandwich because beef is not inspected).

LA POSADA DEL PINTOR AND THE CIRCUS BAR, Calle Los Arboles. No phone.
Cuisine: INTERNATIONAL.
$ Prices: Pizza Q16–Q30 ($3.20–$6); full meals Q15–Q25 ($3–$5). No credit cards.
Open: Daily noon–midnight.

Perhaps the most interesting place in the center of town is on the section of Calle Santander across Calle Principal (that is, in the direction away from the beach). It's a rustic bar with stools, plus dining tables spread with blue-and-white-checked cloths. The walls are covered in old circus posters, and quiet jazz issues from speakers here and there, filling the dining rooms and the small courtyard. In addition to pizza, there are many more interesting dishes on the menu, including shrimp thermidor, potato salad, steaks, pasta, and desserts. If you drop by for just a drink, expect to pay Q5 ($1) for a straight drink and Q7 ($1.40) to Q14 ($2.80) for a cocktail. There's live entertainment in the bar some evenings.

EXCURSIONS

There are regularly scheduled boats to many of the villages that perch on the shores of Lake Atitlán, but by far my favorite is the following.

SANTIAGO ATITLÁN

The village of Santiago Atitlán, across the lake from Panajachel on the southern shore, provides the destination for a nice cruise on the lake. The attractions of the town are its traditional life-style, its huipiles (blouses) embroidered with brilliantly colored flocks of birds, and its unusual history.

Several boats ply between Panajachel and Santiago Atitlán: The most convenient are those leaving from the main beach, which is down at the end of Calle Rancho Grande. Daily departures are at 8:35, 9, and 9:30am and 3 and 4pm; the return trips from Santiago Atitlán leave daily at 6 and 11:45am and 12:30, 1, 2, and 5pm. The one-way fare is Q10 ($2). (There are also boats to San Pedro La Laguna, San Antonio Palopó, and San Lucas Tolimán with departures between 8:30 and 9:30am.) The outbound trip across the lake takes about 1¼ hours; the return trip takes 1¼ to 1½ hours, depending on the wind.

While cruising across the lake, admire the perfect volcanoes and consider that Lake Atitlán is a caldera, formed by the tremendous eruption of an enormous volcano that eons ago literally blew its top off, creating the lake basin.

At the wharf in Santiago Atitlán, children from the town will greet you, selling souvenirs such as little embroidered strips of cloth and penny whistles made of clay. Leave the boat, turn left, and walk until you come to a town street paved in stone blocks.

Up the street on the right, is a sign that says "Visite la casa de la escultura y pintura," visit the house of sculpture and paintings." If you follow the sign's admonition, you will see the works of Diego Chavez and his two sons, Diego and Nicolas, three of the village's self-trained artists. Besides the paintings, there are wood carvings: figurines and bas-reliefs.

Along this street, which is strolled by every tourist coming up from the docks, are most of the town's shops, which sell huipiles and other craft items. The cloth is truly gorgeous, with days of beautiful and painstaking handwork invested in each piece.

Up the hill a bit farther is the town square, the town office, and the huge old church. Within the stark, echoing church are some surprising sights. Along the walls are wooden statues of the saints, each of whom gets a new shawl, embroidered by local women, every year. On the carved wooden pulpit, note the figures of corn (from which humans were formed, according to Mayan religion); the quetzal bird reading a book; and Yum-Kax, the Mayan god of corn. There is similar carving on the back of the priest's chair. The walls of the church bear paintings, now covered by a thin layer of plaster. A memorial plaque at the back of the church commemorates Fr. Stanley Francis Rother, a missionary priest from Oklahoma who was beloved by the local people but despised by ultrarightist elements, who murdered him right here in the church during the troubled year of 1981.

Where to Stay

HOTEL TZUTUHIL, Santiago Atitlán. Tel. 502/62-7174. 22 rms (12 with bath).

$ Rates: Q15 ($3) single without bath, Q25 ($5) single with bath; Q30 ($6) double without bath, Q35 ($7) double with bath. No credit cards.

Located two blocks downhill from the church in the middle of town, this economical hotel is easy to find—it's the tallest building in town. Economical and basic with small rooms, the Tzutuhil is above a hardware store, which is where you should go to ask about a room. Try to get room 17, which has a good view. If you can't get a room with a view, you can hang out on the rooftop patio and enjoy the views from there. There is a little *comedor* (dining room) on the ground floor.

POSADA DE SANTIAGO, Santiago Atitlán. Tel. 502/62-7168 or 62-7158 (messages). Fax 502/962-7132. 6 bungalows.

$ Rates (including continental breakfast): Q100 ($20) single; Q125 ($25) double; Q150 ($30) triple. No credit cards.

Built and owned by an American couple who have been living in Santiago Atitlán for a while, this cozy lodge is a great place to get away from it all. The bungalows are tucked amid a beautiful garden on a hillside above the lake. From the moment you open the intricately carved door to your room, you'll know that a lot of thought and care went into these rooms. There are stone walls and high ceilings, plenty of windows, and hammocks on each individual patio. Fireplaces and Momostecan handwoven blankets will keep you warm on chilly winter nights. One bungalow even has a stone-sided platform bed. You can relax in the garden or just drink in the view from a thatch-roofed observation deck. The hotel's restaurant is furnished with rustic tables and chairs. The menu even features a bit of Mayan cooking (chicken and pork pibil). Prices range from Q8 to Q12 ($1.60 to $2.40) for lunch and Q20 to Q25 ($4 to $5) for dinner. This is one of my favorite hotels in the whole country.

Where to Eat

RESTAURANT EL GRAN SOL, uphill from boat dock. No phone.

$ Prices: Breakfast Q6–Q8 ($1.20–$1.60), main dishes Q6–Q10 ($1.20–$2).

There is a great view over the lake from the palapa-shaded terrace of this restaurant, the nicest in Santiago Atitlán. Bamboo and thatch provide the proper tropical atmosphere to accompany the splendid view. This is a lovely place to sit and watch folks go by.

IXIMCHÉ

A short distance east of the Los Encuentros crossroads on the Pan American Highway, on the way toward Chimaltenango, there is a turnoff for the town of Tecpan and signs point the way through the town to the ancient Mayan city of Iximché. If you have a car, make the detour to see this beautiful archeological site.

As you enter the site, you pass a small building, the museo, on your right. Then you enter the city itself, past some grass-covered mounds and into the main complex of plazas. On many of the pyramids here, the outer coating of plaster is visible in places. When you come to the first uncovered buildings, look for traces of painting on the low structure to the left.

Iximché was selected as the site for the capital city of the Cakchiquel Maya partly because of its natural defenses, as it is on a promontory surrounded on three sides by ravines. It was the Cakchiquel capital when the conquistadores came in the early 1500s, having been founded only a half-century before. The Cakchiquels formed an alliance with the Spaniards, who founded Tecpan nearby and who used Tecpan as their center of operations for the governing of Guatemala. But later these two warlike peoples had a falling out; in the ensuing battles, the Cakchiquels lost to the Spaniards. Still, the Cakchiquel capital city escaped massive destruction and stands today as a fascinating monument to that people.

3. CHICHICASTENANGO

75 miles NW of Guatemala City; 50 miles NE of Quetzaltenango;
25 miles N of Panajachel

GETTING THERE   By Bus   To reach Chichicastenango by bus, you must first get to the crossroads called Los Encuentros, which is on the Pan American Highway between Chimaltenango and Cuatro Caminos. Almost every bus traveling through the highlands on the Pan American Highway drives by Los Encuentros. If you are coming from Panajachel, on Thursday and Sunday mornings at 6:45am there is a direct bus to Chichicastenango. You can also take the first bus headed up to Los Encuentros. From Antigua, you must first take a bus to Chimaltenango and then catch another bus to Los Encuentros. From Los Encuentros, a bus to Chichicastenango will cost Q1.50 (30¢).

Several travel agencies offer trips from Antigua or Panajachel by van. These trips go over in the morning on market days and return in the afternoon. Ceprotours, 4a Calle Poniente No. 1, Antigua (tel. 322-974), charges Q75 ($15) per person and leaves from Antigua's Central Park at 8:30am. This same company offers an overnight trip with one night in Panajachel before continuing to Chichicastenango.

By Car   If you're coming from Guatemala City or Quetzaltenango, the turnoff from the highway is at Los Encuentros. There's a small open market here where people from the surrounding hills sell produce and entrepreneurs from the towns sell locally made clothes. There's also a gas station and a postal and telephone office.

The road to Chichicastenango is scenic, even dramatic, diving down into a deep ravine and then climbing steeply up the other side. Along the way are the inevitable cornfields and local women weaving beautiful clothes near their modest homes.

DEPARTING   Buses arrive and leave from various points around the market; several lines are based near the Hotel Santo Tomas. Just say the name of your destination to any bus driver or policeman and you'll be directed to the proper corner. There are direct buses to Quetzaltenango, Panajachel, and Guatemala City. If you can't find a direct bus that's headed in your direction, catch any bus out to Los Encuentros, and wait there for a bus that's going to the right place.

ESSENTIALS   Orientation   The center of town is, of course, the central square, where the market is held. Coming into town from Los Encuentros, you must turn left at the Hotel Santo Tomas and go down a few blocks. The square will then be two blocks or so over to your left. Note that Chichicastenango is a small town, with few street signs or numbers, so you have to ask around to find everything.

Fast Facts   The post office (correos) is at 7a Avenida 8-47, two blocks northwest of the Hotel Santo Tomas on the road into town. Very near it is the Guatel telephone office, at 7a Avenida 8-21, on the corner of 8a Calle. Market days are Sunday and Thursday. Feast days are December 18 to 21 and Holy Week.

Once a sleepy Indian village, Santo Tomas Chichicastenango (alt. 6,650 feet; pop. 6,500) is today one of Guatemala's most popular tourist destinations. They come for the same reason that Indians have come here for centuries—to shop at the market. Although the market is still where local women buy the necessities of life and local farmers sell their produce, it is also where foreigners come to get the best deals on Guatemalan textiles. Every Sunday and Thursday, the town's central square becomes a maze of stalls selling both traditional and modern textiles, machine- and handmade.

Facing the market square is the Santo Tomas Church, which figures prominently in the religion, both pagan and Christian, of the region. On the circular stone steps of the church, women sell flowers in the morning; throughout the day, Indians approach the massive doors of the church swinging censers made from old coffee cans. The fragrant incense smoke rises in clouds and drifts over the heads of the shoppers pushing their way among the stalls. Amid the chatter of vendors and shoppers, you can hear the chanting of a petitioner at the doors. The ritual is centuries old; the language is Quiché.

Don't expect to be the only gringo witnessing these rituals. On market days huge tour buses roar in to deliver several hundred curious cloth buyers. You can avoid the crowds and still see the local weaving by coming on a nonmarket day, when a few stands are always open and the whole town is a lot quieter.

WHAT TO SEE & DO

Chichicastenango certainly isn't what you'd call an exciting place, except on market days, and that's its very fascination. Unless you're an anthropologist or a textile expert, you won't spend more than an afternoon looking over the marvelous handwoven and embroidered cloths for which the district is famous. Chichicastenango's other claim to fame, its much-vaunted paganism, involves things that you can't look for, although you may happen on them: On a rainy night, a young man swings a censer swiftly back and forth before the locked doors of the Santo Tomas Church, barking admonitions and chants at a woman kneeling in prayer on the bare stones. The symbols, paraphernalia, and words are Christian, but the inspiration is clearly pagan.

On Sunday, the service in the Church of Santo Tomas presents a fascinating vignette: Within the church, Christian mass is in progress, while behind the church, pagan rites are being held. The church dates from the mid-1500s. Its significance and power are not those of the Catholic church so much as of the local male groups known as **cofradías**. Each of these associations pays homage to its own patron saint and has religious and civic duties. In effect, the cofradías are as important as the local Catholic and municipal authorities; among the local people, they're more important. If you're in Chichicastenango on a major church holiday or on one of the cofradías' saints' days, you may see a cofradía procession, led by its alcalde (chief) and a ragtag band, winding through the town and the market.

For a look at more of this town's Pre-Christian culture, take a short hike to the Shrine of Pascual Abaj, on the outskirts of town. Facing the Santo Tomas Church, turn right, walk down the hill on 5a Avenida to 9a Calle, and turn right. Go down the hill on 9a Calle, around the bend to the left; when the road turns sharply to the right, bear left and follow a path through the cornfields, keeping the ditch on your left-hand side. Proceed along the dirt path to the top of the hill covered in fragrant pines. At the very top is a clearing, and in it is the primitive carved-stone head of the idol, surrounded by little fireplace altars. Chances are good that a local man or woman will be chanting and praying at one or more of the altars and burning pungent incense. You can observe the rites without disturbing them. Before heading up here by yourself, ask at your hotel to make sure it is safe. In recent years a number of people have been robbed when they ventured up here on their own. To be safe, you can hire a guide to bring you up. There always seems to be someone on the main square offering to take you to see Pascual Abaj.

Chichicastenango has a museum facing the main square, the **Museo Regional**. Admission is free, although the museum never seems to be open when I am in town. The two large exhibit rooms have plain glass-fronted cabinets in best 19th-century museum style. In the left room are objects, figurines, and necklaces of jade, as well as clay incense burners, effigy pots and plainer vessels, metates (grindstones for corn), flint and obsidian arrowheads and spearheads, clay figurines, and copper axheads. In the right room are polychrome pots and those with relief work on them. Some of these are particularly nice.

WHERE TO STAY

DOUBLES FOR LESS THAN Q40 [$8]

HOTEL CASA DE HUESPEDES GIRON, 5a Calle 4-52, Santo Tomás Chichicastenango. Tel. 502/561-156. 11 rms (none with bath).
$ Rates: Q12–Q20 ($2.40–$4) single; Q20–Q30 ($4–$6) double; Q30 ($6) triple.
You'll find this basic lodging behind the modern shopping center building that houses the Restaurante El Torito. Rooms are small and spartan but usually clean and your right in the thick of things so you don't have far to walk when you become loaded down with purchases from the market.

DOUBLES FOR LESS THAN Q100 [$20]

PENSIÓN CHUGUILÁ, Santo Tomás Chichicastenango. Tel. 502/56-1134. 27 rms (23 with bath).
$ Rates: Q40 ($8) single without bath, Q75 ($15) single with bath; Q60 ($12) double without bath, Q95 ($19) double with bath; Q80 ($16) triple without bath, Q115 ($23) triple with bath. No credit cards.

The budget traveler's version of the Mayan Inn is a charming old place a few blocks off the square. You enter from the cobbled street to find a cobbled courtyard (partly filled with parked cars) and a very pleasant portico paved in tiles and furnished with easy chairs, coffee tables, and tropical plants. The simple but pleasant dining room is to the left as you approach the reception desk. Some of the guest rooms have fireplaces; a few two-room suites have a bedroom and sitting room with fireplace. Furnishings are colonial in style, with accents of local cloth.
Breakfast in the dining room costs Q15 ($3). Lunch and dinner go for Q25 ($5).

MAYA LODGE, 6 Calle A 4-08, Santo Tomás Chichicastenango. Tel. 502/56-1167. 13 rms (all with bath).
$ Rates: Q117 ($23.40) single; Q152.10 ($30.40) double; Q187.20 ($37.45). No credit cards.
If you'd like to be right near the action on market day, this is the place for you. It's right on the main square where the market is held, and you'll have to weave your way through the maze of vendors to get in or out of the hotel. The rates are reasonable, and the accommodations are fairly comfortable. Try to get one of the cozy rooms with a fireplace (*chimenea*). Although rather bare compared to the town's other hostelries and perhaps a bit dark, this hotel is still a far cry from basic, though it is a bit overpriced. The clean, presentable rooms have their own tables and chairs in the long narrow courtyard.
Breakfast in the simple little comedor costs Q15 ($3). Lunch and dinner go for Q20 ($4).

WORTH THE EXTRA BUCKS

Chichicastenango is an excellent place to let go of your budget and indulge yourself, because a little more money buys such an unforgettably beautiful experience.

MAYAN INN, 8a Calle and 3a Avenida, Santo Tomás Chichicastenango. Tel. 502/56-1176. In Guatemala City, tel. 502/231-0213. Fax 502/231-5919. 30 rms (all with bath).
$ Rates: Q321.75 ($64.35) single; Q386.10 ($77.20) double; Q450.45 ($90.10) triple. AE, MC, V.

⭐ The best in town, and perhaps the most enjoyable hotel in Guatemala, is this lovely old lodge on a quiet side street a few blocks from the bustling main market square. The inn was started in 1932 by Alfred S. Clark (of Clark Tours fame); it's composed of several colonial buildings, and the guest rooms are arranged under red-tile porticoes around courtyards planted with beautiful tropical gardens and lush grass. Parrots squawk and whistle here and there, and in the afternoons a local marimba band provides pleasant entertainment. The guest rooms are simple but absolutely charming, with antique furnishings, including carved-wood bedsteads, headboards painted with country scenes, heavily carved armoires, and rough-hewn tables, many of which were found by Mr. Clark himself. Each room has a little fireplace, with split logs laid ready to burn and a few sticks of *ocote* (fat wood) with which to kindle. Everywhere throughout the hotel are those gorgeous local textiles: window curtains, bedspreads, even shower curtains! Private bathrooms are tiled and, if a bit old-fashioned, also spacious and decently kept up; many have tubs.

I must mention that virtually all the staff at the Mayan Inn are dressed in local costumes, including colorful headdress, sash, black tunic with colored embroidery, half-length trousers, and squeaky leather *caites* (sandals). The costume is not purely Mayan, but a Spanish farmer's costume brought over by the conquistadores and adapted by the Guatemalans to their own culture. Although a stay at the Mayan Inn is technically out of your budget range, I urge you to stay here if at all possible—and it may not be possible for you to get reservations. But try.

The hotel has its own cozy colonial bar with fireplace (of course), and two dining rooms with pale-yellow walls, beamed ceilings, red-tile floors, stocky colonial-style tables and chairs, and more local cloth. You can order à la carte, but it makes the most sense to have the daily table d'hôte meals, which cost Q25 ($5) at breakfast, Q50 ($10) at lunch or dinner, plus tip and drinks. A typical dinner might be cream of tomato soup; roast lamb, broiled beef, or beef tongue in a savory sauce; followed by salad; and rhum baba or ice cream for dessert.

HOTEL SANTO TOMAS, Santo Tomás Chichicastenango. Tel. 502/56-1061 or 56-1316. Fax 502/056-1306. 43 rms (all with bath).
$ Rates: Q292.50 ($58.50) single; Q351 ($70.20) double; Q409.50 ($81.90) triple. DC, MC, V.

The most modern hotel in town, the Santo Tomas has become very popular with tour groups and is now even trying to lure conferences to Chichicastenango. You can't miss it as you come into town on the main road, but ask anyone to direct you if you have trouble. Colonial in style, it's modern in facilities. The rooms are arranged on two levels around two courtyards, each with its own fountain, gardens, and menagerie of parrots. Many of the rooms are filled by tour group participants, and the hotel is often abustle with guests arriving, leaving, heading out on shopping excursions, or returning from the same. If you want to stay here, you must reserve as far ahead as possible. The large, cheery rooms are decorated with local cloths and blankets and have private bathrooms and fireplaces. Most have twin beds. Pet parrots and macaws squawk and talk in the courtyard all day, and throughout the hotel are pieces of local upper-class art—fancy robes, church statuary, antique altars, and so forth.

Dining/Entertainment: There is a large, attractive colonial-style dining room and also some tables set out under the arcade for courtyard dining. A table d'hôte breakfast here is priced at Q30 ($6), and lunch and dinner cost Q45 ($9), with drinks, tax, and tip included. The hotel's nice bar has two rooms. A marimba band plays at lunch.

Facilities: Solar-heated swimming pool, Jacuzzi, sauna, and exercise room on the terrace out back.

WHERE TO EAT

Meal possibilities are best in the above hotels, but if you're out for adventure and want to save money, take a look at the little comedors (dining spots) in the market and near the post office and Guatel office on the road into town (7a Avenida). There are also several restaurants around town that cater almost exclusively to the tour-bus trade.

Their menus are primarily international, with a few Guatemalan favorites thrown in for good measure.

RESTAURANTE EL TORITO, Comercial Giron, 2nd floor. No phone.
   Cuisine: GUATEMALAN.
$ **Prices:** Complete meal Q12–Q24 ($2.40–$4.80). No credit cards.
   Open: Daily 7am–9pm.
"The Little Bull," as its name implies, is primarily a steak house; however, you can also get chicken, fish, shrimp, chorizo, and pork chops. All the meals come with soup, potatoes, rice, and bread or tortillas. It is on the second floor of a new shopping arcade and has a few tables on the balcony overlooking the courtyard. The restaurant's main room is huge, obviously designed to accommodate busloads of diners. Light streams in through a wall of windows during the day.

RESTAURANTE TZIGUAN TINAMIT, 5a Avenida and 6a Calle. No phone.
   Cuisine: GUATEMALAN.
$ **Prices:** Breakfast Q8–Q10 ($1.60–$3); main dishes Q18–Q20 ($3.60–$4). MC, V.
   Open: Daily 7am–9pm.
Located on the corner just down from the Pensión Chuguilá, this simple restaurant serves good, inexpensive meals, especially breakfasts. For lunch and dinner there are steaks, fried chicken, fried fish, and pizza. Guatemalan textiles accent the Spartan dining room.

EXCURSIONS

Called simply **Quiché** by the natives, the provincial capital is only 20 miles farther along the road from Chichicastenango. A day trip will hold no great thrills, but you can take a look at its famous church, watch the local women weave straw hats as they walk (distances here are measured in hat-making time!), or have a shave and a haircut in the barbershop by the market. There are some ruins 2 miles from town at Ciudad Gumarcaan (no public transportation), once the royal city of King Quiché. Nothing's been excavated or rebuilt, and the grass-covered stone mounds give you the eerie feeling that you're walking in a dead city.

   You can continue past Quiché by bus over a bumpy and dusty (or muddy) road for a good number of miles to **Nebaj.** The few *norteamericanos* who venture into Nebaj come to see the exquisitely beautiful costumes and headdresses of the Nebaj women, said by crafts experts to be the most beautiful in all of Guatemala. The trip is a fairly long one.

---

4. QUETZALTENANGO

49 miles S of Huehuetenango; 161 miles NW of Guatemala City;
96 miles NW of Panajachel

GETTING THERE By Bus Keep in mind that almost all buses use an abbreviation of Quetzaltenango's Indian name. Look for the word Xela or Xelaju on the windshield. Buses from Guatemala City leave from 7a Av. 19-44, Zona 1 (tel. 23-661) daily at 5:30, 8:30, and 11am and 1, 2:30, 5:30, 7, and 9pm. Duration: 4 hours. Fare: Q15.45 ($3.10). From Chichi or Panajachel, take a bus to Los Encuentros crossroad and flag down a Quetzaltenango bus. Coming from Antigua, you must first take a bus to Chimaltenango and then flag down a Quetzaltenango bus.

By Car If you're coming from the Pacific Highway, take the Quetzaltenango toll road turnoff just past Mazatenango. Coming from Huehuetenango or Guatemala City, turn south at Cuatro Caminos, the intersection just north of Quetzaltenango.

DEPARTING At the main bus terminal on 13a Avenida and 4a Calle, Zona 3 (near

Parque Minerva), there are second-class buses leaving regularly for cities all over Guatemala. These buses usually leave when they are full and are always very crowded. However, they leave much more frequently than the first-class buses of the companies mentioned below. Ticket prices are also slightly less. There are buses out here from the main plaza, or you can take a taxi for Q10 ($2).

To reach Chichicastenango, take a second-class bus from the Zona 3 bus terminal. There are no direct buses to Panajachel. Take any bus headed toward Guatemala City and get off at Los Encuentros. From here you can get a bus down to Panajachel.

Rutas Lima, 11 Av. 4-07, Zona 1 (tel. 2023), with another office next to the Pensión Bonifaz at 2a Calle 1-07, Zona 1, has buses daily to Guatemala City at 5:15 and 7:30am and 2:15 and 7:15pm.

Transportes Galgos, 2a Calle 5-66, Zona 2, and Autobuses Americas, 2a Calle 3-33, are both about a mile northeast of the Parque Centro America, and inconvenient to reach except by taxi. They have daily service to Guatemala City.

Transportes Higueros, 12a Avenida and 7a Calle, Zona 1 (tel. 2233), is beneath the tourist office in the Casa de la Cultura building (facing the building, go around to the right-hand side). Buses for Guatemala City leave at 4am and 3:30pm.

All of these buses take about four hours and charge Q13 to Q15 ($2.60 to $3).

Any bus headed to the Mexican border will stop in Huehuetenango. Duration: 2½–3 hours. Fare: Q5 ($1). You can also get second-class buses to Huehuetenango from the Zona 3 bus terminal.

ESSENTIALS Orientation   The Parque Centro America is the center of town; most of the principal buildings face it, including the new municipal market, the Tourism Office and town hall, the church, the museum, and several hotels and restaurants. The streets are not well marked in this town, so keep track of where you're going.

Fast Facts   Many of the city's banks face the Parque Centro America. Normal hours of operation are Monday to Friday from 8:30 or 9am to 2 or 2:30pm. The Banco Industrial, on the Parque in the Palacio Municipal, at 11a Avenida and 5a Calle (tel. 61-2258 or 61-2288), is open on weekdays until 7pm and Saturdays from 8:30am to 5:30pm.

Take your laundry to the Lavanderia Mini-Max, 14a Avenida C-47, at 1a Calle, facing the plaza with the classical Teatro Municipal, and next to the Taberna de Don Rodrigo.

The **Tourist Office** (tel. 61-4931) is in the Casa de la Cultura (also called the Museo de Historia Natural) at the lower end of the Parque Centro America—open daily from 8am to noon and 2 to 5pm.

Market day is every day. Feast days are September 12 to 18.

Named by the Aztecs for what is now the national bird, Quetzaltenango is the country's second-largest town (alt. 7,800 feet; pop. 80,000). It was built on the site of the Quiché Maya Indian ancient capital of Xelaju, and the Indians still call it by this name. Quetzaltenango is a booming, growing city—but the countryside surrounding it is marvelously beautiful. In the marketplace, men and women wear traditional costumes of heavily embroidered cloth. These are not costumes in the sense that they're put on for special occasions, but rather they're the normal, everyday clothing in this traditional rural culture. The Indian garb contrasts strikingly with the Italianate columns and monuments in the main square, the Parque Centro America.

WHAT TO SEE & DO

Quetzaltenango is not really a sightseer's town, but rather a way station on the highway, at least as far as tourists are concerned. While you're here, though, take a look at the **Museo de Historia Natural,** with a collection of exhibits that might most kindly be termed "eclectic." Also have a look in the **cathedral** and the

Palacio Municipal (city hall). All three of these prominent buildings are on the Parque Centro America.

Walk north on 14a Avenida to 1a Calle, and you'll come face-to-face with the city's impressive neoclassical **Teatro Municipal.** If there's a performance, rehearsal, or meeting in progress when you visit, you'll have to be content with the view from the outside. Inside, however, are three tiers of seating, the lower two of which have private boxes for theatergoers. The boxes were rented by prominent families by the season or the year; each is equipped with a vanity for women.

There is a small **market** to the left of the museum, at the southeastern corner of the Parque Centro America. Although you'll find a few food stalls and shops selling everyday items on the lower level, much of the space here is tourist oriented. Guatemalan fabrics have been used to make dresses and other garments according to North American styles. It's worth a walk through.

The city's large market is the **Mercado La Democracia**, in Zona 3, about ten blocks northwest of the Parque Centro America. To get there, walk along 14a Avenida to 1a Calle. Turn left, walk to 16a Avenida, then turn right. Walk along 16a Avenida, cross Calle Rodolfo Robles (the first major cross-street you encounter), and the market will be on your right. It extends for about two blocks.

La Democracia is the people's market, with fruits, vegetables, tortillas, beans, chickens, shoes, children's clothing, and fabrics for sale. The selection of fabrics is not large, but the prices are fairly good.

Less than a mile west of the Parque Centro America is the **Parque Minerva**, and its neoclassical **Templo de Minerva**, built to honor the classical goddess of education and to inspire Guatemalan youth to new heights of learning.

WHERE TO STAY

DOUBLES FOR LESS THAN Q50 [$10]

CASA SUIZA, 14a Avenida "A" 2-36, Zona 1, Quetzaltenango. Tel. 502/61-4350. 18 rms (12 with bath).
$ Rates: Q17 ($3.40) single without bath, Q35 ($7) single with bath; Q29 ($5.80) double without bath, Q47 ($9.40) double with bath; Q41 ($8.20) triple without bath, Q53 ($10.60) triple with bath. No credit cards.
Swiss in name only, this very basic pension is located across the street from the Hotel Modelo (below). Walk through the street-side doors, and you'll find yourself in a colorfully painted courtyard. All the rooms have high ceilings that make them seem very spacious. The bathrooms, which were obviously added on long after the building was constructed, are housed within glass-and-metal booths in the corners of the rooms. The señorita who runs the pension is very friendly. A fixed-price menu is served in the dining room—Q8 ($1.60) for breakfast and Q12 ($2.40) for lunch.

HOTEL RÍO AZUL, 2a Calle 12-15, Zona 1, Quetzaltenango. No phone. 16 rms (all with bath).
$ Rates: Q35 ($7) single; Q45 ($9) double; Q55 ($11) triple. No credit cards.
Parking: Q2 (40¢).

A new choice in town, the Río Azul is conveniently located close to the Parque Centro America and many good restaurants. The owner of the hotel, who speaks little English, is nevertheless a wealth of information about the area and can help you organize your tour of Guatemala. The rooms are simple, but the red-tile floors give them a rustic appeal. Some rooms have nice views, and all have very clean bathrooms. Security is tight here, so you don't have to worry much about your belongings.

DOUBLES FOR LESS THAN Q90 [$22.50]

GRAN HOTEL AMERICANO, 14a Avenida 3-45, Zona 1, Quetzaltenango. Tel. 502/61-8118 or 61-8219. 12 rms (all with bath). TV
$ Rates: Q70.20 ($14.05) single; Q81.90 ($16.40) double; Q92.60 ($18.50) triple. No credit cards.

In the middle of the restaurant district of Quetzaltenango, you'll probably hear the computerized cacophony of a video arcade. Don't rush by: Upstairs you'll find one of the better hotel deals in town. Luckily, the video games are shut off by 11pm, and upstairs you can barely hear them even when they are going full blast. All the rooms are carpeted, although few have windows. The bathrooms are tiny but adequate, and the beds are comfortable. Generally, this is a convenient place to get a good night's sleep before moving on. Downstairs there is a restaurant that serves excellent breakfasts.

HOTEL DEL CAMPO, Km 224, Camino a Cantel, Quetzaltenango. Tel. 502/61-2064 or 61-8082. 108 rms (all with bath).
$ Rates: Q117–Q146.25 ($23.40–$29.25) single; Q146.25–Q181.35 ($29.25–$36.30) double; Q175.50–Q216.45 ($35.10–$43.30) triple. DC, MC, V.

Although it is a bit out of the way, on a side road off of the Pan American Highway, the del Campo is Quetzaltenango's largest, most modern, and most comfortable place to stay. Constructed in the 1970s, it has a decor that features natural wood and red brick. The guest rooms have private baths (showers) done in linoleum and are generally bright and nice. Avoid the bottom-floor rooms because they can be dark; ask for a room numbered in the 50s. Some rooms have TVs, but these cost a bit more.

There are two restaurants here done in a rustic mountain decor, with large windows letting in lots of light. The prices are very reasonable, averaging Q14 to Q20 ($2.80 to $4). A small bar provides a comfortable gathering spot and there's a heated indoor swimming pool and game room.

HOTEL MODELO, 14a Avenida "A" 2-31, Zona 1, Quetzaltenango. Tel. 502/61-2715 or 61-2529. 22 rms (all with bath).
$ Rates: Q93.60 ($18.70) single; Q117 ($23.40) double; Q140.40 ($28.10) triple. MC, V.

This solid, dependable, moderate-price leader is located on a narrow, short street between 14a and 15a avenidas. An obliging family operates the hotel, and they will welcome you in the high-ceilinged lobby with its big fireplace. When they show you one of the guest rooms, you'll find it decorated with solid-color bedspreads, gaily colored Guatemalan huipiles (blouses) drawn on frames, and contemporary paintings. The rooms have hardwood floors and are equipped with small private bathrooms with tiled showers. Some rooms also have small black-and-white TVs.

There's a small but good restaurant located off the lobby serving breakfast (7:30 to 9:30am), lunch (1 to 4pm), and dinner (7 to 9pm) daily. Breakfast will cost around Q8 ($1.60), and lunch and dinner may be had for Q16 ($3.20). You'll also find a small bar just off the lobby.

CASA KAEHLER, 13a Avenida 3-33, Zona 1, Quetzaltenango. Tel. 502/61-2091. 7 rms (1 with bath).
$ Rates: Q27.50 ($5.50) single without bath, Q33 ($6.60) single with bath; Q33 ($6.60) double without bath, Q38.50 ($7.70) double with bath; Q38.50 ($7.70) triple without bath; Q44 ($8.80) quad without bath. No credit cards.

Before World War II, most of the coffee fincas (farms) on Guatemala's Pacific Slope were run by Germans, hence the German flavor of this city. It's very apparent in the name of this little place, which resembles a modest, old-fashioned European family pension. The guest rooms are very simple and plain but clean and quite cheap. For a bit more comfort, request room no. 7 (*cuarto numero siete*), which has a private bathroom and a double bed. Regardless of which room you stay in, you can make use of the beautiful sitting room with its rocking chairs and stained-glass windows. It's very homey and quiet here (and popular with young people studying Spanish in Quetzaltenango).

WORTH THE EXTRA BUCKS

HOTEL PENSIÓN BONIFAZ, 4a Calle 10-50, Zona 1, Quetzaltenango. Tel. 502/61-4241 or 61-2959. 63 rms, 2 suites (all with bath) TV

$ Rates: Q234 ($46.80) single; Q263.25 ($52.65) double; Q321.75 ($64.35) suite. AE, DC, MC, V.

⭐ The Bonifaz, the city's long-running favorite, is at the upper end of the Parque Centro America. This is the most comfortable place downtown, within walking distance of almost everything. Half of the rooms here (and these are preferable) are in the older, original building. They have French doors leading onto small balconies overlooking the street and are quite spacious. The furnishings are fairly new, and the bathrooms are quite large. The rest of the rooms are in a modernized addition with wood paneling and Danish modern furniture. Not really fancy, the rooms are large, the bathrooms are done in tile (some with only showers), and a number of rooms have two double beds. The second-floor lounge has a beautiful view of the mountains and the city, and there is also a small, but very pleasant garden in the back of the hotel. Facilities include a gift shop, Mexican consulate, and parking lot.

Dining/Entertainment: The hotel has three dining rooms, all of which serve the same excellent food. El Patio is a covered courtyard filled with potted plants and chrome furniture. The light here during the day is beautiful. El Restaurante and Los Balcones are the two formal dining rooms, both done in colonial decor, with wrought-iron chandeliers and a fireplace in one of them. The waitresses are dressed in traditional highland costumes. The service is efficient and very pleasant, and the restaurants are generally very quiet. The food here is primarily Continental, with such offerings as stroganoff, filet mignon, spaghetti, and breaded shrimp. Prices are in the Q20 to Q40 ($4 to $8) range for entrées. Don't miss the tempting pastry cart. There's a small selection of wines to accompany your meal. Just inside the front door is a sedate but cheery bar.

WHERE TO EAT

The best place to dine is in the dining room of the Pensión Bonifaz, where you can start with a fruit cocktail or a bowl of savory black-bean soup; go on to filet mignon, smoked pork chops, or roast chicken; and finish up with cake or pie—for about Q50 ($10) per person, including tax, tip, and a beverage. Lighter fare, including a very substantial club sandwich, can be had, with a drink, for only half that much.

The dining room in the Hotel Modelo is also worth your consideration at mealtime. For a stroll past many of this city's eligible eateries, make your way to the corner of 14a Avenida and 3a Calle, then walk uphill along 14a Avenida.

PASTELERÍA BOMBONIER, 14a Avenida 2-20, Zona 1. Tel. 6225.
   Cuisine: SANDWICHES/PIZZA/PASTRIES.
$ Prices: Q2.75–Q15 (55¢–$3). No credit cards.
   Open: Daily 9am–9pm.
This is a tiny family-run snack place with only a handful of tables—but with hamburgers priced at less than a dollar, it's a real bargain for a light meal.

TABERNA DE DON RODRIGO, 14a Avenida C-45. Tel. 2963.
   Cuisine: SANDWICHES.
$ Prices: Q3.50–Q11.25 (70¢–$2.25). No credit cards.
   Open: Daily 10am–9:30pm.
Across the street from the plaza with the impressive Teatro Municipal you will find a place where local young people like to gather, chat, and consume hamburgers, cheeseburgers, hot dogs, cakes, Cokes, lemonade, coffee, and draft beer. To the local people it's a stylish place, but a light meal here will not cost more than a dollar or two. The specialty is a giant sandwich called the Don Rodrigo super sandwich. Order one of these and a beer for a total bill of less than Q17.50 ($3.50), and you've got a very filling and very cheap meal.

CAFETERÍA EL KOPETIN, 14a Avenida 3-31, Zona 1. Tel. 2401.
   Cuisine: GUATEMALAN/INTERNATIONAL.
$ Prices: Main dishes Q10–Q20 ($2–$4). DC, MC, V.
   Open: Daily 11am–10pm.

⭐ In this dark, modern, family-run place with red tablecloths and natural wood, the specialty is outstanding appetizers. A person could make a meal on just an assortment of some of these delicious starters. Try the *quesos fundidos* (melted cheese) or one of the spicy *chorizo* sausage appetizers, both under Q7 ($1.40). The *parillada* for Q19 ($3.80) is a carnivore's delight that includes five different meats, potatoes, and vegetables. The menu also lists everything from shrimp and fish to filet mignon, all priced around Q14–Q19 ($2.80–$3.80), but there are burgers and sandwiches for much less. El Kopetin is only two blocks off the Parque Centro America.

POLLO FRITO ALBAMAR, 4a Calle 14-16, Zona 1 and 4a Calle 13-84, Zona 3. Tel. 6124 or 6224.
   Cuisine: GUATEMALAN/INTERNATIONAL.
$ **Prices:** Q7–Q19 ($1.40–$3.80). No credit cards.
   Open: Daily 10am–10pm.

Ⓢ Primarily fried-chicken restaurants, these two family fast-food places also serve a variety of other meals, including filet mignon and some delicious *típico* favorites. And you can't beat the prices—even a steak will cost you only Q19 ($3.80). The one in Zona 3 is more family oriented than the one downtown. At the former, you'll find a huge slide to keep your kids entertained while you enjoy your meal. Meals are served either in a large dining room or on tables outside by the slide. The downtown restaurant is very conveniently located a block away from Parque Centro America.

PIZZA RICCA, 14a Avenida 2-52, Zona 1. Tel. 8162.
   Cuisine: PIZZA.
$ **Prices:** Pizzas Q8–Q33 ($1.60–$6.60). No credit cards.
   Open: Daily 11:30am–9:30pm.
This is a tidy little place with cozy booths and a busy wood-fired oven filled with pizzas bubbling and baking. The white-uniformed staff tends the fires and the pies. Order your pizza small, medium, or large; have a beer or soft drink; and the bill will come to about Q12 ($2.40) per person.

RESTAURANT SHANGHAI, 4a Calle 12-22, Zona 1. Tel. 4154.
   Cuisine: CHINESE.
$ **Prices:** Main dishes Q8.75–Q15.50 ($1.75–$3.10). No credit cards.
   Open: Daily 8am–10pm.
Chinese restaurants are common throughout Guatemala, and whenever you get tired of rice and beans and meat, you can always head to one for a big plate of steaming vegetables. The food is far from authentic and the staff seems to be 100% Maya (not Chinese), but the restaurant does add variety to your dining. The combination plates are priced even less than most main dishes. And in very un-Chinese fashion, there is a tempting array of cakes displayed in the front of the restaurant, occasionally including Guatemalan-style cheesecake.

EXCURSIONS

There are dozens of Indian villages in the vicinity of Quetzaltenango, all of which have markets one or more days a week. These markets are excellent places to shop for local crafts and to see Indians in their colorful attire. The following is a list of nearby villages with their market and festival days. On festival days you may get to see the traditional dances, such as the Dance of the Conquest, the Dance of the Moors, or the **palo volador** (flying pole).
   Salcaja: Market day is Tuesday; festival is August 25.
   San Cristóbal Totonicapan: Market day is Sunday; festival is July 26.
   Totonicapan: Market days are Tuesday and Saturday; festival is the last week of September.
   Almolonga: Market days are Wednesday and Saturday; festival is July 27.
   Cantel: Market day is Sunday; festival is August 15.
   Zunil: Market day is Monday; festival is November 25.

San Juan Ostuncalco: Market days are Thursday and Sunday; festival is from January 29 to February 3.
San Pedro Sacatepequez: Market days are Tuesday, Thursday, and Sunday; festival is June 24 to 30.
San Marcos: Market days are Tuesday and Friday; festival is April 22 to 27.
Olintepeque: Market day is Tuesday; festival is June 24.

SAN FRANCISCO EL ALTO & MOMOSTENANGO

Quetzaltenango is high in the mountains, but you can go even higher (660 feet higher, to be exact) to visit the small town of San Francisco El Alto, famous for its Friday market featuring handwoven wool blankets. The town is only a mile off the Pan American Highway over a paved road (or 2 miles over a dirt road, the back way). Buses run from Quetzaltenango three or four times a day. The view from the large, cobblestone municipal plaza where the market is held is fabulous (if you get a clear day). The town itself is very quiet, with virtually no action and very few people in evidence, except on Friday.

Past San Francisco El Alto, 10 miles from the Pan American Highway, is the small town of Momostenango (market day is Sunday), famous throughout Guatemala for its *chamarras* (woolen blankets). Buses from Quetzaltenango chug and bash over the rough dirt road daily, winding up through the forests and down through the valleys. The road may be impassable during parts of the rainy season. On the way into town, the road passes little shops advertising blankets and woolen goods for sale, retail and wholesale.

For meals there are several modest cafés, one attached to the Casa de Huespedes Paclom. There is little to do here but interact awkwardly with the citizenry and buy blankets. Chamarras, serapes, and other fine things all are made by hand here, and the local people in this high-altitude place know what warm blankets mean at night. Look for interesting designs and fine-quality wool.

Buses leave for Totonicapan and San Francisco El Alto from around the Parque Centro America. Ask at the tourist office or your hotel for the exact location.

ZUNIL & FUENTES GEORGINA

For sheer eye-popping brilliance, no other traditional attire in Guatemala is as colorful as that worn by the women of Zunil. This small village is only a few miles south of Quetzaltenango on the road down to Retalhuleu, but it seems a world away. Built on a steep hillside above a little river, Zunil is almost always cool and damp. To stay warm and dry, the women of the village cover themselves with cloaks of shocking pink, magenta, violet, and lavender. As they hurry down the cobblestone streets with their cloaks swaying behind them, they are like apparitions of a long-forgotten civilization.

Zunil is also home to one of the Maximón effigies that are found in a few villages here in the highlands. Maximón (also known as San Simón), is a thinly disguised Mayan god, Mam. He is revered by the local population for his powers to answer prayers and heal the sick. Maximón, who lives in a small house on the hill behind the church, consists of a mannequin wearing a mask, jacket and pants, hat, and dozens of scarves. He sits in state on a large chair, where he meets with those seeking his favors. The traditional way to worship Maximón is to blow cigar smoke in his face and pour liquor into his mouth. The Indians believe devoutly in Maximón, and if you should wish to meet with him, be sure to take him an offering (a few quetzales is acceptable, but some liquor and cigars are preferable).

Just past Zunil on the left is an alternate route into Quetzaltenango. If you turn up this road and then turn right on the first dirt road, you'll be heading for **Fuentes Georginas,** one of the most enchanting places in Guatemala. Several miles up this rough and muddy dirt road, at the head of a valley that begins on the flanks of Zunil Mountain, is a **hot springs complex** that feels at times like the most remote spot on earth. Clouds of steam rise from the pale-blue sulfurous waters and drift up a steep hillside that is draped with fronds of giant ferns. Beside the pool is a bar and tiny restaurant where you can order simple meals. There are a few basic cabins here, with tubs that can be filled with water from the hot springs. If you're looking for the ultimate low-budget spa, this is it. Cabins rent for less than $15 per night.

Just up the road from Zunil toward Quetzaltenango in the village of Los Baños (The Baths) are several dozen less appealing hot springs bathing facilities. If you want to warm up, hop off the bus and check out a few until you find one that meets your standards. My favorite is **Los Chorros** at the lower end of town. This place is open daily from 6am to 7pm and has private tub rooms and a warm-water pool. It costs Q5 ($1) to use a big tub and Q1 (20¢) per person to use the pool. Best of all is the amazing paint job that's been done on the buildings surrounding the swimming pool. You have to see it to believe it!

5. HUEHUETENANGO

160 miles NW of Guatemala City; 52 miles SE of La Mesilla (Mexican border); 51 miles N of Quetzaltenango

GETTING THERE By Bus Buses from Guatemala City to Huehuetenango leave from 7a Avenida 15-27 daily at 7am and 2pm. Duration: 5 hours. Fare: Q18 ($3.60). If you're coming from the border, there'll be a bus there to meet your Mexican bus.

By Car From the Mexican border, it is a fairly easy 52 miles. Watch for the turnoff for Huehuetenango, which is about 4 miles off the highway. If you're coming from Guatemala City, continue going straight through the intersection known as Cuatro Caminos (Four Roads), which is the turnoff for Quetzaltenango. Watch for the Huehuetenango turnoff from the highway.

DEPARTING You can catch a bus to Quetzaltenango either near the market downtown or at the bus terminal, which is a mile or so outside town on the road to Quetzaltenango. Duration: 2½–3 hours. Fare: Q5 ($1).

Buses for Guatemala City leave throughout the day from the bus terminal on the road to Quetzaltenango. Duration: 7 hours. Fare: Q18 ($3.60).

ESSENTIALS Orientation Huehuetenango's main square, reference point for everything in town, is bounded by 2a and 3a calles and by 4a and 5a avenidas.

Fast Facts Banco g&t, 2a Calle 4-66, Zona 1 (across the street from the relief map in the central park), is open Monday through Friday from 8am to 8pm and Saturday from 10am to 2pm.

Market day is every day. Feast days are July 12 to 18.

Huehuetenango, although it is miles from the Mexican border, has the feel of a border town. It is the first major settlement on the road into Guatemala from Mexico and is the provincial capital of Huehuetenango (alt. 6,240 feet; pop. 37,000). There isn't much to keep you here, but the ruins of Zaculeu are only a few miles from town, and there's an assortment of hotels and restaurants, all within your price range. If you've taken a car or a bus from San Cristóbal, Mexico, this is the logical place to spend the night.

This town might be your first glimpse of Guatemalan culture, and you'll be pleasantly surprised the farther you go into the country. The costumes seem to get more and more colorful and unusual as you head southeast through the highlands. Notice that throughout this region, it's traditional for women to wear aprons all the time—they come in all sizes, shapes, and colors. No matter what sort of apron she has, every woman must have one.

On the road from Huehuetenango, the vistas continue: old men, young boys, teenage girls—literally everyone is on foot and carrying something. The men use a "tump line" (a rope or strap from the backpack load to the forehead) to distribute the weight of the huge bundles they carry, or they put their packs in a large piece of cloth, tying the ends so that they can loop it over their foreheads and carry the load on their backs. It's a constant reminder that horses were not found in this hemisphere before the Conquest and that the Indian civilizations knew nothing about the wheel. It also shows how little Indian culture has changed from that day to this.

WHAT TO SEE & DO

First, there's the **market,** a nice one that's busy every day. It's located at 3a Avenida and 4a Calle, and its four great walls hold a busy collection of fruit stands, candle sellers, cloth shops, basket sellers, dried chile sellers, and even a bottle shop where you can purchase an old instant-coffee jar (nothing goes to waste in this town!). Shopkeepers are very obliging—most are friendly, all are curious—and they expect you to bargain for their merchandise.

Besides the market, you'll want to take a look at the **ruins of Zaculeu.** Avoid self-appointed "guides" and take one of the very battered minibuses that depart from in front of the Hotel Maya and the Rico MacPolo at the corner of 3a Avenida and 4a Calle, near the entrance to La Plaza market. The bus fare is only 40 centavos (8¢). Alternatively, you can take a taxi for around Q35 ($7) for the round-trip. You can also walk—it's a pleasant hike of about 45 minutes—and chances are better than not that someone will stop to give you a lift.

If you drive, head out of town on 9a Avenida and keep following the signs on this 2½-mile ride, even though they seem to be leading you on a wild goose chase. You may have to ask directions a few times despite the signs. The ruins at Zaculeu date from the Postclassic Period just before the Spanish Conquest. The Postclassic Period began in A.D. 900, when the Mayan civilization began to fade out and become absorbed by the Mexican tribes that were moving down from the north. Out of this assimilation of Mexican and Mayan cultures arose three powerful nations, one of which was the Mam, who settled in the area around Huehuetenango and made their capital at Zaculeu. The Mayan culture had been greatly diffused by this time, so you will see very little similarity between the Mayan ruins of Yucatán and Petén and those at Zaculeu.

This site was restored in 1940 by the United Fruit Company "as a contribution to Guatemalan culture." The site is small, however, and there are several mounds that have not been uncovered; at present there are no plans for further excavation. The restoration was so complete, down to the coat of mortar that covered the temples, that it appears as a reconstruction rather than a restoration: "perfect temples" down to the manicured lawns. The surroundings are beautiful, and the ruins are worth a visit. There is a small but interesting museum on the premises. Entrance is free to the ruins and museum.

WHERE TO STAY
DOUBLES FOR LESS THAN Q40 [$10]

AUTO HOTEL VASQUEZ, 2a Calle 6-67, Huehuetenango. Tel. 502/641-338. 20 rms (11 with bath).
$ Rates: Q11.70 ($2.35) single without bath, Q26.40 ($5.30) single with bath; Q23.40 ($4.70) double without bath, Q28.80 ($5.75) double with bath. No credit cards.

Small but modern, the Hotel Vasquez is two blocks from the main plaza. If you happen to arrive when they are drying the laundry in the parking lot, it may not seem too appealing, but never fear—the rooms, although small, are not bad. It's not the place to stretch out though, since the tiny rooms here are almost completely filled by their furnishings.

HOTEL MARY, 2a Calle 3-52. Huehuetenango. Tel. 502/641-569. 25 rms (11 with bath).

$ Rates: Q17.55 ($3.50) single without bath; Q29.25 ($5.85) double without bath, Q40.95 ($8.20) double with bath; Q52.65 ($10.55) triple with bath. No credit cards.

The Hotel Mary is a small hotel only a block from the main plaza and directly across the street from Guatel and the post office. The rooms are on four floors (no elevator), with open-air hallways that run the length of the building. It's very basic, but clean. You'll find a bit of off-street parking underneath the hotel by the reception desk. There is a small restaurant on the second floor, where meals average Q10 ($2).

DOUBLES FOR LESS THAN Q80 [$20]

HOTEL ZACULEU, 5a Avenida 1-14, Zona 1, Huehuetenango. Tel. 502/ 641-086 or 641-575. 16 rms (all with bath).
$ Rates: Q40.95–Q117 ($8.20–$23.40) single; Q58.50–Q175.50 ($11.70–$35.10) double. No credit cards.

The long-time favorite of travelers passing through Huehuetenango is a colonial-style hotel a block away from the town's main plaza. Many of the rooms are decorated with local handcrafts—handwoven cloth, tin candlesticks, and clay water pitchers. Some rooms are truly charming, others are not. The older rooms at the front of the hotel open onto a beautiful courtyard filled with flowers and bordered by a colonial arcade. Although these rooms have more of a Guatemalan flavor to them, they are also closer to the street and therefore are noisier than the rooms in back. The new rooms, built in 1990, are done in a modern Spanish style—with bright bathrooms, carpets, and TVs. The higher prices are for these new rooms. Additional facilities include a private parking lot and the best restaurant in town.

OTHER SUPER-BUDGET CHOICES

Besides these modest hostelries, Huehuetenango has half a dozen even more modest places where the price for a bed is about Q15 ($3) per person. They're respectable, with the bare necessities.

WHERE TO EAT

Your best bet for a meal in Huehuetenango will likely be your hotel. If you should want to try someplace else, the following restaurant is convenient.

EBONY RESTAURANT, 2a Calle 5-11. No phone.
  Cuisine: GUATEMALAN/INTERNATIONAL.
$ Prices: Q2.50–Q6 (50¢–$1.20). No credit cards.
  Open: Daily 6am–11pm.
Around the corner from the main plaza you'll find a small, dark restaurant popular with the young generation in Huehuetenango. The walls and ceiling are made of split bamboo, and there are wicker baskets for lampshades. The overall effect is that of a tropical beach hangout, even though you're a long way from the ocean. On the menu are chicken, pork chops, steaks, and chorizo, all for Q6 ($1.20) and a variety of breakfasts for the same price. Delicious fresh fruit licuados are only Q2 (40¢).

6. RETALHULEU

113 miles W of Guatemala City; 32 miles S of Quetzaltenango;
75 miles E of Tapachula, Mexico

GETTING THERE By Bus A bus from the Mexican border into town takes about an hour and will cost about Q3 (60¢). Buses bound from Guatemala City to the

Mexican border at either Tecún Umán or El Carmen stop at Retalhuleu en route. Galgos, 7a Avenida 19-44, Zona 1 (tel. 23-661), has departures at 5:30, 9, and 10am, noon, and 3:30 and 5:15pm. Duration: 4 hours. Fare: Q18 ($3.60). Fortaleza, 19 Calle 8-70, Zona 1 (tel. 517-994), has departures every hour from 4am to 5pm for about the same price.

By Car   You can cross the border at either El Carmen or Tecún Umán. From Tecún Umán it is about 50 miles on the highway; from El Carmen it is about 19 miles to the intersection with the highway from Tecún Umán, where you turn left for Retalhuleu.

DEPARTING   There are several buses a day from Retalhuleu to Guatemala City. The Pacific Highway itself bears right at the Quetzaltenango junction and heads out to Mazatenango, a bustling farm and industrial town right astride the highway with lots of activity. From there the highway goes up hill and down through sugarcane fields and by little fincas (farms or plantations).

Buses for the border leave regularly throughout the day.

ESSENTIALS   Orientation   The town of Retalhuleu is a couple of miles off the highway, but there are two hotels right on the highway that are better than those in town.

Retalhuleu is a quiet small town with little to recommend it other than a number of acceptable hotels that are the best for some miles around. Though the town is on the wide flat plain near the Pacific Coast, I include it in this chapter because it's a gateway to the highlands for travelers coming from or going to the lowlands of Mexico. There is no reason to stay more than a night. The three downtown hotel choices are close to the pretty main square in front of the church.

Just 3 miles out of town is the junction with the toll road to Quetzaltenango, an exciting drive that winds up 2 miles in altitude in only an hour's time. The road is good, and the scenery is exceptional: Four of the highest volcanoes in Guatemala flank the macadam strip, two on either side. Every now and then an exceptionally beautiful ceiba tree will catch your eye, huge and of fine proportion, its bladelike roots standing as much as 20 feet high at its base. At the cloth-weaving town of Zunil, there's a turnoff to the famous hot springs of Fuentes Georgina, which are up the side of a volcano on a rough dirt road (see the Quetzaltenango section for details).

WHERE TO STAY & EAT

HOTEL ASTOR, 5a Calle 4-68, Zona 1, Retalhuleu. Tel. 502/71-0475. 6 rms (4 with bath).

$ Rates: Q80 ($16) double without bath, Q70 ($14) double with bath. No credit cards accepted.

This hotel is an old mansion in which the grand rooms have been split down the middle to make bedrooms for guests. Even so, the spaces are larger than those in most modern luxury hotels. The rooms are entered from a verdant courtyard surrounded by a colonnade.

A small dining room looks onto the courtyard, and meals here are very substantial. Breakfast is served from 7 to 9am; lunch is served from noon to 2pm; dinner is served from 7 to 9pm. A typical dinner might be delicious black beans, potatoes, filet steak smothered in onions and tomatoes, plus fried bananas and mangoes (from the tree out back) for dessert, for only Q25 ($5) per person.

HOTEL LA COLONIA, Km 178 Carretera al Pacífico, San Sebastián, Retalhuleu. Tel. 502/71-0038 or 71-0054. 46 rms (all with bath).

$ Rates: Q125 ($25) single; Q155 ($31) double. DC, MC, V.

Most of the rooms at this motel-style accommodation have air conditioning to help you beat the heat if the two pools aren't enough to cool you off.

The restaurant, which leans heavily toward steak and seafood, is open from 6am to 10pm.

POSADA DE DON JOSÉ, 5a Calle 3-67, Zona 1, Retalhuleu. Tel. 502/71-0180 or 71-0841. 30 rms (all with bath). A/C TEL.

$ **Rates:** Q125–Q155 ($25–$31) single; Q151–Q185 ($31–$37) double; Q185 ($37) triple. AE, DC, V. **Parking:** Free.

A modern and luxurious downtown choice, the Don José is only a few blocks away from the Astor. This is the most comfortable downtown hotel, and you may feel that you owe it to yourself, after the arduous border crossing, to sit back and enjoy the air conditioning or the swimming pool. Try to get a room on the second floor overlooking the plaza. These rooms are quite large, and the view is pleasant.

HOTEL MODELO, 5a Calle 4-53, Zona 1, Retalhuleu. Tel. 71-0256. 7 rms (all with bath). TEL

$ **Rates:** Q25 ($5) single; Q40 ($8) double; Q55 ($11) triple. No credit cards.

This small hotel is directly across the street from the Astor, and although it is not as atmospheric, it is still a good choice. All the rooms have fans to help you sleep through the steamy nights. The rooms are set around a flowered courtyard, and all have hardwood floors and high ceilings. You might even find a small black-and-white TV in the room. Throughout the hotel there are framed huipiles (colorful blouses worn by Indian women) and contemporary paintings by local artists.

The small restaurant and bar are just off the tile-floored lobby. Offerings and prices are comparable to those at the Astor.

HOTEL SIBONEY, Cuatro Caminos, San Sebastián, Retalhuleu. Tel. 502/71-0149. 24 rms (all with bath). A/C TV TEL

$ **Rates:** Q140.40 ($28.10) single; Q157.95 ($31.60) double; Q175.50 ($35.10) triple. DC, MC, V.

This is the first hotel that you'll come to near Retalhuleu, on the left at the intersection leading into town. Large trees shade the parking area. The rooms come with two double beds and color cable TVs so that you can watch all your favorite shows.

There's a huge restaurant with screen walls that let in every least tropical breeze. Steaks and seafood are the specialties.

CHAPTER 11

EL PETÉN

1. FLORES & SANTA ELENA

2. TIKAL

El Petén is Guatemala's vast, wild, low-lying jungle province—a land of dirt roads and four-wheel-drive vehicles, of mammoth Mayan ceremonial centers and towering temples. In its dense jungle cover you'll hear the squawk of parrots, the chatter of monkeys, and the rustling of strange animals moving through the bush. The landscape here is as different from Guatemala's highlands as night is from day.

There are three reasons to penetrate El Petén. First and foremost is to visit Tikal, the greatest Mayan religious center yet uncovered (Caracol in Belize is said to be much larger but has not yet been fully excavated). The second is birds: The jungles of Petén are home to a wondrous variety of exotic birds, and some bird-watchers go to Tikal just to fill up their life lists. The third reason to go into El Petén is to see a different Guatemala, one of small farming villages and hamlets, without paved roads or colonial architecture, but with the same smiling inhabitants that you no doubt encountered in the highlands.

Note: When you are in El Petén, it is imperative that you sleep in an enclosed room with screens on the windows or beneath a mosquito net. This region is home to vampire bats that frequently carry rabies. The bats are nocturnal, and although they prefer cattle, they have been known to bite humans, especially on the toes and nose. The bite of a vampire bat is entirely painless, but an anticoagulant in the bat's saliva will cause a bite to bleed freely. The greatest risk is not from loss of blood, but from rabies. If not treated immediately, rabies is always fatal. Seek medical attention as soon as possible if you are bitten by a bat or by any mammal for that matter.

1. FLORES & SANTA ELENA

280 miles NE of Guatemala City; 84 miles W of the Belizean border

GETTING THERE **By Air** The two small airlines that fly daily between Guatemala City's La Aurora Airport and Flores are **Aerovias,** La Aurora Airport, Avenida Hincapié and 18 Calle, Zona 13 (tel. 325-686, 319-663, or 316-935 and **TAPSA,** Avenida Hincapié and 18 Calle, Zona 13 (tel. 314-860). *Note:* These airlines leave from the national airport terminal on the opposite side from the international terminal. Be sure to tell your taxi driver this (there are no convenient buses to this terminal). The one-way fare is Q267.50 ($53.50). You can buy your ticket from a travel agency in Guatemala City or Antigua or directly from the airlines. If you plan to buy your ticket at the airport, note that the ticket counters are attended only at breakfast time and in the late afternoon. Because these flights are so popular with tourists, they are often booked weeks or months in advance—so make your reservation as early as possible. Schedules are liable to change, but generally there are flights out in the morning, with return flights in the afternoon. **Aviateca,** 10 Calle 6-39, Zona 1 (tel. 81-479), also flies to Flores, but they charge about $13 more than Aerovias or Tapsa, and leave from the international terminal. At the Flores Airport, minibuses, taxis, and tour buses will whisk you out to Tikal, about an hour's drive away.

By Bus Going by bus is very cheap compared to going by plane, but it is extremely tiring, time consuming, and unpleasant. However, if your money is low and your stamina is high, you can get there from Guatemala City by bus. Certainly, you'll never forget the ride. Keep in mind that if you want to get on the Flores-bound bus in Río Dulce (or anywhere other than Guatemala City), you may not get a seat. In fact, you may even have to ride on the roof (not recommended). The bus trip from Guatemala City to Flores takes 14 hours when the road is in good condition and costs Q35 ($7) or Q50 ($10) for a comfortable deluxe bus. Contact **Fuente del Norte,** 17a Calle 8-46, Zona 1 (tel. 513-817), in Guatemala City. The journey from Guatemala City to the Río Dulce bridge is fine, over a fairly well-maintained paved highway. But for the last 126 miles or so (six or eight hours), from just north of Río Dulce to Flores, the road is a battlefield of potholes and ruts, especially during the rainy season (May through Oct). Be prepared for an awful lot of jostling, banging, and bone crunching.

From Belize, it is slightly less difficult and time consuming, although the road is just as bad for several hours of the trip. The schedules change, but there are presently several buses a day leaving for Flores from Melchor de Mencos on the Guatemala side of the border. Thus you should plan to be at the border as early as possible in the morning and allow an hour or two for border formalities. If you leave Belize City for San Ignacio or Benque Viejo by 8 or 9am, you should reach the border in time to catch the 1pm bus.

If you're in a rush to get to Tikal, you can get off the bus at El Cruce (Ixlu), where a road turns right for Tikal, and hope to flag down a passing minibus. However, these minibuses tend to be heading back to Flores in the afternoon and not to Tikal, so it is probably best just to head straight to Flores.

By Car   There is no Pan American Highway crossing El Petén. Going by private car is not as bad as going by the bus, but it is almost as bad. The trip from Guatemala City or Belize is over the same roads the bus takes, but you have the luxury of stopping along the way. For the trip from Guatemala City, I'd recommend spending the night at the Hotel Izabal Tropical near the Río Dulce bridge (see Chapter 12) and starting for Flores bright and early. An alternative is to make it along the bad road as far as Poptún and camp at the Finca Ixobel, where there are some services, including showers and meals.

The journey from the Belizean-Guatemalan border point at Benque Viejo (Belize) and Melchor de Mencos (Guatemala) to Flores takes about three hours by car. The road has lots of potholes and ruts from Melchor to El Cruce, and the average speed is probably 20 miles per hour. It's a rough trip, worse in the rainy season, but it doesn't last all that long—at least not compared to the grueling ride from Guatemala City to Flores. After El Cruce (Ixlu), the road is paved and fast all the way to Tikal or Flores.

It is also possible to talk with a travel agent or taxi driver in San Ignacio and hire a taxi or minibus and driver to take you to Flores and/or Tikal. This will be quite expensive, but if you find others with whom to split the cost, it might be worth it.

By Boat and Bus   A newly developing route is the overland one from Palenque in Chiapas, Mexico, to Flores by bus and boat. It's an adventurous route for the hardy only, because you will have to endure long hours in beat-up buses on bad roads and spend the night in a jungle village short on services. I have not yet taken this route. The following information was gleaned from travelers on the road.

Start out from Palenque by taking a 9am bus to Emiliano Zapata, then another bus from Zapata to Tenosique. At Tenosique, catch a 1pm bus to La Palma, where a boat will be waiting. Pack yourself and your belongings into the little boat and hope that the engine doesn't die. The boat will head down the Río San Pedro to El Naranjo, which is within Guatemala. There is one small, utterly basic hotel in El Naranjo where you can try to grab a little sleep—if there are beds available. As it is the only place in town, it gets away with charging Q25 ($5) for a double. There may be little bedding provided and it can get cold here, so have some camping gear or warm clothes. A bus departs from El Naranjo for Flores at 3am, and this, too, can be a very chilly journey (believe it or not). The entire trip from Palenque to Flores can be done for under $25 per person, including your sleep break at the Posada San Pedro.

DEPARTING   Flying is by far the preferable way to go back to Guatemala City. Aerovias and Tapsa both depart Flores Airport for Guatemala City at 4pm. Duration:

1 hour. Fare: Q267.50 ($53.50) one way. Aviateca also flies between Flores and Guatemala leaving at 8am and 5pm. Fare: Q334.50 ($66.90) one way. There are also flights to Belize City, Belize.

Fuente del Norte buses bound for Guatemala City leave from the Santa Elena market daily at 5 and 11am and 3:45, 10, and 11pm. Duration: 14–16 hours. Fare: Q35 ($7) regular, Q50 ($10) express.

Buses for Melchor de Mencos, on the Belize border, leave from the market, with a stop at Hotel San Juan, at 5, 8, 10, and 11am and 2, 3:30, and 6pm. Duration: 3½ hours. Fare Q8 ($1.60). If you want to be sure of getting a seat, get the bus at the market. From the border, there are buses and taxis to take you on into Belize.

A minibus to Belize City leaves from Hotel San Juan daily at 5am. Duration: 5 hours. Fare Q100 ($20). This minibus sometimes continues on to Chetumal, Mexico. Fare (from Flores): Q150 ($30).

If you are the adventurous type and want to head toward Palenque, Mexico, there are buses to Naranjo at 5am and 12:30pm. You can stay at the inexpensive and very basic Posada San Pedro in El Naranjo before catching the boat down the Río San Pedro.

ORIENTATION

CITY LAYOUT   Now primarily known as Flores, this town actually consists of three smaller towns that have merged. Flores, on an island out in Lake Petén Itzá, is connected to the mainland by a long causeway. On the mainland are Santa Elena (nearest the airport) and San Benito (closer to the bus terminal and market). Whether you arrive by air or by bus from Guatemala City or Belize, you will come into town from the east. The road in from the airport leads straight through Santa Elena to the market and bus terminal, while the causeway to Flores is a turn to the right in the middle of Santa Elena. In Flores, all the hotels can be found on the road that circles the island.

FAST FACTS   There is a bank in Flores proper, open Monday to Friday from 8:30am to 2:30pm (to 3:30pm on Friday). You may be able to change money at your hotel.

There is a post office in Santa Elena. It's just down the street from the Hotel San Juan and is open Monday to Friday from 8am to 4:30pm.

GETTING AROUND

BY CAR   Rental cars, some of them four-wheel-drive Suzukis, are offered by several businesses in town, including the Hotel San Juan (tel. 500-041). **Koka** (tel. 501-233) will rent you a car, minibus, four-wheel-drive vehicle, or pickup truck or will arrange for a taxi tour to Tikal or anywhere else. Basic rates for a four-wheel-drive car are about Q385 ($77) per day, including free mileage. Most hotels can also help you rent a Suzuki four-wheel-drive vehicle for about the same price.

Flores is not much more than a tourist way station, but this tiny island played an important role in Guatemalan and Spanish colonial history. In 1697, Flores (then known as Tayasal) was the last Mayan city to be conquered by the Spanish. Hernán Cortés passed through the area in 1525, but he didn't try to subjugate the local Itzá Indians who had a reputation as fierce warriors. But Cortés left a dying horse in Tayasal and the Itzás, who had never seen a horse before, worshiped the strange beast, bringing it many offerings. When the horse died, a statue of it was carved and the horse worship continued for 100 years until some missionaries descended on Tayasal and destroyed the statue.

Although the town of Flores is built on a small island in Lake Petén Itzá and is connected to the mainland by a rock-and-dirt causeway, it is a hot and dusty town with nothing to recommend it. If it weren't for the nearby ruins at Tikal, this would be a forgotten little village surrounded by jungle. However, there are some nice views of Flores from the mainland town of Santa Elena, which is even less appealing than Flores. For some strange reason, the paved road that leads to Tikal stops the moment it reaches the town limits of Santa Elena. A fine gray limestone powder covers the trees, grass, and houses here. It is all too easy to imagine the dust coating you if you stay too long in town. It's best to head out to Tikal immediately and avoid spending any more time here than necessary.

If you're stuck in town for some reason, you can hire a boat and boatman to take you around this section of the large lake for Q50 ($10). Included in your 2-hour boat tour will be stops at La Guitarra, an island with a small and depressing zoo and a tourist center, and La Mirador, a point from which you can view a nearby Mayan ruin. On the causeway is a shop that rents kayaks for Q10 ($2) per hour. Also, ask around about renting a dugout canoe and paddle yourself around the lake. Be careful, though: Winds pick up in the afternoon and can whip up the waters.

If you're a spelunker, you might want to explore the Aktun Kan, Cave of the Serpent, a large cavern just outside of Santa Elena. The cave takes its name from a legend about a giant snake living there. But don't worry, it's only a legend. To reach the cave, either walk out of Santa Elena on the road that crosses the causeway from Flores or ask a taxi to take you out there. The fare should be around Q10 ($2). Although there are lights in the cave, be sure to bring a flashlight just in case.

You may notice flooded buildings along the lakeshore as you stroll around Flores or Santa Elena. For more than 15 years now Lake Petén Itzá has been inexplicably rising. What were once waterfront buildings are now underwater buildings. Despite this phenomenon, developers continue to build hotels right on the banks of the lake. Several newer hotels are already having to build dikes or abandon their lower rooms.

WHERE TO STAY

Lodging possibilities are rapidly improving here, but so is the tourist traffic, so you may find rooms in short supply. If you want to stay at one of the comfortable hotels, it'd be a good idea to try and reserve a room in advance or at least to call ahead to see how busy the hotel is.

DOUBLES FOR LESS THAN Q50 [$10]
In Santa Elena

HOTEL/RESTAURANT LEO FU LO, Santa Elena, Petén. No phone. 14 rms (1 with bath).
$ Rates: Q15 ($3) single; Q25 ($5) double; Q35 ($7) triple. No credit cards.
Just before you reach the causeway to Flores, you'll see the sign for this very basic backpacker hotel. The rooms are little more than cells, and the parking area is always strung with drying laundry. However, if you're looking for a very cheap room, this place is fairly clean, and it has a very unusual elevated open-air bar and a Chinese restaurant. There's a view of the lake and Flores from the restaurant. Meals cost between Q12 and Q30 ($2.40 and $6).

HOTEL SAN JUAN, Santa Elena, Petén. Tel. 502/500-562. 48 rms (30 with bath).
$ Rates: Q20 ($4) single without bath; Q25 ($5) double without bath, Q50 ($10) with bath, Q100 ($20) with bath and A/C; Q60 ($12) triple with bath. AE, DC, MC, V.

This modest hotel near the causeway to Flores has plain, clean, large rooms with two or three beds, rather large bathrooms with tile showers, cold water (hot on occasion), perhaps toilet seats, and—of all things—TVs! The two-story building is undistinguished but utilitarian. The owner has recently added 18 rooms with air conditioning. Keep in mind that the San Juan acts as a bus stop for buses to various other towns in El Petén, so buses begin leaving (with much shouting, revving of engines, and blowing of horns) around 5am. It's almost impossible to sleep through this cacophony, so you need to be a heavy sleeper to stay here (or you can plan to take an early bus yourself). There's a comedor (dining spot) off the courtyard parking lot, and in the lobby you'll find all sorts of information on getting around El Petén. This is also the place to book tickets on express minibuses to the Belize border and Mexico.

In Flores

POSADA EL TUCAN, Calle Centroamericana no. 45, Flores, Petén. Tel. 501-380. 4 rms (none with bath).
$ Rates: Q33 ($6.60) double; Q49.50 ($9.90) triple. No credit cards.

This backpackers' delight opened early in 1990 and was an instant success. It's built on the water, with a pleasant garden and two little piers for sunning or swimming. There are several tables in the garden where you can relax over a cold beer and a good book. The rooms are spacious with double or twin beds, all sharing a single large bathroom which has hot water (something places in this price range rarely offer). If you're traveling on a shoestring budget, this should be your first choice. The hotel is behind a very attractive little restaurant with a bar in one corner. The decor is tropical jungle, and the meals are Mexican and American standards.

DOUBLES FOR LESS THAN Q150 [$30]

In Santa Elena

COSTA DEL SOL, Santa Elena, Petén. Tel. 502/501-1336 or 500-172. 35 rms (all with bath).
$ Rates: Q117 ($23.40) single; Q140.40 ($28.10) double; Q163.80 ($32.75) triple. No credit cards.

About a block away from the market and bus park is the Costa del Sol, one of Santa Elena's better choices in the budget category. You don't have a lake view, but you do get a swimming pool and you're close to the bus station, which is a plus if you arrive after dark on the bus from Guatemala City. Several of the rooms here have air conditioning, and the large family rooms come with small refrigerators. Let them know in advance, and they'll pick you up at the airport. Family run, the Costa del Sol seems to cater primarily to vacationing Guatemalan families.

The restaurant is a spacious and simple affair with a stuffed jaguar at one end. Meals here range from Q10 ($2) to Q20 ($4).

JAGUAR INN SANTA ELENA, Calzada Rodríquez Macal 8-79, Zona 1, Santa Elena, Petén. Tel. 502/500-002. 18 rms (all with bath).
$ Rates: Q87.75 ($17.55) single; Q117 ($23.40) double. AE, DC, MC, V.
This somewhat new hotel is operated by the same couple that operates the Jaguar Inn at the ruins of Tikal. Watch for their sign on the left as you come into town from the airport. Guest rooms have high ceilings and tile floors and are decorated with Guatemalan textiles and art. Art deco wall sconces add a touch of class in the wilderness, as do the TVs and hot water. There's a garden in the courtyard and an open-air restaurant and lounge with a few comfortable sofas where guests can chat with other jungle explorers. Meals range from Q12.50 ($2.50) for breakfast to Q25 ($5) for dinner.

In Flores

LA CASONA DE LA ISLA, Ciudad Flores, Petén. Tel. 502/500-662, 500-692, or 501-318. Fax 502/500-662 or 501-258. 27 rms (all with bath).
$ Rates: Q77 ($15.40) single; Q88 ($17.60) double; Q125 ($25) triple. AE, DC, MC, V.
Owned by the same people who run the Hotel Petén, La Casona shows the same attention to quality at economical rates. To find the hotel, just watch for the big pink building a few doors past the Hotel Petén. The guest rooms here are fairly small and

lack any semblance of decor, but they do have hot water, ceiling fans, and large, though basic, bathrooms. Between the lobby and the lake, there is a pretty little garden filled with elephant ear plants. There's no restaurant here, but the Hotel Petén's terrace dining room is only a few doors away.

HOTEL PETÉN, Flores, Petén. Tel. 502/500-692. Fax 502/500-662. 21 rms (all with bath).
$ Rates: Q100 ($20) single; Q125 ($25) double; Q150 ($30) triple. AE, DC, MC, V.
From the street, this hotel looks like a very modest Caribbean town dwelling; enter the doorway, and you'll find a small courtyard with tropical plants and a nice brick-and-stucco building of several floors. The friendly manager will show you a comfy if plain room with a fan and an electric hot water showerhead in the bathroom and perhaps a balcony overlooking the water. Most of the rooms here have been recently remodeled, but try to get a room on the top floor (nos. 33, 34, and so on) with a view of the lake. If you can't, be aware that the hotel's roof is actually a terrace that enjoys that same view. There's a restaurant on the ground floor with lakeside terrace dining.

HOTEL YUM KAX, Flores, Petén. Tel. 502/081-1686. 42 rms (all with bath).
$ Rates: Q50–Q75 ($10–$15) single; Q75–Q100 ($15–$20) double; Q100–Q125 ($20–$25) triple; Q125–Q150 ($25–$30) quad. DC.
This old Flores standard was in the midst of a complete remodeling when I last visited and new rates had not yet been set so expect them to be about what I have listed or a little more.

The name is pronounced "Yum Kash," and the hotel is to the left as you cross the causeway. Don't worry—it looks better inside than it does from the causeway vantage point. The guest rooms are bare but not bad—with fans, good cross ventilation to catch breezes on the lake, twin beds, toilet seats, and tile showers. The higher prices are for rooms with air conditioning. Yum Kax, by the way, is the Mayan god of corn. The hotel has a restaurant with a nice view of the water, and there are several others nearby.

DOUBLES FOR LESS THAN Q175 [$35]
In Santa Elena

HOTEL MAYA INTERNACIONAL, Santa Elena, Petén. Tel. 502/501-276. Fax 502/500-032. In Guatemala City, 2a Avenida 7-78, Zona 10, Guatemala City. Tel. 502/319-876, 311-927, or 248-136. Fax 502/346-237. 34 rms (all with bath).
$ Rates: Q140.40 ($28.10) single; Q163.80 ($32.75) double; Q187.20 ($37.45) triple. AE, DC, MC, V.
Built on the banks of the lake quite a few years ago, this hotel has had to contend with the rising lake waters. Several rooms have been abandoned over the years as they became inundated with water, while others built on stilts are still dry. The hotel's newest rooms are set back from the lake a bit and are slightly more substantial, though less romantic, than the older rooms. Still there are balconies and tile floors in the new rooms. The old rooms are not very soundproof, so you'll have to listen to your neighbors. Despite these caveats, the lakeside setting is excellent and a little bay full of water lilies has formed in between the hotel's bungalows.

The hotel dining room is in a separate, larger thatched structure at the end of a short causeway out in the lake. All three meals are served, rough and ready but tasty enough. Breakfast is around Q19 ($3.80), and dinner is about Q45 ($9).

WORTH THE EXTRA BUCKS
In Santa Elena

HOTEL DEL PATIO-TIKAL, Santa Elena, Petén. Tel. 502/501-229 or 500-104. In the U.S., toll free tel. 800/327-3573. In Guatemala City, 4a Calle 5-16, Zona 9, Guatemala City. Tel. 502/323-365. Fax 502/237-4313. 20 rms (all with bath). TV

$ Rates: Q292.50 ($58.50) single or double; Q327.60 ($65.50) triple. AE, DC, MC. V.

Located across the street from the Hotel Maya Internacional, the Del Patio-Tikal is one of the newer hotels in town and consequently is very clean and modern. It is built in colonial Spanish style around a grassy central courtyard with a fountain in the middle. Lounge chairs in the garden are a great place to relax after an exhausting day of hiking from one ruin to the next. Each of the rooms has large closets, a color TV, a ceiling fan, tile floors, and an immaculate tiled bathroom.

The restaurant/bar serves international and típico Guatemalan meals in the Q25 to Q50 ($5 to $10) range. For Q35 ($7), they'll also fix you a box lunch for you to take on your day's outing to the ruins at Tikal. It's hard to beat a picnic atop a Mayan pyramid. The box lunch saves you the hassle of walking all the way out to the little comedores near the parking lot at the ruins. The hotel also has laundry service.

HOTEL TZIQUINAHA, Santa Elena, Petén. Tel. 502/501-359 or 501-216. Fax 502/500-175. 36 rms (all with bath). A/C TV
$ Rates: Q257.40 ($51.50) single; Q292.50 ($58.50) double; Q327.60 ($65.50) triple. AE, DC, MC, V.

On the outskirts of Santa Elena, on the road to the airport and Tikal, is this moderately priced hotel, with modern concrete-and-stucco buildings arranged on landscaped lawns. There's also a swimming pool at the center of the complex, although the water is not always clean. There are some rough edges here, because Santa Elena is not exactly cosmopolitan, but basically the staff is willing and the rooms are comfortable and carpeted, if a bit musty from the damp jungle air. Each room has a tile bath (shower), one double and one twin bed and a minirefrigerator. The hotel caters mostly to tour groups and tends to fill up quickly, so try to make reservations as far in advance as possible.

The restaurant/bar serves all three meals with prices ranging from Q15 ($3) for breakfast to Q30 ($6) for lunch and dinner. There is a TV in the bar that plays American cable stations. Other facilities include a swimming pool, tennis court, car-rental office, and gift shop.

NEARBY PLACES TO STAY

If you'd like to spend some time exploring this area, the following lodge makes a great base of operations for a few days. If you feel like a splurge there is also the Hotel Camino Real Tikal, a luxurious and very expensive new hotel just beyond El Gringo Perdido which caters to tour groups visiting Tikal.

Also, some local folks in the nearby village of El Remate have been operating inexpensive mountain bike, motorcycle, and canoe tours in the area. If you're out this way, it's worth checking to see if these trips are still being operated. Check at the Posada el Mirador del Duende across from the Artesania Ecologica.

EL GRINGO PERDIDO, "THE LOST GRINGO," Flores, Petén. Tel. (in Guatemala City) 502/20-605 or 25-811. 40 beds (none with bath).
$ Rates: Q60–Q75 ($12–$15) per person per night. No credit cards.

Two miles off the Tikal highway, along a rough dirt road from the hamlet of El Remate (which is north of El Cruce-Ixlu on the Tikal road, 22 miles from Flores), you'll find one of Guatemala's only jungle lodges. The name means "The Lost Gringo"; it's a little offbeat paradise arranged along the lakeshore, with shady, rustic hillside gardens, a little restaurant, a bucolic camping area, and simple but pleasant guest quarters. A bungalow has four beds (two sets of bunks), a shower, a toilet, and a patio with palapa cover and hammock. A camarote is a smaller room with a toilet and washbasin and two sets of bunks; it's a little cheaper than the bungalow. Beds in the dormitory (eight beds to a room) are cheaper still. The place calls itself a Parado Ecologico (Ecological Inn), which it is. The very friendly staff will welcome you. El Gringo Perdido offers good swimming in the lake, 3 kilometers of nature trails, quiet times, and tranquillity. The Biotopo Cerro Cahui, a preserve for the endangered Petén turkey, is just across the road, and down the road a short walk are several swampy areas where you might see a few caymans (a Central American relative of the alligator). Access is by taxi from Santa Elena or the airport; once you're here, you'll be here for a while, unless you have your own wheels.

WHERE TO EAT

Most of the hotels listed in this section also have restaurants. Some of the better ones include the lakeside terrace dining room at the Hotel Petén, the elevated lake-view Chinese restaurant at the Hotel Leo Fu Lo, the thatched-roof lakeside dining room at the Hotel Maya Internacional, and the rustic, jungly dining room of the Hotel El Tucan, which serves good Mexican food.

In Flores

RESTAURANT GRAN JAGUAR, Calle Centroamerica. No phone.
   Cuisine: GUATEMALAN/INTERNATIONAL.
$ **Prices:** Entrées Q15–Q30 ($3–$6). No credit cards.
   Open: Mon–Sat 11am–10pm.

⭐ Not far from the Hotel Petén, this is an unusual restaurant with a bold jungle decor. The walls are made from rough-hewn slabs of wood with the bark still on them, and there are abundant plants, both real and artificial. The interesting menu lists a brochette of venado (venison), the most expensive item on the menu at Q30 ($6). Otherwise there are hamburgers, fish, steaks, spaghetti, and lots of drinks. This may be the most expensive place on the island.

Not to be missed is the Gran Jaguar's new lakeside restaurant and swimming area across the lake from Flores. It's called Gran Jaguar del Lago, and a boatman will take you over for only Q4 (80¢). The ride back is free. Service can be slow, so it's a good idea to go for a swim after you place your order.

RESTAURANT LA JUNGLA, Calle Centroamerica. No phone.
   Cuisine: GUATEMALAN/INTERNATIONAL.
$ **Prices:** Entrées Q15–Q25 ($3–$5). No credit cards.
   Open: Daily 10am–10pm.

You have to fight your way through the dense wall of hanging plants in the doorway to enter this aptly named restaurant. Animal skins, including jungle cats, snakes, birds, turtles, and alligators, cover the walls here. There is even an out-of-place painting of a moose done on deerskin and a few dried giant mushrooms to complete the motif. Also included are a tiny street-side terrace with two tables and a standard Petén burgers/spaghetti/venison menu.

RESTAURANT LA MESA DE LOS MAYAS, Flores. Tel. 501-240.
   Cuisine: GUATEMALAN/INTERNATIONAL.
$ **Prices:** Q10–Q35 ($2–$7). DC, MC, V.
   Open: Daily 7am–midnight.

This restaurant, just up a side street from La Jungla, is a popular place with two dining areas and plenty of tables—simple but pleasant enough here in the jungle. The menu is similar to those in the other restaurants, but it also includes wild turkey, venison, and tepezquintle (a jungle rodent the size of a rabbit).

---

2. TIKAL

338 miles NE of Guatemala City; 40 miles N of Flores

GETTING THERE   By Car   The ride from Flores to Tikal along a good paved road takes less than an hour by private car. Head north out of Santa Elena, past the airport, and keep going straight. This road dead-ends at Tikal. Watch out for pedestrians and animals (both domestic and wild) on the roadway.

By Minibus   If you don't have a car, the best way to get to Tikal is by minibus.

Minibuses from Flores and Santa Elena, and from the airport, leave at 6, 8, and 10am and return at 2, 4, and 5pm. You can get a minibus at almost any hotel. If your hotel doesn't offer one, go to the Hotel San Juan in Santa Elena. Duration: 1 hour. Fare: Q30 ($6) per person, one way.

By Bus If you want to take the bus (slow and inconvenient), go to the Hotel San Juan in Santa Elena the night before you want to travel, buy your ticket, and be on the spot the next day at 6am or noon, which is when the buses leave. Duration: 2–3 hours. Fare: Q6 ($1.20).

By Taxi A taxi from the town or the airport to Tikal costs Q180 ($36) or Q210 ($42) total, round-trip, for up to three people.

DEPARTING Minibuses return from Tikal to Flores at 2, 4, and 5pm. Be sure to arrange your return time when you buy your ticket, especially if you plan to stay the night. See the Flores section for information on departing the Petén.

ESSENTIALS Orientation The road from Flores ends in the parking lot of Tikal National Park. There are two museums, three hotels, a campground, and three little comedores (dining spots) here. The ruins are a 20- to 30-minute walk through the forest from the parking lot.

There is a post office and telegraph office on the left as you arrive at the parking area.

Tikal is the most spectacular of the many Mayan ceremonial centers throughout this region. Over 3,000 buildings have been located and mapped in the immediate area of the famous Great Plaza, and there must be thousands more in the rest of the 200-square-mile Parque Nacional Tikal. Almost as impressive as the ruins is the jungle setting, filled with exotic birds, spider monkeys, howler monkeys, ocelots, and other wildlife. Tikal is a "must" for visitors to Guatemala.

Be sure to have enough quetzals for your stay. There are no banks here, and the hotels offer a lousy rate for changing traveler's checks. The last resort is to bus down to Flores, 40 miles away, to cash a check.

Another thing you should bring to Tikal is insect repellent. All year round, but especially in the rainy season (May–Oct), you'll need the stuff. Don't come without it.

Because all of Tikal is a national park, you will have to pay a Q5 ($1) entry fee on the road into the park. The ticket is normally good for one 24-hour overnight stay.

Important Warning: Reports of guerrilla activity near the Tikal National Park continue. From what I have heard, on the Flores-Tikal road there is an incident every now and then in which armed men stop a tourist bus, lecture the tourists on the rightness of the rebel cause, request a small donation, and release them unharmed. There have been no reports of physical harm. Most visitors to Tikal do not look on this as a significant danger.

Of more immediate concern are the armed robberies that have been taking place with increasing frequency along the road between Tikal and Belize. Tourist minibuses and taxis seem to be singled out, so you may be safer riding the local bus. It might be a good idea to entrust your valuables to the management of your hotel before setting out on the road to Tikal.

These incidents may well have ceased by the time you read this. If you have doubts, you can call the **U.S. Department of State's Citizens' Emergency Service** (tel. 202/647-5225) in Washington, D.C., on weekdays from 8:15am to 10pm, for an up-to-date report. Or if you're already in Guatemala when you read this, inquire at your embassy in Guatemala City or ask the locals in Flores for news on the current situation.

WHAT TO SEE & DO
THE RUINS AT TIKAL

Tikal is the largest of the Mayan ceremonial centers. So far, archeologists have mapped about 3,000 constructions, 10,000 earlier foundations beneath surviving structures, 250 stone monuments (stelae and altars), and thousands of art objects found in tombs and cached offerings. There is evidence of continuous construction at Tikal from 200 B.C. through the 9th century A.D., with some suggestion of occupation as early as 600 B.C. The Maya reached their zenith in art and architecture during the Classic Period, which began about A.D. 250 and ended abruptly about A.D. 900, when for some reason Tikal was abandoned. Most of the visible structures at Tikal date from the Late Classic Period, A.D. 600 to 900.

No one's sure just what role Tikal played in the history of the Maya: was it mostly a ceremonial center for priests, artisans, and the elite? Or was it a city of industry and commerce as well? In the 6 square miles of Tikal that have been mapped and excavated, only a few of the buildings were domestic structures; most were temples, palaces, ceremonial platforms, and shrines. Workers are now beginning to excavate the innumerable mounds on the periphery of the mapped area, and they have been finding modest houses of stone and plaster with thatched roofs. Just how far these settlements extended beyond the ceremonial center and how many people lived within the domain of Tikal is still to be determined. At its height, Tikal may have covered as much as 25 square miles.

Tikal is such an immense site that you will need several days to see it thoroughly, but you can visit many of the greatest temples and palaces in one day. To do it properly, you should have a copy of the excellent guidebook to the ruins—*Tikal*, by William Coe, written under the auspices of the University Museum of the University of Pennsylvania. Archeologists from the university, working in conjunction with Guatemalan officials, did most of the excellent excavation work at Tikal from 1956 to 1969. Write to the museum in Philadelphia for a copy of the guide or pick one up in Flores or at Tikal ($16). One of the best features of the guide, and a real necessity given the size of the Tikal complex, is a very detailed map of the area. Don't take a chance on getting lost from site to site.

The best time to visit the ruins is early in the morning if you can manage it. The ruins open at 6am, and from then until 11am they're uncrowded. The ruins close at 5:30pm, but you can get a special pass at the park headquarters building to visit the temples when they're bathed in moonlight—an unforgettable vision.

Walking along the road that goes west from the museum toward the ruins, turn right at the first intersection to get to Twin Complexes Q and R. Seven of these twin complexes are known at Tikal, but their exact purpose is still a mystery. Each complex has two pyramids facing east and west; at the north is an unroofed enclosure entered by a vaulted doorway and containing a single stela and altar; at the south is a small palacelike structure. Of the two pyramids here, one has been restored and one has been left as it was found, and the latter will give you an idea of just how overgrown and ensconced in the jungle these structures had become.

At the end of the Twin Complexes is a wide road called the Maler Causeway. Turn right (north) onto this causeway to get to Group P, another twin complex, a 15-minute walk; turn left (south) onto the causeway to get to the Great Plaza.

Some restoration has been done at Complex P, but the most interesting points are the stela (no. 20) and altar (no. 8) in the north enclosure. Look for the beautiful glyphs next to the carving of a warrior on the stela, all in very good condition. The altar shows a captive bound to a carved-stone altar, his hands tied behind his back—a common scene in carvings at Tikal. Both these monuments date from about A.D. 751. As for Temple IV, it's said to be the tallest structure surviving from the Pre-Columbian era, standing 212 feet from the base of its platform to the top. The first glimpse you get of the temple from the Maudslay Causeway is awesome, for the temple has not been restored, and all but the temple proper (the enclosure) and its roof comb are covered in foliage. The stairway is occluded by earth and roots, but if you're adept at scrambling, you can make your way to the top of the temple from its northeast corner. Do it if you can: The view of the setting and layout of Tikal—and all of the Great Plaza—is magnificent. From the platform of the temple, you can see in all directions and get an idea of the extent of the Petén jungle, an ocean of lush greenery. Temple III is in the foreground to the east; Temples I and II are farther on at the Great Plaza. To the right of these is the South Acropolis and Temple V. The courageous and nonacrophobic can get even a better view by clambering up a metal ladder on the south side of the temple to the base of the roof comb.

Temple IV, and all the other temples at Tikal, are built on this plan: A pyramid is built first, and on top of it is built a platform; the temple proper rests on this platform and is composed of one to three rooms, usually long and narrow and not for habitation but rather for priestly rites. Most temples have beautifully carved wooden lintels above the doorways, but the one from Temple IV is now in a museum in Basel, Switzerland. The temple is thought to date from about A.D. 741. Ladders allow you to climb to the top of this one.

From Temple IV, walk east along the Tozzer Causeway to get to the Great Plaza, about a 10-minute walk. Along the way you'll pass the twin-pyramid Complex N, the Bat Palace, and Temple III. Take a look at the altar and stela in the complex's northern enclosure—two of the finest monuments at Tikal—and also the altar in front of Temple III, showing the head of a deity resting on a plate. By the way, the crisscross pattern shown here represents a woven mat, a symbol of authority to the Mayas.

THE GREAT PLAZA

Entering the Great Plaza from the Tozzer Causeway, you'll be struck by the towering stone structure that is Temple II, seen from the back. It measures 125 feet tall now, although it is thought to have been 140 feet high when the roof comb was intact. Also called the Temple of the Masks, from a large face carved in the roof comb, the temple dates from about A.D. 700.

Temple I, the most striking structure in Tikal, reaches 145 feet above the plaza floor. The temple proper has three narrow rooms with high corbeled vaults (the Mayan "arch") and carved wooden lintels made of zapote wood, which is rot resistant. One of the lintels has been removed for preservation in a museum. The whole structure is made of limestone, as are most others at Tikal. It was within this pyramid that one of the richest tombs in Tikal was discovered, containing some 180 pieces of jade, 90 bone artifacts carved with hieroglyphic inscriptions, numerous pearls, and objects in alabaster and shell.

The North Acropolis (north side of the Great Plaza) is a maze of structures from various periods covering an area of 21 acres. Standing today 30 feet above the limestone bedrock, it contains vestiges of more than a hundred different constructions dating from 200 B.C. to A.D. 800. At the front-center of the acropolis (at the top of the stairs up from the Great Plaza) is a temple numbered 5D-33. Although much of the 8th-century temple was destroyed during the excavations to get to the Early Classic Period temple (A.D. 300) underneath, it's still a fascinating building. Toward the rear of it is a tunnel leading to the stairway of the Early Classic temple, embellished with two 10-foot-high plaster polychrome masks of a god—don't miss these.

Directly across the plaza from the North Acropolis is the Central Acropolis, which covers about four acres. It's a maze of courtyards and palaces on several levels, all connected by an intricate system of passageways. Some of the palaces had five floors, connected by exterior stairways, and each floor had as many as nine rooms arranged like a maze. Look for the graffiti on some of the palace walls.

Before you leave the Great Plaza, be sure to examine some of the 70 beautiful stelae and altars right in the plaza. You can see the full development of Mayan art in them, for they date from the Early Classic Period right through to the Late Classic. There are three major stylistic groups: the stelae with wraparound carving, on the front and sides with a text on the back; those with a figure carved on the front and a text in glyphs on the back; and those with a simple carved figure on the front, a text in hieroglyphs on the sides, and a plain back. The oldest stela is no. 29 (now in the Tikal museum), dating from A.D. 292; the most recent is no. 11 in the Great Plaza, dating from A.D. 879.

THE MUSEUM

The museum contains a good collection of pottery, mosaic masks, incense burners, etched bone, and stelae that is chronologically displayed—beginning with the Preclassic objects on up to the Late Classic ones. Of note are the delicate 3- to 5-inch mosaic masks made of jade, turquoise, shell, and stucco. There is a beautiful cylindrical jar from about A.D. 700 depicting a male and female seated in a typical Maya pose. The drawing is of fine quality, and the slip colors are red, brown, and black. Also on exhibit are a number of jade pendants, beads, and earplugs as well as the famous stela no. 31, which has all four sides carved. On the two sides are spear throwers, each wearing a large feathered headdress and carrying a shield in his left hand; on the front is a complicated carving of an individual carrying a head in his left arm and a chair in his right. It is a most amazing stela from the Early Classic Period, considered one of the finest. Admission to the museum is Q1 (20¢).

WHERE TO STAY

There are only three lodging places at Tikal in the national park. Rooms are often difficult to get, and making reservations is not easy. However, if you really want to stay at Tikal (an unforgettable experience), here are your choices.

JAGUAR INN, Tikal, Petén. Tel. 502/500-002. 2 bungalows (with bath), 3 tents.
$ Rates: Q100 ($20) double in bungalows, Q50 ($10) double in tents. No credit cards.
The Jaguar Inn is a tiny place on the other side of the old museum. It offers the lowest rates of any of the hotels here at the ruins and has only two airy thatched cottages with wood and native-cloth furnishings and simple bathrooms and three large tents, each of which has two beds. The management here is English. To reserve a room, send a telegram, then follow it with a deposit when you get a confirmation. Meals can be had in the quiet screen-walled dining room for Q12.50 ($2.50) for breakfast, Q20 to Q25 ($4 to $5) for lunch, and Q25 ($5) for dinner. You may order à la carte as well. The restaurant hours are 7am to 8:30pm.

JUNGLE LODGE, 29a Calle 18-01, Zona 12, Guatemala City. Tel. 502/760-294. 32 rms (all with bath).
$ Rates: Q150 ($30) single; Q200 ($40) double. No credit cards.
Parts of the complex here were built to house the archeological teams working at Tikal, but with the recent remodeling, all the vestiges of these old and rustic accommodations are gone. It's the biggest establishment here at the ruins. You'll stay either in one of the tin-roofed bungalows or in the thatched and half-timbered main building, which also houses the dining room, bar, and reception desk. The bungalow rooms are the better choice because they are very spacious, with large bathrooms, hot water, skylights, high ceilings, and two double beds. Each comes with its own little porch and lounge chairs. Unfortunately, despite the louvered windows, these rooms have little airflow and can get hot in the day. Try for a room here first, even though it may be filled by a tour group. Three meals a day in the dining room will run you about Q105 ($21).

HOTEL TIKAL INN, Tikal, Petén. No phone. 15 rms (all with bath).
$ Rates (including breakfast and dinner): Q175–Q200 ($35–$40) single; Q350–Q400 ($70–$80) double. No credit cards.
⭐ This is the most pleasant of the three hotels at the ruins. Set back amid the trees, it's the farthest from the museum as you walk down the old airstrip. Several large thatched-roof huts, a swimming pool, and a somewhat dramatic main building make this place look a little grand for the jungle setting. The

accommodations are quite simple but clean. The bungalows have hardwood floors and are very nicely decorated with típico fabrics. To facilitate airflow, the walls of these rooms don't go all the way to the ceiling, and consequently these rooms don't have much conversational privacy. The smaller rooms in the main building have cement floors but the same attention to decor. All the rooms are airy and cool. To make a reservation, write or send a telegram.

CAMPING

Just off the parking lot at the end of the road and the airstrip is a nice lawn with some trees for shade, marked and designated as the camping area. It has simple plumbing and cooking facilities and charges Q15 ($3) for use of the showers. If you have the gear, this is the place for you. You can also rent hammocks and pitch them under palapas for an additional Q15 ($3). Keep in mind, however, that in this area there are vampire bats, even though they don't often bite humans. Be sure to use a tent or mosquito net to keep the bats off while you sleep.

WHERE TO EAT

Besides the hotels above, there are several little eateries (comedores) between the main open area and the gate at the beginning of the road to Flores. As you arrive at Tikal from Flores, you'll see them on the right side: **Comedor Imperio Maya, Comedor Corazon de Jesus,** and **Comedor Tikal & Tienda Angelita.** All are similar in comfort and style (there is none), all are rustic and pleasant, all are run by local women, and all serve huge plates of fairly tasty food at low prices. I had a huge piece of roast chicken, with rice, beans, melon, and a soft drink for Q10 ($2). You may get little choice; what's cooking that day (usually chicken) is what there is. If you have a friend with you, be sure to order a fruit plate for Q9 ($1.80), the largest and most delicious fruit plate I've ever encountered.

Another choice is the **snack bar** behind the new Stelae Museum, the big building on the left as you pull into the parking area. It is in a large covered area with several tables and is open daily from 7am to 8pm. A steak and salad here will run you around Q35 ($7).

Within the area of the ruins there are picnic tables beneath shelters and itinerant soft-drink peddlers, but no snack stands. If you want to spend all day at the ruins without having to walk back to the settlement for lunch, take sandwiches.

EXCURSIONS
EL CEIBAL & OTHER MORE REMOTE RUINS

If your life's passion is Mayan ruins or you simply crave more adventure than you have had so far on your visit to El Petén, maybe you should visit some of the more remote ruins of this region. In addition to exploring seldom-visited Mayan ruins, you'll be traveling by river through uninhabited jungles where you'll likely encounter a great deal of wildlife, which might include coatimundis, howler monkeys, anteaters, tapirs, and possibly even jaguars.

El Ceibal is the most accessible of these other ruins. To reach El Ceibal, first take a bus the 40 miles from Flores to Sayaxche, which is a good-sized town for El Petén (it even has a few basic hotels). From Sayaxche, you must hire a boat to carry you 11 miles up the Río de la Pasión. El Ceibal is a Late Classic ruin (A.D. 600 to 900) known for having the only circular temple in all of El Petén. There are also several well-preserved stelae arranged around one small temple structure on the central plaza. Many of the designs at El Ceibal indicate that the city had extensive contact with cities in the Yucatán, but whether this contact was due to trade or to warfare is unclear.

In order to visit ruins such as **Yaxchilan, Piedras Negras,** and **Altar de los Sacrificios,** you'll have to spend days camping on remote rivers. The best way to visit these would be on an organized trip; this way you would not have to leave anything to chance. Contact **Tropical Tours,** 4a Calle 2-50 "A," Zona 10, Guatemala City (tel. 502/323-748, 345-893, or 345-894), or **Expedicion**

Panamundo, 3a Av. 16-52, Zona 10 (tel. 502/681-315 or 683-010), for information on organized river trips through this region. If you try it on your own, you'll have to rely on someone's recommendation to find a reliable boatman, arrange for several days' meals, bring your own tent, and make sure there is enough fuel to get you there and back. In short, you'll have to mount your own small-scale river expedition into the jungle. However, it can be done, and if you set out to try it, you'll certainly meet other like-minded adventurers with whom to share the costs.

As more and more people venture into the Petén, tours and services are expanding. On my last visit, there was a company offering transportation by minibus and boat to El Ceibal for Q150 ($30) or a 2-day trip for $90. This latter trip included visits to Ceibal and Aguateca, another ruin. For more information on this trip, ask at your hotel or at Hotel La Casona de la Isla in Flores.

CHAPTER 12

THE ATLANTIC HIGHWAY

1. COBÁN

• **WHAT'S SPECIAL ABOUT THE ATLANTIC HIGHWAY**

2. COPÁN [HONDURAS]

3. QUIRIGUÁ

4. RÍO DULCE & LAKE IZABAL

5. LÍVINGSTON & PUERTO BARRIOS

Heading east from Guatemala City, you'll leave the cool highlands and descend first into dry rolling hills and then, as you approach the coast, into lush tropical vegetation. The roads branching off this highway tend to be in excellent shape. The Carretera al Atlántico (Atlantic Highway), which has been undergoing much-needed major repairs in the past few years, leads to several interesting destinations, including the mountainous state of Alta Verapaz and its capital, Cobán; the Mayan ruins at Copán, Honduras; the great pilgrimage church at Esquipulas, famous throughout Central America; the marvelous Mayan stelae and zoomorphs at Quiriguá; the Río Dulce and Lake Izabal, on the road to Tikal; and Guatemala's Caribbean port and laid-back hideaway, Puerto Barrios and Lívingston.

When leaving Guatemala City by private car, be prepared to pay a few small tolls at points along the Atlantic Highway. The tolls (for which you get a receipt) are only a few cents each—more of a bother than an expense.

1. COBÁN

132 miles NE of Guatemala City; 214 miles W of Puerto Barrios

GETTING THERE   By Bus   Buses from Guatemala City leave from 8a Av. 15-16, Zona 1 (tel. 511-878), daily between 4am and 5pm. Duration: 4 hours. Fare: Q11.25 or Q16 ($2.25 or $3.20).

By Car   Take the Carretera al Atlántico to El Rancho, then turn left for Cobán.

DEPARTING   Buses for Guatemala City leave frequently throughout the day from 2a Calle 3-77, Zona 4 (tel. 511-952). Duration: 4 hours. Fare: Q11.25 or Q16 ($2.25 or $3.20).

To reach Puerto Barrios first take a bus to the junction with the Atlantic Highway at El Rancho and then catch one of the frequent buses bound for Puerto Barrios.

ESSENTIALS   Orientation   Cobán is situated on a hill with the city sloping steeply away from the central plaza and cathedral. All of the hotels and restaurants listed here are within a few blocks of the central plaza. Some of the roads around town are one way so pay attention if you are driving.

Fast Facts   The Banco del Agro, where you can change money and traveler's checks, is two blocks from La Posada on the road leading to Guatemala City. The Guatel office is on the main plaza. Feast days are Holy Week and August 4.

Although the road east from Guatemala City rapidly carries you down to hot dusty lowlands where cactus and other desert plants abound, a side trip north to the area of Alta Verapaz will take you into the most beautiful region of the country. High in

WHAT'S SPECIAL ABOUT THE ATLANTIC HIGHWAY

Mayan Ruins
- ☐ Copán (actually in Honduras), nearly as impressive as Tikal.
- ☐ Quiriguá, known for its intricately carved stelae (record-keeping stones).

Natural Spectacles
- ☐ Semuc Champey cataracts and the quetzal preserve near Cobán.

Religious Shrines
- ☐ The basilica in Esquipulas, with a statue of Christ that is the object of a massive pilgrimage every year.

these cloud-shrouded mountains, iridescent birds flit among trees draped with orchids, bromeliads, and ferns. The valleys are given over to pastures, and the lower mountain slopes are covered with coffee plantations (once owned by Germans) and farms that grow decorative tropical plants for export as houseplants to colder climes. These tropical-plant farms are often hidden under acres of canvas, which protects the plants from the burning rays of the tropical sun. It is shocking to see entire hillsides hidden beneath these sheets.

Even though Cobán (alt. 4,290 feet; pop. 15,000) has a long history, dating back to colonial times, it is the countryside surrounding the city that is the main attraction here. Alta Verapaz abounds in natural wonders, and Cobán is an excellent base for exploring the rest of the region. There are several excellent and very inexpensive hotels, which offer some of the best values in all of Guatemala.

WHAT TO SEE & DO

In Cobán itself there is very little to do. Activity focuses on the central plaza and the market behind the cathedral. The Catedral de Santo Domingo, founded in 1687, is rather spartan both inside and out. The cracked bell just inside the front door is not a Guatemalan Liberty Bell but a church bell that fell when the bell tower was struck by lightning. Also facing the central plaza is the art deco Palacio Municipal and another government office building with a two-story facade of long porticoes in the colonial style. In the plaza itself is a very modern-looking band shell that is the site of evening concerts in the dry season.

If you head out of town on the road to Guatemala City for a few blocks, you'll see a church high on a hill to your right. This is El Calvario, a small church in the middle of an old cemetery. The church is reached by a long flight of steps that lead up the hill. As you climb, you'll see little alcoves where offerings are made by the devout. At the top there are beautiful views of the surrounding valley and mountains. Behind El Calvario is a forest park that offers some good bird watching.

Near the village of Tactic, about 20 miles before you reach Cobán, is an unusual natural phenomenon: the Pozo Vivo (Living Well), a pool of water formed by a spring that bubbles up from the ground in the middle of a beautiful green pasture. It derives its name from the way the sand at the bottom of the pool dances while the surface remains smooth as glass. It would hardly be worth stopping for, but it offers a chance to take a short stroll through this beautiful valley. Unfortunately, the well has not been very lively in recent years. There is an attractive colonial church in the town of Tactic itself, and excellent silver and gold jewelry is made and sold here. From the peak of Chi-Ixim hill, just outside of town, there is an excellent view of the town and its surrounding fields.

Nearby San Pedro Carchá, which is about 8 miles from Cobán, is another town famous for its silver filigree work. Situated atop a hill, the town has a large colonial church. During the town's feast days (June 24–29), masked dances are performed in the streets. If you're a member of the Polar Bear Club and enjoy swimming in ice-cold waters, you'll want to pay a visit to Las Islas, a nearby waterfall with a large pool at its base.

Both Tactic and San Pedro Carchá can be reached by frequent bus or minibus service from the market in Cobán. Several interesting excursions (details below) also are possible from Cobán.

WHERE TO STAY

DOUBLES FOR LESS THAN Q75 [$15]

HOTEL COBÁN IMPERIAL, 6a Avenida 1-12, Zona 1, Cobán, Alta Verapaz. Tel. 502/511-131. 7 rms (all with bath).
$ Rates: Q35.10 ($7) single; Q52.65 ($10.55) double; Q70.20 ($14.05) triple. No credit cards.
This rather nondescript hotel is simple but clean and conveniently located close to the Parque Central and El Calvario on the corner of 1a Calle. Rooms here are quite large and have been recently repainted, though the carpets and beds are still old and dreary. Surprisingly, rooms have their own TVs. There is a small restaurant serving very inexpensive meals just off the lobby.

HOTEL MANSION ARMENIA, Avenida del Calvario 2-18, Zona 1, Cobán, Alta Verapaz. Tel. 502/512-284. 22 rms (all with bath).
$ Rates: Q58.50 ($11.70) single; Q70.20 ($14.05) double; Q81.90 ($16.40) triple. No credit cards accepted.
On the street leading to the base of El Calvario (The Calvary), Cobán's little chapel and cemetery, is this two-story neocolonial motel, which offers an excellent value. All the small rooms have arched windows facing onto a parking lot that is locked up at night. The tile floors are squeaky clean, and there are double beds, tables, and wardrobes in most of the rooms. Because of its location off the main street, it's a very quiet place for a good night's sleep. There is a small restaurant at the back of the hotel that serves three meals a day.

DOUBLES FOR LESS THAN Q110 [$22]

HOTEL LA POSADA, 1a Calle 4-12, Zona 2, Cobán, Alta Verapaz. Tel. 502/511-495. 14 rms (all with bath).
$ Rates: Q81.90 ($16.40) single; Q105.30 ($21.05) double; Q128.70 ($25.75) triple. No credit cards. **Parking:** Free.
This rustic colonial hotel may be the best deal in all of Guatemala, perhaps because gringos as a whole have not yet discovered this beautiful region. Although the hotel is wedged between the two busiest streets in town and is consequently noisy, it still manages to maintain a rural atmosphere. You enter the hotel through a large gate and find yourself in a well-tended garden. Along the portico to the left is the office, where you can play table tennis if you like. The floors throughout are wood, and antique wooden benches line the portico. Traditional masks hang from the walls; and *santos,* little statues of saints, are seemingly everywhere. There is a TV lounge with wide-plank floors and shocking-pink furniture. The guest rooms have beamed ceilings, old or antique furniture, and private baths with hot water. You'll spot signs for La Posada on your left just as you approach the Parque Central. There is a cozy restaurant with a fireplace.

HOTEL RABIN AJAU, Calzada Minerva 5-37, Zona 1, Cobán, Alta Verapaz. Tel. 502/512-296. 14 rms (all with bath).

$ Rates: Q35 ($7) single; Q45 ($9) double; Q55 ($11) triple. No credit cards.
Parking: Free.

With two restaurants and a disco, this basic hotel is the closest Cobán has to a resort, which it definitely is not. In Guatemalan terminology, it is a *turicentro,* just down the street from La Posada as you head out of town on the road to Guatemala City. Wood paneling throughout the hotel gives it a rustic, mountain-lodge appeal. Oil paintings by a local artist hang in the small lobby. The service is nothing exceptional here, but then you aren't paying much either. One of the restaurants is a pizzeria, and the other serves typical Guatemalan meals. Prices range from Q8 to Q20 ($1.60 to $4).

WHERE TO EAT

EL GANADERO, 1a Calle 4-11, Zona 1. Tel. 299-4049.
  Cuisine: STEAKS/GUATEMALAN.
  $ Prices: Main dishes Q15–Q33 ($3–$6.60). DC, MC, V.
  Open: Daily 11am–11pm.

This newly opened branch of a popular Guatemala City restaurant serves up excellent steaks in a thatched-roof building set back from the street. It is actually in the courtyard of an older building and is reached by a short hallway hung with contemporary local art. There are more interesting paintings hanging behind the bar in this brightly lit restaurant. Waiters in black vests and bow ties take your order and make sure that all is as it should be during your meal. Try the steak with three sauces—it's delicious. And absolutely do not miss the garlic bread—I had to order two baskets of it.

CAFÉ EL TIROL, 1a Calle 3-13. No phone.
  Cuisine: COFFEE/SANDWICHES.
  $ Prices: Coffee Q2–Q5 (40¢–$1); sandwiches Q3.50–Q5 (70¢–$1). No credit cards.
  Open: Daily 11am–9pm.

Directly across the street from the fountain at the south end of the Parque Central is a new café that is a showcase for Guatemalan coffees. Cobán is coffee-growing country, and you probably saw a great deal of it on your way up here. Don't miss the opportunity to tap into it at its source. If you're a coffeeholic, you'll find the assortment here absolutely mouth watering: coffee "as black as midnight"; café americano; coffee with cocoa and whipped cream; espresso with cardamom; espresso with chocolate, sweet cream, and cinnamon; and even an assortment of coffees with different liquors. Tea and cocoa drinkers are not shunned either. To accompany your coffee, there are delicious pastries and some simple sandwiches. This is a great place for a late-night cup and cake or a light lunch. Have your repast on the portico surrounded by brilliantly colored bougainvillea vines.

EXCURSIONS

MARIO DARY RIVERA BIOTOPO

Located at kilometer 163 on the road leading to Cobán (about an hour from Cobán), this nature reserve is one of the last places in the country where Guatemala's national bird, the resplendent quetzal, is still found. In Pre-Columbian times, the most expensive garments, those worn by kings and princes, were often made from thousands of bird feathers. The most highly prized feathers of all were those of the quetzal, a pigeon-sized bird of the Central American cloud forests. Both the male and the female quetzal sport iridescent green and brilliant red feathers. This beautiful coloring alone would be enough to label them the most beautiful birds in the world, but to add to this display of color, the male of the species also has two willowy tail feathers that can reach almost a yard in length—the most highly prized feathers in Pre-Columbian times.

The male quetzal's tail feathers resemble the fronds of epiphytic ferns that cling to the branches of trees in its cloud-forest habitat. Cloud forests, which form only at high elevations, are similar to lowland rain forests. They are perpetually damp, but the moisture here is not generally in the form of rain. The warm trade winds that pick up moisture as they cross the Caribbean Sea are forced up into colder elevations by Guatemala's mountain ranges. As the moist air cools, it forms dense clouds that blanket the mountains for most of the year, keeping the forests damp. Thousands of species of plants have evolved to make the most of this damp environment. Branches of trees are covered with orchids, ferns, bromeliads, and other epiphytic plants. A stroll along the trails of this nature reserve is certain to elicit gasps from those unfamiliar with the dense tangle of vegetation that comprises a cloud forest. Among the most interesting plants are the tree ferns, which can grow up to twenty feet tall with huge feathery crowns. Many plants that are sold as houseplants in the north grow wild here.

Hundreds of species of birds call this forest home, and a sharp-eyed bird-watcher can easily spot several dozen, perhaps even a quetzal, in a hike through the reserve. Because of the density of the forest, the mammals that inhabit the reserve are much more difficult to spot. Among those that you might see are monkeys and ocelots.

Where to Stay & Eat

POSADA MONTAÑA DEL QUETZAL, Km 156 Ruta a Cobán, Baja Verapaz. In Guatemala City, 6a Ave. 0-60, Zona 4, Torre Profesional 1, Oficina 303, Tel. 502/351-805. 8 rms, 10 bungalows (all with bath).
$ Rates: Q93.60 ($18.70) single; Q163.80 ($32.75) double; Q198.90 ($39.80) triple; Q247 ($49.40) quad; higher rates are for weekends. DC, MC, V.

Located about 2½ miles from the quetzal preserve, this is the most luxurious hotel in the entire region. The hotel, situated on manicured grounds surrounded by forests, is a popular weekend destination for wealthy citizens of Guatemala City who come for the cool, clean country atmosphere. There are trails through the nearby forests, where you might even spot a quetzal, and exotic plants, such as tree ferns, are abundant on the grounds themselves. The bungalows are considerably larger than the rooms and are a particularly good deal. Each comes with two bedrooms, a separate living room, and a fireplace, which keeps the rooms very cozy on cold nights. A great place for a long relaxing stay. Highly recommended.

There are two restaurants and an open-air thatched-roof bar. One restaurant looks onto the parking lot and is a good place to stop for breakfast or lunch if you're just passing through. The other restaurant has a wall of windows looking onto the swimming pool. Breakfast is served from 7 to 10am, lunch from noon to 3pm, and dinner from 6 to 9pm. Meal prices range from Q10 ($2) for breakfast up to Q30 ($6) for dinner. You have a choice of numerous dishes, primarily Guatemalan and international cuisine, at every meal.

Facilities include a swimming pool, children's pool, playground, fishing pond, and hiking trails.

HOSPEDAJE EL RANCHITO DEL QUETZAL, Km 163, Baja Verapaz. No phone. 16 beds (none with bath).
$ Rates: Q15 ($3) single; Q30 ($6) double. No credit cards.
For those who would like to be as close to the *biotopo* as possible and don't have much money to spend, this is your only choice. There are two very rustic cabins here, each with eight beds. It's just a step above camping, but the log cabins beneath tall trees are picturesque. Bring your own food or buy meals at the comedor right here.

LANQUÍN CAVES & SEMUC CHAMPEY

Northeast of Cobán 42 miles on a rough dirt road is the village of Lanquín and its nearby caves. The drive to this area is difficult and time consuming, so leave early in the morning. Don't even think about trying it in the rainy season. Even in the dry season, you'll need a four-wheel-drive vehicle if you want to go as far as Semuc Champey. You might be able to hire a taxi in Cobán to bring you out here.

The mountains throughout this region are limestone and consequently are laced with caverns and sinkholes. Of the caves in the region, those at Lanquín are the most famous, extending for several miles into a mountain, with the Lanquín River running through immense halls. You can find a guide in the village who will turn on the lights in the caves and lead you through. The going is often slippery, so be sure to wear shoes with good traction. It's also a good idea to carry a couple of flashlights in case the power should go off.

Another 6 miles beyond Lanquín is Semuc Champey, a startlingly beautiful ravine that is also a result of the limestone of this region. Pools of icy water collect in bowls carved out of the limestone by torrents of water. Amazingly, each pool is a different shade of turquoise. All around are steep cliffs and lush vegetation. However, these jewel-like pools are only part of the magic of Semuc Champey. Just upstream from the pools, the Cahabón River cascades through a narrow gorge and suddenly disappears into a sinkhole. Further downstream, after passing under a natural bridge on top of which are several turquoise pools, the river reemerges. After the difficult journey to reach this remote and rugged area, you'll certainly want to stay far longer than you had originally planned. If you have camping gear with you, there is a place here to pitch a tent; otherwise, the nearest lodging is in Lanquín, but it is very basic.

---

2. COPÁN [HONDURAS]

112 miles E of Guatemala City; 68 miles S of Río Hondo

GETTING THERE **By Bus**   You take a bus first to Chiquimula, then take another to the border at El Florido. Chiquimula-bound buses leave Guatemala City from 19a Calle 8-18, Zona 1 (tel. 537-282), every 30 minutes from 4am to 6pm. From the central park in Chiquimula, there are buses to the border at 7 and 10am and 12:30pm. If you leave Guatemala City at 7am or earlier, you can make the 11am bus and be at the Honduran border by 3pm (unfortunately the ruins close at 4pm). You can take a minibus or hire a taxi or motorcycle to take you the remaining 9 miles to the ruins. Alternatively, you can hire a taxi in Chiquimula to take you to the border, but this will cost around Q400 ($80) for the day, which includes having the taxi wait for you at the border. Guatemalan taxis will not go into Honduras because the roads are too bad. If you'd like to leave all the planning to someone else, there are tours that leave from Antigua. Check the notice boards around Antigua for current information and rates. This might be the best bet if there are four of you.

By Car   If you're driving, it'll take you four or five hours to reach Copán from Guatemala City. Turn off the Atlantic Highway at Río Hondo and take CA 12 south past Zacapa and Chiquimula. Just south of Chiquimula is a small sign pointing to a dirt road on the left. Take it—it may be a bad road, but it's all you've got. The distance to the border is 40 miles, over mountains, through streams and villages.

DEPARTING   Throughout the morning and on into the early afternoon, trucks and buses leave the town of Copán for the Guatemalan border. From El Florido, on the border, there are buses to Chiquimula several times between 8am and 4pm.

ESSENTIALS   If you needed a visa to get into Guatemala and are planning only to visit Copán and return to Guatemala, be sure your visa is good for multiple entries, otherwise, the nearest Guatemalan consulate is in San Pedro Sula. If you have a Tourist Card, try to convince the guards to give you a temporary exit stamp if you just want to go to the ruins, otherwise you'll have to pay another Q25 ($5) for a new Tourist Card. When crossing from Guatemala into Copán, you'll have to pay a Q5 ($1) exit tax, and then $3 to enter Honduras. Expect to pay between $10 and $20 each way to cross the border if you are driving your own car.

Though the Mayan ruins of Copán are across the border in Honduras, they are so close to Guatemala that I am including them in this book. Few people make the time-consuming journey to visit Copán, but it is certainly worth the effort if you have an interest in *El Mundo Maya* (The Mayan World). The temples and pyramids of Copán are not as impressive as those at Tikal, but the city's sculptural legacy is fascinating. The sculptors of Copán were perhaps the greatest in the Mayan realm, and many of their well-preserved works of art are on display here at the ruins.

WHAT TO SEE & DO

THE RUINS AT COPÁN

Copán is in a valley about 2,000 feet high, right on the Copán River. The area is lush and fertile, good for growing tobacco but cooler than most Mayan sites (which are in sea-level jungle). As with most early cities, Copán has had several locations in its 1,500 years of existence. The first settlement (Early Classic, about A.D. 400) was where the village of Copán is today. By the Late Classic Period (about A.D. 700), most of the area in the Copán valley had been occupied at one time or another. But the Main Structure, about a mile east of Copán village, did not become the religious and governmental center until the middle of the 8th century A.D.; and not until this time did the Mayan artisans of Copán reach their highest level of achievement.

As you enter the village, you'll see signs to the parking lot and a bit farther on a booth where you buy a ticket for the ruins and museum. The museum is on the main plaza in town and has the standard collection of stelae, sculptures, a tomb complete with skulls, and many small jade and stone objects. You can purchase a guidebook to the ruins, which is not really worth it, but the area is so large that a guide is almost a necessity.

From the museum it's about a half-hour walk to the Main Structure, a mile east, and you'll need at least a full day to see these ruins. Plan to spend another day if you want to dig around the other sites: Copán cemetery, quarry beds, and the stone buildings outside Santa Rita. There are vestiges of settlements everywhere in the valley.

The Main Structure is in the center of the valley, north of the Copán River, and covers 62 acres: five plazas surrounded by temples, pyramids, and platforms, all built at different times between A.D. 730 and 850. The largest complex, 130 feet high from the plaza floor, is at the southern end. Called the Acropolis, it was the center for religious life in the city. On the Acropolis's northeast corner (left as you face it from the plaza) is the famous Hieroglyphic Stairway, decorated with some 2,500 glyphs on the 63 stairs that lead up to Temple 26. (The stairs have been restored—a landslide in the 19th century toppled all but 15 of them.) Unfortunately, they won't let you get close enough to the stairs to have a good look at the glyphs.

The stairs on the north side of the Acropolis lead to the Eastern and Western Courts. Archeologists think the Eastern Court was the most sacred spot at Copán because it contains Temple 22 (north side of the court), the most magnificent structure in Copán. Much of the work on the facade has been destroyed, but you can tell from the vestiges of mosaic and sculpture how grand it was. Note the two giant death's-heads intermeshed with squatting figures and grotesque monsters over the

IMPRESSIONS

The only sounds that disturbed the quiet of this buried city were the noise of monkeys moving among the tops of the trees . . . It was the first time we had seen these mockeries of humanity, and, with the strange monuments around us, they seemed like wandering spirits of the departed race guarding the ruins of their former habitations.
—J.L. STEPHENS, *INCIDENTS OF TRAVEL IN CENTRAL AMERICA, CHIAPAS AND YUCATAN,* 1841

door to the sanctuary. The Western Court is less impressive, although Temple 16, a stepped-platform type, is impressive enough. When Maudslay began excavations in 1885, he found fragments of sculpture that had once decorated this temple strewn all over the Western Court.

The Great Plaza at the northern end of the Main Structure is similar in layout to the Great Plaza at Tikal. From dates on the 20 stelae and 14 altars found here, archeologists think that the Great Plaza was the first complex built in the Main Structure. The center of life may have shifted to the Acropolis area once that part was finished.

Be sure to notice the special artistry that Copán's sculptors exhibited in carving the glyphs here, for Copán's glyphs are the finest examples of this Maya "writing." Also, the unusual sculptures, unique in Mayan art, owe a lot of their beauty to the greenish volcanic stone found only at Copán.

WHERE TO STAY & EAT

Copán is primarily a day-trip excursion and few people choose to stay here. The village near the ruins does, however, have a handful of absolutely basic hotels where you can get a room for between $4 and $10. There are also a couple of basic little restaurants in the village.

AN EXCURSION

If you have an interest in colonial or religious history, you might want to make a side trip to **Esquipulas,** which is beyond Chiquimula on the CA 12 highway. Esquipulas is not much different from any other Guatemalan town, except for its basilica—which is very special, indeed. Called by some the "Basilica of all Central America," it was ordered built by the first archbishop of Guatemala, Pedro Pardo de Figueroa, in 1759. The archbishop wanted such a grand place to house the sacred statue of Christ Crucified that had been made in 1594 by Quirio Cantano. The statue had had a long history of miraculous events connected with it even before the church was built: In 1740 it was said to have perspired profusely, a miracle authenticated by the then bishop of Guatemala.

Devout Catholics visit the basilica throughout the year, but the rites during Holy Week attract a larger-than-average crowd, as does the Festival of the Holy Name of Jesus (January 6 to 15). At times such as these, it's possible for visitors to file past the statue and even to kiss it, although the lines are unbelievably long.

Besides the statue, which is quite small and housed in the glass case above the altar, the church boasts the largest bell in Central America, installed in 1946. And the building itself is impressive, simple (for the style of the time) but harmonious, with four tall corner towers and beautiful grounds.

The market just outside the church is especially active during the two festivals mentioned; in fact, it takes on a carnival atmosphere: stalls selling snacks, such as fried banana slices; games of skill and chance; and the normal market activities of selling handwoven blankets and—here in Esquipulas—religious articles and trinkets. There are even fireworks displays during the festivals.

Because Esquipulas is a popular pilgrimage site, you will find dozens of economical hotels and restaurants around town should you decide to stay the night.

3. QUIRIGUÁ

136 miles E of Guatemala City; 67 miles W of Puerto Barrios;
56 miles S of Río Dulce

GETTING THERE By Bus Any bus headed to Puerto Barrios will drop you off at the junction with the road to the ruins or in the village of Quiriguá. From here it is possible to walk or hire a motorcycle to take you the remaining 2½ miles to the ruins.

By Car   The ruins of Quiriguá are 2½ miles south of the Atlantic Highway at kilometer 205 on a dirt road that leads through a banana plantation.

DEPARTING   Buses for Puerto Barrios and Guatemala City pass by on the highway frequently throughout the day. If you are heading to El Petén, you can catch a bus as far as the turnoff for Río Dulce or wait for one of the direct buses.

Though Quiriguá is not one of the more spectacular ruin sites in Guatemala, it is noteworthy for its well-preserved large stone carvings. These carvings, called stelae, were not just works of art but records of historic events. Through the study of such carvings much has been learned about Mayan culture and history. Though close to the Atlantic Highway, Quiriguá is not very convenient to visit unless you are traveling by car. If you are traveling by bus, you can stay in the village of Quiriguá or at one of the nearby cheap hotels and bus, walk, or cycle to and from the ruins. You almost have to stay overnight in the area, and to spend so much time on this small site may only be worthwhile to serious students of the Mayas. If you have your own car, it's much easier to visit and is certainly worth pulling off the highway for an hour or two.

WHAT TO SEE & DO
THE RUINS

Quiriguá is a Late Classic Mayan city, dating from A.D. 692 to 900. It was a dependency of Copán, and it was here that the Mayan methods of quarrying and carving great pieces of stone reached the height of excellence. The area around Quiriguá was once a dense forest of ceiba, mahogany, and palm, but at the turn of this century, the trees and bush were cleared to make way for the farms and plantations of the United Fruit Company. All that remains of the forest is the 75-acre park in which the ruins are set, about a mile south of the highway through the banana plantation.

The ruins were discovered in 1840, and Maudslay took an interest in them later (1881–1894); after the turn of the century, several teams came and excavated at Quiriguá. The site has been restored by the University of Pennsylvania, sponsored by the National Geographic Society.

Quiriguá has three sites, but only the one most lately occupied (A.D. 751–900) is of interest. This is the one in the excellent park, reached by crossing the railroad tracks, going through the parking lot, and then walking along a path to the southwest. From the great plaza (about 1,500 feet long, north to south), it's an awesome sight: a lofty, lush grove with a gigantic ceiba tree in the middle. A yellow-billed ticu may poke its head out of a hole in a dead tree, or you may see a 2-foot-long brilliant-green iguana moving slowly in the grass.

At the southern end of the plaza is the largest of the complexes, a temple plaza raised above ground level and surrounded by six temple-palace structures built at different times between A.D. 750 and 810. Take a look at the structure on the east side, which has two altars, designated Q and R by archeologists, in front of the west doorway. Both these altars represent human figures seated cross-legged. Also look at the 9-foot-high mosaic head over the doorway in the north facade of "Structure 2," on the southwest corner of the plaza. Another sculpture mask with huge teeth is on the southwest corner of the same structure. And on Structure 1, at the far southern end of the plaza, look at the beautiful hieroglyphic inscriptions around the doors.

To me, Quiriguá is synonymous with the grand stelae the Mayas did so well. As you enter the park, you'll pass several of these, carved from brown sandstone, 13 to 35 feet tall. The most famous is 35-foot Stela "E," the tallest stone shaft in Mesoamerica, which is about one-fourth of the way down the plaza as you walk south. (There are two stelae side by side here; facing south, "E" is the one on your right.) Both the front and the back are carved with a man standing on a platform and holding in his right hand a manikin scepter (a Mayan ceremonial wand depicting a long-nosed god). The northern face is the best preserved. On the sides are glyphs that archeologists have used to date this stela at A.D. 771. Most of the other stelae here have similar figures, many having beards that seemed to come into fashion with the Maya for a 30-year period. Stela "D," at the far north end of the plaza, has a figure with a beard; some of the glyphs on the sides have been deciphered, indicating that this figure is "Two-armed Sky," a ruler of Quiriguá in A.D. 766 and a native of Copán.

Look also at the "zoomorphs," huge boulders carved into monsters. Zoomorph "B," behind Stela "E," is one such monster who has a human torso and head protruding from (or, rather, disappearing into) his mouth. Another good one is at the far southern end of the plaza, on the east side: A crouched man is covered by a shield (looking like a human turtle); the shield, seen from the top, is clearly the face of a deity with two large earplugs, and the crouched figure has a face at each end. There are several more of these zoomorphs; to see them well you have to take your time and look at them from every possible angle.

A note on the sandstone used here: The Mayas were lucky in that the beds of this stone in the nearby River Motagua had cleavage planes good for cutting large pieces and that the stone, when freshly cut, was very soft and hardened only after some exposure to the air. No wonder the highly skilled Mayan craftsmen picked Quiriguá for their most impressive sculpture.

WHERE TO STAY & EAT

HOTEL DOÑA MARÍA, Km 181, Carretera al Atlántico at Doña María Bridge. No phone. 22 rms (all with bath).
$ Rates: Q15 ($3) single; Q25 ($5) double; Q35 ($7) triple. No credit cards.
It looks quite forlorn from the front, but behind the facade of this hotel is an airy dining and sitting area with a fine view of the river and the emerald-green grass and tall palm trees that line its banks. A small dam creates a swimming area where children and adults from Guatemala City splash on the weekend. The rooms here are a bit musty, dark, and claustrophobic, but if you spend all of your waking hours swimming in the river, hiking in the mountains, and touring Quiriguá, it might be worth it.

HOTEL ROYAL, Quiriguá. No phone. 15 rms (2 with bath).
$ Rates: Q10 ($2) per person without bath, Q20 ($4) per person with bath. No credit cards.
The only place to stay in this little dirt-street hamlet several miles from the ruins is a short drive off the highway. It's a Caribbean-style wood structure with numerous large, high-ceilinged, well-ventilated rooms. Each room has a concrete floor on which four or five beds are arranged, a cold-water washbasin and, if you're lucky, a shower and a toilet, perhaps with a seat. The walls are painted green. If business is slow, you may be able to rent one of the large bathless rooms entirely for yourself. Although severely plain, the rooms are clean, and the family who runs the place is friendly enough. A little comedor here is the only place for basic meals.

HOTEL SANTA MONICA, Km 200, Carretera al Atlántico, Los Amates, Izabel. No phone. 8 rms (all with bath).
$ Rates: Q20 ($4) single; Q40 ($8) double. No credit cards.
Although it is located behind a Texaco gas station and a 24-hour convenience store, this small, new hotel is very clean and comfortable. The rooms are large, carpeted, and come with two beds each. There is a restaurant next door to the hotel where you can get inexpensive Guatemalan meals.

4. RÍO DULCE & LAKE IZABAL

180 miles E of Guatemala City; 62 miles NW of Puerto Barrios;
56 miles N of Quiriguá

GETTING THERE   By Bus   Buses bound for Flores leave Guatemala City from

17a Calle 8-46, Zona 1 (tel. 513-817), at 1, 2, 3, and 7am and 9pm, stopping in Río Dulce about 5 hours later.

By Car The turnoff for Río Dulce is just past the town of Morales.

DEPARTING Warning: If you plan to proceed from Río Dulce to Flores by bus, be aware that you are very unlikely to get a seat on the bus when it arrives in Río Dulce. In fact many people (usually backpacking travelers) end up riding on the roof because there isn't any standing room on the bus. The road from Río Dulce to Flores is one of the worst in the country, and the trip is very uncomfortable even if you have a seat. If you want to be sure of getting a seat on the bus, you may have to go back to Guatemala City.

ESSENTIALS Orientation The town of Río Dulce is little more than a cluster of market stalls and shops located at the foot of the toll bridge over the river at the mouth of Lake Izabal. The road to Castillo de San Felipe is a narrow muddy lane to the left after you cross the bridge. Boats for Lívingston can be hired at the docks to the right after you cross the bridge.

Thirty miles northwest of the Atlantic Highway lie Lake Izabal and the Río Dulce, which connects the lake with the Gulf of Honduras and the Caribbean Sea. The lake and its jungle-and-forest setting are quite beautiful, but swimming is not recommended in the beaches near the road because the water's not very clean. It's very good for powerboating, however, and on weekends the wealthy citizens of the capital come to the lake and exercise the glittering craft stored on the shore. The lake was famous as a refuge for pirates in days gone by, and its entrance was protected by the picturesque fortress called the Castillo de San Felipe, on the northern shore, a 2½ mile walk from the bridge. Today, most people who come to the lake, if not out for the boating, are on their way to Tikal by road.

WHAT TO SEE & DO

Ask down at the docks to find a boatman who's willing to ferry you to the **Castillo de San Felipe.** The minimum for a trip is two fares, and the boatman will rarely rush you to get through the castle. Plan to spend about a half hour there, about two hours for the entire trip.

The castle was built in the 1600s by the Spaniards to keep pirates out of Lake Izabal, which was being used as a shipping point for gold that had been collected by the conquistadores. Restored in the 1950s, the fort is the only one of its kind in Guatemala. It is in a beautiful, tranquil setting on the banks of the lake, with palm trees waving in the breezes and clouds billowing overhead. You're likely to be the only visitors to the fort and can play at fighting off marauding pirates as you wander through the maze of damp chambers that comprise the fort.

A **boat trip** you can make is down the Río Dulce to Lívingston or Puerto Barrios. The trip will take between two and three hours. You first travel past luxurious vacation homes on the shores of El Golfete, another large lake that begins at the bridge. Then, as you travel farther from the bridge, the houses disappear, and all you see are distant forested mountains. At the far end of El Golfete, the river narrows and passes between steep cliffs. Here and there along this section of the river are tiny huts that are the homes of local families who fish the river by night. The river is still their only link with the outside world, and you have a sense of being far from civilization as you motor past their simple huts.

An added bonus of going downriver is a chance to visit the Chocon Machacas Manatee Preserve. You aren't likely to see any manatees because of the motor on the boat, but there is a short trail through the forest where you are likely to see leaf-cutter ants, pacas (small rabbitlike rodents), and lots of birds.

Every Tuesday and Friday at 6am, a mail boat leaves Río Dulce for Lívingston. The cost is only Q50 ($10). If you want to hire a boat to take you down to Lívingston, expect to pay around Q50 ($10) per person with a five person minimum. The mail boat returns from Lívingston on Tuesday and Friday at 11am. It's best to be on hand at least half an hour early to be sure that you get a seat. In Río Dulce the mail boat leaves from the north side of the bridge. If you hire a boat, be sure to say that you want to stop at the preserve.

WHERE TO STAY & EAT

Although there are a couple of small hotels near the bridge, your best low-budget choice in the area is out by the Castillo. You can hire a boat to take you there, or you can walk or drive the 2½ mile road.

HOTEL DON HUMBERTO, Río Dulce. No phone. 11 rms (all with bath).
$ Rates: Q20 ($4) single; Q25 ($5) double; Q30 ($6) triple. No credit cards.
A 5-minute walk down a quiet path from the Castillo de San Felipe is this tranquil little budget hotel. This neighborhood was once the haunt of pirates, but today it is primarily given over to vacation homes for the wealthy of Guatemala City. The location is very quiet, and the park surrounding the Castillo is very pretty. If you want to get away from it all and not spend much money, this would be a great place to do it. The rooms are very basic but have private baths (showers). The hotel even has its own little dock down on the lake shore, which is only about 100 yards away. The open-air restaurant serves meals from 7am to 8pm.

WORTH THE EXTRA BUCKS

HOTEL IZABAL TROPICAL, Costado, Castillo de San Felipe, Lago de Izabal. Tel. 502/0478-401. In Guatemala City, tel. 502/680-746. 12 rms (all with bath).
$ Rates: Q150–Q250 ($30–$50) single; Q175–Q275 ($35–$55) double; Q200–Q300 ($40–$60) triple; Q225–Q325 ($45–$65) quad. AE, DC, MC, V.
A former Peace Corps volunteer clued me in to this great deal, located very close to the Hotel Don Humberto and reached by taking the dirt road to the left shortly after you cross the bridge over the Río Dulce. Follow the signs even though they lead you down an increasingly rugged road. Eventually, after about 2½ miles, you will reach the hotel. It's built on the edge of the lake and is very popular with boaters. Thatch bungalows with bamboo walls look out over the water. The grounds are neatly manicured, with colorful tropical flowers in bloom year round. By the two swimming pools (one for adults, one for children), there are thatched sunshades to save your skin from getting too burned. Beside the piers is a circular thatched-roof bar where rock music blares and young people gather.
    Slightly higher than the bar is a circular open-air dining room that is much more sedate. You can enjoy spectacular views across the lake to the mountains in the distance while savoring delicious international meals at prices that range from Q20 to Q50 ($4 to $10).

5. LÍVINGSTON & PUERTO BARRIOS

185 miles E of Guatemala City; 67 miles E of Quiriguá;
62 miles SE of Río Dulce

GETTING THERE   By Bus   Buses leave Guatemala City from 15a Calle 10-42, Zona 1 (tel. 27-578), every hour on the hour from 6am to 5pm. Duration: 6 hours. Fare: Q22 ($4.40) regular or Q30 ($6) express.

By Car   Puerto Barrios is at the end of the Atlantic Highway. From here, it is necessary to take a boat to Lívingston.

By Boat   The only way to get to Lívingston is by boat, either from Puerto Barrios or from Río Dulce. From Puerto Barrios, the ferry takes about 1½ hours, leaving daily at 10am and 5pm and returning daily at 5am and 2pm. The one-way fare is Q3.50 (70¢). For Q15 ($3), you can take a fast launch that will get you there in about half the time. These small boats leave only when they have at least five passengers, so you might have to wait for a while. If you don't feel like waiting or have a group, you can simply charter one of these boats for a little more than you would otherwise pay.

See the Río Dulce section for information on boats between Lívingston and Río Dulce.

DEPARTING   The ferry from Lívingston to Puerto Barrios leaves at 5am and 2pm daily. Duration: 1½ hours. Fare: Q3.50 (70¢).

Buses for Guatemala leave almost hourly from 6a Avenida between 9a and 10a calles. Duration: 6 hours. Fare: Q22 ($4.40) regular or Q30 ($6) express.

A passenger ferry leaves on Tuesday and Friday at 8am for Punta Gorda in southern Belize. Duration: 3 hours. Fare: Q21.40 ($4.30). Be sure to buy your ticket the day before the ferry leaves because it is usually full by the time it departs and people sometimes get turned away. Also remember to get your passport stamped at the immigration office at the end of Calle 9, a couple of hundred yards down the dirt road to the right of the ferry dock as you face the water.

The mail boat leaves Lívingston every Tuesday and Friday at 11am. Duration: 3 hours. Fare: Q50 ($10). You can also hire a boat to take you up river. The going rate is around Q200 ($40) for the boat or Q50 ($10) per person.

ESSENTIALS   Orientation   Puerto Barrios is laid out in a grid similar to those used throughout Guatemala. Calles run toward the water, with the ferry to Lívingston located at the end of 12a Calle. The post office is at the corner of 3a Avenida and 7a Calle. The Guatel office is at 10a Calle and 8a Avenida.

Guatemala's Atlantic shore is a narrow strip of land wedged between Honduras and Belize on Amatique Bay. The main town on this coast is Puerto Barrios, which along with the nearby town of Santo Tomas comprises Guatemala's east coast port facilities. These towns have very little to attract the foreign traveler though the mountainous countryside outside of town sweeps down to the bay and is very picturesque.

While Puerto Barrios is crowded, noisy, and busy, across the mouth of the Río Dulce is the much quieter and more laid-back town of Lívingston. Lívingston is a Guatemalan anomaly—a Caribbean town settled by people of African and Indian descent. In many ways it is similar to the other Creole and Garifuna towns along the Central American coast from Belize to Panama. This black Caribbean culture, with its reggae rhythms, has for many years attracted young travelers. However, Lívingston has become distinctively seedy and unfriendly over the years, and I can only recommend a visit if you have no plans to visit Belize, where the people are generally much more friendly. Thefts and armed robberies have been commonplace in Lívingston for so many years that it's hard to believe there is any police force here. Hotel and restaurant personnel are almost universally surly, so don't expect friendly smiles and pleasant service. The waters and beach are filthy, and it is a 3-mile walk to the nearest clean beach. The trip up the Río Dulce to the town of Río Dulce is perhaps the only good reason to spend a night in Lívingston.

Adventurous types might want to check our Punta Manabique, a peninsula across Amatique Bay from Puerto Barrios and Lívingston. I don't know too much about this spot yet, but there are some vacation houses for rent and at least one very basic place with thatched-roof huts renting for Q15 ($3) per person. For more information, phone 502/946-950 in Guatemala City.

WHERE TO STAY & EAT

There aren't too many recommendable places to stay in Lívingston. I suggest that you stay in Puerto Barrios and visit Lívingston as a day trip.

PUERTO BARRIOS
Doubles for Less than Q60 [$12]

HOTEL DEL NORTE, 7a Calle and 1a Avenida, Puerto Barrios. Tel. 502/480-087 or 482-116. 29 rms (16 with bath).
$ Rates: Q41–Q70 ($8.20–$14) single; Q58.50–Q105 ($11.70–$21) double. No credit cards.

My favorite place to stay in Puerto Barrios is this Caribbean classic, which will transport you into a Hemingway frame of mind. The huge cream-colored wooden building with green trim is right on the water, and long wide verandas stretch the length of the building on both floors. You can sit out here and sip a beer and watch the banana boats sail away for northern ports. Inside, the high ceilings and the wide hallways help to keep the old building cool in the summer. The rooms, however, are small, with twin beds, but the high ceilings make them seem much larger than they really are.

The dining room has a very old-fashioned air about it, with a huge old sideboard taking up most of one wall. Here you'll find a variety of seafoods, including lobster for Q40 ($8). Other seafood meals range from Q16 to Q40 ($3.20 to $8). There's also a bar where you can relax in a leather chair and sip a tropical cocktail.

HOTEL EL REFORMADOR, 16a Calle and 7a Avenida no. 159, Puerto Barrios, Izabal. Tel. 502/480-533 or 481-531. 36 rms (all with bath).
$ Rates: Q35–Q82.50 ($7–$16.50) single; Q58.50–Q105 ($11.70–$21) double; Q81.90 ($16.40) triple; Q105 ($21) quad. No credit cards.

In a very modern building near the center of town, the Reformador is just off the main road as you come into town from Guatemala City. The guest rooms are built around two small, sunny courtyards full of potted plants. There are rooms with air conditioning, but the showers have cold water only, so you're better off sticking to a fan and saving some money. Some of the rooms even have TVs (you have your choice of black-and-white or color, but either one costs extra).

The small restaurant on the second floor gets a lot of sunlight and serves meals that range from Q10 to Q30 ($2 to $6).

Doubles for Less than Q100 [$20]

HOTEL HENRY BERRISFORD, 9a Avenida and 17a Calle, Puerto Barrios, Izabal. Tel. 502/481-557 or 481-030. In Guatemala City, Avenida La Reforma 1-64, Zona 9, Guatemala City. Tel. 502/317-866 or 317-858. 30 rms (all with bath). A/C TV
$ Rates: Q58.50–Q78 ($11.70–$15.60) single; Q76.05–Q119.05 ($15.20–$23.80) double; Q93.60–Q145.60 ($18.70–$29.10) triple. DC, MC, V.

About a block away from the Reformador is this slightly nicer hotel that is still very reasonably priced. The three-story cement building is not very attractive, even though a balcony surrounds most of the second and third floors. However, in back of the main building, you'll find an unusual covered recreation area that includes two pools, a bar, arcade games, and, of all things to find in this sweltering climate, a hot tub. The rooms here are comfortable, and most have large windows so that they get plenty of sunlight. If you want a hot shower (rarely necessary around here), you'll have to ask for one of the rooms with hot water.

The hotel's restaurant serves international, Guatemalan, and Caribbean meals at reasonable prices.

LÍVINGSTON
Doubles for Less than Q60 [$12]

HOTEL CARIBE, Lívingston, Izabal. Tel. 502/48-1073. 27 rms (10 with bath).
$ Rates: Q8–Q12 ($1.60–$2.40) single; Q15–Q20 ($3–$4) double; Q22 ($4.40) triple. No credit cards.

One of the better budget choices in Lívingston, the Caribe is up the street to the left when you get off the ferry from Puerto Barrios. The two-story building is set into a shady hillside on the water, and if you get a room at the back, you can listen to the waves lapping on the beach. The rooms are very basic, with twin beds. The bathrooms (cold water only) are down the hall and are kept tolerably clean.

HOTEL RÍO DULCE, Calle Central just up the hill from the main dock, Lívingston. No phone. 10 rms (none with bath).
$ Rates: Q16 ($3.20) single; Q32 ($6.40) double. No credit cards.

This hotel's building is a classic example of Caribbean architecture—a pale-blue wood-frame house with a white picket fence and a big front porch. Around back are some thatch-roofed huts to further the tropical ambience. Hammocks under the palm trees and hibiscuses blooming in the yard complete the scene. This is a backpackers' favorite in Lívingston, even though the rooms are small and very basic, with shared cold-water showers—just as you'd expect.

Worth the Extra Bucks

HOTEL TUCAN DUGU, Lívingston, Izabal. Tel. 502/481-588 or 481-572. In Guatemala City, Avenida Reforma 13-70, Zona 9. Tel. 502/347-813 or 345-242. Fax 502/245-242. 45 rms, 5 suites, 4 bungalows (all with bath).
$ Rates: Q240 ($48) single or double bungalow; Q265 ($53) single, Q360 ($72) single suite; Q290 ($58) double, Q400 ($80) double suite; Q415 ($83) triple, Q465 ($93) triple suite; Q600 ($120) quad suite. DC, MC, V.

Although most accommodations in Lívingston are what you might anticipate based on the Caribbean life-style, the Tucan Dugu is quite different. This is Guatemala's only resort on the Caribbean Coast. Modern but still definitely Caribbean in style, it has many conveniences and comforts. You'll see the hotel on a low hill beside the ferry dock as your boat pulls into town. The two-story white building has a thatch-covered roof to give it a properly rustic appeal. The Tucan Dugu offers three types of rooms: standard, suite, and bungalow. My favorites are the bungalows, even though these are the only rooms that don't have hot water. They are built into the hillside below the main building and are reached by wooden stairs and elevated walkways. You can sit on your porch or balcony no matter which type of room you choose and gaze off across the Gulf of Honduras.

There are two restaurants here, one serving deluxe breakfasts and elegant seafood dinners for between Q15 and Q45 ($3 and $9). The circular dining room has a high thatched roof and louvered windows that leave no doubt that you are in the tropics. The other restaurant is less expensive and more casual, located in the bar adjacent to the swimming pool.

Possible activities here are scuba diving, waterskiing, sailboarding, sailing, boating, and sportfishing in both freshwater and saltwater.

CHAPTER 13

GETTING TO KNOW BELIZE

I f you learned your geography before 1973, you may never have even heard of this tiny country. Before that, Belize was known as British Honduras, a colony whose sole purpose was to supply hardwoods and other wood products throughout the British empire. Consequently, Belize is a Central American anomaly: It is an English-speaking nation surrounded by Spanish-speaking neighbors. With a population of only about 200,000 people, it is also the least-populated country in all Central America. The importance of this statistic is only now becoming significant as environmentalists discover the vast undisturbed wilderness of Belize, where jaguars still roam the jungle in search of tapirs and macaws still screech in the treetops. Add to this the dozens of tiny islands set amid the world's second-longest barrier reef (which offers excellent diving and fishing opportunities) and a population that is more than 60% black Creoles and Garifunas (people of black and Indian ancestry), and you have what is ostensibly a Caribbean island nation on the Central American mainland. The most important British legacy left to Belize, however, is a stable political environment in a region of constant turmoil. To understand Belize, you have to go see it for yourself because, as the Belizeans say, "Seeing is Belizing!"

1. GEOGRAPHY, HISTORY & POLITICS

GEOGRAPHY

Belize is a narrow strip of land on the Caribbean Coast of Central America, located due south of Mexico's Yucatán Peninsula. It covers an area of 9,000 square miles, about the same size as the state of Massachusetts, and is bordered on the west and south by Guatemala and on the east by the Caribbean. Offshore from mainland Belize are hundreds of tiny islands, known as cayes (pronounced "keys"), that rise up from the world's second-longest barrier reef, which extends for more than 180 miles along the Belizean coast. From the wide, flat coastal plains, Belize rises up to mountain peaks of more than 3,000 feet, the source of the many rivers that wind through the country, which were for years the only means of transport within Belize.

REGIONS IN BRIEF

The Cayes Belize's offshore islands lie between the coast of the mainland and the protection of the 180-mile long Barrier Reef. The reef, easily visible from many of the

WHAT'S SPECIAL ABOUT BELIZE

Beaches
☐ Placencia, the longest and best beach in Belize.

Natural Spectacles
☐ The barrier reef off the coast of Belize, the second longest in the world.
☐ The Blue Hole on the Hummingbird Highway, a sinkhole filled with clear water.
☐ Mountain Pine Ridge, a forest reserve with waterfalls and caves.

Zoo
☐ The Belize Zoo, small but with an extremely well-treated menagerie.

Ancient Ruins
☐ Xunantunich, a Mayan pyramid that is one of the tallest buildings in Belize.
☐ Caracol, excavated though not restored, thought to be the largest Mayan city ever discovered.

☐ Altun Ha Mayan ruins, with several excavated temples.

Islands
☐ Dozens of small islands off the coast of Belize, including Caye Caulker and Ambergris Caye, which have small hotels.

Parks
☐ The Cockscomb Basin Wildlife Preserve, the only jaguar preserve in the world.
☐ The Community Baboon Sanctuary, an unusual program in which local farmers help protect baboons.

Activities
☐ Canoeing and horseback riding in the Cayo District.
☐ Bird watching anywhere in the country.
☐ Scuba diving on the barrier reef.

---

cayes, offers some of the world's most exciting snorkeling, diving (visibility is up to 200 feet), and fishing. The more developed cayes offer various day and overnight trips to explore this lively underwater world.

For those whose main sport is catching rays, not fish, it should be mentioned that the cayes, and Belize in general, lack wide, sandy beaches. Although the water is as warm and clear blue as it's touted to be, most of your sunbathing will be on docks or on deck chairs.

Cayo District This mountainous district near the Guatemalan border has become Belize's second most-popular destination. Here you'll find some of Belize's most beautiful countryside and most fascinating natural and man-made sights. The limestone mountains of this region have produced numerous caves, sinkholes, jagged peaks, and waterfalls. There are clear flowing rivers that are excellent for swimming and canoeing as well as mile after mile of unexplored forest full of wild animals. This was also the site of several major Mayan settlements more than 1,000 years ago. Caracol is said to be the largest Mayan city known, but it has not yet been fully excavated. Xunantunich and Cahal Pech are smaller, but still impressive pyramid-and-temple complexes not far from the town of San Ignacio.

DATELINE

- **2000 B.C.–A.D. 1000** Mayan civilization flourishes.
- **1638** Shipwrecked English *(continues)*

HISTORY

Before the arrival of the first Europeans (shipwrecked English sailors), this was the land of the enigmatic Mayas. Although most people think of Mexico's Mayan cities in the Yucatán and Guatemala's Tikal when they hear the word "Mayas," recent discoveries suggest that what is today known as Belize was once the center of the Mayan

BELIZE

MEXICO

GUATEMALA

Chetumal
Santa Rita
Corozal Town

Orange Walk Town

San Pedro

Blue Creek Village

Crooked Tree

Altun Ha

Uaxactún

Blue Creek

Rio Bravo

International Airport

Ladyville
Belize City

Tikal

Spanish Lookout

Hattieville

San Ignacio

Belmopan

Belize River

Western Highway

Northern Lagoon

Hummingbird Highway

Southern Lagoon

Caracol

Mountain Pine Ridge

Gales Point

Maya Mountains

Cockscomb Range

South Stann Creek

Dangriga

Monkey River

Placencia

Southern Highway

Punta Gorda

Caribbean Sea

Mobo River

Barranco

Temash River

Gulf of Honduras

Sarstoon River

Livingston

Castillo de San Felipe

Lake Izabal

Río Dulce

Puerto Barrios

Quiriguá

CA9

Morales

Rio Hondo

HONDURAS

0   50 km   31 mi

DATELINE

sailors establish the first European settlement.

- **1783** English settlement rights are recognized.
- **1786** Settlements become self-governing. British superintendent takes up residence.
- **1798** The last Spanish attack is beaten off by the British.
- **1859** The border between Guatemala and British Honduras is established.
- **1862** The area officially becomes the colony of British Honduras.
- **1931** Hurricane destroys Belize City.
- **1948** Guatemala, laying claim to British Honduras, closes border.
- **1957** First Mennonite farmers arrive from Mexico.
- **1964** The new constitution provides for self-government, but Guatemalan claims to the country delay independence.
- **1973** British Honduras renamed Belize.
- **1981** Belize becomes an independent nation.

Empire. River and coastal trade routes connected dozens of cities and small towns throughout this region to the now better known and more frequently visited cities of Mexico and Guatemala. Caracol, a recently discovered city in the Cayo District of western Belize, is said to be the largest Mayan city yet discovered. Unfortunately, very little of this amazing discovery has been excavated or is likely to be excavated. The funds for massive restorations, such as those done at Tikal and Chichén Itzá, simply are not available.

Corozal Town, in northern Belize, is built on the site of the last Mayan city still occupied when this area was discovered by a Spanish expeditionary force in the 1530s. By the time those first unlucky sailors washed ashore, the Mayan civilization was a mere remnant of its former glory.

Belize likes to play up the fact that it was founded by pirates and buccaneers, and, indeed, these unsavory characters were some of the first to make this region their base of operations, but they were hardly a civilizing influence. By the mid-17th century, British loggers were settling along the coast and making their way up the rivers and streams in search of mahogany for shipbuilding and other types of wood for making dyes. When it formally became the colony of British Honduras in 1862, it was firmly established as a major source of wood for the still-expanding British empire. The forests were exploited, but agriculture was never encouraged. The British needed their colony to remain dependent on the mother country, so virtually all the necessities of life were imported. Few roads were built, and the country remained unexplored and undeveloped with a tiny population, mostly clustered along the coast.

During the 18th and 19th centuries, African slaves were brought to British Honduras, and black Caribs also migrated here from the Caribbean Islands. They established their own villages and culture along the coast. In the mid-19th century, many Mexican and Guatemalan refugees fled across the borders into British Honduras and founded such towns as Corozal Town and Benque Viejo.

In the early 1960s, groundwork was laid for granting British Honduras independence. However, based on 16th-century Spanish claims to all Central America, Guatemala claimed that the territory belonged to them. Fearful of an invasion by Guatemalan forces, the British delayed granting independence until an agreement could be reached with Guatemala. Although the 1964 constitution granted self-government to the British colony, it was not until September 21, 1981, that Belize, which had changed its name in 1973, actually gained its independence. Due to continuing hostility between Guatemala and Belize, the British maintain a protective force in Belize. Fortunately, the mere threat of having to do battle with the British has deterred Guatemala from acting on its claim. Thus Belize is Central America's newest nation.

? DID YOU KNOW . . . ?

- Belize has the second-longest barrier reef in the world.
- Belize is the newest nation in Central America. It gained its independence from the United Kingdom in 1981.
- Nearly 65% of Belize is uninhabited wilderness.
- Belize has the world's first and only jaguar preserve.
- English is the official language of this Central American nation.
- Belize has a sizable population of Mennonite farmers who speak an archaic form of German.
- Belize City has been destroyed by hurricanes several times.
- Belize was first settled by pirates.
- Belize has some of the best scuba diving in the world.

The British legacy in Belize is a stable government with a parliamentary system and regular elections that are contested by two major parties and several smaller parties. The country's small newspapers are mouthpieces for the various parties and are frequently filled with stories disparaging the actions of the other parties. They make fun reading.

2. CULTURAL & SOCIAL LIFE

Art and Architecture Belize was set up as a colony to provide wood and wood products to the British empire. With its tiny population and isolation from the outside world, it did not develop any outstanding artists, writers, or architects. There are only one or two tiny natural history museums in the country and the same number of colonial buildings of any interest in Belize City. Clapboard houses built on stilts were typical and quite a few of these buildings, often painted in the pastel colors that are so popular throughout the Caribbean, remain in small towns. There are, however, a number of excavated Mayan ruins scattered around the countryside. Xunantunich, near the town of San Ignacio, is a pyramid that is still one of the tallest artificial structures in the country.

The People Modern Belize (pop. 200,000) is a very unlikely mixture of peoples and cultures: Although the descendants of the Maya still populate the western and southern jungle areas, the majority of Belizeans are black Caribs or Creoles, descendants of slaves shipwrecked in transit from Africa, who established their own African-type culture in the Caribbean. The first Europeans to settle in Belize were pirates turned loggers, but today they have been joined by Britons and North Americans, Chinese, Lebanese, and the adherents of a German Protestant sect called Mennonites. All these people live in apparent harmony and mutual respect, divided by no great differences in wealth or power. English is the official language of the country, but Indian languages, Spanish, German, Arabic, Chinese, and Creole patois also are spoken depending on the district.

Evening Entertainment Nightlife is limited. There are only a handful of movie theaters in the country. Bars, which occasionally have live bands, are about the extent of the nightlife scene in Belize.

Sports and Recreation Soccer is the national sport, but the two most popular recreational activities are scuba diving and sportfishing. Belize has the best of both. The offshore coral reef is the second-longest barrier reef in the world, while the waters, both offshore and inland, teem with such popular game fish as tarpon, snook, bonefish, barracuda, and snapper. Many companies in Belize offer fishing and diving trips.

3. FOOD & DRINK

Food   Don't expect gourmet food during your visit to Belize. Even the most basic meals in restaurants are much more expensive than they would be in Guatemala or Mexico. Belize has little in the way of its own cuisine, so you'll find burgers, pizzas, fried fish, and Chinese food—and, if you look hard, even a little local food. Because Belize only recently began to grow its own beef and crops, the country relied for a long time on wild game. A favorite is gibnut, a large forest rodent that looks like a cross between a rat and a deer. Another popular wild animal found prepared in restaurants is the sea turtle, endangered all over the world, including in Belize. It's not yet illegal to sell sea turtle within Belize, but international agreements prohibit its export. Please don't order gibnut, turtle steak, or other wild game. Belize is struggling to preserve its natural environment, and as long as people order wild game, it will show up on menus.

Belize has also been a major exporter of lobster for many years, but overfishing has caused the population to decline. It is still available and quite inexpensive, but there is a season on lobster. Please do not order lobster between March 15 and July 15.

Drinks   Much of the **drinking water** in Belize is rainwater. People use the roof of their house to collect water in a cistern which supplies them for the year. Always ask for drinking water at your hotel. Tap water generally is not considered safe to drink. Most major brands of soft drinks are available. Also popular in Belize are fresh lime juice and orange juice.

Belikin beer and Belikin stout are local beers, but a few other imported brands also are available. Several commercially bottled fruit wines are produced in Belize using native fruits. These wines are very sweet and are more a novelty than anything else. In remote parts of the country, you'll find homemade fruit wines that are a bit like hard cider. Most restaurants serve mixed drinks, with a variety of domestic and imported liquors available.

4. RECOMMENDED FILMS & RECORDINGS

Although it wasn't a box office hit, you might want to rent a copy of *The Mosquito Coast* (1986), which was filmed in Belize. Starring Harrison Ford and directed by Peter Weir, the film is about an inventor who relocates his family to the Central American jungle. Another film shot in Belize is *Dogs of War* (1980), which features Christopher Walken.

If you're taken by the pounding beat of soca music (a Caribbean music akin to calypso) and Belize's own punta rock (a kind of reggae-rock fusion), you can pick up cassette tapes in Belize City.

CHAPTER 14

PLANNING A TRIP
TO BELIZE

More and more intrepid explorers are discovering Belize's natural and historic wonders: bird, monkey, and jaguar sanctuaries; Mayan ruins; mahogany forests; and huge limestone caves. The interior does not give itself up easily, though, and that's why it has remained so special and undeveloped. Belize is probably the most expensive country in Central America, but there are still bargains to be had. This chapter will tell you all you need to know about your trip, including how to snag the cheapest airfares, how to map your itinerary, what things cost, and how to stretch your dollars without cramping your style.

1. INFORMATION, ENTRY REQUIREMENTS & MONEY

SOURCES OF INFORMATION

The **Belize Tourist Board,** 15 Penn Plaza, 415 Seventh Ave., 18th floor, New York, NY 10001 (tel. 212/268-8798, or toll free 800/624-0686; Fax 212/695-3018) will send you a package of information about the country. You can also contact the **Belize Tourist Bureau,** 89 North Front St., P.O. Box 325, Belize City (tel. 501/277213, 77490, or 73255)— open Monday to Friday from 8am to noon and 1 to 5pm. Whether your interest is pirate lore or bird identification, you'll find books of interest in the shops on Ambergris Caye.

ENTRY REQUIREMENTS

DOCUMENTS   If you are a citizen of the United States or a Commonwealth country, you need only a valid passport to enter Belize. All other visitors must also have a visa, available from a Belizean consulate. Visas and entry stamps are issued for up to 30 days.

CUSTOMS   Visitors may bring 200 cigarettes (one carton) and a fifth of liquor into Belize.

MONEY

CASH/CURRENCY   The unit of currency in Belize is the Belizean dollar, abbreviated B$. Denominations of B$1, B$5, B$10, B$20, B$50, and B$100 are available. Coins come in 1B¢, 5B¢, 10B¢, 25B¢, 50B¢, and B$1 denominations. On the black market, $1 U.S. equals B$2. Although it is officially illegal, the black market is where everyone changes money because the banks charge a 2% to 3% commission. Never change money with someone who approaches you on the street. Always ask at your hotel where you can change money. If they can't make the transaction themselves, they'll tell you who will.

CURRENCY EXCHANGE CHART

B$	U.S. $
1	.50
2	1.00
3	1.50
4	2.00
5	2.50
6	3.00
7	3.50
8	4.00
9	4.50
10	5.00
50	25.00
100	50.00

TRAVELER'S CHECKS   Traveler's checks are almost as readily convertible as cash dollars anywhere in Belize, so it pays to take the precaution of carrying your money in this more secure form.

CREDIT CARDS   Credit cards are generally not accepted at the low end hotels and restaurants, however, there are exceptions to this rule on Ambergris Caye. American Express, MasterCard, and VISA are the most readily accepted cards in Belize.

WHAT THINGS COST IN BELIZE	U.S. $
Taxi from the airport to the city center	15.00
Local telephone call	0.50
Double at Ramon's Reef Hotel (deluxe)	120.00
Double at Barrier Reef Hotel (moderate)	68.25
Double at Ruby's Hotel (budget)	26.00
Lunch for one at Elvi's Kitchen (moderate)	10.00
Lunch for one at The Pizza Place (budget)	5.00
Dinner for one, without wine at Paradise Hotel (deluxe)	30.00
Dinner for one, without wine at Lily's (moderate)	12.50
Dinner for one, without wine at Marino's (budget)	7.00
Bottle of beer	1.15
Coca-Cola	0.50
Cup of coffee	0.75
Roll of ASA 100 Kodacolor film, 36 exposures	8.50
Admission to the Xunantunich ruins	1.50

2. WHEN TO GO — CLIMATE & HOLIDAYS

CLIMATE The climate of Belize is very similar to that of southern Florida. In the summer months, it is very hot (temperatures in the shade can approach 100°F), with rain almost daily from June to December. The amount of rainfall varies considerably with the regions. In the south, there may be more than 150 inches per year, while in the north there is rarely more than 50 inches per year. The dry season extends from January to May, with temperatures dipping down as low as 40°F in the mountains of the Cayo District. There is also a brief dry period in August. Although temperatures on the coast can climb quite high in the summer, the constant trade winds offer a bit of relief.

AVERAGE MONTHLY TEMPERATURES AND RAINFALL IN BELIZE

	Temp. (F)	Temp. (C)	Days of Rain
Jan	73.4	23	12
Feb	76.1	24.5	6
Mar	77.9	25.5	4
Apr	79.7	26.5	5
May	81.5	27.5	7
Jun	81.5	27.5	13
Jul	81.5	27.5	15
Aug	81.5	27.5	14
Sep	80.6	27	15
Oct	78.8	26	16
Nov	75.2	24	12
Dec	74.3	23.5	14

HOLIDAYS Official holidays in Belize include January 1, New Year's Day; March 9, Baron Bliss Day; Good Friday, Holy Saturday, Easter Monday; May 1, Labor Day; May 24, Commonwealth Day; September 10, St. George's Caye Day; September 21, Independence Day; October 12, Columbus Day; November 19, Garifuna Settlement Day; December 25, Christmas; December 26, Boxing Day; December 31, New Year's Eve.

3. HEALTH, INSURANCE & OTHER CONCERNS

See Chapter 2, "Planning a Trip to Costa Rica," for information.

4. WHAT TO PACK

See Chapter 2, "Planning a Trip to Costa Rica," for information on what to pack. In addition, bring a bathing suit and plenty of sunscreen. If you have your own snorkeling or scuba-diving equipment, you should bring this as well.

5. TIPS FOR THE DISABLED, SENIORS, SINGLES & STUDENTS

For the Disabled   Few streets in Belize have sidewalks, and on the cayes there are really no streets at all, only sandy lanes and paths. Consequently, disabled visitors to Belize have a difficult time.

For Seniors   Don't expect to find senior-citizen discounts here. The tourism industry is still a fledgling in Belize, and seniors are treated the same as anyone else. But you may be able to save 10% on your airline ticket. If you don't think you have the energy required for a visit to a jungle lodge, think again. The jungle lodges of Belize offer a wide variety of activities that people of all ages will find enjoyable. You're never too old to explore the jungles!

For Singles   As in most places, the single traveler is at a disadvantage in Belize. Some hotels do have single rooms though they usually do not have private baths and are generally quite small. If you don't plan to spend much time in your room, you can save money with one of these. Unfortunately, single room rates are usually higher than what each person would pay in a double room. In San Ignacio, Eva's Restaurant serves as a meeting ground for lone travelers seeking other adventurers to help cut the cost of taxis, canoe rentals, and tour rates. Tell Bob behind the counter what you're interested in doing, and he'll put your name on a list with other people interested in the same activity.

For Students   Check with the airlines when purchasing a ticket; there are sometimes special fares for students.

6. ALTERNATIVE/ADVENTURE TRAVEL

ECOTOURS

Much of Belize is still unspoiled forest inhabited by hundreds of species of birds and rare animals, including the world's largest population of jaguars. There are several tour companies that operate natural history tours to Belize. These trips usually include visits to wildlife preserves, hikes in the jungle, bird watching, and visits to Mayan ruins, and, just to balance things out, spending a few days on the beach. **Great Trips,** 1616 W. 139th St., Burnsville, MN 55337 (tel. 612/890-4405, or toll free 800/552-3419; Fax 612/894-9862), offers several different tours. **International Expeditions,** 1776 Independence Court, Suite 104, Birmingham, AL 35216 (tel. 205/870-5550, or toll free 800/633-4734), and **Sea & Explore,** 1809 Carol Sue Ave., Suite E, Gretna, LA 70056 (tel. 504/366-9985, or toll free 800/345-9786; Fax 504/366-9986), also operate similar nature tours to Belize.

If you're a member of the Sierra Club, Smithsonian Institution, or Audubon Society, you might look into their programs—all three offer annual trips to Belize.

KAYAK TRIPS

If you're interested in an active vacation, consider sea kayaking through the cayes with **Island Expeditions Co.,** 368-916 W. Broadway, Vancouver, B.C. V5Z 1K7, Canada (tel. 604/687-2428; fax 604/684-3255). Prices range from $775 for an 8-day trip to $1,199 for a 12-day trip. If bicycling is more your speed and you can tolerate heat and humidity, contact **Paradise Bicycle Tours,** P.O. Box 1726, Evergreen, CO 80439 (tel. 303/670-1842).

7. GETTING THERE

BY PLANE

Even though it is only two hours by air from Miami, Belize is relatively expensive to reach—one reason it has not yet been overdeveloped. Daily flights to Belize City run from New York, Los Angeles, Miami, Houston, and New Orleans, with additional flights from Mexico City, Mérida, Guatemala City, and Tikal. Carriers flying from the United States include **TACA** (tel. toll free 800/535-8780), **Sahsa** (tel. toll free 800/327-1225), **Continental** (tel. toll free 800/231-0856), and **American** (tel. toll free 800/433-7300). **Aerovias** (tel. 305/883-1345), a small Guatemalan airline, has flights from Guatemala City by way of Tikal.

BEST FOR THE BUDGET   See "Best-for-the-Budget Fares" in Chapter 1 for details on airfares to Belize and the rest of Central America.

REGULAR AIRFARES   At the time of this writing, the regular airfares, which have no restrictions, are between $650 and $750 in coach and around $1,200 in first class.

BY BUS

There are only two land routes into Belize—from Chetumal, Mexico, and from Flores, Guatemala. Both routes offer daily service, although the road from Guatemala can become impassable in the rainy season. Buses from Mexico cross the border and proceed into Corozal Town. From Corozal Town, you can catch a bus to Belize City or fly to San Pedro on Ambergris Caye.

Buses from Flores, Guatemala, drop passengers in Melchor de Mencos at the bridge that separates Guatemala and Belize. You must then cross the bridge and catch

---

Ⓕ FROMMER'S SMART TRAVELER: AIRFARES

1. Check the Sunday travel sections of major-city newspapers for companies selling discounted airline tickets that can be $100 to $200 less than the lowest standard airfare.
2. See if you can get a discounted ticket from your departure city to a Central American gateway city (Miami, New Orleans, Houston, or Los Angeles), and combine this with a discount ticket from one of those cities to Belize City.
3. Check airfares to Cancún, including air-and-hotel packages, which are often substantially less than flights to Belize City, which is only a day's bus ride away from Cancún.
4. Shop all the airlines that fly to Belize, including the small Central American airlines that travel agents don't usually check.
5. Even if you are on a tight budget, don't overlook the flights from Belize City to Caye Caulker and Ambergris Caye; these flights are almost as cheap as going by boat.
6. Always ask for the lowest-priced fare, which will usually be a midweek departure.
7. If you're a senior citizen, check to see if you can get a discount.

a Belizean bus or take a taxi. The first town in Belize is Benque Viejo, which has few services or accommodations and is less than a mile from the border. Your best bet is to continue another 8 miles into San Ignacio by either bus or taxi. If you arrive early in the day, you can share a taxi for only B$4 ($2); otherwise, you'll have to pay about B$20 ($10) to hire a taxi to San Ignacio. The bus from the border to San Ignacio is B$1 (50¢). From San Ignacio, you can catch a bus to Belize City.

See "By Car" below for details on crossing the border.

BY CAR

If you're driving from Chetumal, you must hand in your Mexican Tourist Card (and/or car papers, if you have them) at the Mexican border station. You'll be issued new ones if you reenter Mexico. If you have Mexican auto insurance, get the policy stamped by an official so that you can get a rebate for the days you're outside Mexican territory. Cross the bridge over the Río Hondo and you're in Belize.

Both Mexican and Belizean border stations seem to be open during daylight hours all week, with no breaks for lunch.

Your entry permit is the rubber stamp put on your passport (other forms of identification are not accepted), and it will show how long you're allowed to stay. To be on the safe side, ask for a few more days than you think you'll need; the cayes can be very enticing.

Be sure to get a Temporary Import Permit for your car, even if no one tells you a thing about it. Ask for the Customs official if he's not there and get the permit, or you'll be held up at the border when you leave the country. Also required is Belizean auto insurance, which you can buy in the restaurant across the road from the border station.

After they've stamped your passport, issued your auto permit, and inspected your car (a process that ranges from a glance through the window to a good search), and after you've bought auto insurance, you're on your way. The money changers at the border will give the standard two-to-one for your U.S. dollars. *However, don't change pesos here because you'll lose a tremendous amount.* There are banks in Corozal Town (open Monday to Thursday from 8am to 1pm, Friday from 8am to 1pm and 3 to 6pm) 7 miles down the road, where you'll get a better rate on pesos but a worse rate on dollars.

BY SHIP

For adventurous travelers, there's a ferry from Puerto Barrios, Guatemala, to Punta Gorda, Belize, on Tuesday and Friday at 8am. The one-way fare for the 3-hour trip is Q21.40 ($4.30). You can buy your ticket at the Immigration Office on 9a Calle, where you should be sure to get your passport stamped before leaving. Secure a ticket the day before your departure. After arriving in Punta Gorda, take the bus north (along a rough dirt road) or fly to Belize City.

PACKAGE TOURS AND CRUISES

U.S. companies specializing in package tours to Belize are **Great Trips,** 1616 W. 139th St., Burnsville, MN 55337 (tel. 612/890-4405, or toll free 800/552-3419; Fax 612/894-9862); **International Expeditions,** 1776 Independence Court, Suite 104, Birmingham, AL 35216 (tel. 205/870-5550, or toll free 800/633-4734); and **Sea & Explore,** 1809 Carol Sue Ave., Suite E, Gretna, LA 70056 (tel. 504/366-9985, or toll free 800/345-9786; Fax 504/366-9986).

Small cruise ships, primarily geared for scuba divers, have also begun plying the turquoise waters of Belize and, if you're a diver, this may be the best way to see the country's underwater wonders. **American Canadian Caribbean Line, Inc.** (tel. toll free 800/556-7450), offers 12-day cruises for as little as $1,622.

8. SUGGESTED ITINERARIES

HIGHLIGHTS

The following are Belize's most important destinations.

1. Ambergris Caye
2. Caye Caulker
3. Placencia
4. Cayo District

PLANNING YOUR ITINERARY

IF YOU HAVE ONE WEEK

Days 1 through 3: Fly directly to Ambergris Caye and relax on the beach, go snorkeling or scuba diving at Hol Chan Marine Reserve, and sail to Caye Caulker.
Day 4: Take the boat from Caye Caulker to Belize City and continue west to San Ignacio in the Cayo District, stopping at the Belize Zoo on your way. Visit Xunantunich or Cahol Pech ruins in the afternoon.
Day 5: Take a canoe trip on the Macal River, visiting the Panti Medicine Trail.
Day 6: Spend the day in the Mountain Pine Ridge, visiting waterfalls and caves and enjoying the tropical scenery.
Day 7: Head back to Belize City, stopping at Guanacaste Park and making a side trip to the Blue Hole.

IF YOU HAVE TWO WEEKS

Days 1 through 4: Your first four days should be spent in the mountainous Cayo District. Use your first day to reach San Ignacio, with a stop at the Belize Zoo. Spend one day canoeing the Macal River and visiting the Panti Medicine Trail. Spend another day in Mountain Pine Ridge visiting waterfalls and caves. On the fourth day go horseback riding in the morning and visit Xunantunich and Cahal Pech ruins in the afternoon.
Days 5 and 6: Journey into Guatemala to visit the impressive ruins of Tikal, spending the night either at Tikal or in Flores.
Days 7 and 8: Travel to Placencia on the southern coast, with stops at Guanacaste Park, the Blue Hole, St. Herman's Caves, and the Cockscomb Basin Jaguar Preserve. Spend a day lazing on the beach and snorkeling, perhaps hiring a boat to take you to the cayes.
Day 9: Go back up the coast to Belize City.
Days 10 through 12: Catch the early boat to Caye Caulker. Hang out and/or go snorkeling, scuba diving, or fishing. Sail to Ambergris Caye on your third day.
Days 13 and 14: Enjoy more fun in the sun until you have to fly back to the mainland to catch your flight.

IF YOU HAVE THREE WEEKS

Days 1 through 4: Explore the Cayo District by foot, horse, canoe, or Jeep. During your time here, you should visit the Xunantunich ruins, the Panti Medicine Trail, and Mountain Pine Ridge. On your way here from Belize City, stop at the Belize Zoo and Guanacaste Park.
Days 5 through 7: Spend two days exploring Tikal ruins in Guatemala, returning to San Ignacio on your third day.
Days 8 through 11: Continue on to Placencia, stopping at the Blue Hole, St. Herman's Caves, and the Cockscomb Basin Jaguar Preserve. Spend the next two

days relaxing on the beach, swimming, snorkeling, scuba diving, and fishing. On the eleventh day, proceed back up the coast to Belize City.

Day 12: Using Belize City as a base, make a trip to Altun Ha and the Community Baboon Sanctuary.

Days 13 through 16: Catch the early boat to Caye Caulker and spend the next three days enjoying the laid-back atmosphere. Snorkel, scuba dive, or go fishing. Read a good book. On your last day, sail to Ambergris Caye and stop at Hol Chan Marine Reserve to go snorkeling.

Days 17 through 21: Relax in the sun. If you didn't visit the Altun-Ha ruins already, you can do so by boat from here. Try an excursion to the Mexican Rocks for snorkeling or rent a sailboard. Fly back to Belize City to catch your flight home.

THEMED CHOICES

Although many people see Belize as just another Caribbean resort, it has much more to offer, especially to naturalists and bird-watchers. A trip focusing on the natural parks would include stops at the Cockscomb Basin Jaguar Preserve, the Community Baboon Sanctuary, the Crooked Tree Wildlife Sanctuary, Mountain Pine Ridge, Guanacaste Park, the Hol Chan Marine Reserve, and the Belize Zoo.

Would-be archeologists and those fascinated by the Mayas can see ruins as well as present day Mayan villages. Among the ruins that can be easily visited are Cahal Pech, Xunantunich, Pacbitun, Chechem Hah, Altun Ha, Lamanai, Lubaantun, Nim Li Punit, and Santa Rita. With a bit more effort and money, it is possible to visit Caracol, which is thought to have been one of the largest Mayan cities. Down in southern Belize, there are several villages that are populated by latter-day Mayas whose life-style has changed little with the passing of time.

9. GETTING AROUND

BY PLANE Because of the lack of decent roads in most of Belize, flying is recommended as a means of getting around. There are flights between Corozal Town and San Pedro and between Belize City and Corozal Town, San Pedro, Caye Caulker Dangriga, Big Creek, and Punta Gorda. Except for the flights to the Cayes, the flights are not cheap, but they will save you many hours of travel over very bad roads.

BY BUS Buses run between all the main towns in Belize, with Belize City acting as the hub for most routes. However, the bus service is not always frequent. The fares are low, and the buses are generally in good condition.

BY CAR Most roads in Belize are not paved, and so you must have a very sturdy vehicle, preferably with four-wheel drive (especially in the rainy season). There are really only two paved highways—the Northern Highway and the Western Highway. The Hummingbird, or Southern, Highway was partially paved at one time, but now it is a battlefield of potholes that is slowly being repaved. You'll be thankful for plain old dirt after driving this road. If you're driving your own car, install heavy-duty shocks. Also keep your eyes peeled for "sleeping policemen"—speed bumps (usually unmarked)—that can be found as you enter any populated area.

BY RV There are a few campgrounds scattered around Belize. You can also camp at the Cockscomb Basin Jaguar Preserve. You'll need an overnight permit, available at the preserve headquarters.

BY FERRY Boats make regular runs to Caye Caulker and Ambergris Caye from Belize City; others operate between Big Creek and Placencia, which is not an island but a long spit of land.

HITCHHIKING You can hitchhike in Belize, but the buses are easier and quite cheap. The only time you might wish to hitchhike is if you're trying to get to some of

FROMMER'S FAVORITE
BELIZE EXPERIENCES

A Sailboat Trip to Hol Chan Marine Reserve   The barrier reef off the coast of Belize is the second longest in the world, and the wooden sailboats that sail from Caye Caulker will take you to the protected waters of the Hol Chan Marine Reserve off Ambergris Caye. After a couple of hours of sailing, you can snorkel or scuba dive, then visit San Pedro on Ambergris Caye before sailing back to Caye Caulker.

Canoeing on the Macal River   Three-foot-long iguanas bask along the rocky banks and skitter for cover as canoes float past. Women wash their laundry while standing knee-deep in the river, and children swing from ropes and splash into the water. A day spent paddling quietly along the course of the Macal River is a day well spent.

A Visit to the Cockscomb Basin Wildlife Preserve   This preserve was created to protect the world's largest concentration of jaguars. Trails lead through the jungle, and it's even possible to camp or rent a bunk here.

A Day Trip to the Mountain Pine Ridge   Deep in the mountains of western Belize's Cayo District is a rugged forest reserve of pine forests and jungles with spectacular 1,000 Foot Falls, the Río Frio caves, and the Río On pools. A day spent exploring caves and swimming in mountain rivers is unforgettable.

the remote parks and preserves without taking a tour or hiring a car. Remember there is little traffic on Belize's back roads.

10. ENJOYING BELIZE ON A BUDGET

SAVING MONEY ON ACCOMMODATIONS

The best way to save money on accommodations in Belize is to travel during the off season, which is roughly June to October. Not all hotels offer discounts during the off season but many do, and some start offering discounts as early as May. Taking a room with a shared bathroom will also save you quite a bit. Avoid staying in Belmopan, where all the hotels are relatively expensive. You'll also save money on your beach visit if you choose to stay someplace other than Ambergris Caye. Generally speaking, the smaller and more remote coastal villages and inhabited cayes tend to have less expensive (though likewise less luxurious) accommodations. One of the best ways to save money is to read bulletin boards. The newest budget hotels (those that haven't gotten into any guidebooks yet) often have the best rates and tend to post notices on any bulletin boards they can find.

SAVING MONEY ON MEALS

The cheapest food in Belize is found on the street. In almost every town, women cook up their specialties such as coconut buns, chicken tacos, or tamales wrapped in banana leaves and sell them on the street. Often Mom will set up her food stand in a park or near a bus terminal, and the kids will walk around with buckets full of baked goodies. Never let one of these bun boys pass you by without finding out what he's selling. Tacos in Belize are a breakfast dish and consist of a chicken stew rolled in a steamed corn tortilla. You can usually get three tacos or two buns for B$1 (50¢).

SAVING MONEY ON SIGHT-SEEING

Check bulletin boards for notices advertising inexpensive tours. Enterprising folks are always setting up their own little tour companies in Belize, and often their prices are lower than the established competition. You can be sure that if you go to a travel agent in Belize, you will be paying top price for a tour. The walls of Eva's restaurant in San Ignacio are covered with posters and notices for various tours, many of which are surprisingly economical (at least for Belize). You'll almost always save money by getting a group of people together to share taxi or boat expenses.

SAVING MONEY ON SHOPPING

One of the best buys in Belize is Melinda's hot sauce, which comes in three degrees of spiciness and is made with the eye-watering habanero pepper. A small bottle can be had for less than B$2 ($1). If you've developed a taste for reggae and soca music, the record and tape stores in Belize City have very reasonable prices.

SAVING MONEY ON TRANSPORTATION

Taxis, especially those in the Cayo District, are ridiculously expensive. Likewise, the rental cars here are the most expensive that I have encountered anywhere in the world. A 15-year-old gas-guzzling Detroit tank rents for almost $100 per day. Add to this gasoline at $2 per gallon. Save money by taking very inexpensive local buses, or, if you absolutely must hire a taxi, try to get together with several other people and share the expense. Eva's Restaurant in San Ignacio is a good place to meet people with whom to share a cab to some of the more interesting sites in the area. Just tell Bob at the counter what you're interested in doing.

SAVING MONEY ON SERVICES AND OTHER TRANSACTIONS

Tipping   Bell hops: B$1 per bag. Waiters/waitresses: 10 to 15%, but only in better restaurants. Taxi drivers: none. Porters: B$1 per bag.

Money Changing and Credit Cards   Although it is officially illegal, changing money on the black market (at a hotel or with someone recommended by your hotel manager) will save you the 2 to 3% bank service charge. Credit cards are not widely accepted at restaurants, but they are accepted at hotels. Using your credit cards will get you the official two-to-one rate without having to pay a service charge.

Telephone Calls   There are direct-dial AT&T phones at the Belize International Airport and at the main phone office in downtown Belize City. A few phones in San Pedro also offer this service.

FAST FACTS   *BELIZE*

American Express   Belize's only American Express office is in Belize City, upstairs from Belize Global Travel Services, 41 Albert St. (tel. 2-77363). Open Monday to Friday from 8am to noon and from 1 to 4:30pm, Saturday from 8am to noon.

Business Hours   Banks are open Monday through Thursday from 8am to 1pm and Friday from 8am to 1pm and 3 to 6pm. Offices are open from 8am to noon and 1 to 5pm. Restaurants are generally open daily from 11am to 2pm and again from 6 to 10pm. Stores are open daily 8am to noon, 1 to 4pm, and 7 to 9pm (many are only open in the morning on Wednesday).

Camera/Film   Film is available in Belize, but it's very expensive. Bring plenty from home. Remember to bring spare camera batteries also.
Climate   See "When to Go" in this chapter.
Country Code   The country code when dialing Belize is 501.
Crime   See *"Safety,"* below.
Currency   See "Information, Entry Requirements & Money" in this chapter.
Documents Required   See "Information, Entry Requirements & Money" in this chapter.
Driving Rules   See "Getting Around" in this chapter.
Drug Laws   Although marijuana is grown in Belize, it's illegal, and the penalties for its possession are stiff. The same goes for cocaine. Be sure to bring along copies of any prescription medicine that you might need because this can save you problems with Customs officials and help you get prescriptions filled while you're here.
Drugstores   You'll find licensed pharmacies in most towns in Belize.
Electricity   Current is 110 volts.
Embassies and Consulates   United States Embassy, 20 Gabourel Lane, Belize City (tel. 02-77161); Canada Consulate, 89 North Front Street. Belize City (tel. 02-31060); British High Commission, Embassy Square, Belmopan (tel. 08-22146 or 08-22147). Keep in mind that there is no Guatemalan embassy or consulate in Belize. If you need a Guatemalan visa (citizens of Canada, Ireland, the United Kingdom, and Australia need them), the nearest consulate is in Chetumal, Mexico.
Emergencies   Fire and ambulance, dial 90; for the police, dial 72222 in Belize City, 22222 in Belmopan, 2022 in San Ignacio, Benque Viejo or San Pedro, 23129 in Placencia, 2120 in Caye Caulker, 22022 in Dangriga, Orange Walk, or Corozal Town.
Hitchhiking   See "Getting Around" in this chapter.
Holidays   See "When to Go" in this chapter.
Information   See "Information, Entry Requirements & Money" in this chapter. Also see individual city chapters for local information offices.
Language   English is the official language, although Spanish, several Indian dialects, and Creole also are spoken.
Laundry   For listings of laundromats, see individual town and island chapters.
Liquor Laws   You must be 18 years old to purchase alcoholic beverages in Belize.
Mail   Letters take about a week to reach the United States. A postcard to the United States costs 30B¢ (15¢) and a letter costs 60B¢ (30¢). You can usually buy stamps at your hotel and in stores selling postcards as well as at the post office. Post offices are open from Monday to Thursday from 8am to 5pm, Friday from 8am to 4:30pm. It is best to ship parcels from the Parcel Post Office, North Front Street, in Belize City. Open Monday to Thursday from 8am to noon and 1 to 4:30pm, Friday from 8am to noon and 1 to 4pm.
Maps   The Belize Tourist Authority information center in Belize City has several different maps—some free, others for a few dollars. If you plan to drive, I recommend the *Driver's Guide to Beautiful Belize,* a small book that takes you mile by mile down every road with many small maps. It's available at Tropical Books, 9 Regent St., Belize City for B$10 ($5).
Newspapers/Magazines   The *Miami Herald* and *USA Today* are the most readily available international newspapers in Belize and can be found at larger hotels throughout the country. The Belizean newspapers are profoundly lacking in hard news, being primarily mouthpieces for the many political parties in the country.
Passports   See "Information, Entry Requirements & Money" in this chapter.
Pets   If you want to bring your pet along, you must have a recent veterinarian's certificate of good health and inoculation against rabies.
Police   See "Emergencies," above.
Radio/TV   Radio stations in Belize play mostly reggae and soca music. Satellite TV is available at most hotels.
Restrooms   In hotels and restaurants only.

Safety   Belize City has a reputation for being a dangerous place. Whenever you're traveling in an unfamiliar city or country, stay alert. Be aware of your immediate surroundings. Wear a money belt and keep a close eye on your possessions. Be particularly careful with cameras, purses, and wallets—all favorite targets of thieves and pickpockets.

Taxes   There is a B$22.50 ($11.25) departure tax when you leave the country by air. The hotel room tax is 5%, which I have included in the rates listed in this book.

Telephone   Pay phones can be found on the street. They accept coins of different denominations but do not give change. The dial tone is similar to that in the United States. If you make a call from a pay phone and nothing happens, try dialing 8 and then the number. Phone numbers in Belize differ in the number of digits that they have. However, whenever dialing within Belize, you must always dial a zero first; when calling from outside Belize, you don't use the zero. Each town or region has its own prefix, starting with zero. There's only one phone book for all of Belize. The main telephone office in Belize City is on Bishop Street, just around the corner from Albert Street. You'll find direct-dial AT&T phones here. A 3-minute call to the U.S. costs B$9.60 ($4.80).

Time   Belize is on Central Standard Time, or six hours behind Greenwich Mean Time.

Tipping   See "Saving Money on Services and Other Transactions" in this chapter.

Tourist Offices   See "Information, Entry Requirements & Money" in this chapter. Also see individual city chapters.

Visas   See Information, Entry Requirements & Money in this chapter.

Water   On the cayes, avoid tap water, which is often from shallow wells. In Belize City and other towns tap water is heavily chlorinated and safe to drink. Throughout the country people rely on cisterns to collect rainwater for drinking. At your hotel, ask for a pitcher of drinking water; otherwise, bottled water is available.

CHAPTER 15

BELIZE CITY AND THE CAYES

Belize City is no longer the capital of Belize, but as the largest city in the country, it is the business and transportation hub. Sooner or later you're going to have to spend some time here, unless you do all your in-country traveling by air or have a very well-planned itinerary. Whether you are just passing through or spending a day or two here, this chapter will make Belize City a breeze for you.

The cayes, on the other hand, are hard to leave. With their trade winds and coral reefs, cheap lobster and rum punch, they can seduce the most hardened of tropical travelers. The Belizean cayes epitomize life in the slow lane and offer everything from kicked back to laid back to flat on your back soaking up the sun.

1. BELIZE CITY

103 miles S of the Mexican border; 82 miles E of the Guatemalan border

GETTING THERE   By Air   Continental, American, TACA, Tan Sahsa, Aerovias, and several local airlines serve Belize City's two airports. See Chapter 14, "Planning a Trip to Belize," for details.

By Bus   Belize City is well served by about half a dozen different bus lines that run to all corners of the country that have roads. See Chapter 15, "Planning a Trip to Belize," for more details.

By Car   There are only two highways into Belize City—the Northern Highway, which leads to the Mexican border, and the Western Highway, which leads to the Guatemalan border.

By Boat   The *Andrea* and *Andrea II* make the run between San Pedro, Ambergris Caye, and Belize City Monday to Saturday. There also are boats that run between Caye Caulker and Belize City daily.

DEPARTING   Belize City's bus stations are about ten blocks from the Swing Bridge. From Albert Street between the Swing Bridge and the Central Park, walk up Orange Street, cross a canal, continue to the far side of the next canal and turn left for Novelos, located on West Collet Canal (tel. 2-77372); Batty Bros., on Mosul Street (tel. 2-77146), is to the right one block before you cross the second canal. The last two companies, Venus (tel. 2-73354) and Z-Line (tel. 2-73937), are farther away, off Orange Street; turn right onto Magazine Road to find them.

Batty Bros. runs four buses a day to San Ignacio: at 6:30 (this is the only one that goes to Melchor de Mencos, Guatemala), 8, 9, and 10am. The trip takes 1½ hours to Belmopan, where there's a brief stop, then another 1½ hours to San Ignacio. Novelos buses leave for San Ignacio every hour on the hour from 11am through 6pm. The schedule is pared down a bit on Sunday. Transportes del Carmen also runs a few buses out to San Ignacio. Venus and Z-Line serve Dangriga, Mango Creek, Placencia, and Punta Gorda. Batty Bros. and Venus split the northern route to Chetumal; between the two of them, a bus runs every hour.

"The stereo speakers are as big as houses" exclaimed a recent visitor to Belize City (pop. 50,000), and even though that is a bit of an exaggeration, Belize City does rock to a Caribbean beat. Maybe all the rocking is due to the city's shaky foundations. Legend has it that the city was founded 300 years ago by pirates and built out of the marshes on a foundation of empty rum bottles. Whether that is true or not, Belize City is surrounded on three sides by water, and at high tide it is nearly swamped. Several hurricanes have inundated the city over the years, causing extensive damage each time and affecting the creation of two other towns—Belmopan and Hattieville. Belmopan, at the geographical center of the country, may be the capital of Belize, but Belize City is the cultural and commercial center. It's a strange, fascinating warren of narrow streets and canals (the latter being little more than open sewers and pretty pungent in hot weather), modern stores, dilapidated shacks, and quaint wooden mansions. It's not the kind of place that you want to hang around any longer than necessary, but if you happen to be stuck here for a day or two, explore a bit—you might be surprised by what you find.

ORIENTATION

ARRIVING When you fly into Belize, you'll land at the Philip S. W. Goldson International Airport, which is located 10 miles northwest of the city on the Northern Highway. At the airport you'll find the Belize Bank, open daily from 8 to 11am and from noon to 4pm, just outside the terminal entrance. There are also car-rental desks and an information desk that is actually more of a travel agency providing reservations at the more expensive hotels and lodges around the country. A taxi into town will cost B$30 ($15). When I was last in Belize City, someone had started a shuttle bus to the International airport charging B$2 ($1) each way. Buses in from the airport were scheduled for 6, 8, and 10:30am, and 4 and 6pm. Phone 2-73977 or 2-77811 to find out if this shuttle is still operating when you arrive. If you fly in from somewhere else in Belize, you'll land at the Municipal Airport, which is on the edge of town. A taxi from here should be no more than B$8 ($4).

If you arrive in town by bus, you'll be somewhere on the west side of town, depending on where you came from and which bus line you used. All the bus stations are within 10 blocks of Albert Street, which is an easy walk in the day, but it is not recommended after dark. A taxi from the bus station to any hotel in town will cost B$4 ($2) for one person or B$3 ($1.50) per person for two or more people.

If you arrive by car from the north, keep on the road into town, paying close attention to one-way streets, and you'll end up at the Swing Bridge. If you're arriving on the Western Highway, stay on it after it becomes Cemetery Road, and you'll end up at the intersection with Albert Street, a block away from the Swing Bridge.

INFORMATION The **Belize Tourist Board**, 89 North Front St. (tel. 277213, 73255, or 77490) is open Monday to Thursday from 8am to noon and 1 to 5pm, to 4:30pm on Friday; closed on weekends. Travel agencies are another good source of information.

CITY LAYOUT Belize City is surrounded on three sides by water, with the murky waters of the Haulover Creek dividing the city in two. The Swing Bridge, near the mouth of Haulover Creek, is the main route between the two halves of the city. At the south end of the bridge is the market and the start of Regent Street and Albert Street, where you'll find most of Belize City's shops and offices. To the east of these two major roads is a grid of smaller roads lined with dilapidated wooden houses. On the north side of the bridge and to the right, you'll find a pleasant neighborhood of old mansions. This is where you'll find the U.S. embassy, a couple of guest houses, and several expensive hotels. Cemetery Road heads out of town to the west and becomes the Western Highway, and Freetown Road becomes the Northern Highway.

GETTING AROUND

The only way to get around town is on foot or by taxi, unless you have your own car.

BY TAXI A taxi is B$4 ($2) for one person between any two points in town and B$3 ($1.50) per person for two or more people. You'll find taxis waiting on the Market Square near the Swing Bridge, or you can call **Caribbean Taxi Garage** (tel. 2-72888) or **Cinderella Plaza Taxi** (tel. 2-45240).

BY CAR   Car Rentals I don't know of anyplace in the world where it is more expensive to rent a car. It seems that anyone who can get a couple of old Detroit eight-cylinder bombs down here from Texas can open up a car-rental agency. You can count on these cars guzzling expensive gas and breaking down at some point (not my idea of a fun way to spend my vacation).
    A much better bet is to rent a small four-wheel-drive vehicle that will likely get better mileage and be reliable even though it costs a bit more per day. International car-rental agencies with offices in Belize include **Avis** (tel. toll free in the U.S. 800/331-1212), with branches at the Esso station at the corner of Cork and Fort streets (tel. 2-31987), the Radisson Fort George Hotel (tel. 2-77400), and Philip S.W. Goldson International Airport (tel. 2-52385); **Budget Rent-a-Car** (tel. toll free in the U.S. 800/527-0700), 771 Bella Vista (tel. 2-32435); and **National Car Rental** (tel. toll free in the U.S. 800/227-7368), Philip S.W. Goldson International Airport (tel. 2-31586).
    The most economical four-wheel drive vehicles (Suzuki Samurais) rent for around $85, taxes and insurance included. If you go with a local agency, you're likely to get stuck with one of the old Detroit bombs. Try to make a reservation several weeks in advance with one of the international companies. You'll be glad you did.

 BELIZE CITY

American Express The office is located upstairs from Belize Global Travel Services, 41 Albert St. (tel. 2-77363). Open Monday to Friday from 8am to noon and 1 to 4:30pm, Saturday 8am to noon.
    Area Code The area code for Belize City is 501-2.
    Bookstores The Book Center, 144 North Front St. (tel. 2-77457), sells magazines and classic books and is open Monday to Friday from 8am to noon, 1 to 5pm, and 7 to 9pm; Saturday 8am to noon, 1 to 4:30pm, and 7 to 9pm. The Belize Bookshop, Regent and Rectory streets (tel. 2-72054), sells books, magazines, and local and U.S. newspapers and is open Monday, Tuesday, Thursday, and Friday from 8am to noon and 1:30 to 5pm; Wednesday and Saturday 8am to noon.
    Business Hours See "Fast Facts: Business Hours" in Chapter 14.
    Car Rentals See "Getting Around" in this chapter.
    Climate See "When to Go" in Chapter 14.
    Crime See "Safety" below.
    Currency See "Information, Entry Requirements & Money" in Chapter 14.

Currency Exchange All banks are around the Central Park, though few people use banks for changing money because they charge a commission. Ask your hotel manager about changing money. If the hotel can't help you, they can point you in the right direction. Banks are open Monday to Thursday from 8am to 1pm, and Friday 8am to 1pm and 3 to 6pm.

Dentist Contact your embassy for the name of a reliable dentist.

Doctors Contact your embassy for the name of a reliable doctor.

Drugstores Brodie's Pharmacy, Regent Street at Market Square (tel. 2-77070, ext. 266), is open Monday, Tuesday, Thursday, and Saturday from 8:30am to 7pm; Wednesday 8:30am to 12:30pm; Friday 8:30am to 9pm; and Sunday 9am to 12:30pm.

Embassies and Consulates United States Embassy, 29 Gabourel Lane (tel. 02-77161); Canada Consulate, 89 North Front St. (tel. 02-31060); Mexico Embassy, 20 North Park St (tel. 2-30193).

Emergencies Fire and ambulance call 90; police call 72222.

Eyeglasses The Belize Vision Center, 9 Daly St. (tel. 2-45038), can repair or replace your glasses. Open Monday to Friday 8am to noon and 4 to 7pm, Saturday 8am to noon.

Holidays See "When to Go" in Chapter 14.

Hospitals St. Francis Hospital and Diagnostic Center, 28 Albert St. (tel. 2-77068 or 2-75658), has a 24-hour emergency room.

Information See "Information" in this chapter.

Laundry/Dry Cleaning Your best bet is to ask at the front desk of your hotel. If the hotel doesn't do laundry, the staff should be able to refer you to a place nearby.

Luggage Storage/Lockers Ask at your hotel; otherwise, there's no place to leave luggage in Belize City.

Lost Property The best you can do is contact the police.

Newspapers/Magazines The *Miami Herald, USA Today, Time,* and *Newsweek* are available at the bookstores mentioned above.

Photographic Needs Venus Photo, corner of Albert and Bishop streets (tel. 2-73596), sells film (expensive). Open Monday to Saturday from 8am to 5pm and 7 to 9pm. A 36-exposure roll of ASA 100 print film costs B$15 ($7.50).

Police See "Emergencies," above.

Post Office The main post office is on North Front Street at the north end of the Swing Bridge (tel. 2-72201). Open Monday to Thursday from 8am to 5pm, and Friday from 8am to 4:30pm. The parcel post office next door is open Monday to Thursday from 8am to noon and 1 to 4:30pm, Friday 8am to noon and 1 to 4pm.

Radio/TV Local radio stations primarily play reggae, soca, and rap music. Satellite cable TV is what most people here watch.

Religious Services Among the denominations with churches in Belize City are Anglican, Baptist, Presbyterian, Jehovah's Witness, and Seventh Day Adventist. Check the Belize telephone book for addresses and phone numbers.

Restrooms You'll find them in restaurants and hotels, but that's about it.

Safety Like any big city, Belize City has its share of criminals and dangers, although with a bit of caution and common sense, you shouldn't have any problems. You'll hear that you shouldn't go out alone at night in Belize City, but there's nothing that should prevent you from walking from a restaurant to your hotel in pairs, down well-lit main streets. Look like you know where you're going and don't flash money. If someone tries to engage you in conversation not to your liking, excuse yourself politely. Invariably, people who get ripped off are participating in illicit exchanges. You certainly won't have any problems on the cayes, where life never exceeds a snail's pace, but it's still a good idea not to leave valuables in your room.

Taxes There is a 5% tax on hotel rooms.

Taxis See "Getting Around" in this chapter.

Telephone For all your long-distance needs, head to the Belize Telecommuni-

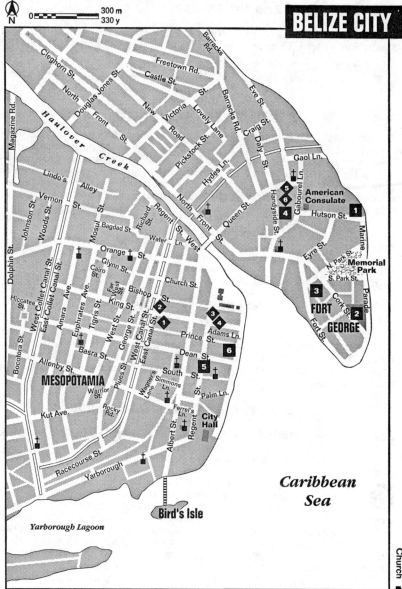

BELIZE CITY

N
0 ——— 300 m
——— 330 y

Caribbean Sea

Haulover Creek

Yarborough Lagoon

Bird's Isle

American Consulate

Memorial Park

FORT GEORGE

MESOPOTAMIA

City Hall

Church ■ ✝

Belize City ★

BELIZE

ACCOMMODATIONS:

Belize Guest House **1**
El Centro **2**
Fort Street Guest House **3**
Mom's Triangle Inn **4**
Mopan **5**
Seaside Guest House **6**

RESTAURANTS:

Dit's ◆
GG's ◆
Macy's ◆
Mom's ◆
Pearl's ◆
Pop 'n' Taco ◆

cations Ltd. office at 1 Church St. Open Monday to Saturday from 8am to 9pm, Sunday 8am to 6pm. There are two AT&T USA direct phones here.

WHAT TO SEE & DO

A walk around town is all that you need to entertain you in Belize City because the fascination never seems to end. Turn right as you come off the northeast end of the Swing Bridge, before the post office, and follow the street southeast to the Fort George Lighthouse and Baron Bliss Memorial. Baron Bliss, who visited Belize on his yacht in the 1920s, left Belize City most of his fortune (a few million dollars, in fact) when he died on the yacht in the harbor, and many of the city's public buildings derive from his bequest.

The Supreme Court building, off the small Central Park, is a real prize of English colonial architecture (à la Caribbean). If you walk down to the end of Regent Street, you'll come to Government House, built in 1814 by the British, who ruled Belize for many years. Across the street is the Anglican Cathedral of St. John the Baptist. In the 19th century, three kings of the Mosquito Coast were crowned here. Also along Regent Street are several old buildings that were once slave quarters.

WHERE TO STAY

Accommodations in Belize City can be a problem: The cheapest hotels are not recommended because of the danger of theft, and the expensive hotels often commit a similar offense by charging too much for what you get. I've listed only safe choices. Remember: When dialing the following phone numbers from within Belize, drop the country code and dial 0 before the first digit.

DOUBLES FOR LESS THAN B$40 [$20]

SEASIDE GUEST HOUSE, 3 Prince St., Belize City. Tel. 501/2-78339. 6 rms.
$ Rates: B$15.75 ($7.90) dorm beds; B$26.25 ($13.15) single; B$36.75 ($18.40) double. No credit cards.

One of Belize City's most popular low-budget lodgings, the Seaside is located on a very quiet street just off Southern Foreshore. This typical Caribbean wood-frame house is a haven for the backpack crowd, and it's very difficult to secure space on the first day that you're in town. If you want to stay here, call and make a reservation. There are only two singles, three doubles, and a five-bed dorm here—but they're all clean. And there are lots of maps of Belize on the walls for those interested in exploring the interior. Breakfasts are served at an additional cost, and there is a coffee shop upstairs.

DOUBLES FOR LESS THAN B$100 [$50]

BELIZE GUEST HOUSE, 2 Hutson St., Belize City. Tel. 501/2-77569 or toll free 800/538-6802. Fax 501/2-77569. 7 rms (2 with bath).
$ Rates: B$66 ($33) single; B$88 ($44) double. AE, MC, V.

This guest house is in my favorite Belize City neighborhood, in which the shady streets are lined with stately old homes that once housed the British officials who governed Belize. Today, the neighborhood is home to embassies, doctors, and lawyers. Although this is not one of the more attractive homes in the neighborhood, it is the closest to the water. In fact, the Belize Guest House claims that it is only 5 feet from the water. The rooms are large but not luxuriously furnished.

Some have air conditioning, while others have only fans. However, if you get too hot, you can always step out on the veranda, which looks directly over the Caribbean and catches the nearly constant trade winds. You can arrange to rent a Suzuki four-wheel-drive vehicle here at rates lower than at other rental agencies in town. There is no restaurant here, but complimentary coffee and drinks are available. A large lounge with dark wood-paneled walls is a great place to relax and read one of the books from the guest house's library. Laundry service and air ticketing available.

COLTON HOUSE, 9 Cork St., Belize. Tel. 501/2-44666. 3 rms (1 with bath).
$ Rates: B$63 ($31.50) single without bath, B$73 ($36.50) single with bath; B$73.50 ($36.75) double without bath, B$83.50 ($41.75) double with bath; B$84 ($42) triple without bath, B$94 ($47) triple with bath. No credit cards.

Located in Belize City's most attractive historic neighborhood, Colton House is directly across the street from the much pricier Radisson Fort George Hotel. A lushly planted yard, a wide veranda, hardwood floors, shuttered windows, and big rooms with high ceilings and overhead fans all add up to a tropical colonial atmosphere, although the furnishings lack the tropical style of the building. If you can afford to spend a bit more, you can't do much better than this. It's easy to forget you're in Belize City.

MOM'S TRIANGLE INN, 11 Handyside St., P.O. Box 332, Belize City. Tel. 501/2-45073 or 2-45523. 6 rms (all with bath).
$ Rates: B$52.50 ($26.25) single, B$73.50 ($36.75) single with A/C; B$63 ($31.50) double, B$84 ($42) double with A/C; B$10.50 ($5.25) per extra person; kids under 12 free. DISC, MC, V.

This is perhaps the best all-around choice in Belize City. All the rooms are fairly spacious and have private baths and carpeting. There's a comfortable lounge for socializing. After the first day, you'll have access to the refrigerator. Lockers can be rented for $1 a day. Mom's is renowned for its commitment to travelers. Unfortunately, this is not one of the city's better neighborhoods. There is laundry service.

WORTH THE EXTRA BUCKS

FORT STREET GUEST RESTAURANT & GUESTHOUSE, 4 Fort St., P.O. Box 3, Belize City. Tel. 501/2-45638. Fax 501/2-78808. 6 rms (none with bath).
$ Rates (including full breakfast): B$100.80 ($50.40) single; B$113.40 ($56.70) double. DISC, MC, V.

⭐ There aren't too many old homes left in Belize City—repeated hurricanes have made sure of that—so it is a special treat to stay in this, one of the city's old gems. Even though all the rooms here share one bathroom (a definite drawback), you won't find accommodations like these anywhere else in town. Situated on a triangular corner lot with a grassy front yard, the lovely, restored 1928 house has a long flight of steps leading up to the first floor, where you'll find a gift shop selling many Guatemalan típicos. The guest rooms are located on the second floor, where you'll also find two wicker sitting areas. The table settings of crystal goblets and linen cloths set a very romantic mood in the first-floor dining room. The woodwork is dark and rich; it's right out of an old New England village, with a dash of Caribbean thrown in. You place your breakfast order the night before by leaving a note in a bottle outside the door of your room. Lunch, served from 11am to 2pm, is a good value at B$7 ($3.50) to B$13 ($6.50). Dinner is pricey at B$22.50 ($11.25) to $27 ($13.50).

ORCHIDIA GUEST HOUSE & CAFÉ, 56 Regent St., Belize City. Tel. 501/2-74266 or toll free 800/447-2931. Fax 501/2-75200. 8 rms (5 with bath).
$ Rates (including breakfast): B$78.75 ($39.40) single; B$110.25 ($55.15) double; B$120.75 ($60.40) triple; B$131.25 ($65.65) quad. AE, MC, V.

If you crave a bit of comfort while you are in Belize City, try this conveniently located bed-and-breakfast. The Orchidia is housed in an old colonial Caribbean building, though recent modifications have hidden many of the original lines. All the rooms are different. Some have air conditioning while others have only fans. The café here serves some of the best food in town, so if you can't afford to stay here, at least have a meal at the Orchidia.

WHERE TO EAT

MEALS FOR LESS THAN B$15 [$7.50]

DIT'S, 50 King St. Tel. 73330.
  Cuisine: CAKES.
  $ Prices: Slice of cake 50B¢–B$1 (25¢–75¢); meals B$2–B$7 ($1–$3.50).
  Open: Mon–Sat 7am–9pm, Sun 8am–4pm.
When a cake craving strikes you in Belize City, search out this little place. A tempting assortment of cakes and pies are displayed in a glass case at the counter, with many Central American specialties that you may never have encountered before—such as cow pie, raisin pie, three-milks cake, and coconut tarts. Dit's also serves simple meals and, on Friday and Saturday, cow's-foot soup.

GG'S CAFE, 2-B King St. Tel. 2-74378.
  Cuisine: INTERNATIONAL.
  $ Prices: B$5–B$18 ($2.50–$9). No credit cards.
  Open: Lunch Mon–Sat 11:30–2pm; dinner Mon–Thurs 5:30–9pm, Fri–Sat 5:30–10pm.
If you've been in Belize a while and you miss the California life-style, stop by GG's for a bit of *al fresco* dining. Though the menu is typically Belizean with lots of burgers, fried chicken, and fish, there is a shady garden dining area where you can enjoy a romantic dinner. The restaurant's owner, George Godfrey, has an extensive collection of music that he plays for his customers.

MACY'S, 18 Bishop St. Tel. 73419.
  Cuisine: BELIZEAN.
  $ Prices: B$8–B$12 ($4–$6). No credit cards.
  Open: Lunch Mon–Sat 11:30am–4pm; dinner Mon–Sat 6–9:30pm.
For authentic Belizean cooking, try this tiny local place. The food is consistent, the service is friendly, and the dining room is cool and cozy. Order a fish filet with rice and beans for B$8 ($4), or be more daring and try one of their daily chalkboard specials. You may want to skip the wild game to help preserve Belize's wildlife. A tall glass of cold, fresh-squeezed orange juice is a bargain in the Belizean heat at B$2.50 ($1.25).

PEARL'S FINE FOODS, 13 Handyside St. Tel. 31120.
  Cuisine: ITALIAN.
  $ Prices: Pizza B$16 ($8); spaghetti B$8–B$9 ($4–$4.50); subs B$5–B$6 ($2.50–$3). No credit cards.
  Open: Mon–Sat 10am–10pm.
Right next door to the ever-popular Mom's, this is another popular spot with travelers. The main menu is just what you would expect in a little neighborhood Italian restaurant, but there are also daily specials such as beef-and-cheese burritos, chili con carne, barbecued chicken, and beef burgundy. The decor is a merging of Italian bistro and tropical styling, and there's a bit of travel information posted on the walls.

POP 'N TACO, 24 Regent St. Tel. 73826.
  Cuisine: CHINESE.
  $ Prices: B$2–B$19 ($1–$9.50). No credit cards.
  Open: Mon–Sat 9am–9pm, Sun 8:30am–1:30pm.
Despite its Mexican name, this is primarily a Chinese restaurant popular with folks from the surrounding neighborhood (which happens to house several budget hotels). There are a few tables in the simple restaurant, or you can get your food to go. Most dishes are priced at around B$9 ($4.50).

IMPRESSIONS

If the world had any ends British Honduras [Belize] would certainly be one of them.
—ALDOUS HUXLEY, *BEYOND THE MEXIQUE BAY*, 1934

MEALS FOR LESS THAN B$25 [$12.50]

MOM'S, 11 Handyside St. Tel. 45073 or 45523.
   Cuisine: AMERICAN/CREOLE/MEXICAN.
$ Prices: Sandwiches B$3–B$8 ($1.50–$4); main meals B$10–B$25 ($5–$12.50). DISC, MC, V.
   Open: Sun–Fri 6am–10pm.
Mom's still reigns supreme as the gathering place for travelers, despite the slow service. The bulletin boards are jammed with information and messages, and the glass door is constantly sliding open and closed as hungry folks wander in and out throughout the day. With 15 tables, Mom's can accommodate quite a few people. Don't be deceived by the run-down appearance of Handyside Street. Mom's has been here for many years and continues its high standards of quality.

EVENING ENTERTAINMENT

The numerous bars in Belize City can be rough places and are not recommended unless you have a local guide to take you to places he knows. If you just want to relax over a drink, try the second-floor bar at the **Bellevue Hotel** on Southern Foreshore. It looks over the water and occasionally has live bands on the weekends.
   The **Baron Bliss Institute, 1 Bliss Promenade. Tel. 02-77267,** named for and financed by Belize City's benefactor, is the city's cultural center, where you'll find a public library, three Mayan stelae, and occasional cultural performances, including the annual Festival of the Arts.

EXCURSIONS

ALTUN HA RUINS

About 30 miles north of Belize City on the Old Northern Highway are the ruins of Altun Ha, an ancient Mayan city thought to have existed here since about A.D. 250. Watch for the turnoff to the right just past Sand Hill. Once you're on the Old Northern Highway, watch for a small and rather inconspicuous sign for the Maruba Resort on the right side of the road. From the highway, it's a bumpy 2¼ miles to the ruins. About 1½ miles in, the road forks—take the right fork.
   Altun Ha flourished during the Classic Period of Mayan civilization, up to the 800s. It was an important trading center linking the coastal and interior settlements. Only a few of the most imposing temples, tombs, and pyramids have been uncovered and rebuilt; hundreds more lie under the jungle foliage. The unique jade-head sculpture of Kinich Ahau (the Mayan sun god), the largest well-carved jade from the Mayan era, was discovered here. Today, it's kept in a bank vault in Belize City out of public view. The site was named after the village in which it's situated—Rockstone Pond, the literal Mayan translation meaning "stone water." The archeological work was done principally by the Royal Ontario Museum beginning in 1964 and although restoration has resulted in some anachronistic juxtapositions, it's a beautiful ruined city, well worth the visit. Open daily from 8am to 5pm, admission is B$3 ($1.50), children under 12 are free. There is no public transport to Altun Ha, so you'll need to take a tour, a taxi, your own wheels, or hitchhike.
   A soft-drink stand and picnic area are available. Don't go too far off the beaten track in this area. (You wouldn't want to stumble on someone's private marijuana plantation.) If you're an intrepid explorer of lost ruins, get a guide.

Where to Stay & Eat

MARUBA RESORT, 40½ Old Northern Highway, Maskall Village. Tel. 501/03-22199. P.O. Box 300703, Houston, Texas 77230. Tel. 713/799-2031. Fax 713/795-8573. 10 rms, 1 suite (all with bath).

$ Rates: B$201.60–B$225.60 ($100.80–$112.80) single; B$254.40–B$278.40 ($127.20–$139.20) double; various meal plans additional. AE, MC, V.

⭐ This is the only place to stay anywhere near the Altun Ha ruins—it's a major splurge but it's one of the nicest small lodges in Belize. You'd hardly expect to find a luxury resort while driving down this potholed stretch of the Old Northern Highway, but that is just what you'll encounter tucked away on an old farm. Perhaps you'll feel like being pampered after several very hard days on the road—how about a soak in the hot tub, a massage, and a manicure or pedicure? Every room is unique, with such unusual design touches as Guatemalan blankets on the beds, animal skins on the walls, "modern art" doors, four pillows on the beds, and Chinese sandalwood soap in the bathrooms. There is a very attractive little swimming pool with its own waterfall, and around the grounds you'll find many caged wild animals. The only drawback to this otherwise idyllic retreat are the numerous biting insects that appear at different times of year—be sure to bring some insect repellent.

The dining room/bar is equally a work of art. In the lounge, a long built-in sofa has a screen of potted plants separating it from the dining area. The bar itself is made of stone and rough logs with a dugout canoe full of business cards hanging above it. Tables in the dining room are set with porcelain and crystal. Meals here are expensive, but you'll rarely find better in Belize. Breakfast is B$20 ($10), lunch is B$25 ($12.50), and dinner is B$45 ($22.50).

COMMUNITY BABOON SANCTUARY

No, there aren't really baboons in Belize, this is just the local name for the black howler monkeys who reside in this innovative sanctuary. The sanctuary is a voluntary program run by local landowners in eight villages to preserve the local population of these endangered and vociferous primates. There is a visitors' center and natural history museum in the village of Bermudian Landing, and it is here that you can pay your minimal admission fee. The admission fee includes the services of a guide, so don't bother hiring one of the local guides. There are several trails through the preserve and as you walk along, you will undoubtedly hear the whooping and barking of the howler monkeys as they make their way through the treetops feeding on fruits, flowers, and leaves. Most visitors also see a few monkeys, though they are often quite high in the trees. Carry binoculars. Many other species, especially birds, make their homes in this preserve.

Bermudian Landing village, site of the preserve's visitor center, is about 20 miles west of Belize City. If you are driving, head north on the Northern Highway and watch for the Burrel Boom Road turnoff. Buses to Bermudian Landing leave Belize City Monday through Saturday at 12:30pm from the corner of Orange and Mosul street and at 12:30, 1, 3:30, and 5pm from the corner of Orange and George streets. Buses return to Belize City at 5:30 and 6am. The fare is around B$2 ($1). Accommodations are available with local families for B$10 ($5) single and B$16 ($8) double. Three meals will cost an additional B$13 ($6.50) per person. For more information or to make a reservation for accommodations, contact the Belize Audubon Society, 29 Regent St. (P.O. Box 1001), Belize City, (tel. 501/2-77369). Be sure to bring mosquito repellent and/or mosquito coils if you plan to stay overnight.

CROOKED TREE WILDLIFE SANCTUARY

Crooked Tree Wildlife Preserve is a swampy lowland that serves as a resting spot for dozens of species of migratory birds, including kites, hawks, ducks, grebes, pelicans, ospreys, egrets, and herons. However, the preserve was established primarily to protect Belize's main nesting site of the endangered jabiru stork, the largest bird in the western hemisphere. Crooked Tree has rapidly become known as an excellent place to spot other endangered wildlife as well. Crocodiles, iguanas, coatimundi, and howler monkeys are all frequently sighted. The best way to explore the preserve's swamps, lagoons, and waterways is by dugout canoe. Leland Tillet, who lives directly behind the sanctuary's visitor center and administrative building, is one of the better local guides. For a few dollars, he'll paddle you around in his dugout for a few hours.

Crooked Tree is located 33 miles northwest of Belize City. If you are driving, head up the Northern Highway and watch for the turnoff to Crooked Tree. Buses leave for Crooked Tree Village from the Batty Bros. bus terminal on Mosul Street (one block before West Collet Canal) Monday through Friday at 4pm, returning at 7:30am. Another bus company leaves from the same terminal Monday through Saturday at 10:55am and 5:15pm, returning from Crooked Tree at 5:30 and 7am and 2:15pm. The fare is around B$4 ($2). If you'd like to spend the night, accommodations can be arranged with a local family for B$20 ($10) single or B$30 ($15) double. Meals are an additional B$18 ($9) per person. For more information or to make a room reservation, contact the Belize Audubon Society, 29 Regent St. (P.O. Box 1001), Belize City (tel. 501/2-77369).

---

2. AMBERGRIS CAYE

36 miles N of Belize City; 40 miles SE of Corozal Town

GETTING THERE   By Plane   There are dozens of daily flights between Belize City and San Pedro on Ambergris Caye. Flights leave from both the Philip S. W. Goldson International Airport and the Belize City Municipal Airport. If you're coming in on an international flight and heading straight for San Pedro, you should book a flight from the international airport. If you're already in Belize City it's cheaper to fly from the municipal airport, which is also cheaper to reach by taxi. Tropic Air (tel. 2-45671 in Belize City, 26-2012 in San Pedro), Island Air (tel. 2-31140 in Belize City, 26-2435 in San Pedro), and Maya Airways (tel. 2-72312 in Belize City, 26-2611 in San Pedro) are the three main airlines flying to San Pedro. Duration: 20–30 minutes. Fare: between B$33 and B$39 ($16.50 and $19.50) one way and between B$66 and B$70 ($33 and $35) round-trip. Because a taxi into Belize City from the international airport costs B$30 ($15) and the boat to San Pedro costs B$20 ($10), it is only slightly more expensive to fly if you are heading directly to San Pedro after arriving on an international flight.

Island Air has several flights each day between Caye Caulker and Ambergris Caye. Duration: 15 minutes. Fare: B$35 ($17.50) one way, B$60 ($30) round-trip. Contact Dolphin Bay Travel, middle of Front Street (tel. 22-2214), on Caye Caulker to make a reservation.

There are two flights a day between Corozal Town and San Pedro on Tropic Air. Duration: 20 minutes. Fare: B$54 ($27) one way, B$104 ($52) round-trip.

By Boat   The *Andrea* and *Andrea II* ply from Belize City to San Pedro Monday through Saturday, departing from a pier near the Bellevue Hotel on Southern Foreshore at 4pm. Duration: 75 minutes. Fare: B$20 ($10) one way, B$35 ($17.50) round-trip.

If you're going to Ambergris Caye from Caye Caulker, you can arrange for the *Andrea* or *Andrea II* to pick you up on its trip from Belize City to San Pedro. Check at one of Caye Caulker's travel agencies to make a reservation and find out where the boats stop. Duration: 45 minutes. Fare: B$15 ($7.50) one way, B$30 ($15) round-trip.

You can also sail over from Caye Caulker on one of the sailboats that go out to Hol Chan Marine Reserve. These boats usually stop for lunch on Ambergris Caye, and there is nothing to stop you from staying in San Pedro. Fare: B$25 ($12.50). Departures from Caye Caulker are around 10am. Find out about trips by asking in front of the Reef Hotel.

DEPARTING   The *Andrea* and *Andrea II* leave San Pedro Monday through Saturday at 7am, with an additional departure Saturday at 1pm. Their dock is toward the north end of San Pedro on the reef side of the town. Flights leave throughout the day for Belize City's two airports. Boat and plane reservations can be made at any of the travel agencies along Barrier Reef Drive. For plane reservations, walk to the airport and make a reservation in person.

ESSENTIALS Orientation San Pedro (the town on the island of Ambergris Caye) is only three streets wide. The streets, from seaside to lagoonside, are Barrier Reef Drive, Pescador Drive, and Angel Coral Street. The airport is at the south end of town.

Fast Facts Belize Bank, across from the Spindrift Hotel on Barrier Reef Drive is open Monday to Thursday 8am to 1pm and Friday 8am to 1pm and 3 to 6pm. Lopez Drugs, the island's one drugstore, is in a shopping center on Barrier Reef Drive toward the north end of town—open daily 8am to noon, 2 to 5pm, and 7 to 9pm. Emergency numbers: police 2022; fire 2372; medical 90. The post office is located on a cross street near the Atlantic Bank and just around the corner from Barrier Reef Drive.

Long before the British settled Belize, and long before the sun-seeking vacationers and zealous reef divers discovered Ambergris Caye, the Mayas were here. In fact, the Mayas created Ambergris Caye when they cut a channel through the long thin peninsula that extended down from what is now Mexico. The channel was cut to facilitate coastal trading and avoid the dangerous barrier reef that begins not too far north of San Pedro. Today Ambergris Caye is 25 miles long and only half a mile wide.

For many years now the town of San Pedro has been Belize's main sun-and-fun community and it is here that you'll find the country's largest concentration of tourist developments. Though San Pedro once attracted primarily scuba divers and fishermen, it is today popular with a wide range of folks who like the slow-paced atmosphere. People compare the island to the Florida Keys 30 or 40 years ago, though San Pedro is rapidly catching up. The town still has no paved streets, but automobiles are proliferating and wooden Caribbean houses have given way to concrete and cinder-block buildings. Unfortunately, in the process, the town has lost almost all of its shade trees, so be sure to bring a good sun block and sunglasses.

Most of Ambergris Caye is still uninhabited, but nearly all of it has been subdivided and sold to developers. Despite the fact that much of the island is seasonally flooded mangrove forest, and despite laws prohibiting the cutting of mangroves, developers continue to clear this marginal land. Indiscriminate cutting of the mangroves is already having an adverse effect on the nearby barrier reef: Without the mangroves to filter the water and slow the impact of waves, silt is formed and carried out to the reef where it settles and kills the coral. Hopefully, before it is too late, something will be done to stop the destruction of the coral reef—the very reason people come to Ambergris Caye.

WHAT TO SEE & DO

This is a beach resort, so you can expect to find most of the standard activities (on a limited scale). There are no submarine rides, but you can rent a sailboard; there are no sunset dine-and-dance cruises, but you do get a rum punch when you go out on a glass-bottomed boat. Sorry golfers: There are no golf courses here—yet.

First, you should be aware that there really isn't any beach to speak of on Ambergris Caye: There is a narrow strip of sand where the land meets the sea, but even at low tide it isn't wide enough for you to unroll a beach towel in most places. The widest section of sand happens to be right in the middle of town, where all the boats dock (not a pleasant place to hang out). Try walking north or south from town along the water to find a more secluded spot where you can sit and stare out to sea. Otherwise, the beachfront (read "expensive") hotels create their own beaches by building retaining walls and filling them in with sand.

Likewise, swimming is not what you might expect. For a 100 yards or more out from shore, the bottom is covered with sea grass. Beneath the grass is a layer of spongy roots and organic matter topped with a thin layer of white sand. Walking on this spongy sand is most unnerving, and it's easy to trip and stumble. Swimming is best off the pier at the Paradise Resort Hotel, where the management has created a sort of swimming pool in the sea by scooping out a deep spot and clearing away all the grass. All the beaches on the caye are public, and you can probably use the hotel's lounge chairs if it's a slow day. The best swimming is from boats anchored out in the turquoise waters between the shore and the reef.

So why do people bother to come here if there is no beach and you can't go swimming right off the shore? They come for the turquoise waters and the coral reef. Less than a quarter mile offshore is the longest coral reef in the western hemisphere. Only Australia's Barrier Reef is longer than this one.

For reliable scuba diving service and reasonable rates, contact **Out Island Divers,** P.O. Box 7, San Pedro (tel. 26-2151, fax 26-2810), which is across from the Spindrift Hotel on Barrier Reef Drive. This company leads dives to popular nearby sites and also offers a day trip to the famous Blue Hole, a huge offshore sinkhole (collapsed cavern) made famous by Jacques Cousteau. The Blue Hole trip is pricey at B$300 ($150), but it includes a plane trip to an island near the Blue Hole. For nearby dives and rental equipment, try **Bottom Time Dive Shop,** at the Sunbreeze Hotel on the south end of Barrier Reef Drive (tel. 26-2348) where a dive with all equipment included will cost B$120 ($60). The **Holiday Dive Shop,** at the Holiday Hotel (tel. 26-2437) charges around B$80 ($40) for two dives, including tank and weight belt. There's a diving school at Ramon's Reef Hotel, where you can practice in the pool before going out. Snorkeling equipment is available at several locations in town for about B$10 ($5). If you're an independent type, just rent your own snorkeling gear and hop off one of the docks. However, you really need to go out to the reef to see much of anything other than sand and sea grass.

The best snorkeling is at the **Hol Chan Marine Reserve,** which is about four miles southeast of San Pedro. *Hol chan* is a Mayan term meaning "little channel," which is exactly what you'll find here—a narrow channel cutting through the shallow coral reef. The walls of the channel are popular with divers, and the shallower areas are frequented by snorkelers. Some of the exciting residents of the area are several large green moray eels (friendly but dangerous), stingrays (don't touch), and nurse sharks (harmless). The reserve covers 5 square miles and is divided into three zones: the reef, the sea-grass beds, and the mangroves. There's also a small "blue hole," which is a deep well formed by a collapsed cavern. A much larger, deeper, and more famous blue hole is far to the south of here. Don't confuse the two—this is not the blue hole that Jacques Cousteau explored. Nor is it the blue hole on the Hummingbird Highway. There is a B$3 ($1.50) charge for diving at Hol Chan, which is usually not included in the price of the boat excursion.

There are several boats offering trips out here. The ***Reef Seeker Glass-Bottom Boat*** tour for B$25 ($12.50) includes a 1-hour trip, an hour of snorkeling (snorkel gear not included), and a complimentary rum punch. If there are enough people, two trips depart daily at 9:15am and 2pm. ***The Coral Jungle*** makes three stops: one at a sunken boat, one at the blue hole, and one at Hol Chan. It leaves at 9am and 2pm on 2½-hour trips and charges B$24 ($12). Make reservations at the Barrier Reef Hotel. Most of the native fishermen are trustworthy for boat excursions. Decide what you want to do, then check out the people who could take you.

Make arrangements at **Amigo Travel** (tel. 26-2180) on Barrier Reef Drive for a full day on the catamaran, *Me Too,* which is docked at Ramon's Reef. For B$80 ($40), you get snorkeling equipment and instruction, a guide, drinks, and bathroom facilities.

The local windsurfing school is housed at Sun Breeze Beach Resort. Rental rates are B$30 ($15) per hour.

Sportfishing for tarpon and bonefish is among the best in the world around these cayes, and over the years a few record catches have been made. The two travel and tour agencies above can arrange fishing trips for you for between B$550 and B$900 ($275 and $450) per day. However, if this is a bit steep for your budget, stop by Ruby's Hotel where you can arrange a half day of angling for bonefish, tarpon, or reef fish for

B$180 ($90) or a full day for B$270 ($135). Omar Arceo (tel. 26-2410) is a reliable local fishing guide who charges B$160 ($80) for a half day or B$280 ($140) for a full day.

WHERE TO STAY

DOUBLES FOR LESS THAN B$55 ($27.50)

CASA BLANCA HOTEL, Pescador Dr., San Pedro, Ambergris Caye. Tel. 501/26-2360. 12 rms (7 with bath).

$ Rates: B$21 ($10.50) single, B$52.50 ($26.25) single with bath; B$42 ($21) double, B$63 ($31.50) double with bath. AE, MC, V.

Just up the street from Martha's Hotel and grocery store is the fairly new Casa Blanca Hotel and Zetina's Restaurant. As the name implies, this is a "white house." The rooms are on the second floor, upstairs from the restaurant, and there is also a TV lounge. There are tile floors throughout, and each room has a couple of chairs or a couch. Though the rooms are large, the bathrooms are not. This is a step above the basic budget hotel and represents one of the best deals on the island. The restaurant is also excellent, with such meals as conch soup with rice for B$7 ($3.50).

MILO'S, P.O. Box 21, San Pedro, Ambergris Caye. Tel. 501/26-2033. Fax 501/26-2463 10 rms (none with bath).

$ Rates: B$20 ($10) single; B$25 ($12.50) double; B$30 ($15) triple. No credit cards.

Milo's are the cheapest rooms on the island for a few reasons: You'll share a bathroom with someone else, the rooms are rather dark, and there's no atmosphere to speak of. Some people swear by Milo's, though. The question you must answer for yourself is: How much time will I be spending in my room? At least the shared bathrooms here are clean. You can find out about rooms here in the general store downstairs. Milo's is just before the Paradise Hotel on Front Street.

PIRATE'S LANTERN GUEST HOUSE, San Pedro, Ambergris Caye. Tel. 501/26-2146. 5 rms, 1 apartment (all with bath).

$ Rates: B$40 ($20) single; B$50 ($25) double; B$60 ($30) triple. MC, V.

Though it is a bit of a walk south from the airport, this small guest house benefits from being outside of town. There are trees and shrubs out here, and the second-floor rooms overlook a shrubby area that attracts several different species of birds. Rooms have hardwood floors and wicker furniture and there's a veranda across the second floor. There's a restaurant and bar on the first floor where you can listen to live music Monday and Wednesday nights. If you're paying by credit card, add 5% to your bill.

RUBY'S HOTEL, Barrier Reef Dr., P.O. Box 56, San Pedro. Tel. 501/26-2063. Fax 501/26-2434. 18 rms (15 with bath).

 FROMMER'S SMART TRAVELER: HOTELS

1. Consider renting a house for your stay if you're coming here with your family or a group of friends. Most rental houses are in the more attractive parts of the island away from San Pedro. Check with Amigo Travel (tel. 26-2180) on Barrier Reef Drive.

2. If you're on a tight budget, get a room without a private bath. There are only a few of these left on the island, so be sure to make a reservation.

3. Visit the island during the summer (June through Aug), if you can stand the heat, and you'll pay lower rates at most hotels.

4. If you crave peace and quiet, try to get as far away from the airport as possible (though luckily flights only operate during daylight hours).

$ Rates: B$26.25–B$31.50 ($13.15–$15.75) single or double without bath; B$44.10–B$76.65 ($22.05–$38.35) single or double with bath. No credit cards.
Down at the airport end of town, you'll find a place called Ruby's. Most of the rooms overlook the water. In fact, this is definitely the cheapest place on the island with a water view. The floors are wooden, the rooms are simply furnished with a couple of beds and little else, and the showers are generally clean.

DOUBLES FOR LESS THAN B$65 ($32.50)

**HOTEL SAN PEDRANO, Barrier Reef Dr. San Pedro, Ambergris Caye.
Tel. 501/26-2054** or 26-2093. 7 rms, 1 apartment, (all with bath).
$ Rates: B$50 ($25) single; B$60 ($30) double; B$75 ($37.50) triple, B$20 ($10) extra with A/C); B$375 ($187.50) apt. per week. AE, MC, V.
Although few of the rooms here have ocean views, they do have nice wooden floors and well-maintained blue patio furniture. There are a single and a double bed in every room and clean baths with tubs. What views you do have from the wide veranda are over the rooftops of adjacent buildings. The hotel is upstairs from a small gift shop toward the northern end of Front Street.

**TOMAS HOTEL, Barrier Reef Dr. San Pedro, Ambergris Caye. Tel.
501/26-2061.** 8 rms (all with bath).
$ Rates: B$42–B$52.50 ($21–$26.25) single; B$52.50 double, B$63–B$73.50 ($31.50–$36.75) double with A/C; B$63 ($31.50) triple, B$84 ($42) triple with A/C. MC, V.
Toward the north end of Front Street, directly across the street from an old blue wooden house with flower designs on it, you'll spot the sign for the Tomas Hotel. The modern cement building is one of the better budget hotels on the island. All the rooms were recently renovated and have tile floors, very clean bathrooms, and fans. There's a deck on the second floor where you can get a bit of sun.

DOUBLES FOR LESS THAN B$75 ($37.50)

LILY'S, on the beach, San Pedro, Ambergris Caye. Tel. 501/26-2059. 10 rms (all with bath).
$ Rates: B$42–B$52.50 ($21–$26.25) single; B$57.75–B$73.50 ($28.90–$36.75) double. No credit cards.
If you want a private bath and a water view, you'll have to pay for it. Lily's is on the beach, right behind the Tomas Hotel, which is toward the north end of Front Street. The rooms are large and have ceiling and table fans, wood paneling, and typical fluorescent lighting. Get your money's worth by watching the sun rise every morning and listening to the waves lap at your doorstep after the sun sets. You'll find a seating area on the front veranda and lounge chairs on the beach for the guests' use. Don't forget your mosquito repellent. Not all of the rooms here have a water view—be sure to ask.

MARTHA'S, Pescador Dr., San Pedro, Ambergris Caye. Tel. 501/26-2053. 14 rms (all with bath).
$ Rates: B$25–B$46 ($12.50–$23) single; B$45–B$69 ($22.50–$34.50) double; B$60–B$92 ($30–$46) triple; B$80–B$115 ($40–$57.50) quad. MC, V.
It's hard to believe that a hotel located upstairs from a grocery store could be so expensive, but here in San Pedro, nothing is cheap. At least the new rooms here are larger than those at most other hotels. There are reading lights over the two double beds, ceiling fans, and big verandas at either end of the building so that you can watch the sunrise or sunset. You'll find Martha's about halfway down Pescador Drive.

WORTH THE EXTRA BUCKS

**BARRIER REEF HOTEL, Barrier Reef Dr. San Pedro, Ambergris Caye.
Tel. 501/26-2075.** Fax 501/26-2719. 10 rms (all with bath).

$ Rates: B$100.80 ($50.40) single; B$136.50 ($68.25) double; B$157.50 ($78.75) triple. AE, MC, V.

⭐ This pricey little hotel is my favorite building in San Pedro. Directly across the street from the town square, the Barrier Reef is a blindingly white building designed to resemble a traditional Caribbean wooden house. On the second floor is a long veranda, and on the third floor is a small balcony. Three gables extend seaward from the roof to complete the picture. Each room has a double and a single bed with a built-in headboard, tile floors, a fan or air conditioning. The nicest rooms are those facing the water, for the view and for access to the nicest section of veranda. On the first floor, the Navigator restaurant and bar is a very casual place serving pizza for B$16 to B$38 ($8 to $19). Daily specials include such fare as shrimp scampi and fish filet in lemon sauce.

OASIS DE MAR, c/o General Delivery, San Pedro Town, Ambergris Caye. Tel. 501/26-2925. 6 cabins (all with bath).
$ Rates: B$102.90 ($51.45) single or double; B$115.50 ($57.75). No credit cards.
Located just south of the airport on the outskirts of town, this collection of tropical cabins really lives up to its name. Though the frequent flights make this place noisy during the day, the shade trees, flowers, and shrubs make it a genuine oasis in barren San Pedro. The cabins sleep up to four people and are all quite spacious. High ceilings, louvered windows, and ceiling fans help keep the rooms cool and there are kitchenettes. Though the price is high for one or two people, this is a deal for three or four.

LONG-TERM STAYS

San Pedro is Belize's number-one tourist destination, and it has more vacation and retirement homes than anywhere else in the country. Consequently, there are quite a few houses available for rent on a daily, weekly, or monthly basis. Check with Amigo Travel (tel. 26-2180) on Barrier Reef Drive.

WHERE TO EAT

Seafood is, of course, the most popular food on the island, and there's plenty of it around all year. However, please keep in mind that there are seasons for lobster, conch, shrimp, and sea turtles (sea turtles are endangered, and turtle should never be ordered). Lobster is available from July 15 to March 14; conch is available from October 2 to June 30, and shrimp is available from August 15 to April 14. When lobster is in season, it's the best deal on the island, and you can order it for three meals a day and not go bankrupt. However, it is rock lobster and is not as flavorful as northern, cold-water lobster.

MEALS FOR LESS THAN B$10 [$5]

AMBERGRIS DELIGHT, Pescador Dr. No phone.
   Cuisine: BELIZEAN.
   $ Prices: B$6–B$12 ($3–$6). No credit cards.
   Open: Lunch daily 11am–2pm; dinner daily 6–10pm.
Located a block north of Elvi's, Ambergris Delight is popular with locals and offers excellent and inexpensive burgers and seafood. A big blackboard serves as menu and includes occasional specials such as conch soup. The best deals are the combination dinners of rice and beans served with a fish filet, whole fried fish, broiled fish, or chicken for B$10 ($5). There are always a few cakes and pies on the counter.

BARRIER REEF RESTAURANT, Barrier Reef Hotel, Barrier Reef Dr. Tel. 26-2075.
   Cuisine: SEAFOOD/PIZZA.
   $ Prices: Dinners B$14–B$28 ($7–$14); pizza B$16–B$38 ($8–$19). MC, V.
   Open: Sun–Thurs 7am–midnight, Fri–Sat 7am–2am.
As the name implies, the motif here is nautical. Glass Japanese fishing floats hang from

the ceiling, the stern of a small boat juts out from a wall à la the Hard Rock Café, and trophy fish hang on the walls. Aside from these decorations, the restaurant is rather plain, with cement floors and wooden booths. However, the Navigator serves some of the tastiest and most unusual pizza I've ever had. Try a taco pizza, a seafood special with lobster, or perhaps the shrimp BLT pizza. You can also get sandwiches and daily seafood specials, such as shrimp scampi and fish filet in lemon-butter sauce. The salads here are also quite good.

THE PIZZA PLACE, Fido's Courtyard, Barrier Reef Dr. No phone.
   Cuisine: PIZZA.
$ Prices: Whole pizza B$20–B$32 ($10–$16); per slice B$3–B$5 ($1.50–$2.50). No credit cards.
   Open: Dinner Sun–Thurs 6:30–9pm, dinner Fri–Sat 6:30–10pm.
For a light snack any day of the week, try this walk-up window. Sit at bar stools under a palapa hut, or take your meal away. If you want a combo selection, the minimum order is two pieces. Juices and shakes are B$2.50 ($1.25) but aren't very big. A large pizza here is plenty for four people. Don't confuse the seating area with San Pedro's Grill, which is fine for a drink but overpriced for the food served.

MEALS FOR LESS THAN B$20 [$10]

ELVI'S KITCHEN, halfway down Pescador Dr. Tel. 26-2176.
   Cuisine: SEAFOOD/INTERNATIONAL.
$ Prices: Seafood dinners B$10–B$35 ($5–$17.50). AE, MC, V.
   Open: Lunch Mon–Sat 11am–2pm; dinner Mon–Sat 5:30–10pm.

Elvi's is the most popular restaurant on Ambergris Caye, and it may be the only restaurant in all of Belize that ever has a waiting line. Even after they enlarged the dining room, they still couldn't handle the dinner crowds who came for the substantial servings, good prices, and food cooked to order. The restaurant is a thatched, screened-in hut with picnic tables, a tree growing up through the roof, and a floor of crushed shells and sand—very tropical. Fans cool the place nicely. A typical dinner here might include squid, scallops, and shrimps in red sauce with spaghetti, okra, and cream of vegetable soup. Be sure to have a fruit shake (*licuado*) while you're here.

JADE GARDEN, ½ mile south of airstrip. Tel. 26-2126 or 2506.
   Cuisine: CHINESE.
$ Prices: Appetizers B$9–B$12 ($4.50–$6); main dishes B$6–B$33 ($3–$16.50). AE, MC, V.
   Open: Daily 11am–2pm, 6–10pm.

(F) **FROMMER'S SMART TRAVELER:
RESTAURANTS**

1. Order seafood as much as possible—it tends to be less expensive than other entrées.
2. For the best deal, look for combination plates with rice and beans and a meat or fish course.
3. If you're in the mood for a splurge but don't want to bust your budget, have lunch at a resort restaurant. These are on the whole the best restaurants on the island, and prices at lunch are cheaper than dinner.
4. Please don't order lobster during the closed season (Mar 15–July 15), even if it is available. Also please don't order sea turtle; though this is a common dish in Belize, all species of sea turtles are endangered.

Located in a large contemporary house south of the airport, Jade Garden has long been San Pedro's most popular restaurant. Wicker chairs, overhead fans, high ceilings, and a balcony overlooking the sea and garden create the atmosphere, and the kitchen serves up a long menu of well-prepared Chinese standards with the emphasis on seafood. There are also several non-Chinese specialties such as surf-and-turf kebabs, broiled lobster, and T-bone steak. After a big dinner, you can walk back to your hotel and burn up a few calories.

MARINO'S, one block south of Elvi's on Pescador Dr. Tel. 26-2184.
   Cuisine: SEAFOOD/BELIZEAN.
$ Prices: B$7–B$15 ($3.50–$7.50). No credit cards.
   Open: Daily 7:30am–10pm.
While tourists flock to Elvi's, locals go to Marino's. There isn't as much atmosphere, but the prices are a bit lower and you won't have to stand in line to get a table. The restaurant is quite spartan, but there are some works by local artists hanging on the walls. The best deal in the house is the rice and beans with fried fish and potato salad for B$7 ($3.50). If you're especially hungry, start your meal with conch fritters or fish fingers for B$6 ($3). This is where to try local Creole dishes like boil up (pronounced "bile-up"), which is made with pig tail and root vegetables.

WORTH THE EXTRA BUCKS

LILY'S, on the beach in the middle of town. Tel. 26-2059.
   Cuisine: SEAFOOD.
$ Prices: Breakfast B$8 ($4); dinner B$25 ($12.50). MC, V.
   Open: Breakfast 6:30–10:30am; dinner 6–9pm; lunch by request.
Lily's Hotel, on the waterfront, is also home to one of the best restaurants in San Pedro. You don't get much choice here, but if you like seafood, you'll love this place. A fish, lobster, conch, or fish/shrimp combo dinner costs B$25 and is served family style so that you can eat your fill. The delicious food is cooked to order and comes with french fries, cole slaw, and a vegetable. The restaurant itself is brightly lit, but there are candles on the tables and wicker chairs for atmosphere.

COCO PALMS RESTAURANT, Sun Breeze Resort at the south end of Barrier Reef Dr. Tel. 26-2191.
   Cuisine: SEAFOOD/MEXICAN.
$ Prices: Complete meals B$12–B$35 ($6–$17.50). AE, MC, V.
   Open: Daily 6–10pm.
For an elegant and delicious splurge meal, head down to this elegant tropical restaurant behind the Sunbreeze Resort. Comfortable wicker chairs, ceiling fans, and coral-pink and sea-foam-green linen set the mood. The service and food are both excellent. On a hot sunny day, the large windows and air conditioning make this the ideal place for relaxing and enjoying the sight of palm trees. Start your meal with ceviche or a salad, then move on to something like the seafood platter (the most expensive item on the menu, but it comes with generous portions of shrimp, lobster, conch, and fish) or something less pricey, such as Caribbean fish broiled with mayonnaise, lime juice, bell peppers, onions, and tomatoes for B$22 ($11).

EVENING ENTERTAINMENT

THE TACKLE BOX BAR, off Barrier Reef Dr. near the south end of town. No phone.
   The first thing to do is drop in for beer (B$3, $1.50) or a piña colada (B$7, $3.50) here at San Pedro's most famous bar, out at the end of a short pier. Local fishermen and sailors gather here to exchange information. If you want a boat to another caye, the folks behind the bar will be able to set you up with a ride. Nautical motifs decorate the interior, and out behind the back terrace is an enclosed tank full of sharks and giant sea turtles. Don't miss it! The last time I was there, a sign had been posted to the effect that British soldiers were no longer admitted due to their unruly behavior. So don't expect any Hollywood-style brawls here.

BIG DADDY'S, across from the Barrier Reef Hotel and behind the church. No phone.
Nowhere have I ever seen a bar or disco located so close to a church. The saints and sinners seem to be in a competition to see who can play the loudest music. The church often throws its doors open and cranks up the volume on its organ, but there always seems to be more people in the disco. The dress is casual, and the drinks are not overpriced.

EXCURSIONS

If you've been on the island for a while and want to see more of Belize contact **Amigo Travel** (tel. 26-2180) or **Universal Travel & Tours** (tel. 26-2031), both on Barrier Reef Drive. They offer excursions to various locations—including Altun Ha, Xunantunich, Mountain Pine Ridge, and Tikal. The popular day trip to the Mayan ruins at Altun Ha begins on the *Hustler,* a powerful little boat that will whisk you over to the mainland. You'll then take a taxi to the ruins and have lunch before returning to San Pedro for B$130 ($65) per person. Call 026-2538 or 026-2279.

---

3. CAYE CAULKER

20 miles N of Belize City; 10 miles S of Ambergris Caye.

GETTING THERE   By Air   Island Air (tel. 2-31140 in Belize City) has daily flights to Caye Caulker from both the international and municipal airports in Belize City. Duration: 20–30 minutes. Fare: B$35 ($17.50) one way from municipal airport, B$50 ($25) one way from international airport. Island Air (tel. 26-2435 in San Pedro) also flies between Ambergris Caye and Caye Caulker. Duration: 15 minutes. Fare: B$35 ($17.50) one way, B$60 ($30) round-trip. If you just flew in to Belize from another country and are heading directly to Caye Caulker, you might as well fly because the combination taxi into Belize City and boat to Caye Caulker cost B$45 ($22.50), only B$5 less than the plane.

By Boat   High-speed launches leave from behind the Shell gas station on North Front Street. You'll find the gas station about 50 yards west of the Swing Bridge, downtown Belize City's main reference point. Several boats a day leave between 10am and 3pm. Duration: 50 minutes. Fare: B$15 ($7.50). You pay when you arrive at Caye Caulker. Unsavory street guides will offer to take you to the boat to Caye Caulker; these guides are not to be trusted, so don't wander off with one to negotiate any deals.
The *Andrea* and *Andrea II,* which leave from Southern Foreshore near the Bellevue Hotel, primarily serve Ambergris Caye but will stop at Caye Caulker if you arrange it with the captain. These two boats leave Monday through Saturday at 4pm.

DEPARTING   There are daily flights to both Belize City airports and to Ambergris Caye. Contact Dolphin Bay Travel, on Front Street (tel. 22-2214), to make a reservation on Island Air. The boats heading back to Belize City charge only B$10 ($5) rather than the B$15 they charge for getting to the island. Most boats leave Caye Caulker between 6 and 7am. It's a good idea to buy your ticket the day before you plan to leave. If you contact Jan's Travel Service at the north end of Caye Caulker (next door to Jan's Deli), you can arrange for the *Andrea* or *Andrea II* to pick you up on its way to Ambergris Caye. The fare to San Pedro is B$15 ($7.50). You can also sail over to Ambergris Caye on one of the sailboats that go out to the Hol Chan Marine Reserve; these boats usually leave Caye Caulker around 10am and stop for lunch in San Pedro in the afternoon. Instead of sailing back, you can just stay in San Pedro.

ESSENTIALS   Orientation   Most boats dock at the Front Bridge, so named because this is the front side of the island facing the reef (east). The town extends north and south from here. As you debark, you'll be able to see the western side of the island and the Back Bridge/dock. Caye Caulker consists of two main sand roads, a few cross streets, and numerous paths.

Fast Facts   There was no bank on Caye Caulker during my last visit, but you can change money and traveler's checks at most hotels. Even if a bank does open, you'll probably get a better rate at the hotels. Several women on the island take in laundry; watch for their signs around town. The telephone office is about midway along Front Street and is open Monday to Friday 8am to noon and 1 to 4pm, Saturday 8am to noon. If you are calling somewhere else in Belize, remember to dial 0 before the phone number. Though Caye Caulker is still a relatively safe place, it is not advisable to leave money or valuables in your hotel room.

For more than 20 years Caye Caulker was the preferred destination of young backpackers traveling on a very low budget. Rooms and meals were cheap and the atmosphere was truly laid back. Though many new hotels and restaurants and even a few gift shops have sprouted over the years, the island remains basically the same. This may all be changing now that Caye Caulker has its very own airstrip and is connected to both Belize City and San Pedro by air. There are no resorts yet, but hotels on the island have been renovating in anticipation of more well-to-do guests.

On the other hand, some locals and resident foreigners have been trying to enact building codes and establish a nature and marine reserve here. However, pressures from developers are intense. Hopefully the island will not become as overbuilt and shadeless as San Pedro.

One more thing you should know about Caye Caulker—it's home to nasty sand fleas, a tiny insect with a vicious bite that leaves an itchy welt. These sand fleas come out whenever the trade winds die. When this happens, the best solution is to put on socks and long pants, since they tend to bite feet and ankles. Sitting out at the end of a long pier also offers some relief.

WHAT TO SEE & DO

The main activity on Caye Caulker is swimming and sunbathing at The Cut or off the docks. Currents through The Cut can be swift, and only strong swimmers or those with flippers should attempt to swim it. The water is very calm off Back Bridge, making it a good place to practice if you're an inexperienced snorkeler. Take care if you're swimming off a dock. After a swimmer was killed by a boat, a designated swimming area was set aside off the Front Bridge.

Several boats leave from the front-side docks on half-day trips to the reef. For safety's sake, the boat should be in good condition, with a working motor (even on sailboats) in case the seas become rough or in the rare event that a quick rescue is needed. Your guide should be attentive and aware of your experience or inexperience.

Ellen McRae, resident marine biologist and founder of Cari Search, Ltd. (a group dedicated to research and protection of Belize's natural environment), advises that "you'll be safe with just about any of the residents who take people out, but it's still best to find out about the recent experiences of fellow tourists on the island." If you want to know more about what you'll see at the reef, Ellen offers a Reef Ecology Tour that includes a 1-hour lecture in the morning before an afternoon of guided snorkeling for B$24 ($12) with gear rental extra. She also offers 3-hour bird/cayes ecology hikes for B$10 ($5). Bring binoculars if you have them. You can find Ellen at the **Galeria Hicaco** (tel. 022-2178) gift shop, near the Tropical Paradise, which features original artwork made in Belize.

Another local to look for is resident artist Philip Lewis, whose drawings of Belize and detailed map of Caulker are sold in the Galeria. If you'd like to see more than what's on display, Philip (also known by his nickname, "Karate") can usually be found eating the heavenly ice cream at the Tropical in the mornings; he'll be the one carrying the large sketchpad.

Sea-ing is Belizing (open daily from 9am to 5pm) is a gallery which specializes in underwater photography by co-owner James Beveridge, who has been photographing Belize since 1969. Besides selling photographic postcards and framed and unframed prints, the gallery offers a slide show illustrating the reefs and cayes. The program is held regularly at 8pm. It costs B$4 ($2) per person. They also offer T-shirts, books about Belize, and film processing.

Right beside Sea-ing Is Belizing is **Belize Diving Services** (tel. 022-2143), Caye Caulker's only full-service dive center. Open Monday to Saturday from 8am to 5pm; Sunday from 10am to 4pm. A two-tank dive will cost you B$80 ($40). They also offer cave diving to certified cave divers, 4-day scuba-diving courses, and equipment rental.

In terms of shopping, there are only a few shops on the island: a couple of general stores, a few gift shops, and **Jan's Deli,** a good place to pick up bread, cheese, yogurt, drinks, and other staples, open Monday to Saturday from 7am to 1pm and 3 to 7pm, Sunday from 8am to noon.

For evening entertainment, you can stargaze, go for a night dive, or have a drink in one of the island's handful of bars. That's about it for nightlife on Caye Caulker.

WHERE TO STAY

Accommodations on Caye Caulker have improved in recent years, but they're still far from luxurious. In the off-season (May through Aug), it's possible to get substantial discounts. However, you'll have to put up with biting flies in May and mosquitoes in June, July, and August. Besides the hotels listed below, there are furnished houses for rent on Caye Caulker—just walk around, and you'll see signs for them.

DOUBLES FOR LESS THAN B$35 [$17.50]

THE ANCHORAGE, south of the Front Bridge, Caye Caulker. No phone. 4
   rms (all with bath).
$ Rates: B$30 ($15) single or double. No credit cards.
A 10-minute walk south of the Front Bridge, the Anchorage is the sort of place tropical travelers on a very low budget dream about—white sand, coconut palms rustling in the trade winds, turquoise water, and the distant murmur of waves crashing on the barrier reef. There are four whitewashed adobe huts with palm-thatch roofs, each with its own bath (cold-water showers only). American Jo Ann Wilson is the owner here.

**IGNACIO'S BEACH CABAÑAS, south of Front Bridge, Caye Caulker. No
   phone.** 13 rms (all with bath).
$ Rates: B$30 ($15) single, double, or triple. No credit cards.
These are currently the accommodations most popular with the backpack set. Located next to the Anchorage, the cabañas here are brightly painted little wooden boxes that sit right on the sand or up a bit on stilts and give the appearance of a shanty town, but the groups of young people relaxing in hammocks strung between the palm trees indicate that this is a low-budget tropical paradise. The owner, Ignacio, is one of the island's more colorful characters.

JIMENEZ CABAÑAS, Caye Caulker. Tel. 501/22-2175. 4 rms (none with
   bath), 4 cabañas.
$ Rates: B$10 ($5) single; B$15 ($7.50) double; cabañas B$30 ($15) single, B$42
   ($21) double, B$52 ($26) triple, B$63 ($31.50) quad. MC, V.
Across the island from the Tropical Paradise Hotel (below) is this very attractive little grouping of cabañas set in a sunny garden with conch shell–lined walkway. The cabañas are peaceful and secluded, and have palm-trunk walls, thatched roofs, and little porches. Inside each contains one or two double beds, a hammock, and a very basic bathroom with cold water only. The other four rooms are not nearly as nice, so hold out for a hut. The owner was a lobster fisherman for years until the lobster harvest began to decline.

TOM'S HOTEL, south of Front Bridge. Tel. 501/22-21020. 23 rms (5 with
   bath).
$ Rates: B$21 ($10.50) single or double without bath, B$53.50 ($26.75) single,
   double, or triple with bath. No credit cards.

The rooms here are tiny and can get hot and stuffy, but if you spend all your time snorkeling or hanging out elsewhere, you won't mind very much. It's certainly difficult to beat the prices. There is a veranda overlooking the water and a private dock for tanning. The cabañas, with private baths, are much roomier than the rooms in the main building. Consider the rooms last resorts if none of the cabañas are available.

DOUBLES FOR LESS THAN B$70 [$35]

RAINBOW HOTEL, north of Front Bridge, Caye Caulker. Tel. 501/22-2123. 16 rms (all with bath).
$ Rates: B$40–B$50 ($20–$25) single; B$50–B$60 ($25–$30) double; B$60–B$70 ($30–$35) triple; lower rates May–Oct. MC, V.
Located next door to the Reef Hotel, the Rainbow is very similar in appearance to the Reef, both inside and out. Only a few feet from the water it has a veranda and a private dock for guests. The rooms are clean, with tiled showers, ceiling fans, and louvered windows that let in the breezes. Double and twin beds are available. It may be difficult to find the manager; sometimes there's someone around and sometimes there isn't.

SEA BEEZZ, Caye Caulker. Tel. 501/22-2176 or (in the U.S.) 602/451-0040. 6 rms (all with bath).
$ Rates: B$63 ($31.50) single or double. MC, V.
Gray buildings with white trim give this place a bit of Cape Cod styling, but the iron bars on the windows remind you that you are in Central America. Although the guest rooms are modern and clean and have ceiling fans and hot water, they are situated in such a way that they don't catch the breezes. To make up for this, there is a pretty garden with tables in the sand only steps from the water. Sea Beezz also has its own small restaurant and bar that serves excellent (though expensive) margaritas.

TROPICAL PARADISE HOTEL, RESTAURANT, AND ICE CREAM PARLOUR, Caye Caulker. Tel. 501/022-2124. Fax 501/22-2225. 5 rms, 5 cabañas, 5 suites (all with bath).
$ Rates: B$50–B$60 ($25–$30) single; B$55–B$110 ($27.50–$55) double. DISC, MC, V.
This should be your first choice for both a room and a good meal on Caye Caulker. Proprietor Ramon Reyes runs a tight ship: The rooms are very clean and paneled, with a little bit of storage space for your things and a narrow front porch for catching the breeze. The hot water is a bit finicky, however. The cabins and suites are the most expensive and are quite a bit larger than the rooms. But the cabins aren't as breezy as the rooms at the back of the complex behind the restaurant that bears the same name. This is as good as budget accommodations get in Belize. They even have a hot tub.

WHERE TO EAT

As on Ambergris Caye, seafood is popular and plentiful all year but cheaper than in San Pedro. Do remember to abide by the seasons on lobster, conch, shrimp, and don't order turtle steaks (sea turtles are endangered). The seasons are the same for Ambergris Caye. Restaurants are not supposed to serve lobster in the off-season, when the lobsters are breeding. If it's on the menu off-season, please don't order it.

Caye Caulker has a thriving cottage industry of snack bakers. Wander the streets and you're sure to see signs offering yogurt and granola, freshly squeezed juices, hot lobster pie, sweet rolls, chocolate or cheese pie—each B$1 (50¢). Don't be bashful: Just step right up and knock on the door for a homemade treat. You won't be disappointed. (It's also a chance to get a glimpse into a few Belizean homes.) For more substantial meals, try one of the restaurants listed below.

MEALS FOR LESS THAN B$15 [$7.50]

ABERDEEN RESTAURANT, just south of the Hotel Martinez. Tel. 022-2127.

Cuisine: CHINESE.
$ Prices: B$8–B$16 ($4–$8). MC, V.
Open: Daily 6:30am–10pm.

The menu is Chinese, the music is reggae, the servings are generous, and the decor is sparse. You can pick from a long list of all the standards prepared with nearly every type of meat or seafood. How about sweet-and-sour conch or lobster chop suey. The most interesting dishes available are listed on the back of the menu: tempting offerings such as salty pepper shrimp and lobster with peppers and black soy beans. If you've been missing vegetables in your diet, this is the place to eat your fill.

HOTEL MARTINEZ'S RESTAURANT AND BAR, north of Front Bridge near the Reef Hotel. Tel. 022-2113.
Cuisine: SEAFOOD/MEXICAN.
$ Prices: Breakfast B$4–B$5 ($2–$2.50); lunch and dinner B$7–B$12 ($3.50–$6). No credit cards.
Open: Daily 7am–10pm.

Martinez's serves throughout the day, and it's almost always busy with locals and tourists alike. Start your day here with lobster and eggs for B$9 ($4.50); for lunch and dinner, you have your choice of steaks, burgers, lobster, and fish. Do try a fishburger at least once while you're here. Whenever hunger strikes, you can duck in here and get a cheap fast Mexican snack for 75B¢ (40¢). Plus, there's always the old standby of rice and beans or beans and rice. Martinez's popular rum punch is sold by the bottle for B$10 ($5) or by the glass for B$2.50 ($1.25)—it's guaranteed to put you in a tropical frame of mind.

SAND BOX RESTAURANT, on the water just before The Cut. Tel. 022-2200.
Cuisine: SEAFOOD/INTERNATIONAL.
$ Prices: B$8–B$12 ($4–$6). No credit cards.
Open: Daily noon–3pm and 5–10pm.

The old wooden building isn't very big and with sand on the floor of the dining room and a few tables in the sand out front, it is appropriately named. The menu here is rather eclectic and is posted on a little bulletin board that is brought to your table. There are salad plates, crunchy conch fritters, and nachos. Shrimp shows up in curried shrimp, shrimp lasagne, and a delicious bisque. For those with a sweet tooth, there are root beer floats, cheesecake, and tropical fruit ice creams.

TROPICAL PARADISE HOTEL RESTAURANT AND ICE CREAM PARLOR, south of Front Bridge. Tel. 022-2124.
Cuisine: INTERNATIONAL.
$ Prices: Breakfast B$3–B$7 ($1.50–$3.50); dinner B$7–B$15 ($3.50–$7.50). No credit cards.
Open: Daily 8am–2pm and 6–9pm.

The Tropical Paradise stays packed for all three meals. It's so popular because it serves the most consistent food on the island at very good prices. Inside, it's light and breezy and has the feel of a small-town diner. Try one of the dinner specials, such as curried lobster for B$15.50 ($7.75). In the afternoon and evening, everyone on the island comes for soft ice cream, which goes for B$1.50 (75¢) small and B$2 ($1) large. Flavors change daily and include vanilla, blueberry, peach, peanut, and chocolate.

MEALS FOR LESS THAN B$25 [$12.50]

MARIN'S RESTAURANT, located a block west of the Tropical Paradise. Tel. 022-2104.
Cuisine: INTERNATIONAL.
$ Prices: Complete dinner B$8–B$18 ($3.50–$9). MC.
Open: Daily 8am–2pm and 5:30–10pm.

There's plenty of local atmosphere here, with soca music playing all day long. Marin's serves fresh seafood in its outdoor garden or in its mosquito-proof dining room. Try the shrimp or lobster with pineapple (Belizean style, sweet-and-sour) for B$18 ($9) or the catch of the day (steamed, fried, or baked) for B$9 ($4.50). If you're starving, go for the Marin's special, a platter of fried shrimp, conch, and fish.

4. MORE CAYES

As Ambergris Caye and Caye Caulker become more developed and crowded, intrepid travelers in search of unspoiled havens have sought out the more secluded cayes. Luckily the inhabitants of these cayes offer lodges and resorts in various price ranges. If you're searching for tranquillity, then you might want to try one of these more isolated cayes. Though remote cayes can be difficult or expensive to reach, that is the price one must pay for solitude these days.

As one island becomes too pricey, you can bet that another will begin attracting budget travelers—after all, Belize has hundreds of cayes of various sizes. Below are a few of the places that have sprung up in recent years.

NORTHERN LONG CAYE

CASTAWAYS, P.O. Box 1706, Belize City. Tel. (in Belize City) 501/2-32837 or 2-32634. Fax 501/2-75831. 6 rms (all with bath).
$ Rates (including three meals): B$70 ($35) single; B$120 ($60) double (10% discount for stays of 2 or more days). AE, MC, V.

Castaways is located on Northern Long Caye, 16 miles north of Belize City, and can be reached by taking any boat bound for Caye Caulker and telling the boatman where you are headed. The fare is B$12 ($6) each way. Northern Long Caye is about two miles long and is home to a few lobster fishing families and little else but birds, iguanas, mangroves, and palms. Rooms are simply furnished but have fans for hot nights. There are good views from all the rooms, and a large deck for socializing or sipping a cocktail. Meals in the dining room range from American favorites to Belizean standards such as rice and beans. As you may have guessed, there isn't much to do here, but you can snorkel on the reef, bird watch, or work on your tan. A great place to do a lot of reading.

LONG CAYE

GLOVER'S ATOLL RESORT, P.O. Box 563, Belize City. Tel. 501/8-22505. 8 cabins (none with bath).
$ Rates: B$150 ($75) per person for 5 nights; B$244 ($122) per person for 12 nights; B$45 ($22.50) per person for 5 nights camping. No credit cards.

Located on Long Caye, off the central coast southeast of Dangriga, Glover's Atoll Resort is a very rustic sort of place that should appeal to hardy travelers accustomed to camping. Each of the cabins sleeps two and has its own kitchenette. You'll need to bring your own food for the duration of your stay, although you should be able to catch or buy fish while you are here. You'll also have to carry water from a well. The cabins have their own showers and outhouses. The reef here is within swimming distance of the shore, the snorkeling is excellent, and the scuba diving is said to be the second best in Belize—the Blue Hole is considered the best.

Long Caye is reached by a private boat that leaves from Sittee River Village every Sunday at 8am. The boat ride takes five hours and is included in the room rate. The best way to catch the boat is to spend the night in Sittee River Village at the Glover's Atoll Guest House, where a bed is only B$5 ($2.50). To get to Sittee River Village, take the Saturday Z-Line bus that leaves for Punta Gorda at 3pm and be sure to tell the driver that you want to get off at the Sittee River turnoff. From here a truck will take you the rest of the way to Sittee River Village. The bus fare is B$6 ($3) and truck fare is B$4 ($2).

TOBACCO CAYE

Located 12 miles east of the town of Dangriga, Tobacco Caye sits right in the middle of the barrier reef and surrounds a shallow lagoon, so the snorkeling is always good. The island is only about 200 yards by 350 yards, so you'd better bring a few good books if you head out here. Despite the island's small size, it manages to support several modest lodges and a campground. A boat out here from Dangriga costs B$25 ($12.50) per person if there are two or more people and can be arranged by asking at the fish market near The Hub, the guest house at the last Z-Line bus stop in Dangriga, or by contacting Ralph at the Rio Mar Hotel. If there is only one person, the fare is B$50 ($25). The ride out to Tobacco Caye takes about 30 minutes.

FAIRWEATHER & FRIENDS TOBACCO CAYE GUEST HOUSE, Tobacco Caye. No phone. 10 rms (all with bath).
$ Rates (including three meals): B$50 ($25) per person. No credit cards.
Elwood Fairweather's place is sort of a motel-style hotel that seems a bit out of place on this tiny island, but the low rates do make it attractive. Rooms are very basic.

OCEAN'S EDGE, Tobacco Caye, P.O. Box 10, Dangriga. Tel. 501/5-22142 or 5-22171. 4 cabins (all with bath).
$ Rates (including three meals): B$80 ($40) single; B$150 ($75) double. No credit cards.
Operated by Marlo Jackson, the Ocean's Edge offers the most interesting accommodations on the island. The four cabins are all about seven feet off the ground and are attached to one another by an elevated walkway. There are fans to keep you cool and screens to keep out the insects. Water for showers is provided by a rainwater cistern. The room rates here also include snorkeling and fishing equipment and a ride out to the reef.

REEF'S END LODGE, Tobacco Caye, P.O. Box 10, Dangriga. Tel. 501/5-22142 or 5-22171. 4 rms (all with bath).
$ Rates (including three meals): B$80 ($40) single; B$130 ($65) double. No credit cards.
Operated by a former lobsterman, the Reef's End Lodge is a small place with a Caribbean feel. The rooms are in a wooden building with a long veranda across the front. Electricity is provided by photovoltaic cells. The lodge's dining room is built on a pier on the lagoonside of the island, and there's even a ladder leading down from the kitchen into the water. The room rates here also include use of snorkeling equipment, fishing gear, and even a boat ride out to the reef.

REMOTE CAYES

If you are really looking for a Robinson Crusoe adventure, then the cayes listed above might not quite satisfy you. However, if you keep your eyes open whenever you see a bulletin board or a notice pinned on a wall, you will find advertisements for the tiniest of cayes. Places where there may be three palm trees, a hut, and nothing else. Maybe there won't even be the palm trees. Such island getaways are popping up all over, and I've seen notices for little huts on cayes off Ambergris Caye, Caye Caulker, Long Caye, and Placencia. What they all have in common is a small hut where you'll be the only guests. You do your own cooking and stay for a prearranged number of days. If you decide a 30-foot-long island is just too quiet even for you, tough luck, the boat won't be back until the day you told it to return!

CHAPTER 16

ELSEWHERE IN BELIZE

1. BELMOPAN

2. PLACENCIA

3. PUNTA GORDA

4. SAN IGNACIO & THE CAYO DISTRICT

5. COROZAL TOWN & THE NORTHERN HIGHWAY

As is often the case in places blessed with beautiful islands, warm waters, and colorful coral reefs, areas away from the water can be overlooked. When you've had enough sunshine and swimming out on the cayes, spend some time exploring the rest of Belize. Once the heart of the Mayan Empire, Belize has many excavations scattered throughout the country.

In western Belize's Cayo District, a densely forested region of limestone mountains and clear-running rivers, Caracol is the largest Mayan city yet discovered. Though Caracol has not been turned into a major tourist destination like the Mayan ruins in Mexico or Guatemala, it's worth seeing for serious students of Mesoamerican cultures. The mountains here are laced with caves, several of which can be explored.

Wildlife abounds throughout Belize, though it is increasingly endangered. The Belize Zoo, near the capital city of Belmopan, is dedicated to educating the public about the benefits of preserving Belize's wild heritage. South of Belmopan is the Cockscomb Basin Wildlife Preserve, the world's first jaguar preserve. North of Belmopan are the Community Baboon Sanctuary (a howler monkey preserve) and the Crooked Tree Wildlife Sanctuary, another preserve that is home to many rare species of tropical birds.

If you find yourself in need of another dose of beach life, Placencia, in southern Belize, offers the best beach in the country. Miles of sand stretch northward from this tranquil little village at the tip of a long peninsula.

And way down at the isolated southern end of the country, near the town of Punta Gorda, there are numerous villages where Mayan Indians farm the land much as they did 1,000 years ago. If you're interested in staying in a Mayan home to learn more about these indigenous people, this chapter will tell you how.

1. BELMOPAN

52 miles W of Belize City; 30 miles E of San Ignacio; 90 miles N of Placencia

GETTING THERE   By Bus   Batty Bros., Novelos, Z-Line, and Venus all run buses to Belmopan frequently throughout the day. Duration: 1½ hours. Fare: B$2.75 ($1.38).

By Car   From Belize City, take Cemetery Road to the Western Highway.

DEPARTING   Buses run frequently to San Ignacio, Belize City, and Dangriga. From Dangriga you can get a bus to Placencia if you arrive before 3pm on Monday, Wednesday, Friday, or Saturday. It's about 1½ hours to either Belize City or San Ignacio and 3 hours to Dangriga.

ESSENTIALS Orientation Belmopan is a planned city with a ring road and wide deserted streets. There is only one road in or out of the city. It branches off the Hummingbird (Southern) Highway 2½ miles south of the Western Highway.

Conceived as the dynamic center of a growing Belize, Belmopan (pop. 4,000), the capital of Belize, is actually a sleepy place 2½ miles in from the Western Highway. Modest government buildings are laid out according to a master plan, and small residential areas are enclosed by a ring road. Business seems limited to a gas station, a few little food shops, and three modest hostelries. The facilities here that you may find useful are a bank, post office, hospital, and microwave telephone installation.

Belmopan is a model city designed and built from scratch in the jungle at the geographical center of the country. Unfortunately, the planners who designed it didn't count on the people's resistance to moving here. Belmopan has yet to see any substantial growth, and Belize City remains the country's largest city.

The Western Highway to Belmopan (about 50 miles) is sometimes good, sometimes bad. The road to the new capital takes you into the foothills of the Maya Mountains and through farming country that's quite pretty. Onward from Belmopan, the road climbs slowly into the Maya Mountains, and the seamy, ramshackle way of life in Belize's coastal towns gives way to cooler, less humid air, a workaday farming life, and greater natural beauty. The area is home to macaws, mahogany, mangoes, jaguars, and orchids.

WHAT TO SEE & DO

If you're in town on Monday, Wednesday, or Friday morning, you may be able to arrange a guided tour of the vault in the basement of the **Archeology Department** (near the bus station). Since Belize doesn't yet have a museum the many Mayan artifacts found at sites around the country are displayed here.

What follows are several possible excursions that can be made with Belmopan as a base.

By the time you finally get around to visiting the **Belize Zoo,** you'll already be familiar with the zoo's most famous resident—April the tapir—because her picture appears on posters all over the country. April is just one of dozens of species of animals native to Belize that are housed in this zoo. Among the most popular are a variety of indigenous Belizean cats and other wild animals in natural surroundings. The animals here are some of the liveliest and happiest looking that I've ever seen in a zoo. It's obvious that they're well cared for. All the exhibits have informative signs accompanying them.

The entrance is a mile in from the Western Highway. Any bus traveling between Belize City and Belmopan or San Ignacio will drop you off at the zoo entrance. Do a bit of calculating as to when the next bus will be coming by, or plan on hitching to your next destination.

Admission is B$10 ($5). Open daily 9:30am to 4pm, the zoo is at mile 28 Western Highway.

Guanacaste Park, a 50-acre park located where the Hummingbird Highway turns off of the Western Highway, about 2½ miles north of Belmopan, is an excellent introduction to tropical forests. The park is named for a huge old guanacaste tree that is found within the park. Guanacaste trees were traditionally preferred for building dugout canoes, but this particular tree, which is about 100 years old, was spared the boat-builders' ax because it has a triple trunk that makes it unacceptable for canoe building. More than 35 species of epiphytes (plants that grow on other plants), including orchids, bromeliads, ferns, mosses, lichens, and philodendrons cover its trunk and branches.

There are nearly 2 miles of trails in the park, with several benches for sitting and observing wildlife. The park is bordered on the west by Roaring Creek and on the north by the Belize River. Among the animals you might see are more than 100 species of birds, large iguanas, armadillos, kinkajous, deer, agoutis (large rodents that are a favorite game meat in Belize), and jaguarundis (small jungle cats). A map and a brochure about the park are available from the Belize Audubon Society in Belize City.

The Maya Mountains are primarily limestone and consequently, laced with caves—that's why this region of Belize is known as Cave Branch. About 11 miles from Belmopan on the Hummingbird Highway, you'll come across a dirt road to the right. About half a mile down this road is the entrance to **St. Herman's Cave,** one of the largest and most easily accessible caves in Belize. You'll need at least two good flashlights and sturdy shoes to explore this undeveloped ½-mile long cave.

Equally fascinating is the **Blue Hole,** a collapsed cavern just off the Hummingbird Highway, 12½ miles from Belmopan. After locking your car and placing any valuables in the trunk, walk down the cement steps. Dense jungle surrounds a small natural pool of a deep turquoise. A limestone cliff rises up from the edge of the pool on two sides. The water flows for only about 100 feet on the surface before disappearing into a cave. This is a great place for a quick dip on a hot day because the water is refreshingly cool and clear. You can clearly see fish swimming around the edges of the Blue Hole.

WHERE TO STAY & EAT

BANANA BANK RANCH, Box 48, Belmopan. Tel. 501/8-23180 or 8-22677. Fax 501/8-22366. 10 rms (4 with bath).

$ Rates: B$73.50 ($36.75) single without bath, B$115.50–B$136.50 ($57.75–$68.25) single with bath; B$105 ($52.50) double without bath, B$136.50–B$157.50 ($68.25–$78.75) double with bath; B$126 ($63) triple without bath, B$178.50 ($89.25) triple with bath; B$147 ($73.50) quad, B$199.50 ($99.75) quad with bath. Meals extra $26 per person per day. No credit cards.

The turnoff for this fascinating lodge is at Mile 47 on the Western Highway, not far past the turnoff for Belmopan. From here it is about 1¼ miles to the ranch. Owners John and Carolyn Carr moved to Belize from the United States nearly 15 years ago. Carolyn is an artist and John is a cowboy from Montana. Together, they operate one of the oldest cattle ranches in Belize and for several years have been taking in paying guests. The guest quarters are on the banks of the Belize River. Each of the two cabins comes complete with a sleeping loft, room for six people, a private bathroom, two bedrooms, queen-size beds, and plenty of space to spread out and make yourself at home. These cabins also have their own private patios overlooking the river. One room in the main house even has a water bed. On the property you can visit a Mayan ruin and meet the Carr's pet jaguar, Tika. Horseback riding, canoeing, and even horse-drawn buggy rides can be arranged at additional cost. Meals are served in a small dining room. The house specialty is barbecued pork spare ribs, served with all the trimmings.

BULL FROG INN, 25 Half Moon Ave., P.O. Box 28, Belmopan. Tel. 501/8-22111. Fax 501/8-23155. 25 rms (all with bath). A/C TV

$ Rates: B$89.25 ($44.65) single; B$131.25 ($65.65) double; B$157.50 ($78.75) triple. MC, V.

The only other budget lodging in town is just a couple of doors down from the Circle A Hotel. The higher prices are for the new rooms, which are larger and much nicer than the old rooms. The old rooms, although small, have air conditioning, fans, TVs, and carpeting. The new rooms have more light, balconies, phones, and very nice bathrooms with tubs. There's a cool open-air restaurant attached to the hotel serving breakfast for B$7 ($3.50) and lunch and dinner for B$14 to B$16 ($7 to $8).

CIRCLE A HOTEL, 37 Half Moon Ave., Belmopan. Tel. 501/8-22296. 14 rms (all with bath).

$ Rates: B$52.50 ($26.25) single; B$63 ($31.50) double. MC, V.

There aren't too many reasons to come to Belmopan, unless you have business at one of the government ministries. However, if you do stay over, this is the place to check first. To reach the Circle A, take a taxi or drive around the circle road that goes left from the bus station. If you want to walk, it'll take about 10 minutes along the path behind the market to the right; when the path forks, bear left and follow it to the end. A shopping center will be on your right and Half Moon Avenue will be on your left. Most of the rooms here are carpeted, and some have TVs. The restaurant next door is open from 7am to 10pm and serves Chinese food for B$8 ($4) to B$16 ($8).

CAMPING

MONKEY BAY WILDLIFE SANCTUARY, Mile 32 Western Highway, P.O. Box 187, Belmopan. No phone.
About 1½ miles down a dirt road off the Western Highway, four miles west of the Belize Zoo, is a tranquil spot where you can park your RV or pitch a tent. There are no monkeys and no bay, but there are beautiful big trees, acres of pasture, a creek, a river nearby, and plenty of solitude. The privately owned sanctuary is only just being developed and so the facilities are primitive. Register with the caretaker, Pedro Reyes, who lives in the little house on the other side of the fence. The fee for camping is B$5 ($2.50) per night.

2. PLACENCIA

150 miles S of Belize City (120 miles by New Belize Road); 100 miles SE of Belmopan; 55 miles NE of Punta Gorda

GETTING THERE   By Plane   There are six flights daily between Big Creek (across the bay from Placencia) and Belize City on Maya Airways. Fare: B$84 ($42) one way, B$156 ($78) round-trip.

By Bus   On Monday, Wednesday, Friday, and Saturday there is bus service between Dangriga and Placencia. Buses depart Dangriga around 4pm and from Placencia at 6am. Fare: B$7.50 ($3.75). Alternatively, there are several buses daily that operate between Dangriga and Mango Creek (Z-Line and Williams Bus) and between Belize City and Mango Creek (Williams Bus Service from the Pound Yard Bridge and Z-Line from Magazine Road). Fares: from Belize City B$14 ($7), from Dangriga B$5 ($2.50). From Mango Creek, you must take a boat across Placencia Lagoon—see "By Boat" below for details.

By Car   Take the Western Highway from Belize City. Around Mile 30, watch for the New Belize Road turnoff for Democracia and points south. This good dirt road now has a bridge where it was once necessary to ford a river, which was possible only in the dry season. The road cuts 30 miles off the drive to Placencia but bypasses Belmopan, the Blue Hole, St. Herman's Cave, and Guanacaste Park. At the end of the New Belize Road turn left onto the Hummingbird Highway. In 1½ miles, you'll come to the turnoff for the Southern Highway (Dangriga is 6 miles farther). After 22½ miles on the Southern Highway, turn left onto the road to Riversdale and Placencia. From this turnoff it's another 20 miles to Placencia. Be sure to fill your tank in Dangriga.

By Boat   Outboard-powered skiffs, which can carry up to six people, can be hired for the trip across Placencia Lagoon from Big Creek or Mango Creek for B$30 ($15), one way, for one or two people. For three or more, its B$10 ($5) per person.

DEPARTING   The bus for Dangriga leaves Monday, Wednesday, Friday, and Saturday at 6am from Placencia. Buses also leave from Mango Creek several times daily for Dangriga, Belize City, and Punta Gorda. There are also daily flights from Big Creek to Belize City.

ESSENTIALS   Orientation   There's only one road in Placencia, and it ends at the dock and gas station at the south end of town. The town's main thoroughfare is the Sidewalk, a narrow cement path that parallels the beach beginning at the Fishermen's Co-op by the dock.
The post office is at the gas station at the south end of town. Open Monday to

Friday from 8am to noon and 1 to 4pm, Saturday from 8am to 1pm. The village's public phone is at the post office/gas station.

Located at the southern tip of a long, sandy peninsula that is separated from the mainland by a narrow lagoon, Placencia is a tiny Creole village of pastel-colored houses on stilts. The town's main thoroughfare is a sidewalk, which will give you some idea of how laid back and quiet this place is. If you're looking for lots to see and do, you're better off going to Ambergris Caye. The people here are still friendly to tourists, and you don't have the hassles that come with a stay on Caye Caulker. Best of all is that Placencia has one of the only "real" beaches in Belize—16 miles of white sand backed with dense vegetation, although at high tide the beach disappears.

WHAT TO SEE & DO

There isn't much to do in Placencia, which is exactly why people come here. You just can't help slowing down and relaxing. Sit back, sip a seaweed punch, and forget your cares. Nobody ever seems to get up early (except maybe the fishermen), and most people spend their days reading books and eating seafood. The beach, although narrow, is just about the only real beach I know of in Belize. You can walk for miles and see hardly a soul. North of town a mile or two, there's good snorkeling right off the beach.

If you're serious about diving or snorkeling, you'll want to get a group together and hire a boat to take you out to the dozens of little offshore cayes. It's between 10 and 25 miles out to the reef here, so a snorkeling or dive trip is not cheap. At **Placencia Dive Shop** (Kitty's Place), north of town (tel. 06-22027), scuba divers pay between B$130 and B$150 ($65 and $75) for a two-tank dive; snorkelers B$70 to B$90 ($35 to $45) for trips including equipment, food, drinks, and a guide. Bring a lot of sunscreen. More adventurous types can organize overnight boat trips to remote rivers where the wildlife is said to be spectacular. These trips are B$80 ($40) per person at Placencia Dive Shop, although less expensive day trips also are available. If you ask around town, you can probably arrange a trip out to the reef or cayes for much less than what Kitty charges. Snorkeling trips (including equipment, lunch, and drinks) can be arranged at the Jene's Restaurant for B$30 ($15).

Fishing around here is some of the best in Belize. A day's fishing expedition will cost B$400 to B$450 ($200 to $225) for a boat. Grouper, tarpon, bonefish, and snook are the popular gamefish.

WHERE TO STAY

DOUBLES FOR LESS THAN B$35 [$17.50]

PARADISE VACATION HOTEL, Placencia. Tel. 501/6-23118 or 6-23179. 16 rms (4 with bath).

$ Rates: B$20 ($10) single without bath; B$35 ($17.50) double without bath; B$40 ($20) triple without bath; B$50 ($25) single/double/triple with bath. No credit cards.

Although it hardly lives up to its glorious name, the Paradise Vacation Hotel is Placencia's best and most popular true budget hotel. You'll find everyone from backpackers to vacationing lodge owners here. The ground-floor rooms have private baths and are slightly more spacious than the rooms without baths. The eight rooms on the second floor get more breezes and share two moderately clean bathrooms downstairs and at the back of the building. The calm waters of the bay lap at your doorstep, and there's a pier that is great for sunning and swimming.

Tentacles restaurant next door serves good seafood and is a popular place to hang out and meet interesting people. Meals range from B$8 to B$18 ($4 to $9).

SEASPRAY, Placencia. Tel. 501/6-23148. 6 rms (4 with bath).
$ Rates: B$21 ($10.50) single without bath, B$26.25–B$42 ($13.15–$21) single with bath; B$31.50 ($15.75) double without bath, B$36.75–B$52.50 ($18.40–$26.25) double with bath; B$47.25 ($23.65) triple without bath, B$63 ($31.50) triple with bath. No credit cards.

The rooms here are small and lack any semblance of style, but they're inexpensive and conveniently located in the middle of town. Fans help you stay cool at night, and, if you're traveling in a group, you might appreciate the bunk beds. The rooms are arranged on either side of a wide hallway, which serves as the lounge and library.

DOUBLES FOR LESS THAN B$100 [$50]

SONNY'S RESORT, Placencia. Tel. 501/6-2046, ext. 103. 11 rms (all with bath).
$ Rates: B$70 ($35) single; B$45 ($90) double; B$120 ($60) single or double cabaña. MC, V.

One of the older hotels in Placencia, Sonny's was started with a couple of mobile homes that had been divided into three guest rooms each. Over the years, screened porches were added to them, giving them a more permanent feel, and although they have seen better days, they still suffice. However, there are also six spacious wooden cabins raised up on stilts. Each has a large porch and is situated to make the most of the prevailing trade winds. They also have small refrigerators, coffee makers, reading lamps, and high ceilings with fans.

The hotel's restaurant is a casual diner-style place with a small bar where fishermen swap stories in the evening. It's open 7am to 10pm daily. Prices range from B$6 to B$15 ($3 to $7.50).

WORTH THE EXTRA BUCKS

RANGUANA LODGE, Placencia. Tel. 501/6-23112. 5 cabins (all with bath).
$ Rates: B$90 ($45) single; B$180 ($90) double; B$200 ($100) triple. No credit cards.

⭐ Although the five cabins here are packed together on a tiny piece of sand in the middle of town, they're still very attractive inside. The water is only a few steps away. Nearly everything in these cozy cabins is made of hardwood—walls, floors, ceilings, even the louvered windows. Each has a little refrigerator and coffee maker, porch, tub, and table.

Just outside your door, you'll find a little thatch-roofed open-air bar where folks (both local and foreign) love to sit around all day gabbing and drinking and soaking up the sun. The Kingfisher serves as the restaurant for the Ranguana Lodge. It's a big screened-in room right on the water, where a meal will cost anywhere from B$12 to B$25 ($6 to $12.50).

WHERE TO EAT

JENE'S RESTAURANT, across from Seaspray Hotel. Tel. 6-23112.
Cuisine: BELIZEAN/INTERNATIONAL.
$ Prices: B$8–B$30 ($4–$15). No credit cards.
Open: Tues–Sun 7:30am–11pm.

Jene's is a long-time favorite in Placencia. The small dining room has hardwood paneling, floors, and ceiling. Paper money from countries all over the world adorns one wall—a testimonial to the diverse backgrounds of visitors who've discovered Placencia. Another wall features a large map of Belize. You can plan your upcoming jungle expeditions while you dine on lobster, fish filets, conch, or shrimp. All meals can be fried, boiled, or broiled and come with french fries and a vegetable. Hamburgers, fishburgers, and veggie burgers also available. Refreshing fresh juices are sometimes available.

KINGFISHER RESTAURANT, behind Ranguana Lodge. No phone.
Cuisine: BELIZEAN/SEAFOOD.

$ Prices: B$8–B$25 ($4–$12.50). No credit cards.
   Open: Fri–Wed 7am–2pm, 6–11pm.
Situated on the beach, the Kingfisher is a large, open room with screen walls that let in the sea breezes. The big porch out front is a great place to relax with a drink and meet fellow travelers. Inside, the decor is early jungle rustic, with a jaguar skin nailed to the wall. Fish, shrimp, conch, and lobster make up the bulk of the short menu, with pork chops, fried chicken, and steaks also available. There are daily seafood specials for around B$15–B$18 ($7.50–$9), which make this one of the best places to find inexpensive seafood.

TENTACLES, next door to Paradise Vacation Hotel. Tel. 6-23156.
   Cuisine: SEAFOOD.
$ Prices: B$8–B$18 ($4–$9). No credit cards.
   Open: Thurs–Tues 7:30am–10pm.
It's hard to beat the view from the second-floor deck of this restaurant at the very southern end of Placencia. There are more tables outside than there are inside, but no matter where you sit, you'll be among friendly locals, tourists, businesspeople, and boaters in from the sailboats moored offshore. The conversation is usually lively. You'll find all the Belizean standards on the menu. If the food isn't memorable, the setting certainly is: The mangrove swamps begin a few steps away, while several little islands dot the far horizon; sailboats rock gently at anchor while skiffs race back and forth to the mainland. It's positively bewitching when the moon sparkles on the waves.

AN EXCURSION

Weighing up to 200 pounds and measuring more than six feet from nose to tip of tail, jaguars are king of the new-world jungle. Nocturnal predators, jaguars prefer to hunt peccaries (wild piglike animals), deer, and other small mammals. The **Cockscomb Basin,** a wildlife sanctuary established in 1986 as the world's first jaguar reserve, covers nearly 150 square miles of rugged forested mountains and has the greatest density of jaguars in the world. It is part of the even larger Cockscomb Basin Forest Reserve, which was created in 1984.

The forests within the preserve are home to other wild cats as well, including pumas, ocelots, and margays, all of which are very elusive, so don't get your hopes of seeing them too high. Few people do. Other mammals that you might spot if you're lucky include otters, coatimundis, kinkajous, deer, peccaries, anteaters, and armadillos.

The largest land mammal native to Central America—the tapir—is also resident. Locally known as a "mountain cow," the tapir is the national animal of Belize. A tapir can weight up to 600 pounds and is related to the horse, although its protruding upper lip is more like an elephant's trunk.

Much more easily spotted in the dense vegetation surrounding the preserve's trails are nearly 300 species of birds, including the scarlet macaw, the keel-billed toucan, the king vulture, and the great curassow.

Great caution should be exercised when visiting the preserve—in addition to jaguars, which can be dangerous, there are also poisonous snakes, including the deadly fer-de-lance. Always wear shoes, preferably boots, when hiking the trails here.

Visitors' facilities include an information center, picnic area, campground, and a few primitive cabins costing B$12 ($6) per person per night. Drinking water is available. For more information on the preserve, contact the **Belize Audubon Society,** P.O. Box 1001, 29 Regent St., Belize City (tel. 2-77369).

3. PUNTA GORDA

205 miles S of Belize City; 100 miles S of Dangriga

GETTING THERE   By Plane   Maya Airways (tel. 2-72312 or 2-77215 in Belize

City) flies several times a day from Belize City to Punta Gorda. Duration: 1 hour. Fare: B$108 ($54) one way. The Punta Gorda airport is on the west edge of town within walking distance of the town's hotels and guest houses.

By Boat   There is a ferry between Puerto Barrios, Guatemala, and Punta Gorda, Belize, every Tuesday and Friday leaving Puerto Barrios at 8am. Buy your ticket the day before departure at the green ferry ticket office. Duration: 2–3 hours. Fare: Q21.40 ($4.28). When you arrive, be sure to get your passport stamped at the immigration office just up from the dock.

By Bus   Z-Line buses leave from the Magazine Road bus terminal in Belize City Monday to Saturday at 8am; Monday, Wednesday, and Saturday at 3pm; and Sunday at 10am. Duration: 8 hours. Fare: B$20 ($10).

By Car   It is a long and grueling road to Punta Gorda. The Southern Highway, which starts in Dangriga, is unpaved for 100 miles and, though fairly good in the dry season, can get very muddy in the wet season. Any time of year you'll have to take it slowly. Coming from Belize City, you can take the Manatee Road turnoff just past the Belize Zoo or continue on to Belmopan and turn south on the Hummingbird Highway. Neither road is very good, but the Hummingbird Highway is infamous for its killer potholes (though it's supposed to be repaved). Avoid it if you can.

DEPARTING   Buses for Mango Creek (Placencia), Dangriga, Belmopan, and Belize City leave at 5 and 10am daily with additional 1pm departures on Tuesday and Friday. Planes depart daily for Mango Creek, Dangriga, and Belize. The ferry to Puerto Barrios, Guatemala, leaves Tuesday and Friday at 2pm. Be sure to buy your ticket the day before at the Maya de Indita store half a block north from the northwest corner of the central park. Duration: 2–3 hours. Fare: B$10.70 ($5.35). Launches also make the trip across to Puerto Barrios on an irregular basis. They usually leave between 8am and noon from the main wharf and charge between B$20 and B$30 ($10 and $15). Ask around at the wharf for a boat.

ESSENTIALS   Punta Gorda is a small coastal town, and the road into town runs right along the water before angling a bit inland. There is a Belize Bank on the town's central park; it's open Monday to Thursday 8am to 1pm, Friday 8am to 1pm and 3 to 6pm. The central park is also where you can catch buses to nearby Mayan villages.

Punta Gorda, Belize's southernmost town, is a quiet place with clean paved streets, lush vegetation, and hardly a soul about after the sun goes down. Although it is right on the Caribbean, there is no beach and the water is rather murky. However, the surrounding scenery is as verdant as you'll find anywhere in Belize (due to nearly 200 inches of rain a year). The surrounding Toledo District is home to several Mayan ruins and numerous villages that are still peopled by Maya Indians who migrated here from Guatemala during the last century.

Settled by Black Caribs in 1823, Punta Gorda was only accessible by boat for many years, and even though the Southern Highway now connects the town with points north, the 100 miles of bad gravel road ensure that the town is still isolated. As the administrative center for the Toledo District, Punta Gorda has an active market and bus services to the many surrounding Mayan villages, although connections are not very good. Most travelers do little more than pass through Punta Gorda on their way to or from Guatemala by way of the Puerto Barrios ferry. However, there is plenty to keep the adventurous traveler busy for several days.

WHAT TO SEE & DO

A stroll through Punta Gorda is the best way to enjoy the Caribbean atmosphere. If you've come down from the north, you'll likely be surprised at what a clean and quiet town Punta Gorda is compared with Dangriga or Belize City. It's a welcome relief and worth savoring for a day or two.

Most people who spend any time in Punta Gorda are interested in learning more about Mayan village life or sustainable agriculture, although there are also several Mayan ruins that attract a few hardy Mayaphiles. For information on a nearby permaculture (sustainable agriculture) farm and how to arrange staying in a Mayan Village, see the listings below for Dem Dats Doin and Nature's Way Guest House.

The largest of the nearby Mayan ruins is **Lubaantun** (Place of Fallen Rock), which is about 20 miles from Punta Gorda and about 1 mile from the village of San Pedro Columbia. From the main road it is a 20-minute walk to the ruins. This Late Classic Maya ruin is unusual in that the structures were built using a technique of cut-and-fitted stones rather than the usual limestone-and-rock construction technique used elsewhere by the Mayans. Lubaantun is perhaps most famous as the site where a crystal skull was discovered by a Canadian woman in 1926. Kept in a vault in Canada, the skull has been surrounded with controversy. What was it used for? How could such a hard stone have been carved in such a detailed manner? Where did it come from? Some stories claim a light emanates from the skull, others attribute magical powers to it.

Nim Li Punit (Big Hat), off the Southern Highway 25 miles north of Punta Gorda, is the site of the largest Maya stela (carved record stone) known in Belize. It measures almost 30 feet tall and is one of more than two dozen stelae found here.

Other ruins in the area include **Uxbenka** near Santa Cruz and **Pusilha** near Aguacate. There is no charge to visit any of these ruins, yet, and the resident guards will even give you free guided tours.

Though the ruins were abandoned centuries ago, Mayan Indians still live in this region. The villages of the Toledo District are populated by two groups of Maya Indians—the Kekchi and the Mopan—who have both different languages and agricultural practices. The Mopan are upland farmers, while the Kekchi farm the lowlands. Both groups are thought to have migrated into southern Belize from Guatemala less than 100 years ago. San Antonio, the largest Mopan Maya village, is known for its annual festival on June 13th in honor of the village's patron saint. The festival includes masked dances similar to those performed in the Guatemalan highlands. In San Antonio, you can stay at Bol's Hilltop Hotel, a very basic place with great views that charges B$10 ($5) for a single and B$20 ($10) for a double.

Mayan culture, past and present, may be the main attractions of Punta Gorda, but it also boasts natural attractions. About 2½ miles before the village of San Antonio is one of the most beautiful swimming holes in all of Belize. Flowing out of a cave in a limestone mountain, the aptly named **Blue Creek** is a cool stream with striking deep turquoise water. Lush rain forest shades the creek, creating an idyllic place to spend an afternoon. You can cool off by swimming up into the mouth of the cave from which the stream flows. Blue Creek is a privately owned park charging a B$4 ($2) admission.

Near the village of Big Falls, which is near a waterfall on the Rio Grande, there is a natural **hot spring** that's a popular weekend picnic spot. You can have a refreshing swim in the river at the falls and then warm your muscles in the hot spring. There are also some attractive small waterfalls near the village of San Antonio.

There are buses from Punta Gorda to San Antonio, Big Falls, and Blue Creek, and buses headed north to Belize City pass by Nim Li Punit. However, some of these buses only run every other day, so making connections can take time. It's also possible to hitchhike, though not always reliable. Check with the Toledo Visitor Information Center at the wharf in Punta Gorda to find out about current bus schedules. If you have more money than time, you might want to consider arranging a tour either through Nature's Way Guest House or Dem Dats Doin. If you get a group of five or six people together, the tours become relatively economical—about B$60 ($30) for a 1-day tour that includes a village visit, a tour of Dem Dats Doin, and a stop at Blue Creek.

WHERE TO STAY

DEM DATS DOIN, P.O. Box 73, Punta Gorda. Tel. 501/7-22470. 1 rm.
$ Rates: B$30 ($15) single; B$40 ($20) double. No credit cards.
Dem Dats Doin bills itself as an energy sufficient low-input organic minibiosphere, in

other words, it's a self-sufficient organic farm. As part of the farm, owners Alfredo and Yvonne Villoria have a single bedroom available as a bed-and-breakfast (lunch and dinner also available for B$10 to B$12 ($5 to $6) per person per meal). The farm is primarily visited by people fascinated by sustainable agriculture (permaculture). Electricity and cooking fuel come from the sun and biogas, and there are more than 1,000 varieties of tropical plants as well as a collection of butterflies and insects on the farm. The farm is within walking distance of the Kekchi Maya village of San Pedro Columbia and Lubaantun ruins.

If you'd just like to visit and see what's doin', 2-hour tours are available for B$10 ($5). The Villorias also operate a homestay program in several of the nearby Maya villages. They charge a B$20 ($10) registration fee and the room and board cost B$22 ($11) per person. If you're interested in spending a night with a Mayan family, register at the Villoria's Toledo Visitors Information Center on Front Street at the main wharf (where the Puerto Barrios ferry docks). The information center is open Monday through Wednesday and Friday and Saturday from 8am to noon.

GOYO'S INN, Main Middle St., Punta Gorda. Tel. 501/7-22086. 8 rms (all with bath).
$ Rates: B$31.50 ($15.75) single; B$36.75–B$42 ($18.40–$21) double; B$52.50–B$63 ($26.25–$31.50) triple. No credit cards.
Located right on the central park, Goyo's is convenient if you arrive in town after dark and don't want to wander around an unfamiliar town looking for a room. The main drawback here is that the adjacent clock tower tolls the hours all night long. Light sleepers beware. There is a small restaurant on the first floor, and behind this is a TV lounge. Rooms vary considerably; some are large and clean, with cement floors, while others are smaller, darker, and not as clean.

NATURE'S WAY GUEST HOUSE, 65 Front St., Punta Gorda. Tel. 501/7-22119. 8 rms (none with bath).
$ Rates: B$15 ($7.50) single; B$25 ($12.50) double; B$35 ($17.50) triple. No credit cards.
Located three blocks south of the central park and across the street from the water, Nature's Way is a long-time favorite of budget travelers and should be your first choice in Punta Gorda. Even though the rooms do not have private bathrooms, the shared baths are large, clean, and modern. The guest house is operated by an American named William "Chet" Smith who moved down here more than 20 years ago to promote sustainable agricultural practices. Chet is a wealth of information about the area and helped start a village guest house program which allows visitors to stay in the nearby Mayan villages. At B$228 ($114) per person, the charge for this program seems a bit high, but it includes transportation to the village, lodging, three meals, a tour, and a music and dance performance; 33% of the money goes to community development and agricultural programs.

ST. CHARLES INN, 23 King St., Punta Gorda. Tel. 501/7-22149. 13 rms (all with bath).
$ Rates: B$32 ($16) single; B$50 ($25) double. No credit cards.
Located two blocks north of the central park, the St. Charles is part of a small general store, which is where you should go to ask about a room. The guest rooms are in two buildings, and the second floor is a bit nicer since it has a veranda and overlooks a small green yard. The small rooms have louvered windows and fans for cooling. Some of the rooms have carpeting and TVs.

WHERE TO EAT

MAN MAN'S 5 STAR RESTAURANT, no address. No phone.
Cuisine: BELIZEAN.
$ Prices: Full meal B$10–B$12 ($5–$6). No credit cards.
Open: Dinner daily 6–9pm.
This is Punta Gorda's most famous eating establishment, and if you're lucky, Man Man will still be cooking up a storm when you pass through town. To find the

restaurant, walk two blocks east (away from the water) from the north side of the central park and then turn right. In the middle of the block you should see a sign for the restaurant hanging in a tree. Behind the sign is a tiny shack: inside there is one table to the side of the tiny kitchen. Man Man does the cooking and the menu is whatever he happens to be fixing that night, which is frequently delicious fresh fish. Portions are huge, and if he isn't busy, Man Man will sit and chat with you over your meal. Don't miss this rare dining experience.

SHAIBA TROPICAL RESTAURANT, 6 Front St. Tel. 7-22370.
   Cuisine: CREOLE.
$ **Prices:** Main dishes B$5–B$20 ($2.50–$10). No credit cards.
   Open: Daily 7am–2pm and 6–11pm.
With a rustic front room decorated with jaguar skins and paintings by owner "Pino" Sierra, a very competent, self-taught artist, and a TV lounge in the back, Shaiba is another Punta Gorda gem. Pino's wife Lila does the cooking—the menu changes daily but usually includes the likes of conch soup, pork chops, fish filets, butter conch, and turtle steaks. This is Creole cooking at its very best and no meal is complete without lots of freshly made Creole sauce. Lila also makes jams and wines from local fruits and ginger. If you'd like to try some, ask what's available. Don't miss the seaweed punch either; it's a bit like eggnog.

---

4. SAN IGNACIO & THE CAYO DISTRICT

72 miles W of Belize City; 40 miles W of Belmopan;
9 miles E of the Guatemalan border

GETTING THERE   By Bus   Novelos and Batty Bros. buses leave frequently from their Collet Canal stations in Belize City (the station is actually one block before the canal down a side street to the right. Duration: 3 hours. Fare: B$4 ($2). There's also frequent daily service from Belmopan. Duration: 1½ hours. Fare: B$2 ($1).

By Car   Take the Western Highway from Belize City.

DEPARTING   Novelos and Batty Bros. operate buses to Belmopan and Belize City between 4am and 4pm. Duration: 1½ hours to Belmopan, 3 hours to Belize City. Fare: B$2 ($1) to Belmopan, B$4 ($2) to Belize City.
   If you are heading for Tikal in Guatemala, get an early start. Batty's buses leave for the border at 8:30 and 9:30am (B$1 [50¢]), although there are buses throughout the day to Benque Viejo, which is only a mile from the border. You can also take a taxi from San Ignacio to the border for B$20 ($10) or from Benque Viejo B$4 ($2). If you leave early enough, you can catch the 11am bus from Melchor de Mencos, the Guatemalan town just across the border. This bus takes three hours to Flores and costs Q8 ($1.60). Another bus leaves Melchor de Mencos at 1pm.
   Be sure to leave at least an hour for border formalities. Leaving Belize, you'll have to fill out a departure card and turn in your temporary entry permit if you're driving your own car. Entering Guatemala, you will have to pay Q25 ($5) for a Tourist Card, and you may also be asked to pay a few quetzales to have your bags cursorily inspected. If you're driving a car, expect to pay around $10 depending on the whims of the border guards. This payment covers required papers, fumigation of your tires and possibly the inside of your car, and most likely a bribe. You can keep border-crossing costs to a minimum by crossing during regular business hours, which are Monday through Friday 8am to noon and 2 to 6pm. Outside these hours, and especially after dark, you can expect to be asked for additional unexplained payments (bribes). There are always several money changers working here at the border, so be

sure to change your Belize dollars for quetzales (usually a bad exchange rate) and $50 to $100 U.S. dollars to see you through Tikal where the lodges offer notoriously bad exchange rates.

Note: If you're a citizen of the U.K., Ireland, Canada, or Australia, you'll need a visa to get into Guatemala. The nearest Guatemalan consulate is in Chetumal, Mexico.

Once you've passed through Guatemalan border formalities, cross the bridge and walk up the hill to the gas station to find out when the next bus leaves for Flores. There are usually five or six buses a day between 3am and 4pm. If you're in a hurry to reach Tikal, take the bus to El Cruce (also called Ixlu), which is the turnoff for Tikal and is about two hours away over a horrendously rutted road. Unfortunately, buses headed to Tikal pass fairly early in the morning, so your only option may be to try hitchhiking. A safer plan is to take the bus all the way to Flores, spend the night there, and continue to Tikal the next day.

Other options for getting to Tikal are to go back to Belize City and fly Aerovias Airlines to Flores for B$100 ($50) plus the international departure tax of B$22.50 ($11.25). This flight leaves Belize City at 1:30pm daily. If you have a group of four or five people, you can hire a taxi to take you to Tikal for around B$100 ($50) per person. However, in early 1992 there was a spate of armed robberies of carloads of gringo tourists on the road between Melchor de Mencos and Tikal. Check at Eva's restaurant before traveling by taxi or hired vehicle to Tikal. You might be safer on the local bus.

ESSENTIALS Orientation San Ignacio is on the banks of the Macal River, on the far side of an old metal bridge. Just across the bridge is a traffic circle. Downtown San Ignacio is to the right on Burns Avenue, and the San Ignacio Hotel is to the left on Buena Vista Road. Most of the hotels and restaurants are on or within a block of Burns Avenue.

See Bob at Eva's Restaurant on Burns Avenue for information about the area. He can help you arrange tours and accommodations.

Fast Facts There is a drugstore downstairs from the Venus Hotel on Burns Avenue. The police emergency phone number is 2022. The telephone office is across from the Venus Hotel on Burns Avenue. Open Monday to Friday 8am to noon and 1 to 4pm, Saturday 8am to noon.

I n the foothills of the mountains, close to the Guatemalan border, lie the twin towns of Santa Elena and San Ignacio (pop. 7,100) on either side of a beautiful, calm, clear river (good for a swim). San Ignacio is the administrative center for the Cayo District, a region of cattle ranches and dense forests, of clear rivers and Mayan ruins. If you've come from Guatemala, you'll sense immediately that you are now in a Caribbean country. If you've come up from the coast, you might be surprised by how cool it can get up here in the mountains. Cayo and the cayes are worlds apart. While the cayes cater to those looking for fun in the sun, Cayo caters to those interested in nature. This area makes a good first stop in Belize; you can get in a lot of activity before heading to the beach to relax.

WHAT TO SEE & DO

High on a hill to the southwest of downtown San Ignacio are the Mayan ruins of **Cahal Pech.** This former royal residence was recently restored with the help of the United States Agency for International Development and San Diego State University. The restoration has created a bit of controversy in town because parts of the ruins were restored to the way they looked when they were first built, which is a bit more polished and modern-looking than most people like their ruins. However, the setting is beautiful, with tall old trees shading the site's main plaza and pyramid/castle. The name Cahal Pech means the "Place of the Family of Pech" (Pech means tick in Mayan). The name was given to the site in the 1950's when there were quite a few ticks in the area. The ruins date back to between A.D. 650 and 900, though there are indications that the site was used prior to this time as well.

A **museum** displays a collection of artifacts recovered from the site and provides insight into the Cahal Pech social structure. Admission to the museum and ruins is B$3 ($1.50). Be sure to ask for a copy of the very informative guide to the site. To reach Cahal Pech, walk up toward the San Ignacio Hotel continuing on around the curve for a few hundred yards until you see the sign pointing up a dirt road to the ruins. It's about a 15-minute walk.

After a visit to the ruins, or any time for that matter, nothing feels better than a swim in San Ignacio's **Macal River.** Though you can join the locals right in town where the river is treated as a free laundry, car wash, horse and dog wash, and swimming hole, you'll do better to head upstream a few hundred yards above the bridge to a swimming hole complete with rope swing and cliffs for high divers.

Another alternative is to head downriver about 1½ miles to a spot called **Branch Mouth,** where the different-colored waters of the Macal and Mopan rivers converge. Branch Mouth is a favorite picnic spot, with shady old trees clinging to the river banks. There's even a rope swing from one of the trees. The road is dusty, so you'll be especially happy to go for a swim here.

One option is to hang out by the pool at the San Ignacio Hotel. The pool is open to the public for B$5 ($2.50) per adult.

For much of Belize's history, the rivers were the highways. The Mayans used them for trading, and British loggers used them to get mahogany. If you're interested, you can explore the Cayo District's two rivers by canoe. In fact, you can paddle as far as the coast if you're so inclined. The waters in these rivers have a few riffles, but you don't need white-water experience. The trips are leisurely, with stops for swimming or land excursions. **Tony's Adventure Tours** (tel. 92-2267) offers regular day-long guided canoe trips up the Macal River as far as Chaa Creek Cottages and the Panti Medicine Trail. These trips cost B$25 ($12.50) per person. Along the way, you're likely to see iguanas, snakes, toucans, and other wildlife. There are always plenty of stops to cool off in the water, and you can have lunch at Chaa Creek and then tour the Panti Trail (both of these cost extra).

If your preferred activity is **mountain biking,** you should be able to find a bike to rent if you ask at Eva's Restaurant, or check at the Red Rooster Inn, 2 Far West St. (tel. 92-3016). However, let me warn you that the hills here are steep and the heat and humidity can be overwhelming. Take (and drink) lots of water, and try to avoid pedaling during the middle of the day. Rental rates when I last visited were B$5 ($2.50) per hour. The Red Rooster Inn also offers rafting trips, though the rivers here are often so low that rafting is not very exciting.

If you enjoy horseback riding, contact **Mountain Equestrian Trails,** Mile 8 Mountain Pine Ridge Road, Central Farm P.O., Cayo (tel. 8-23180). Although not cheap, they provide excellent horseback tours of the area, including visits to caves and waterfalls. A half-day trip costs B$110 ($55) per person; a full-day trip costs B$140 ($70). **Guacamallo Treks,** Maya Ranch, Mile 4½ Mountain Pine Ridge Road (tel. 92-2188), also offers various horseback riding trips. A half-day ride is B$80 to B$90 ($40 to $45), while full-day trips range from B$130 to B$190 ($65 to $95). Rides are not offered every day so be sure to call in advance. Another alternative is to contact one of the lodges outside of San Ignacio to see if you can arrange a few hours of riding. Places to try include Las Casitas Resort, Clarissa Falls Cottages, and Nabitunich, all of which are listed below.

WHERE TO STAY

Good accommodations in San Ignacio are scarce: There are lots of choices that are outside your budget and several that are more basic than you'll probably want, but little in between. Still, there are a few options in this beautiful neck of the Belizean woods.

DOUBLES FOR LESS THAN B$30 ($15)

HI-ET, corner of Waight and West streets, San Ignacio, Cayo. Tel. 501/92-2828. 6 rms (none with bath).
$ Rates: B$10 ($5) single; B$20 ($10) double. No credit cards.
The water is cold and you have to share a bathroom, but the Hi-Et is family run, clean, and secure. This is the best of the backpacker-frequented hotels in San Ignacio. Unfortunately, it's almost always full.

VENUS HOTEL, 29 Burns Ave., San Ignacio, Cayo District. Tel. 501/92-2186. 29 rms (11 with bath).
$ Rates: B$21 ($10.50) single without bath, B$36.75 ($18.40) single with bath; B$26.25 ($13.15) double without bath, B$47.25 ($23.65) double with bath. AE, MC, V.
The Venus Hotel, which opened in 1990, fills a gap in the San Ignacio hotel scene. Previously, there were high- and low-end hotels but nothing in the middle. Make this your first choice now. The rooms are large, clean, and bright. There are two TV lounges and a long veranda from which you can observe life in the street below. Although the cheapest rooms are quite basic (just beds), the larger rooms are quite nice, with wallpaper, attractive curtains, new vinyl floors, and ceiling fans. The only drawback here is that the rooms can be quite stuffy. The Venus is located upstairs from the Venus Store and down the street from Eva's Restaurant.

DOUBLES FOR LESS THAN B$70 ($35)

HOTEL MAXIMA, Hudson St., San Ignacio, Cayo District. Tel. 501/92-2265. 14 rms (all with bath).
$ Rates: B$35–B$50 ($17.50–$25) single; B$45–B$60 ($22.50–$30) double. No credit cards.
Located just around the corner from Burns Avenue (San Ignacio's main street), the Maxima is one of the newer hotels in town and as such is one of the better choices. However, don't expect luxury or quality workmanship here. Though some of the halls are carpeted, it is questionable whether this is a benefit or a liability in this climate. However, the rooms in this 3-story hotel are clean. The pricier rooms have air conditioning and televisions.

PLAZA HOTEL, Burns Ave., San Ignacio, Cayo District. Tel. 501/92-3332, 92-3374, or 92-3375. 12 rms (all with bath).
$ Rates: B$36.75–B$63 ($18.40–$31.50) single; B$52.50–B$78.75 ($26.25–$39.40) double. No credit cards.
Rooms at the Plaza are almost identical to those at the Maxima, though here there are phones in the rooms, but no TVs. If you want to watch the tube, there is one in the lobby lounge. Walls are painted in Caribbean colors, so despite the cinder-block construction, there is a hint of the tropics here. Higher priced rooms have air conditioning.

WORTH THE EXTRA BUCKS

HOTEL SAN IGNACIO, San Ignacio, Cayo. Tel. 501/92-2034. 25 rms (all with bath).
$ Rates: B$52.50–B$136 ($26.25–$68) single; B$63–B$157.50 ($31.50–$78.75) double; B$74–B$178.50 ($37–$89.25) triple. AE, MC, V.
The Hotel San Ignacio is up the steep hill just past the police station, at the west end of the bridge into town. Because it's situated on Buena Vista Road, it has magnificent views of the jungle. The hotel is a welcome oasis in this country of generally substandard accommodations, but it's often full by sundown. Although it's a bit expensive, it's clean and comfortable.
There's a good restaurant and bar with decent food and great views from its terrace. A full breakfast costs B$7 to B$12 ($3.50 to $6). A complete dinner of chicken on a skewer, fried, or in a stew ranges from B$8 to B$12 ($4 to $12).

CAMPING

Cosmos Camping is a campground on the road leading out toward Branch Mouth and Las Casitas, where you can park your van or pitch your tent for B$10 ($5) per day. It has a cold-water shower and an outhouse, but there isn't much other than that. The river is just across a field, which makes this a rather nice spot.

WHERE TO EAT

EVA'S RESTAURANT & BAR, 22 Burns Ave. Tel. 92-2267.
Cuisine: BELIZEAN/INTERNATIONAL.
$ Prices: B$4.50–B$10 ($2.25–$5). No credit cards.
Open: Daily 7am–midnight.

What Mom's is to Belize City, Eva's is to San Ignacio. A postcard collection covers a few walls, the tabletops are Formica, and the conversation is lively. Although it's short on atmosphere, Eva's is long on information. Owner Bob Jones is a wealth of information about the area and acts as the local branch of the tourist board. If you want to get a group of people together to rent a taxi or canoe or to defray the costs of a tour, let Bob know—he'll try to put you in touch with other like-minded folks. Rice, beans, and chicken cost B$6 ($3); fish and fries cost B$9 ($4.50). There are daily specials (usually local dishes) that are always good choices.

MAXIM'S CHINESE RESTAURANT, corner of Far West and Bullet Tree roads. Tel. 92-2282.
Cuisine: CHINESE.
$ Prices: B$6–B$16 ($3–$8). No credit cards.
Open: Lunch Mon–Sat 11:30am–2:30pm; dinner daily 5:30pm–midnight.

For delicious Chinese food, try this casual place. Various plates of fried rice range from B$5.75 ($2.90) to B$10 ($5), and sweet-and-sour dishes cost B$8 ($4) to B$10 ($5). There's also a host of vegetarian dishes. Try the Belikin Stout if you like dark beer with a bite. The owner goes into Belize City once a week to secure fish and other ingredients. (The owner will also change traveler's checks as a favor.) Take-out is also available.

SERENDIB RESTAURANT, 27 Burns Ave. Tel. 92-2302.
Cuisine: SRI LANKAN.
$ Prices: B$8–B$16 ($4–$8). No credit cards.
Open: Mon–Thurs 9:30am–3pm and 6:30–11pm.

This pleasant little restaurant is an unexpected surprise in the tiny town of San Ignacio. Owner Hantley Pieris is from Sri Lanka and came to Belize years ago with the British army. He now runs a restaurant serving excellent curries in the style of his native country. You can get beef or chicken curry with yellow or fried rice, potatoes, and a salad for B$9.50 ($4.75). There are also sandwiches, burgers, chow mein, and fried fish on the menu for B$3 to B$15 ($1.50–$7.50).

NEARBY PLACES TO STAY & EAT

If you've made it this far, you're probably the adventurous type, and I'm sure you'd like to know about some wonderful splurges in the Cayo District. Within a few miles of San Ignacio are several **jungle lodges** where you can canoe down clear rivers past 4-foot iguanas sunning themselves on the rocks, ride horses to Mayan ruins, hike jungle trails, and spot dozens of beautiful birds and, occasionally, other wild animals. I highly recommend that you stay at one of the jungle lodges listed below while you're in the area. A few of the lodges can be reached by public bus from San Ignacio though you may have a 20-minute walk after getting off the bus. All the lodges will arrange trips to various sites in the area—such as Mountain Pine Ridge, Xunantunich, and Tikal. You can also hire a taxi, though this is quite expensive: B$50 ($25) to Chaa Creek and B$60 ($30) to duPlooy's.

DOUBLES FOR LESS THAN B$100 [$50]

BLACK ROCK, P.O. Box 48, San Ignacio, Cayo District. Tel. 501/92-2341. 6 tent cabins (none with bath).
$ Rates (including three meals): B$79–B$94 ($39.50–$47) double. No credit cards.

So, you *really* want to get away from it all? Well, this is the place. To reach Black Rock, you travel six miles down a dirt road and then hike for a mile along the Macal River. Accommodations are in large tents, but there are plans for more permanent structures soon. What do you do at Black Rock? Why, nothing of course! Just enjoy the river, with its rapids, waterfalls, and cliffs. The only electricity out here is from photovoltaic cells, so at night it's just you and the stars and all those strange noises. The higher rates are for the plan that includes better meals. If you're on a tight budget, you'll have to opt for the rice-and-beans econo trip. Transportation out here will set you back a bit, but, if you ask me, it's worth it. No drop-ins please, reservations only.

CLARISSA FALLS COTTAGES, P.O. Box 44, San Ignacio, Cayo. Tel. 501/93-2462 or 93-2424. 3 cabins (none with bath).
$ Rates (without meals): B$15 ($7.50) single; B$30 ($15) double; B$45 ($22.50) triple; B$5 ($2.50) per person to camp. No credit cards.

Clarissa Falls and the jade green waters of the Mopan River are the backdrop for this, my favorite budget lodging in Cayo. Situated on an 800-acre working cattle ranch, these three cottages are quite basic, with cement floors and beds and little else. However, the spartan decor is more than compensated for by the beautiful surroundings of hilly pastures and river. An open-air restaurant serving meals for between B$10 ($5) and B$15 ($7.50) sits atop a Mayan ruin. Boats and inner tubes can be rented and horseback riding is available. If you'd like to just visit for the day, you can swim in the river and picnic for B$2 ($1), which is a very popular activity on weekends (if you crave peace and tranquillity, visit on a weekday). Clarissa Falls Cottages are about 1½ miles off the highway about 4 miles west of San Ignacio. The bus to Benque Viejo will drop you at the turnoff.

MIDA'S RESORT, Branch Mouth Rd., San Ignacio. Tel. 501/92-3172, 92-2101, or 92-2737. 4 cabins (2 with bath).
$ Rates (without meals): B$42 ($21) single without bath, B$63 ($31.50) single with bath; B$52.50 ($26.25) double without bath, B$73.50 ($36.75) double with bath; B$84 ($42) triple without bath; B$10 ($5) per person to camp. No credit cards.

Though Mida's is just a short walk from downtown San Ignacio, it feels a world away. The round Mayan-style cottages are set in a sunny garden but have thatch roofs and screen walls so they stay cool. The Macal River is only a stroll away down a grassy lane, and you can spend the day lounging on the little beach on the river bank. There's no restaurant here, but it only takes a few minutes to walk into San Ignacio. To reach Mida's, walk out of town across the fields behind San Ignacio's combination bus terminal and public park. A dirt road leads past Mida's toward Branch Mouth.

RANCHO LOS AMIGOS, San José Succotz Village. Tel. 501/93-2483. 4 cabins (none with bath).
$ Rates (including breakfast and dinner): B$50 ($25) single; B$100 ($50) double; B$150 ($75) triple; B$30 ($15) per person to camp. No credit cards.

If you don't mind using a pit toilet and bathing in a spring-fed pool, Rancho Los Amigos may just be your idea of paradise. This rustic retreat is an economical place to experience all the best of the Cayo District. Xunantunich ruins and the Mopan River are only a mile or so away, and if you have more energy, you can walk to Black Rock on the Macal River. The cabins here are rustic but comfortable and the Jenkins family, refugees from Southern California, will make you feel right at home. Excellent meals (including vegetarian) are cooked up in an open-air kitchen atop a Mayan ruin. The lack of electricity here adds to the rustic appeal. If you happen to have any aches or pains, you might even get Ed Jenkins to perform a bit of acupuncture on you.

DOUBLES FOR LESS THAN B$200 [$100]

LAS CASITAS, 56 Burns Ave., San Ignacio. Tel. 501/92-2506, or 92-2999. Fax 501/92-2475. 6 rms (5 with bath).

$ Rates (including two meals and two hours horseback riding or canoeing): B$105 ($52.50) single; B$157.50 ($78.75) double (rates without meals or activities are lower). No credit cards.

Located 1½ miles outside of San Ignacio at Branch Mouth—the confluence of the Mopan and Macal rivers—Las Casitas is accessible by boat or taxi. The guest rooms are in screen-walled cabins, and there is a three-story thatched-roof lookout tower that serves as restaurant and lounge. Hammocks are slung from trees by the river where you can take a refreshing dip. The rooms have all been recently refurnished and have somewhat new beds. This is a popular spot with backpackers and younger travelers. Stop by the lodge's office in San Ignacio to arrange transportation.

NABITUNICH, Benque Viejo Rd., Cayo District. Tel. 501/93-2309. Fax 501/93-2096. 12 rms. (all with bath).

$ Rates (including three meals): B$126 ($63) single; B$168 ($84) double. No credit cards.

With the rapid rise in room rates at the Cayo District's jungle lodges, Nabitunich has become the best deal around. This former farm/ranch is owned by Rudy and Margaret Juan. Rudy's family has owned the land for years, and Margaret is a nurse from England. Easy accessibility from the highway makes this my favorite choice in the area. You can take a taxi out here (expensive) or catch a bus bound for the border and ask to be let off when you see the Nabitunich sign. The cottages are set on a gently sloping hillside with pastures all around. Down at the bottom of the hill, you'll find the Mopan River and a trail through the forest (both areas are great for bird watching). Each cottage is different from the others—some are of white stucco and some are of stone, but all have thatched roofs. There are orchids all around the grounds; off in the distance you can see the ruins of Xunantunich. Equestrian-types can ride for hours on nearby bridle trails.

The dining room is spacious, and there's a bar on the patio of the dining hall.

WORTH THE EXTRA BUCKS

CHAA CREEK COTTAGES, P.O. Box 53, San Ignacio, Cayo. Tel. 501/92-2037. Fax 501/92-2501. 17 rms (all with bath).

$ Rates (including three meals): B$139.20 ($69.60) single without bath, B$218.40 ($109.20) single with bath; B$190.20 ($95.10) double without bath, B$321.20 ($160.60) double with bath. AE, MC, V.

Much loving care has gone into creating the beautiful grounds and cottages here; if you decide to spend the extra money, I'm sure you'll be glad you did. This is one of the oldest of the jungle lodges in the Cayo District and is located on the Macal River. To reach the cottages, drive 5 miles west from San Ignacio and watch for the sign on your left. It's another couple of miles down a very rough dirt road from the main highway. All of the thatched-roof cottages are artistically decorated with Guatemalan textiles and handcrafts and have private baths with hot water. There are canoes available at an additional charge, and horseback rides can always be arranged. For those seeking a real jungle experience, several-day hiking trips through the jungle can be arranged. Mick and Lucy Fleming are the engaging hosts here.

A separate bar and dining room provide plenty of space for socializing.

DUPLOOY'S, San Ignacio, Cayo District. Tel. 501/92-3301. Fax 501/92-3301. 15 rms (8 with bath).

$ Rates (including three meals): B$119.50 ($59.75) single without bath, B$186.50 ($93.25) double without bath; B$184 ($92) single with bath, B$276 ($138) double with bath. MC, V.

You'll certainly think that you're lost long before you reach this remote lodge, but keep following the rutted road. When you finally top a very steep hill and gaze down into the pastured valley below, you won't ever want to leave. The lodge is situated overlooking the Macal River, with jungle-covered limestone cliffs opposite. Jungle covers the surrounding hills. Ken and Judy duPlooy, who moved here a few years ago from South Carolina, are your hosts. Their lodge is a bit more luxurious than the others in the area; this, combined with the stunning location, make duPlooy's my favorite of Cayo's jungle lodges. The nine rooms are in three stone-and-stucco buildings with tile roofs. Each has a screened porch and a private bath. There's a beach on the river, and canoes and snorkeling and fishing equipment are available for rent. If you're paying by credit card, add 5% to your bill. Follow the directions for Chaa Creek Cottages. DuPlooy's is a bit farther on the same dirt road, but be sure to take the right fork and follow the signs.

Breakfast is served in the rooms, and lunch and dinner are served in a small open-air restaurant overlooking the Macal River.

EXCURSIONS
XUNANTUNICH

Although you may not be able to pronounce it (say "Shoo-nahn-too-nitch"), you can visit it. Xunantunich is a Mayan ruin 6½ miles past San Ignacio on the road to Benque Viejo. The name translates as "maiden of the rocks." Open daily from 8am to 4pm. The admission is B$3 ($1.50).

At 127 feet, this pyramid is one of the tallest structures in Belize, despite the new glass-tower addition to the Fort George Hotel in Belize City. The panorama from the top is amazing. Don't miss it. On the east side of the pyramid, near the top, is a remarkably well-preserved stucco frieze.

Down below, under the protection of a thatched palapa in the temple forecourt, are three magnificent stelae portraying rulers of the region. Xunantunich was a thriving Mayan city about the same time as Altun Ha, in the Classic Period, about A.D. 600 to 900.

Take a bus bound for Benque Viejo and get off in San José Succotz. To reach the ruins, you must cross the Mopan River aboard a tiny hand-cranked car-ferry in the village of San José Succotz. You're bound to see colorfully dressed women washing clothes in the river as you are cranked across by the ferryman. After crossing the river, it is a short walk to the ruins. You can also take a taxi, but it's very expensive—unless you share one for B$4 ($2) to the border and ask the driver to drop you off at the ferry.

IX CHEL FARM & THE PANTI MAYAN MEDICINE TRAIL

Located adjacent to Chaa Creek Cottages, Ix Chel Farm is a tropical plant research center operated by Drs. Greg Shropshire and Rosita Arvigo. Rosita studied traditional herbal medicine for five years with a local Mayan medicine man. Here on the farm she has built a trail through the forest to share with visitors the fascinating medicinal values of many of the tropical forest's plants. If you have a group of six people, you can spend a day touring the Panti Trail with Rosita as your guide. After a natural-food vegetarian lunch and a swim in the Macal River, you'll learn about the farm and traditional healing in Belize. The price is B$70 ($35) per person. You can also simply tour the trail with a guide for B$15 ($7.50) per person or use Rosita's guidebook to the trail available for B$10 ($5).

Contact your lodge owner or Bob at Eva's Restaurant for information on scheduling a visit.

MOUNTAIN PINE RIDGE & CARACOL

Few people think of pine trees as being a tropical species, but you'll see plenty of them in Belize, especially in these rugged mountains. This 3,400-foot ridge is complete with a secret waterfall, wild orchids, parrots, keel-billed toucans, and other exotic flora and fauna. Mountain Pine Ridge, Hidden Valley Falls (also called Thousand Foot Falls), and the Río On and Río Frío Caves are off the Western Highway near Georgeville.

These roads are nearly impassable in the wet season and are pretty bad even in the dry season, so don't even think about attempting the trip in anything less than a four-wheel-drive vehicle. All the lodges offer tours to the area, with prices ranging from B$60 to B$90 ($30 to $45) per person if you have a group of four or five people. You can arrange a trip for B$35 ($17.50) if you arrange your trip through Bob at Eva's Restaurant. He'll put your name on a list with other people who are interested in going.

Caracol is believed to be the largest of the Mayan ruins. It's not set up as a tourist sight, but if you have the interest, stamina, and vehicle to make it, you can visit. It's on the same road as Mountain Pine Ridge, several very rough miles farther south. Don't try it in the rainy season. Also, ask for a German fellow named Chris at Eva's Restaurant; he may be taking groups to Caracol.

CHECHEM HAH

Ten miles south of Benque Viejo, on a dirt road that is recommended only for four-wheel-drive vehicles, is the cave of Chechem Hah, which was only rediscovered a few years ago. When the cave was explored, a cache of Mayan artifacts was discovered within the cave. The Mayas believed that caves were a direct avenue to the underworld gods; caves filled with offerings have been found throughout Mayan territory. Chechem Hah is privately owned and there is an admission charge of B$50 ($25) per group for a tour of the cave where you can see many of the Mayan relics just as they were found. It is also possible to stay on a farm near the cave. Also in the vicinity is **Vaca Fall,** a beautiful and remote waterfall that's a popular day trip with horseback riders. Check at Eva's for more information on visiting Chechem Hah.

5. COROZAL TOWN & THE NORTHERN HIGHWAY

96 miles N of Belize City; 31 miles N of Orange Walk; 8 miles S of the Mexican border

GETTING THERE **By Air** Maya Airways operates two flights daily from San Pedro. Duration: 20 minutes. Fare: B$54 ($27) one way, B$104 ($52) round-trip.

By Bus Both Batty Bros. and Venus bus lines run several buses daily from Belize City. Duration: 3 hours. Fare: B$6 ($3). Buses originating from Chetumal, Mexico, go into town daily every hour from 4am to 6pm.

By Car Corozal Town is the last town on the Northern Highway before you reach the Mexican border. Take Freetown Road out of Belize City to connect with the Northern Highway. If you want to visit the Altun Ha ruins, take the Old Northern Highway. The turnoff is 22 miles from Belize City, on the right. If you're driving in from Mexico, you'll reach a fork in the road 3 miles from the border; bear left to reach Corozal Town.

DEPARTING Buses leave throughout the day for both Chetumal, Mexico, and Belize City. The fare for the 9-mile trip to Chetumal is B$2.50 ($1.25). Expect to spend 30 to 45 minutes going through border formalities. Bus fare to Belize City is B$7.50 ($3.75).

ESSENTIALS The bus station is located two blocks west of the town's central park. Three of the four hotels listed here are at the south end of town where the Northern Highway runs alongside the bay.

Nine miles from the Mexican border, Corozal Town (pop. 8,700) is for many people their first glimpse of Belize. There isn't much to see or do in Corozal. It's mostly just a stopping point for weary travelers. However, it sits on the shores of the **Bay of Chetumal,** which has the most amazing turquoise-blue water. The town was settled in the mid-19th century by refugee Mestizos from Mexico, and Spanish is still the principal language spoken here. Before the 1850s, the area had been one of the last centers of the Mayan civilization.

WHAT TO SEE & DO

If you've just come from Mexico, swim in the bay, or walk around town and marvel at the difference between Mexican culture and Belizean culture. The countries are so close and yet worlds apart. Belize is truly a Caribbean country, with frame houses built on high stilts to provide coolness, protection from floods, and shade for sitting. Farming and growing sugarcane are what Corozal survives on, plus a little fishing.

If you haven't yet had your fill of Mayan ruins, there are a couple to visit in the area. If you look across the water from the shore in Corozal Town, you can see **Cerros** or **Cerro Maya** on the far side of the Bay of Chetumal. It's that little bump in the forest, but up close it seems much larger. Cerros was an important coastal trading center during the Late Preclassic Period. Some of the remains of this city are now under the waters of the bay, but there's still a 65-foot-tall **pyramid** that you can visit. By asking around town, you should be able to find someone willing to take you by boat to the ruins.

Right in town is another small ruin called **Santa Rita.** Corozal Town is actually built on the ruins of Santa Rita, which was an important Late Postclassic Mayan town and was still occupied at the time of the Spanish Conquest. The only excavated building is a small temple across the street from the Coca-Cola bottling plant. To reach it, head north past the bus station and, at the curve to the right, take the road straight ahead that leads up a hill. You'll see the building one block over to the right.

WHERE TO STAY & EAT

Three of the listings below are at the southern end of the town. Ask the bus driver to drop you off or take a taxi from the bus station.

DOUBLES FOR LESS THAN B$25 [$12.50]

CARIBBEAN MOTEL, Cabins and Trailer Park, south end of town on Belize Highway, Corozal Town. No phone. 6 rms (all with bath).
$ Rates: B$25 ($12.50) single or double. No credit cards.

On the bay, in an idyllic location shaded by lofty palms and with a swimming dock across the street, this is the traditional place to stay. Even though it has seen better days, the Caribbean is still a great deal and may provide the cheapest room with private bath that you'll find in Belize. Quaint and primitive thatched bungalows are built according to traditional Mayan designs and are almost identical (from the outside) to the ones that you see all over the Yucatán.

The owner, Jo, serves up the biggest and best salads (a real treat, especially if you've been in Mexico for a while) and burgers in town, each for B$6 ($3). Ask anyone in town to attest to it. The restaurant is open every day except Tuesday (try to time your stay accordingly, other choices for food aren't as good) and serves all three meals.

NESTOR'S HOTEL, 123 Fifth Ave., Corozal Town. Tel. 501/4-22354. 25 rms (all with bath).
$ Rates: B$15 ($7.50) single; B$17–B$20 ($8.50–$10) double. No credit cards.

The cheapest prices in town are to be found here, on the corner of Fifth Avenue and Fourth Street. Jake's rooms are basic, with solar-heated showers, and the plumbing tends to act up now and then in the back rooms, but he'll fix it if you let him know. Jake's been in Belize a long time and will gladly give you a few pointers.

DOUBLES FOR LESS THAN B$50 [$25]

HOTEL MAYA, P.O. Box 112, Corozal Town. Tel. 501/4-22082. 17 rms (all with bath).
$ Rates: B$33 ($16.50) single; B$44 ($22) double; B$66 ($33) triple. MC, V.
Located on the shore road south of town, the Maya is probably your best bet. The

rooms are very clean and basic, and all have private showers with hot and cold running water. This place tends to be popular with American businesspeople who come to negotiate deals, so you may find no rooms available. Unfortunately, it can also get a little bit noisy. You can get a big breakfast for B$8.50 ($4.25), including meat, beans, orange juice, coffee, and toast, or johnnycakes. Dinner runs B$7 to B$10 ($3.50 to $5).

WORTH THE EXTRA BUCKS

TONY'S MOTEL, south end, Corozal Town. Tel. 501/4-22055. 26 rms (all with bath).
$ Rates: B$70–B$120 ($35–$60) single; B$90–B$140 ($45–$70) double; B$10–B$20 ($5–$10) cheaper in summer months; children under 12 stay free in parents' room. AE, MC, V.

The rooms here are newer and larger than those in the above hostelries, and consequently this place is popular with group tours and conferences. Tony's is on the left just past the Caribbean Motel on the shore road south of town. The grounds are nicely landscaped, with lawn chairs that overlook the ocean. There's even a little beach. The rooms come with mahogany furniture, tile floors, attractive floral-print bedspreads, and potted plants. The rooms with air conditioning also come with cable color TVs. Although the prices in the restaurant here are high, especially if you've been traveling in Mexico, it's certainly a welcome oasis of cool air during the summer.

EN ROUTE TO BELIZE CITY

Between Corozal Town and Belize City, the only other town of any size is Orange Walk. There's nothing much of interest here to tourists, but it can make a good base for visiting several surrounding attractions if you have your own car. Sites that could be visited include the Altun Ha and Lamanai ruins and the Crooked Tree Wildlife Sanctuary. For information on Altun Ha and Crooked Tree, see the "Excursions" section of Chapter 15. There really isn't any convenient way to visit Altun Ha by public transportation from Orange Walk, but you could hitch a ride. If you're driving, be sure to take the turnoff for the old Northern Highway as you head south toward Belize City.

Lamanai is an even more difficult ruin to visit—time and money are required to rent a boat to take you down the New River from either Guinea Grass or Shipyard, two small villages near Orange Walk. Ask around in Orange Walk before heading out and you might be able to arrange a tour straight from Orange Walk. Expect to pay around B$150 ($75) for a boat to take you upriver to the ruin (boats usually carry four people, so the price could be reasonable). During the dry season it's possible to drive to Lamanai if you have a four-wheel-drive vehicle. From Orange Walk, take the road to San Felipe.

Lamanai (submerged crocodile in Mayan) is one of the largest Mayan sites in Belize; it was occupied from around 1500 B.C. until the Spanish arrived in the 16th century. In addition to the numerous pyramids and temples, there are also ruins of two churches built by the Spanish. Lamanai's most striking feature is the 12-foot-high stone-and-mortar face set into the side of one of the temples. Most of the ruins here have not been cleared and are surrounded by dense rain forest. The trails leading between temples offer excellent bird watching.

Where to Stay

HOTEL BARONS, Belize-Corozal Rd., Orange Walk. Tel. 501/32-2518 or 032-2364. 31 rms (all with bath).
$ Rates: B$42 ($21) single; B$47.25 ($23.63) double, B$84 ($42) double with A/C. No credit cards.

Spacious, clean rooms with tile floors and hot and cold water await you here, a surprisingly nice hotel on an otherwise dreary section of road, if you just can't go any farther. You'll also find a cool swimming pool with a tiled patio around it. The restaurant serves Belizean and Chinese food at reasonable prices.

CHAN CHICH LODGE, P.O. Box 37, Belize City, Tel. 501/2-75634. Fax 501/2-75635. In the U.S., P.O. Box 1088, Vineyard Haven, MA 02568. Tel. toll free 800/343-8009. Fax 508/693-6311. 12 cabins (all with bath).

$ Rates: B$136.50 ($68.25) single; B$168 ($84) double; B$189 ($94.50) triple; B$210 ($105) quad. AE, MC, V.

It is hard to imagine a more spectacular setting for a lodge. Chan Chich ("Little Bird" in Mayan) sits in the plaza of an ancient Mayan ruin. Overgrown pyramids and temples surround the thatched-roof cabins, and beyond the ruins there is dense jungle. The cabins cluster around the dining room and bar, and each cabin has a veranda that completely surrounds the room itself. There are plenty of louvered windows to let in the breezes and ceiling fans as well. Queen size beds and writing desks are luxurious little touches for such a remote location. Meals are an additional B$60 ($30) per adult per day, B$40 ($20) for children. Activities available (at additional cost) include canoeing, horseback riding, guided hikes, and night walks.

Chan Chich is surrounded by 250,000 acres of wilderness and is a bit difficult to reach. It's a 4-hour drive from Belize City, or a plane can be chartered. If you're driving, head north to Orange Walk and then turn west toward Blue Creek, continuing on to Gallon Jug. Blue Creek is the last place to get gasoline. Don't let your tank get low.

APPENDIX

METRIC MEASURES

Length

1 millimeter (mm)	=	.04 inches (*or* less than ¹⁄₁₆ in.)
1 centimeter (cm)	=	.39 inches (*or* just under ½ in.)
1 meter (m)	=	39 inches (*or* about 1.1 yards)
1 kilometer (km)	=	.62 miles (*or* about ⅔ of a mile)

To convert kilometers to miles, multiply the number of kilometers by .62. Also use to convert kilometers per hour (kmph) to miles per hour (m.p.h.).

To convert miles to kilometers, multiply the number of miles by 1.61. Also use to convert speeds from m.p.h. to kmph.

Capacity

1 liter (l)	=	33.92 fluid ouncees	=	2.1 pints	=	1.06 quarts
	=	.26 U.S. gallons				
1 Imperial gallon	=	1.2 U.S. gallons				

To convert liters to U.S. gallons, multiply the number of liters by .26.

To convert U.S. gallons to liters, multiply the number of gallons by 3.79.

To convert Imperial gallons to U.S. gallons, multiply the number of Imperial gallons by 1.2.

To convert U.S. gallons to Imperial gallons, multiply the number of U.S. gallons by .83.

Weight

1 gram (g)	=	.035 ounces (*or* about a paperclip's weight)
1 kilogram (kg)	=	35.2 ounces = 2.2 pounds
1 metric ton	=	2,205 pounds = 1.1 short ton

To convert kilograms to pounds, multiply the number of kilograms by 2.2.

To convert pounds to kilograms, multiply the number of pounds by .45.

Area

1 hectare (ha)	=	2.47 acres		
1 square kilometer (km²)	=	247 acres	=	.39 square miles

To convert hectares to acres, multiply the number of hectares by 2.47.

To convert acres to hectares, multiply the number of acres by .41.

To convert square kilometers to square miles, multiply the number of square kilometers by .39.

To convert square miles to square kilometers, multiply the number of square miles by 2.6.

Temperature

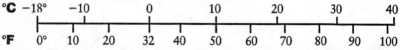

To convert degrees Celsius to degrees Fahrenheit, multiply °C by 9, divide by 5 and add 32 (example: 20°C × 9/5 + 32 = 68°F).

To convert degrees Fahrenheit to degrees Celsius, substract 32 from °F, multiply by 5, then divide by 9 (example: 85°F − 32 × 5/9 = 29.4°C).

INDEX

GENERAL INFORMATION

BELIZE

COSTA RICA

GUATEMALA

DESTINATIONS

BELIZE

KEY TO ABBREVIATIONS: * = Author's favorite; $ = Special savings; *Cg* = Campgrounds; *W* = Worth the extra bucks

COSTA RICA

IRAZÚ VOLCANO, 55-6

JACÓ BEACH, 93-7
accommodations, 94-6
  Apartamentos El Mar (W), 96
  Apartotel Gaviotas (W*), 96
  Cabinas Alice,$ 94
  Cabinas el Bohio, 94
  Cabinas Gaby, 94-5
  Cabinas Las Palmas, 95
  Chalet Santa Ana, 95
  El Hicaco (Cg), 96
  Hotel Cocal, 95
  Hotel Zabamar, 95-6
  Madrigal (Cg), 96
  Pochote Grande (W), 96
  Villas Miramar, 95
getting to, 93
orientation, 93
restaurants, 96-7
sights and activities, 94
tourist information, 93

KÉKOLDI INDIAN RESERVATION, 125

LA FORTUNA, 67-70
LAKE ARENAL (NORTH END), 65-7
LIBERIA, 70-3
LIMÓN, 111-13

MANUEL ANTONIO NATIONAL PARK, 98-105
see also QUEPOS
MANZANILLO, 125
MONTEVERDE, 59-65
accommodations, 62-5
  El Bosque, 63
  El Establo, 64
  El Iman, 62
  El Sapo Dorado, 65
  Hotel Belmar,* 64
  Hotel de Montaña Monteverde, 64-5
  Hotel Fonda Vela, 64
  Hotel Tucan, 62-3
  Pensión El Quetzal,* 63-4
  Pensión Flor Mar, 63
  Pensión Monteverde Inn,$ 63
getting to, 59-60
orientation, 60
Reserva Biologica Bosque Nuboso Monteverde, 60-2
restaurant, 65
sights and activities, 61-2

NORTHWEST, 59-88
La Fortuna, 67-70
Lake Arenal (North End), 65-7
Liberia, 70-3
Monteverde, 59-65
Playa Brasilito, Flamingo, Potrero & Pan de Azucar, 77-80
Playa del Coco, 73-5
Playa Hermosa, 75-7
Playa Montezuma, 85-8
Playa Nosara, 83-5
Playa Sámara, 83-5
Playa Tamarindo, 80-3
Tilaran, 65-7
what's special about, 60
see also specific places

OROSI VALLEY, 56
OSA PENINSULA, 107-9

PACIFIC COAST, 89-110
Dominical, 105-7
Drake Bay, 107-9
Jacó Beach, 93-7
Manuel Antonio National Park, 98-105
Osa Peninsula, 107-9
Puntarenas, 89-93
Quepos, 98-105
what's special about, 90
see also specific places

PLAYA BRASILITO, 77-80
PLAYA DEL COCO, 73-5
PLAYA ESTERILLOS, 97
PLAYA FLAMINGO, 77-80
PLAYA HERMOSA, 75-7, 97
PLAYA HERRADURA, 97
PLAYA MONTEZUMA, 85-8
accommodations, 86-8
  Amor de Mar, 87
  Casablanca, 87
  El Sano Banano, 87-8
  Hotel Montezuma, 87
  Hotel Montezuma Pacific, 87
  Pensión Arenas, 86-7
getting to, 85-6
restaurants, 88
sights and activities, 86
PLAYA NOSARA, 83-5
PLAYA PAN DE AZUCAR, 77-80
PLAYA POTRERO, 77-80
PLAYA SÁMARA, 83-5
PLAYA TAMARINDO, 80-3
POÁS VOLCANO, 56-7
PUERTO VIEJO, 120-5
accommodations, 121-4
  Cabinas Black Sands,* 122
  Cabinas Chimuri,* 122
  Cabinas Jacaranda,$ 121
  Cabinas Playa Negra, 122
  El Pizote (W*), 122-3
  Escape Caribeño, 123
  Hotel Maritza, 121
  Hotel Puerto Viejo, 121
  Hotel Pura Vida, 121-2
  Las Palmas Resort (W), 123
  Miraflores Lodge, 123
  Playa Chiquita Lodge (W), 124
excursion areas, 125
getting to, 120
orientation, 120
restaurants, 124-5
sights and activities, 120-1
PUNTARENAS, 89-93
PUNTA UVA, 125

QUEPOS, 98-105
accommodations, 100-4
  Apartotel el Colibri (W*), 103
  Cabinas Espadilla, 101
  Cabinas Los Almendros,$ 101
  Cabinas Manuel Antonio, 101
  Cabinas Pedro Miguel, 101
  Cabinas Piscis, 101-2
  Cabinas Ramirez, 102
  Cabinas Vela-Bar, 102
  Hotel Ceciliano,$ 100
  Hotel Divisamar (W), 103
  Hotel Malinche, 100
  Hotel Mirador del Pacifico, 102-3
  Hotel Plinio,* 102
  Hotel Quebos,$ 100-1
  Karahé (W), 103-4
  La Quinta (W), 104
  long-term stays, 103
Fast Facts, 98
getting to, 98
orientation, 98
restaurants, 104-5
  Barba Roja (seafood/continental; W*), 105
  La Tortuga (seafood), 104-5
  Restaurant Isabel (steaks/Costa Rican), 104
  Restaurant Mar y Sombra (Costa Rican,$), 105
sights and activities, 99-100
transportation, 98

RESERVA BIOLOGICA BOSQUE NUBOSO MONTEVERDE, 60-2

SAN JOSÉ, 28-58
accommodations, 35-40

GUATEMALA

324 • INDEX

Now Save Money On All Your Travels by Joining
FROMMER'S ™ TRAVEL BOOK CLUB
The World's Best Travel Guides at Membership Prices

FROMMER'S TRAVEL BOOK CLUB is your ticket to successful travel! Open up a world of travel information and simplify your travel planning when you join ranks with thousands of value-conscious travelers who are members of the FROMMER'S TRAVEL BOOK CLUB. Join today and you'll be entitled to all the privileges that come from belonging to the club that offers you travel guides for less to more than 100 destinations worldwide. Annual membership is only $25 (U.S.) $35 (Canada and all foreign).

The Advantages of Membership

1. Your choice of three free FROMMER'S TRAVEL GUIDES (you can pick two from our FROMMER'S COUNTRY and REGIONAL GUIDES and one from our FROMMER'S CITY GUIDES).
2. Your own subscription to **TRIPS AND TRAVEL** quarterly newsletter.
3. You're entitled to a **30% discount** on your order of any additional books offered by FROMMER'S TRAVEL BOOK CLUB.
4. You're offered (at a small additional fee) our **Domestic Trip Routing Kits.**

Our quarterly newsletter **TRIPS AND TRAVEL** offers practical information on the best buys in travel, the "hottest" vacation spots, the latest travel trends, world class events and much, much more.

Our **Domestic Trip Routing Kits** are available for any North American destination. We'll send you a detailed map highlighting the best route to take to your destination—you can request direct or scenic routes.

Here's all you have to do to join:
Send in your membership fee of $25 ($35 Canada and foreign) with your name and address on the form below along with your selections as part of your membership package to **FROMMER'S TRAVEL BOOK CLUB, P.O. Box 473, Mt. Morris, IL 61054-0473**. Remember to select 2 FROMMER'S COUNTRY and REGIONAL GUIDES and 1 FROMMER'S CITY GUIDE on the pages following.

If you would like to order additional books, please select the books you would like and send a check for the total amount (please add sales tax in the states noted below), plus $2 per book for shipping and handling ($3 per book for all foreign orders) to:

FROMMER'S TRAVEL BOOK CLUB
P.O. Box 473
Mt. Morris, IL 61054-0473
1-815-734-1104

[ ] **YES**. I want to take advantage of this opportunity to join FROMMER'S TRAVEL BOOK CLUB.

[ ] **My check is enclosed**. Dollar amount enclosed _____*

Name _____

Address _____

City _____ State _____ Zip _____

To ensure that all orders are processed efficiently, please apply sales tax in the following areas: CA, CT, FL, IL, NJ, NY, TN, WA and CAN.

*With membership, shipping and handling will be paid by FROMMER'S TRAVEL BOOK CLUB for the three free books you select as part of your membership. Please add $2 per book for shipping and handling for any additional books purchased ($3 per book for all foreign orders).

Allow 4-6 weeks for delivery. Prices of books, membership fee, and publication dates are subject to change without notice.

FROMMER GUIDES

	Retail Price	Code		Retail Price	Code
Alaska 1990–91	$14.95	C001	Jamaica/Barbados 1993–94	$15.00	C105
Arizona 1993–94	$18.00	C101	Japan 1992–93	$19.00	C020
Australia 1992–93	$18.00	C002	Morocco 1992–93	$18.00	C021
Austria/Hungary 1991–92	$14.95	C003	Nepal 1992–93	$18.00	C038
Belgium/Holland/ Luxembourg 1993–94	$18.00	C106	New England 1992	$17.00	C023
Bermuda/Bahamas 1992–93	$17.00	C005	New Mexico 1991–92	$13.95	C024
			New York State 1992–93	$19.00	C025
Brazil 1991–92	$14.95	C006	Northwest 1991–92	$16.95	C026
California 1992	$18.00	C007	Portugal 1992–93	$16.00	C027
Canada 1992–93	$18.00	C009	Puerto Rico 1993–94	$15.00	C103
Caribbean 1993	$18.00	C102	Puerto Vallarta/ Manzanillo/		
The Carolinas/Georgia 1992–93	$17.00	C034	Guadalajara 1992–93	$14.00	C028
Colorado 1993–94	$16.00	C100	Scandinavia 1991–92	$18.95	C029
Cruises 1993–94	$19.00	C107	Scotland 1992–93	$16.00	C040
DE/MD/PA & NJ Shore 1992–93	$19.00	C012	Skiing Europe 1989–90	$14.95	C030
			South Pacific 1992–93	$20.00	C031
Egypt 1990–91	$14.95	C013	Switzerland/Liechten- stein 1992–93	$19.00	C032
England 1993	$18.00	C109	Thailand 1992–93	$20.00	C033
Florida 1993	$18.00	C104	USA 1991–92	$16.95	C035
France 1992–93	$20.00	C017	Virgin Islands 1992–93	$13.00	C036
Germany 1993	$19.00	C108	Virginia 1992–93	$14.00	C037
Italy 1992	$19.00	C019	Yucatán 1992–93	$18.00	C110

FROMMER $-A-DAY GUIDES

	Retail Price	Code		Retail Price	Code
Australia on $45 a Day 1993–94	$18.00	D102	Israel on $45 a Day 1993–94	$18.00	D101
Costa Rica/Guatemala/ Belize on $35 a Day 1991–92	$15.95	D004	Mexico on $50 a Day 1993	$19.00	D105
Eastern Europe on $25 a Day 1991–92	$16.95	D005	New York on $70 a Day 1992–93	$16.00	D016
England on $60 a Day 1993	$18.00	D107	New Zealand on $45 a Day 1993–94	$18.00	D103
Europe on $45 a Day 1993	$19.00	D106	Scotland/Wales on $50 a Day 1992–93	$18.00	D019
Greece on $45 a Day 1993–94	$19.00	D100	South America on $40 a Day 1991–92	$15.95	D020
Hawaii on $75 a Day 1993	$19.00	D104	Spain on $50 a Day 1991–92	$15.95	D021
India on $40 a Day 1992–93	$20.00	D010	Turkey on $40 a Day 1992	$22.00	D023
Ireland on $40 a Day 1992–93	$17.00	D011	Washington, D.C. on $40 a Day 1992	$17.00	D024

FROMMER CITY $-A-DAY GUIDES

	Retail Price	Code		Retail Price	Code
Berlin on $40 a Day 1992–93	$12.00	D002	Madrid on $50 a Day 1992–93	$13.00	D014
Copenhagen on $50 a Day 1992–93	$12.00	D003	Paris on $45 a Day 1992–93	$12.00	D018
London on $45 a Day 1992–93	$12.00	D013	Stockholm on $50 a Day 1992–93	$13.00	D022

FROMMER TOURING GUIDES

Amsterdam	$10.95	T001	New York	$10.95	T008
Australia	$10.95	T002	Paris	$ 8.95	T009
Barcelona	$14.00	T015	Rome	$10.95	T010
Brazil	$10.95	T003	Scotland	$ 9.95	T011
Egypt	$ 8.95	T004	Sicily	$14.95	T017
Florence	$ 8.95	T005	Thailand	$12.95	T012
Hong Kong/Singapore/ Macau	$10.95	T006	Tokyo	$15.00	T016
Kenya	$13.95	T018	Turkey	$10.95	T013
London	$12.95	T007	Venice	$ 8.95	T014

FROMMER'S FAMILY GUIDES

California with Kids	$16.95	F001	San Francisco with Kids	$17.00	F004
Los Angeles with Kids	$17.00	F002	Washington, D.C. with Kids	$17.00	F005
New York City with Kids	$18.00	F003			

FROMMER CITY GUIDES

Amsterdam/Holland 1991–92	$ 8.95	S001	Miami 1991–92	$ 8.95	S021
Athens 1991–92	$ 8.95	S002	Minneapolis/St. Paul 1991–92	$ 8.95	S022
Atlanta 1991–92	$ 8.95	S003	Montréal/Québec City 1991–92	$ 8.95	S023
Atlantic City/Cape May 1991–92	$ 8.95	S004	New Orleans 1993–94	$13.00	S103
Bangkok 1992–93	$13.00	S005	New York 1992	$12.00	S025
Barcelona/Majorca/ Minorca/Ibiza 1992	$12.00	S006	Orlando 1993	$13.00	S101
Belgium 1989–90	$ 5.95	S007	Paris 1993–94	$13.00	S109
Berlin 1991–92	$10.00	S008	Philadelphia 1991–92	$ 8.95	S028
Boston 1991–92	$ 8.95	S009	Rio 1991–92	$ 8.95	S029
Cancún/Cozumel/ Yucatán 1991–92	$ 8.95	S010	Rome 1991–92	$ 8.95	S030
Chicago 1991–92	$ 9.95	S011	Salt Lake City 1991–92	$ 8.95	S031
Denver/Boulder/ Colorado Springs 1990–91	$ 7.95	S012	San Diego 1993–94	$13.00	S107
Dublin/Ireland 1991–92	$ 8.95	S013	San Francisco 1993	$13.00	S104
Hawaii 1992	$12.00	S014	Santa Fe/Taos/ Albuquerque 1993–94	$13.00	S108
Hong Kong 1992–93	$12.00	S015	Seattle/Portland 1992–93	$12.00	S035
Honolulu/Oahu 1993	$13.00	S106	St. Louis/Kansas City 1991–92	$ 9.95	S036
Las Vegas 1991–92	$ 8.95	S016	Sydney 1991–92	$ 8.95	S037
Lisbon/Madrid/Costa del Sol 1991–92	$ 8.95	S017	Tampa/St. Petersburg 1993–94	$13.00	S105
London 1993	$13.00	S100	Tokyo 1992–93	$13.00	S039
Los Angeles 1991–92	$ 8.95	S019	Toronto 1991–92	$ 8.95	S040
Mexico City/Acapulco 1991–92	$ 8.95	S020	Vancouver/Victoria 1990–91	$ 7.95	S041
			Washington, D.C. 1993	$13.00	S102

Other Titles Available at Membership Prices—
SPECIAL EDITIONS

	Retail Price	Code		Retail Price	Code
Bed & Breakfast North America	$14.95	P002	Marilyn Wood's Wonderful Weekends (within 250-mile radius of New York City)	$11.95	P017
Caribbean Hideaways	$16.00	P005			
Honeymoon Destinations	$14.95	P006	New World of Travel 1991 by Arthur Frommer	$16.95	P018
			Where to Stay USA	$13.95	P015

GAULT MILLAU'S "BEST OF" GUIDES

Chicago	$15.95	G002	New England	$15.95	G010
Florida	$17.00	G003	New Orleans	$16.95	G011
France	$16.95	G004	New York	$16.95	G012
Germany	$18.00	G018	Paris	$16.95	G013
Hawaii	$16.95	G006	San Francisco	$16.95	G014
Hong Kong	$16.95	G007	Thailand	$17.95	G019
London	$16.95	G009	Toronto	$17.00	G020
Los Angeles	$16.95	G005	Washington, D.C.	$16.95	G017

THE REAL GUIDES

Amsterdam	$13.00	R100	Morocco	$14.00	R111
Barcelona	$13.00	R101	Nepal	$14.00	R018
Berlin	$11.95	R002	New York	$13.00	R019
Brazil	$13.95	R003	Able to Travel (avail April '93)	$20.00	R112
California & the West Coast	$17.00	R102	Paris	$13.00	R020
Canada	$15.00	R103	Peru	$12.95	R021
Czechoslovakia	$14.00	R104	Poland	$13.95	R022
Egypt	$19.00	R105	Portugal	$15.00	R023
Florida	$14.00	R006	Prague	$15.00	R113
France	$18.00	R106	San Francisco & the Bay Area	$11.95	R024
Germany	$18.00	R107			
Greece	$18.00	R108	Scandinavia	$14.95	R025
Guatemala/Belize	$14.00	R109	Spain	$16.00	R026
Holland/Belgium/ Luxembourg	$16.00	R031	Thailand	$17.00	R114
			Tunisia	$17.00	R115
Hong Kong/Macau	$11.95	R011	Turkey	$13.95	R116
Hungary	$12.95	R012	U.S.A.	$18.00	R117
Ireland	$17.00	R110	Venice	$11.95	R028
Italy	$13.95	R014	Women Travel	$12.95	R029
Kenya	$12.95	R015	Yugoslavia	$12.95	R030
Mexico	$11.95	R016			